I0161374

Ancient Hebrew Torah Lexicon

Ancient Hebrew Torah Lexicon

~~~~~~~~~~~~~~~~~~~~~~~~~~~~~~

Jeff A. Benner
~~~~~~~~~~~~~~~~~~~~~~~~~~~~~~

Cover design by Jeff A. Benner

"Ancient Hebrew Torah Lexicon," by Jeff A. Benner. ISBN 978-1-949756-52-4.

Published 2019 by Virtualbookworm.com Publishing. P.O. Box 9949, College Station, TX 77842, US.

Manufactured in the United States of America.

Table of Contents

About the Lexicon

The translations in this lexicon are derived from the author's Mechanical Translation of the Torah (http://www.mechanical-translation.org).

Words in all upper case letters are the translation of Hebrew words. These words can also be found in the Dictionary of Hebrew Words, which provides a definition of the word as well as this words identifying number in the author's *Ancient Hebrew Lexicon of the Bible* (AHLB) and *Strong's Dictionary*. Note that some of the entries in this lexicon may have more than one translation due to one Hebrew word that may have multiple meanings.

Words in all lower case letters are affixes (prefixes, suffixes and infixes) that are added to the root stem. These words are found in the Dictionary of affixes where each affix is defined.

Words where only the first letter is capitalized are names and they can be found in the Dictionary of Names where a translation of the name is provided.

About the Hebrew Language

The language of the Ancient Hebrews is closely related to their agricultural and nomadic lifestyle. Each word must be understood through this culture rather than from our own modern western Greco-Roman culture. As an example, the Hebrew word 𐤌𐤑𐤅𐤄 (*mitsvah*) is usually translated as a command or commandment in most other translations but hebraically means the directions given to guide one on the journey. Hence, this word will be translated in the MT as "direction."

Hebraic thought differs from our own process of thinking, in that the Hebrews were concrete thinkers in contrast to our own abstract way of thinking. Concrete thought relates all words, concepts and ideas to something that can be sensed by the five senses. For instance, the Hebrew word 𐤀𐤐 (*aph*) is the nose or nostrils, but is the same word for anger, since one who is angry will flare the nostrils.

At times you are going to come across a word in this translation that seems to make absolutely no sense. This is mostly due to the differences between our modern Greco-Roman perspective of thought and that of the ancient Hebrew's. Also keep in mind that each Hebrew word is translated exactly the same way every time, so there will be instances when the word seems out of context. What you will need to do is study that word and the context in which it is used, so you can better understand its Hebraic meaning. Once this has been done, the word and the verse itself will come to life in ways never before perceived.

Hebrew words, verbs, nouns, adjectives, etc., are best defined through a visual action. The Hebrew root 𐤏𐤒𐤁 is used for the noun *eqev* meaning the heel, the verb *aqav* meaning to restrain in the sense of grabbing the heel to hold one back, and the adjective *eyqev* meaning 'because' or 'since,' through the concept of one idea in a sentence being on the heel of another idea within the sentence.

The Root System of Hebrew Words

The vocabulary of the Hebrew language is a system of roots and words. The most basic root is the parent or two-letter root. An example is the parent root 𐤀𐤋 (E.L. el), which means "mighty one." This word is often translated as "God" or "god" in other translations.

Child or three-letter roots are derived by placing an *aleph* (𐤀), *hey* (𐤄), *vav* (𐤅) or *yud* (𐤉)[1] in front, in the middle or at the end of the parent root. An example of a child root derived from the parent root 𐤀𐤋 (E.L *el*) is 𐤀𐤋𐤄 (*A.L.H*) from which the verb 𐤀𐤋𐤄 (*A.L.H*) meaning "to take an oath" and 𐤀𐤋𐤄 (*a'lah*) meaning an "oath" are derived. Another child root derived from the same parent root is 𐤀𐤉𐤋 (*A.Y.L*) from which the noun 𐤀𐤉𐤋 (*ayil*) meaning a "buck" and 𐤀𐤉𐤋𐤄 (*ay'ya'lah*) meaning a "doe" are derived. Another form of child root is where the last letter of the parent root is doubled, so that from the parent root 𐤀𐤋 (*el*) would come the child root 𐤀𐤋𐤋 (*A.L.L*); however, this root is not used in the Hebrew Bible.

Another three-letter root is the adopted root, which is derived by adding a Hebrew consonant to the parent root in the same way that the child root does. An example of an adopted root is the root 𐤀𐤋𐤐 (*A.L.P*), which is derived from the parent root 𐤀𐤋 (*el*) by adding the consonant 𐤐 (*p*) to the end. From this adopted root comes the verb 𐤀𐤋𐤐 (*A.L.P*) meaning "to learn," the noun 𐤀𐤋𐤐

[1] In Ancient Hebrew these four letters doubled as consonants or vowels, as does the letter "y" in the English language. The "y" can be used as a consonant, as in the word "yellow," or as a vowel, as in the word "fly."

(*eleph*) meaning a bovine, and the noun אלוף (*aluph*) meaning a "chief."

When studying Hebrew words, it is essential that you understand a word within the context of its roots to provide a much clearer picture of the meaning of the word. This is the purpose of the lexicon included in this book, which groups all of the Hebrew words found in the *Torah* according to their root words.

The Verb

A verb describes an action, such as the word "cut" in the sentence, "Jacob cut a tree." Each Hebrew verb can be written with different moods and voices. For example, the active voice of the verb ראה (*ra'ah*) means to "see" but, the passive voice, identified by the prefix "*be~*," means "be seen" but is translated as "appeared" in the RMT. As another example, the simple mood of the verb בוא (*bo*)means to "come" but, the causative mood, identified by the prefix "*make~*," means "make come" but, is translated as "bring" in the RMT.

Tense

There are four tenses in Hebrew verbs, perfect, imperfect, participle and imperative. In the English language the verb tenses are related to time; past, present and future, while the Hebrew verbs are all related to action. The perfect tense is a completed action and in most cases is related to the English past tense (he cut). The imperfect tense is an incomplete action and is closely related to the English present and future tenses (he cuts or he will cut). The participle can be a current action or one who performs the action (a cutting or cutter). The imperative identifies the action, similar to a command, with no reference to the subject (cut!). When the prefix ו (*waw*) meaning "and" is attached to the verb, the verb tense (perfect or imperfect) reverses. For this reason this letter, when used in this context, is called the reversing or consecutive *waw*.

Below are a few common verb conjugations of the Hebrew verb (*Sh-M-Ah*)[2]. The bold letters are the prefixes and suffixes which identify the tense, person, and gender of the subject of the verb.

Table 1 – Perfect Tense Verbs

	shama**tiy**	**I** heard
	shama**ta**	**you** heard
	shama	**he** heard
	shama**h**	**she** heard

Table 2 – Imperfect Tense Verbs

	eshma	**I will** hear
	tishma	**you will** hear
	yishma	**he will** hear
	tishma	**she will** hear

[2] I should note that Hebrew verb stems, such as , are not actual words and cannot be pronounced until they are conjugated. Therefore, I will simply transliterate each letter of the verb stems. For the verb stem this will be "Sh" for the letter *shin* ( ), "M" for the letter *mem* ( ) and "Ah" for the letter *ayin* ( ).

Voice

Each Hebrew verb includes voice of which there are three: active, passive or reflexive. The active voice identifies the action of the verb as coming from the subject (he cut). The passive voice does not identify the origin of action placed on the subject of the verb (he was cut). The reflexive voice places the action of the verb onto the subject (he cut himself).

Mood

Each verb also includes mood of which there are three: simple, intensive or causative. The simple mood is simple action of the verb (he cut). The intensive mood implies force or emphasis on the verb (he slashed or hacked). The causative mood expresses causation to the verb ("he made a cut" or "he caused a cut").

The voice and mood of a verb is identified by seven different forms as shown in the table below:

Table 3 – Verb Forms

Form	Mood	Voice	Example
Pa'al[3]	Simple	Active	He cut
Niphal	Simple	Passive	He was cut
Pi'el	Intensive	Active	He slashed
Pu'al	Intensive	Passive	He was slashed
Hiphil	Causative	Active	He made cut
Hophal	Causative	Passive	He was made cut
Hitpa'el	Intensive	Reflexive	He slashed himself

Below are a few common suffixes (in bold letters) that identify the object of a verb.

Table 4 – Suffixes

𐤔𐤋𐤇𐤍𐤉	shelahha**niy**	he sent **me**
𐤔𐤋𐤇𐤊	shal'hhe**kha**	he sent **you**
𐤔𐤋𐤇𐤅	shelahh**o**	he sent **him**

Besides the "simple" verbs (called *qal* verbs) used above, seven other verb forms are used that slightly change the meaning of the verb. However, we will only look at the three most common. The niphil is the passive form and adds the prefixed letter 𐤍 (*ni*). The *hiphil* is the causative form and adds the prefixed letter 𐤄 (*hi*) and

[3] Also called the "*qal*" form.

the letter (*iy*) as an infix. The *Hitpa'el* is the reflexive form and adds the prefixed letters (*hit*).

Table 5 – Niphil, *Hiphil* and *Hitpa'el* verb forms

Niphil		niq'dash	he was special
Hiphil		hiq'diysh	he caused to be special
Hitpa'el		hit'qa'desh	he made himself special

A few other verb forms differ from those we have previously discussed. The first is the infinitive verb, which does not include a tense (perfect or imperfect), subject or object of the verb. It only identifies the action, such as "listen." The second is the imperative, which like the infinitive, does not include a tense or object, but it does identify the gender and number of the subject as well as the action of the verb, but more as a command, such as "listen!." The third is the participle, which is used much like our present tense verbs in English, such as "listening." Below are examples of these verb forms.

Table 6 – Infinitive, Imperative and Participle verb forms

Infinitive		shamo	**listen**
Imperative		shema	**listen!**
Participle		shomey	**listening**

While all of this appears complex and confusing at first, it should be noted that the majority of the Hebrew verbs in the Bible are written in the *pa'al* form and in the perfect tense, third person, masculine, singular.

The Verb, Subject and Object

In English, the general order of words is: subject of the verb, verb and then object of the verb. As an example, using the RMT from Genesis 1:12, we have the sentence, "and the land brought out grass." The word "land" is the subject of the verb, "brought out" is the verb" and "grass" is the object of the verb. In Hebrew, this order is slightly different. The general order of Hebrew sentences is: verb, subject of the verb and then the object of the verb. The Hebrew behind the English sentence above is ותוצא הארץ דשא. The first word, ותוצא, is the verb, the second word, הארץ, is the subject of the verb and the third word, דשא, is the object of the verb.

Hebrew gender

All Hebrew pronouns will be translated as "he" or "she." This may appear strange at first, as a word like "ground," a feminine word, will be identified as a "she" (see 4:12). This is an important issue as knowing the correct gender of a pronoun can influence interpretation. A classic example is found in 4:7 where most translations read, ."..sin is crouching at the door; its desire is for you." It is usually assumed the word "its" is referring to the word "sin" but, knowing that the word "sin" is a feminine word and "its" is a masculine pronoun we discover that the word "its" cannot be referring to the "sin."

Hebrew genders should not be viewed in the same manner we view gender. For instance, the word "beast" is a feminine word and any pronoun associated with this word will be a "she" with no regard to the actual gender of the beast.

Hebrew grammar uses the masculine form of nouns and pronouns for a group of mixed genders. For instance, in 36:25 the "sons" (masculine plural) of Anah are identified as Dishon (a male) and Ahalivamah (a female).

The Noun

The most common noun form is the use of the two or three letter root. From the parent root אב (*av*), meaning a tent pole, comes the noun אב (*av*) meaning "father." As was mentioned previously, all nouns are action oriented and the full understanding of the noun אב is "the one who holds up the tent/house." Just as the tent pole supports the tent, the father supports the family within the tent. The root פתח (*P.T.Hh*) is the base for the verb פתח (*patahh*) meaning "to open" and the noun פתח (*petahh*) meaning a door.

Noun Derivatives

Additional nouns are also formed out of the base root by adding specific letters as prefixes, infixes and suffixes, in specific places within the root. The noun derivative מפתח (*maph'teach*) meaning 'a key' is formed by adding the letter מ to the front of the noun פתח (*petahh* - a door). Some of the most common noun derivatives are formed by placing a מ (*m*) or ת (*t*) before the root or a י (*i*) or ו (*o* or *u*) within the root.

Feminine Derivatives

In Hebrew all nouns are either masculine or feminine. In most cases the nouns and noun derivatives are masculine and are converted into feminine nouns by adding one of four suffixes; ה (*ah*), ת (*et*), ות (*owt*), or ית (*iyt*). Generally, masculine nouns are concrete while feminine nouns are abstract.

Combination Derivatives

Additional noun derivatives are formed by combining different prefixes, infixes and suffixes. The four feminine suffixes can also be added to any of the other noun derivatives resulting in a wide variety of possible nouns.

Plural Nouns

Nouns are made plural by adding the suffix ים (*iym*) or ות (*ot*). Generally the ים is used for masculine nouns and ות for feminine nouns. In some cases masculine words, usually very ancient words, will use the ות suffix. The Hebrew words אב (*av* - father) and אור (*or* - light) are masculine words but are written as אבות and אורות in the plural. In all modern languages the plural is always quantitative, while in Ancient Hebrew a plural can be quantitative or qualitative. An example of this is the word בהמות (*behemoth* – see Job 40:15). This word is the plural form of the singular בהמה (*behemah*), meaning beast, but refers to a very large beast rather than more than one beast. One of the most common uses of the qualitative plural is the word אלהים (*elohiym*) which can be translated as "gods" (quantitative) or as "God" (qualitative).

Grammatical Tools

Hebrew uses nouns for other functions within the sentence. They can be used as adjectives, adverbs, prepositions, conjunctions, etc. The noun עקב (*eqev*) can be the "heel" of the foot but, it can also mean "because" in the sense of being on the heel of the previous phrase. Because the Ancient Hebrew language does not make distinctions between these types of words, the Lexicon lists them all as nouns and noun derivatives.

Articles, Conjunctions and Prepositions

Specific letters are used in Hebrew to represent the article, conjunction, and preposition and are prefixed to nouns (and sometimes verbs). Below are all of these prefixes (in bold) attached to the Hebrew noun ארץ (*erets*, Strong's #776):

Table 7 – Articles, Conjunctions and Prepositions

Article	הארץ	**ha**'arets	**the** land
Conjunction	וארץ	**va**'arets	**and** a land

Preposition	לארץ	**la**'arets	**to** a land
Preposition	בארץ	**be**'erets	**in** a land
Preposition	מארץ	**me**'erets	**from** a land
Preposition	כארץ	**ke**'erets	**like** a land

Adjectives

An adjective is a word that provides description to a noun. For instance, the Hebrew word טוב (good) is a common adjective that can be found in the following phrase meaning "good day."

יום טוב (*yom tov*)

Notice that in Hebrew the adjective follows the noun which it describes. If the noun is prefixed by the article ה (*ha*), then the adjective will be as well, such as we see in the next phrase meaning "the good mountain."

ההר הטוב (*hahar hatov*)

The adjective will also match the gender of the noun. In the last two examples, the words יום and הר are masculine nouns therefore; the masculine form טוב is used. The word ארץ (land) is a feminine word so the feminine adjective טובה is used in the following phrase meaning "good land."

ארץ טובה (*erets tovah*)

The adjective will also match the number (singular or plural) of the noun. In each of our previous examples, the singular form of the word טוב is being used because the nouns it describes are singular. In the phrase, meaning "good houses," the word בית (house) is written in the plural form, therefore the adjective is as well.

(batiym toviym)

Hebrew Pronunciation

Vowels

Four of the Hebrew letters double as consonants and vowels. These are the (*aleph*), (*hey*), (*waw*) and the (*yud*). The *aleph* can be a glottal stop (silent pause) or the vowel sound "a." The letter *hey* has an "h" sound as a consonant or an "e" sound as a vowel. The *waw* is a "w" as a consonant or an "o" or "u" as a vowel. The *yud* is a "y" as a consonant or an "i' as a vowel. The *waw* and the *yud* are the two most commonly used as vowels in Hebrew words. When the *waw* appears at the beginning of a syllable, it will use the consonantal "w" sound. The same is true for the *yud*, which will use the consonantal "y" when at the beginning of a syllable.

Another type of vowel is the implied vowel sounds. This means that the vowel is not written but is necessary in order to pronounce the word. An example of this is the word (grain) which consists of the two consonant B and R and cannot be pronounced without a vowel between them. In most cases the implied vowel will be an "a" or an "e." In this case the implied vowel is the "a" and the word is pronounced *"BaR."*

Spirants and Stops

A spirant is a letter whose sound can be prolonged. Some examples of this from the English language are the v, z, f, and sh. A stop is a letter whose sound ends abruptly such as the b, p, d and t. A few of the Hebrew letters will have a different pronunciation depending on their position within the word. The letter will usually be pronounced as a stop (*b*) when at the beginning of the word, and as a spirant (*v*) when it is anywhere else in the word. For example, the word is pronounced *"bar"* while the word is pronounced *"rav."* Another letter that will change is the letter *kaph* – . When at the beginning of a word it will be pronounced as a stop (*k*). Otherwise it will be pronounced as a spirant (*kh* – pronounced like the *ch* in the name *Bach*). The only other letter that will change is the letter *peh* – פ. When at the beginning of a word, it will be a stop (*p*); otherwise it will be a spirant (*ph*).

Syllables

There are two types of syllables, open and closed. A closed syllable will include a consonant-vowel-consonant combination while an open syllable will have a vowel-consonant combination. The vowel may be one of the four consonant/vowel letters, usually the *yud* (י) or the *waw* (O or U) or an implied vowel. In most cases the final syllable will be a closed syllable. The word ברית (covenant) will have two syllables. The first is ב, an open syllable pronounced "be," and the second is רית a closed syllable pronounced *"riyt."*

Generally, a word with three consonants will be divided as Cv-CvC. A word with four consonants will be divided as Cv-Cv-CvC or CvC-CvC. When a word includes five consonants, the breakdown is usually Cv-Cv-Cv-CvC or CvC-Cv-CvC.

If the word includes one of the four consonant/vowel letters, its position within the word will determine if it is used as a consonant or a vowel. Generally, when the consonant/vowel is placed at the beginning of a syllable or the end of a closed syllable, it will take on the consonantal sound. When it is in the middle of a closed syllable or the end of an open syllable, it will take on the vowel sound.

Ancient Hebrew Speech

Each culture has its own unique style of speech where words and phrases are used that are not meant to be literal and can only be understood correctly if one is familiar with the style of speech used. If these unique words and phrases are heard or read literally, a completely different meaning will be assumed that was not intended by the author.

Idioms

An idiom is defined as "a manner of expression peculiar to a given language, culture or people whose meanings cannot be understood through the context of the words alone." We use idiomatic words and phrases all the time without realizing that we are doing it. Below are just a few examples of idioms peculiar to the English language of America involving parts of the body.

I bent over backwards. (I tried everything.)
Let me give you a hand. (Let me help.)
I put my nose to the grindstone. (I worked hard.)
I spilled his guts. (I told everything.)
You're pulling my leg. (You're joking.)
He's shooting his mouth off. (He's saying too much.)
Break a leg. (Good luck.)
My ears are burning. (Someone is talking about me.)
My head is spinning (This is too much for me to think about.)
I have a hollow leg. (I eat a lot.)
I'm dragging my feet (I'm procrastinating.)
I'm pulling my hair out. (I'm frustrated.)
Hold your tongue. (Don't say anything.)

When someone from another culture hears or reads these idioms, there is no possible way to comprehend the meaning unless an outside source is consulted for interpretation. To demonstrate how difficult it is to interpret an idiom, consider the following idiom from Mexico, "The farmer went into the field and hung up his tennis shoes."

When we read that sentence we envision a farmer going out into the field and hanging his shoes up in a tree or fence post or something like that. It's impossible for us to understand this passage without an outside source. The phrase "hung up his tennis shoes" is equivalent to our idiom "kicked the bucket." In other words, he died.

Below are a few idioms found within the *Torah*.

face fell = sad (Genesis 4:5)
heart lifted up = proud (Deuteronomy 8.14)
knew no quiet in the belly = greedy (Job 20.20)
open the ear = inform (Job 33.16)
right hand = mighty (Psalms 89.13)
hide the face = refuse to answer (Ps 102.2)
bad eye = stingy (Proverbs 28.22)
good eye = generous (Proverbs 22.9)
hard forehead = stubborn (Ezekiel 3.7)

Euphamisms

A euphemism is the use of one word in place of another such as the common Euphemisms used today in our culture.

dough = money

Just as in the case of idioms, the true meaning in Hebrew cannot be understood unless one is familiar with the euphemism. For example, take Psalms 24:7 which reads:

"Lift up your heads, O you gates"

How does a gate lift up its head? The word "gate" is a euphemism for a "judge." The cities in Israel were often surrounded by walls. At the gates of these walls the judges would hold court. Hence, the judges were called "gates."

Gender

All Hebrew nouns, verbs, adjectives and most pronouns identify gender, either masculine or feminine, such as we can see in the first two verses of Genesis:

In the beginning God (m.) created (m.) the sky (m.) and the land (f.) and the land (f.) was (f.) empty and void and the Spirit (f.) of God (m.) hovered (f.) over the face (m.) of the deep.

The identity of a word's gender is essential in translation as well as in interpretation. Take Genesis 4:7 as an example:

> *If thou doest well, shall it not be lifted up? and if thou doest not well, sin coucheth at the door: and unto thee shall be its desire, but do thou rule over it. (ASV, Genesis 4:7)*

The most common interpretation of this verse is that Cain is told that he must control the sin. While this verse is translated appropriately, this interpretation is incorrect because the translation has erased the genders of the verse. Below is the same verse, but adding the gender according to the Hebrew:

> *If thou doest well, shalt thou not be accepted? and if thou doest not well, sin lieth at the door. And unto thee shall be his desire, and thou shalt rule over him. (KJV, Genesis 4:7)*

While the ASV uses the word "it" the Hebrew would literally be translated as "him" as seen in the KJV. There is no "it" in Hebrew; all things are either a "him/he" or a "her/she." The verse says that Cain is to control "him," and since "sin" is a feminine word, sin cannot be the "him."

Ancient Hebrew Styles of Writing

Just as it is important to understand how the Hebrews thought and spoke, it is just as important to know how they wrote. Their style of writing is different from what we are used to, yet we attempt to read the ancient Hebrew texts as if they were written by one of our contemporary writers. This again causes a mistranslation as well as misinterpretations of the text. Therefore, it is essential to learn the unique styles of writing employed by the Hebrews in order to read the texts correctly.

Hebrew Poetry

There are several different types of Hebrew poetry.

As Hebrew poetry differs greatly from our own Western style of poetry, many do not recognize the poetry when they read it. This can cause problems when translating or interpreting these passages.

Approximately 75% of the Tenakh (Old Testament) is poetry. All of Psalms and Proverbs are Hebrew poetry. Even the book of Genesis is filled with Poetry. The Hebrews used poetry for several reasons. Much of the *Torah* was sung and was easier to sing. Also, poetry and songs are easier to memorize than straight texts. Parallel poetry (as in Genesis 1) emphasizes something of great importance, as is the creation story. The rabbis believed that "if something is worth saying, it is worth saying beautifully." There is much more poetry in the Bible than most people realize because most do not recognzize or understand it.

Parallelism

Parallelism is most commonly found in the book of Psalms and Proverbs but is found throughout the entire Hebrew Bible. Parallelism is the expression of one idea in two or more ways.

> "Your word is a lamp to my feet and a light for my path." (Psalms 119:105)

The above example of a simple parallel and can be written in this manner;

> Your word is;
>
> 1. a lamp to my feet
> 2. a light for my path

Here we see that the words "lamp" and "light" are paralleled as well as the words "my feet" and "my path." Below is another example of this style of poetry.

> "My son, my teachings you shall not forget and my commands your heart shall guard." (Proverbs 3:1)

In this verse the words "my teachings" is paralleled with "my commands" and "you shall not forget" is paralleled with "your heart shall guard" and can be written as follows.

My son;

1. my teachings you shall not forget
2. my commands your heart shall guard

Below is Psalm 15:1-3 broken down into its poetic sequences. In this example each thought is represented by the letters A, B, C and D. Each expression of a thought is represented by the numbers 1 and 2.

A1. Lord, who may <u>dwell</u> in your *sanctuary*?
    A2. Who may <u>live</u> on your *holy hill*?
B1. He whose <u>walk</u> is *blameless*
    B2. and who <u>does</u> what is *righteous*.
C1. who speaks the <u>truth</u> from his *heart*
    C2. and has <u>no</u> <u>slander</u> on his *tongue*.
D1. who does his <u>neighbor</u> *no wrong*
    D2. and casts *no slur* on his <u>fellow</u> <u>man</u>.

Another common form of parallelism is the use of negatives where two opposing ideas are stated, as we see in Proverbs 11:19:

A1. Righteousness brings one to life
    A2. Pursuit of evil brings one to his death.

In Genesis 12:1 we can see the poetry of God's command to Abraham to leave his hometown in three different ways:

Leave
    a. from your land
    b. and from your people
    c. and from the house of your father
and go to the land I will show you.

And

In the Western style of writing, an account is broken up into sentences. Each thought is written and closed with a period. The Eastern style of writing on the other hand continues a sentence dividing each thought with the word "and." Below is a translation of Genesis 1:3-8 retaining the "and" as found in the Hebrew:

> ***and*** *God said let there be light* ***and*** *there was light* ***and*** *God saw that the light was good* ***and*** *God separated between the light* ***and*** *the darkness* ***and*** *God called the light day* ***and*** *the darkness he called night* ***and*** *there was an evening* ***and*** *there was a morning a first day* ***and*** *God said let there be an expanse between the water* ***and*** *let there be a separation between the waters from the waters* ***and*** *God made the expanse* ***and*** *God separated between the waters under the expanse* ***and*** *the waters above the expanse* ***and*** *it was so* ***and*** *God called the expanse sky* ***and*** *it was evening* ***and*** *it was morning a second day.*

The use of the word "and" within the text must be kept in mind when reading Biblical accounts, as it may influence the interpretation of the story. For example, in Exodus 17:7 we read:

> *And he called the name of the place Massah, and Meribah, because of the chiding of the children of Israel, and because they tempted the LORD, saying, Is the LORD among us, or not? (KJV)*

In most translations this verse ends the paragraph and a new paragraph begins with verse 8:

> *Then came Amalek, and fought with Israel in Rephidim. (KJV)*

The format of these two passages implies two separate events. But, if the word "and," as found in the Hebrew, is inserted between the two, the passages become related, as we see here.

> *And he called the name of the place Massah, and Meribah, because of the chiding of the children of Israel, and because they tempted the LORD, saying, Is the LORD among us, or not? And Amalek came and fought with Israel in Rephidim.*

When read the passage in this manner, it appears that Amalek came and attacked as a result of their "chiding" and "tempting" of God.

While the removal of the word "and" can cause some misinterpretations of the text, misinterpretations can also be made when it remains in the translation:

> *So he drove out the man; and he placed at the east of the garden of Eden Cherubims, and a flaming sword which turned every way, to keep the way of the tree of life. (KJV, Genesis 3:24)*

The use of the word "and" between "Cherubims" and "a flaming sword" suggest two objects guarding the tree of life. Hebrew, on the other hand, will frequently use the word "and" between two identifiers of the same thing such as in the following passage:

> *Hearken unto the voice of my cry, my King, and my God: for unto thee will I pray. (KJV, Psalm 5:2)*

In this passage, the words "king" and "God" are two names for one person. In the same manner the words "Cherubim" and "flaming sword" are two words for the same thing. It should also be noted that the Hebrew for Cherubim and sword are almost identical.

Lexicon of Hebrew Words

I~will~SPIT.UPON(V) :
FATHER :
he~did~PERISH(V) | >~much~PERISH(V) :
she~did~PERISH(V) | LOST.THING :
>~PERISH(V)~you(ms) :
we~did~PERISH(V) :
you(ms)~did~PERISH(V) | LOST.THING :
he~did~CONSENT(V) :
I~will~COME(V) :
>~PERISH(V) :
FATHER~s :
FATHER~s~me :
FATHER~s~him :
FATHER~s~you(ms) :
FATHER~s~you(mp) :
FATHER~s~us :
FATHER~s~you(mp) :
FATHER~s~them(m) :
I~will~CHOOSE(V) :
FATHER~of | FATHER~me :
I~will~make~COME(V) :
I~will~make~COME(V)~him :
GREEN.GRAIN :
Avidan :
FATHER~her :
Aviyhu :
FATHER~them(m) :
FATHER~them(f) :
FATHER~him :
NEEDY :
NEEDY~s :
NEEDY~you(ms) :
Avihha'il :
FATHER~you(ms) | FATHER~you(fs) :
FATHER~you(mp) :
FATHER~you(fp) :
Aviyma'el :
Aviymelekh :
FATHER~us :
VALIANT :
you(mp)~did~CONSENT(V) :
Aveyl-Hashit'tim :
Aveyl-Mitsrayim :
NEVERTHELESS | MOURNING :
STONE :
SASH :
SASH~s :
STONE~s :
STONE~s~her :
STONE~s~him :
STONE~s :
PUSTULE~s :
DUST :
Avraham :
BEND.THE.KNEE :
I~will~much~KNEEL(V)~you(ms) :
I~will~much~KNEEL(V)~them(m) :
Avram :
FEATHER~him :
I~will~MAGNIFY(V) :
BUNCH :
I~will~IMMIGRATE(V) :
POOL~s~them(m) :
I~will~much~CAST.OUT(V)~him :
I~will~much~SPEAK(V) :
Edom :
RED :
Edom~of :
Adonai | LORD~s~me | LORD~me | LORD~s :
LORD~s~her :
LORD~s~him :

LORD~s~you(ms) : אדניך
EMINENT~s : אדירים
HUMAN : אדם
REDDISH : אדמדם
REDDISH~s : אדמדמות
REDDISH : אדמדמת
GROUND | Admah : אדמה
RUDDY : אדמוני
GROUND : אדמת
GROUND~him : אדמתו
GROUND~you(ms) : אדמתך
GROUND~you(mp) : אדמתכם
GROUND~them(m) : אדמתם
GROUND~us : אדמתנו
FOOTING~s : אדני
FOOTING~s~her : אדניה
FOOTING~s~them(m) : אדניהם
FOOTING~s~him : אדניו
FOOTING~s : אדנים
I~will~KNOW(V) : אדע
I~will~KNOW(V)~& : אדעה
I~will~SEEK(V) : אדרש
Ed're'i : אדרעי
I~will~SEEK(V)~him : אדרשנו
he~did~LOVE(V) : אהב
he~did~LOVE(V)~him : אהבו
he~did~LOVE(V)~you(ms) : אהבך
you(ms)~did~LOVE(V) : אהבת
I~did~LOVE(V) : אהבתי
LOVE(V)~ed(fs) : אהובה
I~will~EXIST(V) | Ehyeh : אהיה
TENT~him : אהלו
TENT~her : אהלוה
TENT~s : אהלי
Ahaliyav : אהליאב
Ahalivamah : אהליבמה
TENT~s~them(m) : אהליהם
Aharon : אהרן
OR : או
NECROMANCER : אוב
PERISH(V)~ing(ms) : אובד
I~will~make~ THROW.THE.HAND(V) : אודה
CONCERNING~s | CONCERNING : אודות
CARNELIAN : אודם
LOVE(V)~ing(mp) : אוהבים

LOVE(V)~ing(fs) : אוהבת
TENT : אוהל
TENT~you(ms) : אוהלך
TENT~s : אוהלים
Uzal : אוזל
EAR : אוזן
TAKE.HOLD(V)~ing(fs) : אוחזת
OH | Ewi : אוי
ATTACK(V)~ing(ms) : אויב
ATTACK(V)~ing(ms)~s~me : אויבי
ATTACK(V)~ing(ms)~s~ them(m) : אויביהם
ATTACK(V)~ing(ms)~s~him : אויביו
ATTACK(V)~ing(mp)~s~ you(ms) : אויביך
ATTACK(V)~ing(mp)~ you(mp) : אויבכם
ATTACK(V)~ing(ms)~you(ms) : אויבך
ATTACK(V)~ing(ms)~you(ms) : אוייבך
I~will~BE.ABLE(V) | I~will~EAT(V) | EAT(V)~ing(ms) | FOODSTUFF | EAT(V)~ ed(ms) : אוכל
EAT(V)~ing(fs) | I~will~EAT(V)~& : אוכלה
EAT(V)~ing(mp)~him : אוכליו
EAT(V)~ing(fs) : אוכלת
POSSIBLY : אולי
TRIBE~s : אומות
INDEED : אומנם
I~will~SAY(V) | Omar | SAY(V)~ ing(ms) : אומר
SAY(V)~ing(mp) : אומרים
On | BARRENNESS : און
VIGOR~him : אונו
VIGOR~me : אוני
Onan : אונן
I~will~make~ADD(V) : אוסיף
ADD(V)~ing(ms) : אוסף
TIE.UP(V)~ing(ms)~me : אוסרי
BAKE(V)~ing(ms) : אופה
Ophir : אופיר
WHEEL : אופן
I~will~make~GO.OUT(V) : אוציא
I~will~make~GO.OUT(V)~& : אוציאה
SUPPLY.HOUSE~him : אוצרו
LIGHT : אור
BRAID(V)~ing(ms) : אורג
PATH : אורח

CARAVAN : אורחת
Uriy : אורי
I~will~make~POSSESS(V) : אוריש
LENGTH : אורך
she~did~be~much~BETROTH(V) : אורסה
SPIT.UPON(V)~ing(mp)~you(ms) : אורריך
SIGN | DESIRE : אות
AT~her | SIGN~her : אותה
AT~him : אותו
SIGN~s : אותות
SIGN~s~me : אותותי
SIGN~s~him : אותותיו
AT~me | SIGN~me : אותי
AT~you(ms) | AT~you(fs) : אותך
AT~you(mp) | AT~you(ms) : אותכה
AT~them(m) : אותם
AT~them(f) : אותנה
AT~us : אותנו
AT.THAT.TIME : אז
HYSSOP : אזוב
I~will~REMEMBER(V) : אזכור
I~will~make~REMEMBER(V) : אזכיר
MEMORIAL~her : אזכרתה
she~did~WAVER(V) : אזלת
EAR~him : אזנו
TOOLS~you(ms) : אזנך
EAR~them(m) : אזנם
I~will~ENRAGE(V) : אזעום
I~will~much~DISPERSE(V) : אזרה
BROTHER : אח
UNIT : אחד
UNIT~s : אחדים
TAKE.HOLD(V)~ed(ms) : אחוז
HOLDINGS : אחוזה
HOLDINGS : אחוזת
HOLDINGS~him : אחוזתו
HOLDINGS~you(mp) : אחוזתכם
HOLDINGS~them(m) : אחוזתם
I~will~PROVIDE.PROTECTION(V) : אחון
BACK : אחור
BACK~s | BACK~s~me : אחורי
BACKWARD : אחורנית
SISTER : אחות
SISTER~her : אחותה
SISTER~him : אחותו
SISTER~me : אחותי
SISTER~you(ms) : אחותך
SISTER~them(m) : אחותם
SISTER~us : אחותנו
he~did~TAKE.HOLD(V) : אחז
I~will~SEIZE(V) : אחזק
I~will~much~FAIL(V)~her : אחטנה
BROTHER~me | BROTHER~of | BROTHER~s~me | BROTHER~s | Eyhhiy : אחי
BROTHER~her | BROTHER~s~her : אחיה
Ahhihud : אחיהוד
BROTHER~s~them(m) : אחיהם
BROTHER~him | BROTHER~s~him : אחיו
BROTHER~you(ms) | BROTHER~s~you(ms) : אחיך
BROTHER~you(mp) | BROTHER~s~you(mp) : אחיכם
BROTHER~s : אחים
Ahhiman : אחימן
BROTHER~s~us | BROTHER~us : אחינו
Ahhiysamahh : אחיסמך
Ahhi'ezer : אחיעזר
Ahhira : אחירע
I~will~make~DRILL(V) : אחל
I~will~much~DISTRIBUTE(V) : אחלק
I~will~much~DISTRIBUTE(V)~them(m) : אחלקם
OTHER | AFTER | he~did~much~DELAY(V) : אחר
LAST~s : אחרונים
OTHER~s : אחרות
AFTER | AFTER~me : אחרי
AFTER~her : אחריה
AFTER~them(m) : אחריהם
AFTER~them(f) : אחריהן
AFTER~him : אחריו
AFTER~you(ms) : אחריך
AFTER~you(mp) : אחריכם
OTHER~s : אחרים
AFTER~us : אחרינו
END : אחרית
END~me : אחריתי
END~them(m) : אחריתם

OTHER :𐤀𐤇𐤓𐤕
UNIT :𐤀𐤇𐤕
WHERE :𐤀𐤉
HOSTILITY :𐤀𐤉𐤁𐤄
I~will~BUILD(V) :𐤀𐤉𐤁𐤍𐤄
CALAMITY~them(m) :𐤀𐤉𐤃𐤌
WHERE :𐤀𐤉𐤄
I~will~be~APPOINT(V) :𐤀𐤉𐤅𐤏𐤃
I~will~make~DO.WELL(V) :𐤀𐤉𐤈𐤉𐤁
ISLAND~s :𐤀𐤉𐤉
BUCK :𐤀𐤉𐤉𐤋
WITHOUT :𐤀𐤉𐤉𐤍
HOW :𐤀𐤉𐤊
WHERE~you(ms) | HOW :𐤀𐤉𐤊𐤄
!(mp)~EAT(V)~him :𐤀𐤉𐤊𐤋𐤅𐤄𐤅
Eyl-Paran :𐤀𐤉𐤋-𐤐𐤀𐤓𐤍
BUCK :𐤀𐤉𐤋
DOE :𐤀𐤉𐤋𐤄
Eylon :𐤀𐤉𐤋𐤅𐤍
BUCK~s :𐤀𐤉𐤋𐤉
BUCK~s :𐤀𐤉𐤋𐤉𐤌
Eyliym~unto :𐤀𐤉𐤋𐤉𐤌𐤄
MUTE :𐤀𐤉𐤋𐤌
IF :𐤀𐤉𐤌
TERROR | MOTHER~her :𐤀𐤉𐤌𐤄
MOTHER~him :𐤀𐤉𐤌𐤅
MOTHER~me :𐤀𐤉𐤌𐤉
MOTHER~you(ms) :𐤀𐤉𐤌𐤊
I~will~be~SLIP.AWAY(V) :𐤀𐤉𐤌𐤋𐤈𐤄
!(fs)~SAY(V) | STATEMENT~s :𐤀𐤉𐤌𐤓𐤉
SPEECH~me :𐤀𐤉𐤌𐤓𐤕𐤉
SPEECH~you(ms) :𐤀𐤉𐤌𐤓𐤕𐤊
TERROR :𐤀𐤉𐤌𐤕𐤄
TERROR~me :𐤀𐤉𐤌𐤕𐤉
WITHOUT :𐤀𐤉𐤍
he~did~much~APPROACH(V) :𐤀𐤉𐤍𐤄
WITHOUT~you(ms) :𐤀𐤉𐤍𐤊
WITHOUT~you(mp) :𐤀𐤉𐤍𐤊𐤌
WITHOUT~her :𐤀𐤉𐤍𐤍𐤄
WITHOUT~him :𐤀𐤉𐤍𐤍𐤅
WITHOUT~me :𐤀𐤉𐤍𐤍𐤉
BOND :𐤀𐤉𐤎𐤓
I'ezer :𐤀𐤉𐤏𐤆𐤓
I~will~GIVE.ADVICE(V)~you(ms) :𐤀𐤉𐤏𐤑𐤊
EYPHAH :𐤀𐤉𐤐𐤄
WHERE :𐤀𐤉𐤐𐤅𐤄
EYPHAH :𐤀𐤉𐤐𐤕
I~will~be~MEET(V) :𐤀𐤉𐤒𐤓𐤄
I~will~POSSESS(V)~her :𐤀𐤉𐤓𐤔𐤍𐤄
MAN :𐤀𐤉𐤔
I~will~be~SWEAR(V) :𐤀𐤉𐤔𐤁𐤏
WOMAN | MAN~her | FIRE.OFFERING :𐤀𐤉𐤔𐤄
FIRE~him :𐤀𐤉𐤔𐤅
MAN~me | FIRE.OFFERING~s :𐤀𐤉𐤔𐤉
MAN~you(fs) :𐤀𐤉𐤔𐤊
they~did~much~HAPPY(V)~me :𐤀𐤉𐤔𐤓𐤅𐤍𐤉
WOMAN~him :𐤀𐤉𐤔𐤕𐤅
WOMAN~me :𐤀𐤉𐤔𐤕𐤉
WOMAN~you(ms) :𐤀𐤉𐤔𐤕𐤊
AT~her :𐤀𐤉𐤕𐤄
AT~him :𐤀𐤉𐤕𐤅
AT~me :𐤀𐤉𐤕𐤉
AT~you(fs) | AT~you(ms) :𐤀𐤉𐤕𐤊
AT~you(mp) :𐤀𐤉𐤕𐤊𐤌
AT~them(m) :𐤀𐤉𐤕𐤌
Iytamar :𐤀𐤉𐤕𐤌𐤓
CONSISTENCY :𐤀𐤉𐤕𐤍
AT~us :𐤀𐤉𐤕𐤍𐤅
SURELY :𐤀𐤊
I~will~be~BE.HEAVY(V) :𐤀𐤊𐤁𐤃
I~will~much~BE.HEAVY(V)~you(ms) :𐤀𐤊𐤁𐤃𐤊
>~EAT(V) :𐤀𐤊𐤅𐤋
CRUEL :𐤀𐤊𐤆𐤓
>~EAT(V) | he~did~EAT(V) :𐤀𐤊𐤋
I~will~much~FINISH(V) | !(ms)~EAT(V) :𐤀𐤊𐤋𐤄
they~did~EAT(V) | >~EAT(V)~him :𐤀𐤊𐤋𐤅
you(ms)~>~EAT(V) | I~will~much~FINISH(V)~you(ms) | FOODSTUFF~you(ms) :𐤀𐤊𐤋𐤊
I~will~much~SUSTAIN(V) :𐤀𐤊𐤋𐤊𐤋
>~EAT(V)~you(mp) :𐤀𐤊𐤋𐤊𐤌
FOODSTUFF~them(m) :𐤀𐤊𐤋𐤌
he~did~EAT(V)~me :𐤀𐤊𐤋𐤍𐤉
you(ms)~will~EAT(V) :𐤀𐤊𐤋𐤕
she~did~EAT(V)~him :𐤀𐤊𐤋𐤕𐤄𐤅
I~did~EAT(V) :𐤀𐤊𐤋𐤕𐤉
you(mp)~did~EAT(V) :𐤀𐤊𐤋𐤕𐤌

SURELY : אכן
I~will~make~HIT(V)~him : אכנו
I~will~make~BE.ANGRY(V)~them(m) : אכעיסם
I~will~much~COVER(V)~& : אכפרה
El-Elohey-Yisra'eyl : אל־אלוהי־ייסראל
El-Beyt-El : אל־בית־אל
El-Ra'iy : אל־ראי
TO | DO.NOT | MIGHTY.ONE : אל
I~will~BRING.FORTH(V) : אלד
Eldad : אלדד
THESE | OATH | Eylah : אלה
TO~them(m) : אלהם
TO~them(f) : אלהן
POWER : אלוה
Elohiym | Elohiym~me : אלוהי
Elohiym~them(m) : אלוהיהם
Elohiym~them(f) : אלוהיהן
Elohiym~him : אלוהיו
Elohiym~you(ms) : אלוהיך
Elohiym~you(mp) : אלוהיכם
Elohiym | POWER~s : אלוהים
Elohiym~him : אלוהימו
Elohiym~us : אלוהינו
BOUND.SHEAF~s~you(mp) : אלומותיכם
BOUND.SHEAF~s : אלומים
BOUND.SHEAF~me : אלומתי
Alon-Bakhut : אלון־בכות
GREAT.TREE : אלון
GREAT.TREE~s : אלוני
CHIEF : אלוף
CHIEF~s : אלופי
CHIEF~s~them(m) : אלופיהם
OATH~s : אלות
TO~me | MIGHTY.ONE~me : אלי
Eli'av : אליאב
Elidad : אלידד
TO~her : אליה
TO~them(m) : אליהם
TO~them(f) : אליהן
TO~him : אליו
TO~you(fs) : אלייך
TO~you(ms) : אליך
TO~you(mp) : אליכם
WORTHLESS~s : אלילים
BUCK~s : אלים
TO~us : אלינו
Elyasaph : אליסף
Eli'ezer : אליעזר
Eliphaz : אליפז
Elitsur : אליצור
Elitsaphan : אליצפן
Eliysheva : אלישבע
Elishah : אלישה
Elishama : אלישמע
I~will~WALK(V) : אלך
I~will~WALK(V)~& : אלכה
TO~you(mp) : אלכם
Almodad : אלמודד
WIDOW : אלמנה
WIDOW~s : אלמנות
WIDOWHOOD~her : אלמנותה
Elasar : אלסר
Elazar : אלעזר
Elaley : אלעלא
THOUSAND : אלף
THOUSAND~s : אלפי
THOUSAND~s2 : אלפיים
BOVINE~s~you(ms) : אלפיך
THOUSAND~s : אלפים
El'tsaphan : אלצפן
MOTHER : אם
FOREARM | BONDWOMAN : אמה
FIRMNESS : אמון
FIRMNESS : אמונה
!(ms)~SAY(V) | >~SAY(V) : אמור
Emor~of : אמורי
I~will~DIE(V) | FOREARM~s : אמות
I~will~DIE(V)~& : אמותה
I~will~WIPE.AWAY(V) : אמחה
I~will~WIPE.AWAY(V)~him : אמחנו
Eym~s : אמים
I~will~make~DIE(V) : אמית
I~will~much~FILL(V) : אמלא
SO.BE.IT : אמן
SURE : אמנה
I~will~FIND(V) : אמצא
he~did~SAY(V) : אמר
she~did~SAY(V) : אמרה
they~did~SAY(V) : אמרו
Amraphel : אמרפל
you(ms)~did~SAY(V) : אמרת

I~did~SAY(V) :
you(mp)~did~SAY(V) :
LAST.NIGHT :
TRUTH :
BONDWOMAN~her :
BONDWOMAN~him :
GRAIN.SACK~s :
GRAIN.SACK~s~ you(mp) :
GRAIN.SACK~s~us :
GRAIN.SACK :
GRAIN.SACK~him :
BONDWOMAN~me :
FOREARM~s2 :
BONDWOMAN~you(ms) :
PLEASE :
WHEREVER :
I :
I~will~FLEE(V) :
Enosh :
WE :
I :
SHIP~s :
I~will~TEST(V)~him :
MAN~s :
MAN~s~him :
MAN~s :
I~will~LIFT.UP(V) :
HARM :
!(ms)~GATHER(V) :
TIE.UP(V)~ed(ms) | I~will~ TURN.ASIDE(V) :
I~will~TURN.ASIDE(V)~& :
TIE.UP(V)~ed(mp) :
TIE.UP(V)~ed(mp) :
I~will~make~OVERTAKE(V) :
I~will~PLACE(V) :
I~will~PLACE(V)~& :
I~will~PLACE(V)~you(ms) :
I~will~PLACE(V)~him :
Asiyr :
Asnat :
he~did~GATHER(V) :
?~!(ms)~GATHER(V) | I~will~ make~CONSUME(V) :
she~did~TIE.UP(V) :
BOND~s~her :

I~will~make~HIDE(V) :
I~will~make~HIDE(V)~& :
I~will~be~HIDE(V) :
I~will~SERVE(V)~you(ms) :
I~will~CROSS.OVER(V) :
I~will~CROSS.OVER(V)~& :
I~will~make~CROSS.OVER(V) :
I~will~CROSS.OVER(V)~& :
I~will~LEAVE(V)~you(ms) :
I~will~GO.UP(V) | I~will~make~ GO.UP(V) :
I~will~make~GO.UP(V)~you(ms) :
I~will~DO(V) :
I~will~much~ GIVE.A.TENTH(V)~him :
I~will~BARTER(V)~him :
I~will~make~INTERCEDE(V) :
MOREOVER | NOSE :
I~will~make~ BLOW.AWAY(V)~them(m) :
I~will~RANSOM(V) :
he~did~BAKE(V) | NOSE~her :
NOSE~him | !(mp)~BAKE(V) :
THEN :
EPHOD :
EPHOD~him :
NOSE~me :
NOSE~s2 :
NOSE~s~you(ms) :
LATE~s :
NOSE~you(ms) :
THICK.GLOOMINESS :
NOSE~them(m) :
he~did~COME.TO.AN.END(V) | FAR.END :
FAR.END~s :
ASH :
CHICK~s :
I~will~SPREAD.OUT(V) :
Ephrayim :
Ephrat :
Ephrat~unto :
I~will~GO.OUT(V) :
FINGER :
FINGER~him :
I~will~make~ BE.STEADFAST(V) :

I~will~much~DIRECT(V) :אצוה
I~will~much~DIRECT(V)~you(ms) :אצוך
I~will~much~DIRECT(V)~him :אצונו
I~will~make~ :אציגה
LEAVE.IN.PLACE(V)~&
LEADER~s :אצילי
COMPEL(V)~ing(mp) :אצים
BESIDE :אצל
BESIDE~her :אצלה
BESIDE~me :אצלי
you(ms)~did~SET.ASIDE(V) :אצלת
ARMLET :אצעדה
Eytser :אצר
I~will~much~SET.APART(V) | I~ :אקדש
will~be~SET.APART(V)
I~will~HOLLOW.OUT(V) :אקוב
I~will~TAKE(V) :אקח
/ I~will~TAKE(V)~you(ms) :אקחך
I~will~make~RISE(V) :אקים
I~will~make~ :אקניאם
BE.ZEALOUS(V)~them(m)
I~will~CALL.OUT(V) :אקרא
I~will~make~BE.HARD(V) :אקשה
I~will~SEE(V) | I~will~be~SEE(V) :אראה
I~will~make~SEE(V)~you(ms) :אראך
I~will~SEE(V)~him :אראנו
I~will~make~INCREASE(V) | :ארבה
SWARMING.LOCUST
FOUR :ארבע
FOUR :ארבעה
FOUR~s :ארבעים
FOUR :ארבעת
Argov :ארגוב
PURPLE :ארגמן
I~will~GO.DOWN(V) | Ard :ארד
I~will~GO.DOWN(V)~her :ארדה
I~will~PURSUE(V) :ארדוף
!(ms)~SPIT.UPON(V)~& :ארה
BOX :ארון
SPIT.UPON(V)~ed(ms) :ארור
SPIT.UPON(V)~ed(ms) :ארורה
CEDAR :ארז
I~will~much~ :ארחם
HAVE.COMPASSION(V)
LION :אריה
Aryokh :אריוך
I~will~make~SMELL(V) :אריח

I~will~make~DRAW.OUT(V) :אריק
SLOW :ארך
LENGTH~her :ארכה
they~did~PROLONG(V) | :ארכו
LENGTH~him
Aram- :ארם־נהריים
Nahara'im
Aram :ארם
Aram~of :ארמי
Arnon :ארנון
he~did~much~BETROTH(V) :ארס
I~will~FEED(V) :ארעה
I~will~HEAL(V) :ארפא
Arpakhshad :ארפכשד
LAND :ארץ
LAND~unto | LAND~her :ארצה
LAND~him :ארצו
LAND~me :ארצי
LAND~you(ms) :ארצך
LAND~you(mp) :ארצכם
LAND~them(m) :ארצם
he~did~much~SPIT.UPON(V)~ :אררה
her
Ararat :אררט
FIRE :אש
I~will~DRAW.WATER(V) :אשאב
I~will~make~CEASE(V)~& :אשביתה
RAVINE~s :אשדות
Eyshdat :אשדת
I~will~TURN.BACK(V) :אשוב
I~will~TURN.BACK(V)~& :אשובה
>~BE.GUILTY(V) :אשום
Ashur :אשור
Ashur~unto :אשורה
Ashur~s :אשורים
I~will~LOOK.UPON(V)~him :אשורנו
I~will~make~DAMAGE(V) :אשחית
I~will~make~TURN.BACK(V) :אשיב
I~will~make~ :אשיבנה
TURN.BACK(V)~her
I~will~make~ :אשיבנו
TURN.BACK(V)~him
I~will~SING(V)~& :אשירה
I~will~SET.DOWN(V) :אשית
TESTICLES :אשך
Eshkol :אשכול
I~will~make~BE.DRUNK(V) :אשכיר

I~will~BE.CHILDLESS(V) :אשכל
CLUSTER~s :אשכלות
CLUSTER~s~her :אשכלותיה
/ Ashkanaz :אשכנז
TAMARISK :אשל
I~will~much~SEND(V) :אשלח
I~will~much~SEND(V)~you(ms) :אשלחך
I~will~much~MAKE.RESTITUTION(V) :אשלם
GUILT | he~did~BE.GUILTY(V) :אשם
GUILT :אשמה
GUILT~him :אשמו
I~will~SAFEGUARD(V) :אשמור
GUILT~s :אשמים
GUILT~them(m) :אשמם
I~will~HEAR(V) :אשמע
GUILTINESS~him :אשמתו
I~will~make~DRINK(V) :אשקה
WHICH | Asher :אשר
GROVE :אשרה
GROVE~s~him :אשריו
HAPPY~you(ms) :אשריך
WOMAN :אשת
AT | YOU :את
YOU :אתה
AT~them(m) :אתהם
AT~them(f) :אתהן
I~will~self~KNOW(V) :אתודע
SHE-DONKEY~him :אתונו
SHE-DONKEY~s :אתונות
SHE-DONKEY~you(ms) :אתונך
AT~you(mp) :אתכם
YOU | Eytam :אתם
/ I~will~GIVE(V) :אתן
I~will~self~LEAD(V)~& :אתנהלה
WAGES :אתנן
I~will~GIVE(V)~her :אתננה
he~did~COME(V) | COME(V)~ing(ms) :בא
in~FATHER~s~you(ms) :באבותיך
in~STONE | in~the~STONE :באבן
in~SASH :באבנט
in~the~STONE~s :באבנים
in~the~GOBLET~s :באגנות
in~FIST :באגרוף
in~Edom :באדום
in~the~HUMAN | in~HUMAN :באדם
in~GROUND :באדמה

in~Ed're'i :באדרעי
she~did~COME(V) :באה
in~AFFECTION :באהבתו
in~TENT~him :באהלו
in~TENT~s :באהלי
in~TENT~s~you(mp) :באהליכם
they~did~COME(V) :באו
in~Ovot :באובות
in~the~TENT | in~TENT :באוהל
in~TENT~s~you(ms) :באוהליך
in~BARRENNESS~me :באוני
in~SUPPLY.HOUSE~s~me :באוצרותי
in~Ur :באור
in~LENGTH | in~the~LENGTH :באורך
COME(V)~ing(fp) :באות
in~SIGN~s :באותות
in~EAR~him :באזנו
in~EAR~s2 | in~EAR~s2~me :באזני
in~EAR~s2~them(m) :באזניהם
in~EAR~s2~you(mp) :באזניכם
in~NATIVE :באזרח
in~UNIT :באחד
in~the~MARSH.GRASS :באחו
in~SISTER~her :באחותה
in~BROTHER~him :באחיו
in~BROTHER~you(ms) :באחיך
in~the~LAST :באחרונה
in~END :באחרית
in~END~you(ms) :באחריתך
in~UNIT :באחת
COME(V)~ing(mp) :באי
in~HOSTILITY :באיבה
in~BUCK :באיל
COME(V)~ing(mp) :באים
in~the~MAN | in~MAN :באיש
in~MAN~her :באישה
in~WOMAN~him :באישתו
in~CONSISTENCY :באיתן
in~>~EAT(V) :באכול
in~>~EAT(V)~you(mp) :באכלכם
in~>~EAT(V)~them(m) :באכלם
in~>~EAT(V)~us :באכלנו
in~MIGHTY.ONE :באל
in~THESE :באלה
in~Elohiym :באלוהים

in~GREAT.TREE~s :
in~Alush :
in~the~MIGHTY.ONE~s :
in~the~FOREARM :
in~>~SAY(V) :
in~FOREARM :
in~GRAIN.SACK~s~you(mp) :
in~GRAIN.SACK~s~us :
in~GRAIN.SACK :
in~GRAIN.SACK~me :
we~did~COME(V) :
in~the~SHIP~s :
in~MAN~s :
in~MAN~s :
in~BARN~s~you(ms) :
in~>~GATHER(V)~you(ms) :
in~>~GATHER(V)~you(mp) :
in~NOSE :
in~NOSE~him :
in~NOSE~me :
in~NOSE~s2~him :
in~NOSE~you(ms) :
in~the~THICK.GLOOMINESS :
in~NOSE~them(m) :
in~FINGER :
in~FINGER~him :
in~FINGER~you(ms) :
Be'er-Lahhiy-Ro'iy :
B'er-Sheva :
WELL | he~did~much~EXPLAIN(V) | >~much~EXPLAIN(V) :
in~the~SWARMING.LOCUST :
in~FOUR :
in~FOUR :
in~FOUR~s :
B'er-Sheva~unto :
B'er~unto :
in~the~BOX :
WELL~s :
Be'eri :
in~the~LAND | in~LAND :
in~LAND~him :
in~LAND~s :
in~LAND~s~them(m) :

in~LAND~you(ms) :
in~LAND~you(mp) :
in~LAND~them(m) :
in~the~FIRE :
in~NIGHT.WATCH :
in~WHICH :
in~HAPPINESS~me :
you(fs)~did~COME(V) :
I~did~COME(V) :
you(mp)~did~COME(V) | in~Eytam :
in~GARMENT | in~the~GARMENT :
in~STRAND :
in~the~BEAST :
in~BEAST :
in~the~BRIGHT.SPOT :
>~COME(V) | in~>~COME(V) :
in~>~COME(V)~him :
in~>~COME(V)~me :
in~>~COME(V)~you(ms) :
in~>~COME(V)~you(mp) :
in~>~COME(V)~them(m) :
in~>~COME(V)~them(f) :
in~the~MORNING :
in~the~CISTERN :
in~GARMENT~him :
in~WOMB~her :
in~WOMB~you(fs) :
in~the~HOUSE | in~HOUSE :
in~the~LEVEL.VALLEY :
in~HOUSE :
in~HOUSE~him :
in~HOUSE~you(ms) :
in~DAUGHTER~them(m) :
Bavel :
in~SON~s~you(ms) :
in~SON~s~us :
in~the~FLESH :
in~Ba'al-Pe'or :
in~the~CATTLE :
in~>~FLEE.AWAY(V)~him :
in~>~FLEE.AWAY(V)~you(ms) :
in~>~much~KNEEL(V)~him :
in~Bashan :
in~DAUGHTER :
in~HOUSE~s~you(mp) :

in~the~BARE.SPOT :
in~BARE.SPOT~him :
in~FORTUNE | GARMENT :
in~the~GREAT :
GARMENT~s~him :
GARMENT~s :
in~GREAT~you(ms) :
in~NATION :
in~NATION~s~them(m) :
in~the~NATION~s | in~NATION~s :
in~LOT :
in~Goren-Ha'atad :
in~PLUCKING :
in~the~STEEP.VALLEY :
in~the~STEEP.VALLEY :
in~SINEW :
in~Gil'ad :
in~>~DRAW.NEAR(V)~them(m) :
in~the~CAMEL ~s :
in~GARDEN :
in~ARCH ~him :
in~the~IMMIGRANT :
in~the~AX :
in~>~DRAW.NEAR(V) :
STRAND :
in~>~much~SPEAK(V) | in~the~EPIDEMIC | in~the~WORD :
in~>~much~SPEAK(V)~him :
in~>~much~SPEAK(V)~me :
in~>~much~SPEAK(V)~you(mp) :
in~>~much~SPEAK(V)~them(m) :
Bedad | ALONE :
in~MANDRAKES~s :
in~the~GENERATION :
in~GENERATION~s~him :
in~Dotan :
STRAND~s :
in~Dibon-Gad :
in~WORD~s :
STRAND~s~him :
STRAND~s :
in~Dinah :
in~>~THRESH(V) :
in~the~BLOOD | in~BLOOD :

in~Daphqah :
in~ROAD | in~the~ROAD :
in~her :
in~>~be~GRAPPLE(V)~him :
in~>~make~PROLONG(V) :
in~VANITY~s~them(m) :
in~>~PUSH.AWAY(V) :
in~>~make~GO.OUT(V)~him :
in~>~make~GO.OUT(V)~me :
in~>~make~GO.OUT(V)~you(ms) :
in~Hor :
in~>~be~SHAPE(V)~them(m) :
/ in~>~be~BRING.FORTH(V) :
in~>~make~DO.WELL(V)~him :
in~>~be~BE.HEAVY(V)~me :
in~>~be~SNIP.OFF(V) :
in~>~be~make~SNIP.OFF(V)~him :
in~>~be~ASSEMBLE(V) :
in~>~self~GATHER(V) :
in~>~self~KNOW(V) :
in~>~self~PROVIDE.PROTECTION(V)~him :
in~>~make~HIT(V)~me :
DISMAY :
in~Ham | in~them(m) :
BEAST | in~THEY :
BEAST~s :
BEAST :
BEAST~her :
BEAST~him :
BEAST~you(ms) :
BEAST~you(mp) :
BEAST~them(m) :
BEAST~us :
in~them(f) :
in~them(f) :
in~>~make~INHERIT(V) :
in~>~make~REST(V) :
in~>~make~GO.UP(V)~you(ms) :

in~>~OVERTURN(V) : בהפוך
in~>~make~DIVIDE.APART(V)~him : בהפרידו
in~>~make~STRUGGLE(V)~them(m) : בהצותם
in~>~make~COME.NEAR(V)~you(mp) : בהקריבכם
in~>~make~COME.NEAR(V)~them(m) : בהקריבם
in~>~make~BE.HARD(V)~her : בהקשותה
in~the~HILL | in~HILL : בהר
BRIGHT.SPOT~s : בהרות
in~HILL~s : בהרי
in~HILL~s : בהרים
in~>~make~RAISE.UP(V)~you(mp) : בהרימכם
in~MOUNT~them(m) : בהררם
BRIGHT.SPOT : בהרת
in~>~be~make~DESOLATE(V) : בהשמה
in~him : בו
!(ms)~COME(V) | >~COME(V) : בוא
!(mp)~COME(V) | >~COME(V)~him : בואו
>~COME(V)~me : בואי
>~COME(V)~you(ms) : בואך
>~COME(V)~you(ms)~& : בואכה
in~>~COME(V)~you(mp) : בואכם
>~COME(V)~them(m) : בואם
>~COME(V)~us : בואנו
THUMB : בוהן
RASH : בוהק
Buz : בוז
CLING(V)~ing(ms) : בוטח
WEEP(V)~ing(ms) : בוכה
WEEP(V)~ing(mp) : בוכים
BUILD(V)~ing(ms) : בונה
SWEET.SPICE : בוסם
BURN(V)~ing(ms) : בוער
Buqi : בוקי
MORNING : בוקר
CISTERN : בור
FLEE.AWAY(V)~ing(ms) : בורח
FLEE.AWAY(V)~ing(fs) : בורחת
she~did~be~much~BOIL(V) : בושלה
he~did~much~BE.ASHAMED(V) : בושש
in~ARROGANCE : בזדון

in~THIS | he~did~DISDAIN(V) : בזה
in~the~GOLD : בזהב
in~THIS : בזאת
in~DISCHARGE~him : בזובו
we~did~PLUNDER(V) : בזונו
they~did~PLUNDER(V) : בזזו
we~did~PLUNDER(V) : בזזנו
in~SWEAT : בזעת
in~BEARD : בזקן
in~BE.STRANGE(V)~s : בזרים
in~SEED~him : בזרעו
in~SEED~you(ms) : בזרעך
in~SEED~them(m) : בזרעם
in~Hhevron : בחברון
in~FEAST : בחג
in~FEAST~you(ms) : בחגך
in~NEW.MOON~him : בחדשו
in~the~COUPLING : בחוברת
in~the~NEW.MOON | in~NEW.MOON : בחודש
in~GRASP : בחוזק
/ in~the~SAND : בחול
in~MORTAR : בחומר
in~WANTING : בחוסר
in~the~OUTSIDE : בחוץ
in~CUSTOM : בחוקת
in~CUSTOM~s~me : בחוקתי
in~Hhor-Hagidgad : בחור הגידגד
CHOOSE(V)~ed(ms) : בחור
in~Hhorev : בחורב
in~BREASTPLATE : בחושן
in~>~FAIL(V)~& : בחטאה
in~FAILURE~him : בחטאו
in~RIDDLE~s : בחידות
in~LIVING~me : בחיי
in~LIVING~her : בחייה
in~LIVING~s~you(ms) : בחייך
in~LIVING~s : בחיים
in~HASTE : בחיפזון
in~BOSOM~him : בחיקו
in~BOSOM~you(ms) : בחיקך
in~SKILL : בחכמה
in~the~FAT : בחלב
in~the~DREAM : בחלום
in~DREAM~me : בחלומי
in~DRILLED : בחלל
in~the~DONKEY~s : בחמורים

in~the~FIVE :
in~the~FIVE~s :
in~PITIFUL :
in~the~SLIME :
in~FURY :
in~KINDNESS~you(ms) :
in~the~ STRAIGHT.TRUMPET :
in~HALF :
in~Hhats'tson- Tamar :
in~COURTYARD :
in~Hhatsarot :
in~COURTYARD~s~ them(m) :
in~Hhatsariym :
!(ms)~CHOOSE(V) | he~did~ CHOOSE(V) :
in~SWORD | in~the~SWORD :
in~the~DRIED.OUT :
in~SWORD~me :
in~Hharadah :
they~did~CHOOSE(V) :
in~the~ENGRAVING.TOOL :
in~the~MAGICIAN :
in~the~FLAMING :
in~PLOWING :
in~Hharan :
in~DECORATIVE.BAND :
in~Hheshbon :
in~Hhashmonah :
in~the~RING~s | in~RING~s :
in~the~CLEAN :
in~CLEANSING~him :
in~the~FUNCTIONAL | in~ FUNCTIONAL :
in~DIRTY :
in~DIRTY~them(m) :
SAFELY :
in~DIRTY :
in~much~DIRTY~you(mp) :
in~>~BE.DIRTY(V)~them(m) :
WOMB :
in~the~REED-BASKET :
PISTACHIO :
in~the~BABIES :
in~BEFORE :

in~me :
in~the~STREAM :
in~B'er-Sheva :
in~BEAST :
in~FIRSTBORN :
in~WEEPING :
in~UNAWARE :
in~SON~him :
in~DAUGHTER~s :
in~B'ney- Ya'aqan :
in~SON~s :
in~FLESH :
in~FLESH~her :
in~FLESH~you(mp) :
in~MASTER~s~him :
in~CATTLE~you(ms) :
in~COVENANT :
in~the~DRY.GROUND :
in~the~DRY.LAND :
in~VIRGINITY~s~her :
in~BORDER :
in~BORDER~him :
in~BORDER~s :
in~BORDER~you(ms) :
GARMENT~him :
in~GREAT :
GARMENT~s :
GARMENT~s~them(m) :
GARMENT~s~you(mp) :
in~SORROW :
in~EXPIRE(V) :
in~ON.ACCOUNT.OF :
in~ON.ACCOUNT.OF~you(fs) | in~ON.ACCOUNT.OF~you(ms) :
in~ON.ACCOUNT.OF~ you(mp) :
in~THEFT~him :
in~Gerar :
in~HAND :
in~WORD :
in~HONEY :
in~FISH :
in~HAND~her :
in~HAND~him :
/ in~HAND~me :
in~HAND~s~her :

in~HAND~s2~him :
in~HAND~you(ms) | in~HAND~you(fs) :
in~HAND~you(mp) :
in~HAND~them(m) :
in~LIKENESS :
in~LIKENESS~him :
in~BLOOD~s :
in~HAND~us :
in~ROAD~s~him :
in~YHWH :
in~>~EXIST(V) :
in~>~EXIST(V)~them(m) :
in~the~JUBILEE :
in~the~DAY | in~DAY :
in~DAY~him :
in~SETTLE(V)~ing(ms) :
in~TAIL~him :
in~ARM :
in~Yatvatah :
WOMB~her :
WOMB~you(fs) | WOMB~you(ms) :
in~the~WINE :
in~Yisra'eyl :
in~Yits'hhaq :
HOUSE :
in~HEAVINESS :
in~ARMAMENT~me :
FIRSTFRUIT~s :
FIRSTFRUIT~s~you(ms) :
FIRSTFRUIT~s :
in~Keziv :
in~UTENSIL :
in~UTENSIL~s~you(mp) :
in~WING~s~him :
in~HEART~him :
in~HEART~you(ms) :
in~HEART~them(m) :
in~the~BOY :
in~>~much~BRING.FORTH(V)~them(f) :
Bilhah :
Bilhan :
APART.FROM :
Bilam :
EXCEPT :

in~the~SEA :
in~MANY :
in~the~GENITALS~s~him :
in~much~INSCRIBE(V)~ing(ms) :
in~DAY~s :
in~DAY~s~him :
in~the~SEA~s | in~the~DAY~s :
in~RIGHT.HAND~him :
in~BUSINESS :
in~CAVE :
in~DEPTH~s :
in~AREA :
in~AREA~us :
in~CONTENTION :
in~>~DRAW(V) :
in~MORTAL.MAN~s :
BETWEEN | SON :
in~FREEWILL.OFFERING :
BETWEEN~him | !(mp)~UNDERSTAND(V) :
BETWEEN~s~us :
BETWEEN~them(m) :
in~>~EXTEND(V)~me :
BETWEEN~me :
Binyamin :
BETWEEN~s~us | BETWEEN~us :
BETWEEN~you(ms) | SON~you(ms) :
in~>~JOURNEY(V) :
in~YOUNG.AGE~her :
in~YOUNG.MAN~s~us :
in~>~LIFT.UP(V) :
in~FIELD :
in~Sedom :
in~WAGE~him :
in~LEFT.HAND :
in~LIP :
in~LIP~s2 :
in~Ya'aqov :
in~the~FOREST :
I~did~much~BURN(V) :
in~JUDGE~s :

in~FACE~s~you(mp) :
in~>~REGISTER(V) :
in~PRODUCE :
in~CORD :
in~AMBUSH :
EGG~s :
in~BURIAL.PLACE~them(m) :
in~ASSEMBLY :
in~ASSEMBLY~them(m) :
in~Qe'hey'latah :
PUNISHMENT :
LEVEL.VALLEY :
LEVEL.VALLEY :
in~EXTREMITY :
in~NEAR~s~me :
he~did~much~SEARCH.OUT(V) :
in~>~SEE(V)~them(m) :
in~FOURTH :
in~the~TENT.WALL :
in~TENT.WALL~s :
in~GOODS :
PRESENT~s :
KNEE~me | KNEE~s :
KNEE~s~him :
PRESENT :
PRESENT~me :
in~the~FLANK~s2 :
PRESENT~you(ms) :
in~>~FEED(V)~him :
in~Rephiydiym :
in~SHEET :
Birsha :
in~SWEARING :
in~SWEARING :
in~ERROR :
in~Yeshurun :
in~BOILS :
in~>~DWELL(V) :
in~Shekhem :
in~TITLE~him :
in~>~HEAR(V) :
in~TITLE~s~them(m) :
in~TITLE~me :
in~TITLE~you(ms) :
in~TWO :
in~TWO :

in~YEAR :
in~GATE~s~you(ms) :
in~JUDGMENT~s :
in~IMAGINATION :
in~TWO | in~WARP :
Beyt-El :
Beyt-Haran :
Beyt-Lehhem :
Beyt-Nimrah :
Beyt-Pe'or :
HOUSE :
in~INTELLIGENCE :
HOUSE~unto | HOUSE~her | DAUGHTER~her :
HOUSE~him | DAUGHTER~him :
HOUSE~me | DAUGHTER~me :
HOUSE~you(ms) | DAUGHTER~you(ms) :
DAUGHTER~us :
in~SECURITY.DEPOSIT :
CUT.PIECE~him :
in~OFFERING :
in~you(fs) | in~you(ms) :
in~the~SHEEP~s :
he~did~WEEP(V) :
in~the~ADMINISTRATOR~s :
in~the~STRENGTH | in~STRENGTH :
in~STRENGTH~him :
in~STRENGTH~you(ms) :
in~ALL | in~the~ALL :
in~the~COVERING :
FIRSTBORN :
BIRTHRIGHT :
FIRSTBORN~him :
FIRSTBORN~me :
FIRSTBORN~you(ms) :
BIRTHRIGHT~him :
BIRTHRIGHT~me :
BIRTHRIGHT~you(ms) :
in~TUNIC~s~them(m) :
WEEPING :
in~BAG~you(ms) :
TIME.OF.WEEPING~him :
you(mp)~did~WEEP(V) :
in~ALL :

in~you$^{(mp)}$:
in~Kena'an~of :
in~WING~s~them$^{(m)}$:
in~the~SHEEP~s :
in~SILVER :
in~PALM :
in~PALM~him :
in~>~much~COVER$^{(V)}$~you$^{(ms)}$:
in~DEPRESSION :
in~VINEYARD :
in~the~WRITE$^{(V)}$~ed$^{(mp)}$:
in~the~SHOULDER.PIECE :
in~HEART :
in~Lavan :
in~GLIMMERING :
in~>~BRING.FORTH$^{(V)}$:
in~BLAZING~s~them$^{(m)}$:
they~did~WEAR.OUT$^{(V)}$:
in~NOT :
in~Luz :
in~Lot :
MIX$^{(V)}$~ed$^{(ms)}$:
in~the~LOOP~s :
MIX$^{(V)}$~ed$^{(fs)}$:
MIX$^{(V)}$~ed$^{(fp)}$:
I~>~WEAR.OUT$^{(V)}$:
in~the~BREAD :
in~BREAD~him :
in~SECRET~s~them$^{(m)}$:
UNAWARE :
in~HEART~him :
in~Livnah :
in~>~BRING.FORTH$^{(V)}$~her :
in~the~NIGHT | in~NIGHT :
Beli'ya'al | UNAWARE~&~ he~will~Gain$^{(V)}$:
in~>~WALK$^{(V)}$~you$^{(ms)}$:
he~did~MIX$^{(V)}$:
Bela :
Balaq :
she~did~WEAR.OUT$^{(V)}$:
in~them$^{(m)}$:
in~HUNDRED :
in~the~PESTILENCE :
in~the~ MORTAR.AND.PESTLE :
in~WHAT :
in~the~BRANCH :
in~Moseyrot :
in~APPOINTED :
in~APPOINTED~him :
in~APPOINTED~s~ you$^{(mp)}$:
in~APPOINTED~them$^{(m)}$:
in~>~FIND$^{(V)}$~you$^{(mp)}$:
in~SETTLING~them$^{(m)}$:
in~Mosheh :
in~DEATH | Bamot | PLATFORM~s :
in~DEATH~him :
PLATFORM~s :
PLATFORM~s~you$^{(mp)}$:
PLATFORM~s~them$^{(m)}$:
in~DEATH~them$^{(m)}$ | PLATFORM~s~them$^{(m)}$:
in~the~JOINT :
in~the~VISION :
in~the~CAMP :
in~the~SEARCHING :
in~the~BRANCH :
in~BRANCH~him :
in~BRANCH~you$^{(ms)}$:
in~WATER~s2 :
in~CHOSEN :
in~ FORTIFICATION~s :
in~the~WILDERNESS | in~ WILDERNESS :
in~the~MEASUREMENT :
in~Mid'yan :
in~the~ALTAR :
in~BEST :
in~the~WATER~s2 | in~ WATER~s2 :
in~the~SINGE.SCAR :
in~ROOF.COVERING :
in~WORTH :
in~SETTING~s~ them$^{(m)}$:
in~the~BATTLE :
in~the~DEPOSIT :
in~POVERTY :
in~NUMBER :
in~NUMBER~them$^{(m)}$:

in~Mits'rayim :
in~LIVESTOCK :
in~LIVESTOCK~you(mp) :
in~LIVESTOCK~you(ms) :
in~CHARIOT :
in~DECEIT :
in~LYING.PLACE~her :
in~LYING.PLACE~him :
in~CUSTODY | in~the~CUSTODY :
in~CUSTODY~s~them(m) :
in~CHARGE :
in~NARROW.WAY :
in~STAVE~s~them(m) :
in~the~DECISION | in~DECISION :
in~DECISION~s~me :
in~the~WEIGHT :
in~WEIGHT~him :
in~Mitqah :
in~Makhpelah :
in~the~PLACE.OF.LODGING :
in~the~SALT :
in~KING :
in~LOAD :
in~Mas'sah :
in~TRIAL~s :
in~the~HIGHWAY :
in~ABDOMEN~s~you(ms) :
in~STAIR.STEP~s :
in~TRANSGRESSION~them(m) :
in~WORK :
in~the~CAVE :
in~the~SMACKED | in~SMACKED :
in~Maqheylot :
in~the~AREA | in~AREA :
in~the~ROD :
in~the~ROD~s :
in~ROD~me :
in~the~APPEARANCE :
in~REFLECTION~s :
in~Marah :
in~the~BOILING.POT :
in~the~AWL :
in~DIE(V)~ing(ms) | in~the~DIE(V)~ing(ms) :
in~SUM~her :
in~WAIST~him :
Ben-Oni :
Ben-Amiy :
SON :
in~the~SOUTH :
in~the~TOUCH | in~TOUCH :
in~>~TOUCH(V)~him :
in~>~SMITE(V)~him :
SON~her | !(ms)~BUILD(V) | he~did~BUILD(V) :
SON~him | they~did~BUILD(V) | in~us | !(mp)~BUILD(V) :
in~PLUMAGE~her :
DAUGHTER~s :
DAUGHTER~s~me :
DAUGHTER~s~her :
DAUGHTER~s~them(m) :
DAUGHTER~s~him :
DAUGHTER~s~you(ms) :
DAUGHTER~s~you(mp) :
DAUGHTER~s~us :
DAUGHTER~s~them(m) :
in~WADI | in~the~WADI :
in~INHERITANCE :
in~INHERITANCE :
in~INHERITANCE~him :
in~INHERITANCE~you(ms) :
in~INHERITANCE~you(mp) :
in~INHERITANCE~them(m) :
B'ney-Ya'aqan :
SON~s | SON~me | SON~s~me :
in~CARCASS :
in~CARCASS~her :
in~CARCASS~them(m) :
in~REMOVAL :
in~REMOVAL~her :
SON~s~her :
SON~s~them(m) :
SON~s~him :
SON~s~you(ms) :
in~CRAFTINESS~s~them(m) :

SON~s~you(mp) :
SON~s :
in~FISSURE :
you(ms)~did~BUILD(V) :
SON~you(fs) :
SON~us :
in~>~JOURNEY(V)~them(m) :
in~the~SOUL | in~SOUL :
in~SOUL~him :
in~SOUL~s~them(m) :
in~>~PIERCE.THROUGH(V)~him :
in~the~WOMAN~s :
in~USURY :
in~the~ELEVATION :
in~NET :
in~the~FIELD | in~FIELD :
in~FIELD~you(ms) :
in~RAM :
in~CONFIDENCE~them(m) :
in~the~BOOTH~s | in~Suk'kot :
in~the~HORSE~s :
in~the~REEDS :
in~Suphah :
in~GRAY-HEADED :
in~BURDEN~s~them(m) :
in~the~LIME :
in~REJOICING :
in~APPAREL~s~them(m) :
in~HATE :
in~HATE :
in~the~WICKER.BASKET | in~WICKER.BASKET :
in~OUTER.GARMENT~him :
in~the~CLIFF :
SWEET.SPICE :
SWEET.SPICE~s :
Basmat :
in~the~SIGHTLESSNESS :
in~Se'iyr :
in~the~BASIN :
in~the~SCROLL | in~SCROLL :
in~SACK~him :
FLESH :
FLESH~her :
FLESH~him :
FLESH~you(ms) :
FLESH~them(m) :
FLESH~us :
in~the~HIDING :
in~THICK :
in~SERVANT~me :
in~SERVANT~you(ms) :
in~the~SERVICE :
in~the~SERVICE :
in~the~PLEDGE~him :
in~the~CROSS.OVER(V)~ed(ms) | in~CROSS.OVER(V) | in~>~CROSS.OVER(V) :
in~the~CROSS.OVER(V)~ed(ms)~her :
in~the~CROSS.OVER(V)~ed(ms)~you(ms) | in~the~CROSS.OVER(V)~ed(ms)~you(fs) :
in~the~CROSS.OVER(V)~ed(ms)~them(m) :
in~OTHER.SIDE :
in~Evronah :
in~>~CROSS.OVER(V)~you(ms) :
in~>~CROSS.OVER(V)~you(mp) :
in~the~CART~s :
in~UNTIL :
in~the~COMPANY :
in~UNTIL~him :
in~UNTIL~me :
in~UNTIL~you(ms) :
in~UNTIL~them(m) :
in~Eden :
in~the~COMPANY :
in~YET.AGAIN :
in~YET.AGAIN~him :
in~YET.AGAIN~me :
in~the~EXCEED(V)~ing(ms) :
in~TWISTEDNESS :
in~YOKE :
MARRY(V)~ed(fs) :
in~the~OMER :
in~the~TWISTEDNESS~s :
in~the~TWISTEDNESS~them(m) :
in~DO(V)~ing(mp) :
in~the~FLYER :
Be'or | in~SKIN | in~the~SKIN :

in~SKIN~him :בעורו
in~NECK :בעורף
in~BOLDNESS~you(ms) :בעזך
in~HELP~me :בעזרי
in~HELP~you(ms) :בעזרך
in~the~GOAT~s :בעיזים
in~Iyey-Ha'a'variym :בעיי העברים
in~EYE :בעין
in~EYE~him :בעינו
in~EYE~s2 | in~EYE~s2~me :בעיני
in~EYE~s2~her :בעיניה
in~EYE~s2~them(m) :בעיניהם
in~EYE~s2~him :בעיניו
in~EYE~s2~you(fs) :בעינייך
in~the~Eynayim :בעיניים
in~EYE~s2~you(ms) :בעיניך
in~EYE~s2~you(mp) :בעיניכם
in~EYE~s2~us :בעינינו
in~EYE~you(ms) :בעינך
in~HARDSHIP~you(ms) :בעיצבון
in~the~CITY | in~CITY :בעיר
CATTLE~her :בעירוה
CATTLE~you(mp) :בעירכם
CATTLE~them(m) :בעירם
in~APPOINTED.TIME~him :בעיתו
in~APPOINTED.TIME~them(m) :בעיתם
Ba'al-Hhanan :בעל־חנן
Ba'al-Me'on :בעל מעון
Ba'al-Pe'or :בעל פעור
Ba'al-Tsephon :בעל צפון
Ba'al-Tsephon :בעל־צפון
MASTER | Ba'al :בעל
MASTER~her :בעלה
in~>~GO.UP(V)~me :בעלותי
in~>~GO.UP(V)~you(ms) :בעלותך
MASTER~s :בעלי
MASTER~s~him :בעליו
in~Almon-Divlatayim :בעלמון דיבלתימה
in~the~PEOPLE | in~PEOPLE :בעם
in~>~STAND(V)~him :בעמדו
in~PILLAR :בעמוד
in~PEOPLE~me :בעמי
in~PEOPLE~s~him :בעמיו
in~PEOPLE~s~you(ms) :בעמיך
in~the~PEOPLE~s :בעמים
in~the~NEIGHBOR~him :בעמיתו
in~PEOPLE~you(ms) :בעמך
in~the~Amaleq :בעמלק
in~VALLEY | in~the~VALLEY :בעמק
in~AFFLICTION~me :בעניי
in~CLOUD :בענן
in~>~much~CONJURE(V)~me :בענני
in~the~TENTH.ONE | in~TENTH.ONE :בעשור
in~>~DO(V)~her :בעשותה
in~the~TENTH :בעשירי
in~TEN~s :בעשרים
in~DIRT :בעפר
in~Ephron :בעפרון
in~the~TREE :בעץ
in~DISTRESSING.PAIN :בעצב
in~Etsi'on-Gaver :בעציון גבר
in~BONE | in~the~BONE :בעצם
in~HEEL :בעקב
in~Ar :בער
in~the~EVENING | in~MIXTURE | in~the~MIXTURE :בערב
in~the~DESERT :בערבה
in~DESERT~s :בערבות
she~did~BURN(V) :בערה
in~CITY~s :בערי
in~CITY~s~them(m) :בעריהם
in~CITY~s~you(mp) :בעריכם
in~CITY~s :בערים
in~ARRANGEMENT~you(ms) :בערכך
in~SUBTLETY :בערמה
in~ONE :בעשתי
in~Ashterot-Qar'nayim :בעשתרות־קרניים
in~Ashterot :בעשתרות
in~the~APPOINTED.TIME | in~APPOINTED.TIME :בעת
in~Padan-Aram :בפדן־ארם
in~Punon :בפונון
in~AWE :בפחד
in~MOUTH | in~MOUTH~me :בפי
in~>~REACH(V)~him :בפיגעו
in~MOUTH~her :בפיה
in~MOUTH~them(m) :בפיהם

in~MOUTH~him : בפיו
in~MOUTH~you(ms) : בפיך
in~DEPOSITED : בפיקדון
in~the~FLAX~s : בפישתים
in~FACE~s~her : בפניה
in~FACE~s~him : בפניו
in~FACE~s~you(ms) : בפניך
in~FACE~s : בפנים
in~the~FOOTSTEP | in~FOOTSTEP : בפעם
in~BULL : בפר
in~the~SKILLET : בפרור
in~WHIP : בפרך
in~Paroh : בפרעה
in~OPENING : בפתח
in~INSTANT : בפתע
in~>~GO.OUT(V) : בצאת
in~>~GO.OUT(V)~him : בצאתו
in~>~GO.OUT(V)~me : בצאתי
in~>~GO.OUT(V)~you(ms) : בצאתך
in~>~GO.OUT(V)~you(mp) : בצאתכם
in~>~GO.OUT(V)~them(m) : בצאתם
in~the~ARMY : בצבא
in~STEADFAST : בצדק
in~the~GLISTENING~s2 : בצהריים
in~FLOCKS | in~the~FLOCKS : בצואן
in~FLOCKS~you(ms) : בצואנך
in~FLOCKS~us : בצואננו
in~Tso'ar : בצוער
in~the~BOULDER : בצור
FENCE.IN(V)~ed(fp) : בצורות
in~SIDE~her : בצידה
in~SIDE~s~you(mp) : בצידיכם
in~STEADFASTNESS~me : בצידקתי
in~STEADFASTNESS~you(ms) : בצידקתך
VINTAGE : בציר
in~SHADOW : בצל
Betsaleyl : בצלאל
in~IMAGE : בצלם
in~IMAGE~him : בצלמו
in~Tsalmonah : בצלמונה
in~IMAGE~us : בצלמנו
in~the~THIRST : בצמא
in~the~WOOL : בצמר

PROFIT : בצע
in~the~VEIL : בצעיף
in~the~FROG~s : בצפרדעים
she~did~SWELL.UP(V) : בצקה
DOUGH~him : בצקו
in~the~NARROW | Betser : בצר
in~GRAVE | in~the~GRAVE : בקבר
in~Qadesh : בקדש
in~the~SPECIAL~s : בקדשים
in~the~SPECIAL | in~SPECIAL : בקודש
in~VOICE : בקול
in~VOICE~her : בקולה
in~VOICE~him : בקולו
in~VOICE~me : בקולי
in~VOICE~you(mp) : בקולכם
in~VOICE~us : בקולנו
in~HANDFUL~him : בקומצו
in~>~SEVER(V)~you(ms) : בקוצרך
in~>~TAKE(V)~him : בקחתו
in~Qivrot-Hata'awah : בקיברות-התאוה
in~GRAVE~me : בקיברי
in~ZEALOUSNESS~me : בקינאתי
in~INSIDE~her : בקירבה
in~INSIDE~him : בקירבו
in~INSIDE~me : בקירבי
in~INSIDE~you(ms) : בקירבך
in~INSIDE~you(mp) : בקירבכם
in~INSIDE~us : בקירבנו
in~WALL~s : בקירות
in~Qiryat-Arba : בקירית-ארבע
in~the~GRAIN.STALK : בקמה
in~RISE(V)~ing(mp)~them(m) : בקמיהם
in~GRAIN.STALK : בקמת
in~>~much~BE.ZEALOUS(V)~him : בקנאו
in~STALK | in~the~STALK : בקנה
BEQA : בקע
in~EXTREMITY~him : בקצהו
CATTLE : בקר
in~INSIDE : בקרב
in~>~COME.NEAR(V)~them(m) : בקרבתם
in~the~BALD.SPOT : בקרחת
in~BALD.SPOT~him : בקרחתו
in~CONTRARY : בקרי

CATTLE~you(ms) :
CATTLE~you(mp) :
CATTLE~them(m) :
in~HORN~s~him :
in~the~HOOK~s :
in~BOTTOM :
GRAIN :
he~did~SHAPE(V) :
he~did~SHAPE(V)~them(m) :
in~HEAD~s~you(mp) :
in~PRIME :
I~did~SHAPE(V) :
in~Ravah :
in~FOOT :
in~FOOT~s~me :
in~FOOT~s~them(m) :
in~FOOT~s~you(ms) :
in~FOOT~s~you(mp) :
in~FOOT~you(ms) :
Bered | HAILSTONES :
in~>~PURSUE(V)~them(m) :
in~>~GO.DOWN(V) :
in~TROUGH~s :
>~SHAPE(V) :
in~HEAD :
in~HEAD~him :
in~HEAD~them(m) :
in~WIND :
in~WIDTH :
in~WIND~you(ms) :
KNEEL(V)~ed(ms) :
IRON :
!(ms)~FLEE.AWAY(V) | he~did~ FLEE.AWAY(V) :
in~the~STREET :
in~the~MILLSTONE~s :
in~Rahhel :
SHAPE :
FED.FAT~s :
in~the~FIRST :
in~the~FIRST :
in~DISPUTE~him :
in~>~GO.DOWN(V)~him :
in~AROMA :
WOOD.BAR~s~him :
WOOD.BAR~s :
WOOD.BAR~s~him :
WOOD.BAR~s :
in~VEHICLE~him :
in~Rimon-Perets :
in~Risah :
Beri'ah :
in~WAYWARDNESS :
COVENANT :
COVENANT~him :
COVENANT~me :
in~Ritmah :
>~much~KNEEL(V) | he~did~ much~KNEEL(V) | he~will~much~ KNEEL(V) :
PRESENT :
he~did~much~KNEEL(V)~him :
he~did~much~KNEEL(V)~you(ms) :
!(ms)~much~KNEEL(V)~me :
you(ms)~did~much~KNEEL(V) :
I~did~much~KNEEL(V) :
you(ms)~did~much~ KNEEL(V)~me :
Barneya :
Bera | in~the~DYSFUNCTIONAL | in~DYSFUNCTIONAL :
in~the~HUNGER | in~HUNGER :
in~DYSFUNCTIONAL :
in~COMPANION~him :
in~LOUD.NOISE :
in~COMPANION~you(ms) :
in~DYSFUNCTIONAL~me :
FLASH :
in~WEEK~s~ you(mp) :
in~the~STAFF :
in~the~CAPTIVE :
in~the~CAPTIVITY :
in~SEVEN :
in~the~GRAIN.SEEDS :
in~CEASING~him :
in~CEASING~s~ you(mp) :
in~which~ALSO :
in~ Shaweh-Qiryatayim :
in~OX :
in~the~BOILS :
in~the~CONSUMPTION :

in~>~much~DAMAGE$^{(V)}$:
in~the~CAPTIVE :
in~SEVEN :
in~SEVEN~s :
in~>~CRACK$^{(V)}$~me :
in~>~SETTLE$^{(V)}$~you$^{(ms)}$:
in~>~SETTLE$^{(V)}$~you$^{(mp)}$:
in~SETTLE$^{(V)}$~us :
in~MADNESS :
in~Shitiym :
in~>~LIE.DOWN$^{(V)}$~her :
in~WATERING.TROUGH~s :
in~BOILED :
!$^{(mp)}$~BOIL$^{(V)}$ | !$^{(mp)}$~much~BOIL$^{(V)}$:
in~COMPLETENESS :
in~>~much~SEND$^{(V)}$:
in~>~much~SEND$^{(V)}$~me :
in~>~much~SEND$^{(V)}$:
in~TITLE :
in~TITLE~s :
in~the~SKY~s2 :
in~the~OIL | in~OIL :
in~>~HEAR$^{(V)}$~him :
in~TOOTH | Bashan :
in~the~YEAR | in~YEAR :
in~the~YEAR~s :
in~GATE :
in~GATE~s~you$^{(mp)}$:
in~SHEQEL :
in~the~SWARMER :
in~the~WARP :
DAUGHTER :
in~the~VESSEL :
in~the~PRODUCTION :
in~PATTERN~them$^{(m)}$:
Betu'el :
in~MIDST | in~the~MIDST :
in~MIDST~her :
in~MIDST~him :
in~MIDST~you$^{(mp)}$:
in~MIDST~them$^{(m)}$:
in~MIDST~us :
VIRGIN :
VIRGINITY~s :
VIRGINITY~s | VIRGIN~s :
in~KERMES :

VIRGIN :
in~DISGUSTING~s :
in~TAMBOURINE :
in~TAMBOURINE~s :
in~TEACHING~me :
in~the~FIRST.TIME :
in~Tahhat :
in~LOWER.PART :
HOUSE~s :
HOUSE~s~them$^{(m)}$:
HOUSE~s~you$^{(ms)}$:
HOUSE~s~you$^{(mp)}$:
HOUSE~s :
HOUSE~s~us :
in~NINE :
in~>~GIVE$^{(V)}$~him :
in~>~GIVE$^{(V)}$~you$^{(ms)}$:
in~the~BLUE :
in~MATURE :
in~the~OVEN | in~OVEN :
he~did~CUT.IN.TWO$^{(V)}$:
in~Terahh :
in~>~GIVE$^{(V)}$:
he~did~RISE.UP$^{(V)}$:
Ge'u'eyl :
>~RISE.UP$^{(V)}$:
>~REDEEM$^{(V)}$:
REDEMPTION :
REDEMPTION :
REDEMPTION~him :
MAJESTY :
MAJESTY~you$^{(ms)}$:
PRIDE~you$^{(ms)}$:
you$^{(ms)}$~did~REDEEM$^{(V)}$:
HIGH~her :
BORDER :
BORDER~him :
BORDER~s :
BORDER~you$^{(ms)}$:
BORDER~you$^{(mp)}$:
BRAVERY :
ARCH ~s :
BOWL :
BOWL~me :
BOWL~s~her :
BOWL~s :
OWNER :

FEMALE.OWNER~her : גבירתה
FEMALE.OWNER~me : גבירתי
FEMALE.OWNER~you$^{(fs)}$: גבירתך
they~did~BOUND$^{(V)}$: גבלו
EDGING : גבלות
WARRIOR : גבר
they~did~OVERCOME$^{(V)}$: גברו
ROOF~him : גגו
Gad | CORIANDER : גד
BAND : גדוד
GREAT : גדול
GREAT : גדולה
GREAT~s : גדולות
GREAT~s : גדולים
MALE.KID | Gad'diy : גדי
Gad'di'eyl : גדיאל
MALE.KID~s : גדיי
TASSEL~s : גדילים
STACK : גדיש
he~did~MAGNIFY$^{(V)}$ | >~much~MAGNIFY$^{(V)}$: גדל
she~will~MAGNIFY$^{(V)}$: גדלה
MAGNIFICENCE~him : גדלו
MAGNIFICENCE~you$^{(ms)}$: גדלך
FENCE : גדר
REDEEM$^{(V)}$~ing$^{(ms)}$: גואל
REDEEM$^{(V)}$~ing$^{(ms)}$~him : גואלו
MAGNIFICENCE : גודל
SHEAR$^{(V)}$~ing$^{(mp)}$: גוזזי
YOUNG.PIGEON~s~him : גוזליו
NATION : גוי
NATION~s : גויי
Goyim | NATION~s : גויים
BODY~us : גויתנו
Golan : גולן
BULRUSH : גומא
Gomer : גומר
STEAL$^{(V)}$~ing$^{(ms)}$: גונב
I~did~be~much~STEAL$^{(V)}$: גונבתי
>~be~much~STEAL$^{(V)}$: גונוב
he~did~EXPIRE$^{(V)}$: גוע
we~did~EXPIRE$^{(V)}$: גוענו
GOPHER : גופר
!$^{(ms)}$~IMMIGRATE$^{(V)}$ | WHELP : גור
LOT : גורל
LOT~s : גורלות
Goren-Ha'atad : גורןהאטד

FLOOR : גורן
CAST.OUT$^{(V)}$~ing$^{(ms)}$: גורש
they~did~be~much~CAST.OUT$^{(V)}$: גורשו
Goshen : גושן
Goshen~unto : גושנה
FLEECE : גז
PLUCK.AWAY$^{(V)}$~ed$^{(ms)}$: גזול
HEWN.STONE : גזית
he~did~PLUCK.AWAY$^{(V)}$: גזל
they~did~PLUCK.AWAY$^{(V)}$: גזלו
UNINHABITED : גזרה
BELLY : גחון
BELLY~you$^{(ms)}$: גחונך
EMBER~s : גחלי
Gahham : גחם
COURAGEOUS : גיבור
BARE.SPOT : גיבח
HUNCHBACK : גיבן
BUDDING : גיבעול
KNOLL~s : גיבעות
SINEW : גיד
Gidoni : גידעוני
FENCE~s : גידרות
Giyhhon : גיחון
he~did~much~REMOVE.THE.COVER$^{(V)}$: גילה
IDOL~s~them$^{(m)}$: גילוליהם
IDOL~s~you$^{(mp)}$: גילוליכם
Gil'ad : גילעד
Gil'ad~unto : גילעדה
she~did~much~REMOVE.THE.COVER$^{(V)}$: גילתה
RAIN.SHOWER~s~you$^{(mp)}$: גישמיכם
>~DRAW.NEAR$^{(V)}$~him : גישתו
MOUND : גל
Galeyd : גלעד
/ ALSO : גם
they~did~YIELD$^{(V)}$~you$^{(ms)}$: גמלוך
Gemali : גמלי
Gamli'eyl : גמליאל
CAMEL ~s~him : גמליו
CAMEL ~s~you$^{(ms)}$: גמליך
CAMEL ~s : גמלים
we~did~YIELD$^{(V)}$: גמלנו
GARDEN : גן

you[ms]~did~STEAL[V] :
she~did~STEAL[V]~them[m] :
STEAL[V]~ed[ms] | >~STEAL[V] :
STEAL[V]~ed[fs] :
she~did~CAST.AWAY[V] :
I~did~CAST.AWAY[V]~ them[m] :
Gatam :
GRAPEVINE :
GRAPEVINE~them[m] :
BRIMSTONE :
IMMIGRANT | he~did~ IMMIGRATE[V] :
Gera :
IRRITATION :
GERAH | CUD :
they~did~IMMIGRATE[V] | IMMIGRANT~him :
CAST.OUT[V]~ed[fs] :
AX :
Gerizim :
IMMIGRANT~s :
CARTILAGE :
BEATEN.GRAIN :
Gerar :
Gerar~unto :
>~much~CAST.OUT[V] | BROUGHT.OUT :
Gershom :
Gershon :
you[ms]~did~much~ CAST.OUT[V] :
you[ms]~did~IMMIGRATE[V] :
I~did~IMMIGRATE[V] :
![ms]~DRAW.NEAR[V] :
![ms]~DRAW.NEAR[V]~& :
![mp]~DRAW.NEAR[V] :
TOUGHNESS~you[ms] :
Devorah :
WORD | ![ms]~much~SPEAK[V] | EPIDEMIC | >~much~SPEAK[V] :
>~much~SPEAK[V]~him | ![mp]~ much~SPEAK[V] | WORD~him :
WORD~s~me | WORD~me :
WORD~s~him :
WORD~s :
>~much~SPEAK[V]~you[ms] :

HONEY :
FISH :
FISH~s :
BANNER :
CEREAL :
CEREAL~you[ms] :
Dedan :
SPEAK[V]~ing[ms] :
SPEAK[V]~ing[fp] :
SPEAK[V]~ing[mp] :
UNCLE :
MANDRAKES~s :
MANDRAKES~s :
UNCLE~him :
UNCLE~s~them[f] :
AUNT~him :
AUNT~you[ms] :
ILLNESS :
GENERATION :
GENERATION~s~you[mp] :
SEEK[V]~ing[ms] :
>~ILL[V]~her :
Dotan~unto :
SUFFICIENT :
SLANDER :
Dibon :
he~did~much~SPEAK[V] :
she~did~much~SPEAK[V] :
they~did~much~SPEAK[V] | he~did~much~SPEAK[V]~him :
WORD~s | Divriy :
WORD~s~them[m] :
WORD~s~you[mp] :
we~did~much~SPEAK[V] :
you[ms]~did~much~SPEAK[V] :
I~did~much~SPEAK[V] :
you[mp]~did~much~ SPEAK[V] :
SLANDER :
SLANDER~them[m] :
BANNER~him :
THRESHING :
SUFFICIENT~them[m] :
I~did~much~ RESEMBLE[V] :
BLOOD~you[mp] :
PLEA :

Dinah :דינה
Dinhavah :דינהבה
Diqlah :דיקלה
Dishon :דישון
Dishan :דישן
BROKEN :דכא
they~did~GROUND.TO.PIECES$^{(V)}$:דכו
HELPLESS :דל
he~did~DRAW.UP$^{(V)}$:דלה
>~DRAW.UP$^{(V)}$:דלוה
HELPLESS~s :דלות
you$^{(ms)}$~did~INFLAME$^{(V)}$:דלקת
DOOR~s :דליתים
BLOOD :דם
BLOOD~her :דמה
BLOOD~him :דמו
BLOOD~s :דמי
BLOOD~s~her :דמיה
BLOOD~s~them$^{(m)}$:דמיהם
BLOOD~s~him :דמיו
BLOOD~s :דמים
BLOOD~them$^{(m)}$:דמם
Dameseq :דמסק
Dan | MODERATE$^{(V)}$~ing$^{(ms)}$:דן
he~did~MODERATE$^{(V)}$~me :דנני
!$^{(ms)}$~KNOW$^{(V)}$:דע
De'u'eyl :דעואל
DISCERNMENT :דעת
I~did~KNOW$^{(V)}$:דעתי
SCRAWNY | he~did~BEAT.SMALL$^{(V)}$:דק
SCRAWNY :דקה
SCRAWNY~s :דקות
FREE.FLOWING :דרור
>~SEEK$^{(V)}$:דרוש
ROAD | he~did~TAKE.STEPS$^{(V)}$:דרך
ROAD~him :דרכו
ROAD~me :דרכי
ROAD~s~him :דרכיו
ROAD~s~you$^{(ms)}$:דרכיך
ROAD~s :דרכיכם
ROAD~s :דרכים
ROAD~you$^{(ms)}$:דרכך
he~did~SEEK$^{(V)}$:דרש
GRASS :דשא
Datan :דתן
~ ? :ה
LO :הא

the~LOST.THING :האבדה
the~FATHER~s :האבות
the~MELON~s :האבטיחים
the~GREEN.GRAIN :האביב
>~make~PERISH$^{(V)}$~him :האבידו
the~NEEDY :האביון
the~MOURNING :האבל
the~STONE :האבן
the~SASH :האבנט
the~STONE.STOOL :האבניים
the~STONE~s :האבנים
the~POOL~s :האגמים
the~RED :האדום
the~LORD :האדון
the~LORD~s :האדונים
the~HUMAN :האדם
the~GROUND :האדמה
the~LOVE$^{(V)}$~ed$^{(fs)}$:האהובה
the~NECROMANCER~s :האובות
the~TENT :האוהל
the~TENT~unto :האוהלה
the~FOODSTUFF :האוכל
the~EAT$^{(V)}$~ing$^{(mp)}$:האוכלים
the~EAT$^{(V)}$~ing$^{(fs)}$:האוכלת
the~SECURE$^{(V)}$~ing$^{(ms)}$:האומן
?~INDEED :האומנם
the~SAY$^{(V)}$~ing$^{(ms)}$:האומר
the~GATHER$^{(V)}$~ing$^{(ms)}$:האוסף
the~BAKE$^{(V)}$~ing$^{(mp)}$:האופים
the~LIGHT :האור
the~Uriym :האורים
the~SIGN :האות
the~SIGN~s :האותות
the~HYSSOP :האזוב
he~did~make~WEIGH.OUT$^{(V)}$:האזין
!$^{(ms)}$~make~WEIGH.OUT$^{(V)}$~& :האזינה
!$^{(mp)}$~make~WEIGH.OUT$^{(V)}$:האזינו
!$^{(fp)}$~make~WEIGH.OUT$^{(V)}$:האזנה
the~Azni~of :האזני
the~NATIVE :האזרח
the~UNIT :האחד
the~TAKE.HOLD$^{(V)}$~ed$^{(ms)}$:האחוז
?~BROTHER~s~you$^{(mp)}$:האחיכם
the~Ahhiram~of :האחירמי
the~LAST :האחרון

the~OTHER :
the~UNIT :
the~HAWK :
the~BUCK :
the~BUCK :
the~BUCK~s :
?~IF :
the~Eym~s :
the~I'ezer~of :
the~EYPHAH :
the~MAN :
the~WOMAN | the~ FIRE.OFFERING :
the~>~be~EAT(V) :
I~did~make~EAT(V) :
the~THESE | the~MIGHTY.ONE :
the~THESE | the~OAK | the~ OATH :
the~Elohiym :
the~GREAT.TREE :
the~Eylon~of :
the~OATH~s :
the~RUMP :
the~WORTHLESS~s :
?~I~will~WALK(V) :
the~THOUSAND :
the~THOUSAND~s :
the~MOTHER :
the~BONDWOMAN | the~ FOREARM :
the~BONDWOMAN~s :
the~Emor~of :
the~Eym~s :
he~did~make~SECURE(V) :
he~did~make~SAY(V)~ you(ms) :
you(mp)~did~make~ SECURE(V) :
you(ms)~did~make~SAY(V) :
the~TRUTH | ?~TRUTH :
?~I :
the~HERON :
the~MAN~s :
the~GATHERING :
the~PRISONER~s :
>~be~GATHER(V) :
!(mp)~be~GATHER(V) :
!(mp)~be~TIE.UP(V) :
the~Asri'eyl~of :
?~MOREOVER | the~NOSE :
the~EYPHAH :
the~EPHOD :
the~CHICK~s :
the~Areliy :
the~SWARMING.LOCUST :
the~FOUR~s :
the~Argov :
the~PURPLE :
the~Ard~of :
the~Arwad~of :
the~BOX :
the~CEDAR :
the~Aram~of :
the~HARE :
the~LAND :
the~LAND~s :
the~FIRE :
the~Ashbeyl~of :
the~CLUSTER :
the~GUILT :
the~YOU :
the~SHE-DONKEY :
the~Atariym :
the~COME(V)~ing(ms) | !(ms)~make~ COME(V) :
the~COME(V)~ing(fs) :
the~COME(V)~ing(fp) :
the~COME(V)~ing(mp) :
the~WELL :
the~WELL~s :
you(ms)~did~make~COME(V) :
I~did~make~COME(V) :
you(mp)~did~make~COME(V) :
the~GARMENT :
the~GARMENT~s :
the~STRAND :
the~AMBER :
the~TIN :
the~STRAND~s :
!(ms)~PROVIDE(V)~& :
the~BEAST :
the~BRIGHT.SPOT :
!(mp)~PROVIDE(V) :
?~>~COME(V) :

the~SWEET.SPICE : הבושם
the~MORNING : הבוקר
the~CISTERN : הבור
the~CISTERN~unto : הבורה
the~CISTERN~s : הבורות
the~PLUNDER : הבז
!(ms)~make~STARE(V) : הבט
he~did~make~COME(V) | >~ make~COME(V) : הביא
!(ms)~make~COME(V) : הביאה
!(mp)~make~COME(V) | they~ did~make~COME(V) | he~did~make~ COME(V)~him : הביאו
we~did~make~ COME(V)~them(m) : הביאונום
I~did~make~COME(V)~ him : הביאותיו
you(ms)~did~make~ COME(V)~us : הביאותנו
>~make~COME(V)~you(mp) : הביאכם
he~did~make~COME(V)~ me : הביאני
the~HOUSE : הביית
the~FIRSTFRUIT~s : הביכורים
the~EGG~s : הביצים
the~KNEE~s2 : הבירכיים
the~HOUSE~unto : הביתה
the~FIRSTBORN : הבכור
the~BIRTHRIGHT : הבכורה
the~FIRSTBORN.FEMALE : הבכירה
the~Bekher~of : הבכרי
Hevel : הבל
the~Bela~of : הבלעי
?~in~CAMP~s : הבמחנים
the~SON : הבן
the~DAUGHTER~s : הבנות
the~SON~s : הבנים
the~FLESH : הבשר
the~BURNING : הבערה
the~ONION~s : הבצלים
the~DOUGH : הבצק
the~CATTLE : הבקר
the~HAILSTONES : הברד
the~IRON : הברזל
the~FED.FAT~s : הבריאות
the~WOOD.BAR : הבריח
the~WOOD.BAR~s : הבריחים

the~Beri'ah~of : הבריעי
the~COVENANT : הברית
?~PRESENT | the~PRESENT : הברכה
the~PRESENT~s : הברכות
the~Bashan : הבשן
?~DAUGHTER | the~DAUGHTER : הבת
the~VIRGIN : הבתולה
the~VIRGIN~s : הבתולות
the~HOUSE~s : הבתים
the~HIGH~s : הגבהות
the~HIGH~s : הגבוהים
the~BORDER : הגבול
the~BOWL : הגביע
!(ms)~make~BOUND(V) : הגבל
the~KNOLL~s : הגבעות
the~WARRIOR : הגבר
the~WARRIOR~s : הגברים
the~GREAT : הגדול
the~GREAT : הגדולה
the~GREAT~s : הגדולות
the~GREAT~s : הגדולים
the~MALE.KID | the~Gad~of : הגדי
the~REDEEM(V)~ing(ms) : הגואל
the~Gudgodah : הגודגודה
the~NATION | ?~NATION : הגוי
the~NATION~s : הגויים
the~Guni : הגוני
the~LOT : הגורל
the~FLOOR : הגורן
the~PLUCKED : הגזלה
the~DIVIDED.PART~s : הגזרים
the~STEEP.VALLEY : הגיא
the~COURAGEOUS : הגיבור
the~COURAGEOUS~s : הגיבורים
the~KNOLL : הגיבעה
!(ms)~make~ BE.FACE.TO.FACE(V)~& : הגידה
!(mp)~make~ BE.FACE.TO.FACE(V) : הגידו
!(fs)~make~ BE.FACE.TO.FACE(V) : הגידי
/ the~Gilgal : הגילגל
the~Gil'ad : הגילעד
the~Gil'ad~of : הגילעדי
the~Girgash~of : הגירגשי
!(ms)~make~ DRAW.NEAR(V)~& : הגישה

the~MOUND :
?~ALSO :
!(fs)~make~GUZZLE(V)~me :
the~CAMEL :
the~CAMEL ~s :
the~GARDEN :
the~THIEF :
the~THEFT :
Hagar | the~IMMIGRATE(V)~ing(ms) | the~IMMIGRANT :
the~CUD :
the~IMMIGRATE(V)~ing(mp) :
the~Gershon~of :
the~Geshur~of :
the~RAIN.SHOWER :
the~VULTURE :
the~BEE~s :
the~FASTENER~s :
the~WORD | the~EPIDEMIC :
the~WORD~s :
the~FISH :
Hadad :
the~SPEAK(V)~ing(ms) :
the~GROUSE :
the~GENERATION :
Hadoram :
the~DOOR :
the~BLOOD :
the~DISCERNMENT :
he~did~PUSH.AWAY(V)~him :
>~make~BEAT.SMALL(V) :
the~SCRAWNY~s :
Hadar | HONOR :
the~ROAD :
the~FATNESS :
the~HE | ?~HE :
the~WALK(V)~ing(ms) :
the~WALK(V)~ing(mp) :
the~WALK(V)~ing(fs) :
the~SHE :
the~HIYN :
?~he~did~make~PROSPER(V) :
the~THEY :
the~THEY :
?~>~make~BENEFIT(V) :
the~OVERTURNING :
the~HILL :
the~HILL~unto :
the~HILL~s :
?~>~make~TURN.BACK(V) :
HE :
he~did~make~TAKE.UPON(V) :
I~will~make~TAKE.UPON(V) :
he~did~be~make~COME(V) :
they~did~be~make~COME(V) :
she~did~be~make~COME(V) :
>~make~KNOW(V) :
>~make~KNOW(V)~you(ms) :
!(ms)~make~KNOW(V)~me :
he~did~be~make~KNOW(V) :
you(ms)~did~make~KNOW(V)~me :
!(ms)~BE(V) :
he~did~be~make~DRILL(V) :
she~did~be~make~BE.DIRTY(V) :
EXIST(V)~ing(fs) :
>~self~WASH(V) :
he~did~be~make~HIT(V) :
>~make~REBUKE(V) :
you(ms)~did~make~REBUKE(V) :
he~did~make~REBUKE(V) :
>~be~make~BRING.FORTH(V) | you(ms)~did~make~BRING.FORTH(V) :
he~did~make~BRING.FORTH(V) :
>~make~BRING.FORTH(V)~him | they~did~make~BRING.FORTH(V) :
he~did~make~WALK(V)~you(ms) :
WALK(V)~ing(ms) :
WALK(V)~ing(fp) :
WALK(V)~ing(mp) :
he~did~be~make~WAVE(V) :
he~did~be~make~TURN.ASIDE(V) :
he~did~make~BE.BRIGHT(V) :
!(mp)~make~GO.OUT(V) :
you(ms)~did~make~GO.OUT(V) :
I~did~make~GO.OUT(V) :

I~did~make~GO.OUT$^{(V)}$~you$^{(ms)}$: הוצאתיך
you$^{(mp)}$~did~make~GO.OUT$^{(V)}$: הוצאתם
you$^{(ms)}$~did~make~GO.OUT$^{(V)}$~us : הוצאתנו
he~did~make~GO.OUT$^{(V)}$: הוציא
!$^{(mp)}$~make~GO.OUT$^{(V)}$: הוציאו
!$^{(mp)}$~make~GO.OUT$^{(V)}$~her : הוציאוה
he~did~make~GO.OUT$^{(V)}$~you$^{(ms)}$: הוציאך
!$^{(mp)}$~make~GO.OUT$^{(V)}$~them$^{(m)}$ | he~did~make~GO.OUT$^{(V)}$~them$^{(m)}$: הוציאם
he~did~make~GO.OUT$^{(V)}$~us : הוציאנו
he~did~be~make~RISE$^{(V)}$: הוקם
Hor : הור
KILL$^{(V)}$~ing$^{(ms)}$: הורג
he~did~be~make~GO.DOWN$^{(V)}$ | !$^{(ms)}$~make~GO.DOWN$^{(V)}$: הורד
we~did~make~GO.DOWN$^{(V)}$: הורדנו
CONCEIVE$^{(V)}$~ing$^{(mp)}$~me : הורי
!$^{(mp)}$~make~GO.DOWN$^{(V)}$: הורידו
!$^{(mp)}$~make~GO.DOWN$^{(V)}$~him : הורידהו
he~did~make~POSSESS$^{(V)}$~him : הורישו
he~did~be~make~RAISE.UP$^{(V)}$: הורם
he~did~be~make~TURN.BACK$^{(V)}$ | !$^{(ms)}$~make~SETTLE$^{(V)}$: הושב
I~did~be~make~TURN.BACK$^{(V)}$: הושבתי
Hosheya : הושע
he~did~make~LEAVE.BEHIND$^{(V)}$: הותיר
the~ISSUE$^{(V)}$~ing$^{(ms)}$: הזב
the~Zevulun~of : הזבולני
the~SACRIFICE : הזבח
the~THIS | ?~THIS | !$^{(ms)}$~make~SPATTER$^{(V)}$: הזה
the~GOLD : הזהב
the~THIS : הזאת
the~Zuz~s : הזוזים
the~BE.A.HARLOT$^{(V)}$~ing$^{(mp)}$: הזונים

the~SPRINKLE$^{(V)}$~ing$^{(ms)}$: הזורק
the~REMEMBRANCE : הזיכרון
>~make~DEDICATE$^{(V)}$~him : הזירו
the~MALE : הזכר
the~MALE~s : הזכרים
the~BEARD : הזקן
the~BEARD~s : הזקנים
the~ARM : הזרוע
the~Zerahh~of : הזרחי
the~SEED : הזרע
the~Hhevron~of : החברוני
the~Hhever~of : החברי
the~GRASSHOPPER : החגב
the~Hhagi : החגי
the~CHAMBER~unto : החדרה
the~COUPLING : החוברת
the~NEW.MOON : החודש
the~Hhawilah : החוילה
the~ORDINARY : החול
the~WEASEL : החולד
the~CAMP$^{(V)}$~ing$^{(mp)}$: החונים
the~Hhupham~of : החופמי
the~OUTSIDE~unto : החוצה
the~CUSTOM : החוקה
the~CUSTOM~s : החוקים
the~Hhur~of : החורי
the~Hhor~s : החורים
/ the~DARKNESS : החושך
the~BREASTPLATE : החושן
the~SEAL : החותמת
the~CHEST : החזה
the~CHEST : החזות
the~SWINE : החזיר
?~FORCEFUL : החזק
the~FORCEFUL : החזקה
the~FAILURE~s : החטאים
the~FAILURE : החטאת
the~LIVING : החי
the~LIVING : החיה
!$^{(mp)}$~make~LIVE$^{(V)}$: החיו
the~Hhiw~of : החיוי
the~FORCE : החייל
the~LIVING~s : החיים
I~did~make~LIVE$^{(V)}$: החייתי
?~you$^{(mp)}$~>~did~LIVE$^{(V)}$: החייתם
you$^{(ms)}$~did~make~LIVE$^{(V)}$~us : החייתנו

you(ms)~did~make~DRILL(V) : החילות
I~did~make~DRILL(V) : החילותי
>~make~DRILL(V)~them(m) : החילם
the~Hhirot : החירות
the~Hhet~of : החתי
the~SKILLED.ONE~s : החכמים
he~did~make~DRILL(V) | !(ms)~ make~DRILL(V) : החל
the~FAT : החלב
the~FAT~s : החלבים
the~PIERCED.BREAD : החלה
the~DREAM : החלום
the~DREAM~s : החלומות
the~WINDOW : החלון
the~DRILLED : החלל
the~DRILLED~s : החללים
the~QUARTZ : החלמיש
!(mp)~be~EXTRACT(V) : החלצו
the~Hheleq~of : החלקי
the~PLEASANT~s : החמודות
the~Hhamul~of : החמולי
the~DONKEY : החמור
the~DONKEY~s : החמורים
the~FIVE : החמישה
the~FIFTH : החמישי
the~FIVE~s : החמישים
the~FIFTH : החמישית
the~SKIN.BAG : החמת
the~Hhamat~of : החמתי
the~RIPEN(V)~ed(mp) : החנוטים
the~Hhanokh~of : החנוכי
the~KINDNESS : החסד
the~KINDNESS~s : החסדים
the~STORK : החסידה
he~did~make~DIMINISH(V) : החסיר
the~Hheypher~of : החפרי
the~HERBAGE : החציר
the~COURTYARD : החצר
the~Hhetsron~of : החצרוני
the~COURTYARD~s : החצרות
the~COURTYARD~s : החצרים
the~SWORD : החרב
the~LEAPING.LOCUST : החרגל
the~MAGICIAN~s : החרטמים
he~did~make~ KEEP.SILENT(V) : החריש
the~ASSIGNED | >~make~ PERFORATE(V) | the~PERFORATED : החרם
the~Hharmah : החרמה
>~make~KEEP.SILENT(V) : החרש
he~did~make~SEAL(V) : החתים
the~SLAUGHTERING~s : הטבחים
the~RING~s : הטבעות
the~RING : הטבעת
the~CLEAN : הטהור
the~CLEAN : הטהורה
the~FUNCTIONAL : הטוב
the~FUNCTIONAL | ?~ FUNCTIONAL : הטובה
the~FUNCTIONAL~s : הטובות
the~ROW : הטור
!(fs)~make~EXTEND(V) : הטי
the~DEW : הטל
the~DIRTY : הטמא
the~DIRTY : הטמאה
the~DIRTY~s : הטמאים
the~REED-BASKET : הטנא
the~BABIES : הטף
?~BEFORE : הטרם
the~TORN : הטרפה
SHE : היא
the~STREAM : היאור
the~STREAM~unto : היאורה
the~STREAM~s : היאורים
he~did~make~STINK(V) : היבאיש
you(mp)~did~make~ STINK(V) : היבאשתם
he~did~make~ SEPARATE(V) : היבדיל
!(mp)~be~SEPARATE(V) : היבדלו
I~did~make~ SEPARATE(V) : היבדלתי
the~Yevus~of : היבוסי
he~did~make~STARE(V) : היביט
>~be~SHAPE(V)~them(m) : היבראם
the~DRY.GROUND : היבשה
they~did~make~BOIL(V) : היבשילו
you(ms)~did~make~ BE.FACE.TO.FACE(V) : היגדת
I~did~make~ BE.FACE.TO.FACE(V) : היגדתי
he~did~make~ BE.FACE.TO.FACE(V) : היגיד

>~be~YIELD(V) :
the~HAND | ?~HAND :
?~>~KNOW(V) :
the~HAND~s :
he~did~make~ DRIVE.OUT(V)~you(ms) :
?~you(mp)~did~KNOW(V) :
he~did~EXIST(V) | !(ms)~EXIST(V) :
they~did~EXIST(V) | >~EXIST(V) | !(mp)~EXIST(V) :
SHE :
the~JUBILEE :
the~BRING.FORTH(V)~ing(fs) :
the~DAY :
the~DOVE :
the~SUCKLE(V)~ing(ms) :
>~be~FOUND(V)~her :
the~GO.OUT(V)~ing(ms) :
the~GO.OUT(V)~ing(mp) :
the~GO.OUT(V)~ing(fs) :
the~GO.OUT(V)~ing(fp) :
the~GO.DOWN(V)~ing(ms) :
the~SETTLE(V)~ing(ms) :
the~SETTLE(V)~ing(mp) :
>~EXIST(V) :
>~EXIST(V)~you(mp) :
the~LOBE :
the~Yahh'le'el :
the~Yahhtse'el~of :
>~make~DO.WELL(V) :
>~be~PLASTER(V) :
he~did~make~DO.WELL(V) :
they~did~make~ DO.WELL(V) :
!(fs)~EXIST(V) :
the~KNOWER~s :
he~will~DO.WELL(V) :
the~WINE :
the~BIRTHED :
the~Yimnah :
we~did~EXIST(V) :
the~Yisra'eyl~of :
the~Yisra'eyl~of :
?~he~did~be~ PERFORM(V) :
the~Yits'har~of :
the~Yetser~of :
he~will~MEET(V)~you(ms) :
the~Yishwiy :
?~THERE.IS~you(mp) :
the~ Yishma'el~s :
you(ms)~did~EXIST(V) :
I~did~EXIST(V) :
you(mp)~did~EXIST(V) :
I~did~make~ BE.HEAVY(V) :
he~did~make~HIT(V) :
he~did~make~HIT(V)~him :
they~did~make~HIT(V) :
?~>~BE.ABLE(V) :
the~Yakhin~of :
he~did~make~ RECOGNIZE(V) :
he~did~make~ RECOGNIZE(V)~him :
they~will~ RECOGNIZE(V)~him :
you(ms)~did~make~HIT(V) :
you(ms)~did~make~ HIT(V)~me :
>~be~CUT(V) :
she~did~make~ WEAR(V) :
the~BOY :
the~GIRL :
the~BOY~s :
SHINING~s :
!(ms)~be~FIGHT(V) :
make~!(fs)~WALK(V) :
?~he~will~WALK(V) :
the~SEA :
the~SEA~unto :
>~be~SNIP.OFF(V) :
he~did~make~ PRECIPITATE(V) :
the~DAY~s | the~YEMIM :
the~RIGHT.HAND :
the~Yamin~of :
>~be~SELL(V)~him :
!(ms)~be~SLIP.AWAY(V) :
the~RIGHT :
>~be~FIND(V) :

they~did~make~ :
FIND(V)
>~be~SMEAR(V) :
HIYN :
LOOK :
he~did~make~ :
GUIDE(V)~me
she~did~make~ :
SUCKLE(V)
LOOK~you(fs) | LOOK~you(ms) :
LOOK~us :
LOOK~me :
!(fs)~be~ACQUIT(V) :
the~EARED.OWL :
he~did~make~SHUT(V) :
he~did~make~ :
SHUT(V)~them(m)
she~did~make~ :
OVERTAKE(V)
they~did~make~ :
OVERTAKE(V)
you(ms)~did~make~ :
CONFIDENT(V)
I~did~make~ :
BENEFIT(V)
>~self~TURN.ASIDE(V) :
the~SHOVEL~s :
the~OWL :
he~did~make~ :
REGISTER(V)
!(ms)~be~DIVIDE.APART(V) :
he~did~make~ :
DIVIDE.APART(V)
she~did~make~ :
CLEAVE(V)
they~did~make~ :
CLEAVE(V)
he~did~make~ :
REPRODUCE(V)~me
you(ms)~did~make~ :
STAND.UP(V)
they~did~make~STRUGGLE(V) :
he~did~make~DELIVER(V) :
he~did~make~ :
DELIVER(V)~them(m)
he~did~make~ :
DELIVER(V)~us

he~did~make~ :
PROSPER(V)
you(ms)~did~make~ :
DELIVER(V)
the~WINE.TROUGH :
!(mp)~be~ :
GATHER.TOGETHER(V)
I~did~make~ :
SET.APART(V)
they~did~make~ :
ASSEMBLE(V)
the~SUBSTANCE :
he~did~make~ :
BURN.INCENSE(V)
they~did~make~ :
SCRAPE.OFF(V)
>~make~SCRAPE.OFF(V) :
you(ms)~did~make~ :
SNAP(V)
you(mp)~did~make~ :
SNAP(V)
he~did~make~MEET(V) :
he~did~make~ :
COME.NEAR(V)
they~did~make~ :
COME.NEAR(V)
they~did~make~ :
COME.NEAR(V)~them(m)
he~did~make~BE.HARD(V) :
the~FEAR(V)~ing(ms) :
he~did~make~INCREASE(V) :
!(mp)~KILL(V) :
the~Yarden :
the~Yarden~unto :
the~MOON :
he~did~make~WIDEN(V) :
they~did~make~ :
BE.FAR(V)
the~TENT.WALL :
the~TENT.WALL~s :
the~MIDSECTION :
the~GREEN :
?~THERE.IS :
he~did~make~ :
REMAIN(V)
we~did~make~ :
REMAIN(V)

he~did~make~SWEAR(V) :
he~did~make~SWEAR(V)~you(ms) :
he~did~make~SWEAR(V)~me :
>~be~SWEAR(V) :
!(ms)~be~SWEAR(V)~& :
the~Yashuv~of :
he~did~make~DAMAGE(V) :
he~did~make~DECEIVE(V)~me :
the~DESOLATE.WILDERNESS :
he~did~make~THROW.OUT(V) :
>~be~DESTROY(V) :
>~be~DESTROY(V)~you(ms) :
>~be~DESTROY(V)~them(m) :
he~did~make~DESTROY(V) :
he~did~make~DESTROY(V)~him :
they~did~make~DESTROY(V)~them(m) :
>~make~DESTROY(V)~you(ms) :
he~did~make~HEAR(V)~you(ms) :
!(ms)~be~SAFEGUARD(V) :
!(mp)~be~SAFEGUARD(V) :
>~be~CHANGE(V) :
she~did~make~DRINK(V) :
the~STRAIGHT :
they(m)~will~self~YEARN(V) :
he~did~self~SNORT(V) :
he~did~self~SHAVE(V)~him :
the~TENT.PEG~s :
she~did~EXIST(V) :
he~did~self~WALK(V) | !(ms)~self~WALK(V) :
they~did~self~WALK(V) :
I~did~self~WALK(V) :
!(ms)~self~STAND.UP(V) :
!(mp)~self~STATION(V) :
we~did~self~LINGER(V) :
>~self~INHERIT(V) :
I~did~self~FALL(V) :
they~did~make~WANDER(V) :
you(fs)~did~self~WORK.OVER(V) :
I~did~self~WORK.OVER(V) :
they~did~self~STRIVE(V) :
!(ms)~self~DECORATE(V) :
!(ms)~self~PLEAD(V) :
!(mp)~self~TEAR.OFF(V) :
they(m)~will~self~SET.APART(V) :
the~HEAVY :
the~ARMAMENT :
the~SHEEP :
the~SHEEP~s :
>~make~HIT(V) :
the~ADMINISTRATOR :
the~ADMINISTRATOR~s :
the~STAR~s :
the~ALL :
the~CUP | the~LITTLE.OWL :
the~Kush~of :
>~make~HIT(V) :
>~make~HIT(V)~him :
the~TUNIC :
>~make~HIT(V)~me :
?~like~BE.A.HARLOT(V)~ing(fs) :
?~GIVEN.THAT :
the~FURNACE :
the~CAULDRON :
the~ROUNDNESS | the~KIKAR :
I~did~make~PREPARE(V) :
the~GNAT~s :
the~GNAT~s :
the~SEAT :
the~ATONEMENT~s :
the~UTENSIL :

the~KIDNEY~s :הכליות
the~UTENSIL~s :הכלים
the~Kena'an~of :הכנעני
the~Kena'an~s :הכנעניות
the~WING :הכנף
the~SHEEP :הכשב
the~SHEEP~s :הכשבים
the~HIP~s :הכסלים
the~SILVER :הכסף
the~PALM :הכף
the~LID :הכפורת
the~PALM~s :הכפות
the~like~YELL~her :הכצעקתה
!(ms)~make~RECOGNIZE(V) :הכר
the~KERUV~s :הכרובים
the~VINEYARD :הכרם
the~Karmi :הכרמי
the~VINEYARD~s :הכרמים
the~LEG~s2 :הכרעיים
the~WRITE(V)~ed(fs) :הכתובה
the~WRITE(V)~ed(mp) :הכתובים
the~TUNIC :הכתונת
the~TUNIC~s :הכתנות
the~SHOULDER.PIECE :הכתף
FURTHER :הלאה
the~HEART :הלבב
the~FRANKINCENSE :הלבונה
?~to~SON | the~WHITE :הלבן
the~BRICK :הלבנה
the~BRICK~s :הלבנים
?~to~>~KILL(V)~me :הלהרגני
?~NOT :הלוא
?~NOT :הלוה
the~SLAB~s :הלוחות
the~Lewi :הלוי
the~Lewi~s :הלויים
>~WALK(V) :הלוך
the~LOOP~s :הלולאות
AT.THIS.POINT :הלום
THIS.ONE :הלזה
the~BREAD :הלחם
the~SQUEEZING :הלחץ
the~Liyvniy :הליבני
the~NIGHT :הלילה
you(mp)~did~make~MURMUR(V) :הלינותם
he~did~WALK(V) :הלך

they~did~WALK(V) :הלכו
we~did~WALK(V) :הלכנו
you(ms)~did~WALK(V) :הלכת
I~did~WALK(V) :הלכתי
you(mp)~did~WALK(V) :הלכתם
!(ms)~make~PROVIDE.FOOD(V)~me :הלעיטני
the~TORCH~s :הלפידים
THEY :הם
the~be~much~BE.RED(V)~ing(mp) :המאדמים
the~LUMINARY :המאור
the~LUMINARY~s :המאורות
the~be~much~BETROTH(V)~ing(fs) :המאורשה
the~HUNDRED~s :המאות
the~make~EAT(V)~ing(ms)~you(ms) :המאכילך
the~KNIFE :המאכלת
the~SPITTING :המארה
the~much~SPIT.UPON(V)~ing(mp) :המאררים
the~FLOOD :המבול
the~make~BURN(V)~ing(ms) :המבעיר
the~much~SEARCH.OUT(V)~ing(mp) :המבקשים
the~PESTILENCE :המגפה
the~much~SPEAK(V)~ing(ms) :המדבר
the~much~SPEAK(V)~ing(mp) :המדברים
THEY :המה
the~TUMULT :המהומה
the~BAR :המוט
the~be~make~HIT(V)~ing(ms) | the~be~make~HIT(V)~ing(fs) :המוכה
?~make~WALK(V)~ing(ms)~you(ms) :המוליכך
the~Molekh :המולך
MULTITUDE :המון
the~WONDER~s :המופתים
FIND(V)~ing(mp) :המוצאים
the~make~GO.OUT(V)~ing(ms) | ?~make~GO.OUT(V)~ing(ms) :המוציא
the~make~GO.OUT(V)~ing(ms)~you(ms) :המוציאך
the~FEARING :המורא

the~Moriyah : המוריה
the~DISOBEY(V)~ing(mp) : המורים
the~be~make~ TURN.BACK(V)~ing(ms) : המושב
the~Mushiy : המושי
the~REGULATE(V)~ing(ms) : המושל
the~REGULATE(V)~ing(mp) : המושלים
the~DEATH : המות
the~DOORPOST : המזוזה
the~DOORPOST~s : המזוזות
the~PAN : המחבת
the~much~FAIL(V)~ing(ms) : המחטא
the~SICKNESS : המחלה
the~Mahh'liy : המחלי
the~CAMP : המחנה
the~CAMP~s : המחנות
the~HALF.THE.SPOILS : המחצה
the~MORROW : המחרת
the~FIRE.PAN : המחתה
the~FIRE.PAN~s : המחתות
the~BRANCH : המטה
the~much~BE.CLEAN(V)~ing(ms) : המטהר
the~BRANCH~s | the~ BRANCH : המטות
the~DELICACY~s : המטעמים
the~PRECIPITATION : המטר
?~from~UNAWARE : המיבלי
the~FORTIFICATION : המיבצר
the~HEADDRESS : המיגבעות
the~TOWER : המיגדל
the~REPROVE : המיגערת
the~WILDERNESS : המידבר
the~WILDERNESS~unto : המידברה
the~Mid'yan~of : המידיני
the~Mid'yan~s : המידינים
the~Mid'yan~of : המידינית
the~ALTAR : המיזבח
the~ALTAR~unto : המיזבחה
the~ALTAR~s : המיזבחות
the~FORK~s : המיזלגות
the~SPRINKLING.BASIN : המיזרק
the~ SPRINKLING.BASIN~s : המיזרקות
the~BED : המיטה
to~the~make~ BE.CLEAN(V)~ing(ms) : המיטהר
the~WATER~s2 : המיים
the~SINGE.SCAR : המיכוה
the~much~ BRING.FORTH(V)~ing(fp) : המילדות
the~much~ BRING.FORTH(V)~ing(fs) : המילדת
the~ INSTALLATION~s : המילואים
the~BATTLE : המילחמה
the~WATER~s2~unto : המימה
?~FROM : המין
the~DEPOSIT : המינחה
the~RIM : המיסגרת
the~SCAB : המיספחת
the~DIRECTIVE : המיצוה
the~DIRECTIVE~s : המיצות
the~TURBAN : המיצנפת
the~Mits'rayim~of : המיצרי
the~Mits'rayim~s : המיצריות
the~Mits'rayim~s : המיצרים
the~Mits'rayim~of : המיצרית
the~SANCTUARY : המיקדש
the~REFUGE : המיקלט
the~LIVESTOCK : המיקנה
the~BUTTRESS~s : המיקצועות
the~PLAIT~s : המישבצות
the~PLAIN : המישור
the~OINTMENT : המישחה
the~LYING.PLACE : המישכב
the~DWELLING : המישכן
the~DOUBLE : המישנה
the~DECISION : המישפט
the~DECISION~s : המישפטים
the~ SADDLEBAG~s : המישפתיים
>~make~DIE(V) : המית
the~self~YEARN(V)~ing(mp) : המיתאוים
the~self~ OVERTURN(V)~ing(fs) : המיתהפכת
>~make~DIE(V)~him : המיתו
you(mp)~did~make~DIE(V) : המיתם
make~HIT(V)~ing(ms) : המכה
the~Makhir~of : המכירי
the~TRIBUTE : המכס

the~much~COVER.OVER(V)~ing(ms) :המכסה
the~Makhpelah :המכפלה
the~RIPE.FRUIT :המלאה
the~MESSENGER :המלאך
the~BUSINESS :המלאכה
the~MESSENGER~s :המלאכים
?~>~REIGN(V) :המלוך
the~PLACE.OF.LODGING :המלון
the~SALT :המלח
the~make~MIMIC(V)~ing(ms) :המליץ
the~KING :המלך
the~Malki'el~of :המלכיאלי
the~KING~s :המלכים
the~BOOTY :המלקוח
the~KINGDOM~s :הממלכות
the~make~BE.LESS(V)~ing(ms) :הממעיט
the~Mahn :המן
the~OASIS :המנוחה
the~LAMPSTAND :המנורה
the~SACRIFICIAL.BOWL :המנקיות
the~Menasheh :המנשה
the~Menasheh~of :המנשי
they~did~make~MELT.AWAY(V) :המסו
the~HOOD :המסוה
the~TRIAL~s :המסות
the~CANOPY :המסך
?~SMALL.AMOUNT | the~SMALL.AMOUNT :המעט
the~CLOAK :המעיל
the~make~GO.UP(V)~ing(ms) :המעלה
make~GO.UP(V)~ing(ms)~you(ms) :המעלך
the~WORK :המעשה
the~WORK~s :המעשים
the~TENTH.PART :המעשר
the~CAVE :המערה
the~RANK :המערכה
the~IN.LINE :המערכת
the~MONUMENT :המצבה
the~be~much~INFECT(V)~ing(ms) :המצורע
the~UNLEAVENED.BREAD~s :המצות
the~make~SET.APART(V)~ing(ms) :המקדיש
the~AREA :המקום
the~AREA~s :המקומות
the~be~much~TIE(V)~ing(fp) :המקשרות
the~ROD~s :המקלות
the~much~BELITTLE(V)~ing(ms) :המקלל
?~much~BE.ZEALOUS(V)~ing(ms) :המקנא
the~make~COME.NEAR(V)~ing(ms) :המקריב
>~make~CONVERT(V) :המר
the~APPEARANCE :המראה
the~make~INCREASE(V)~ing(ms) :המרבה
the~BITTER~s :המרים
the~SADDLE :המרכב
the~AWL :המרצע
the~Merari :המררי
the~make~EXCHANGE(V)~ing(ms) :המשביר
the~SMEAR(V)~ed(mp) :המשוחים
the~make~DAMAGE(V)~ing(ms) :המשחית
the~SMEARED :המשיח
the~DRINKING :המשקה
the~LINTEL :המשקוף
the~make~DRINK(V)~ing(mp) :המשקים
the~DIE(V)~ing(ms) :המת
the~DIE(V)~ing(mp) :המתים
THOUGH :הן
the~be~EAT(V)~ing(fs) :הנאכלת
the~be~SECURE(V)~ing(ms) :הנאמן
the~ANNOUNCER :הנביא
the~ANNOUNCER :הנביאה
the~SOUTH :הנגב
the~SOUTH~unto :הנגבה
the~TOUCH :הנגע
the~STRIKING :הנגף
THEY | TO.THIS.POINT :הנה
the~RIVER :הנהר
the~RIVER~s :הנהרות
the~COMMIT.ADULTERY(V)~ing(ms) :הנואף
the~PUSH(V)~ing(mp) :הנוגשים
the~TOUCH(V)~ing(ms) :הנוגע
the~TOUCH(V)~ing(fs) :הנוגעת
the~MAKE.A.VOW(V)~ing(ms) :הנודר

the~be~BRING.FORTH(V)~ing(ms) :
the~be~BRING.FORTH(V)~ing(mp) :
the~LIFT.UP(V)~ing(ms) :
the~LIFT.UP(V)~ing(mp) :
the~be~APPOINT(V)~ing(mp) :
the~FALL(V)~ing(ms) :
the~be~FEAR(V)~ing(fp) :
the~BITE(V)~ing(ms) :
the~GIVE(V)~ing(ms) :
the~be~LEAVE.BEHIND(V)~ing(ms) :
the~be~LEAVE.BEHIND(V)~ing(fp) :
the~be~LEAVE.BEHIND(V)~ing(mp) :
the~be~LEAVE.BEHIND(V)~ing(fs) :
the~DEDICATED :
the~ORNAMENTAL.RING :
the~ORNAMENTAL.RING~s :
the~COPPER :
>~make~INHERIT(V)~him :
the~WADI :
the~INHERITANCE :
the~WADI~s :
the~SERPENT :
the~SERPENT~s :
the~be~SHATTER(V)~ing(mp) :
the~EXTEND(V)~ed(fs) :
he~did~make~FORBID(V) :
the~be~DRAW.NEAR(V)~ing(mp) :
the~REMOVAL :
?~he~did~be~EXIST(V) :
!(fs)~make~REST(V) :
!(mp)~make~REST(V) :
the~SWEET :
the~be~BE.HEAVY(V)~ing(ms) :
be~FIGHT(V)~ing(ms) :
?~he~did~be~FIND(V) | the~be~FIND(V)~ing(ms) :
the~be~FIND(V)~ing(fp) :
he~did~make~FLEE(V) :
?~he~did~much~TEST(V) :
the~be~HIDE(V)~ing(fp) :
he~did~make~WAVE(V) :
>~make~WAVE(V)~you(mp) :
the~be~STAND.UP(V)~ing(mp) :
the~be~FASTEN(V)~ing(mp) :
the~be~SEE(V)~ing(ms) :
the~be~REMAIN(V)~ing(ms) :
the~be~REMAIN(V)~ing(mp) :
the~be~REMAIN(V)~ing(fs) :
?~he~did~be~HEAR(V) :
the~be~LOOK.DOWN(V)~ing(ms) :
the~FOREIGNER :
the~FOREIGNER :
the~Nemu'eyl~of :
the~STANDARD :
the~CAPTAIN~s :
the~POURING :
the~SANDAL :
the~Na'amah~of :
the~YOUNG.MAN | the~YOUNG.WOMAN :
the~YOUNG.WOMAN :
the~YOUNG.MAN~s :
the~Nephilim~s :
the~SOUL :
the~SOUL~s :
you(ms)~did~make~WAVE(V) :
the~FALCON :
the~SPECKLED~s :
the~INNOCENT :
the~LAMP~s :
the~THIGH.MUSCLE :
the~BITE(V)~ed(ms) :
the~WOMAN~s :
the~EAGLE :
the~PIECE~s :

the~ERUPTION : הנתק
the~PLENTY : הסבע
the~FIELD : הסדה
the~FIELD~s : הסדות
the~RAM : הסה
the~GO.AROUND(V)~ing(ms) : הסובב
the~PRISON : הסוהר
the~BOOTH~s : הסוכות
the~REEDS : הסופ
the~Sidim : הסידימ
the~SHRUB : הסיחימ
the~APPAREL : הסימלה
the~Sin~of : הסיני
!(mp)~make~TURN.ASIDE(V) : הסירו
the~POT~s : הסירות
!(ms)~make~POUR(V) : הסכ
!(ms)~make~TAKE.HEED(V) : הסכת
the~WICKER.BASKET : הסל
the~QUAIL : הסלו
the~WICKER.BASKET~s : הסלימ
the~CLIFF : הסלע
the~LOCUST : הסלעמ
the~LEFT.HAND : הסמאלית
the~LEFT.HAND : הסמואל
the~AROMATIC.SPICE~s : הסמימ
the~THORN.BUSH : הסנה
the~HATE(V)~ed(fs) : הסנואה
the~BARLEY : הסעורה
the~HAIRY.GOAT : הסעיר
the~HAIRY.GOAT~s : הסעירימ
the~LAPIS.LAZULI : הספיר
>~make~TURN.ASIDE(V) : הסר
the~BRAIDED.WORK : הסרד
the~Sered~of : הסרדי
the~CREMATE(V)~ing(mp) : הסורפימ
the~TWIG~s : הסריגימ
the~CREMATING : הסרפה
the~VENOMOUS~s : הסרפימ
>~make~HIDE(V) : הסתר
the~SERVANT : העבד
the~SERVANT~s : העבדימ
the~SERVICE : העבודה
the~PLEDGE : העבוט
the~THICK.WOVEN~s : העבותות
he~did~make~CROSS.OVER(V) : העביר
>~make~CROSS.OVER(V)~us : העבירנו
the~Ever~s : העברימ
the~BULLOCK : העגל
the~HEIFER : העגלה
the~CART~s : העגלות
!(ms)~make~WRAP.AROUND(V) | the~WITNESS : העד
the~COMPANY : העדה
the~Adulam~of : העדולמי
the~EVIDENCE | the~WITNESS~s : העדות
you(ms)~did~make~WRAP.AROUND(V)~& : העדותה
the~WITNESS~s : העדימ
he~did~make~EXCEED(V) : העדיפ
the~DROVE~s : העדרימ
the~SERVE(V)~ing(ms) : העובד
the~CROSS.OVER(V)~ing(ms) : העובר
?~YET.AGAIN : העוד
?~YET.AGAIN~them(m) : העודמ
?~YET.AGAIN~him : העודנו
the~EXCEED(V)~ing(ms) : העודפ
the~EXCEED(V)~ing(mp) : העודפימ
the~EXCEED(V)~ing(fs) : העודפת
the~ASCENSION.OFFERING : העולה
the~GO.UP(V)~ing(fp) : העולות
the~GO.UP(V)~ing(mp) : העולימ
the~STAND(V)~ing(ms) : העומד
the~STAND(V)~ing(mp) : העומדימ
the~OMER | the~SHEAF : העומר
the~ANSWER(V)~ing(ms) : העונה
the~DO(V)~ing(ms) : העוסה
the~DO(V)~ing(fp) : העוסות
the~DO(V)~ing(mp) : העוסימ
the~FLYER : העופ
the~LEAD : העופרת
the~SKIN : העור
the~RAVEN : העורב
the~OPPRESSION : העושק
the~RICHES : העושר
!(ms)~make~BE.BOLD(V) : העז
the~Uziy'eyl~of : העזיאלי
the~OSPREY : העזניה
the~TURN.OVER(V)~ed(mp) : העטופימ
the~BAT : העטלפ

the~Ay :העי
the~Ever~of :העיברי
the~Ever~of~her :העיבריה
the~Ever~s :העיבריות
the~Ever~s :העיבריים
the~Ever~s :העיברים
he~did~make~ WRAP.AROUND(V) :העיד
I~did~make~ WRAP.AROUND(V) :העידותי
the~BLIND :העיור
the~GOAT~s :העיזים
the~BIRD.OF.PREY :העייט
the~EYE :העיין
the~EYE~unto :העיינה
?~EYE~s2 :העייני
the~CITY :העיר
the~CITY~unto :העירה
!(ms)~make~GO.UP(V) :העל
he~did~make~GO.UP(V) :העלה
!(mp)~be~GO.UP(V) :העלו
they~did~make~GO.UP(V)~ you(ms) :העלוך
to~>~be~GO.UP(V) :העלות
>~be~GO.UP(V)~him :העלותו
the~UPPER :העליון
you(ms)~did~make~GO.UP(V) :העלית
you(mp)~did~make~ GO.UP(V)~us :העליתונו
you(ms)~did~make~ GO.UP(V)~us :העליתנו
>~make~BE.OUT.OF.SIGHT(V) :העלם
the~YOUNG.MAIDEN :העלמה
he~did~make~GO.UP(V)~us :העלנו
the~PEOPLE :העם
I~did~make~STAND(V)~ you(ms) :העמדתיך
the~PILLAR~s :העמודים
the~PEOPLE~s :העמים
the~Amaleq~of :העמלקי
the~Amram~of :העמרמי
the~GRAPE~s :הענבים
the~AFFLICTION :העני
>~make~ENCOMPASS(V) :העניק
the~CLOUD :הענן
the~Anaq :הענק
the~DO(V)~ed(ms) :העשוי

the~DO(V)~ed(fs) :העשויה
the~TENTH :העשירי
the~TEN :העשרה
the~TEN~s :העשרים
the~DIRT :העפר
the~TREE :העץ
the~SPINE :העצה
the~TREE~s :העצים
the~STRIPED~s :העקודים
the~EVENING | the~MIXTURE :הערב
the~DESERT :הערבה
the~TOKEN :הערבון
the~EVENING~s2 :הערביים
he~did~make~UNCOVER(V) :הערה
the~HORDE :הערוב
the~BEHEAD(V)~ed(fs) :הערופה
the~Eyriy :הערי
the~CITY~s :הערים
the~ARRANGEMENT~you(ms) :הערכך
the~UNCIRCUMCISED :הערל
the~Eyran~of :הערני
the~THICK.DARKNESS :הערפל
the~Araq~of :הערקי
the~RICH :העשיר
I~did~make~BE.RICH(V) :העשרתי
the~MALE.GOAT~s :העתודים
!(mp)~make~INTERCEDE(V) :העתירו
the~EDGE~s :הפאות
the~CORPSE~s :הפגרים
the~REDEEMED~s :הפדויים
the~SUET :הפדר
the~Pun~of :הפוני
the~RANSOM.PRICE :הפידיום
the~ CONCUBINE~s :הפילגשים
the~Pisgah :הפיסגה
he~did~make~ SCATTER.ABROAD(V)~you(ms) :הפיצך
he~did~make~ SCATTER.ABROAD(V)~them(m) :הפיצם
the~DEPOSITED :הפיקדון
the~FLAX~s :הפישתים
he~did~OVERTURN(V) :הפך
she~did~OVERTURN(V) :הפכה
>~OVERTURN(V)~me :הפכי
the~Palu~of :הפלואי
the~ESCAPED :הפלטה

the~ESCAPED : הפליט
the~FACE~s : הפנים
the~Pesahh : הפסח
the~WRIST~s : הפסים
the~Pe'or : הפעור
the~FOOTSTEP : הפעם
the~BELL~s : הפעמונים
he~did~be~make~REGISTER(V) | !(ms)~make~REGISTER(V) : הפקד
the~REGISTER(V)~ed(mp) : הפקודים
he~did~make~BREAK(V) | the~BULL | >~make~BREAK(V) : הפר
the~COW : הפרה
the~TENT.CURTAIN : הפרוכת
the~COW~s : הפרות
the~VILLAGE : הפרזי
the~Perez~of : הפריזי
the~BULL~s : הפרים
he~did~make~BREAK(V)~them(m) : הפרם
the~BEARDED.VULTURE : הפרס
the~HOOF : הפרסה
the~Perets~of : הפרצי
the~HORSEMAN~s : הפרשים
the~OPENING : הפתח
the~OPENING~unto : הפתחה
the~ARMY : הצבא
the~GAZELLE : הצבי
>~make~LEAVE.IN.PLACE(V) : הצג
the~HUNT(V) : הצד
the~STEADFAST.ONE : הצדיק
the~STEADFAST.ONE~s : הצדיקים
the~YELLOW : הצהוב
the~FLOCKS | ?~FLOCKS : הצואן
the~MUSTER(V)~ing(fp) : הצובאות
the~MUSTER(V)~ing(mp) : הצובאים
the~SPRING.UP(V)~ing(ms) : הצומח
the~BOULDER : הצור
the~PRESS.IN(V)~ing(ms) : הצורר
>~make~DELIVER(V) : הציל
!(ms)~make~DELIVER(V)~me : הצילני
he~did~make~FLOAT(V) : הציף
the~BIRD : הציפור
the~HORNET : הצירעה
the~RIB : הצלע

the~WHIRRING.LOCUST : הצלצל
the~THIRST : הצמאה
the~BRACELET~s : הצמידים
the~WOOL : הצמר
the~Tsemar~of : הצמרי
the~VEIL : הצעיף
the~LITTLE.ONE : הצעיר
the~LITTLE.ONE : הצעירה
the~Tsaphon~of : הצפוני
>~make~CONCEAL(V)~him : הצפינו
the~FROG : הצפרדע
the~FROG~s : הצפרדעים
the~NARROW : הצר
the~PERSECUTION : הצרה
the~INFECT(V)~ed(ms) : הצרוע
the~INFECTION : הצרעת
the~PELICAN : הקאת
the~UNIQUE : הקדוש
the~FEVER : הקדחת
the~EAST.WIND : הקדים
the~EAST : הקדם
the~Qadmon~of : הקדמוני
the~PROSTITUTE : הקדשה
the~SPECIAL~s : הקדשים
!(mp)~make~ASSEMBLE(V) : הקהילו
the~ASSEMBLY | !(mp)~make~ASSEMBLE(V) : הקהל
the~Qehat~of : הקהתי
the~Qehat~s : הקהתים
the~HUT : הקובה
the~SPECIAL : הקודש
the~VOICE : הקול
the~VOICE~s : הקולות
the~PURCHASE(V)~ing(ms) : הקונה
the~MEET(V)~ing(fp) : הקורות
the~SMALL : הקטון
the~INCENSE.SMOKE : הקטורת
the~SMALL : הקטן
the~SMALL : הקטנה
>~make~RISE(V) | he~did~make~RISE(V) : הקים
I~did~make~RISE(V) : הקימותי
the~Qayin~of : הקיני
the~OUTER : הקיצונה
the~WALL : הקיר
the~CUCUMBER~s : הקישואים

?~they~did~BELITTLE(V) :הקלו
the~LIGHTWEIGHT :הקלוקל
the~ANNOYANCE :הקללה
the~ANNOYANCE~s :הקללות
!(ms)~make~RISE(V) :הקם
the~GRAIN.STALK :הקמה
the~RISE(V)~ing(mp) :הקמים
the~ZEALOUSNESS~s :הקנאות
the~Qenaz~of :הקניזי
the~STALK~s :הקנים
the~JUG~s :הקסות
the~PLATTER :הקערה
the~PLATTER~s :הקערות
the~EXTREMITY :הקצה
the~EXTREMITY~s :הקצות
the~HARVEST :הקציר
the~SPLINTER :הקצף
!(ms)~make~COME.NEAR(V) | the~INSIDE :הקרב
!(ms)~make~MEET(V) :הקרה
the~NEAR :הקרוב
the~NEAR :הקרובה
the~NEAR~s :הקרובים
the~Qorahh~of :הקרחי
>~make~COME.NEAR(V) :הקריב
>~make~COME.NEAR(V)~him :הקריבו
the~HOOK~s :הקרסים
the~BOARD :הקרש
the~BOARD~s :הקרשים
the~HARD :הקשה
the~BOW :הקשת
HILL :הר
he~did~make~SEE(V) :הראה
the~Re'uven~of :הראובני
>~be~SEE(V) :הראות
>~be~SEE(V)~him :הראותו
>~make~SEE(V)~you(ms) :הראותך
you(ms)~did~be~make~SEE(V) :הראית
I~did~make~SEE(V)~you(ms) :הראיתיך
he~did~make~SEE(V)~you(ms) :הראך
he~did~make~SEE(V)~us :הראנו
!(ms)~make~SEE(V)~me :הראני
you(ms)~did~be~make~SEE(V) :הראת
the~ABUNDANT :הרב
>~make~INCREASE(V) :הרבה
!(mp)~make~INCREASE(V) :הרבו
the~>~INCREASE(V) :הרבות
the~ABUNDANT~s :הרבים
the~FOURTH :הרביעי
the~FOURTH :הרביעת
he~did~KILL(V)~him | they~did~KILL(V) :הרגו
!(ms)~KILL(V)~me :הרגני
you(ms)~did~KILL(V) :הרגת
I~did~KILL(V) :הרגתי
I~did~KILL(V)~you(fs) :הרגתיך
HILL~unto | PREGNANT :הרה
the~TROUGH~s :הרהטים
the~Re'uven~of :הרואובני
the~SEE(V)~ing(fp) :הרואות
the~SEE(V)~ing(mp) :הרואים
the~HEAD :הרואש
>~KILL(V) :הרוג
!(mp)~KILL(V) :הרוגו
the~WATERED :הרוה
the~WIND :הרוח
the~RESPITE :הרוחה
the~WIND~s :הרוחות
!(mp)~be~LIFT(V) :הרומו
the~TREAD(V)~ing(ms) :הרומס
the~TREAD(V)~ing(fs) :הרומסת
the~FEED(V)~ing(ms) :הרועה
the~FEED(V)~ing(mp) :הרועים
the~HEAL(V)~ing(mp) :הרופאים
the~MURDER(V)~ing(ms) :הרוצח
the~DISTANCE :הרחוקות
the~DISTANCE~s :הרחוקים
the~MILLSTONE~s :הרחיים
the~GIER-EAGLE :הרחם
the~GIER-EAGLE :הרחמה
>~make~BE.FAR(V) :הרחק
HILL~s :הרי
the~FIRST :הריאשון
the~FIRST~s :הריאשונות
the~FIRST~s :הריאשונים
the~DISPUTE :הריב
the~Rivlah :הריבלה
HILL~s :הרים
they~did~make~RAISE.UP(V) :הרימו
the~POMEGRANATE~s :הרימונים

I~did~make~RAISE.UP(V) : הרימותי
I~did~CONCEIVE(V) : הריתי
the~TENDER : הרך
the~VEHICLE : הרכב
the~TENDER : הרכה
the~GOODS : הרכוש
!(ms)~make~RAISE.UP(V) : הרם
the~RAISE.UP(V)~ing(mp) : הרמים
the~TREADER : הרמס
Haran : הרן
!(mp)~make~SHOUT.ALOUD(V) : הרנינו
>~much~CAST.DOWN(V) : הרס
he~did~make~BE.DYSFUNCTIONAL(V) | the~DYSFUNCTIONAL : הרע
the~HUNGER : הרעב
the~DYSFUNCTIONAL : הרעה
you(ms)~did~make~BE.DYSFUNCTIONAL(V) | the~DYSFUNCTIONAL~s : הרעות
you(ms)~did~make~BE.DYSFUNCTIONAL(V)~& : הרעותה
I~did~make~BE.DYSFUNCTIONAL(V) : הרעותי
you(mp)~did~make~BE.DYSFUNCTIONAL(V) : הרעותם
the~DYSFUNCTIONAL~s : הרעים
!(ms)~make~SINK.DOWN(V) : הרף
the~Rapha~s : הרפאים
?~FRAIL : הרפה
?~ONLY : הרק
the~THIN~s | the~EMPTY~s : הרקות
the~SHEET : הרקיע
the~HILL~s : הררי
the~LOST : הרשע
the~LOST~s : הרשעים
the~NETTING : הרשת
she~did~CONCEIVE(V) : הרתה
the~Sha'ul~of : השאולי
!(ms)~make~TURN.BACK(V) | the~TURN.BACK(V)~ing(ms) : השב
the~SWEARING : השבועה
the~WEEK~s : השבועות
the~STAFF : השבט
the~CAPTIVE : השבי
the~SEVENTH : השביעי
the~SEVENTH : השביעית
>~make~SWEAR(V) | the~SEVEN : השבע
the~GRAIN.SEEDS : השבר
the~CEASING : השבת
the~DRAW.WATER(V)~ing(fp) : השואבות
the~ERR(V)~ing(fs) : השוגגת
the~ONYX : השוהם
the~RAM.HORN : השופר
the~BRIBE : השוחד
the~Shuhham~of : השוחמי
the~OFFICER ~ing(mp) : השוטרים
the~LIE.DOWN(V)~ing(ms) : השוכב
the~DWELL(V)~ing(ms) : השוכן
the~TABLE : השולחן
the~GARLIC~s : השומים
the~HEAR(V)~ing(ms) : השומע
the~HEAR(V)~ing(mp) : השומעים
?~SAFEGUARD(V)~ing(ms) : השומר
the~Shuni~of : השוני
?~DECIDE(V)~ing(ms) | the~DECIDE(V)~ing(ms) : השופט
the~DECIDE(V)~ing(mp) : השופטים
the~Sheshupham~of : השופמי
the~RAM.HORN : השופר
the~THIGH~s2 : השוקיים
the~WATERING.TROUGH : השוקת
the~OX : השור
the~SWARM(V)~ing(ms) : השורץ
the~SWARM(V)~ing(fs) : השורצת
the~Shutelahh : השותלחי
the~SLAY(V)~ed(fs) : השחוטה
the~BOILS : השחין
>~make~DAMAGE(V)~you(ms) : השחיתך
the~SEAGULL : השחף
the~CONSUMPTION : השחפת
the~DAWN : השחר
>~make~DAMAGE(V) : השחת
he~did~make~TURN.BACK(V) | >~make~TURN.BACK(V) : השיב
we~did~make~TURN.BACK(V) : השיבנו
the~EAR.OF.GRAIN~s : השיבלים
the~Shekhem~of : השיכמי

the~Shalem~of :
the~Shimon~of :
the~Shiymiy :
the~Shimron~of :
the~MAID :
the~SONG :
the~SIX :
the~SIXTH :
the~SIXTH :
!$^{(mp)}$~make~DEPART.EARLY$^{(V)}$:
?~COMPLETENESS :
the~THREE :
the~THREE :
the~GOVERNOR :
!$^{(ms)}$~make~ THROW.OUT$^{(V)}$~him :
!$^{(mp)}$~make~THROW.OUT$^{(V)}$:
the~THIRD :
the~THIRD :
the~CORMORANT :
the~SPOIL :
the~ OFFERING.OF.RESTITUTION~s :
the~Sheylah~of :
the~TITLE :
!$^{(ms)}$~make~DESTROY$^{(V)}$:
>~be~make~DESOLATE$^{(V)}$~ her :
the~Shemida~of :
the~RELEASE :
the~SKY~s2 :
the~SKY~s2~unto :
the~EIGHTH :
the~EIGHTH :
the~OIL :
?~OIL :
?~he~did~HEAR$^{(V)}$:
the~SUN :
the~YEAR :
the~SECOND | the~SCARLET :
the~YEAR~s :
the~SECOND :
the~SPLIT.IN.TWO$^{(V)}$~ed$^{(fs)}$:
the~GATE~unto :
the~MAID~s :
the~RABBIT :
!$^{(mp)}$~make~DRINK$^{(V)}$:

!$^{(fs)}$~make~DRINK$^{(V)}$~me :
!$^{(ms)}$~make~ LOOK.DOWN$^{(V)}$~& :
the~SHEQEL :
the~SWARMER :
the~MINISTRY :
the~LINEN :
the~WARP :
FIG~s :
the~VESSEL :
the~PRODUCTION :
the~STRAW :
the~THANKS :
the~Tola~of :
the~KERMES :
the~Tumiym :
the~DISGUSTING :
the~DISGUSTING~s :
the~TAMBOURINE :
the~TEACHING :
the~TEACHING~s :
the~TURTLEDOVE~s :
the~SETTLER~s :
the~NIGHTHAWK :
the~Tahhan~of :
the~BADGER :
the~BADGER~s :
?~UNDER :
the~MIDDLEMOST :
the~Teyman~of :
the~IBIS :
the~HE.GOAT~s :
?~you$^{(ms)}$~will~ SAFEGUARD$^{(V)}$:
the~BLUE :
he~did~make~ DEAL.DECEITFULLY$^{(V)}$ | >~make~ DEAL.DECEITFULLY$^{(V)}$:
the~TROUBLE :
?~you$^{(fs)}$~will~WALK$^{(V)}$:
the~CONTINUALLY :
the~DATE.PALM~s :
the~WAVING :
the~CROCODILE~s :
they~did~self~REGISTER$^{(V)}$:
the~OFFERING :
the~SHOUT :

the~SCOUT(V)~ing(mp) :
the~FAMILY.IDOL~s :
?~you(ms)~will~make~ DAMAGE(V) :
the~NINTH :
the~NINTH :
and~I~will~make~ SEPARATE(V) :
and~you(mp)~did~PERISH(V) :
and~I~will~COME(V) :
and~I~will~COME(V)~& :
and~FATHER~s :
and~FATHER~s~you(ms) :
and~FATHER~of :
and~I~will~make~COME(V) :
and~Aviyasaph :
and~Avida :
and~FATHER~her :
and~Aviyhu :
and~FATHER~them(m) :
and~FATHER~him :
and~NEEDY :
and~FATHER~you(fp) :
and~Aviymelekh :
and~Aviram :
and~STONE :
and~SASH :
and~STONE~s :
and~Avraham :
and~I~will~much~KNEEL(V) :
and~I~will~much~KNEEL(V)~ & :
and~I~will~much~ KNEEL(V)~him :
and~I~will~much~KNEEL(V)~ you(ms) :
and~I~will~much~ KNEEL(V)~you(ms)~& :
and~I~will~much~KNEEL(V)~ them(m) :
and~Avram :
and~I~will~MAGNIFY(V) :
and~I~will~make~ BE.FACE.TO.FACE(V)~& :
and~I~will~much~ CAST.OUT(V)~him :
and~MIST :
/ and~Adbe'el :
and~I~will~much~SPEAK(V) :
and~I~will~much~SPEAK(V)~ & | and~I~will~much~SPEAK(V) :
and~LORD~me | and~ LORD~s :
and~HUMAN :
and~Admah :
and~GROUND~us :
and~FOOTING~s~ / them(m) :
and~FOOTING~s~him :
and~I~will~KNOW(V)~& :
and~I~will~KNOW(V)~you(ms) :
and~Ed're'i :
and~he~did~LOVE(V)~you(ms) :
and~you(ms)~did~LOVE(V) :
and~you(mp)~did~LOVE(V) :
and~I~will~EXIST(V) :
and~Ahaliyav :
and~Ahalivamah :
and~I~will~KILL(V) :
and~Aharon :
and~LOVE(V)~ing(ms) :
and~Ohad :
and~TENT~s :
and~ATTACK(V)~ ing(mp)~us :
and~I~will~EAT(V) :
and~I~will~EAT(V) | and~I~ will~EAT(V)~& :
and~EAT(V)~ing(mp)~him :
and~I~will~make~WALK(V) :
and~BUT :
and~I~will~SAY(V) :
and~I~will~SAY(V)~& :
and~On :
and~Onam :
and~Onan :
and~BRAID(V)~ing(ms) :
and~Uriym~you(ms) :
and~I~will~make~ POSSESS(V)~him :
and~LENGTH :
and~SPIT.UPON(V)~ing(mp)~ you(ms) :
and~AT~her | and~SIGN~her :

and~AT~him :
and~AT~me :
and~AT~you(fs) :
and~AT~them(m) :
and~AT~us :
and~AT.THAT.TIME :
and~HYSSOP :
and~I~will~REMEMBER(V) :
and~EAR~s :
and~I~will~WITHDRAW(V) :
and~UNIT :
and~!(ms)~TAKE.HOLD(V) :
and~Ahhuzat :
and~SISTER :
and~BROTHER~of | and~BROTHER~s~me :
and~I~will~much~LIVE(V) :
and~BROTHER~s~him | and~BROTHER~him :
and~BROTHER~s~you(ms) :
and~BROTHER~s~you(mp) :
and~BROTHER~us :
and~AMETHYST :
and~I~will~KEEP.BACK(V) :
and~AFTER | and~I~will~DELAY(V) :
and~AFTER :
and~AFTER~him :
and~END~him :
and~you(mp)~did~much~PERISH(V) :
and~HOSTILITY :
and~I~will~be~BUILD(V) :
and~I~did~ATTACK(V) :
and~WHERE | and~Ayah :
and~WHERE~him :
and~I~will~make~DO.WELL(V)~& :
and~BUCK :
and~HOW :
and~I~will~be~BE.HEAVY(V)~& :
and~!(mp)~EAT(V) :
and~!(mp)~EAT(V)~him~& :
and~BUCK~s :
and~BUCK~s :
and~IF :

and~MOTHER~her :
and~MOTHER~him :
and~I~will~make~GO.RIGHT(V)~& :
and~MOTHER~you(ms) :
and~he~did~much~BE.STRONG(V) :
and~!(mp)~BE.STRONG(V) :
/ and~WITHOUT :
and~WITHOUT~him :
and~EYPHAH :
and~I~will~AWAKE(V) :
and~I~will~FEAR(V) :
and~MAN :
and~WOMAN | and~FIRE.OFFERING | and~MAN~her :
and~WOMAN~him :
/ and~WOMAN~you(ms) :
and~AT~him :
and~AT~you(mp) :
and~Iytamar :
and~AT~us :
and~SURELY | and~I~will~make~HIT(V) :
and~Akad :
and~>~EAT(V) :
and~I~will~SMASH(V) :
and~he~did~EAT(V) :
and~!(ms)~EAT(V) | and~she~did~EAT(V) | and~I~will~much~FINISH(V) | and~he~did~EAT(V)~her :
and~they~did~EAT(V) :
and~they~did~EAT(V)~him :
and~I~will~much~FINISH(V)~them(m) :
and~you(ms)~did~EAT(V) :
and~I~did~EAT(V) :
and~you(mp)~did~EAT(V) :
and~I~will~WRITE(V) :
and~TO | and~DO.NOT | and~MIGHTY.ONE :
and~Elda'ah :
and~THESE :
and~TO~them(m) :
and~Elohiym :
and~Elohiym :
and~Eylon :

and~TO~him :
and~TO~you(ms) :
and~I~will~WALK(V)~& :
and~WIDOW :
and~Elazar :
and~Elaley :
and~THOUSAND :
and~THOUSAND~s2 :
and~El'tsaphan :
and~Elqanah :
and~FOREARM | and~BONDWOMAN :
and~BONDWOMAN~s~him :
and~BONDWOMAN~s~you(mp) :
and~I~will~GROPE(V) :
and~I~will~WIPE.AWAY(V) :
and~TRUTH~him :
and~I~will~much~FILL(V) :
and~!(ms)~BE.STRONG(V) :
and~!(ms)~much~BE.STRONG(V)~him :
and~he~did~SAY(V) :
and~she~did~SAY(V) :
and~they~did~SAY(V) :
and~we~did~SAY(V) :
and~Amraphel :
and~you(ms)~did~SAY(V) :
and~I~did~SAY(V) :
and~you(mp)~did~SAY(V) :
and~TRUTH :
and~BONDWOMAN~him :
and~FOREARM~s2 :
and~BONDWOMAN~you(ms) :
and~WHEREVER :
and~I~will~make~ABIDE(V)~him :
and~I :
and~WE :
and~I :
and~MAN~s :
and~MAN~s :
and~I~will~LIFT.UP(V) :
and~I~will~PRESS(V) :
and~I~will~PLACE(V) :
and~I~will~PLACE(V)~& :
and~I~will~PLACE(V)~them(m) :
and~I~will~make~LEFT.HAND~& :
and~he~did~GATHER(V) :
and~you(ms)~did~GATHER(V) :
and~you(ms)~did~GATHER(V)~him :
and~she~did~TIE.UP(V) | and~BOND~her :
and~I~will~CREMATE(V) :
and~Asri'eyl :
and~BOND~s~her :
and~I~will~make~WITNESS~& :
and~I~will~make~GO.UP(V) :
and~I~will~DO(V) :
and~I~will~DO(V)~& :
and~I~will~DO(V)~you(ms) :
and~MOREOVER | and~NOSE :
and~you(ms)~did~GIRD(V) :
and~they~will~BAKE(V) :
and~EPHOD :
and~I~will~make~SCATTER.ABROAD(V)~them(m) :
and~you(ms)~did~BAKE(V) :
and~I~did~TURN(V) :
and~I~did~TURN(V) :
and~FAR.END :
and~I~will~SCULPT(V) :
and~I~will~REGISTER(V) :
and~ASH :
and~Ephrayim :
and~Etsbon :
and~I~will~much~DIRECT(V) :
and~I~will~much~DIRECT(V) :
and~I~will~much~DIRECT(V)~him :
and~I~did~SET.ASIDE(V) :
and~Eytser :
and~I~will~BURY(V)~& | and~I~will~BURY(V)~her :
and~WILD.GOAT :
and~I~will~BOW.THE.HEAD(V) :
and~I~will~LOATHE(V) :
and~I~will~TAKE(V) :
and~I~will~TAKE(V)~her :

and~I~will~BELITTLE(V) :ואקל
and~I~will~CALL.OUT(V) :ואקרא
and~I~will~COME.NEAR(V) :ואקרב
and~I~will~SEE(V) | and~I~will~be~SEE(V) :וארא
and~I~will~SEE(V) :ואראה
and~Areliy :ואראלי
and~I~will~SEE(V)~him :ואראנו
and~he~did~AMBUSH(V) :וארב
and~I~will~make~INCREASE(V) :וארבה
and~FOUR :וארבע
and~FOUR :וארבעה
and~FOUR~s :וארבעים
and~PURPLE :וארגמן
and~Ard | and~I~will~GO.DOWN(V) :וארד
and~CHIMNEY~s :וארבות
and~Arodiy :וארודי
and~I~will~much~RAISE.UP(V)~him :וארוממנהו
and~BOX :וארון
and~SPIT.UPON(V)~ed(ms) :וארור
and~Aryokh :ואריוך
and~Erekh :וארך
and~Aram :וארם
and~Aran :וארן
and~Arpakhshad :וארפכשד
and~LAND :וארץ
and~FIRE :ואש
and~I~will~INQUIRE(V) :ואשאל
and~I~will~SETTLE(V) :ואשב
and~I~will~CRACK(V) :ואשבור
and~I~will~make~SWEAR(V)~you(ms) :ואשביעך
and~Ashbeyl :ואשבל
and~Eshban :ואשבן
and~I~will~CRACK(V)~them(m) :ואשברם
and~BANKS :ואשד
and~I~will~TURN.BACK(V)~& :ואשובה
and~Ashur :ואשור
and~GROVE~them(m) :ואשירהם
and~CLUSTER :ואשכול
and~I~will~SEND(V) :ואשלח
and~I~will~SEND(V)~& | and~I~will~much~SEND(V)~& :ואשלחה
and~I~will~much~SEND(V)~you(ms) | and~I~will~SEND(V)~you(ms) :ואשלחך
and~I~will~THROW.OUT(V) :ואשליך
and~I~will~make~THROW.OUT(V)~him :ואשליכהו
and~I~will~make~THROW.OUT(V)~them(m) :ואשליכם
and~he~did~BE.GUILTY(V) :ואשם
and~she~did~BE.GUILTY(V) :ואשמה
and~they~did~BE.GUILTY(V) :ואשמו
and~I~will~make~DESTROY(V)~them(m) :ואשמידם
and~I~will~make~HEAR(V)~them(m) :ואשמיעם
and~I~will~HEAR(V)~& :ואשמעה
and~WHICH | and~Asher :ואשר
and~GROVE~s~them(m) :ואשריהם
and~WOMAN | and~I~will~GULP(V) :ואשת
and~I~will~GULP(V) :ואשתה
and~I~will~self~BEND.DOWN(V) :ואשתחוה
and~AT | and~YOU :ואת
and~YOU | and~he~did~ARRIVE(V) :ואתה
and~AT~them(f) :ואתהן
and~SHE-DONKEY~s :ואתנות
and~I~will~make~self~PROVIDE.PROTECTION(V) :ואתחנן
and~AT~you(mp) :ואתכם
and~YOU :ואתם
and~I~will~GIVE(V) :ואתן
and~I~will~GIVE(V)~& | and~YOU | and~I~will~GIVE(V) :ואתנה
and~I~will~self~FALL(V) :ואתנפל
and~I~will~SEIZE.HOLD(V) :ואתפוס
and~I~will~make~self~PLEAD(V) :ואתפלל
and~he~did~COME(V) :ובא
and~in~SASH :ובאבנט
and~in~the~STONE~s :ובאבנים
and~in~Aharon :ובאהרן
and~they~did~COME(V) :ובאו
and~in~TENT :ובאוהל
and~in~SIGN~s :ובאותות
and~in~the~HYSSOP :ובאזוב

and~in~NATIVE :ובאזרח
and~in~BROTHER~him :ובאחיו
and~in~BROTHER~s~you(mp) :ובאחיכם
and~in~Eyliym :ובאילים
and~in~WOMAN~him :ובאישתו
and~in~THESE :ובאלה
and~in~Elohiym~them(m) :ובאלוהיהם
and~in~OATH~him :ובאלתו
and~in~FOUR :ובארבע
and~in~the~PURPLE :ובארגמן
and~in~LAND | and~in~the~LAND :ובארץ
and~in~LAND~you(mp) :ובארצכם
and~he~did~STINK(V) :ובאש
and~in~WOMAN :ובאשת
and~you(ms)~did~COME(V) :ובאת
and~you(mp)~did~COME(V) :ובאתם
/ and~in~the~BEAST :ובבהמה
and~in~>~COME(V) :ובבוא
and~in~the~MORNING :ובבוקר
and~in~HOUSE :ובבית
and~in~DAUGHTER~her :ובביתה
and~in~SON~s~her :ובבניה
and~in~HOUSE~s~them(m) :ובבתיהם
and~in~HOUSE~s~you(ms) :ובבתיך
and~in~PRIDE~him :ובגאותו
and~GARMENT :ובגד
and~GARMENT~s~him :ובגדיו
and~GARMENT~s :ובגדים
and~in~the~NATION~s :ובגויים
and~in~the~GRAPEVINE :ובגפן
and~in~the~IMMIGRANT :ובגר
and~in~the~IRRITATION :ובגרב
and~in~the~WORD :ובדבר
and~in~the~INFLAMMATION :ובדלקת
and~in~the~DOOR :ובדלת
and~in~BLOOD :ובדם
and~in~DISCERNMENT :ובדעת
and~in~ROAD :ובדרך
and~in~her :ובה
and~in~>~make~PROLONG(V) :ובהאריך
and~BEAST :ובהמה
and~BEAST~you(ms) :ובהמתך

and~in~>~make~TURN.OVER(V) :ובהעטיף
and~in~>~make~GO.UP(V) | and~in~>~be~GO.UP(V) :ובהעלות
and~in~>~make~GO.UP(V)~him :ובהעלותו
and~>~make~ASSEMBLE(V) :ובהקהיל
and~in~the~HILL :ובהר
and~in~him :ובו
and~!(mp)~COME(V) :ובואו
and~!(fs)~COME(V) :ובואי
and~UNFILLED :ובוהו
and~MORNING :ובוקר
and~CISTERN :ובור
and~CISTERN~s :ובורות
and~in~GOLD :ובזהב
and~in~the~PITCH :ובזפת
and~in~SEED~you(ms) :ובזרעך
and~in~FEAST :ובחג
and~in~CHAMBER :ובחדר
and~in~the~NEW.MOON :ובחודש
and~in~WANTING :ובחוסר
and~in~SHORE :ובחוף
and~in~CUSTOM~s~them(m) :ובחוקותיהם
and~in~Hhorev :ובחורב
and~in~the~LIVING :ובחיה
and~in~FURY :ובחמה
and~in~the~DONKEY :ובחמור
and~in~the~DONKEY~s :ובחמורים
and~in~the~FIVE :ובחמישה
and~in~FURY~him :ובחמתו
and~in~>~CAMP(V) :ובחנות
and~in~the~SWORD :ובחרב
and~in~the~ENGRAVING :ובחרושת
and~in~the~BURNING.FLAME :ובחרחור
and~in~the~ITCH :ובחרס
and~you(ms)~did~CHOOSE(V) :ובחרת
and~in~FUNCTIONAL :ובטוב
and~in~ROW.OF.TENTS~s~them(m) :ובטירותם
and~in~BEFORE :ובטרם
and~in~BEAST~you(ms) :וביבהמתך
and~in~SON~her :וביבנה

and~in~DAUGHTER~s~us :
and~in~FLESH~them(m) :
and~in~CATTLE~us :
and~GARMENT~s :
and~GARMENT~s~you(mp) :
and~in~ON.ACCOUNT.OF :
and~in~HAND :
and~in~the~JUBILEE :
and~in~the~DAY | and~in~DAY :
and~in~STRAIGHTNESS :
and~in~BEARD~us :
and~in~ARM :
and~in~ARM~you(ms) :
and~in~the~WINE :
and~in~HEART~you(ms) :
and~in~BRICK~s :
and~APART.FROM~you(ms) :
and~Bilam :
and~in~DANCE~s :
and~in~>~FILL(V) :
and~in~AREA :
and~BETWEEN :
and~BETWEEN~you(ms) :
and~BETWEEN~you(mp) /
and~Binyamin :
and~BETWEEN~you(ms) | and~SON~you(ms) :
and~in~>~JOURNEY(V) :
and~UNDERSTANDING~you(mp) :
and~in~SEEING.AS :
and~he~did~much~BURN(V) :
and~you(ms)~did~much~BURN(V) :
and~in~PRODUCE :
and~you(mp)~did~much~SEARCH.OUT(V) :
and~in~SELF-WILL~them(m) :
and~in~the~MILDEW :
and~they~did~much~BOIL(V) :
and~in~>~SEND(V) :
and~you(ms)~did~much~BOIL(V) :
and~in~TITLE~him :
and~in~SCARLET :
and~in~GATE~s~you(ms) :
and~in~JUDGMENT~s :
and~HOUSE :
and~in~INTELLIGENCE :
and~DAUGHTER~her :
and~HOUSE~him | and~DAUGHTER~him :
and~HOUSE~me :
and~HOUSE~you(ms) | and~DAUGHTER~you(ms) :
and~HOUSE~you(mp) :
and~in~REMAINDER :
and~in~you(fs) | and~in~you(ms) :
and~in~you(ms) :
and~in~ALL :
and~FIRSTBORN~s :
and~in~HARP :
and~in~ALL :
and~in~UTENSIL~s~him :
and~in~the~SILVER :
and~Bekher :
and~in~VINEYARD :
and~she~did~WEEP(V) :
and~in~HEART :
and~in~the~BREAD :
and~in~NIGHT :
and~in~>~WALK(V)~you(ms) :
and~she~did~SWALLOW(V) :
and~Balaq :
and~in~WHAT :
and~in~APPOINTED~s~you(mp) :
and~in~WONDER~s :
and~in~FEARING :
and~in~FEARING~s :
and~in~Mosheh :
and~in~the~WILDERNESS :
and~in~the~WATER~s2 :
and~in~BATTLE :

and~in~TURBAN : ובמיצנפת
and~in~LIVESTOCK : ובמיקנה
and~in~KNEADING.BOWL~s~you(ms) : ובמישארותיך
and~in~CLAN~him : ובמישפחתו
and~in~the~LAMPSTAND : ובמנורה
and~in~Mas'sah : ובמסה
and~in~the~QUANTITY : ובמסורה
and~in~STRESS : ובמצוק
and~in~GREAT.NUMBER : ובמרבית
and~in~SUM : ובמתכונתו
and~SON : ובן
and~in~the~SOUTH : ובנגב
and~in~>~REST(V)~her : ובנוחוה
and~DAUGHTER~s : ובנות
and~DAUGHTER~s~him : ובנותיו
and~DAUGHTER~s~you(ms) : ובנותיך
and~DAUGHTER~s~you(mp) : ובנותיכם
and~in~the~COPPER : ובנחושת
and~in~the~WADI~s : ובנחלים
and~SON~s : ובני
and~in~CARCASS~them(m) : ובניבלתם
and~SON~s~them(m) : ובניהם
and~SON~s~him : ובניו
and~SON~s~you(ms) : ובניך
and~SON~s~you(mp) : ובניכם
and~SON~s : ובנים
and~in~INNOCENCE : ובניקיון
and~you(ms)~did~BUILD(V) : ובנית
and~in~the~FIELD : ובשדה
and~in~the~WICKER.BASKET : ובסל
and~in~SWEET.SPICE~s : ובשמים
and~Basmat : ובשמת
and~in~Se'iyr : ובשעיר
/ and~FLESH : ובשר
and~FLESH~him : ובשרו
and~FLESH~me : ובשרי
and~FLESH~them(m) : ובשרם
and~in~SERVANT~s~you(ms) : ובעבדיך
and~in~the~CROSS.OVER(V)~ed(ms) : ובעבור
and~in~UNTIL : ובעד
and~Be'on : ובעון

and~in~FLYER | and~in~the~FLYER : ובעוף
and~in~BLINDNESS : ובעיורון
and~in~the~GOAT~s : ובעיזים
and~in~EYE~s2 : ובעיני
and~in~NAKED : ובעירום
and~CATTLE~them(m) : ובעירם
and~CATTLE~us : ובעירנו
and~MASTER : ובעל
and~he~did~MARRY(V)~her : ובעלה
and~you(ms)~did~MARRY(V)~her : ובעלתה
and~in~PILLAR : ובעמוד
and~in~PEOPLE~you(ms) : ובעמך
and~in~CLOUD : ובענן
and~in~HERB : ובעשב
and~in~TENTH.ONE : ובעשור
and~in~the~TUMOR~s : ובעפלים
and~in~TREE : ובעץ
and~in~the~TREE~s : ובעצים
and~in~the~EVENING : ובערב
and~in~Perez~of : ובפריזי
and~in~HORSEMAN~s~him : ובפרשיו
and~in~>~GO.OUT(V)~him : ובצאתו
and~in~the~FLOCKS : ובצואן
and~in~FLOCKS~you(ms) : ובצואנך
and~FENCE.IN(V)~ed(fp) : ובצורות
and~in~the~BIRD : ובציפור
and~VINTAGE : ובציר
and~Betsaleyl : ובצלאל
and~in~THIRST : ובצמא
and~in~the~FEVER : ובקדחת
and~in~VOICE : ובקול
and~in~VOICE~him : ובקולו
and~in~>~RISE(V)~her : ובקומה
and~in~>~RISE(V)~you(ms) : ובקומך
and~in~>~SEVER(V)~you(mp) : ובקוצרכם
and~in~the~SMALL : ובקטון
and~in~Qivrot-Hata'awah : ובקיברות-התאוה
and~!(ms)~CLEAVE.OPEN(V)~him : ובקעהו
and~LEVEL.VALLEY~s : ובקעות
and~in~HARVEST : ובקציר

and~in~SPLINTER :
and~CATTLE :
and~in~>~COME.NEAR$^{(V)}$~ them$^{(m)}$:
and~CATTLE~you$^{(ms)}$:
and~CATTLE~you$^{(mp)}$:
and~CATTLE~them$^{(m)}$:
and~in~BOW~me :
and~in~HEAD~s :
and~HAILSTONES :
and~in~>~GO.DOWN$^{(V)}$:
and~in~ABUNDANCE :
and~SPOTTED~s :
and~in~WIND :
and~KNEEL$^{(V)}$~ed$^{(ms)}$:
and~IRON :
and~FED.FAT~s :
and~WOOD.BAR :
and~WOOD.BAR~s~him :
and~Beri'ah :
and~in~ WAYWARDNESS :
and~COVENANT~you$^{(ms)}$:
and~he~did~much~KNEEL$^{(V)}$ | and~!$^{(ms)}$~much~KNEEL$^{(V)}$:
and~he~did~much~KNEEL$^{(V)}$~ you$^{(ms)}$:
and~you$^{(ms)}$~did~much~ KNEEL$^{(V)}$:
and~I~did~much~KNEEL$^{(V)}$:
and~I~did~much~ KNEEL$^{(V)}$~her :
and~I~did~much~ KNEEL$^{(V)}$~you$^{(ms)}$:
and~you$^{(mp)}$~did~much~ KNEEL$^{(V)}$:
and~FLASH~s :
and~EMERALD :
and~in~the~ SEVENTH :
and~in~SEVEN :
and~in~the~ BLASTING :
and~in~INFANT~her :
and~in~SONG~s :
and~in~>~LIE.DOWN$^{(V)}$~ you$^{(ms)}$:

and~in~the~LIQUOR :
and~BOILED :
and~in~TITLE~s :
and~in~the~YEAR :
and~in~the~LOWLAND :
and~in~the~LINEN :
and~DAUGHTER :
and~in~Taveyrah :
and~Betu'el :
and~in~CONFUSION :
and~in~MIDST :
and~in~MIDST~them$^{(m)}$:
and~in~the~KERMES :
and~HOUSE~s :
and~HOUSE~s~you$^{(mp)}$:
and~HOUSE~s :
and~in~ ASTONISHMENT :
and~in~OVEN~s~ you$^{(ms)}$:
and~he~did~REDEEM$^{(V)}$:
and~I~did~REDEEM$^{(V)}$:
and~BORDER :
and~he~did~OVERCOME$^{(V)}$:
and~MAGNIFIED :
and~FENCE :
and~FENCE~s :
and~YOUNG.PIGEON :
and~NATION :
and~STEAL$^{(V)}$~ing$^{(ms)}$ | and~he~ did~be~much~STEAL$^{(V)}$:
and~Guni :
and~LOT :
and~PLUCK.AWAY$^{(V)}$~ed$^{(ms)}$:
and~FENCE~s :
and~he~did~much~ REMOVE.THE.COVER$^{(V)}$:
and~he~did~much~SHAVE$^{(V)}$:
and~she~did~much~ SHAVE$^{(V)}$:
and~REMOVE.THE.COVER$^{(V)}$~ ed$^{(ms)}$:
and~they~will~ROLL$^{(V)}$:
and~ALSO :
and~CAMEL ~s~ them$^{(m)}$:
and~CAMEL ~s :

and~STEAL(V)~ed(fs) :
and~she~did~CAST.AWAY(V) :
and~Gatam :
and~GRAPEVINE :
and~IMMIGRANT :
and~CUD :
and~CAST.OUT(V)~ed(fs) :
and~IMMIGRANT~you(ms) :
and~she~did~much~CAST.OUT(V) :
and~I~did~much~CAST.OUT(V) :
and~I~did~much~CAST.OUT(V)~him :
and~you(ms)~did~much~CAST.OUT(V)~them(m) :
and~Getar :
and~BROODING :
and~he~did~ADHERE(V) :
and~they~did~ADHERE(V) :
and~WORD :
and~WORD~s~him :
and~WORD~s :
and~HONEY :
and~CEREAL :
and~Dedan :
and~Dodan~s :
and~Dumah :
and~GENERATION :
and~SEEK(V)~ing(ms) :
and~Di-Zahav :
and~Dibon :
and~he~did~much~SPEAK(V) :
and~they~did~much~SPEAK(V) :
and~you(ms)~did~much~SPEAK(V) :
and~I~did~much~SPEAK(V) :
and~you(mp)~did~much~SPEAK(V) :
and~FRUIT.PRESS~you(ms) :
and~Dishon | and~ANTELOPE :
and~ANTELOPE :
and~they~did~much~MAKE.FAT(V) :

and~HELPLESS :
and~BLOOD :
and~!(mp)~KNOW(V) :
and~we~did~BEAT.OUT(V)~them(m) :
and~SCRAWNY~s :
and~THISTLE :
and~SOUTHERN :
and~they~did~SEEK(V) :
and~you(ms)~did~SEEK(V) :
and~he~did~MAKE.FAT(V) :
and~Datan :
and~you(ms)~did~make~PERISH(V) :
and~I~did~make~PERISH(V) :
and~you(ms)~did~make~PERISH(V)~them(m) :
and~he~did~make~PERISH(V) :
and~the~STONE :
and~the~STONE~s :
and~the~HUMAN :
and~the~GROUND :
and~the~FOOTING~s :
and~the~TENT :
and~the~EAT(V)~ing(ms) :
and~the~BAKE(V)~ing(ms) :
and~the~SIGN~s :
and~you(ms)~did~make~WEIGH.OUT(V) :
and~the~UNIT :
and~!(mp)~be~TAKE.HOLD(V) :
and~the~UNIT :
and~he~did~make~LIGHT(V) :
and~the~MAN :
and~the~WOMAN :
and~the~Elohiym :
and~the~RUMP :
and~the~WIDOW :
and~the~MOTHER :
and~the~FOREARM :
and~the~Emor~of :
and~he~will~make~SECURE(V) :
and~they~did~make~SECURE(V) :

and~the~HERON : והאנפה
and~the~FERRET : והאנקה
and~the~MAN~s : והאנשים
and~!$^{(ms)}$~be~GATHER$^{(V)}$: והאסף
and~the~MIXED.MULTITUDE : והאספסף
/ and~the~PURPLE : והארגמן
and~you$^{(ms)}$~did~make~PROLONG$^{(V)}$: והארכת
and~you$^{(mp)}$~did~make~PROLONG$^{(V)}$: והארכתם
and~the~LAND : והארץ
and~the~FIRE : והאש
and~Waheyv : והב
and~the~COME$^{(V)}$~ing$^{(ms)}$: והבא
and~the~COME$^{(V)}$~ing$^{(mp)}$: והבאים
and~you$^{(ms)}$~did~make~COME$^{(V)}$: והבאת
and~you$^{(ms)}$~did~make~COME$^{(V)}$~her : והבאתה
and~I~will~make~COME$^{(V)}$: והבאתי
and~you$^{(mp)}$~did~make~COME$^{(V)}$: והבאתם
and~the~GARMENT : והבגד
and~the~BEAST : והבהמה
and~the~CISTERN : והבור
and~he~did~make~COME$^{(V)}$: והביא
and~!$^{(ms)}$~make~COME$^{(V)}$ | and~he~did~make~COME$^{(V)}$~her | and~she~did~make~COME$^{(V)}$: והביאה
and~!$^{(mp)}$~make~COME$^{(V)}$ | and~they~did~make~COME$^{(V)}$: והביאו
and~they~did~make~COME$^{(V)}$~them$^{(m)}$: והביאום
and~I~did~make~COME$^{(V)}$~him : והביאותיו
and~he~did~make~COME$^{(V)}$~you$^{(ms)}$: והביאך
and~I~did~make~COME$^{(V)}$: והביאתי
and~Hevel : והבל
and~the~SON~s : והבנים
and~the~FLESH : והבשר
and~the~FENCE.IN$^{(V)}$~ed$^{(fp)}$: והבצורות
and~the~CATTLE : והבקר
and~the~HAILSTONES : והברד

and~the~FED.FAT~s : והבריאות
and~the~WOOD.BAR : והבריח
and~the~Girgash~of : והגירגשי
and~the~CAMEL ~s : והגמלים
and~the~IMMIGRANT : והגר
and~the~WORD : והדבר
and~the~FISH : והדגה
and~the~ILLNESS : והדוה
and~the~GROUSE : והדוכיפת
and~the~VULTURE : והדיה
and~the~HELPLESS : והדל
and~the~DOOR : והדלת
and~the~BLOOD : והדם
and~you$^{(ms)}$~did~GIVE.HONOR$^{(V)}$: והדרת
and~the~HILL : וההר
and~HE : והוא
and~he~did~be~make~COME$^{(V)}$: והובא
and~he~did~be~make~BE.FACE.TO.FACE$^{(V)}$: והוגד
and~you$^{(ms)}$~did~make~KNOW$^{(V)}$: והודעת
and~I~did~make~KNOW$^{(V)}$: והודעתי
and~you$^{(mp)}$~did~make~KNOW$^{(V)}$~them$^{(m)}$: והודעתם
and~he~did~be~make~HIT$^{(V)}$: והוכה
and~he~will~make~REBUKE$^{(V)}$: והוכיח
and~WALK$^{(V)}$~ing$^{(ms)}$: והולך
and~he~did~be~make~DIE$^{(V)}$: והומת
and~he~did~be~make~WRAP.AROUND$^{(V)}$: והועד
and~>~make~GO.OUT$^{(V)}$: והוצא
and~you$^{(ms)}$~did~make~GO.OUT$^{(V)}$: והוצאת
and~I~did~make~GO.OUT$^{(V)}$: והוצאתי
and~you$^{(mp)}$~did~make~GO.OUT$^{(V)}$: והוצאתם
and~you$^{(ms)}$~did~make~GO.OUT$^{(V)}$~me : והוצאתני
and~he~did~make~GO.OUT$^{(V)}$: והוציא
and~!$^{(mp)}$~make~GO.OUT$^{(V)}$: והוציאו

and~!(ms)~make~DISLOCATE(V) :והוקע
and~he~did~be~make~GO.DOWN(V) :והורד
and~you(mp)~did~make~GO.DOWN(V) :והורדתם
and~!(mp)~make~GO.DOWN(V) | and~they~did~make~GO.DOWN(V) :והורידו
and~he~did~make~POSSESS(V) :והוריש
and~I~did~make~THROW(V) :והוריתי
and~I~did~make~THROW(V)~you(ms) :והוריתיך
and~you(mp)~did~make~POSSESS(V) | and~you(ms)~did~make~POSSESS(V)~them(m) :והורשתם
and~Hosheya :והושע
and~he~did~make~LEAVE.BEHIND(V)~you(ms) :והותירך
and~>~make~LEAVE.BEHIND(V) :והותר
and~the~ISSUE(V)~ing(ms) :והזב
and~the~BE.STRANGE(V)~ing(ms) :והזר
and~the~ARM :והזרוע
and~the~SNAIL :והחומט
and~the~CAMP(V)~ing(mp) :והחונים
and~the~CUSTOM~s :והחוקים
and~the~DARKNESS :והחושך
and~he~did~make~SEIZE(V) :והחזיק
and~she~did~make~SEIZE(V) :והחזיקה
and~!(ms)~make~SEIZE(V) :והחזיקי
and~you(ms)~did~make~SEIZE(V) :והחזקת
and~the~Hhiw~of :והחיוי
and~the~WHEAT :והחיטה
and~the~Hhet~of :והחיתי
and~he~did~make~PASS.OVER(V) :והחליף
and~!(mp)~make~PASS.OVER(V) :והחליפו
and~the~FURY :והחמה
and~the~SLIME :והחמר
and~the~KINDNESS :והחסד
and~the~STORK :והחסידה
and~he~did~make~KEEP.SILENT(V) :והחריש
and~I~did~make~ASSIGN(V) :והחרמתי
and~we~did~make~DO.WELL(V) :והטבנו
and~the~CLEAN :והטהור
and~the~FUNCTIONAL :והטוב
and~the~ROW :והטור
and~the~SPOT(V)~ed(fs)~s :והטלואות
and~the~SPOT(V)~ed(ms)~s :והטלואים
and~the~BABIES :והטף
and~SHE :והיא
and~she~did~make~SEPARATE(V) :והיבדילה
and~he~did~make~SEPARATE(V)~him :והיבדילו
and~you(ms)~did~make~SEPARATE(V) :והיבדלת
and~you(mp)~did~make~SEPARATE(V) :והיבדלתם
and~the~Yevus~of :והיבוסי
and~he~did~make~STARE(V) :והיביט
and~they~did~make~STARE(V) :והיביטו
and~you(ms)~did~make~BOUND(V) :והיגבלת
and~you(ms)~did~make~BE.FACE.TO.FACE(V) :והיגדת
and~I~did~make~BE.FACE.TO.FACE(V) :והיגדתי
and~you(mp)~did~make~BE.FACE.TO.FACE(V) :והיגדתם
and~he~did~make~BE.FACE.TO.FACE(V) :והיגיד
and~they~did~make~BE.FACE.TO.FACE(V) :והיגידו
and~he~did~make~DRAW.NEAR(V)~her :והיגישה
and~he~did~make~DRAW.NEAR(V)~him :והיגישו
and~you(mp)~did~make~TOUCH(V) :והיגעתם
and~the~HAND :והיד
and~the~HAND~s2 :והידיים

and~he~did~EXIST(V) | and~!(ms)~EXIST(V)

and~they~did~EXIST(V)

and~SHE

and~the~GO.OUT(V)~ing(ms)

and~the~SETTLE(V)~ing(ms)

and~he~did~make~SPATTER(V)

and~you(ms)~did~make~ILLUMINATE(V)

and~he~did~make~DEDICATE(V)

and~you(ms)~did~make~SPATTER(V)

and~you(ms)~did~make~REMEMBER(V)~me

and~they~did~make~BE.A.HARLOT(V)

and~you(mp)~did~make~DEDICATE(V)

and~!(mp)~make~BE.CLEAN(V) | and~they~did~be~make~BE.CLEAN(V)

and~he~did~make~DO.WELL(V)~you(ms)

and~we~did~EXIST(V)

and~you(ms)~did~EXIST(V)

and~I~did~EXIST(V)

and~he~did~make~HIT(V)

and~he~did~make~HIT(V)~him

and~they~did~make~HIT(V)~me

and~I~did~make~KEEP.SECRET(V)~him

and~you(ms)~did~make~HIT(V)

and~I~did~make~HIT(V)

and~you(mp)~did~make~HIT(V) | and~you(ms)~did~make~HIT(V)~them(m)

and~he~did~make~HIT(V)~me

and~she~did~make~CUT(V)

and~I~did~make~CUT(V)

and~you(ms)~did~make~WEAR(V)

and~you(ms)~did~make~WEAR(V)~them(m)

and~you(ms)~did~make~JOIN(V)

and~the~DAY~s

and~Heymam

and~she~did~make~BE.LESS(V)

and~HIYN

and~LOOK

and~LOOK~him

and~!(ms)~be~COMFORT(V)

and~you(ms)~did~make~REST(V)

and~you(ms)~did~make~REST(V)~him

and~you(ms)~did~make~REST(V)~them(m)

and~he~did~make~REST(V)

and~he~did~make~REST(V)~him

and~he~did~make~REST(V)~them(m)

and~make~!(fs)~SUCKLE(V)~him

and~LOOK~you(mp)

and~LOOK~them(m)

and~LOOK~me

and~he~did~make~SHUT(V)

and~he~did~make~SHUT(V)~him

and~you(ms)~did~make~OVERTAKE(V)~them(m)

and~they~did~make~LIFT.UP(V)

and~he~did~make~OVERTAKE(V)

and~she~did~make~OVERTAKE(V)

and~he~did~make~OVERTAKE(V)~him

and~they~did~make~OVERTAKE(V)~you(ms)

and~I~did~make~HIDE(V)
and~he~did~make~FALL(V)~him
and~he~did~make~PERFORM(V)
and~he~did~make~BE.DISTINCT(V)
and~I~did~make~BE.DISTINCT(V)
and~I~did~make~REGISTER(V)
and~I~did~make~REPRODUCE(V)
and~I~did~make~REPRODUCE(V)
and~he~did~make~STRIP.OFF(V)
and~I~did~make~LEAVE.IN.PLACE(V)~him
and~they~did~much~BE.STEADFAST(V)
and~they~did~make~DELIVER(V)
and~he~did~make~PROSPER(V)
and~I~did~make~DELIVER(V)
and~you(ms)~did~make~ASSEMBLE(V)
and~he~did~make~BURN.INCENSE(V)
and~they~did~make~BURN.INCENSE(V) | and~he~did~make~BURN.INCENSE(V)~him
and~he~did~make~BURN.INCENSE(V)~them(m)
and~you(ms)~did~make~BURN.INCENSE(V)
and~you(ms)~did~make~COME.NEAR(V)
and~you(mp)~did~make~COME.NEAR(V)
and~he~did~make~COME.NEAR(V)
and~he~did~make~COME.NEAR(V)~her | and~she~did~make~COME.NEAR(V)
and~they~did~make~COME.NEAR(V) | and~he~did~make~COME.NEAR(V)~him
and~you(mp)~did~make~COME.NEAR(V)
and~I~did~make~INCREASE(V)
and~I~did~make~INCREASE(V)~you(ms)
and~he~did~make~INCREASE(V)~you(ms)
and~!(mp)~KILL(V)
and~the~Yarden
and~the~MOON
and~I~did~make~WIDEN(V)
and~she~did~make~ACCEPT(V)
and~they~did~make~DEPART(V)
and~he~did~make~SWEAR(V)
and~I~did~make~CEASE(V)
and~you(mp)~did~make~CEASE(V)
and~you(mp)~did~make~DAMAGE(V)
and~you(mp)~did~make~DEPART.EARLY(V)
and~I~did~make~SEND(V)
and~he~did~make~THROW.OUT(V)
and~they~did~make~THROW.OUT(V)
and~I~did~make~DESTROY(V)
and~he~did~make~DESTROY(V)~you(ms)
and~!(ms)~be~LEAN(V)
and~he~did~make~DRINK(V) | and~he~did~make~DRINK(V)~her

and~they~did~make~ :והישקו
DRINK(V)
and~they~did~ :והישקינו
make~DRINK(V)
and~you(ms)~did~ :והישקית
make~DRINK(V)
and~the~STRAIGHT :והישר
and~they~did~self~ :והישתחוו
BEND.DOWN(V)
and~you(ms)~did~ :והישתחוית
self~BEND.DOWN(V)
and~you(mp)~ :והישתחויתם
did~self~BEND.DOWN(V)
and~you(mp)~did~ :והיתאויתם
self~POINT.OUT(V)
and~he~did~self~ :והיתברך
KNEEL(V)
and~they~did~self~ :והיתברכו
KNEEL(V)
and~he~did~self~ :והיתגלח
SHAVE(V)
and~!(ms)~self~MEDDLE(V) :והיתגר
and~she~did~EXIST(V) :והיתה
and~he~did~self~ :והיתהלך
WALK(V)
and~I~did~self~ :והיתהלכתי
/ WALK(V)
and~he~did~self~ :והיתודה
THROW.THE.HAND(V)
and~they~did~self~ :והיתודו
THROW.THE.HAND(V)
and~the~ORPHAN :והיתום
and~you(mp)~did~ :והיתחזקתם
self~SEIZE(V)
and~!(mp)~self~ :והיתחתנו
BE.AN.IN-LAW(V)
and~!(ms)~self~ :והיתיצב
STAND.UP(V)
and~!(mp)~self~ :והיתיצבו
STATION(V)
and~you(mp)~did~ :והיתמכרתם
self~SELL(V)
and~you(mp)~will~ :והיתנחלתם
self~INHERIT(V)
and~you(ms)~did~ :והיתעלמת
self~BE.OUT.OF.SIGHT(V)

and~he~did~self~ :והיתעמר
BUNDLE(V)
and~!(fs)~self~ :והיתעני
AFFLICT(V)
and~you(mp)~ :והיתקדישתם
did~self~SET.APART(V)
and~!(ms)~make~HIT(V) :והך
and~>~make~BE.HEAVY(V) :והכבד
and~the~ADMINISTRATOR :והכוהן
and~the~ :והכוהנים
ADMINISTRATOR~s
and~the~CHAMELEON :והכוח
and~the~SPELT :והכוסמת
and~they~did~make~ :והכינו
PREPARE(V)
and~the~KIDNEY~s :והכליות
and~!(ms)~make~PREPARE(V) :והכן
and~the~Kena'an~of :והכנעני
and~the~SHEEP~s :והכסבים
and~the~LEG~s2 :והכרעיים
and~FURTHER :והלאה
and~the~Levanon :והלבנון
and~the~SLAB~s :והלוחות
and~the~Lewi :והלוי
and~the~Lewi~s :והלויים
and~the~JAW~s2 :והלחייים
and~the~LIZARD :והלטאה
and~she~did~WALK(V) :והלכה
and~we~did~WALK(V) :והלכנו
and~you(ms)~did~WALK(V) :והלכת
and~I~did~WALK(V) :והלכתי
and~you(mp)~did~WALK(V) :והלכתם
and~THEY :והם
and~the~HUNDRED~s :והמאות
and~the~ :והמאתיים
HUNDRED~s2
and~the~FLOOD :והמבול
and~the~PESTILENCE :והמגפה
and~the~Mid'yan~s :והמדינים
and~THEY :והמה
and~the~Mo'av~s :והמואבים
and~the~WONDER :והמופת
and~the~WONDER~ :והמופתים
s
and~the~DEATH :והמות
and~I~did~CONFUSE(V) :והמותי
and~the~BRANCH :והמטה

and~the~ALTAR~s :
and~the~WATER~s2 :
and~the~THING.WRITTEN :
and~the~DIRECTIVE :
and~the~Mitspah :
and~the~DECISION~s :
and~he~did~make~DIE(V) :
and~you(fp)~did~make~DIE(V) :
and~the~much~COVER.OVER(V)~ing(ms) :
and~the~FULL~s :
and~the~BUSINESS :
and~the~KING~s :
and~he~did~ROAR(V)~them(m) :
and~the~make~BE.LESS(V)~ing(ms) :
and~the~Mahn :
and~the~LAMPSTAND :
and~the~CANOPY :
and~the~Ma'akhah~of :
and~the~CAVE :
and~the~much~SEND(V)~ing(ms) :
and~the~DIE(V)~ing(ms) :
and~you(ms)~did~make~DIE(V) :
and~THOUGH :
and~the~ANNOUNCER :
and~the~TOUCH :
and~the~RIVER :
and~the~COMMIT.ADULTERY(V)~ing(fs) :
and~the~PUSH(V)~ing(mp) :
and~the~TOUCH(V)~ing(ms) :
and~the~LIFT.UP(V)~ing(ms) :
and~the~be~FEAR(V)~ing(ms) | ?~the~be~FEAR(V)~ing(ms) :
and~be~LEAVE.BEHIND(V)~ing(ms) | and~the~be~LEAVE.BEHIND(V)~ing(ms) :
and~the~be~LEAVE.BEHIND(V)~ing(fs) :
and~!(ms)~make~REST(V) :
and~the~SERPENT :
and~the~be~REMOVE.THE.COVER(V)~ing(fp) :
and~he~did~make~REST(V) :
and~I~did~make~REST(V) :
and~the~be~HIDE(V)~ing(mp) :
and~he~did~WAVE(V) :
and~the~be~REMAIN(V)~ing(ms) :
and~the~be~REMAIN(V)~ing(mp) :
and~the~FOREIGNER :
and~the~CAPTAIN~s :
and~the~YOUNG.MAN | and~the~YOUNG.WOMAN :
and~the~SOUL :
and~you(ms)~did~make~WAVE(V) :
and~the~WOMAN~s :
and~the~CREMATE(V)~ing(ms) :
and~he~did~make~TURN.ASIDE(V) :
and~she~did~make~TURN.ASIDE(V) :
and~I~did~make~TURN.ASIDE(V) :
and~the~THORN.BUSH :
and~the~HATE(V)~ed(fs) :
and~the~BARLEY :
and~the~HAIRY.GOAT :
and~>~make~MAKE.A.PLEDGE(V) :
and~you(ms)~did~make~MAKE.A.PLEDGE(V) :
and~they~did~make~CROSS.OVER(V) :
and~you(ms)~did~make~CROSS.OVER(V) :
and~you(mp)~did~make~CROSS.OVER(V) :
and~the~Awi~s :
and~the~ASCENSION.OFFERING :
and~the~OMER :

and~the~FLYER : והעוף
and~OSPREY : והעזניה
and~the~BAT : והעטלף
and~the~Ay : והעי
and~the~CITY : והעיר
and~the~MOUSE : והעכבר
and~!(ms)~make~GO.UP(V) : והעל
and~he~did~make~GO.UP(V) : והעלה
and~!(ms)~make~GO.UP(V)~him : והעלהו
and~you(ms)~did~make~GO.UP(V) : והעלית
and~you(mp)~did~make~GO.UP(V) : והעליתם
and~the~PEOPLE : והעם
and~you(ms)~did~make~STAND(V) : והעמדת
and~the~Amon~s : והעמונים
and~he~did~make~STAND(V) : והעמיד
and~he~did~make~STAND(V)~her : והעמידה
and~he~did~make~STAND(V)~him : והעמידו
and~the~Amaleq~of : והעמלקי
and~the~SOFT : והענוג
and~the~SOFT : והענוגה
and~the~CLOUD : והענן
and~the~TREE~s : והעצים
and~the~DESERT : והערבה
and~he~did~make~ARRANGE(V) : והעריך
and~he~did~make~ARRANGE(V)~him : והעריכו
and~the~CITY~s : והערים
and~the~THICK.DARKNESS : והערפל
and~!(mp)~INTERCEDE(V) : והעתירו
and~I~did~make~INTERCEDE(V) : והעתרתי
and~he~did~make~RANSOM(V)~her | and~>~be~much~RANSOM(V) : והפדה
and~the~RANSOM(V)~ing(ms)~you(ms) : והפודך
and~he~did~make~SCATTER.ABROAD(V) : והפיץ
and~he~did~make~SCATTER.ABROAD(V)~you(ms) : והפיצך
and~the~FLAX : והפישתה
and~he~did~make~BREAK(V) : והפר
and~the~Perez~of : והפרזי
and~the~BEARDED.VULTURE : והפרס
and~!(ms)~make~STRIP.OFF(V) : והפשט
and~the~CORD~s : והפתילים
and~the~TORTOISE : והצב
and~the~FLOCKS : והצואן
and~>~make~DELIVER(V) : והצל
and~the~BRACELET~s : והצמידים
and~the~LITTLE.ONE : והצעיר
and~the~LITTLE.ONE : והצעירה
and~he~did~make~PRESS.IN(V) : והצר
and~the~INFECT(V)~ed(ms) : והצרוע
and~the~PELICAN : והקאת
and~the~STOMACH : והקבה
and~!(ms)~make~ASSEMBLE(V) : והקהל
and~the~VOICE : והקול
and~the~VOICE~s : והקולת
and~the~SMALL : והקטן
and~the~INCENSE.SMOKE : והקטורת
and~he~did~make~RISE(V) : והקים
and~they~did~make~RISE(V) : והקימו
and~I~did~make~RISE(V) : והקימותי
and~!(ms)~make~BELITTLE(V) : והקל
and~the~ANNOYANCE : והקללה
and~!(ms)~make~RISE(V) : והקם
and~you(ms)~did~make~RISE(V) : והקמות
and~the~INSIDE | and~!(ms)~make~COME.NEAR(V) : והקרב
and~the~TIE(V)~ed(mp) : והקשורים
and~HILL : והר
and~he~did~be~make~SEE(V) | and~the~KITE : והראה
and~>~make~INCREASE(V) : והרבה
and~they~did~KILL(V) : והרגו
and~they~did~KILL(V)~me : והרגוני
and~you(ms)~did~KILL(V) : והרגת
and~I~did~KILL(V) : והרגתי

and~PREGNANCY~you(fs) :
and~he~did~make~ RAISE.UP(V) :
and~I~did~make~ DRAW.OUT(V) :
and~the~GOODS :
and~you(ms)~did~make~ RAISE.UP(V) :
and~you(mp)~did~make~ RAISE.UP(V) :
and~Haran :
and~the~HUNGER :
and~the~DYSFUNCTIONAL~s :
and~you(mp)~did~make~ SHOUT(V) :
and~>~make~TURN.BACK(V) :
and~you(ms)~did~make~ TURN.BACK(V) :
and~you(ms)~did~make~ TURN.BACK(V)~him :
and~the~SEVENTH :
and~the~LIE.DOWN(V)~ing(ms) :
and~the~TABLE :
and~the~DECIDE(V)~ ing(mp) :
and~the~OX :
and~he~did~make~ TURN.BACK(V) :
and~they~did~make~ TURN.BACK(V) :
and~I~did~make~ TURN.BACK(V) :
and~I~did~make~ TURN.BACK(V)~you(ms) :
and~he~did~make~ TURN.BACK(V)~you(ms) :
and~!(ms)~make~ TURN.BACK(V)~me :
and~the~SEVEN~s :
and~I~did~make~ SUBSIDE(V) :
and~I~did~make~ DESOLATE(V) :
and~!(ms)~make~ THROW.OUT(V) :
and~the~ OFFERING.OF.RESTITUTION~s :

and~the~TEACHING :
and~the~TEACHING~s :
and~the~IBIS :
and~PEG~s :
and~PEG~s~them(m) :
and~PEG~s :
and~Zevulun :
and~they~did~SACRIFICE(V) :
and~SACRIFICE~s :
and~we~did~SACRIFICE(V) :
and~you(ms)~did~SACRIFICE(V) :
and~you(mp)~did~ SACRIFICE(V) :
and~THIS :
and~GOLD :
and~THIS :
and~SACRIFICE~s~ you(mp) :
and~Zikh'riy :
and~MUSIC :
and~BEARD~s :
and~BEARD~s~ you(mp) :
and~OLIVE~s :
and~you(ms)~did~ REMEMBER(V) :
and~I~did~REMEMBER(V) :
and~you(mp)~did~ REMEMBER(V) :
and~MOUNTAIN-SHEEP :
and~he~did~BE.A.HARLOT(V) :
and~they~did~BE.A.HARLOT(V) :
and~Za'awan :
and~BE.STRANGE(V)~ing(ms) :
and~ARM~him :
and~Zerahh | and~he~did~ COME.UP(V) :
and~SEED :
and~SEED~him :
and~SEED~you(ms) :
and~you(mp)~did~SOW(V) :
and~he~did~SPRINKLE(V) :
and~he~did~SPRINKLE(V)~him | and~they~did~SPRINKLE(V) :
and~you(ms)~did~SPRINKLE(V) :
/ and~FINGER.SPAN :
and~Hhevron :

and~you$^{(ms)}$~did~SADDLE$^{(V)}$:
and~FEAST :
and~you$^{(mp)}$~did~HOLD.A.FEAST$^{(V)}$:
and~Hhagi :
and~Hhaglah :
and~you$^{(ms)}$~did~GIRD.UP$^{(V)}$:
and~he~did~TERMINATE$^{(V)}$:
and~you$^{(ms)}$~did~TERMINATE$^{(V)}$:
and~he~did~be~much~COUPLE$^{(V)}$ | and~COUPLE$^{(V)}$~ing$^{(ms)}$:
and~Hhawilah :
and~Hhul :
and~HOT | and~BLACK :
and~VINEGAR :
and~Hhupim :
and~OUTSIDE~unto :
and~CUSTOM~s~him :
and~CUSTOM~s~him :
and~Hhur :
and~WINTER :
and~THINK$^{(V)}$~ing$^{(ms)}$:
and~THINK$^{(V)}$~ing$^{(mp)}$:
and~DARKNESS :
and~CHEST :
and~FORCEFUL :
and~!$^{(ms)}$~much~SEIZE$^{(V)}$~him :
and~FAILURE :
and~FAILURE~s :
and~FAILURE :
and~I~did~FAIL$^{(V)}$:
and~FAILURE~them$^{(m)}$ | and~you$^{(mp)}$~did~FAIL$^{(V)}$:
and~he~did~LIVE$^{(V)}$ | and~he~will~LIVE$^{(V)}$ | and~LIVING :
and~you$^{(ms)}$~did~much~COUPLE$^{(V)}$:
and~!$^{(ms)}$~LIVE$^{(V)}$ | and~she~did~LIVE$^{(V)}$:
and~!$^{(mp)}$~LIVE$^{(V)}$:
and~I~did~much~SEIZE$^{(V)}$:
and~he~did~much~FAIL$^{(V)}$:
and~he~did~much~FAIL$^{(V)}$~him :
and~you$^{(ms)}$~did~much~FAIL$^{(V)}$:

and~you$^{(ms)}$~did~LIVE$^{(V)}$:
and~FORCE~him :
and~you$^{(ms)}$~did~much~DRILL$^{(V)}$:
and~they~did~much~EXTRACT$^{(V)}$:
and~he~did~much~TAKE.A.FIFTH$^{(V)}$:
and~ARROW~s :
and~Hhiyrah :
and~he~did~much~THINK$^{(V)}$:
and~he~did~much~ATTACH$^{(V)}$:
and~she~did~LIVE$^{(V)}$:
and~LIVING~him :
and~TREMBLING.IN.FEAR~you$^{(mp)}$:
and~SKILLED.ONE :
and~FAT :
and~GALBANUM :
and~they~did~TWIST$^{(V)}$:
and~PIERCED.BREAD~s :
and~INFIRMITY~s :
and~DRILLED :
and~she~did~EXTRACT$^{(V)}$:
and~DISTRIBUTION :
and~PIERCED.BREAD :
and~Hham | and~he~did~BE.WARM$^{(V)}$:
and~Hhamul :
and~DONKEY :
and~DONKEY~him :
and~DONKEY~s~them$^{(m)}$:
and~DONKEY~s :
and~DONKEY~you$^{(ms)}$:
and~ARM.FOR.BATTLE~ed$^{(mp)}$:
and~FIVE :
and~FIVE~s :
and~FIFTH~him :
and~FIFTH~s~him :
and~FIVE :
and~FIVE :
and~SKIN.BAG :
and~they~did~CAMP$^{(V)}$:
and~Hhanokh :

and~PROTECTIVE : וחנון
and~I~did~PROVIDE.PROTECTION$^{(V)}$: וחנותי
and~>~DIMINISH$^{(V)}$: וחסור
and~Hheypher : וחפר
and~you$^{(ms)}$~did~DIG.OUT$^{(V)}$~& : וחפרתה
and~they~did~DIVIDE$^{(V)}$: וחצו
and~STRAIGHT.TRUMPET~s : וחצוצרות
and~HALF : וחצי
and~you$^{(ms)}$~did~DIVIDE$^{(V)}$: וחצית
and~Hhetsron | Hhetsron : וחצרוון
and~Hhatsarot : וחצרות
and~CUSTOM : וחק
and~you$^{(ms)}$~did~EXAMINE$^{(V)}$: וחקרת
and~SWORD : וחרב
and~DRIED.OUT : וחרבה
and~SWORD~him : וחרבו
and~SWORD~me : וחרבי
and~he~did~FLARE.UP$^{(V)}$: וחרה
and~SICKLE : וחרמש
and~he~did~MAKE.HASTE$^{(V)}$: וחש
and~DECORATIVE.BAND : וחשב
and~Hheshbon : וחשבון
and~BINDER~s~them$^{(m)}$: וחשוקיהם
and~you$^{(ms)}$~did~ATTACH$^{(V)}$: וחשקת
and~!$^{(ms)}$~BUTCHER$^{(V)}$: וטבוח
and~he~did~BUTCHER$^{(V)}$~him : וטבחו
and~he~did~DIP$^{(V)}$: וטבל
and~you$^{(mp)}$~did~DIP$^{(V)}$: וטבלתם
and~RING : וטבעת
and~CLEAN : וטהורה
and~he~did~BE.CLEAN$^{(V)}$: וטהר
and~she~did~BE.CLEAN$^{(V)}$: וטהרה
and~CLEAN~them$^{(m)}$: וטהרתם
and~FUNCTIONAL | and~he~did~DO.WELL$^{(V)}$: וטוב
and~FUNCTIONAL~s : וטובות
and~DIP$^{(V)}$~ing$^{(ms)}$: וטובל
and~FUNCTIONAL~them$^{(m)}$: וטובתם
and~DIRTY~him : וטומאתו
and~he~did~PLASTER$^{(V)}$: וטח
and~they~did~GRIND$^{(V)}$: וטחנו
and~he~did~much~BE.CLEAN$^{(V)}$: וטיהר
and~he~did~much~BE.CLEAN$^{(V)}$~him : וטיהרו
and~you$^{(ms)}$~did~much~BE.CLEAN$^{(V)}$: וטיהרת
and~he~did~much~BE.DIRTY$^{(V)}$: וטימא
and~he~did~much~BE.DIRTY$^{(V)}$~him : וטימאו
and~SPOT$^{(V)}$~ed$^{(ms)}$: וטלוא
and~the~SPOT$^{(V)}$~ed$^{(ms)}$: וטלואים
and~he~did~BE.DIRTY$^{(V)}$: וטמא
and~she~did~BE.DIRTY$^{(V)}$: וטמאה
and~they~did~BE.DIRTY$^{(V)}$: וטמאו
and~DIRTY~s : וטמאים
and~FLAVOR~him : וטעמו
/ and~BABIES~you$^{(mp)}$: וטפכם
and~BABIES~them$^{(m)}$: וטפם
and~BABIES~us : וטפנו
and~he~did~TEAR.INTO.PIECES$^{(V)}$: וטרף
and~TORN : וטרפה
and~he~will~much~PERISH$^{(V)}$~them$^{(m)}$: ויאבדם
and~he~will~be~GRAPPLE$^{(V)}$: ויאבק
and~he~will~LOVE$^{(V)}$: ויאהב
and~he~will~LOVE$^{(V)}$~her : ויאהבה
and~he~will~PITCH.TENT$^{(V)}$: ויאהל
and~they$^{(m)}$~will~be~TAKE.HOLD$^{(V)}$: ויאחזו
and~they$^{(m)}$~will~make~COMPEL$^{(V)}$: ויאיצו
and~Ya'ir : ויאיר
and~he~will~make~EAT$^{(V)}$~you$^{(ms)}$: ויאכילך
and~he~will~be~EAT$^{(V)}$: ויאכל
and~they$^{(m)}$~will~make~SECURE$^{(V)}$: ויאמינו
and~he~will~make~SECURE$^{(V)}$: ויאמן
and~they$^{(m)}$~will~be~SECURE$^{(V)}$: ויאמנו
and~they$^{(m)}$~will~SIGH$^{(V)}$: ויאנחו
and~he~will~GATHER$^{(V)}$: ויאסוף
and~he~will~TIE.UP$^{(V)}$: ויאסור
and~he~will~be~GATHER$^{(V)}$: ויאסף
and~they$^{(m)}$~will~GATHER$^{(V)}$: ויאספו

and~he~will~GIRD(V) :
and~he~will~make~SET.ASIDE(V) :
and~he~will~make~LIGHT(V) :
and~he~will~make~COME(V) :
and~he~will~make~SEPARATE(V) :
and~he~will~COME(V) :
and~they(m)~will~COME(V) :
and~they(m)~will~PLUNDER(V) :
and~PRODUCT~her :
and~he~will~make~COME(V)~her :
and~he~will~make~COME(V)~him :
and~they(m)~will~make~COME(V) :
and~he~will~make~COME(V)~us :
and~he~will~WEEP(V) :
and~!(ms)~DO.THE.MARRIAGE.DUTY(V) :
and~he~will~CLEAVE.OPEN(V) :
and~he~will~much~SEARCH.OUT(V) :
and~he~will~much~KNEEL(V) | and~he~will~make~KNEEL(V) :
and~he~will~much~KNEEL(V)~him :
and~they(m)~will~much~KNEEL(V) :
and~he~will~much~KNEEL(V)~you(ms) :
and~he~will~much~KNEEL(V)~them(m) :
and~he~will~much~KNEEL(V)~me :
and~DRY~s :
and~he~will~CUT.IN.TWO(V) :
and~Yagbahah :
and~he~will~make~BE.FACE.TO.FACE(V) :
and~he~will~make~BE.FACE.TO.FACE(V)~you(ms) :
and~he~will~SWEEP(V) :
and~they(m)~will~make~BE.FACE.TO.FACE(V) :
and~they(m)~will~make~DRAW.NEAR(V) :
and~he~will~ROLL(V) | and~he~will~much~REMOVE.THE.COVER(V) :
and~he~will~much~SHAVE(V) :
and~WEARY :
and~he~will~IMMIGRATE(V) :
and~he~will~much~CAST.OUT(V) :
and~they(m)~will~CAST.OUT(V)~them(m) :
and~he~will~make~DRAW.NEAR(V) :
and~HAND :
and~he~will~make~ADHERE(V) :
and~he~will~much~SPEAK(V) :
and~they(m)~will~much~SPEAK(V) :
and~HAND~him :
and~KNOW(V)~ed(mp) :
and~HAND~s2 :
and~HAND~s2~him :
and~they(m)~will~make~DRIVE.OUT(V) :
and~HAND~us :
and~he~will~KNOW(V) :
and~they(m)~will~KNOW(V) | and~they~did~KNOW(V) :
and~you(ms)~did~KNOW(V) :
and~you(mp)~did~KNOW(V) :
and~Yehudah :
and~YHWH :
and~Yehoshu'a :
and~he~will~EXIST(V) :
and~you(mp)~did~EXIST(V) :
and~FLINT :
and~they(m)~will~much~SHINE(V) :
and~he~will~CONFUSE(V) :
and~he~will~SILENCE(V) :
and~he~will~OVERTURN(V) :
and~he~will~be~OVERTURN(V) :
and~they(m)~will~be~OVERTURN(V) :
and~he~will~KILL(V)~him :

and~they(m)~will~KILL(V) : ויהרגו
and~he~will~KILL(V) : ויהרוג
and~they(m)~will~PERISH(V) : ויאבדו
and~he~will~EAT(V) : ויאכל
and~they(m)~will~EAT(V) : ויאכלו
and~he~will~make~TAKE.UPON(V) : ויאל
and~he~will~SAY(V) : ויאמר
and~they(m)~will~SAY(V) : ויאמרו
and~they(m)~will~BAKE(V) : ויאפו
and~Yov : ויוב
and~he~will~be~make~BE.FACE.TO.FACE(V) : ויוגד
and~he~will~make~KNOW(V) | and~KNOW(V)~ing(ms) : ויודע
and~they(m)~will~be~make~HIT(V) : ויוכו
and~he~will~make~REBUKE(V) : ויוכח
and~they(m)~will~make~REBUKE(V) : ויוכיחו
and~he~will~make~BRING.FORTH(V) : ויולד
and~you(fs)~did~BRING.FORTH(V) : ויולדת
and~he~will~make~WALK(V) : ויולך
and~DAY : ויום
and~DAYTIME : ויומם
and~Yawan : ויון
and~they(m)~will~make~ADD(V) : ויוסיפו
and~he~will~make~ADD(V) | and~Yoseph : ויוסף
and~he~will~make~GO.OUT(V) : ויוצא
and~he~will~make~GO.OUT(V) : ויוציא
and~he~will~make~GO.OUT(V)~her : ויוציאה
and~they(m)~will~make~GO.OUT(V)~him | and~they(m)~will~make~GO.OUT(V) : ויוציאו
and~they(m)~will~make~GO.OUT(V)~him : ויוציאהו
and~he~will~make~GO.OUT(V)~you(ms) : ויוציאך
and~he~will~make~GO.OUT(V)~us | and~he~did~make~GO.OUT(V)~us : ויוציאנו
and~GO.DOWN(V)~ing(mp) : ויורדים
and~he~will~make~THROW(V)~him : ויורהו
and~they(m)~will~make~GO.DOWN(V) : ויורידו
and~POSSESS(V)~ing(ms) : ויורש
and~he~will~make~SETTLE(V) | and~he~will~be~make~TURN.BACK(V) : ויושב
and~he~will~make~RESCUE(V)~them(f) : ויושיען
and~he~will~make~RESCUE(V) : ויושע
and~they(m)~will~make~LEAVE.BEHIND(V) : ויותירו
and~LOBE : ויותרת
and~he~will~make~SPATTER(V) : ויז
and~he~will~make~SIMMER(V) : ויזד
and~he~will~much~ATTACK.THE.REAR(V) : ויזנב
and~he~will~SADDLE(V) : ויחבוש
and~he~will~much~EMBRACE(V) : ויחבק
and~he~will~much~EMBRACE(V)~him : ויחבקהו
and~he~will~much~COUPLE(V) : ויחבר
and~he~will~GIRD.UP(V) : ויחגור
and~TOGETHER : ויחדו
and~they(m)~will~TERMINATE(V) : ויחדלו
and~they(m)~will~HOLD.A.FEAST(V) : ויחוגו
and~he~will~PROVIDE.PROTECTION(V)~you(ms) : ויחונך
and~they(m)~will~PERCEIVE(V) : ויחזו
and~they(m)~will~make~SEIZE(V) : ויחזיקו
and~he~will~SEIZE(V) | and~he~will~make~SEIZE(V) | and~he~will~much~SEIZE(V) : ויחזק
and~he~will~much~FAIL(V) : ויחטא

and~he~will~much~FAIL(V)~him :
and~he~will~LIVE(V) :
and~!(mp)~LIVE(V) :
and~he~will~TWIST(V) | and~he~will~make~DRILL(V) | and~he~will~much~TWIST(V) :
and~Yahh'le'el :
and~he~will~DREAM(V) :
and~he~will~WEAKEN(V) :
and~they(m)~will~DREAM(V) : /
and~he~will~much~PASS.OVER(V) :
and~he~will~be~DISTRIBUTE(V) :
and~they(m)~will~HEAT(V) :
and~ROEBUCK :
and~they(m)~will~HEAT(V) :
and~they(m)~will~CAMP(V) :
and~they(m)~will~RIPEN(V) :
and~they(m)~will~DIMINISH(V) :
and~he~will~DIG.OUT(V) :
and~he~will~much~SEARCH(V) :
and~they(m)~will~DIG.OUT(V) :
and~he~will~DIVIDE(V) :
and~he~will~TREMBLE(V) :
and~they(m)~will~TREMBLE(V) :
and~he~will~make~ASSIGN(V) :
and~he~will~THINK(V)~her :
and~he~will~EXTEND(V) :
and~he~will~STINK(V) :
and~he~will~DISDAIN(V) :
and~they(m)~will~be~WATCH.OVER(V) :
and~he~will~CHOOSE(V) :
and~they(m)~will~WEEP(V) :
and~he~will~SWALLOW(V) :
and~he~did~much~DO.THE.MARRIAGE.DUTY(V)~her :
and~he~will~BUILD(V) :
and~they(m)~will~BUILD(V) :
and~he~will~KICK(V) :

and~they(m)~will~be~CLEAVE.OPEN(V) :
and~he~will~SHAPE(V) :
and~he~will~FLEE.AWAY(V) :
and~they(m)~will~OVERCOME(V) :
and~he~will~MAGNIFY(V) :
and~they(m)~will~MAGNIFY(V) :
and~he~will~EXPIRE(V) :
and~he~will~SMITE(V) :
and~he~will~YIELD(V) :
and~he~will~be~YIELD(V) :
and~he~will~STEAL(V) :
and~he~will~TOUCH(V) :
and~he~will~REPROVE(V) :
and~he~will~DRAW.NEAR(V) :
and~they(m)~will~DRAW.NEAR(V) :
and~they(m)~will~AMPLIFY(V) :
and~he~will~BE.SILENT :
and~KNOWER :
and~he~will~PIERCE(V) :
and~he~will~MAKE.A.VOW(V) :
and~they(m)~will~EXIST(V) :
and~he~will~be~BRING.FORTH(V) :
and~they(m)~will~be~BRING.FORTH(V) :
and~he~will~be~LEAVE.BEHIND(V) :
and~he~will~SACRIFICE(V) :
and~they(m)~will~SACRIFICE(V) :
and~he~will~REMEMBER(V) :
and~they(m)~will~YELL.OUT(V) :
and~he~will~DISPERSE(V) :
and~he~will~SPRINKLE(V) :
and~he~will~COME.UP(V) :
and~he~will~SOW(V) :
and~he~will~SPRINKLE(V)~him :

and~he~will~BE.AMAZED(V) :
and~he~will~TWIST(V) :
and~he~will~CAMP(V) :
and~he~will~FLARE.UP(V) :
and~he~will~DO.WELL(V) | and~he~will~make~DO.WELL(V) :
and~they(m)~will~DO.WELL(V) :
and~he~will~DIP(V) :
and~they(m)~will~DIP(V) :
and~he~will~LEAVE.ALONE(V) :
and~he~will~GRIND(V) :
and~he~will~SUBMERGE(V) :
and~he~will~SUBMERGE(V)~him :
and~he~will~PLANT(V) :
and~WINE :
and~he~will~BE.HEAVY(V) :
and~they(m)~will~be~DENY(V) :
and~he~will~be~RESTRICT(V) :
and~they(m)~will~FINISH(V) :
and~they(m)~will~DIG(V) :
and~they(m)~will~CUT(V) :
and~they(m)~will~WRITE(V) :
and~he~will~WRITE(V)~them(m) :
and~he~will~WRITE(V) :
and~they(m)~will~BE.IMPATIENT(V) :
and~they(m)~will~be~JOIN(V) :
and~they(m)~will~be~MURMUR(V) :
and~he~will~be~FIGHT(V) :
and~they(m)~will~be~MURMUR(V) :
and~they(m)~will~TRAP(V) :
and~they(m)~will~TRAP(V)~her :
and~he~will~TRAP(V) :
and~they(m)~will~PICK.UP(V) :
and~they(m)~will~be~SNIP.OFF(V) :
and~he~will~WIPE.AWAY(V) :
and~they(m)~will~be~WIPE.AWAY(V) :
and~he~will~SELL(V) :
and~they(m)~will~SELL(V) :
and~he~will~be~FILL(V) :
and~they(m)~will~FILL(V) :
and~he~will~REIGN(V) :
and~they(m)~will~be~COMMIT(V) :
and~he~will~FIND(V) | and~he~will~be~FIND(V) :
and~he~will~FIND(V)~her :
and~he~will~FIND(V)~him :
and~they(m)~will~FIND(V) :
and~he~will~FIND(V)~them(m) :
and~he~will~SMEAR(V) :
and~he~will~SMEAR(V)~them(m) :
and~they(m)~will~DRAW(V) :
and~they(m)~will~TASTE.SWEET(V) :
and~he~will~PROVOKE(V) :
and~he~will~DRIVE(V) :
and~they(m)~will~be~DEDICATE(V) :
and~he~will~be~COMFORT(V) :
and~he~will~BREATHE.DEEPLY(V) :
and~they(m)~will~be~STRUGGLE(V) :
and~he~will~LIFT.UP(V) :
and~they(m)~will~LIFT.UP(V) :
and~they(m)~will~LIFT.UP(V)~him :
and~they(m)~will~LIFT.UP(V)~them(m) :
and~he~will~SHUT(V) :

and~he~will~GO.AROUND(V) :
and~they(m)~will~TRADE(V) :
and~he~will~HOLD.A.GRUDGE(V) :
and~they(m)~will~HOLD.A.GRUDGE(V)~him :
and~they(m)~will~be~SHUT(V) :
and~he~will~PLACE(V) :
and~he~will~SUPPORT(V) :
and~they(m)~will~SUPPORT(V) :
and~he~will~HATE(V)~her :
and~they(m)~will~HATE(V) :
and~he~will~JOURNEY(V) :
and~they(m)~will~JOURNEY(V) :
and~they(m)~will~LAMENT(V) :
and~he~will~CLASP(V) :
and~Yisra'eyl :
and~they~did~much~CORRECT(V) :
and~he~will~CREMATE(V) :
and~I~did~much~CORRECT(V) :
and~Yis'sas'khar :
and~he~will~REACH(V) :
and~they(m)~will~REACH(V) :
and~he~will~ENCOUNTER(V)~him :
and~he~will~RANSOM(V)~you(ms) :
and~he~will~FALL(V) :
and~he~will~EXHALE(V) :
and~they(m)~will~FALL(V) :
and~he~will~TURN(V) :
and~they(m)~will~TURN(V) :
and~he~will~SCULPT(V) :
and~he~will~PRESS.HARD(V) :
and~they(m)~will~PRESS.HARD(V) :
and~he~will~REGISTER(V)~them(m) :
and~he~will~REGISTER(V) :
and~he~will~OPEN.UP(V) :
and~they(m)~will~DIVIDE.APART(V) :
and~they(m)~will~REPRODUCE(V) :
and~he~will~SPREAD.OUT(V) :
and~he~will~BREAK.OUT(V) :
and~he~will~OPEN(V) :
and~they(m)~will~OPEN(V) :
and~he~will~INTERPRET(V) :
and~they(m)~will~MUSTER(V) :
and~he~will~PILE.UP(V) :
and~they(m)~will~PILE.UP(V) :
and~Yits'har | and~FRESH.OIL :
and~FRESH.OIL~you(ms) :
and~he~will~POUR.DOWN(V) :
and~he~will~LAUGH(V) | and~Yits'hhaq :
and~he~will~THIRST(V) :
and~he~will~be~FASTEN(V) :
and~he~will~CRY.OUT(V) :
and~they(m)~will~CRY.OUT(V) :
and~he~will~MOLD(V) :
and~he~will~GATHER.TOGETHER(V) :
and~he~will~BURY(V) :
and~they(m)~will~GATHER.TOGETHER(V) :
and~he~will~be~BURY(V) :

and~they[m]~will~BURY[V]
and~they[m]~will~BOW.THE.HEAD[V]
and~he~will~be~SET.APART[V]
and~they[m]~will~SET.APART[V]
and~he~will~be~ASSEMBLE[V]
and~they[m]~will~be~ASSEMBLE[V]
and~he~will~PIERCE.THROUGH[V]
and~he~will~BOW.THE.HEAD[V]
and~he~will~TAKE[V]
and~he~will~TAKE[V]~her
and~they[m]~will~TAKE[V]~him
and~they[m]~will~TAKE[V]
and~they[m]~will~TAKE[V]~him
and~he~will~TAKE[V]~them[m]
and~he~will~PURCHASE[V]
and~he~will~PURCHASE[V]~him
and~he~will~AWAKE[V]
and~he~will~SNAP[V]
and~he~will~MEET[V]
and~he~will~CALL.OUT[V] | and~he~will~be~CALL.OUT[V]
and~they[m]~will~CALL.OUT[V]
and~he~will~COME.NEAR[V]
and~they[m]~will~COME.NEAR[V]
and~he~will~TEAR[V]
and~they[m]~will~TEAR[V]
and~he~will~FEAR[V]
and~he~will~SEE[V]~her
and~they[m]~will~SEE[V] | and~they[m]~will~FEAR[V]
and~they[m]~will~SEE[V]~must

and~FEARFULNESS~you[ms]
and~he~will~INCREASE[V]
and~they[m]~will~INCREASE[V]
and~they[m]~will~KILL.BY.STONING[V]
and~he~did~RULE[V]
and~he~will~PURSUE[V]
and~they[m]~will~PURSUE[V]
and~he~will~PURSUE[V]~them[m]
/ and~he~will~BATHE[V]
and~they[m]~will~BATHE[V]
and~they[m]~will~TIE.ON[V]
and~he~will~SINK.DOWN[V]
and~he~will~HEAL[V]
and~he~will~POSSESS[V]
and~they[m]~will~POSSESS[V]
and~they[m]~will~POSSESS[V]~them[m]
and~he~will~INQUIRE[V]
and~he~will~INQUIRE[V]~him
and~they[m]~will~INQUIRE[V]
and~he~will~be~REMAIN[V]
and~they[m]~will~be~REMAIN[V]
and~he~will~CAPTURE[V]
and~they[m]~will~CAPTURE[V]
and~he~will~EXCHANGE[V]
and~he~will~CEASE[V]
and~he~will~be~SWEAR[V]
and~they[m]~will~be~SWEAR[V]
and~they[m]~will~CEASE[V]

and~Yishwah
and~Yishwiy
and~he~will~SLAY(V)
and~he~will~SLAY(V)~him
and~they(m)~will~SLAY(V)
and~he~will~SLAY(V)~them(m)
and~they(m)~will~SPREAD(V)
and~he~will~LIE.DOWN(V)
and~he~will~DWELL(V)
and~he~will~FORGET(V)~him
and~they(m)~will~DWELL(V)
and~he~will~BE.DRUNK(V)
and~they(m)~will~BE.DRUNK(V)
and~he~will~SEND(V)
and~he~will~SEND(V)~him
and~they(m)~will~SEND(V)
and~he~will~SEND(V)~me
and~he~will~SAFEGUARD(V)
and~he~will~GROW.FAT(V)
and~he~will~HEAR(V)
and~Yishma'el
and~they(m)~will~HEAR(V)
and~he~will~SAFEGUARD(V)~you(ms)
and~he~will~SLEEP(V)
and~he~will~LOOK.WITH.RESPECT(V)
and~he~will~DECIDE(V)
and~he~will~KISS(V)
and~he~will~KISS(V)~him
and~he~will~WEIGH(V)
and~they(m)~will~SWARM(V)
and~they(m)~will~GULP(V)
and~he~will~self~BEND.DOWN(V) | and~they(m)~will~BEND.DOWN(V)
and~they(m)~will~BEND.DOWN(V) | and~they(m)~will~self~BEND.DOWN(V)
and~he~will~self~MOURN(V)
and~they(m)~will~self~MOURN(V)
and~he~will~self~SNORT(V)
and~he~will~self~HOLD.BACK(V)
and~he~will~make~self~REMOVE.THE.COVER(V)
and~he~will~self~WALK(V)
and~he~will~BE.WHOLE(V)
and~he~will~self~WITHDRAW(V)
and~he~will~self~SEIZE(V)
and~they(m)~he~will~self~FAIL(V)
and~they(m)~will~make~BRING.FORTH(V)
and~he~will~self~STATION(V)
and~they(m)~will~be~make~STAND.UP(V)
and~they(m)~will~MARVEL(V)
and~he~will~self~LINGER(V)
and~they(m)~will~BE.WHOLE(V)
and~he~will~UPHOLD(V)
and~he~will~GIVE(V)
and~they(m)~will~self~ANNOUNCE(V)
and~he~will~GIVE(V)~her

and~he~will~GIVE(V)~him :וייתנהו
and~they(m)~will~GIVE(V) :וייתנו
and~they(m)~will~GIVE(V)~them(m) :וייתנום
and~he~will~self~COMFORT(V) :וייתנחם
and~they(m)~will~self~BE.CRAFTY(V) :וייתנכלו
and~he~will~self~RECOGNIZE(V) :וייתנכר
and~he~will~GIVE(V)~them(m) :וייתנם
and~they(m)~will~self~DELIVER(V) :וייתנצלו
and~he~will~self~CROSS.OVER(V) :וייתעבר
and~he~will~self~DISTRESS(V) :וייתעצב
and~they(m)~will~self~DISTRESS(V) :וייתעצבו
and~he~will~self~PLEAD(V) :וייתפלל
and~they(m)~will~SEW.TOGETHER(V) :וייתפרו
and~they(m)~will~self~TEAR.OFF(V) :וייתפרקו
and~he~will~THRUST(V)~him :וייתקעהו
and~they(m)~will~self~CRUSH(V) :וייתרוצצו
and~REMAINDER~them(m) :וייתרם
and~Yitran :וייתרן
and~he~will~ROOT.OUT(V)~them(m) :וייתשם
and~he~will~make~HIT(V) :ויך
and~he~will~make~BE.HEAVY(V) :ויכבד
and~they(m)~will~much~WASH(V) :ויכבסו
and~he~will~make~HIT(V)~him :ויכהו
and~he~will~much~ADORN(V) :ויכהן
and~they(m)~will~make~HIT(V) :ויכו
and~they(m)~will~be~FINISH(V) :ויכולו
and~they(m)~will~make~HIT(V)~them(m) :ויכום
and~he~will~much~PREPARE(V)~you(ms) :ויכוננך
and~they(m)~will~much~COVER.OVER(V) :ויכוסו
and~he~will~much~LIE(V) :ויכזב
and~Yakhin :ויכין
and~they(m)~will~make~PREPARE(V) :ויכינו
and~he~will~make~RECOGNIZE(V)~her :ויכירה
and~he~will~make~RECOGNIZE(V)~them(m) :ויכירם
and~he~will~much~FINISH(V) :ויכל
and~he~will~SUSTAIN(V) :ויכלכל
and~you(ms)~did~BE.ABLE(V) :ויכלת
and~he~will~make~them(m)HIT(V)~them(m) :ויכם
and~he~will~much~COVER.OVER(V) :ויכס
and~he~will~much~COVER.OVER(V)~him :ויכסהו
and~they(m)~will~much~COVER.OVER(V) :ויכסו
and~he~will~much~COVER(V) :ויכפר
and~he~will~make~RECOGNIZE(V) :ויכר
and~they(m)~will~make~SMASH(V) :ויכתו
and~they(m)~will~make~SMASH(V)~them(m) :ויכתום
and~he~will~make~WEAR(V)~them(m) :וילבישם
and~he~will~make~WEAR(V) :וילבש
and~BOY :וילד
and~she~did~BRING.FORTH(V) :וילדה
and~they(m)~will~BRING.FORTH(V) | and~they~did~BRING.FORTH(V) :וילדו
and~BOY~s~her :וילדיה
and~the~BOY~s~them(f) :וילדיהן
and~BORN :ויליד

and~they(m)~will~ STAY.THE.NIGHT(V) :
and~he~will~WALK(V) :
and~they(m)~will~WALK(V) :
and~he~will~much~ LEARN(V)~her :
and~he~will~ STAY.THE.NIGHT(V) :
and~he~will~much~PICK.UP(V) :
and~he~will~much~ REFUSE(V) :
and~SEA~unto :
and~he~will~much~ HURRY(V) :
and~they(m)~will~much~ HURRY(V) :
and~they(m)~will~ MEASURE(V) :
and~he~will~GROPE(V)~ him :
and~he~will~DIE(V) :
and~they(m)~will~DIE(V) :
and~he~will~make~ PRECIPITATE(V) :
and~DAY~s :
and~Yamin :
and~he~will~make~ DIE(V)~him :
and~he~will~SNIP.OFF(V) :
and~he~will~much~FILL(V) :
and~they(m)~will~much~ FILL(V) :
and~they(m)~will~ much~FILL(V)~them(m) :
and~they(m)~will~ make~FIND(V) :
and~they(m)~will~much~ BE.BITTER(V) :
and~they(m)~will~ BE.BITTER(V)~him :
and~he~will~make~GROPE(V) :
and~he~will~much~ GROPE(V) :
and~he~will~DIE(V) | and~he~ will~make~DIE(V) :
and~he~will~much~FADE(V) :
and~he~will~TOUCH(V) :
and~he~will~much~ DRIVE(V)~him :
and~he~will~much~ LEAD(V)~them(m) :
and~they(m)~will~FLEE(V) :
and~they(m)~will~ STAGGER(V) :
and~he~will~REST(V) | and~ he~will~make~REST(V) :
and~he~will~COMFORT(V) :
and~they(m)~will~ FORBID(V) :
and~he~will~make~ DEPOSIT(V)~him | and~he~will~ make~REST(V)~him :
and~they(m)~will~make~ REST(V) :
and~they(m)~will~ make~REST(V)~him :
and~he~will~make~ STAGGER(V)~them(m) :
and~he~will~make~ WAVE(V)~him :
and~they(m)~will~make~ SUCKLE(V) :
and~he~will~FLEE(V) :
and~they(m)~will~much~ TEST(V) :
and~he~will~much~ SHAKE.OFF(V) :
and~he~will~make~WAVE(V) :
and~they(m)~will~much~ DELIVER(V) :
and~they(m)~will~BITE(V) :
and~he~will~much~KISS(V) :
and~he~will~make~ GO.AROUND(V) :
and~he~will~make~ OVERTAKE(V) :
and~they(m)~will~ TURN.ASIDE(V) :
and~they(m)~will~make~ OVERTAKE(V) :
and~he~will~make~ OVERTAKE(V) :
and~he~will~PLACE(V)~ him :

and~they(m)~will~PLACE(V) :
and~he~will~PLACE(V)~me :
and~he~will~make~POUR(V) | and~he~will~FENCE.AROUND(V) :
and~he~will~much~TWIST.BACKWARDS(V) :
and~he~will~PLACE(V) :
and~he~will~JOURNEY(V) :
and~he~will~ADD(V) :
and~they~did~ADD(V) :
and~he~will~much~COUNT(V) :
and~they(m)~will~COUNT(V) :
and~you(ms)~did~ADD(V) :
and~I~did~ADD(V) :
and~he~will~make~TURN.ASIDE(V) :
and~they~did~much~SHUT.UP(V)~them(m) :
and~he~will~make~HIDE(V) :
and~they(m)~will~SERVE(V) :
and~they(m)~will~SERVE(V)~me :
and~he~will~SERVE(V)~me :
and~he~will~SERVE(V) :
and~he~will~CROSS.OVER(V) :
and~they(m)~will~make~SERVE(V) :
and~they(m)~will~make~CROSS.OVER(V) :
and~he~will~make~CROSS.OVER(V)~them(m) :
and~he~will~make~CROSS.OVER(V) :
and~they(m)~will~CROSS.OVER(V) :
and~he~will~LEAVE(V) :
and~Yazeyr :
and~they(m)~will~HELP(V)~you(mp) :
and~he~will~HELP(V)~you(ms) :
and~SHOVEL~s~him :
and~he~will~make~GO.UP(V) | and~he~will~GO.UP(V) :

and~he~will~make~GO.UP(V)~him :
and~they(m)~will~make~GO.UP(V) | and~they(m)~will~GO.UP(V) | and~they(m)~will~be~GO.UP(V) :
and~he~will~make~STAND(V) :
and~they(m)~will~STAND(V) :
and~he~will~STAND(V) :
and~he~will~LOAD(V) :
and~he~will~make~STAND(V)~him :
and~he~will~ANSWER(V) :
and~he~will~much~AFFLICT(V)~her :
and~they(m)~will~ANSWER(V) :
and~they(m)~will~much~AFFLICT(V)~us :
and~he~will~much~AFFLICT(V)~you(ms) :
and~he~will~DO(V) :
and~he~will~DO(V)~her :
and~he~will~DO(V)~him :
and~they(m)~will~DO(V) :
and~they(m)~will~make~PRESUME(V) :
and~they(m)~will~BE.ABUNDANT(V) :
and~he~will~RESTRAIN(V)~me :
and~Ya'aqov :
and~he~will~BIND(V) :
and~he~will~ARRANGE(V) :
and~they(m)~will~ARRANGE(V) :
and~he~will~make~ADVANCE(V) :
and~he~will~INTERCEDE(V) | and~he~will~be~INTERCEDE(V) :
and~he~will~BE.NUMB(V) :
and~BEAUTIFUL :
and~they(m)~will~REFINE(V) :
and~they(m)~will~SCATTER.ABROAD(V) :
and~BEAUTIFUL~s :
and~he~will~make~FALL(V) :

and~he~will~make~SCATTER.ABROAD(V) : ויפץ
and~he~will~much~PEEL(V) : ויפצל
and~he~will~make~REGISTER(V) : ויפקד
and~he~will~make~REGISTER(V)~him : ויפקידהו
and~he~will~make~REPRODUCE(V)~you(ms) : ויפרך
and~he~will~make~STRIP.OFF(V) : ויפשט
and~they(m)~will~make~STRIP.OFF(V) : ויפשיטו
and~Yaphet | and~BEAUTIFUL : ויפת
and~he~will~OPEN(V) : ויפתח
and~he~will~GO.OUT(V) : ויצא
and~she~did~GO.OUT(V) : ויצאה
and~they(m)~will~GO.OUT(V) | and~they~did~GO.OUT(V) : ויצאו
and~you(ms)~did~GO.OUT(V) : ויצאת
and~he~will~make~STAND.UP(V) : ויצב
and~he~will~make~LEAVE.IN.PLACE(V) : ויצג
and~he~will~much~DIRECT(V) : ויצו
and~he~will~much~DIRECT(V)~him : ויצוהו
and~they(m)~will~much~DIRECT(V) : ויצוו
and~he~will~much~DIRECT(V)~them(m) : ויצום
and~he~will~much~DIRECT(V)~us : ויצונו
and~he~will~make~LEAVE.IN.PLACE(V)~them(m) : ויציגם
and~he~will~make~DELIVER(V)~him : ויצילהו
and~he~will~make~DELIVER(V)~them(m) : ויצילם
and~he~will~DELIVER(V)~me : ויצילני
and~he~will~make~DELIVER(V) : ויצל
and~he~will~make~SPRING.UP(V) : ויצמח
and~he~will~much~OVERLAY(V) : ויצף
and~he~will~much~OVERLAY(V)~him : ויצפהו
and~he~will~much~OVERLAY(V)~them(m) : ויצפם
and~he~will~be~BLOOM(V) : ויצץ
and~he~did~POUR.DOWN(V) : ויצק
and~you(ms)~did~POUR.DOWN(V) : ויצקת
and~he~will~MOLD(V) | and~Yetser | and~he~will~SMACK(V) : ויצר
and~he~will~much~SET.APART(V) : ויקדש
and~he~will~much~SET.APART(V)~him : ויקדשהו
and~they(m)~will~make~ASSEMBLE(V) : ויקהילו
and~he~will~ASSEMBLE(V) : ויקהל
and~they(m)~will~RISE(V) : ויקומו
and~they(m)~will~LOATHE(V) : ויקוצו
and~Yaqtan : ויקטן
and~he~will~make~BURN.INCENSE(V) : ויקטר
and~he~will~much~BELITTLE(V) : ויקלל
and~he~will~RISE(V) | and~he~will~make~RISE(V) : ויקם
and~they(m)~will~much~BE.ZEALOUS(V) : ויקנאו
and~he~will~LOATHE(V) : ויקץ
and~he~will~make~COME.NEAR(V) : ויקרב
and~they(m)~will~make~COME.NEAR(V) : ויקריבו
and~Yaq'shan : ויקשן
and~he~will~SEE(V) | and~he~will~be~SEE(V) : וירא
and~he~will~make~SEE(V)~him : ויראהו
and~they~did~FEAR(V) : ויראו
and~they(m)~will~make~SEE(V)~them(m) : ויראום
and~you(ms)~did~FEAR(V) : ויראת
and~he~will~DISPUTE(V) : וירב
and~he~will~make~INCREASE(V)~you(ms) : וירבך
and~they(m)~will~much~TREAD.ABOUT(V) : וירגלו

and~he~will~GO.DOWN$^{(V)}$ | and~he~did~GO.DOWN$^{(V)}$:

and~they$^{(m)}$~will~GO.DOWN$^{(V)}$ | and~they~will~GO.DOWN$^{(V)}$:

and~we~will~GO.DOWN$^{(V)}$:

and~I~did~GO.DOWN$^{(V)}$:

and~he~will~RAISE.UP$^{(V)}$:

and~they$^{(m)}$~will~SHOUT.ALOUD$^{(V)}$:

and~he~will~make~SMELL$^{(V)}$:

and~they$^{(m)}$~will~DISPUTE$^{(V)}$:

and~he~will~RAISE.UP$^{(V)}$~her :

and~they~will~make~RUN$^{(V)}$~him :

and~you$^{(ms)}$~did~POSSESS$^{(V)}$~her :

and~you$^{(mp)}$~did~POSSESS$^{(V)}$ | and~you$^{(ms)}$~did~POSSESS$^{(V)}$~them$^{(m)}$:

and~he~will~make~RIDE$^{(V)}$:

and~he~will~make~RIDE$^{(V)}$~them$^{(m)}$:

and~FLANK~him :

and~he~will~make~RAISE.UP$^{(V)}$:

and~he~will~BE.DYSFUNCTIONAL$^{(V)}$:

and~they$^{(m)}$~will~make~BE.DYSFUNCTIONAL$^{(V)}$:

and~he~will~make~BE.HUNGRY$^{(V)}$~you$^{(ms)}$:

and~he~will~RUN$^{(V)}$:

and~he~will~EMPTY :

and~she~did~SPIT$^{(V)}$:

and~they$^{(m)}$~will~HAMMER$^{(V)}$:

and~they$^{(m)}$~will~HAMMER$^{(V)}$~them$^{(m)}$:

and~he~did~POSSESS$^{(V)}$:

and~they~did~POSSESS$^{(V)}$:

and~we~did~POSSESS$^{(V)}$:

and~you$^{(ms)}$~did~POSSESS$^{(V)}$:

and~THERE.IS :

and~they$^{(m)}$~will~make~INQUIRE$^{(V)}$~them$^{(m)}$:

and~he~will~SETTLE$^{(V)}$ | and~he~will~make~TURN.BACK$^{(V)}$ | and~he~will~make~GUST$^{(V)}$ | and~he~will~TURN.BACK$^{(V)}$ | and~he~did~SETTLE$^{(V)}$:

and~she~did~SETTLE$^{(V)}$:

and~they$^{(m)}$~will~SETTLE$^{(V)}$:

and~he~will~make~SWEAR$^{(V)}$~me :

and~we~did~SETTLE$^{(V)}$:

and~he~will~make~SWEAR$^{(V)}$:

and~he~will~CRACK$^{(V)}$:

and~you$^{(ms)}$~did~SETTLE$^{(V)}$:

and~you$^{(ms)}$~did~SETTLE$^{(V)}$~& :

and~you$^{(mp)}$~did~SETTLE$^{(V)}$:

and~he~will~TURN.BACK$^{(V)}$:

and~they$^{(m)}$~will~TURN.BACK$^{(V)}$:

and~they$^{(m)}$~will~SUBSIDE$^{(V)}$:

and~they$^{(m)}$~will~make~TURN.BACK$^{(V)}$ | and~they$^{(m)}$~will~TURN.BACK$^{(V)}$:

and~he~will~SET.DOWN$^{(V)}$~him :

and~they$^{(m)}$~will~make~DEPART.EARLY$^{(V)}$:

and~he~will~make~DEPART.EARLY$^{(V)}$:

and~he~will~DWELL$^{(V)}$:

and~he~will~much~SEND$^{(V)}$ | and~he~will~SEND$^{(V)}$:

and~he~will~SEND$^{(V)}$~her :

and~he~will~SEND$^{(V)}$~him :

and~they$^{(m)}$~will~much~SEND$^{(V)}$:

and~he~will~much~SEND$^{(V)}$~them$^{(m)}$:

and~he~will~SEND$^{(V)}$~us :

and~he~will~make~THROW.OUT$^{(V)}$~him :

and~they$^{(m)}$~will~make~THROW.OUT$^{(V)}$:

and~he~will~make~THROW.OUT$^{(V)}$~them$^{(m)}$:
and~he~will~make~THROW.OUT$^{(V)}$:
and~they$^{(m)}$~will~make~DESTROY$^{(V)}$~them$^{(m)}$:
and~he~will~make~DESTROY$^{(V)}$~them$^{(m)}$:
and~he~will~make~HEAR$^{(V)}$~us :
and~SLEEPING :
and~JASPER :
and~he~will~make~DRINK$^{(V)}$:
and~they$^{(m)}$~will~make~LOOK.DOWN$^{(V)}$:
and~he~will~make~/ LOOK.DOWN$^{(V)}$:
and~STRAIGHT :
and~he~will~much~MINISTER$^{(V)}$:
and~they$^{(m)}$~will~much~MINISTER$^{(V)}$~you$^{(ms)}$:
and~he~will~GULP$^{(V)}$ | and~he~will~SET.DOWN$^{(V)}$:
and~he~will~ARRIVE$^{(V)}$:
and~TENT.PEG :
and~TENT.PEG~s~her :
and~TENT.PEG~s~them$^{(m)}$:
and~ORPHAN :
and~they$^{(m)}$~will~SCOUT$^{(V)}$:
and~REMAINDER :
and~like~BUCK :
and~like~FOREARM~s2 :
and~like~LION :
and~like~GUILT :
and~like~WHICH :
and~HEAVY :
and~like~>~COME$^{(V)}$:
and~ARMAMENT :
and~SHEEP :
and~SHEEP :
and~JAR~her :
and~like~ROAD :
and~he~did~be~much~WASH$^{(V)}$:
and~IN.THIS.WAY :
and~ADMINISTRATOR :
and~ALL :
and~ALL~him :
and~ARM.BAND :
and~CUP :
and~Kush :
and~like~the~SAND :
and~GIVEN.THAT :
and~he~did~much~WASH$^{(V)}$:
and~they~did~much~WASH$^{(V)}$:
and~you$^{(mp)}$~did~much~WASH$^{(V)}$:
and~!$^{(mp)}$~SUBDUE$^{(V)}$~her :
and~like~BRAVERY~s~you$^{(ms)}$:
and~he~did~much~ADORN$^{(V)}$:
and~they~did~much~ADORN$^{(V)}$:
and~he~did~much~DENY$^{(V)}$:
and~ROUNDNESS :
and~he~did~much~FINISH$^{(V)}$:
and~FAILING :
and~I~will~much~FINISH$^{(V)}$~you$^{(ms)}$:
and~I~did~much~SUSTAIN$^{(V)}$:
and~like~DAY~s~you$^{(ms)}$:
and~like~Menasheh :
and~he~did~much~COVER.OVER$^{(V)}$:
and~he~did~much~COVER.OVER$^{(V)}$~him :
and~they$^{(m)}$~did~much~COVER.OVER$^{(V)}$:
and~we~did~COVER.OVER$^{(V)}$:
and~you$^{(ms)}$~did~COVER.OVER$^{(V)}$:
and~she~did~much~COVER.OVER$^{(V)}$:
and~he~did~much~COVER$^{(V)}$:
and~like~SHOWERS~s :

and~EARTHENWARE~s2 :
and~like~PRODUCTION :
and~like~IN.THIS.WAY :
and~like~ALL :
and~ALL :
and~Kaleyv :
and~like~LIONESS :
and~CONSUMING~s :
and~UTENSIL~s | and~UTENSIL :
and~ENTIRELY :
and~Kalneh :
and~like~THAT.ONE :
and~like~THAT.ONE~him :
and~like~DECISION~him :
and~like~the~FULL :
and~like~WORK :
and~SO :
and~BASE~him :
and~like~POURING~her :
and~like~POURING~him :
and~Kena'an :
and~SHEEP :
and~SILVER :
and~like~COMPANY~him :
and~like~BONE :
and~PALM~s~him :
and~you$^{(ms)}$~did~DOUBLE.OVER$^{(V)}$:
and~!$^{(ms)}$~much~COVER$^{(V)}$:
and~you$^{(ms)}$~did~COVER$^{(V)}$:
and~KNOB :
and~KERUV :
and~CUT$^{(V)}$~ed$^{(ms)}$:
and~VINEYARD :
and~Karmi :
and~VINEYARD~you$^{(ms)}$:
and~PLANTATION :
and~Keran :
and~LEG~s~him :
and~you$^{(ms)}$~will~CUT$^{(V)}$:
and~like~THIGH :
and~they~did~TOPPLE$^{(V)}$:
and~like~>~HEAR$^{(V)}$~him :
and~he~did~WRITE$^{(V)}$:
and~you$^{(ms)}$~did~WRITE$^{(V)}$:
and~I~did~WRITE$^{(V)}$:
and~you$^{(ms)}$~did~WRITE$^{(V)}$~them$^{(m)}$:
and~WRITING :
and~TUNIC :
and~SMASH$^{(V)}$~ed$^{(ms)}$:
and~to~FATHER~s~you$^{(ms)}$:
and~to~FATHER~s~us :
and~to~FATHER~him :
and~to~NEEDY~you$^{(ms)}$:
and~to~Aviram :
and~to~Avram :
and~to~LORD :
and~to~HUMAN :
and~Le'ah :
and~to~>~LOVE$^{(V)}$:
and~to~Aharon :
and~COMMUNITY :
and~Le'um~s :
and~to~NATIVE :
and~to~SISTER~him :
and~to~BROTHER~him :
and~to~BROTHER~you$^{(ms)}$:
and~to~MOTHER~her :
and~to~MOTHER~him :
and~to~BOND :
and~to~MAN :
and~to~WOMAN~him :
and~to~Iytamar :
and~to~>~EAT$^{(V)}$:
and~to~>~EAT$^{(V)}$~you$^{(mp)}$:
and~to~THESE :
and~to~Elohiym~them$^{(m)}$:
and~to~the~WIDOW :
and~to~Elazar :
and~to~BONDWOMAN~you$^{(ms)}$:
and~to~the~LAND :
and~to~LAND~me :
and~to~LAND~them$^{(m)}$:
and~to~the~GUILT :
and~to~the~WHICH | and~to~Asher :
and~to~the~BEAST :
and~to~BEAST :

and~to~the~BRIGHT.SPOT :ולבהרת
and~to~>~COME(V) :ולבוא
and~FRANKINCENSE :ולבונה
and~to~GARMENT~s :ולביגדי
and~to~the~HOUSE :ולביית
and~to~EXCEPT :ולבילתי
and~to~Binyamin :ולבינימין
and~to~HOUSE :ולבית
and~to~DAUGHTER~him :ולביתו
and~to~HOUSE~you(ms) :ולביתך
and~Lavan | and~WHITE :ולבן
and~to~SON~s~him :ולבניו
and~to~SON~s~you(ms) :ולבניך
and~BRICK~s :ולבנים
and~to~SON~s~us :ולבנינו
and~to~>~much~KNEEL(V) :ולברך
and~he~did~WEAR(V) :ולבש
and~he~did~WEAR(V)~them(m) :ולבשם
and~to~Gad :ולגד
and~to~the~Gad~of :ולגדי
and~to~IMMIGRANT :ולגר
CHILD :ולד
and~to~>~ADHERE(V) :ולדבקה
and~to~Dan :ולדן
and~to~her :ולה
and~to~>~make~SEPARATE(V) :ולהבדיל
and~to~>~make~COME(V)~you(ms) :ולהביאך
and~to~>~make~THROW(V) :ולהורות
and~to~>~make~LIVE(V) :ולהחיות
and~to~>~self~FALL(V) :ולהיתנפל
and~to~them(m) :ולהם
and~to~>~make~GO.UP(V)~him :ולהעלותו
and~to~>~make~INCREASE(V) :ולהרבות
and~to~>~make~TURN.BACK(V) :ולהשיב
and~to~>~make~DESTROY(V) :ולהשמיד
and~to~him | and~WOULD.THAT :ולו
and~NOT :ולוא
and~LOG :ולוג

and~Lud :ולוד
and~HAZEL :ולוז
and~Lot | and~LAUDANUM :ולוט
and~Lewi :ולוי
and~to~SACRIFICE :ולזבח
and~to~REMEMBRANCE :ולזיכרון
and~to~BEARD~s :ולזיקני
and~to~SEED~him :ולזרעו
and~to~SEED~you(ms) :ולזרעך
and~to~SEED~them(m) :ולזרעם
and~FIGHT(V)~ed(mp) :ולחומי
and~to~DARKNESS :ולחושך
and~to~the~BREASTPLATE :ולחושן
and~to~the~FAILURE :ולחטאת
and~to~FAILURE~us :ולחטאתנו
and~to~the~LIVING :ולחיה
and~to~>~much~DRILL(V) :ולחלל
and~BREAD :ולחם
and~to~the~HALF :ולחצי
and~to~COURTYARD :ולחצר
and~to~>~THINK(V) :ולחשוב
and~to~MARKER~s :ולטוטפות
and~Letush~s :ולטושים
and~to~BEAST~you(ms) :וליבהמתך
and~to~>~WEEP(V)~her :וליבכותה
and~to~SON~him :וליבנו
and~to~DAUGHTER~s~me :וליבנותי
and~to~DAUGHTER~s~him :וליבנותיו
and~to~DAUGHTER~s~you(ms) :וליבנותיך
and~to~SON~s :וליבני
and~to~SON~s~them(m) :וליבניהם
and~to~>~GIVE(V)~you(ms) :וליהיותך
and~to~Yoseph :וליוסף
and~to~Zevulun :וליזבולון
and~to~Yisra'eyl :ולייסראל
and~to~Yits'hhaq :ולייצחק
and~to~>~FEAR(V) :ולייראה
and~to~Yishma'el :וליישמעאל
and~NIGHT :ולילה

and~you(mp)~did~much~LEARN(V)
and~to~DAY~s
and~to~much~HATE(V)~ing(mp)~me
and~to~>~REGULATE(V)
and~!(mp)~STAY.THE.NIGHT(V)
and~to~WOMAN~s~you(mp)
and~to~HIRELING~you(ms)
and~to~Ya'aqov
and~to~EDGE
and~to~FACE~s
and~to~PRICKLY.THORN~s
and~to~Qehat
and~to~INCENSE.SMOKE
and~to~GOODS~them(m)
and~to~FLANK~s2
and~to~SWEARING
and~to~>~HEAR(V)
and~to~>~SAFEGUARD(V)
and~to~PIERCING
and~to~MAID~s
and~!(ms)~WALK(V) | and~to~you(ms)
and~to~the~SHEEP~s
and~to~you(ms) | and~!(ms)~WALK(V)~&
and~!(mp)~WALK(V)
and~to~ADMINISTRATOR
/ and~to~ALL
and~to~ALL
and~to~>~much~FINISH(V)~them(m)
and~to~you(mp)
and~to~>~much~COVER(V)
and~to~the~SHOULDER.PIECE
and~to~Le'ah
and~to~Lavan
and~to~Lewi
and~to~>~WALK(V)
and~!(ms)~much~LEARN(V)~her
and~they~did~LEARN(V)
and~you(mp)~did~LEARN(V)
and~to~WHAT
and~to~KINDRED~you(ms)
and~to~KINDRED~us
and~to~APPOINTED~s
and~to~WONDER
and~to~BRANCH
and~to~WHO
and~to~from~HOUSE
and~to~the~ALTAR
and~to~the~SETTING~s
and~to~DEPOSIT~s~you(mp)
and~to~Mits'rayim
and~to~Mits'rayim~s
and~to~COLLECTION
and~to~LIVESTOCK~him
and~to~EXTREMITY
and~Lamekh
and~to~Makhir
and~to~much~DO.SORCERY(V)~ing(mp)
and~to~>~much~FILL(V)
and~to~LOAD
and~to~JOURNEY
and~to~the~SMALL.AMOUNT
and~to~THAT
and~to~VOW
and~to~HEIR~me
and~to~POURING~s~you(mp)
and~to~POSTERITY~me
and~to~YOUNG.MAN
and~to~>~make~FALL(V)
and~to~Naphtali
and~to~the~FEMALE
and~to~the~ERUPTION
and~to~the~ELEVATION
and~to~the~CHOICE.VINE
and~to~the~SCAB

and~to~Sarah : ולשרה
and~to~the~NOBLE~s : ולשרים
and~to~>~SERVE(V)~him : ולעבדו
and~to~SERVANT~s~you(ms) : ולעבדיך
and~to~SERVANT~you(ms) : ולעבדך
and~to~>~SERVE(V) : ולעבוד
and~to~Ever : ולעבר
and~to~Og : ולעוג
and~to~FLYER : ולעוף
and~to~EYE~s : ולעיני
and~to~>~STAND(V) : ולעמוד
and~to~PEOPLE~you(ms) : ולעמך
and~HEMLOCK : ולענה
and~to~>~DO(V) : ולעשות
and~to~the~EVENING : ולערב
and~to~MOUTH : ולפי
and~TORCH : ולפיד
and~to~RIB : ולצלע
and~to~the~WOOL : ולצמר
and~to~INFECTION : ולצרעת
and~to~TOP.OF.THE.HEAD : ולקדקוד
and~he~did~TAKE(V) : ולקח
and~she~did~TAKE(V) | and~he~did~TAKE(V)~her : ולקחה
and~they~did~TAKE(V) : ולקחו
and~we~did~TAKE(V) : ולקחנו
and~you(ms)~did~TAKE(V) | and~to~>~TAKE(V) : ולקחת
and~I~did~TAKE(V) : ולקחתי
and~I~did~TAKE(V)~you(ms) : ולקחתיך
and~you(mp)~did~TAKE(V) : ולקחתם
and~GLEANINGS : ולקט
and~they~did~PICK.UP(V) : ולקטו
and~to~FOOT : ולרגל
and~to~the~Re'uven~of : ולראובני
and~to~WIDTH~her : ולרחבה
and~to~Rivqah : ולרבקה
and~to~VEHICLE~him : ולרכבו
and~to~SAFEGUARD(V)~ing(mp) : ולשומרי
and~to~OFFERING.OF.RESTITUTION~s~you(mp) : ולשלמיכם
and~to~Shem : ולשם
and~to~OIL : ולשמן
and~to~>~SAFEGUARD(V)~her : ולשמרה
and~to~the~SUN : ולשמש
and~to~GATE : ולשער
and~to~Shet : ולשת
and~to~the~SETTLER : ולתושב
and~to~SETTLER~you(ms) : ולתושבך
and~to~DECORATION : ולתיפארת
and~to~>~GIVE(V)~you(ms) : ולתיתך
and~to~>~GIVE(V) : ולתת
and~HUNDRED : ומאה
and~from~AT.THAT.TIME : ומאז
and~from~THESE : ומאלה
and~from~LAND : ומארץ
and~from~WHICH : ומאשר
and~HUNDRED | and~from~AT : ומאת
and~HUNDRED~s2 : ומאתים
and~much~KNEEL(V)~ing(mp)~you(ms) : ומברכיך
and~Magog : ומגוג
and~they~did~MEASURE(V) : ומדדו
and~WHY : ומדוע
and~you(mp)~did~MEASURE(V) : ומדותם
and~Madai : ומדי
and~make~SORROW(V)~ing(fp) : ומדיבות
and~WHAT : ומה
and~from~HILL~s~her : ומהרריה
and~Mo'av~of : ומואבי
and~KINDRED~you(ms) : ומולדתך
and~WONDER~s : ומופתים
and~FEARING~you(mp) : ומוראכם
and~DISOBEY(V)~ing(ms) : ומורה
and~he~did~be~much~SCOUR(V) : ומורק
and~SETTLING : ומושב
and~Mosheh : ומושה
and~Mushiy : ומושי
and~REGULATE(V)~ing(ms) : ומושל
and~!(ms)~DIE(V) : ומות
and~make~SPATTER(V)~ing(ms) : ומזה
and~MEAT : ומזון
and~from~CHAMBER~s : ומחדרים
and~he~did~WIPE.AWAY(V) : ומחה
and~DANCE~s : ומחולות

and~much~INSCRIBE(V)~ing(ms) :
and~Mehhuya'el :
and~PRICE :
and~I~did~WIPE.AWAY(V) :
and~from~FAT~them(f) :
and~he~did~STRIKE.THROUGH(V) :
and~ONE.HALF~her :
and~TOMORROW :
and~FIRE.PAN~s~her :
and~FIRE.PAN~s~him :
and~BRANCH | and~she~did~TOTTER(V) :
and~BRANCH~you(ms) :
and~PRECIPITATION :
and~WATER~s2 | and~WHO :
and~CHOSEN :
and~from~HOUSE :
and~from~Bamot :
and~from~SON :
and~Mivsam :
and~from~HOUSE~s~you(ms) :
and~HEADDRESS~s | and~from~KNOLL~s :
and~TOWER :
and~ORNAMENT~s :
and~from~LOT :
and~from~FLOOR~you(ms) :
and~OPEN.SPACE :
and~OPEN.SPACE~s :
and~OPEN.SPACE~s~them(m) :
and~from~IMMIGRATE(V)~ing(fs) :
and~from~HAND :
and~Meydad :
and~from~BLOOD :
and~you(mp)~did~much~HURRY(V) :
and~from~DAY :
and~Miz'zah | and~from~THIS :
and~FORK~s~him :
and~SUNRISE~unto :
and~SEED~you(ms) :
and~SPRINKLING.BASIN~s~him :
and~from~OUTSIDE :
and~REVIVING :
and~BEST :
and~from~DEW :
and~WATER~s2 :
and~from~Yisra'eyl :
and~from~WINE.TROUGH~you(ms) :
and~from~ALL :
and~from~ALL :
and~UNDERGARMENT~s :
and~ROOF.COVERING :
and~TRIBUTE~them(m) :
and~he~did~much~FILL(V) :
and~!(mp)~FILL(V) :
and~you(ms)~did~much~FILL(V) :
and~from~to~STRAND :
and~Milkah :
and~from~PRECIOUS :
and~from~KINDRED~you(ms) :
and~from~ONE.HALF :
and~from~MORROW :
and~from~WILDERNESS :
and~from~LIVESTOCK :
and~CLAN~them(m) :
and~from~make~CLEAVE(V)~ing(mp) :
and~from~APPEARANCE :
and~from~Matanah :
/ and~FROM :
and~DEPOSIT :
and~from~Nahhali'eyl :
and~from~INHERITANCE :
and~DEPOSIT :

and~DEPOSIT~her :
and~DEPOSIT~him :
and~DEPOSIT~them(m) :
and~from~FIELD :
and~from~HATE~him :
and~from~WICKER.BASKET :
and~from~LEFT.HAND~them(m) :
and~PROVENDER :
and~NUMBER :
and~from~OFFENSE~s~them(m) :
and~from~FACE~s~you(ms) :
and~from~PRODUCE :
and~from~OPENING :
and~from~FLOCKS~you(ms) :
and~DIRECTIVE~s~him :
and~Mits'rayim :
and~SANCTUARY~me :
and~LIVESTOCK :
and~LIVESTOCK~s~me :
and~LIVESTOCK~you(mp) :
and~ACQUIRED :
and~from~EXTREMITY :
and~Mir'yam :
and~KNEADING.BOWL~you(ms) :
and~from~CROPLAND :
and~OINTMENT :
and~from~THERE :
and~from~OIL :
and~from~OIL :
and~from~OIL~s :
and~Mishma :
and~>~SAFEGUARD(V)~him :
and~CHARGE :
and~CHARGE~them(m) :
and~DOUBLE :
and~CLAN :

and~DECISION :
and~DECISION~s~him :
and~DECISION~s :
and~from~DEEP.WATER :
and~from~UNDER :
and~from~REMAINDER :
and~STRING~s~them(m) :
and~he~did~BE.LOW(V) :
and~make~HIT(V)~ing(ms) :
and~>~SELL(V) :
and~Makhir :
and~he~did~SELL(V) :
and~he~did~SELL(V)~him | and~they~did~SELL(V) :
and~much~DO.SORCERY(V)~ing(ms) / and~he~did~SNIP.OFF(V) :
and~FULL :
and~she~did~FILL(V) :
and~they~did~FILL(V) :
and~FILLING :
and~FILLING~her :
and~SALT :
and~KING :
and~Malkiy-Tsedeq :
and~Malki'el :
and~KING~s :
and~he~did~SNAP.OFF(V) :
and~LATE.RAIN :
and~TONG~s~her :
and~you(ms)~did~SNIP.OFF(V) :
and~you(mp)~did~SNIP.OFF(V) :
and~much~HURRY(V)~ing(ms) :
and~Mamre :
and~much~PREDICT(V)~ing(ms) :
and~Manahhat :
and~SACRIFICIAL.BOWL~s~him :
and~Menasheh :
and~Masa :
and~LOAD~you(mp) :
and~CANOPY :
and~CAST.IMAGE :

and~much~HATE(V)~ing(mp)~him :
and~from~SERVANT~s~you(ms) :
and~from~SERVICE :
and~PRESS.FIRMLY(V)~ed(ms) :
and~SMALL.AMOUNT :
and~CLOAK :
and~from~HARDSHIP :
and~UPWARD~unto | and~she~did~TRANSGRESS(V) :
and~from~PEOPLE~him :
and~from~PEOPLE~me :
and~from~PEOPLE~you(ms) :
and~from~TREE :
and~from~Etsi'on-Gaver :
and~he~did~FIND(V) :
and~she~did~FIND(V) | and~he~did~FIND(V)~her :
and~they~did~FIND(V)~him :
and~they~did~FIND(V)~you(ms) :
and~you(ms)~did~FIND(V) :
and~you(ms)~did~FIND(V) :
and~MONUMENT :
and~MONUMENT~s~them(m) :
and~UNLEAVENED.BREAD~s :
and~AREA :
and~ROD~you(mp) :
and~much~BELITTLE(V)~ing(ms) :
and~much~BELITTLE(V)~ing(mp)~you(ms) :
and~APPEARANCE | and~APPEARANCE~her :
and~APPEARANCE~him :
and~APPEARANCE~s~them(f) :
and~BITTER :
and~from~HEAD :
and~from~TENDERNESS :
and~BITTER.HERBS~s :
and~Meriyvah :
and~Merari :
and~Mash :
and~you(ms)~did~SMEAR(V) :
and~Meshek :
and~much~MAKE.RESTITUTION(V)~ing(ms) :
and~you(ms)~did~REGULATE(V) :
and~much~MINISTER(V)~ing(ms)~him :
and~he~did~DIE(V) :
and~she~did~DIE(V) :
and~they~did~DIE(V) :
and~Metusha'el :
and~I~did~DIE(V) :
and~GIFT :
and~we~did~DIE(V) :
and~DECLARE(V)~ed(ms) :
and~he~did~be~EAT(V) :
and~be~SECURE(V)~ing(fp) :
and~be~SECURE(V)~ing(mp) :
and~they~did~be~GATHER(V) :
and~you(ms)~did~be~GATHER(V) :
and~you(mp)~did~be~GATHER(V) :
and~Nevo :
and~we~will~COME(V) :
and~be~UNDERSTAND(V)~ing(ms) :
and~be~UNDERSTAND(V)~ing(mp) :
and~we~will~MIX(V)~& :
and~SOUTH~unto :
and~we~will~make~BE.FACE.TO.FACE(V) :
and~>~TOUCH(V) :
and~they~did~SMITE(V) :
and~NOD(V)~ing(ms) :
and~we~did~KNOW(V) :
and~VOW :
and~VOW~s~her :
and~VOW~s~you(ms) :
and~we~will~EXIST(V) :
and~he~did~be~OVERTURN(V) :

and~they~did~be~OVERTURN(V) :
and~RIVER :
and~we~will~KILL(V)~him :
and~they~did~be~TAKE.HOLD(V) :
and~we~will~EAT(V)~& :
and~we~will~SAY(V) :
and~Novahh :
and~TOUCH(V)~ing(ms) :
and~she~did~be~KNOW(V) :
and~No'ahh :
and~be~REBUKE(V)~ing(fs) :
and~he~did~ADD(V) :
and~she~did~be~ADD(V) :
and~they~did~be~APPOINT(V) :
and~I~did~be~APPOINT(V) :
and~No'ah :
and~PIERCE.THROUGH(V)~ing(ms) :
and~be~FEAR(V)~ing(ms) :
and~you(mp)~did~be~SLEEP(V) :
and~you(mp)~did~be~RESCUE(V) :
and~STEW :
and~ORNAMENTAL.RING :
and~Nahhor :
and~COPPER :
and~we~will~LIVE(V) :
and~INHERITANCE :
and~they~did~INHERIT(V) :
and~we~will~DREAM(V)~& :
and~you(ms)~did~INHERIT(V) :
and~INHERITANCE~him :
and~INHERITANCE~you(ms) :
and~you(ms)~did~INHERIT(V)~us :
and~be~CRAVE(V)~ing(ms) :
and~WE :
and~we~will~make~PERFORATE(V) :
and~he~did~be~THINK(V) :
and~!(ms)~EXTEND(V) | and~he~did~EXTEND(V) :
and~you(mp)~did~PLANT(V) :
and~you(ms)~did~LEAVE.ALONE(V)~her :
and~they~did~much~PROVOKE(V)~me :
and~they~did~be~KNEEL(V) :
and~he~did~be~REDEEM(V) :
and~you(mp)~did~be~SMITE(V) :
and~he~did~be~TAKE.AWAY(V) :
and~she~did~be~TAKE.AWAY(V) :
and~he~did~be~DRAW.NEAR(V) :
and~she~did~be~DRAW.NEAR(V) :
and~they~did~be~DRAW.NEAR(V) :
and~FREEWILL.OFFERING~you(ms) :
and~FREEWILL.OFFERING~s~you(mp) :
and~she~did~be~DRIVE.OUT(V) :
and~you(ms)~did~be~DRIVE.OUT(V) :
and~VOW~s~you(mp) :
and~we~will~EXIST(V) :
and~we~will~SACRIFICE(V)~& :
and~you(mp)~did~be~REMEMBER(V) :
and~she~did~be~SOW(V) :
and~we~will~LIVE(V) :
and~she~did~be~BE.DIRTY(V) :
and~you(mp)~did~be~BE.DIRTY(V) :
and~be~BE.HEAVY(V)~ing(mp) :
and~she~did~be~SUBDUE(V) :

and~he~did~self~ COVER(V)
and~he~did~be~CUT(V)
and~she~did~be~CUT(V)
and~they~did~be~CUT(V)
and~they~did~be~ BE.IMPATIENT(V)
and~they~did~be~JOIN(V)
and~he~did~be~FIGHT(V)
and~we~did~be~ FIGHT(V)
and~we~will~TRAP(V)
and~he~did~be~SELL(V)
and~we~will~SELL(V)~ him
and~he~did~be~FIND(V)
and~they~did~be~ FIND(V)
and~he~did~be~ DRAIN(V)
and~Nimrah
and~he~did~be~LIFT.UP(V)
and~you(mp)~did~be~ TEAR.AWAY(V)
and~POURING~her
and~POURING~them(m)
and~POURING~him
and~POURING~her
and~POURING~s~ them(m)
and~he~did~be~ FORGIVE(V)
and~we~will~JOURNEY(V)
and~we~will~ CREMATE(V)~&
and~she~did~be~HIDE(V)
and~we~did~be~ BE.DISTINCT(V)
and~they(f)~did~be~ OPEN.UP(V)
and~we~will~OPEN(V)~ &
and~they~did~be~ STAND.UP(V)
and~you(ms)~did~be~ STAND.UP(V)

and~you(mp)~did~ much~DELIVER(V)
and~we~will~CRY.OUT(V)
and~he~did~be~ SET.APART(V)
and~I~did~be~ SET.APART(V)
and~he~did~be~ACQUIT(V)
and~we~will~TAKE(V)
and~you(ms)~will~be~ ACQUIT(V)
and~he~did~be~DRY(V)
and~he~did~be~ CALL.OUT(V)
and~he~did~be~ COME.NEAR(V)
and~she~did~be~ ACQUIT(V)
and~we~will~SEE(V)~& | and~he~did~be~SEE(V)
and~she~did~be~SEE(V)
and~we~will~THROW(V)~ them(m)
and~he~did~be~HEAL(V)
and~he~did~be~ ACCEPT(V)
and~we~will~ INQUIRE(V)
and~you(mp)~did~ be~REMAIN(V)
and~he~did~be~ SWEAR(V)
and~he~did~be~CRACK(V)
and~we~will~ EXCHANGE(V)~&
and~we~will~ LIE.DOWN(V)
and~he~did~be~ FORGET(V)
and~I~did~be~ DESTROY(V)
and~we~will~HEAR(V) | and~he~did~be~HEAR(V)
and~we~will~ HEAR(V)~&
and~you(ms)~will~be~ SAFEGUARD(V)

and~you(mp)~will~be~SAFEGUARD(V) :
and~he~did~be~LEAN(V) :
and~she~did~be~LOOK.DOWN(V) :
and~we~will~GULP(V) :
and~we~did~self~BEND.DOWN(V) :
and~he~did~much~DIVIDE.INTO.PIECES(V) :
and~we~will~GIVE(V) :
and~you(mp)~did~much~BREAK.DOWN(V) :
and~you(mp)~did~be~GIVE(V) :
and~we~will~make~HIT(V) :
and~we~will~make~HIT(V)~him :
and~we~will~make~HIT(V) :
and~we~did~WALK(V) :
and~we~will~WALK(V)~& :
and~you(mp)~did~CUT.OFF(V) :
and~he~did~be~MELT.AWAY(V) :
and~he~did~FLEE(V) :
and~he~did~LIFT.UP(V) :
and~they~did~LIFT.UP(V) :
and~I~did~LIFT.UP(V) :
and~you(mp)~did~LIFT.UP(V) :
and~you(ms)~did~LIFT.UP(V)~me :
and~he~did~be~GO.AROUND(V) | and~we~will~GO.AROUND(V) :
and~they~did~FLEE(V) :
and~>~JOURNEY(V) :
and~CAPTAIN :
and~CAPTAIN~s :
and~POURING :
and~POURING~s~her :
and~POURING~s :
and~he~did~JOURNEY(V) :
and~they~did~JOURNEY(V) :
and~we~will~much~COUNT(V) :
and~you(mp)~did~FLEE(V) :
and~we~will~SERVE(V)~& :
and~we~will~be~make~SERVE(V)~them(m) :
and~we~will~CROSS.OVER(V) :
and~we~will~GO.UP(V) :
and~we~will~GO.UP(V)~& | and~he~did~be~GO.UP(V) :
and~SANDAL~s~you(ms) :
and~he~did~be~BE.OUT.OF.SIGHT(V) :
and~Na'aman :
and~we~will~DO(V) :
and~we~will~DO(V)~her :
and~YOUNG.MAN :
and~YOUNG.WOMAN~s~her :
and~Nepheg :
and~he~did~FALL(V) :
and~she~did~FALL(V) :
and~they~did~FALL(V) :
and~you(mp)~did~FALL(V) :
and~we~will~TURN(V) :
and~SOUL :
and~SOUL~him :
and~SOUL~us :
and~Naphtali :
and~FEMALE :
and~>~much~ACQUIT(V) :
and~SPECKLED :
and~we~will~RISE(V)~& :
and~INNOCENT :
and~VENGEANCE :
and~we~will~make~COME.NEAR(V) :
and~we~will~make~TURN.BACK(V) | and~we~will~SETTLE(V) :
and~we~did~TURN.BACK(V) :
and~WOMAN~s :
and~WOMAN~s~them(m) :
and~we~will~make~DESOLATE(V) :
and~he~did~CAST.OFF(V) :
and~we~will~much~SEND(V)~you(ms) :
and~we~will~make~THROW.OUT(V)~him :

and~they~did~be~DESOLATE(V) : ונשמו
/ and~>~GIVE(V) : ונתון
and~DRAW.AWAY(V)~ed(ms) : ונתוק
and~he~did~GIVE(V) : ונתן
and~he~did~GIVE(V)~her | and~she~did~GIVE(V) : ונתנה
and~we~did~GIVE(V) | and~they~did~GIVE(V) | and~he~did~GIVE(V)~him : ונתנו
and~he~did~GIVE(V)~you(ms) : ונתנך
and~he~did~GIVE(V)~them(m) : ונתנם
and~he~did~BREAK.DOWN(V) : ונתץ
and~you(ms)~did~GIVE(V) : ונתת
and~you(ms)~did~GIVE(V)~& : ונתתה
and~I~did~GIVE(V) : ונתתי
and~I~did~GIVE(V)~him : ונתתיו
and~I~did~GIVE(V)~you(ms) : ונתתיך
and~you(mp)~did~GIVE(V) : ונתתם
and~!(ms)~LIFT.UP(V) : ושא
and~ALL.AROUND : וסביב
and~Sevam : ושבם
and~PLENTY | and~he~did~BE.SATISFIED(V) : ושבע
and~they~did~BE.SATISFIED(V) : ושבעו
and~you(ms)~did~BE.SATISFIED(V) : ושבעת
and~Savtah : ושבתה
and~Savtekha : ושבתכא
and~FIELD : ושדה
and~you(ms)~did~DAUB(V) : ושדת
and~RAM : ושה
and~IMBIBE(V)~ing(ms) : וסובא
and~FLOUR : וסולת
and~!(mp)~TRADE(V)~her : וסחרוה
and~!(ms)~PLACE(V) : ושים
and~they~did~PLACE(V) : ושימו
and~he~did~REJOICE(V) : ושימח
and~APPAREL : ושימלה
and~Sitriy : וסיתרי
and~you(ms)~did~FENCE.AROUND(V) : ושכות
and~I~did~FENCE.AROUND(V) : ושכותי
and~HIRELING : ושכיר
and~WICKER.BASKET : וסל

and~you(ms)~will~FORGIVE(V) : וסלחת
and~he~did~PLACE(V) : ושם
and~he~did~PLACE(V)~him | and~they~did~PLACE(V) : ושמו
and~LEFT.HAND : ושמאול
and~LEFT.HAND : ושמאל
and~he~did~REJOICE(V) : ושמח
and~you(ms)~did~REJOICE(V) : ושמחת
and~REJOICING~you(mp) : ושמחתם
and~he~did~SUPPORT(V) : וסמך
and~they~did~SUPPORT(V) : וסמכו
and~you(ms)~did~SUPPORT(V) : וסמכת
and~APPAREL~s : ושמלות
and~you(ms)~did~PLACE(V) : ושמת
and~I~did~PLACE(V) : ושמתי
and~I~did~PLACE(V)~you(ms) : ושמתיך
and~you(mp)~did~PLACE(V)~them(m) | and~you(mp)~did~PLACE(V) : ושמתם
and~he~did~HATE(V)~her : ושנאה
and~!(mp)~HOLD.UP(V) : וסעדו
and~!(mp)~JOURNEY(V) : וסעו
and~BARLEY : ושעורה
and~HAIRY.GOAT : ושעיר
and~HAIRY.GOAT~s : ושעירי
and~HAIR : ושער
and~HAIR | and~HAIR~her : ושערה
and~LIP : ושפה
and~BOARDED.UP(V)~ing(mp) : וספוני
and~!(ms)~COUNT(V) : וספור
and~he~did~COUNT(V) : וספר
and~she~did~COUNT(V) : וספרה
and~you(ms)~did~COUNT(V) : וספרת
and~you(mp)~did~COUNT(V) : וספרתם
and~they~did~STONE(V)~her : וסקלוה
and~they~did~STONE(V)~me : וסקלוני
and~you(ms)~did~STONE(V)~him : וסקלתו
and~you(ms)~did~STONE(V)~them(m) | and~you(mp)~did~STONE(V) : וסקלתם
and~he~did~TURN.ASIDE(V) : וסר
and~Sarah : ושרה
and~they~did~TURN.ASIDE(V) : וסרו
and~Serahh | and~OVERHANG : וסרח

and~SLICING : ושרט
and~Sarai | and~NOBLE~s : ושרי
and~he~did~CREMATE(V) : ושרף
and~they~did~CREMATE(V) : ושרפו
and~you(ms)~did~CREMATE(V) : ושרפת
and~you(mp)~did~TURN.ASIDE(V) : ושרתם
and~SERVANT | and~he~did~SERVE(V) : ועבד
and~SERVANT~him | and~he~did~SERVE(V)~him | and~they~did~SERVE(V) : ועבדו
and~they~did~SERVE(V)~you(ms) : ועבדוך
and~they~did~SERVE(V)~them(m) : ועבדום
and~SERVANT~me : ועבדי
and~SERVANT~s~him : ועבדיו
and~SERVANT~s~you(ms) : ועבדיך
and~SERVANT~s~you(mp) : ועבדיכם
and~SERVANT~s : ועבדים
and~SERVANT~you(ms) | and~he~did~SERVE(V)~you(ms) : ועבדך
and~you(ms)~did~SERVE(V) : ועבדת
and~you(mp)~will~SERVE(V) | and~you(ms)~did~SERVE(V)~them(m) : ועבדתם
and~you(ms)~did~SERVE(V)~me : ועבדתני
and~SERVE(V)~ed(fs) | and~SERVICE : ועבודה
and~SERVICE : ועבודת
and~he~did~CROSS.OVER(V) : ועבר
and~I~did~CROSS.OVER(V) : ועברתי
and~WRATH~them(m) | and~you(mp)~did~CROSS.OVER(V) : ועברתם
and~BULLOCK : ועגל
and~UNTIL | and~WITNESS : ועד
and~WITNESS : ועדה
and~WITNESS~s~him : ועדותיו
and~Og : ועוג
and~REED.PIPE : ועוגב
and~YET.AGAIN : ועוד
and~YET.AGAIN~you(ms) : ועודך
and~Uziy'eyl : ועוזיאל
and~ASCENSION.OFFERING : ועולה
and~ASCENSION.OFFERING~s : ועולוות
and~ASCENSION.OFFERING : ועולת
and~COHABITATION~her : ועונתה
and~DO(V)~ing(ms) : ועושה
and~FLYER : ועוף
and~BRAWN : ועוצם
and~SKIN~s : ועורות
and~GOAT | and~STRONG : ועז
and~he~did~LEAVE(V) : ועזב
and~he~did~LEAVE(V)~me : ועזבני
and~I~did~LEAVE(V)~them(m) : ועזבתים
and~LEAVE(V)~ed(ms) : ועזוב
and~HELP : ועזר
and~!(mp)~SERVE(V) : ועיבדו
and~Eyval : ועיבל
and~!(mp)~CROSS.OVER(V) : ועיברו
and~GOAT~s~you(ms) : ועיזיך
and~GOAT~s : ועיזים
and~WITH : ועים
and~WITH~him : ועימו
and~they~did~much~AFFLICT(V) | and~EYE~him : ועינו
and~EYE~s2 : ועיני
and~EYE~s2 : ועיניים
and~EYE~s2~you(ms) : ועיניך
and~EYE~s2~us : ועינינו
and~you(mp)~did~much~AFFLICT(V) : ועיניתם
and~EYE~s2~you(mp) : ועינכם
and~ONE.TENTH : ועישרון
and~CITY : ועיר
and~Irad : ועירד
and~COLT ~s : ועירים
and~UPON : ועל
and~he~did~GO.UP(V) | and~!(ms)~GO.UP(V) : ועלה
and~!(mp)~GO.UP(V) | and~they~did~GO.UP(V) : ועלו
and~TWILIGHT : ועלטה
and~UPON~them(m) : ועליהם
and~UPON~him : ועליו
and~we~GO.UP(V) : ועלינו
and~you(ms)~did~GO.UP(V) : ועלית
and~you(mp)~did~GO.UP(V) : ועליתם
and~she~did~GO.UP(V) : ועלתה
and~he~did~STAND(V) : ועמד
and~they~did~STAND(V) : ועמדו

and~PILLAR :
and~PILLAR~s~him :
and~PILLAR~s :
and~PILLAR~s~ them$^{(m)}$:
and~PILLAR~s~him :
and~SUNKEN :
and~Ghamorah :
and~PEOPLE~me :
and~PEOPLE~you$^{(ms)}$:
and~VALLEY :
and~GRAPE~s :
and~Anah :
and~they~did~ANSWER$^{(V)}$:
and~you$^{(ms)}$~did~ANSWER$^{(V)}$:
and~CLOUD :
and~CLOUD~you$^{(ms)}$:
and~BOUGH :
and~they~did~FINE$^{(V)}$:
and~she~did~ANSWER$^{(V)}$:
and~!$^{(ms)}$~DO$^{(V)}$ | and~he~did~ DO$^{(V)}$:
and~he~did~DO$^{(V)}$~him :
and~!$^{(mp)}$~DO$^{(V)}$ | and~Esaw | and~they~did~DO$^{(V)}$:
and~!$^{(fs)}$~DO$^{(V)}$:
and~we~did~DO$^{(V)}$:
and~TENTH :
and~you$^{(ms)}$~did~DO$^{(V)}$:
and~you$^{(ms)}$~will~DO$^{(V)}$~ them$^{(m)}$ | and~you$^{(mp)}$~did~DO$^{(V)}$:
and~TEN :
and~TEN~s :
and~she~did~DO$^{(V)}$:
and~she~did~DO$^{(V)}$:
and~DIRT | and~Epher :
and~Ephron :
and~TREE :
and~NUMEROUS :
and~NUMEROUS~s :
and~TREE~s :
and~BONE :
and~BONE~s~ them$^{(m)}$:
and~he~did~STOP$^{(V)}$:
and~Aqan :
and~SCORPION :

and~STERILE :
and~WILLOW~s :
and~NAKEDNESS :
and~CITY~s :
and~CITY~s~him :
and~CITY~s~you$^{(mp)}$:
and~CITY~s :
and~he~did~ARRANGE$^{(V)}$:
and~they~did~ARRANGE$^{(V)}$:
and~you$^{(ms)}$~did~ARRANGE$^{(V)}$:
and~UNCIRCUMCISED :
and~you$^{(mp)}$~did~ CONSIDERED.UNCIRCUMCISED$^{(V)}$:
and~CHESTNUT :
and~they~did~BEHEAD$^{(V)}$:
and~NECK~you$^{(mp)}$:
and~THICK.DARKNESS :
and~you$^{(ms)}$~did~ BEHEAD$^{(V)}$~him :
and~YOUNG.SHEEP~s :
and~NOW :
and~MALE.GOAT~s :
and~EDGE :
and~he~did~RANSOM$^{(V)}$:
and~RANSOM$^{(V)}$~ed$^{(ms)}$~him :
and~Pu'a :
and~Put :
and~DEED :
and~INTERPRET$^{(V)}$~ing$^{(ms)}$:
and~AWE :
and~you$^{(ms)}$~did~ SHAKE.IN.AWE$^{(V)}$:
and~BURSTING :
and~MOUTH :
and~!$^{(mp)}$~REACH$^{(V)}$:
and~CORPSE~s~ / you$^{(mp)}$:
and~Pikhol :
and~CONCUBINE~him :
and~they~did~much~ TURN$^{(V)}$:
and~DUNG~him :
and~FLAX~s :
and~you$^{(ms)}$~did~much~ OPEN$^{(V)}$:
and~Palu :
and~OTHERWISE :

and~he~did~TURN(V) :
and~FACE~s~me :
and~FACE~s~them(m) :
and~you(ms)~did~TURN(V) :
and~I~did~TURN(V) :
and~he~did~HOP(V) :
and~I~did~HOP(V) :
Waphsi :
and~SCULPTURE~s :
and~SCULPTURE~s~them(m) :
and~SCULPTURE :
and~BELL~s :
and~she~did~PART(V) :
and~they~did~REGISTER(V) :
and~I~did~REGISTER(V) :
and~you(mp)~did~REGISTER(V) :
and~REGISTER(V)~ed(mp) :
and~REGISTER(V)~ed(mp)~them(m) :
and~REGISTER(V)~ed(mp)~him :
and~OVERSIGHT :
and~BULL :
and~they~did~REPRODUCE(V) :
and~BUD | and~he~did~BURST.OUT(V) :
and~BUD~s~her :
and~FALLEN.GRAPE :
and~PRODUCE :
and~BULL~s :
and~we~will~REPRODUCE(V) :
and~HOOF :
and~they~did~SPREAD.OUT(V) :
and~he~did~LOOSE(V) :
and~Paroh :
and~Perets :
and~you(ms)~did~BREAK.OUT(V) :
and~you(ms)~did~TEAR.OFF(V) :
and~HORSEMAN~s~him :
and~he~did~STRIP.OFF(V) :
and~OFFENSE :
and~OPENING :
and~she~did~OPEN(V) :

and~CORD~you(ms) :
and~TWISTED :
and~!(ms)~GO.OUT(V) :
and~ARMY~him :
and~Tseviim :
and~GAZELLE :
and~she~did~SWELL(V) :
and~STEADFAST.ONE :
and~STEADFAST :
and~STEADFASTNESS :
and~!(ms)~much~DIRECT(V) :
and~FLOCKS :
and~FLOCKS~you(ms) :
and~FLOCKS~you(mp) :
and~FLOCKS~them(m) :
and~!(ms)~HUNT(V) :
and~Tsohhar :
and~Tsiv'on :
and~he~did~much~DIRECT(V) :
and~you(ms)~did~much~DIRECT(V) :
and~I~did~much~DIRECT(V) :
and~he~did~much~DIRECT(V)~you(ms) :
and~Tsilah :
and~NOMAD~s :
and~THIRSTY.LAND :
and~he~did~much~OVERLAY(V) :
and~METAL.PLATING :
and~you(ms)~did~much~OVERLAY(V) :
and~Tselaph'hhad :
and~SPRING.UP(V) :
and~BRACELET :
and~NORTH~unto :
and~PERSECUTION :
and~BALM :
and~they~did~PRESS.IN(V) :
and~you(ms)~did~SMACK(V) :
and~I~did~SMACK(V) :
and~!(ms)~BURY(V) :
and~you(ms)~did~HOLLOW.OUT(V)~him :
and~!(ms)~HOLLOW.OUT(V)~him :

and~you(ms)~did~BURY(V)~me :
and~EAST~unto | Qedmah :
and~Qedar :
and~he~did~SET.APART(V) :
and~ASSEMBLY :
and~Qehat :
and~VOICE :
and~!(ms)~RISE(V) :
and~HEIGHT :
and~!(mp)~RISE(V) :
and~BRAMBLE :
and~COLD :
and~they~did~much~COLLECT(V) :
and~!(ms)~TAKE(V) :
and~!(mp)~TAKE(V) :
and~DESTRUCTION :
and~INCENSE.SMOKE :
and~SMALL :
and~you(ms)~did~CROP.OFF(V) :
and~he~did~much~GATHER.TOGETHER(V)~you(ms) :
and~CASSIA :
and~he~did~much~SET.APART(V) :
and~he~did~much~SET.APART(V)~him :
and~you(ms)~did~much~SET.APART(V) :
and~you(ms)~did~much~SET.APART(V)~him :
and~I~did~much~SET.APART(V) :
and~you(ms)~did~much~SET.APART(V)~them(m) | and~you(mp)~did~much~SET.APART(V) :
and~Qayin :
and~SUMMER :
and~he~did~much~BE.ZEALOUS(V) :
and~ZEALOUSNESS~him :
and~MATERIAL~them(m) :
and~CINNAMON :
and~he~did~SLICE.OFF(V) :
and~INSIDE~him :
and~DEFORM(V)~ed(ms) :
and~ROASTED.GRAIN :
and~ANNOYANCE :
and~SLING~s :
and~he~did~RISE(V) :
and~they~did~RISE(V) :
and~he~did~GRASP(V) :
and~you(ms)~did~RISE(V) :
and~STALK~her | and~STALK :
and~STALK~s~them(m) :
and~Qenaz :
and~JUG~s~him :
and~DIVINATION~s :
and~SCALES :
and~you(ms)~did~SLICE.OFF(V) :
and~HARVEST :
and~you(mp)~did~SEVER(V) :
and~he~did~CALL.OUT(V) :
and~he~did~MEET(V)~him :
and~they~did~CALL.OUT(V) :
and~you(fs)~did~CALL.OUT(V) | and~you(ms)~did~CALL.OUT(V) :
and~I~did~CALL.OUT(V) :
and~you(mp)~did~CALL.OUT(V) :
and~she~did~COME.NEAR(V) :
and~DONATION~him :
and~you(ms)~did~COME.NEAR(V) :
and~he~did~MEET(V)~him :
and~ICE :
and~HORN~s :
and~he~did~TEAR(V) :
and~he~did~much~TOSS.OUT(V) :
and~you(ms)~did~TIE(V)~them(m) | and~you(mp)~did~TIE(V) :
and~BOW~you(ms) :
and~!(ms)~SEE(V) | and~he~did~SEE(V) :
and~he~did~SEE(V)~him :
and~!(mp)~SEE(V) | and~they~did~SEE(V) :
and~you(ms)~did~SEE(V) :
and~you(ms)~did~SEE(V) :
and~I~did~SEE(V) :
and~I~did~SEE(V)~her :
and~you(mp)~did~SEE(V) :

and~you(fp)~did~SEE(V) : וראיתן
and~he~did~SEE(V)~you(ms) : וראך
and~HEAD~s : וראשי
and~PRIME : וראשית
and~ABUNDANT : ורב
and~!(ms)~INCREASE(V) | and~ she~did~INCREASE.IN.NUMBER(V) : ורבה
and~!(mp)~INCREASE(V) | and~ they~did~INCREASE(V) : ורבו
and~FOURTH : ורביעית
and~you(ms)~did~INCREASE(V) : ורבית
and~you(mp)~did~make~ INCREASE(V) : ורביתם
and~she~did~STRETCH.OUT(V) : ורבצה
and~they~did~SHAKE(V) : ורגזו
and~FOOT~s : ורגלי
and~FOOT~s2~them(m) : ורגליהם
and~FOOT~you(ms) : ורגלך
and~they~did~ KILL.BY.STONING(V) : ורגמו
and~they~did~ KILL.BY.STONING(V)~him : ורגמהו
and~!(mp)~RULE(V) | and~they~ did~RULE(V) : ורדו
and~he~did~PURSUE(V) : ורדף
and~they~did~PURSUE(V) : ורדפו
and~they~did~PURSUE(V)~ you(ms) : ורדפוך
and~you(mp)~did~ PURSUE(V) : ורדפתם
/ and~Rosh | and~VENOM : ורואש
and~HEAD~him : ורואשו
and~ABUNDANCE : ורוב
and~they~did~ INCREASE.IN.NUMBER(V) : ורובו
and~PURSUE(V)~ing(ms) : ורודף
and~WIND : ורוח
and~WIDTH : ורוחב
and~RIDE(V)~ing(ms)~him : ורוכבו
/ and~EMBROIDER(V)~ing(ms) : ורוקם
and~WIDE : ורחבה
and~Rahhel : ורחל
and~BOWELS : ורחם
and~he~did~BATHE(V) : ורחץ
and~!(mp)~BATHE(V) | and~they~ did~BATHE(V) : ורחצו
and~you(ms)~did~BATHE(V) : ורחצת

and~DISPUTE~you(mp) : וריבכם
and~Rivqah : וריבקה
and~he~did~much~ HAVE.COMPASSION(V)~you(ms) : וריחמך
and~I~did~much~ HAVE.COMPASSION(V) : וריחמתי
and~MAGGOT : ורימה
and~POMEGRANATE : ורימון
and~Riphat : וריפת
and~TENDER : ורך
and~VEHICLE : ורכב
and~GOODS~him : ורכושו
and~RAISE.UP(V)~ing(ms) | and~ he~did~RAISE.UP(V) : ורם
and~TREADER : ורמס
and~DYSFUNCTIONAL : ורע
and~she~did~ BE.DYSFUNCTIONAL(V) : ורעה
and~DYSFUNCTIONAL~s : ורעות
and~DYSFUNCTIONAL~s : ורעים
and~Ramah : ורעמה
and~>~much~HEAL(V) : ורפוא
and~SELF-WILL : ורצון
and~CRUSH(V)~ed(ms) : ורצוץ
and~he~did~MURDER(V) : ורצח
and~he~did~MURDER(V)~him : ורצחו
and~he~did~BORE.THROUGH(V) : ורצע
and~THIN~s : ורקות
and~THIN.BREAD : ורקיק
and~THIN.BREAD~s : ורקיקי
and~!(mp)~POSSESS(V) : ורשו
and~Sha'ul : ושאול
and~he~did~INQUIRE(V) : ושאל
and~she~did~INQUIRE(V) : ושאלה
and~he~did~INQUIRE(V)~ you(ms) : ושאלך
and~you(ms)~did~INQUIRE(V) : ושאלת
and~!(ms)~SETTLE(V) | and~he~did~ TURN.BACK(V) : ושב
and~she~did~TURN.BACK(V) : ושבה
and~they~did~TURN.BACK(V) : ושבו
and~CAPTIVE~you(mp) : ושביכם
and~you(ms)~did~CAPTURE(V) : ושבית
and~SEVEN : ושבע
and~>~much~CRACK(V) : ושבר
and~I~did~CRACK(V) : ושברתי
and~you(ms)~did~TURN.BACK(V) : ושבת

and~she~did~CEASE(V) :
and~I~did~TURN.BACK(V) :
and~you(mp)~did~TURN.BACK(V) :
and~BLAST(V)~ed(fp) :
and~INQUIRE(V)~ing(ms) :
and~>~TURN.BACK(V) | and~!(ms)~TURN.BACK(V) :
and~!(mp)~TURN.BACK(V) :
and~Shoval :
and~ONYX :
and~BRIBE :
and~he~did~be~much~FLUSH(V) :
and~OFFICER ~s~him :
and~OFFICER ~s~you(mp) :
and~OFFICER ~s :
and~SPLIT.IN.TWO(V)~ing(ms) :
and~SPLIT.IN.TWO(V)~ing(fs) :
and~DECIDE(V)~ing(ms) :
and~DECIDE(V)~ing(mp)~you(ms) :
and~OX :
and~OX~him :
and~OX~you(ms) :
and~he~did~SLAY(V) :
and~they~did~SLAY(V) | and~!(mp)~SLAY(V) | and~he~did~SLAY(V)~him :
and~you(ms)~did~SLAY(V) :
and~ONYCHA :
and~you(ms)~did~PULVERIZE(V) :
and~CAPTIVE :
and~SEVEN :
and~SEVEN~s :
and~SEVEN :
and~you(ms)~did~much~WEAVE(V) :
and~!(mp)~EXCHANGE(V) :
and~you(mp)~did~much~CRACK(V) :
and~he~did~much~DAMAGE(V) :
and~he~did~much~DAMAGE(V)~her :
and~you(mp)~did~much~DAMAGE(V) :
and~she~did~much~BE.CHILDLESS(V) :
and~he~did~much~SEND(V) :
and~he~did~much~SEND(V)~her :
and~you(ms)~did~SEND(V)~her :
and~I~did~much~SEND(V) :
and~Shilem | and~he~did~much~MAKE.RESTITUTION(V) | and~RECOMPENSE :
and~you(ms)~did~much~BE.THREEFOLD(V) :
and~!(mp)~HEAR(V) :
and~Shimon :
and~Shiymiy :
and~Shimron :
and~you(ms)~did~much~WHET(V)~them(m) :
and~he~did~much~SPLIT.IN.TWO(V) :
and~MAID :
and~SIX :
and~SIX~s :
and~he~did~LIE.DOWN(V) :
and~I~did~LIE.DOWN(V) :
and~you(mp)~did~LIE.DOWN(V) :
and~he~did~FORGET(V) :
and~you(ms)~did~FORGET(V) :
and~Shekhem :
and~DWELLER~him :
and~I~did~DWELL(V) :
and~LIQUOR :
and~Sheylah :
and~THREE :
and~THREE :
and~THREE~s :
and~THREE :
and~Shelahh :
and~she~did~SEND(V) :
and~they~did~SEND(V) :
and~I~did~SEND(V) :

and~THIRD~s | and~LIEUTENANT~s :
and~THIRD :
and~SPOIL :
and~TITLE | and~Shem | and~THERE :
and~Shemever :
and~TITLE~her | and~THERE~unto :
and~TITLE~him :
and~EIGHT :
and~EIGHT~s :
and~EIGHT :
and~>~SAFEGUARD(V) :
and~TITLE~me | and~SKY~s2 :
and~Shemida :
and~SKY~s2 :
and~they~did~DESOLATE(V) :
and~OIL :
and~!(ms)~HEAR(V) | and~he~did~HEAR(V) :
and~she~did~HEAR(V) :
and~they~did~HEAR(V) :
and~we~did~HEAR(V) :
and~you(ms)~did~HEAR(V) :
and~I~did~HEAR(V) :
and~I~did~HEAR(V)~him :
and~he~did~SAFEGUARD(V) :
and~they~did~SAFEGUARD(V) :
and~he~did~SAFEGUARD(V)~me :
and~you(ms)~did~SAFEGUARD(V) :
and~I~did~SAFEGUARD(V)~you(ms) :
and~you(mp)~did~SAFEGUARD(V) :
and~TOOTH :
and~TWO | and~SCARLET :
and~SECOND | and~TWO :
and~YEAR~s :
and~SPLITTING :
and~MAID~s :
and~they~did~DECIDE(V) :
and~they~did~DECIDE(V)~them(m) :
and~I~did~DECIDE(V) :
and~you(mp)~did~DECIDE(V) :
and~he~did~POUR.OUT(V) :
and~they~did~POUR.OUT(V) :
and~you(ms)~did~POUR.OUT(V) :
and~LOW :
and~ALMOND :
and~!(ms)~KISS(V)~& :
and~FILTHY :
and~he~did~SWARM(V) :
and~they~did~SWARM(V) :
and~he~did~much~MINISTER(V) :
and~they~did~much~MINISTER(V) :
and~SIX | and~LINEN :
and~SIX :
and~he~did~GULP(V) :
and~>~GULP(V) :
and~TWO | and~I~did~SET.DOWN(V) :
and~TWO :
and~TWO :
and~I~did~GULP(V) :
and~you(mp)~did~GULP(V) :
and~ORYX :
and~FIG :
and~she~will~COME(V) :
and~you(mp)~will~COME(V) :
and~they(f)~will~COME(V) :
and~PRODUCTION :
and~INTELLIGENCE :
and~she~will~make~STARE(V) :
and~she~will~make~COME(V)~him :
and~she~will~WEEP(V) :
and~STRAW :
and~she~will~make~BE.FACE.TO.FACE(V) :
and~you(ms)~will~make~MAGNIFY(V) :
and~you(ms)~will~make~BE.FACE.TO.FACE(V) :
and~she~will~make~TOUCH(V) :

and~she~will~much~SPEAK(V) | and~you(ms)~will~much~SPEAK(V)
and~DEEP.WATER~s
and~she~will~EXIST(V)
and~you(mp)~will~make~SUFFICIENT(V)
and~she~will~CONCEIVE(V)
and~they(f)~will~CONCEIVE(V)
and~she~will~TAKE.HOLD(V)
and~she~will~EAT(V) | and~you(ms)~will~EAT(V)
and~they(f)~will~EAT(V)
and~she~will~SAY(V)
and~you(mp)~will~SAY(V)
and~they(f)~will~SAY(V)
and~they(f)~will~SAY(V)
and~Tuval
and~Togarmah
and~you(ms)~BE.ABLE(V)
and~MEASURED.AMOUNT
and~KERMES
and~she~will~make~ADD(V)
and~she~will~make~GO.OUT(V)
and~TAKE(V)~ed(fs)
and~TURTLEDOVE
and~she~will~make~GO.DOWN(V)
and~TEACHING~s~me
and~TEACHING~you(ms)
and~SETTLER
and~SETTLER~s
and~you(mp)~will~make~SIMMER(V)
and~you(mp)~will~GIRD.UP(V)
and~she~will~SEIZE(V)
and~she~will~LIVE(V)
and~they(f)~will~much~LIVE(V)
and~they(f)~will~DRILL(V)
and~you(ms)~will~much~DRILL(V)~her
and~you(ms)~will~make~PASS.OVER(V)
and~she~will~SHOW.PITY(V)
and~she~will~PASTE(V)
and~she~will~DARKEN(V)
and~UNDER
and~she~will~EXTEND(V)
and~she~will~STINK(V)
and~you(mp)~will~WEEP(V)
and~she~will~SWALLOW(V)
and~she~will~SWALLOW(V)~them(m)
and~they(f)~will~SWALLOW(V)
and~they(f)~will~SWALLOW(V)
and~she~will~BURN(V)
and~she~will~be~CLEAVE.OPEN(V)
and~she~will~FLEE.AWAY(V)
and~she~will~STEAL(V) | and~you(ms)~will~STEAL(V)
and~she~will~DRAW.NEAR(V)
and~they(f)~will~DRAW.NEAR(V)
and~she~will~ADHERE(V)
and~she~will~TOSS(V)
and~they(f)~will~DRAW.UP(V)
and~Tidal
and~they(f)~will~EXIST(V)
and~they(f)~will~EXIST(V)
and~she~will~WALK(V)
and~she~will~BE.DIRTY(V)
and~you(ms)~will~PLANT(V)~them(m)
and~they(f)~will~DIM(V)
and~she~will~self~PREPARE(V)
and~you(ms)~will~be~KEEP.SECRET(V)
and~they(f)~will~FINISH(V)
and~she~will~CUT(V)
and~she~will~WEAR(V)
and~she~will~SQUEEZE(V)
and~Teyma

and~she~will~be~FILL(V) : ותימלא
and~SOUTHWARD~unto : ותימנה
and~Timna : ותימנע
and~she~will~ TRANSGRESS(V) : ותימעול
and~she~will~make~ SUCKLE(V) : ותיניק
and~she~will~self~ LIFT.UP(V) : ותינסא
and~she~will~be~ DELIVER(V) : ותינצל
and~she~will~LIFT.UP(V) : ותיסא
and~she~will~be~SHUT(V) : ותיסגר
and~she~will~be~ CREMATE(V) : ותיסרף
and~she~will~FALL(V) : ותיפול
and~she~will~be~ BEAT(V) : ותיפעם
and~they(f)~will~be~ OPEN.UP(V) : ותיפקחנה
and~she~will~OPEN(V) : ותיפתח
and~she~will~LAUGH(V) : ותיצחק
and~she~will~ CONCEAL(V)~him : ותיצפנהו
and~she~will~be~BURY(V) : ותיקבר
and~she~will~SMOLDER(V) : ותיקד
and~she~will~ASSEMBLE(V) : ותיקהל
and~she~will~TAKE(V) : ותיקח
and~she~will~TAKE(V)~her : ותיקחה
and~she~will~SEVER(V) : ותיקצר
and~she~will~CALL.OUT(V) : ותיקרא
and~they(f)~will~ CALL.OUT(V) : ותיקראן
and~they(f)~will~ CALL.OUT(V) : ותיקראנה
and~you(mp)~will~ COME.NEAR(V)~must : ותיקרבון
and~they(f)~will~ COME.NEAR(V) : ותיקרבנה
and~she~will~TIE(V) : ותיקשור
and~she~will~SEE(V)~him : ותיראהו
and~you(mp)~will~SEE(V) : ותיראו
and~they(f)~will~FEAR(V) : ותיראן
and~she~will~SEE(V)~ me : ותיראני
and~she~will~ STRETCH.OUT(V) : ותירבץ
and~FRESH.WINE : ותירוש
and~FRESH.WINE~you(ms) : ותירושך
and~they(f)~will~ RIDE(V) : ותירכבנה
and~Tiras : ותירס
and~she~will~ BE.HUNGRY(V) : ותירעב
and~they(f)~will~ FEED(V) : ותירעינה
and~she~will~ACCEPT(V) : ותירץ
and~Tirtsah : ותירצה
and~you(ms)~will~ ACCEPT(V)~me : ותירצני
and~she~will~ DRAW.WATER(V) : ותישאב
and~she~will~be~ DAMAGE(V) : ותישחת
and~HE.GOAT~s : ותישים
and~she~will~LIE.DOWN(V) : ותישכב
and~you(ms)~will~ FORGET(V) : ותישכח
and~she~will~SEND(V) : ותישלח
and~she~will~HEAR(V) : ותישמע
and~NINE~s : ותישעים
and~she~will~DROWN(V) : ותישקע
and~they(f)~will~ self~BEND.DOWN(V) : ותישתחוין
and~she~will~BE.WHOLE(V) : ותיתום
and~she~will~self~ COVER.OVER(V) : ותיתכס
and~she~will~GIVE(V) | and~ you(ms)~will~GIVE(V) : ותיתן
and~she~will~self~ WRAP(V) : ותיתעלף
and~she~will~ SEIZE.HOLD(V)~him : ותיתפסהו
and~she~will~much~DENY(V) : ותכחש
and~she~will~much~FINISH(V) | and~she~will~FINISH(V) : ותכל
and~BLUE : ותכלת
and~she~will~much~ COVER.OVER(V) : ותכס
and~she~will~make~WEAR(V) : ותלבש
and~she~will~BRING.FORTH(V) : ותלד
and~they(f)~will~ BRING.FORTH(V) : ותלדן

and~he~did~HANG(V) | and~she~will~FAINT(V) : ותלה
and~she~will~much~BLAZE(V) : ותלהט
and~you(ms)~did~HANG(V) : ותלית
and~she~will~WALK(V) : ותלך
and~they(f)~will~WALK(V) : ותלכנה
and~Talmai : ותלמי
and~he~did~BE.WHOLE(V) : ותם
and~you(ms)~will~much~REFUSE(V) : ותמאן
and~she~will~much~HURRY(V) : ותמהר
and~RESEMBLANCE : ותמונה
and~RESEMBLANCE : ותמונת
and~EXCHANGE~him : ותמורתו
and~she~will~FILL(V) : ותמלא
and~they(f)~will~FILL(V) : ותמלאנה
and~you(mp)~will~make~DISOBEY(V) : ותמרו
and~she~will~DIE(V) : ותמת
and~!(ms)~GIVE(V) : ותן
and~you(ms)~will~much~DRIVE(V) : ותנהג
and~!(mp)~GIVE(V) : ותנו
and~she~will~REST(V) | and~she~will~make~REST(V) : ותנח
and~she~will~make~SUCKLE(V)~him : ותניקהו
and~she~will~PLACE(V)~them(m) : ותשימם
and~she~will~PLACE(V) : ותשם
and~she~will~make~TURN.ASIDE(V) : ותסר
and~>~much~ABHOR(V) : ותעב
and~she~will~CROSS.OVER(V) : ותעבור
and~she~will~GO.UP(V) : ותעל
and~you(mp)~will~GO.UP(V) : ותעלו
and~you(mp)~will~STAND(V)~must : ותעמדון
and~she~will~STAND(V) : ותעמוד
and~they(f)~will~STAND(V) : ותעמודנה
and~she~will~ANSWER(V) : ותען
and~she~will~AFFLICT(V)~her : ותענה
and~you(mp)~will~ANSWER(V) : ותענו
and~she~will~DO(V) : ותעש
and~she~will~be~STOP(V) : ותעצר
and~she~will~much~UNCOVER(V) : ותער
and~he~will~SEIZE.HOLD(V)~her : ותפשה
and~they~will~SEIZE.HOLD(V) : ותפשו
and~she~will~GO.OUT(V) : ותצא
and~they(f)~will~GO.OUT(V) : ותצאן
and~she~will~much~VOMIT(V) : ותקיא
and~she~will~BELITTLE(V) : ותקל
and~she~will~RISE(V) : ותקם
and~she~will~BE.ZEALOUS(V) : ותקנא
and~she~will~DISLOCATE(V) : ותקע
and~they~did~THRUST(V) : ותקעו
and~you(mp)~did~THRUST(V) : ותקעתם
and~she~will~much~BE.HARD(V) : ותקש
and~she~will~SEE(V) : ותרא
and~she~be~SEE(V) : ותראה
and~she~will~INCREASE(V) : ותרב
and~INTEREST : ותרבית
and~you(mp)~will~be~WHISPER(V) : ותרגנו
and~she~will~GO.DOWN(V) : ותרד
and~TRANCE : ותרדמה
and~OFFERING : ותרומה
and~OFFERING : ותרומת
and~the~SHOUT : ותרועת
and~she~will~RAISE.UP(V) : ותרם
and~she~will~RUN(V) : ותרץ
and~Tarshish : ותרשיש
and~she~will~TURN.BACK(V) | and~she~will~SETTLE(V) : ותשב
and~you(mp)~will~SETTLE(V) : ותשבו
and~you(mp)~will~TURN.BACK(V) : ותשובו
and~you(mp)~will~SEND(V)~me : ותשלחוני
and~she~will~THROW.OUT(V) : ותשלך
and~NINE : ותשע
and~she~will~make~DRINK(V) : ותשק
and~she~will~make~DRINK(V)~him : ותשקהו
and~they(f)~will~make~DRINK(V) : ותשקין
and~she~will~GULP(V) : ותשת
and~she~will~WANDER(V) : ותתע

and~she~will~self~STATION(V) : 𐤅𐤕𐤕𐤑𐤁
WOLF : 𐤆𐤀𐤁
ISSUE(V)~ing(ms) : 𐤆𐤁
DOWRY : 𐤆𐤁𐤃
he~did~ENDOW(V)~me : 𐤆𐤁𐤃𐤍𐤉
ISSUE(V)~ing(fs) : 𐤆𐤁𐤄
Zevulun : 𐤆𐤁𐤅𐤋𐤅𐤍
SACRIFICE : 𐤆𐤁𐤇
SACRIFICE~s~you(ms) : 𐤆𐤁𐤇𐤉𐤊
SACRIFICE~s : 𐤆𐤁𐤇𐤉𐤌
SACRIFICE~s~them(m) : 𐤆𐤁𐤇𐤉𐤌𐤅
ISSUE(V)~ing(fs) : 𐤆𐤁𐤕
GRAPE.SKIN : 𐤆𐤂
they~did~SIMMER(V) : 𐤆𐤃𐤅
THIS : 𐤆𐤄
GOLD : 𐤆𐤄𐤁
WHEREIN : 𐤆𐤅
THIS : 𐤆𐤅𐤀𐤕
DISCHARGE : 𐤆𐤅𐤁
DISCHARGE~her : 𐤆𐤅𐤁𐤄
DISCHARGE~him : 𐤆𐤅𐤁𐤅
SACRIFICE(V)~ing(ms) : 𐤆𐤅𐤁𐤇
SACRIFICE(V)~ing(mp) : 𐤆𐤅𐤁𐤇𐤉
SACRIFICE(V)~ing(mp) : 𐤆𐤅𐤁𐤇𐤉𐤌
CRAWL(V)~ing(mp) : 𐤆𐤅𐤇𐤋𐤉
GLUTTON(V)~ing(ms) : 𐤆𐤅𐤋𐤋
WITH.THE.EXCEPTION~of : 𐤆𐤅𐤋𐤕𐤉
BE.A.HARLOT(V)~ing(fs) : 𐤆𐤅𐤍𐤄
BE.A.HARLOT(V)~ing(mp) : 𐤆𐤅𐤍𐤉𐤌
!(ms)~ENRAGE(V)~& : 𐤆𐤅𐤏𐤌𐤄
BE.SAD(V)~ing(mp) : 𐤆𐤅𐤏𐤐𐤉𐤌
SOW(V)~ing(ms) : 𐤆𐤅𐤓𐤏
SPRINKLE(V)~ed(ms) : 𐤆𐤅𐤓𐤒
!(mp)~SACRIFICE(V) | SACRIFICE~him : 𐤆𐤉𐤁𐤇𐤅
SACRIFICE~me | SACRIFICE~s : 𐤆𐤉𐤁𐤇𐤉
SACRIFICE~s~them(m) : 𐤆𐤉𐤁𐤇𐤉𐤄𐤌
SACRIFICE~you(mp) : 𐤆𐤉𐤁𐤇𐤊𐤌
OLIVE : 𐤆𐤉𐤉𐤕
REMEMBRANCE : 𐤆𐤉𐤊𐤓𐤅𐤍
MEMORY~me : 𐤆𐤉𐤊𐤓𐤉
MEMORY~them(m) : 𐤆𐤉𐤊𐤓𐤌
Zilpah : 𐤆𐤉𐤋𐤐𐤄
MISCHIEF : 𐤆𐤉𐤌𐤄
Zimri : 𐤆𐤉𐤌𐤓𐤉
Zimran : 𐤆𐤉𐤌𐤓𐤍

Ziphron~unto : 𐤆𐤉𐤐𐤓𐤅𐤍𐤄
BEARD~s : 𐤆𐤉𐤒𐤍𐤉
BEARD~s~you(mp) : 𐤆𐤉𐤒𐤍𐤉𐤊𐤌
OLD.AGE~her : 𐤆𐤉𐤒𐤍𐤕𐤄
OLIVE : 𐤆𐤉𐤕
OLIVE~s : 𐤆𐤉𐤕𐤉𐤌
OLIVE~you(ms) : 𐤆𐤉𐤕𐤊
REFINED : 𐤆𐤊
REFINED : 𐤆𐤊𐤄
>~REMEMBER(V) | !(ms)~REMEMBER(V) | Zakur : 𐤆𐤊𐤅𐤓
MEN~her : 𐤆𐤊𐤅𐤓𐤄
MEN~you(ms) : 𐤆𐤊𐤅𐤓𐤊
MALE | he~did~REMEMBER(V) | MEMORY : 𐤆𐤊𐤓
we~did~REMEMBER(V) : 𐤆𐤊𐤓𐤍𐤅
you(ms)~did~REMEMBER(V)~me : 𐤆𐤊𐤓𐤕𐤍𐤉
VINE : 𐤆𐤌𐤅𐤓𐤄
Zamzum~s : 𐤆𐤌𐤆𐤅𐤌𐤉𐤌
he~did~PLOT(V) : 𐤆𐤌𐤌
WHOREDOM~you(mp) : 𐤆𐤍𐤅𐤕𐤉𐤊𐤌
she~did~BE.A.HARLOT(V) : 𐤆𐤍𐤕𐤄
he~did~ENRAGE(V) : 𐤆𐤏𐤌
YELL : 𐤆𐤏𐤒𐤕
EXTREME.OLD.AGE~s : 𐤆𐤒𐤅𐤍𐤉𐤌
he~did~BE.OLD(V) | BEARD : 𐤆𐤒𐤍
BEARD~him : 𐤆𐤒𐤍𐤅
BEARD~s~you(ms) : 𐤆𐤒𐤍𐤉𐤊
BEARD~s : 𐤆𐤒𐤍𐤉𐤌
BEARD~you(ms) : 𐤆𐤒𐤍𐤊
BEARD~them(m) : 𐤆𐤒𐤍𐤌
I~did~BE.OLD(V) : 𐤆𐤒𐤍𐤕𐤉
MOLDING | BE.STRANGE(V)~ing(ms) : 𐤆𐤓
Zered : 𐤆𐤓𐤃
BE.STRANGE(V)~ing(fs) | !(ms)~DISPERSE(V) : 𐤆𐤓𐤄
SOWN | ARM : 𐤆𐤓𐤅𐤏
ARM~s : 𐤆𐤓𐤅𐤏𐤕
ARM~s : 𐤆𐤓𐤅𐤏𐤉
ARM~you(ms) : 𐤆𐤓𐤅𐤏𐤊
Zerahh : 𐤆𐤓𐤇
she~did~COME.UP(V) : 𐤆𐤓𐤇𐤄
SEED : 𐤆𐤓𐤏
SEED~her : 𐤆𐤓𐤏𐤄
SEED~him : 𐤆𐤓𐤏𐤅
SEED~you(ms) | SEED~you(fs) : 𐤆𐤓𐤏𐤊

SEED~you(mp) : זרעכם
he~did~SPRINKLE(V) : זרק
FINGER.SPAN : זרת
>~TAKE.AS.A.PLEDGE(V) : חבול
STRIPED.BRUISE : חבורה
REGION : חבל
Hhever | COUPLE : חבר
they~did~COUPLE(V) : חברו
Hhevron : חברון
FEAST : חג
LOIN.WRAP~s : חגורות
GIRD.UP(V)~ed(mp) : חגורים
FEAST~me : חגי
Hhaglah : חגלה
Hhadad : חדד
he~did~TERMINATE(V) | !(ms)~TERMINATE(V) : חדל
NEW : חדש
NEW : חדשה
NEW.MOON~s~you(mp) : חדשיכם
NEW.MOON~s | NEW~s : חדשים
CHERISH(V)~ing(ms) : חובב
Hhovah : חובה
TAKE.AS.A.PLEDGE(V)~ing(ms) : חובל
COUPLE(V)~ed(ms) : חובר
COUPLE(V)~ing(fp) : חוברות
NEW.MOON : חודש
Hhawah : חוה
Hhawot : חוות
TOWN~s~them(m) : חוותיהם
Hhawilah : חוילה
SAND : חול
BE.SICK(V)~ing(ms) : חולה
INFIRMITY : חולי
DREAM(V)~ing(ms) : חולם
BLACK : חום
RAMPART : חומה
RAMPART~s~you(ms) : חומותיך
VINEGAR : חומץ
HHOMER : חומר
CAMP(V)~ing(ms) : חונה
CAMP(V)~ing(fp) : חונים
BLANKET(V)~ing(ms) : חופף
FREEDOM | she~did~be~much~FREE(V) : חופשה
OUTSIDE : חוץ
OUTSIDE~unto : חוצה

Hhutsot : חוצות
CUSTOM : חוק
CUSTOM : חוקה
CUSTOM~s~me : חוקותי
CUSTOM~s~him : חוקותיו
CUSTOM~s : חוקי
CUSTOM~s~him : חוקיו
CUSTOM~s : חוקים
CUSTOM~them(m) : חוקם
CUSTOM : חוקת
Hhur : חור
PARCHING.HEAT | Hhorev : חורב
Hhorev~unto : חורבה
Hhoriy | PALENESS : חורי
CRAFTSMAN : חורש
THINK(V)~ing(ms) : חושב
Hhush~s | MAKE.HASTE(V)~ed(mp) : חושים
DARKNESS : חושך
Hhusham : חושם
BREASTPLATE : חושן
SEAL : חותם
SEAL~you(ms) : חותמך
BE.AN.IN-LAW(V)~ing(ms) : חותן
BE.AN.IN-LAW(V)~ing(ms)~him : חותנו
BE.AN.IN-LAW(V)~ing(ms)~you(ms) : חותנך
BE.AN.IN-LAW(V)~ing(fs)~him : חותנתו
CHEST : חזה
Hhazo : חזו
he~did~SEIZE(V) | FORCEFUL | !(ms)~much~SEIZE(V) | !(ms)~SEIZE(V) : חזק
FORCEFUL : חזקה
NOSE.RING : חח
he~did~FAIL(V) | FAILURE : חטא
FAILURE : חטאה
they~did~FAIL(V) | FAILURE~him : חטאו
FAILURE~s~me : חטאי
FAILURE~s : חטאים
FAILURE~them(m) : חטאם
we~did~FAIL(V) : חטאנו
FAILURE : חטאת
FAILURE~him : חטאתו
I~did~FAIL(V) | FAILURE~me : חטאתי
FAILURE~you(ms) : חטאתך
FAILURE~you(mp) : חטאתכם

you(mp)~did~FAIL(V) | FAILURE~them(m) : חטאתם
FAILURE~s : חטואת
FAILURE~s~you(mp) : חטואתיכם
FAILURE~them(m) : חטואתם
LIVING | he~did~LIVE(V) : חי
he~did~much~COUPLE(V) : חיבר
Hhideqel : חידקל
LIVING : חיה
!(mp)~LIVE(V) : חיו
LIVELY~s | LIVING~s : חיות
!(mp)~SEIZE(V) : חיזקו
WHEAT : חיטה
WHEAT~s : חיטים
LIVING~s | LIVING~s~me : חיי
LIVING~s~them(m) : חייהם
LIVING~s~him : חייו
LIVING~s~you(ms) : חייך
LIVING~s~you(mp) : חייכם
FORCE : חייל
LIVING~s : חיים
FORCE | AGONY : חיל
he~did~much~BE.SICK(V) : חילה
FORCE~him : חילו
he~did~much~DRILL(V) : חילל
he~did~much~DRILL(V)~him : חיללו
you(ms)~did~much~DRILL(V) : חיללת
FORCE~them(m) : חילם
he~did~much~EXTRACT(V) : חילץ
BEAUTY~him : חינו
FREELY : חינם
ARROW~me : חיצי
ARROW~s : חיצים
BOSOM~her : חיקה
BOSOM~him : חיקו
BOSOM~you(ms) : חיקך
Hhiyrah : חירה
LIVING : חית
LIVING~them(m) : חיתם
DREAD : חיתת
DULL.RED : חכלילי
SKILLED.ONE : חכם
SKILL : חכמה
they~did~BE.SKILLED(V) : חכמו
SKILLED.ONE~s : חכמי
SKILLED.ONE~her : חכמיה
SKILLED.ONE~s : חכמים

SKILLED.ONE | SKILL : חכמת
SKILL~you(mp) : חכמתכם
FAT : חלב
FAT~her : חלבה
FAT~them(f) : חלבהן
FAT~him : חלבו
FAT~s : חלבי
FAT~them(m) : חלבם
PIERCED.BREAD : חלה
DREAM : חלום
DREAM~him : חלומו
DREAM~s~him : חלומותיו
DREAM~s~us : חלומותינו
WINDOW | Hheylon : חלון
EXTRACT(V)~ed(ms) : חלוץ
EXTRACT(V)~ed(mp) : חלוצי
EXTRACT(V)~ed(mp) : חלוצים
DEFEAT : חלושה
PIERCED.BREAD~s : חלות
INFIRMITY : חלי
FAR.BE.IT : חלילה
/ REPLACEMENT~s : חליפות
DRILLED : חלל
DRILLED~s~them(m) : חלליהם
DRILLED~s : חללים
he~did~DREAM(V) : חלם
we~did~DREAM(V) : חלמנו
you(ms)~did~DREAM(V) : חלמת
I~did~DREAM(V) : חלמתי
FOR : חלף
SLICK | DISTRIBUTION | he~did~DISTRIBUTE(V) : חלק
DISTRIBUTION~you(ms) : חלקך
DISTRIBUTION~them(m) : חלקם
SMOOTH | PARCEL : חלקת
PIERCED.BREAD : חלת
Hham : חם
CHEESE : חמאה
CHEESE : חמאת
Hhemdan : חמדן
DONKEY | Hhamor : חמור
DONKEY~him : חמורו
DONKEY~s~them(m) : חמוריהם
DONKEY~s : חמורים
DONKEY~s~us : חמורינו
DONKEY~you(ms) : חמורך
FATHER-IN-LAW~her : חמיה

FATHER-IN-LAW~you(fs) :
FIVE :
FIFTH :
FIVE~s :
FIFTH | FIVE :
FIFTH~him | FIVE~him :
SUN.IDOL~s~you(mp) :
VIOLENCE :
VIOLENCE~me :
LEAVENED.BREAD | he~did~BE.SOUR(V) :
SLIME :
SLIME~s | HHOMER~s :
FIVE :
FIVE :
FURY | Hhamat :
FURY~me :
BEAUTY :
they~did~CAMP(V) | !(mp)~CAMP(V) :
Hhanokh :
DEVOTION :
PROTECTIVE :
>~CAMP(V)~us :
Hhani'eyl :
EXPERIENCED~s~him :
he~did~DEVOTE(V)~him :
he~did~PROVIDE.PROTECTION(V) :
he~did~PROVIDE.PROTECTION(V)~me :
KINDNESS :
KINDNESS~him :
KINDNESS~you(ms) | KINDNESS~you(fs) :
KIND.ONE~you(ms) :
they~did~TAKE.REFUGE(V) :
he~did~KEEP.BACK(V) :
you(ms)~did~KEEP.BACK(V) :
you(ms)~did~DIMINISH(V) :
CUPPED.HAND~s~him :
CUPPED.HAND~s2~you(mp) :
he~did~DELIGHT(V) :
you(ms)~did~DELIGHT(V) :
I~did~DELIGHT(V) :
Hheypher :
they~did~DIG.OUT(V) :
they~did~DIG.OUT(V)~her :
I~did~DIG.OUT(V) :
FREE :
you(ms)~did~HEW(V) :
he~did~DIVIDE(V) :
DIVIDE(V)~ed(mp) :
STRAIGHT.TRUMPET~s :
HALF :
HALF~him :
Hhatsar-Adar :
Hhatsar-Eynan :
COURTYARD :
Hhetsron :
Hhatsarot :
Hhatsarmawet :
CUSTOM :
CUSTOM~you(ms) :
CUSTOM~you(mp) :
SWORD :
DRIED.OUT :
they~did~DRY.UP(V) | SWORD~him :
SWORD~me :
SWORD~you(ms) :
TREMBLING :
he~did~FLARE.UP(V) :
PERFORATE(V)~ed(ms) :
FLAMING.WRATH :
FLAMING.WRATH~you(ms) :
CUT.SHARPLY(V)~ed(ms) :
ENGRAVE(V)~ed(ms) :
MAGICIAN~s :
FLAMING :
PLOWING :
ASSIGNED :
Hharmah :
Hhermon :
SICKLE :
Hharan :
Hharan~unto :
CLAY :
DISGRACE :
DISGRACE~me :
SILENT | ENGRAVER :
DECORATIVE.BAND :
he~did~THINK(V)~her :
Hheshbon :
you(mp)~did~THINK(V) :

DARK : 𐤇𐤔𐤊𐤄
he~did~ATTACH(V) : 𐤇𐤔𐤒
she~did~ATTACH(V) : 𐤇𐤔𐤒𐤄
Hhet : 𐤇𐤕
SEAL(V)~ed(ms) : 𐤇𐤕𐤅𐤌
IN.LAW : 𐤇𐤕𐤍
IN.LAW~s~him : 𐤇𐤕𐤍𐤉𐤅
BUTCHER(V)~ed(ms) : 𐤈𐤁𐤅𐤇
Tevahh | SLAUGHTERING : 𐤈𐤁𐤇
RING~s : 𐤈𐤁𐤏𐤅𐤅𐤕
RING~s : 𐤈𐤁𐤏𐤅𐤕
RING~s~them(m) : 𐤈𐤁𐤏𐤅𐤕𐤉𐤄𐤌
RING~s~them(m) : 𐤈𐤁𐤏𐤅𐤕𐤌
RING : 𐤈𐤁𐤏𐤕
RING~him : 𐤈𐤁𐤏𐤕𐤅
CLEAN : 𐤈𐤄𐤅𐤓
CLEAN : 𐤈𐤄𐤅𐤓𐤄
CLEAN~s : 𐤈𐤄𐤅𐤓𐤅𐤕
CLEAN | CLEAN~her | she~did~ BE.CLEAN(V) : 𐤈𐤄𐤓𐤄
CLEAN~him : 𐤈𐤄𐤓𐤕𐤅
FUNCTIONAL : 𐤈𐤅𐤁
FUNCTIONAL : 𐤈𐤅𐤁𐤄
FUNCTIONAL~him : 𐤈𐤅𐤁𐤅
FUNCTIONAL~s : 𐤈𐤅𐤁𐤅𐤕
FUNCTIONAL~me : 𐤈𐤅𐤁𐤉
FUNCTIONAL~s : 𐤈𐤅𐤁𐤉𐤌
they~did~be~much~SINK(V) : 𐤈𐤅𐤁𐤏𐤅
FUNCTIONAL : 𐤈𐤅𐤁𐤕
they~did~SPIN(V) : 𐤈𐤅𐤅
DIRTY : 𐤈𐤅𐤌𐤀𐤄
DIRTY~s~them(m) : 𐤈𐤅𐤌𐤀𐤅𐤕𐤌
DIRTY~her : 𐤈𐤅𐤌𐤀𐤕𐤄
DIRTY~him : 𐤈𐤅𐤌𐤀𐤕𐤅
HAND.SPAN : 𐤈𐤅𐤐𐤇
ROW : 𐤈𐤅𐤓
ROW~s : 𐤈𐤅𐤓𐤉
ROW~s : 𐤈𐤅𐤓𐤉𐤌
TEAR.INTO.PIECES(V)~ed(ms) | he~did~be~much~ TEAR.INTO.PIECES(V) : 𐤈𐤅𐤓𐤐
>~GRIND(V) : 𐤈𐤇𐤅𐤍
he~did~much~BE.DIRTY(V) : 𐤈𐤉𐤌𐤀
they~did~much~BE.DIRTY(V) : 𐤈𐤉𐤌𐤀𐤅
ROW.OF.TENTS~s~them(m) : 𐤈𐤉𐤓𐤅𐤕𐤌
DEW : 𐤈𐤋
DIRTY | he~did~BE.DIRTY(V) : 𐤈𐤌𐤀

DIRTY : 𐤈𐤌𐤀𐤄
DIRTY~s : 𐤈𐤌𐤀𐤉𐤌
SUBMERGE(V)~ed(mp) : 𐤈𐤌𐤅𐤍𐤉
REED-BASKET~you(ms) : 𐤈𐤍𐤀𐤊
FLAVOR~him : 𐤈𐤏𐤌𐤅
!(mp)~PACK(V) : 𐤈𐤏𐤍𐤅
BABIES~you(mp) : 𐤈𐤐𐤊𐤌
BABIES~them(m) : 𐤈𐤐𐤌
BABIES~us : 𐤈𐤐𐤍𐤅
>~TEAR.INTO.PIECES(V) : 𐤈𐤓𐤅𐤐
HEAVY.BURDEN~you(mp) : 𐤈𐤓𐤇𐤊𐤌
BEFORE : 𐤈𐤓𐤌
PREY : 𐤈𐤓𐤐
TORN : 𐤈𐤓𐤐𐤄
he~will~LOVE(V)~me : 𐤉𐤀𐤄𐤁𐤍𐤉
STREAM~s~them(m) : 𐤉𐤀𐤅𐤓𐤉𐤄𐤌
they(m)~will~AGREE(V) : 𐤉𐤀𐤅𐤕𐤅
he~will~much~DELAY(V) : 𐤉𐤀𐤇𐤓
Ya'ir : 𐤉𐤀𐤉𐤓
they(m)~will~make~LIGHT(V) : 𐤉𐤀𐤉𐤓𐤅
he~will~make~EAT(V)~us : 𐤉𐤀𐤊𐤉𐤋𐤍𐤅
he~will~be~EAT(V) : 𐤉𐤀𐤊𐤋
they(m)~will~be~EAT(V) : 𐤉𐤀𐤊𐤋𐤅
they(m)~will~make~ SECURE(V) : 𐤉𐤀𐤌𐤉𐤍𐤅
he~will~BE.STRONG(V) : 𐤉𐤀𐤌𐤑
he~will~be~SAY(V) : 𐤉𐤀𐤌𐤓
he~will~be~GATHER(V) : 𐤉𐤀𐤎𐤐
they(m)~will~be~GATHER(V) : 𐤉𐤀𐤎𐤐𐤅
he~will~be~TIE.UP(V) : 𐤉𐤀𐤎𐤓
he~will~make~LIGHT(V) : 𐤉𐤀𐤓
he~will~make~PROLONG(V) : 𐤉𐤀𐤓𐤉𐤊
they(m)~will~make~ PROLONG(V) : 𐤉𐤀𐤓𐤉𐤊𐤅
they(m)~will~make~ PROLONG(V)~must : 𐤉𐤀𐤓𐤉𐤊𐤅𐤍
he~will~BE.GUILTY(V) : 𐤉𐤀𐤔𐤌
he~will~make~SEPARATE(V) : 𐤉𐤁𐤃𐤉𐤋
he~will~COME(V) : 𐤉𐤁𐤅𐤀
they(m)~will~COME(V) : 𐤉𐤁𐤅𐤀𐤅
he~will~be~much~ BE.FIRSTBORN(V) : 𐤉𐤁𐤅𐤊𐤓
PRODUCT~her : 𐤉𐤁𐤅𐤋𐤄
he~will~much~ UNDERSTAND(V)~him : 𐤉𐤁𐤅𐤍𐤍𐤄𐤅
Yaboq : 𐤉𐤁𐤅𐤒

>~DRY.OUT(V) : יבושת
he~will~CHOOSE(V) : יבחר
he~will~much~UTTER(V) : יבטא
he~will~make~COME(V) : יביא
he~will~make~COME(V)~her : יביאה
he~will~make~COME(V)~him : יביאהו
they(m)~will~make~COME(V) : יביאו
they(m)~will~make~COME(V)~must : יביאון
he~will~make~COME(V)~you(ms) : יביאך
he~will~make~COME(V)~them(m) : יביאם
he~will~make~COME(V)~her : יביאנה
he~will~make~COME(V)~him : יביאנו
he~will~make~STARE(V) : יביט
SISTER-in-law~him : יבמתו
they(m)~will~UNDERSTAND(V)~must : יבינו
they(m)~will~WEEP(V) : יבכו
Yaval : יבל
ULCER : יבלת
BROTHER-IN-LAW~her : יבמה
>~much~DO.THE.MARRIAGE.DUTY(V)~me : יבמי
he~will~BUILD(V) : יבנה
he~will~BURN(V) : יבער
he~will~make~BURN(V) : יבער
he~will~be~FENCE.IN(V) : יבצר
he~will~much~INVESTIGATE(V) : יבקר
he~will~SHAPE(V) : יברא
he~will~much~KNEEL(V) : יברך
he~will~much~KNEEL(V)~you(ms) : יברכך
she~did~DRY.OUT(V) | DRY : יבשה
he~will~be~REDEEM(V) | he~will~REDEEM(V) | Yigal : יגאל
he~will~REDEEM(V)~her : יגאלנה
he~will~REDEEM(V)~him : יגאלנו
he~will~MAGNIFY(V) : יגדל
he~will~INVADE(V) : יגוד
he~will~INVADE(V)~us : יגודנו
he~will~PUSH(V) : יגושׂ

he~will~EXPIRE(V) : יגוע
he~will~SMITE(V) : יגוף
he~will~IMMIGRATE(V) : יגור
you(ms)~did~BE.AFRAID(V) : יגורת
I~did~BE.AFRAID(V) : יגורתי
he~will~GORE(V) : יגח
he~will~make~BE.FACE.TO.FACE(V) : יגיד
they(m)~will~make~BE.FACE.TO.FACE(V) : יגידו
TOIL : יגיע
TOIL~you(ms) : יגיעך
he~will~much~REMOVE.THE.COVER(V) : יגלה
he~will~much~SHAVE(V) : יגלח
they(m)~will~much~SHAVE(V) : יגלחו
he~will~much~SHAVE(V)~him : יגלחנו
Yagli : יגלי
he~will~be~STEAL(V) : יגנב
he~will~STEAL(V) : יגנוב
he~will~TOUCH(V) : יגע
they(m)~will~TOUCH(V) : יגעו
Yegar-Sa'haduta : יגרשׂהדותא
he~will~be~CHEW(V) : יגר
he~will~much~GNAW(V) : יגרם
he~will~TAKE.AWAY(V) | he~will~be~TAKE.AWAY(V) : יגרע
he~will~much~CAST.OUT(V) : יגרש
he~will~much~CAST.OUT(V)~them(m) : יגרשם
he~will~DRAW.NEAR(V) : יגש
they(m)~will~DRAW.NEAR(V) : יגשו
HAND : יד
he~will~DIVE(V) : ידאה
he~will~OFFER.WILLINGLY(V)~him : ידבנו
he~will~ADHERE(V) : ידבק
he~will~make~ADHERE(V) : ידבק
they(m)~will~ADHERE(V) : ידבקו
he~will~much~SPEAK(V) : ידבר
HAND~her : ידה
HAND~him : ידו
he~will~MODERATE(V) : ידון
>~KNOW(V) : ידוע
he~will~MAKE.A.VOW(V) : ידור
HAND~s : ידות

HAND~s~him :
HAND~me | HAND~s2 | HAND~s2~me :
CHERISHED :
HAND~s2~her :
HAND~s2~them(m) :
HAND~s2~him :
HAND~s2 :
HAND~s2~you(ms) :
HAND~s2~you(mp) :
he~will~MODERATE(V) :
HAND~s2~us :
HAND~you(fs) | HAND~you(ms) :
HAND~you(ms) :
HAND~you(mp) :
Yidlap :
HAND~them(m) :
they(m)~will~BE.SILENT :
he~did~KNOW(V) :
he~did~KNOW(V)~her :
they~did~KNOW(V) | they(m)~will~KNOW(V) | he~did~KNOW(V)~him :
they~did~KNOW(V)~them(m) :
they~did~KNOW(V)~must :
KNOWER :
we~did~KNOW(V) :
you(ms)~did~KNOW(V) :
you(ms)~did~KNOW(V)~him :
I~did~KNOW(V) :
I~did~KNOW(V)~him :
I~did~KNOW(V)~you(ms) :
you(mp)~did~KNOW(V) | you(ms)~did~KNOW(V)~them(m) :
you(fp)~did~KNOW(V) :
he~will~SEEK(V)~him :
Yah :
he~will~PUSH.AWAY(V)~him :
Yehudah :
Yehudit :
YHWH-Yireh :
YHWH-Nisiy :
YHWH :
YHWH :
Yehoshu'a :
he~will~EXIST(V) :
he~will~EXIST(V) :
they(m)~will~EXIST(V) :
Yahats~unto :
they(m)~will~KILL(V)~me :
he~will~KILL(V)~me :
they(m)~will~CAST.DOWN(V) :
he~will~CONSENT(V) :
he~will~TAKE.HOLD(V)~them(m) :
he~will~EAT(V) :
they(m)~will~EAT(V) :
they(m)~will~EAT(V)~her :
they(m)~will~EAT(V)~him :
he~will~EAT(V)~must :
he~will~EAT(V)~them(m) :
he~will~EAT(V)~her :
he~will~EAT(V)~him :
he~will~SAY(V) :
they(m)~will~SAY(V) :
he~will~be~make~SPIT.UPON(V) :
he~will~be~make~COME(V) :
Yovav :
Yuval | JUBILEE :
they(m)~will~make~THROW.THE.HAND(V)~you(ms) :
he~will~be~KNOW(V) :
KNOW(V)~ing(ms) :
KNOW(V)~ing(mp) :
KNOW(V)~ing(fs) :
Yokheved :
he~will~BE.ABLE(V) :
they(m)~will~BE.ABLE(V)~must :
BRING.FORTH(V)~ed(ms) :
he~will~be~BRING.FORTH(V) :
BRING.FORTH(V)~ed(fs) :
BRING.FORTH(V)~ed(mp) :
they(m)~will~be~BRING.FORTH(V) :
BRING.FORTH(V)~ing(fs) :
he~will~make~BRING.FORTH(V) :
he~will~make~WALK(V) :
DAY :
DAY~s2 :
DAYTIME :

he~will~be~make~DIE(V) : יומת
they~will~be~make~DIE(V) : יומתו
Yawan : יון
DOVE : יונה
SUCKLE(V)~ing(ms) : יונק
he~will~make~ADD(V) : יוסיף
they(m)~will~make~ADD(V) : יוסיפו
he~will~be~make~POUR(V) : יוסך
Yoseph | he~will~make~ADD(V) | ADD(V)~ing(ms) : יוסף
ADD(V)~ing(mp) : יוספים
he~will~be~make~TURN.ASIDE(V) : יוסר
GO.OUT(V)~ing(ms) : יוצא
GO.OUT(V)~ing(fp) : יוצאות
GO.OUT(V)~ing(mp) : יוצאי
GO.OUT(V)~ing(mp) : יוצאים
GO.OUT(V)~ing(fs) : יוצאת
he~will~be~make~LEAVE.IN.PLACE(V) : יוצג
he~will~make~GO.OUT(V) : יוציא
he~will~make~GO.OUT(V)~them(m) : יוציאם
he~will~be~make~POUR.DOWN(V) : יוצק
he~will~be~much~TAKE(V) : יוקח
he~will~be~make~AVENGE(V) : יוקם
FIRST.RAIN : יורה
they(m)~will~make~THROW(V) : יורו
they(m)~will~make~THROW(V)~you(ms) : יורוך
they(m)~will~make~GO.DOWN(V) : יורידו
he~will~make~POSSESS(V)~her : יורישנה
they(m)~will~make~RAISE.UP(V) : יורם
POSSESS(V)~ing(ms) : יורש
POSSESS(V)~ing(mp) : יורשים
POSSESS(V)~ing(fs) : יורשת
SETTLE(V)~ing(ms) : יושב
SETTLE(V)~ing(mp) : יושבי
SETTLE(V)~ing(mp)~her : יושביה
SETTLE(V)~ing(mp) : יושבים
SETTLE(V)~ing(fs) : יושבת
he~will~SET.DOWN(V)~ed(ms) : יושת
he~will~make~LEAVE.BEHIND(V) : יותיר

he~GIVE(V)~ed(ms) : יותן
he~will~be~much~BREAK.DOWN(V) : יותץ
he~will~be~LEAVE.BEHIND(V) : יותר
he~will~make~LEAVE.BEHIND(V) : יותר
LOBE : יותרת
they(m)~will~SACRIFICE(V) : יזבחו
he~will~RESIDE(V)~me : יזבלני
he~will~make~SPATTER(V) : יזה
he~will~SPATTER(V) : יזה
he~will~ISSUE(V) : יזוב
he~will~be~LOOSEN(V) : יזח
he~will~make~SIMMER(V) : יזד
he~will~make~SIMMER(V)~must : יזידון
he~will~make~DEDICATE(V) : יזיר
he~will~FLOW(V) : יזל
they(m)~will~PLOT(V) : יזמו
he~will~much~JUMP(V) : יזנק
he~will~SPRINKLE(V) : יזרוק
he~will~be~SOW(V) : יזרע
he~will~TAKE.AS.A.PLEDGE(V) : יחבול
he~will~GIRD.UP(V) : יחגור
TOGETHER : יחד
TOGETHER : יחדו
he~will~TERMINATE(V) : יחדל
they(m)~will~TERMINATE(V)~must : יחדלון
he~will~PROVIDE.PROTECTION(V) : יחון
he~will~PERCEIVE(V) : יחזה
he~will~FAIL(V) : יחטא
they(m)~will~make~FAIL(V) : יחטיאו
he~will~LIVE(V) : יחי
SOLITARY~you(ms) : יחידך
he~will~LIVE(V) : יחיה
they(m)~will~much~LIVE(V) : יחיו
he~will~make~DRILL(V) : יחל
he~will~make~PASS.OVER(V)~him : יחליפנו
he~will~much~DRILL(V) : יחלל
they(m)~will~much~DRILL(V) : יחללו
he~will~much~DRILL(V)~her : יחללהו
he~will~much~DRILL(V)~him : יחללנו

he~will~DISTRIBUTE(V) | he~will~be~DISTRIBUTE(V) :
>~much~HEAT(V) | he~will~HEAT(V) :
he~will~CRAVE(V) :
he~will~BE.SOUR(V) :
they(m)~will~CAMP(V) :
he~will~make~BE.FILTHY(V) :
he~will~PROVIDE.PROTECTION(V)~you(ms) :
he~will~DEVOTE(V)~him :
he~will~DEVOUR(V)~him :
he~will~DIMINISH(V) :
they(m)~will~DIMINISH(V) :
he~will~DELIGHT(V) :
Yahhtse'el :
they(m)~will~DIVIDE(V)~must :
he~will~FLARE.UP(V) :
he~will~FLARE.UP(V) :
he~will~make~ASSIGN(V) :
he~will~make~KEEP.SILENT(V) :
he~will~be~make~ASSIGN(V) :
he~will~CUT.SHARPLY(V) :
he~will~be~THINK(V) :
they(m)~will~be~THINK(V) :
Yatvatah :
he~will~BE.CLEAN(V) :
Yetur :
he~will~BE.DIRTY(V) :
they~will~BE.DIRTY(V) :
he~will~much~BE.DIRTY(V)~him :
he~will~TEAR.INTO.PIECES(V) | he~will~be~TEAR.INTO.PIECES(V) :
he~will~DO.WELL(V) :
he~will~make~DO.WELL(V) :
WINE :
WINE~them(m) :
they(m)~will~SUCKLE(V) :
he~will~POUR.DOWN(V) :
he~will~much~CORRECT(V) :
he~will~APPOINT(V)~her :
he~will~be~THROW(V) :
he~will~POSSESS(V) | he~will~much~POSSESS(V) :
they(m)~will~POSSESS(V) :
they(m)~will~POSSESS(V)~her :
they(m)~will~POSSESS(V)~them(m) :
he~will~POSSESS(V)~you(ms) :
he~will~BE.STRAIGHT(V) :
he~will~WASH(V) :
he~will~make~HIT(V) :
he~did~BE.ABLE(V) | >~BE.ABLE(V) :
they~did~BE.ABLE(V) :
>~BE.ABLE(V) :
I~did~BE.ABLE(V) :
he~will~be~much~COVER(V) :
he~will~make~RECOGNIZE(V) :
he~will~make~HIT(V)~you(ms) :
he~will~RESTRICT(V) :
she~did~BE.ABLE(V) :
they~did~BE.ABLE(V) :
he~will~make~HIT(V)~him :
he~will~make~LOWER(V)~them(m) :
he~will~be~LOWER(V) :
they(m)~will~much~COVER.OVER(V)~them(m) :
he~will~much~COVER.OVER(V)~him :
he~will~make~BE.ANGRY(V)~him :
he~will~much~COVER(V) :
he~will~DIG(V) :
he~will~make~CUT(V) :
he~will~be~CUT(V) :
he~will~WEAR(V) :
he~will~WEAR(V)~them(m) :
he~did~BRING.FORTH(V) :
she~did~BRING.FORTH(V) :
they~did~BRING.FORTH(V) :
BOY~s~me :
BOY~s~her :
BOY~s~them(f) :
BOY~s~him :
he~did~BRING.FORTH(V)~you(ms) :
I~did~BRING.FORTH(V) :

he~will~be~JOIN(V) :ילוה
he~will~make~JOIN(V)~you(ms) :ילוך
they(m)~will~much~LICK(V) :ילחכו
will~be~FIGHT(V) :ילחם
BORN :יליד
BORN~s | BOY~s :ילידי
I~did~BRING.FORTH(V)~him :ילידתיהו
he~will~STAY.THE.NIGHT(V) :ילין
he~will~WALK(V) :ילך
they(m)~will~WALK(V) :ילכו
HOWLING :ילל
he~will~LEARN(V) :ילמד
they(m)~will~much~LEARN(V) :ילמדו
they(m)~will~much~LEARN(V) :ילמדו
they(m)~will~LEARN(V)~must :ילמדון
they(m)~will~much~LEARN(V)~must :ילמדון
SKIN.SORE :ילפת
they(m)~will~PICK.UP(V) :ילקטו
SEA :ים
he~will~much~REFUSE(V) :ימאן
SEA~unto :ימה
he~will~HURRY(V)~her :ימהרנה
Yemu'el :ימואל
he~will~BE.LOW(V) :ימוך
he~will~be~SNIP.OFF(V) :ימול
he~will~FEEL(V)~me :ימושני
he~will~DIE(V) | DAY~s :ימות
they(m)~will~DIE(V) :ימותו
they(m)~will~DIE(V)~must :ימותון
he~will~be~WIPE.AWAY(V) :ימחה
he~will~STRIKE.THROUGH(V) :ימחץ
DAY~s | DAY~s~me :ימי
DAY~s~her :ימיה
DAY~s~him :ימיו
DAY~s~you(ms) :ימיך
DAY~s~you(mp) :ימיכם
SEA~s | DAY~s :ימים
DAY~s~unto :ימימה
RIGHT.HAND :ימין
RIGHT.HAND~him :ימינו
RIGHT.HAND~you(ms) :ימינך
he~will~make~CONVERT(V) :ימיר
he~will~make~CONVERT(V)~him :ימירנו
he~will~make~MOVE.AWAY(V) :ימיש
he~will~make~DIE(V) :ימית
he~will~make~DIE(V)~him :ימיתנו
he~will~SELL(V) :ימכור
he~will~SELL(V) | he~will~be~SELL(V) :ימכר
they(m)~will~be~SELL(V) :ימכרו
he~will~much~FILL(V) :ימלא
they(m)~will~FILL(V) :ימלאו
he~will~REIGN(V) :ימלוך
he~will~be~RECKON(V) | Yimnah :ימנה
he~will~be~MELT.AWAY(V) :ימס
he~will~BE.LESS(V) :ימעט
he~will~make~BE.LESS(V) :ימעיט
he~will~be~FIND(V) | he~will~FIND(V) :ימצא
he~will~FIND(V)~him :ימצאהו
they(m)~will~be~FIND(V) :ימצאון
he~will~be~DRAIN(V) :ימצה
they(m)~will~be~ROT(V) :ימקו
he~will~be~HAIR.FELL.OUT(V) :ימרט
he~will~REGULATE(V) :ימשול
they(m)~will~REGULATE(V) :ימשולו
he~will~SMEAR(V) :ימשח
he~will~REGULATE(V) :ימשל
he~will~much~GROPE(V) :ימשש
WINE :יין
he~will~COMMIT.ADULTERY(V) :ינאף
they(m)~will~much~PROVOKE(V)~me :ינאצוני
he~will~much~GORE(V) :ינגח
he~will~much~DRIVE(V) :ינהג
he~will~much~DRIVE(V)~you(ms) :ינהגך
he~will~REST(V) :ינוח
he~will~FLEE(V) :ינוס
they(m)~will~FLEE(V) :ינוסו
he~will~make~INHERIT(V) :ינחיל
he~will~make~INHERIT(V)~you(ms) :ינחילך
he~will~make~INHERIT(V)~her :ינחילנה
they(m)~will~INHERIT(V) :ינחלו

he~will~be~COMFORT(V) : 𐤉𐤍𐤇𐤌

he~will~much~COMFORT(V)~us : 𐤉𐤍𐤇𐤌𐤍𐤅

he~will~make~GUIDE(V)~him : 𐤉𐤍𐤇𐤍𐤅

he~will~make~GUIDE(V)~me : 𐤉𐤍𐤇𐤍𐤉

he~will~much~PREDICT(V) : 𐤉𐤍𐤇𐤔

he~will~make~FORBID(V) : 𐤉𐤍𐤉𐤀

he~will~make~REST(V) : 𐤉𐤍𐤉𐤇

they(m)~will~make~FLEE(V) : 𐤉𐤍𐤉𐤎𐤅

he~will~make~WAVE(V)~him : 𐤉𐤍𐤉𐤐𐤍𐤅

they(m)~will~much~RECOGNIZE(V) : 𐤉𐤍𐤊𐤓𐤅

they(m)~will~be~STRUGGLE(V) : 𐤉𐤍𐤑𐤅

they(m)~will~PRESERVE(V) : 𐤉𐤍𐤑𐤓𐤅

he~will~be~DELIVER(V) : 𐤉𐤍𐤑𐤋

he~will~much~ACQUIT(V) : 𐤉𐤍𐤒𐤄

he~will~be~AVENGE(V) : 𐤉𐤍𐤒𐤌

he~will~be~GIVE(V) : 𐤉𐤍𐤕𐤍

he~will~LIFT.UP(V) : 𐤉𐤎𐤀

he~will~LIFT.UP(V)~him : 𐤉𐤎𐤀𐤄𐤅

they(m)~will~LIFT.UP(V) : 𐤉𐤎𐤀𐤅

he~will~make~SHUT(V)~him : 𐤉𐤎𐤂𐤉𐤓𐤍𐤅

he~will~much~GO.AROUND(V)~him : 𐤉𐤎𐤅𐤁𐤁𐤍𐤄𐤅

BOTTOM.BASE : 𐤉𐤎𐤅𐤃

he~will~PLACE(V) : 𐤉𐤎𐤅𐤌

he~will~TURN.ASIDE(V) : 𐤉𐤎𐤅𐤓

they(m)~will~TURN.ASIDE(V) : 𐤉𐤎𐤅𐤓𐤅

he~will~HOLD.A.GRUDGE(V)~us : 𐤉𐤎𐤈𐤌𐤍𐤅

he~will~make~OVERTAKE(V) : 𐤉𐤎𐤉𐤂

he~will~PLACE(V) : 𐤉𐤎𐤉𐤌

they(m)~will~PLACE(V) : 𐤉𐤎𐤉𐤌𐤅

he~will~PLACE(V)~you(ms) : 𐤉𐤎𐤉𐤌𐤊

he~will~PLACE(V)~them(m) : 𐤉𐤎𐤉𐤌𐤌 /

he~will~SKIP.WITH.JOY(V) : 𐤉𐤎𐤉𐤎

he~will~make~TURN.ASIDE(V) : 𐤉𐤎𐤉𐤓

he~will~make~TURN.ASIDE(V)~her : 𐤉𐤎𐤉𐤓𐤍𐤄

he~will~make~PERSUADE(V)~you(ms) : 𐤉𐤎𐤉𐤕𐤊

Yiskah : 𐤉𐤎𐤊𐤄

they(m)~will~make~CALCULATE(V) : 𐤉𐤎𐤊𐤉𐤋𐤅

he~will~FORGIVE(V) : 𐤉𐤎𐤋𐤇

they(m)~will~SUPPORT(V) : 𐤉𐤎𐤌𐤊𐤅

they(m)~will~JOURNEY(V) : 𐤉𐤎𐤏𐤅

he~did~ADD(V) : 𐤉𐤎𐤐

she~did~ADD(V) : 𐤉𐤎𐤐𐤄

they~did~ADD(V) : 𐤉𐤎𐤐𐤅

he~will~be~COUNT(V) : 𐤉𐤎𐤐𐤓

he~will~be~STONE(V) : 𐤉𐤎𐤒𐤋

they(m)~will~STONE(V)~us : 𐤉𐤎𐤒𐤋𐤅𐤍𐤅

Yisra'eyl : 𐤉𐤎𐤓𐤀𐤋

Yisra'eyl~of : 𐤉𐤎𐤓𐤀𐤋𐤉𐤕

he~will~CREMATE(V) : 𐤉𐤎𐤓𐤅𐤐

they(m)~will~SLICE(V) : 𐤉𐤎𐤓𐤈𐤅

he~will~be~CREMATE(V) : 𐤉𐤎𐤓𐤐

they(m)~will~CREMATE(V) : 𐤉𐤎𐤓𐤐𐤅

Yis'sas'khar : 𐤉𐤎𐤔𐤊𐤓

he~will~be~SERVE(V) : 𐤉𐤏𐤁𐤃

they(m)~will~SERVE(V) : 𐤉𐤏𐤁𐤃𐤅

they(m)~will~SERVE(V)~you(ms) : 𐤉𐤏𐤁𐤃𐤅𐤊

he~will~SERVE(V) : 𐤉𐤏𐤁𐤅𐤃

they(m)~will~SERVE(V) : 𐤉𐤏𐤁𐤅𐤃𐤅

he~will~CROSS.OVER(V) : 𐤉𐤏𐤁𐤅𐤓

he~will~CROSS.OVER(V) : 𐤉𐤏𐤁𐤓

they(m)~will~CROSS.OVER(V) : 𐤉𐤏𐤁𐤓𐤅

he~did~APPOINT(V)~her : 𐤉𐤏𐤃𐤄

he~will~much~FLY(V) : 𐤉𐤏𐤅𐤐𐤐

he~will~much~BLIND(V) : 𐤉𐤏𐤅𐤓

Ye'ish : 𐤉𐤏𐤅𐤔

he~will~LEAVE(V) : 𐤉𐤏𐤆𐤁

he~will~LEAVE(V)~you(ms) : 𐤉𐤏𐤆𐤁𐤊

Yazeyr : 𐤉𐤏𐤆𐤓

he~will~ENWRAP(V) : 𐤉𐤏𐤈𐤄

he~will~make~STIR.UP(V) : 𐤉𐤏𐤉𐤓

Ye'ish : 𐤉𐤏𐤉𐤔

he~will~GO.UP(V) : 𐤉𐤏𐤋

he~will~GO.UP(V) | he~will~be~GO.UP(V) : 𐤉𐤏𐤋𐤄

they(m)~will~GO.UP(V) : 𐤉𐤏𐤋𐤅

they(m)~will~make~BE.OUT.OF.SIGHT(V) : 𐤉𐤏𐤋𐤉𐤌𐤅

Yalam | he~will~make~GO.UP(V)~them(m) : 𐤉𐤏𐤋𐤌

he~will~be~much~STAND(V) : 𐤉𐤏𐤌𐤃

they(m)~will~STAND(V) : 𐤉𐤏𐤌𐤃𐤅

he~will~STAND(V) :יעמוד
SEEING.AS :יען
he~will~ANSWER(V) :יענה
they(m)~will~AFFLICT(V) :יענו
he~will~ANSWER(V)~him :יעננו
he~will~be~FINE(V) :יענש
he~will~DO(V) | he~will~be~DO(V) :יעשה
they~did~be~DO(V) | they(m)~will~DO(V) :יעשו
they(m)~will~DO(V)~must :יעשון
Ya'aqov :יעקוב
he~will~ARRANGE(V) :יערוך
he~will~DROP(V) :יערוף
he~will~make~ARRANGE(V) :יעריך
he~will~make~ARRANGE(V)~him :יעריכנו
he~will~ARRANGE(V)~him :יערכנו
they(m)~will~DROP(V) :יערפו
he~will~SMOKE(V) :יעשן
he~will~REACH(V)~us :יפגענו
he~will~ENCOUNTER(V)~you(ms) :יפגשך
he~will~be~RANSOM(V) :יפדה
BEAUTIFUL :יפה
he~will~FALL(V) :יפול
Yephunah :יפונה
BEAUTIFUL~s :יפות
he~will~make~FALL(V) :יפיל
he~will~be~PERFORM(V) :יפלא
he~will~make~BE.DISTINCT(V) :יפלה
they(m)~will~FALL(V) :יפלו
he~will~make~PERFORM(V) :יפליא
he~will~TURN(V) :יפנה
he~will~SPREAD.ACROSS(V) :יפשה
he~will~be~REGISTER(V) :יפקד
he~will~REGISTER(V) :יפקוד
he~will~make~BREAK(V) :יפר
he~will~be~DIVIDE.APART(V) :יפרד
they~will~be~DIVIDE.APART(V) :יפרדו
he~will~RIP(V) :יפרום
he~will~SPREAD.OUT(V) :יפרוש
he~will~BREAK.OUT(V) :יפרוץ
he~will~BURST.OUT(V) :יפרח
he~will~make~CLEAVE(V) :יפריס
he~will~make~BREAK(V)~him :יפרנו
they(m)~will~SPREAD.OUT(V) :יפרשו
he~will~LOOSE(V) :יפרע
he~will~BREAK.OUT(V) :יפרץ
Yaphet | he~will~make~SPREAD.WIDE(V) | BEAUTIFUL :יפת
he~will~much~SPREAD.WIDE(V) :יפתה
he~will~SPREAD.WIDE(V) :יפתה
he~will~OPEN(V) :יפתח
he~did~GO.OUT(V) | he~will~GO.OUT(V) :יצא
she~did~GO.OUT(V) :יצאה
they~did~GO.OUT(V) | they(m)~will~GO.OUT(V) :יצאו
we~did~GO.OUT(V) :יצאנו
you(ms)~did~GO.OUT(V) :יצאת
I~did~GO.OUT(V) :יצאתי
you(mp)~did~GO.OUT(V) :יצאתם
he~will~make~STAND.UP(V) :יצב
Yits'har | FRESH.OIL :יצהר
he~will~much~DIRECT(V) :יצו
>~GO.OUT(V) :יצוא
he~will~HUNT(V) :יצוד
he~will~much~DIRECT(V) :יצוה
he~will~be~much~DIRECT(V) :יצווה
COUCH~me :יצועי
he~will~POUR.DOWN(V) :יצוק
Yits'hhaq | he~will~LAUGH(V) :יצחק
he~will~make~HARASS(V) :יציק
he~will~SPRING.UP(V) :יצמח
he~will~WIND.AROUND(V) :יצנוף
he~will~CRY.OUT(V) :יצעק
he~will~KEEP.WATCH(V) :יצף
he~did~POUR.DOWN(V) :יצק
he~did~MOLD(V) | THOUGHT :יצר
THOUGHT~him :יצרו
he~will~PRESERVE(V)~him :יצרנהו
WINE.TROUGH :יקב
he~will~much~GATHER.TOGETHER(V)~you(ms) :יקבצך
he~will~make~SET.APART(V) :יקדיש
they(m)~will~make~SET.APART(V) :יקדישו

he~will~SET.APART(V) : יקדש
OBEDIENCE : יקהת
he~will~be~BOUND.UP(V) : יקוו
he~will~RISE(V) : יקום
he~will~RISE(V) : יקום
they(m)~will~RISE(V) : יקומו
they(m)~will~RISE(V)~must : יקומון
he~will~TAKE(V) : יקח
he~will~TAKE(V)~him : יקחהו
they(m)~will~TAKE(V) : יקחו
he~will~TAKE(V)~you(ms) : יקחך
he~will~TAKE(V)~her : יקחנה
he~did~make~BURN.INCENSE(V) : יקטיר
he~will~make~BURN.INCENSE(V)~her : יקטירנה
Yaqtan : יקטן
he~will~make~RISE(V) : יקים
they(m)~will~make~RISE(V) : יקימו
he~will~make~RISE(V)~you(ms) : יקימך
he~will~make~RISE(V)~her : יקימנה
he~will~make~RISE(V)~him : יקימנו
he~will~much~BELITTLE(V) : יקלל
he~will~PURCHASE(V) : יקנה
they(m)~will~make~BE.ZEALOUS(V)~him : יקניאוהו
he~will~SNAP(V) : יקצוף
he~will~make~SCRAPE.OFF(V) : יקציע
he~will~CALL.OUT(V) | he~will~be~CALL.OUT(V) | he~will~be~MEET(V) : יקרא
they(m)~will~be~CALL.OUT(V) | they(m)~will~CALL.OUT(V) : יקראו
he~will~MEET(V)~us : יקראנו
he~will~COME.NEAR(V) : יקרב
they(m)~will~COME.NEAR(V) : יקרבו
he~will~be~MEET(V) : יקרה
he~will~make~MAKE.BALD(V)~her : יקרחה
he~will~make~COME.NEAR(V) : יקריב
they(m)~will~make~COME.NEAR(V) : יקריבו
he~will~make~COME.NEAR(V)~him : יקריבנו
he~will~be~TEAR(V) : יקרע
he~will~BE.HARD(V) : יקשה
Yaq'shan : יקשן
he~did~FEAR(V) | FEARFUL | he~will~SEE(V) | he~will~be~SEE(V) | FEAR(V)~ing(ms) : ירא
he~will~SEE(V) : יראה
she~did~FEAR(V) | he~will~be~SEE(V) : יראה
they(m)~will~SEE(V) : יראו
they~did~FEAR(V) | they(m)~will~be~SEE(V) : יראו
he~will~SEE(V)~her : יראוה
they(m)~will~SEE(V)~must : יראון
FEARFUL~s : יראי
he~will~SEE(V)~her : יראנה
he~will~make~SEE(V)~me : יראני
he~will~SEE(V)~me : יראני
FEARFULNESS : יראת
FEARFULNESS~him : יראתו
I~did~FEAR(V) : יראתי
you(mp)~did~FEAR(V) : יראתם
he~did~INCREASE(V) : ירב
he~will~INCREASE(V) : ירבה
he~will~make~INCREASE(V) : ירבה
they(m)~will~INCREASE(V) : ירבו
they(m)~will~INCREASE(V)~must : ירביון
they(m)~will~SHAKE(V)~must : ירגזון
they(m)~will~KILL.BY.STONING(V) : ירגמו
they(m)~will~KILL.BY.STONING(V)~him : ירגמוהו
Yared | he~will~GO.DOWN(V) | he~did~GO.DOWN(V) : ירד
they~will~GO.DOWN(V) : ירדו
he~will~PURSUE(V) : ירדוף
they(m)~will~PURSUE(V) : ירדופו
Yarden : ירדן
he~will~RULE(V)~him : ירדנו
we~did~GO.DOWN(V) : ירדנו
he~did~THROW(V) : ירה
>~GO.DOWN(V) : ירוד
>~THROW(V) : ירוה

>~SPIT(V) :
HERITAGE :
HERITAGE~him :
Yerahh | MOON :
Ye'rey'hho :
he~will~make~WIDEN(V) :
MOON~s :
he~will~much~FLUTTER(V) :
he~will~BATHE(V) :
they(m)~will~BATHE(V) :
he~will~BE.FAR(V) :
he~did~HAND.OVER(V) :
they(m)~will~DISPUTE(V)~ must :
he~will~make~SMELL(V)~ must :
he~will~make~RAISE.UP(V) :
they(m)~will~make~ RAISE.UP(V) :
TENT.WALL~s :
I~did~THROW(V) :
MIDSECTION | he~will~ BE.SOFT(V) :
he~will~RIDE(V) :
MIDSECTION~her :
MIDSECTION~him :
MIDSECTION~me :
they(m)~will~make~ RIDE(V) :
MIDSECTION~s :
MIDSECTION~you(fs) :
he~will~BE.DYSFUNCTIONAL(V) :
they(m)~will~FEED(V) :
he~will~much~HEAL(V) :
he~will~make~ SINK.DOWN(V)~you(ms) :
he~will~be~ACCEPT(V) :
!(mp)~ACCEPT(V) :
they(m)~will~be~ACCEPT(V) :
he~will~MURDER(V) :
GREEN | he~did~SPIT(V) :
he~will~COMPOUND(V) :
GREENISH :
GREENISH~s :
PROPERTY | !(ms)~POSSESS(V)~ & :
they~did~POSSESS(V) :

he~will~make~ DEPART(V)~must :
we~did~POSSESS(V) :
THERE.IS :
he~will~make~REMAIN(V) :
they(m)~will~make~ REMAIN(V) :
he~will~INQUIRE(V) :
he~will~INQUIRE(V)~you(ms) :
he~did~SETTLE(V) | he~will~ SETTLE(V) :
they(m)~will~SETTLE(V) | they~ did~SETTLE(V) :
they(m)~will~CEASE(V) :
we~did~SETTLE(V) :
he~will~be~SWEAR(V) :
Yish'baq :
he~will~be~CRACK(V) :
they(m)~will~CRACK(V) :
you(mp)~did~SETTLE(V) :
they(m)~will~GO.ASTRAY(V) :
he~will~COPULATE(V)~ her :
he~will~make~OVERLOOK(V) :
he~will~TURN.BACK(V) :
they(m)~will~TURN.BACK(V) :
RELIEF :
RELIEF~him :
he~will~FALL.UPON(V)~ you(ms) :
Yeshurun :
he~will~SLAY(V) | he~will~be~ SLAY(V) :
he~will~SLAY(V)~him :
he~will~make~ DAMAGE(V)~you(ms) :
he~will~be~FLUSH(V) :
he~will~make~ TURN.BACK(V) :
they(m)~will~make~ TURN.BACK(V) :
: DESOLATE.WILDERNESS
he~will~SING(V) :
/ he~will~SET.DOWN(V) :
he~will~BITE(V) :
THERE.IS~you(ms) :

he~will~LIE.DOWN(V) : ישכב
they(m)~will~LIE.DOWN(V) : ישכבו
he~will~DWELL(V) : ישכון
he~will~FORGET(V) : ישכח
THERE.IS~you(mp) : ישכם
he~will~DWELL(V) : ישכן
he~will~CAST.OFF(V) : ישל
he~will~much~SEND(V) : ישלח
he~will~SEND(V) : ישלח
he~will~much~SEND(V)~them(m) : ישלחם
he~will~much~SEND(V)~him : ישלחנו
he~will~much~MAKE.RESTITUTION(V) : ישלם
he~will~much~MAKE.RESTITUTION(V)~her : ישלמנה
he~will~make~DESTROY(V) : ישמיד
he~will~make~DESTROY(V)~them(m) : ישמידם
he~will~HEAR(V) | he~will~be~HEAR(V) : ישמע
Yishma'el : ישמעאל
Yishma'el~s : ישמעאלים
they(m)~will~HEAR(V) : ישמעו
they(m)~will~HEAR(V)~must : ישמעון
he~will~HEAR(V)~me : ישמעני
he~will~SAFEGUARD(V)~him : ישמרנו
SLEEPING : ישן
THERE.IS~him : ישנו
they(m)~will~DO(V) : ישעו
he~will~DECIDE(V) : ישפוט
they(m)~did~DECIDE(V) : ישפוטו
he~will~POUR.OUT(V) : ישפוך
they(m)~will~DECIDE(V) : ישפטו
he~will~be~POUR.OUT(V) : ישפך
he~will~KISS(V) : ישק
he~will~make~DRINK(V) : ישקה
they(m)~will~DRINK(V) : ישקו
he~will~WEIGH(V) : ישקול
STRAIGHT~s : ישרים
they(m)~will~SWARM(V) : ישרצו
they(m)~will~much~MINISTER(V) : ישרתו
they(m)~will~much~MINISTER(V)~him : ישרתוהו
he~will~GULP(V) | he~will~be~GULP(V) : ישתה
they(m)~will~GULP(V) : ישתו
they(m)~will~self~BEND.DOWN(V) : ישתחוו
they(m)~will~self~BE.ASHAMED(V) : יתבוששו
TENT.PEG~s : יתדות
TENT.PEG~s~him : יתדותיו
ORPHAN : יתום
ORPHAN~s : יתומים
he~will~self~FAIL(V) : יתחטא
he~will~self~THINK(V) : יתחשב
he~will~self~STATION(V) : יתיצב
they(m)~will~BE.WHOLE(V) : יתמו
he~will~GIVE(V) : יתן
they(m)~will~GIVE(V) : יתנו
he~will~self~COMFORT(V) : יתנחם
he~will~GIVE(V)~you(ms) : יתנך
he~will~GIVE(V)~her : יתננה
he~will~GIVE(V)~him : יתננו
he~will~self~LIFT.UP(V) : יתנשא
they(m)~will~be~make~SET.APART(V) : יתקדשו
they(m)~will~THRUST(V) : יתקעו
REMAINDER | Yeter : יתר
Yitro : יתרו
Yetet : יתת
like~STONE : כאבן
like~ROBE : כאדרת
like~ALOE~s : כאהלים
like~NATIVE : כאזרח
like~UNIT : כאחד
like~BROTHER~him : כאחיו
like~MAN : כאיש
like~DEEP.BLACK : כאישון
like~MIGHTY.ONE : כאל
like~THESE : כאלה
like~Elohiym : כאלהים
like~Ephrayim : כאפרים
like~CEDAR~s : כארזים
like~LION : כארי
like~LION : כאריה
like~LAND : כארץ
like~FIRE : כאש

like~GUILT :
like~WHICH :
HEAVY | !(ms)~much~BE.HEAVY(V) | >~much~BE.HEAVY(V) :
she~did~BE.HEAVY(V) :
they~did~BE.HEAVY(V) :
HEAVY~s :
>~much~BE.HEAVY(V)~you(ms) :
like~>~COME(V) :
like~>~COME(V)~me :
ARMAMENT :
ARMAMENT~him :
ARMAMENT~me :
ARMAMENT~you(ms) :
like~PRESENT :
like~PRESENT~him :
like~>~much~SWALLOW(V) :
SHEEP :
SHEEP :
SHEEP~s :
like~IRON :
like~the~GREAT :
like~MAGNIFICENCE :
like~the~NATION :
like~GARDEN :
like~GARDEN ~s :
like~the~IMMIGRANT :
like~the~WORD | like~>~much~SPEAK(V) :
like~>~much~SPEAK(V)~her :
like~the~WORD~s :
like~>~much~SPEAK(V)~you(mp) :
like~CEREAL :
JAR~her :
like~SUFFICIENT :
like~WORD~s~you(mp) :
JAR~you(fs) :
like~ROAD :
Kedarla'omer :
DIMNESS :
ADMINISTRATION :
ADMINISTRATION :
ADMINISTRATION~you(mp) :
ADMINISTRATION~them(m) :

like~>~make~GO.OUT(V)~them(m) :
DIMNESS~s :
like~the~DAY :
like~THEY :
like~>~make~RAISE.UP(V)~me :
she~did~DIM(V) :
BE.IN.MISERY(V)~ing(mp) :
IN.THIS.WAY :
ADMINISTRATOR :
ADMINISTRATOR~s :
STRENGTH :
STRENGTH~her :
STRENGTH~me :
STRENGTH~you(mp) :
SINGEING :
STAR :
STAR~s :
ALL :
ALL~her :
ALL~him :
ALL~you(mp) :
ALL~them(m) :
ALL~them(f) :
ALL~us :
they~did~much~PREPARE(V) :
CUP :
COVERING | he~did~be~much~COVER(V) :
CUT(V)~ing(ms) :
Kush :
Kush~of :
TUNIC~s :
TUNIC~him :
Kazbi :
like~THIS :
like~THIS :
like~SEED :
like~GRASSHOPPER~s :
like~SAND :
like~HOT :
like~CUSTOM :
like~the~CHEST :
like~the~FAILURE :
like~FAILURE~s~you(mp) :

like~FAT :
like~DREAM~him :
like~DISTRIBUTION :
like~the~KINDNESS :
like~CENTER :
like~the~FUNCTIONAL :
like~DIRTY :
like~the~DEW :
like~FLAVOR :
GIVEN.THAT :
like~BIRTHRIGHT~him :
he~did~much~WASH(V) :
SHEEP :
like~FLESH~him :
SHORT :
FURNACE :
like~WORD :
like~WORD~you(ms) :
like~HAND~s2 :
like~LIKENESS~us :
like~YHWH :
like~the~DAY :
CAULDRON :
like~SEED :
ROUNDNESS | KIKAR :
DIVERSE.KIND~s2 :
like~HEART~him :
he~did~much~FINISH(V) :
they~did~much~FINISH(V) :
like~>~LICK(V) :
KIDNEY~s :
I~did~much~much~FINISH(V) :
you(mp)~did~much~FINISH(V) :
like~much~HURL(V)~ing(mp) :
like~DAY~s :
like~DAY~s | like~the~DAY~s :
like~SMALL.AMOUNT :
like~much~LAUGH(V)~ing(ms) :
like~much~TREAD.ABOUT(V)~ing(mp) :
like~much~IMITATE(V)~ing(ms) :
HARP :
like~WADI~s :
GNAT~s :
like~YOUNG.AGE~s~her :
Kineret :
SEAT :
SEAT~him :
SHEEP :
like~FIELD :
he~did~much~COVER.OVER(V) :
he~did~much~COVER.OVER(V)~him :
like~HIRELING :
Kislon :
he~did~much~COVER.OVER(V)~them(m) :
like~RAINDROP~s :
she~did~much~COVER.OVER(V) :
they~did~much~BE.ANGRY(V)~me :
ATONEMENT~s :
like~YOUTHFULNESS~him :
like~Re'uven :
like~>~SEE(V) :
like~>~SEE(V)~her :
like~>~SEE(V)~him :
like~GREEN :
like~CAPTURE(V)~ed(fp) :
like~THREE :
like~>~HEAR(V) :
!(mp)~WRITE(V) :
like~PRODUCTION :
Kit~s :
like~YESTERDAY :
SHOULDER.PIECE~s :
like~OFFERING :
like~IN.THIS.WAY :
like~STAR~s :
like~ALL :
like~ALL :
like~>~much~FINISH(V) :
like~>~much~FINISH(V)~him :
like~you(mp) :
like~HOARFROST :

ALL :
!(ms)~RESTRICT(V)~them(m) :
DOG | Kaleyv :
like~LIONESS :
COMPLETION :
!(mp)~much~FINISH(V) :
>~much~FINISH(V) :
>~much~FINISH(V)~him :
>~much~FINISH(V)~them(m) :
Kalahh :
UTENSIL~s | UTENSIL~me | UTENSIL :
UTENSIL~s~her :
UTENSIL~them(m) :
UTENSIL~s~him :
UTENSIL~you(ms) :
UTENSIL~s~you(mp) :
ENTIRELY :
UTENSIL~s :
DAUGHTER-IN-LAW~him :
DAUGHTER-IN-LAW~you(ms) :
like~WHAT :
like~OVERTHROWING :
like~THAT.ONE :
like~THAT.ONE~her :
like~THAT.ONE~him :
like~BRIDE.PRICE :
like~THAT.ONE~you(ms) :
like~THAT.ONE~you(ms) :
like~THAT.ONE~us :
like~THAT.ONE~me :
STORE(V)~ed(ms) :
Kemosh :
like~Mosheh :
like~DEATH :
like~the~PRECIPITATION :
like~the~WATER~s2 :
like~the~THING.WRITTEN :
like~the~DEPOSIT :
like~DEPOSIT :
like~the~NUMBER :
like~NUMBER~them(m) :
like~from~FACE~s :
like~LYING.PLACE :
like~from~THREE :

like~the~DECISION | like~DECISION :
like~DECISION~him :
like~DECISION~them(m) :
like~self~COMPLAIN(V)~ing(mp) :
like~WORK :
like~WORK~him :
like~WORK~s~them(m) :
like~WORK~s~you(ms) :
like~APPEARANCE | like~the~APPEARANCE :
like~make~TURN.BACK(V)~ing(ms) :
like~the~DIE(V)~ing(ms) :
like~CONTRIBUTION :
SO :
like~OPPOSITE~him :
like~TOUCH :
BASE~him :
like~>~REST(V) :
like~DECEIVE(V)~ing(ms) :
like~the~BRASS :
BASE~me :
like~REMOVAL~her :
BASE~s :
like~Nimrod :
BASE~you(ms) :
Kena'an :
Kena'an~of :
WING :
WING~s :
WING~s :
WING~s~him :
WING~s2 :
like~SOUL~you(ms) :
like~the~WOMAN~s :
like~EAGLE :
STOOL :
SHEEP :
SHEEP~s :
Kesed :
Kesed~s :
OUTER.COVERING :
RAIMENT :
RAIMENT~her :

RAIMENT~her :
RAIMENT~you(ms) :
you(ms)~did~COVER.OVER(V) :
like~HIRELING :
Kasluhh~s :
SILVER :
SILVER~him :
SILVER~me :
SILVER~s~them(m) :
SILVER~you(ms) :
SILVER~you(mp) :
SILVER~us :
like~LEAD :
like~EYE :
like~the~Anaq~s :
ANGER :
like~DIRT :
like~ARRANGEMENT~you(ms) :
like~SMOKE :
like~the~APPOINTED.TIME :
PALM :
PALM~her :
PALM~him :
DOUBLE.OVER(V)~ed(ms) :
like~BURST.OUT(V)~ing(fs) :
LID :
PALM~s :
PALM~s~him :
PALM~s2~me | like~MOUTH | PALM~s2 | PALM~me :
PALM~s2~her :
PALM~s2~them(m) :
PALM~s2~him :
like~INTERPRETATION :
like~FOOTSTEP :
!(ms)~much~COVER(V) :
like~Paroh :
KNOB :
KNOB~s~her :
KNOB~s~them(m) :
Kaphtor~s :
like~>~GO.OUT(V) :
like~>~GO.OUT(V)~me :
like~the~GAZELLE :
like~the~STEADFAST.ONE :
like~the~FLOCKS :
like~BOULDER~us :

like~IMAGE~him :
like~WAFER :
like~Qorahh :
like~the~SMALL :
like~SMOKING :
like~>~COME.NEAR(V)~you(mp) :
like~the~STUBBLE :
like~MOMENT :
KERUV :
KERUV~s :
they~did~DIG(V)~her :
like~the~FIRST :
like~the~FIRST :
like~FIRST~s :
like~AROMA :
DEPRESSION~s :
DIVORCE :
/ I~did~DIG(V) :
OUTER.RIM :
OUTER.RIM~him :
VINEYARD :
VINEYARD~him :
VINEYARD~s :
VINEYARD~you(ms) :
PLANTATION :
he~did~STOOP(V) :
LEG~s~him :
LEG~s2 :
like~the~LOST :
he~did~CUT(V) :
they~did~CUT(V) :
I~did~CUT(V) :
like~>~SETTLE(V)~him :
like~the~SNOW :
like~>~much~SEND(V)~him :
like~TITLE :
like~TITLE~s :
like~>~HEAR(V)~him :
like~>~HEAR(V)~you(mp) :
like~>~HEAR(V)~them(m) :
like~SIX :
!(ms)~WRITE(V) :
you(ms)~did~WRITE(V) :
I~did~WRITE(V) :
!(ms)~WRITE(V) | WRITE(V)~ed(ms) :
WRITE(V)~ed(mp) :

like~BIRTHING~s~them(m) :כתולדותם
TUNIC :כתונת
like~DISGUSTING~s :כתועבות
like~BULK~s :כתועפות
like~SETTLER :כתושב
SHOULDER.PIECE~s~him :כתיפיו
SMASHED :כתית
TUNIC~s :כתנות
SHOULDER.PIECE :כתף
SHOULDER.PIECE~s :כתפות
SHOULDER.PIECE~s~him :כתפיו
to~FATHER :לאב
to~FATHER~s~him :לאבותיו
to~FATHER~s~you(ms) :לאבותיך
to~FATHER~s~you(mp) :לאבותיכם
to~FATHER~s~us :לאבותינו
to~FATHER~s~them(m) :לאבותם
to~FATHER~me | to~the~FATHER~of :לאבי
to~FATHER~her :לאביה
to~FATHER~him :לאביו
to~FATHER~you(ms) :לאביך
to~Aviymelekh :לאבימלך
to~FATHER~us :לאבינו
to~STONE :לאבן
to~DUST :לאבק
to~Avraham :לאברהם
to~Avram :לאברם
to~LORD :לאדון
to~Adonai | to~LORD~me :לאדוני
to~LORD~s~her :לאדוניה
to~LORD~s~them(m) :לאדוניהם
to~the~LORD~s~him :לאדוניו
to~HUMAN | to~the~HUMAN :לאדם
to~the~FOOTING :לאדן
Le'ah :לאה
to~>~LOVE(V) :לאהבה
to~TENT~him :לאהלו
to~TENT~s~you(mp) :לאהליכם
to~Aharon :לאהרון
to~LOVE(V)~ing(mp)~me :לאוהבי
to~LOVE(V)~ing(mp)~him :לאוהביו
to~TENT | to~the~TENT :לאוהל
to~TENT~you(ms) :לאוהלך
to~ATTACK(V)~ing(mp)~s~you(ms) :לאויביך

to~TRIBE~s~them(m) :לאומותם
COMMUNITY~s :לאומים
to~Onan :לאונן
to~LIGHT :לאור
to~SIGN :לאות
to~SIGN~s :לאותות
to~MEMORIAL :לאזכרה
to~Azni :לאזני
to~NATIVE :לאזרח
to~UNIT :לאחד
to~HOLDINGS :לאחוזה
to~HOLDINGS :לאחוזת
to~HOLDINGS~him :לאחוזתו
to~BROTHER~s :לאחי
to~BROTHER~her :לאחיה
to~BROTHER~s~him | to~BROTHER~him :לאחיו
to~BROTHER~you(fs) | to~BROTHER~s~you(ms) | to~BROTHER~you(ms) :לאחיך
to~BROTHER~s~you(mp) :לאחיכם
to~Ahhiram :לאחירם
to~the~LAST :לאחרונה
to~END~them(m) :לאחריתם
to~UNIT :לאחת
to~SOFTLY~me :לאיטי
to~the~BUCK :לאייל
to~the~BUCK~s :לאילים
to~MOTHER~him :לאימו
to~MAN | to~the~MAN :לאיש
to~WOMAN | to~MAN~her :לאישה
to~MAN~me | to~FIRE.OFFERING~s~me :לאישי
to~WOMAN~him :לאישתו
to~CONSISTENCY~him :לאיתנו
to~>~EAT(V) :לאכול
to~>~EAT(V) :לאכל
to~FOOD :לאכלה
to~MIGHTY.ONE | La'eyl :לאל
to~THESE | to~OATH :לאלה
to~POWER~s :לאלוהי
to~Elohiym~them(m) :לאלוהיהם
to~Elohiym~them(f) :לאלוהיהן
to~Elohiym~him :לאלוהיו
to~Elohiym~you(mp) :לאלוהיכם

to~Elohiym | to~the~ Elohiym :
to~Elohiym~us :
to~BOUND.SHEAF~me :
to~Elyon :
to~CHIEF~s~them(m) :
to~Eliphaz :
to~Elazar :
to~THOUSAND :
to~THOUSAND~s :
to~the~THOUSAND~s :
to~BONDWOMAN :
to~>~SAY(V) :
to~the~Emor~of :
to~the~BONDWOMAN~ you(ms) :
to~MAN~s :
to~the~MAN~s :
to~>~TIE.UP(V) :
to~the~EPHOD :
to~NOSE~s~him :
to~Ephrayim :
to~Areliy :
to~FOUR :
to~FOUR :
to~Arwad :
to~LENGTH~her :
to~the~LAND | to~LAND :
to~LAND~you(ms) :
to~Ashbeyl :
to~GUILT :
to~GUILTINESS :
to~GUILTINESS :
to~the~WHICH | to~Asher :
to~the~SHE-DONKEY :
HEART :
to~the~WELL :
HEART :
HEART~him :
HEART~me :
HEART~you(ms) :
HEART~you(mp) :
HEART~them(m) :
HEART~us :
to~STRAND :
to~ALONE :
to~STRAND~her :
to~STRAND~them(f) :
to~STRAND~him :
to~STRAND~me :
to~STRAND~s | to~the~ STRAND~s :
to~STRAND~you(ms) :
to~STRAND~you(mp) :
to~STRAND~them(m) :
to~STRAND~them(f) :
to~>~COME(V) :
to~DESPISE(V) :
FRANKINCENSE :
to~FRANKINCENSE~her :
to~the~MORNING :
CLOTHING~him :
to~the~PLUNDER :
to~>~much~UTTER(V) :
to~the~SAFELY :
to~the~HOUSE :
to~Bilam :
to~EXCEPT :
to~Binyamin :
to~SON~you(ms) :
to~Beyt-El :
to~HOUSE :
to~DAUGHTER~him | to~ HOUSE~him :
to~HOUSE~me :
to~DAUGHTER~you(ms) :
to~Bekher | to~>~much~ BE.FIRSTBORN(V) :
to~Bela :
to~Balaq :
Lavan | to~SON | WHITE :
WHITE :
WHITE~s :
to~SON~s~me :
to~SON~s~him :
to~SON~s~you(ms) :
BRICK~s :
to~FLESH :
to~in~CROSS.OVER(V) :
to~Ba'al-Pe'or :
to~>~much~BURN(V) :
to~the~WOOD.BAR~s :
to~>~much~KNEEL(V) :
he~did~WEAR(V) :

to~DAUGHTER : לבת
to~HOUSE~s : לבתים
to~ROOF~you(ms) : לגגך
to~Gad : לגד
to~the~Gad~of : לגדי
to~>~SHEAR(V) : לגוז
to~NATION : לגוי
to~NATION~s~them(m) : לגויהם
to~NATION~s : לגויים
to~the~SKULL : לגולגולת
to~SKULL~them(m) : לגולגלותם
to~Guni : לגוני
to~>~IMMIGRATE(V) : לגור
to~Gil'ad : לגילעד
to~>~much~REMOVE.THE.COVER(V) : לגלות
to~the~CAMEL~s : לגמלים
to~GARDEN : לגן
to~GRAPEVINE : לגפן
to~IMMIGRANT | to~the~IMMIGRANT : לגר
to~Gershon : לגרשון
to~the~Gershon~of : לגרשוני
to~>~much~SPEAK(V) | to~the~WORD : לדבר
to~GENERATION : לדור
to~GENERATION~s : לדורות
to~GENERATION~s~him : לדורותיו
to~GENERATION~s~you(mp) : לדורותיכם
to~GENERATION~s~them(m) : לדורותם
to~BANNER~s~them(m) : לדיגליהם
to~PLEA : לדין
to~BLOOD | to~the~BLOOD : לדם
to~Dameseq : לדמשק
to~Dan : לדן
to~>~KNOW(V) : לדעה
to~>~KNOW(V) : לדעת
to~>~KNOW(V)~her : לדעתה
to~the~ROAD : לדרך
to~ROAD~him : לדרכו
to~ROAD~you(mp) : לדרככם
to~>~much~MAKE.FAT(V)~him : לדשנו
to~Datan : לדתן

to~her : לה
to~>~make~PERISH(V) : להאביד
to~>~make~PERISH(V)~him : להאבידו
to~>~make~LIGHT(V) : להאיר
to~>~make~STINK(V)~me : להבאישני
to~>~make~SEPARATE(V) : להבדיל
GLIMMERING : להבה
to~>~make~COME(V) : להביא
to~>~make~COME(V)~you(ms) : להביאך
to~>~make~COME(V)~them(m) : להביאם
Lehav~s : להבים
to~>~make~BE.FACE.TO.FACE(V) : להגיד
to~>~PUSH.AWAY(V) : להדוף
to~>~make~DRIVE.OUT(V)~you(ms) : להדיחך
to~>~CONFUSE(V)~them(m) : להומם
to~>~make~ADD(V) : להוסיף
to~>~make~GO.OUT(V) : להוציא
to~>~make~GO.OUT(V)~them(m) : להוציאם
to~>~make~GO.OUT(V)~us : להוציאנו
to~>~make~THROW(V) : להורות
to~>~make~THROW(V)~them(m) : להורותם
to~>~make~GO.DOWN(V) : להוריד
to~>~make~POSSESS(V) : להוריש
to~>~make~POSSESS(V)~them(m) : להורישם
to~>~make~RESCUE(V) : להושיע
to~Hosheya : להושע
to~>~make~DEDICATE(V) : להזיר
to~>~make~BE.A.HARLOT(V)~her : להזנותה
to~>~make~LIVE(V) : להחיות
to~>~make~DRILL(V)~him : להחלו
BLAZING : להט
to~>~make~EXTEND(V) : להטות
to~>~make~EXTEND(V)~her : להטותה
to~>~make~DO.WELL(V) : להיטיב
to~>~DO.WELL(V)~you(ms) : להיטיבך

to~>~be~FIGHT$^{(V)}$:להילחם
to~>~be~SNIP.OFF$^{(V)}$:להימול
to~>~make~SLIP.AWAY$^{(V)}$:להימלט
to~>~self~BEND.DOWN$^{(V)}$:להישתחות
to~>~self~HOLD.BACK$^{(V)}$:להיתאפק
to~>~self~ROLL$^{(V)}$:להיתגולל
to~>~self~LINGER$^{(V)}$:להיתמהמה
to~>~self~COMFORT$^{(V)}$:להיתנחם
to~>~self~BE.OUT.OF.SIGHT$^{(V)}$:להיתעלם
to~>~make~HIT$^{(V)}$:להכות
to~>~make~HIT$^{(V)}$~her :להכותה
to~>~make~HIT$^{(V)}$~him :להכותו
to~>~make~BE.ANGRY$^{(V)}$~him :להכעיסו
to~>~make~CUT$^{(V)}$:להכרית
to~>~WALK$^{(V)}$:להלוך
to~them$^{(m)}$:להם
to~>~make~DIE$^{(V)}$:להמית
to~>~make~DIE$^{(V)}$~him :להמיתו
to~>~make~DIE$^{(V)}$~them$^{(m)}$:להמיתם
to~>~make~DIE$^{(V)}$~us :להמיתנו
to~them$^{(f)}$:להן
to~>~make~REST$^{(V)}$~him :להניחו
to~>~make~WAVE$^{(V)}$:להניף
to~>~make~TURN.ASIDE$^{(V)}$:להסיר
to~>~make~CALCULATE$^{(V)}$:להסכיל
to~>~make~CROSS.OVER$^{(V)}$:להעביר
to~>~make~GO.UP$^{(V)}$:להעלות
to~>~make~BREAK$^{(V)}$:להפר
to~>~make~BREAK$^{(V)}$~you$^{(mp)}$:להפרכם
to~>~make~DELIVER$^{(V)}$:להציל
to~>~make~DELIVER$^{(V)}$~him :להצילו
to~>~make~DELIVER$^{(V)}$~you$^{(ms)}$:להצילך
to~>~make~SET.APART$^{(V)}$~me :להקדישני
to~>~make~BURN.INCENSE$^{(V)}$:להקטיר
to~>~make~RISE$^{(V)}$:להקים
to~>~make~COME.NEAR$^{(V)}$:להקריב
to~>~make~SEE$^{(V)}$:להראות
to~>~KILL$^{(V)}$~him :להרגו
to~>~KILL$^{(V)}$~you$^{(ms)}$:להרגך
to~>~KILL$^{(V)}$~us :להרגנו
to~>~KILL$^{(V)}$:להרוג
to~>~make~SMELL$^{(V)}$:להריח
to~>~make~BE.DYSFUNCTIONAL$^{(V)}$:להרע
to~>~make~HEAL$^{(V)}$:להרפא
to~>~make~TURN.BACK$^{(V)}$:להשיב
to~>~make~TURN.BACK$^{(V)}$~him :להשיבו
to~>~make~DESTROY$^{(V)}$:להשמיד
to~>~make~DESTROY$^{(V)}$~him :להשמידו
to~>~make~DESTROY$^{(V)}$~us :להשמידנו
to~>~make~DRINK$^{(V)}$:להשקות
to~>~make~DRINK$^{(V)}$~him :להשקותו
to~him | WOULD.THAT :לו
NOT :לוא
LOG :לוג
Lud~s :לודים
Luz :לוז
Luz~unto :לוזה
SLAB~s :לוחות
SQUEEZE$^{(V)}$~ing$^{(mp)}$:לוחצים
Lot :לוט
Lotan :לוטן
SHARPEN$^{(V)}$~ing$^{(ms)}$:לוטש
Lewi :לוי
UNLESS :לולא
LOOP~s :לולאות
UNLESS :לולי
he~did~be~TAKE$^{(V)}$ | TAKE$^{(V)}$~ing$^{(ms)}$:לוקח
be~TAKE$^{(V)}$~ed$^{(fs)}$:לוקחה
TAKE$^{(V)}$~ing$^{(mp)}$:לוקחי
you$^{(ms)}$~did~be~TAKE$^{(V)}$:לוקחת
!$^{(fs)}$~KNEAD$^{(V)}$:לושי
to~SACRIFICE | to~the~SACRIFICE :לזבח
to~THIS :לזואת
to~BE.A.HARLOT$^{(V)}$~ing$^{(fs)}$:לזונה
to~SACRIFICE~s :לזיבחי
to~REMEMBRANCE :לזיכרון
to~BEARD~s :לזיקני

to~OLIVE~you(ms) :
to~the~MALE :
to~TAIL :
to~AGITATION :
to~BEARD :
to~VOMIT :
to~MOLDING~him :
to~Zerahh :
to~SEED :
to~SEED~him :
to~SEED~you(ms) :
to~SEED~you(mp) :
MOIST :
to~STRIPED.BRUISE~me :
to~>~much~COUPLE(V) | to~Hhever :
to~Hhagi :
to~NEW.MOON~s :
to~Hhovav :
to~the~NEW.MOON :
MOIST~her :
to~MORTAR :
to~the~FIFTH.PART :
to~SHORE :
to~Hhupham :
to~CUSTOM :
to~CUSTOM :
to~BE.AN.IN-LAW(V)~ing(ms)~him :
to~>~much~FAIL(V) :
to~FAILURE | to~the~FAILURE :
to~>~FAIL(V) :
to~>~CARVE(V) :
to~FAILURE :
to~>~much~LIVE(V) :
to~>~much~LIVE(V)~us :
to~LIVING~s :
to~FORCE :
MOIST~s :
to~SKILLED.ONE~s :
to~Hheleq :
BREAD :
BREAD~him :
to~Hhamul :
to~DONKEY~him :
to~DONKEY~s~them(m) :

BREAD~me :
BREAD~you(ms) :
BREAD~you(mp) :
BREAD~us :
to~>~RIPEN(V) :
to~Hhanokh :
to~the~DEVOTION :
to~>~CAMP(V)~you(ms) :
to~FREE :
to~the~HALF :
SQUEEZING~us :
to~the~COURTYARD :
to~Hhetsron :
to~CUSTOM :
to~SWORD :
to~DRIED.OUT :
to~Hhermon :
to~DECORATIVE.BAND :
to~>~THINK(V) :
to~the~CLEAN :
to~>~much~BE.CLEAN(V) :
to~>~much~BE.CLEAN(V)~him :
to~>~much~BE.CLEAN(V)~them(m) :
to~CLEAN~him :
to~the~FUNCTIONAL | to~FUNCTIONAL :
to~FUNCTIONAL :
to~CLEANLINESS :
to~MARKER~s :
to~>~much~BE.DIRTY(V) | to~the~DIRTY :
to~DIRTY~her | to~the~DIRTY :
to~>~much~BE.DIRTY(V)~him :
to~BABIES~you(mp) :
to~BABIES~us :
to~me :
to~BEAST~you(ms) :
to~BEAST~them(m) :
HEART~him :
HEART~me :
HEART~you(ms) :
to~>~WEEP(V) :
HEART~you(mp) :
HEART~them(m) :
HEART~them(f) :

POPLAR : ליבנה
to~SON~him : ליבנו
to~>~BUILD(V) | to~ : ליבנות
DAUGHTER~s
to~DAUGHTER~s~him : ליבנותיו
to~SON~s | Liyvniy : ליבני
to~SON~s~them(f) : ליבניהן
to~SON~s~you(mp) : ליבניכם
to~SON~you(ms) : ליבנך
BRICK : ליבנת
to~MASTER~s~him : ליבעליו
to~>~FLEE.AWAY(V) : ליברוח
to~Beri'ah : ליבריעה
to~COVENANT : ליברית
to~PRESENT : ליברכה
to~DRY.GROUND : ליבשה
to~Betu'el : ליבתואל
to~BORDER : ליגבול
to~BORDER~s~her : ליגבולותיה
to~>~EXPIRE(V) : ליגוע
to~>~SHEAR(V) : ליגזוז
to~CAMEL ~s~you(ms) : ליגמליך
to~HAND~him : לידו
to~>~SEEK(V) : לידרוש
>~BRING.FORTH(V)~her : לידתה
to~Yehudah : ליהודה
to~YHWH : ליהוה
to~Yehoshu'a : ליהושוע
to~>~EXIST(V) : ליהיות
to~the~DAY : ליום
to~Yoseph : ליוסף
to~SETTLE(V)~ing(ms) : ליושב
to~>~SACRIFICE(V) : ליזבוח
to~Zevulun : ליזבולון
to~>~REMEMBER(V) : ליזכור
to~ : ליזנונים
PROSTITUTION~s
to~>~BE.A.HARLOT(V) : ליזנות
to~ : ליזקוניו
EXTREME.OLD.AGE~s~him
to~Yahh'le'el : ליחלאל
to~>~much~HEAT(V)~her : ליחמנה
to~Yahhtse'el : ליחצאל
to~Yimnah : ליימנה
to~Yisra'eyl : ליישראל
to~Yis'sas'khar : לייששכר
to~Yits'hhaq : לייצחק

to~>~FEAR(V) : לייראה
to~Yishwiy : ליישוי
to~ : ליישמעאלים
Yishma'el~s
to~ADMINISTRATION : ליכהונת
to~Yakhin : ליכין
to~>~CUT(V) : ליכרות
to~>~WRITE(V) : ליכתוב
NIGHT : ליל
to~>~MAKE.BRICKS(V) : לילבון
to~>~WEAR(V) : לילבוש
NIGHT : לילה
to~>~PICK.UP(V) : לילקוט
to~TONGUE~him : לילשונו
to~TONGUE~s~ : לילשונותם
them(m)
to~the~SEA : לים
to~LUMINARY~s : לימאורות
to~HUNDRED : לימאת
I~did~much~LEARN(V) : לימדתי
to~PRECIPITATION : לימטר
to~DAY~s : לימים
to~Yamin : לימין
to~BUSINESS : לימלאכה
to~BUSINESS : לימלאכת
to~>~RECKON(V) : לימנות
to~Menasheh : לימנשה
to~>~COMMIT(V) : לימסר
to~>~TRANSGRESS(V) : לימעול
to~SMALL.AMOUNT : לימעט
to~>~FIND(V) : לימצוא
to~AREA~her : לימקומה
to~AREA~him : לימקומו
to~AREA~s~them(m) : לימקומותם
to~CORNER.POST~s : לימקצועות
to~Merari : לימררי
to~>~TOUCH(V) : לינגוע
to~>~SMITE(V) : לינגוף
to~FREEWILL.OFFERING : לינדבה
to~>~DRIVE.OUT(V) : לינדוח
to~MAKE.A.VOW(V) : לינדור
to~VOW~s~her : לינדריה
!(mp)~STAY.THE.NIGHT(V) : לינו
to~>~INHERIT(V) : לינחול
to~>~EXTEND(V) : לינטות
to~Nemu'eyl : לינמואל
to~>~FALL(V) : לינפול

to~PIECE~s~her :
to~PIECE~s~him :
to~>~GO.AROUND(V) :
to~>~CARRY(V) :
to~>~BE.SATISFIED(V) :
to~>~LAMENT(V) :
to~>~COUNT(V) :
to~>~CONSUME(V) :
to~>~much~CORRECT(V)~her :
to~>~much~CORRECT(V)~you(ms) :
to~CREMATING :
to~Ya'aqov :
to~EDGE :
to~ESCAPED :
to~>~TURN(V) :
to~FACE~s :
to~FACE~s~them(m) :
to~FACE~s~you(mp) :
to~REGISTER(V)~ed(mp)~them(m) :
to~>~SPREAD.OUT(V) :
to~Yaphet :
to~>~INTERPRET(V) :
to~>~MUSTER(V) :
to~PERMANENT :
to~Tsaphon :
to~Yetser :
to~>~PRESS.IN(V) :
to~>~BURY(V) :
to~ASSEMBLY :
to~Qehat :
LEARNING~me :
!(mp)~PICK.UP(V) :
to~INCENSE.SMOKE :
to~HANDFUL~s :
to~>~SEVER(V) :
to~>~MEET(V) :
to~>~MEET(V)~her :
to~>~MEET(V)~him :
to~>~MEET(V)~me :
to~>~MEET(V)~you(ms) :
to~>~MEET(V)~them(m) :
to~>~MEET(V)~them(m) :
to~>~MEET(V)~us :
to~>~CALL.OUT(V) :
to~Re'uven :
to~>~SEE(V) :
to~>~SEE(V)~her :
to~SEE(V)~them(m) :
to~>~KILL.BY.STONING(V) :
to~Yarden :
to~HERITAGE~him :
to~the~MOON :
to~>~BATHE(V) :
to~the~FLANK~s2 :
to~>~FEED(V) :
to~SELF-WILL~him :
to~SELF-WILL~you(mp) :
to~>~DRAW.WATER(V) :
to~KIN~him :
to~>~CRACK(V) | to~>~EXCHANGE(V) :
to~STAFF~s~him :
to~STAFF~s~you(ms) :
to~>~EXCHANGE(V) :
to~ERROR :
to~Yashuv :
to~RELIEF :
to~RELIEF~you(ms) :
to~>~SLAY(V) :
to~BOILS :
to~>~LIE.DOWN(V) :
to~>~DWELL(V) :
to~THREE :
to~THREE :
to~THREE :
to~OFFERING.OF.RESTITUTION~s :
to~>~HEAR(V) :
to~>~SAFEGUARD(V) :
to~TITLE~s :
to~TITLE~me :
to~>~SAFEGUARD(V)~you(ms) :
to~TWO :
to~TWO~them(m) :
to~TWO :
to~>~DECIDE(V) :
to~Sheshupham :
to~>~GULP(V) :
to~TWO :
to~ADORATION :

to~the~ORPHAN :ליתום
to~WAVING :ליתנופה
to~OFFERING :ליתרומת
to~you(ms) | to~you(fs) | !(ms)~WALK(V) / :לך
to~ARMAMENT :לכבוד
to~the~SHEEP :לכבס
we~did~TRAP(V) :לכדנו
!(ms)~WALK(V)~& :לכה
to~>~much~ADORN(V) :לכהן
to~>~much~ADORN(V)~him :לכהנו
!(mp)~WALK(V) :לכו
to~the~ADMINISTRATOR :לכוהן
to~the~ ADMINISTRATOR~s :לכוהנים
to~ALL :לכול
to~ALL~them(m) :לכולם
!(fs)~WALK(V) :לכי
to~GNAT~s :לכינים
to~ALL :לכל
to~the~DOG :לכלב
to~>~much~FINISH(V)~ them(m) :לכלותם
to~you(mp) :לכם
to~SO :לכן
to~>~much~COVER.OVER(V) :לכסות
to~>~much~COVER.OVER(V)~ him :לכסותו
to~PALM :לכף
to~>~much~COVER(V) :לכפר
to~Karmi :לכרמי
to~VINEYARD~you(ms) :לכרמך
>~WALK(V)~you(ms) :לכתך
to~the~SHOULDER.PIECE :לכתף
to~Le'ah :ללאה
to~Lavan | to~WHITE :ללבן
to~>~BRING.FORTH(V) :ללדת
to~Lot :ללוט
to~Lewi :ללוי
to~Lewi~s :ללויים
to~>~STAY.THE.NIGHT(V) :ללון
to~BREAD | to~the~BREAD :ללחם
to~>~STAY.THE.NIGHT(V) :ללין
to~>~WALK(V) :ללכת
to~>~much~LEARN(V) :ללמד
to~the~LUMINARY :למאור
to~from~MAN :למאיש

to~NOURISHMENT :למאכל
to~FLOOD :למבול
to~WHAT :למה
to~>~much~HURRY(V) :למהר
to~them(m) :למו
to~Mo'av :למואב
to~the~CIRCUMCISION~s :למולות
to~the~Molekh :למולך
to~the~APPOINTED | to~ APPOINTED :למועד
to~APPOINTED~her :למועדה
to~GOING.OUT~s~ them(m) :למוצאיהם
to~SNARE :למוקש
to~SETTLING~s~ them(m) :למושבותם
to~Mosheh :למושה
to~>~DIE(V) :למות
to~the~CAMP | to~CAMP :למחנה
to~TOMORROW :למחר
to~BRANCH | to~the~BRANCH | to~the~BENEATH :למטה
to~BRANCH :למטות
to~WHO | to~WATER~s2 :למי
to~Migdal-Eyder :למיגדל־עדר
to~the~ALTAR :למיזבח
to~REVIVING :למיחיה
to~the~make~ BE.CLEAN(V)~ing(ms) :למיטהר
to~WATER~s2 :למיים
to~GRATE :למיכבר
to~the~much~ BRING.FORTH(V)~ing(fp) :למילדות
to~the~BATTLE :למילחמה
to~FROM :למין
to~KIND~her :למינה
to~KIND~him :למינהו
to~KIND~them(m) :למינהם
to~KIND~him :למינו
to~the~DEPOSIT | to~ DEPOSIT :למינחה
to~RIM~him :למיסגרתו
to~NUMBER :למיספר
to~DIRECTIVE~s~ him :למיצותיו
to~Mits'rayim :למיצריים
to~REFUGE :למיקלט

to~ACQUIRED :
to~LIVESTOCK~us :
to~MEETING :
to~Mir'yam :
to~LYING.PLACE :
to~the~DWELLING | to~DWELLING :
to~CHARGE :
to~CLAN~s :
to~CLAN~s~them(m) :
to~CLAN~s~him :
to~CLAN~s~you(mp) :
to~CLAN~s~them(m) :
to~CLAN :
to~the~DECISION :
Lamekh :
to~Makhir :
to~>~SELL(V)~her :
to~>~much~FILL(V) :
to~the~BUSINESS :
to~>~much~FILL(V) :
to~KING :
to~Malki'el :
to~REGULATION :
to~SHARE :
to~the~Menasheh~of :
to~TASK.WORK | to~the~TASK.WORK :
to~the~CANOPY :
to~JOURNEY :
to~JOURNEY~s~them(m) :
to~JOURNEY~s~him :
to~UPWARD~unto | to~ASCENT :
to~THAT :
to~THAT~you(mp) :
to~the~AREA :
to~APPEARANCE :
to~BITTER~s :
to~>~SMEAR(V) :
to~DAMAGING :
to~PARABLE :
to~the~DIE(V)~ing(ms) | to~DIE(V)~ing(ms) :
to~HOW.LONG :
he~did~STAY.THE.NIGHT(V) :
to~BE.FACE.TO.FACE(V)~me :
to~BE.FACE.TO.FACE(V)~you(ms) :
to~TOUCH | to~the~TOUCH :
to~us :
to~No'ahh :
to~IN.FRONT :
to~>~FLEE(V) | >~FLEE(V) :
to~Nahhor :
to~>~make~GUIDE(V)~them(m) :
to~INHERITANCE :
to~INHERITANCE :
to~>~much~COMFORT(V)~him :
to~SERPENT :
to~FOREIGNER | to~the~FOREIGNER :
to~STANDARD :
to~>~much~TEST(V)~you(ms) :
to~CAPTAIN :
to~the~POURING :
to~Na'aman :
to~YOUNG.WOMAN | to~YOUNG.MAN :
to~SOUL | to~the~SOUL :
to~SOUL~her :
to~SOUL~s~you(mp) :
to~Naphtali :
to~the~FEMALE :
to~WOMAN~s~him :
to~WOMAN~s :
to~>~much~KISS(V) :
to~>~much~LEAP(V) :
to~>~LIFT.UP(V) :
to~the~RAM :
to~SATISFACTION :
to~MEDITATE(V) :
to~the~TRADE(V)~ing(ms) :
to~>~PLACE(V) :
to~HATE(V)~ing(ms)~him :
to~HATE(V)~ing(mp)~me :

to~HATE(V)~ing(mp)~him :לשונאיו
>~SKIP.WITH.JOY(V) :לשוש
to~HORSE~s~him :לסוסיו
to~OPPONENT :לשטן
to~BURDEN~s~you(mp) :לסיבלותיכם
to~Sihhon :לסיחון
to~STICKERBUSH~s :לשיכים
to~APPAREL~him :לשימלתו
to~the~HATED :לשניאה
to~the~HAIRY.GOAT~s :לשעירים
to~the~HAIR :לשער
to~NOBLE :לשר
to~Sered :לסרד
to~Sarah :לשרה
to~>~SERVE(V)~her :לעבדה
to~SERVANT~s~you(ms) :לעבדיך
to~the~SERVANT~s :לעבדים
to~SERVANT~you(ms) :לעבדך
to~>~SERVE(V)~them(m) :לעבדם
to~>~SERVE(V) :לעבוד
to~the~SERVICE :לעבודה
to~the~>~MAKE.A.PLEDGE(V) :לעבוט
to~the~>~CROSS.OVER(V) :לעבור
to~>~CROSS.OVER(V)~you(ms) :לעברך
to~WITNESS :לעד
to~WITNESS | to~the~COMPANY :לעדה
to~the~EVIDENCE :לעדות
to~the~COMPANY :לעדת
to~TWISTEDNESS~us :לעוננו
to~ASCENSION.OFFERING | to~the~ASCENSION.OFFERING :לעולה
to~ASCENSION.OFFERING~s~you(mp) :לעולותיכם
to~DISTANT :לעולם
to~ASCENSION.OFFERING :לעולת
to~ALONGSIDE :לעומת
to~the~TWISTEDNESS :לעון
to~the~DO(V)~ing(ms) :לעושה
to~the~FLYER :לעוף
to~SKIN~him :לעורו
to~Azazeyl :לעזאזל
to~>~LEAVE(V) :לעזוב
to~Ayin :לעיין
to~EYE~s2 :לעיני
to~EYE~s2~them(m) :לעיניהם
to~EYE~s2~him :לעיניו
to~the~EYE~s2 | to~EYE~s2 :לעיניים
to~EYE~s2~you(ms) :לעיניך
to~EYE~s2~you(mp) :לעיניכם
to~EYE~s2~us :לעינינו
to~the~CITY :לעיר
to~>~GO.UP(V) :לעלות
to~PEOPLE | to~the~PEOPLE :לעם
to~PEOPLE~him :לעמו
to~>~STAND(V) :לעמוד
to~the~PILLAR~s :לעמודים
to~PEOPLE~me :לעמי
to~the~NEIGHBOR~you(ms) :לעמיתך
to~PEOPLE~you(ms) :לעמך
to~Amram :לעמרם
to~>~ANSWER(V) | to~>~much~AFFLICT(V) :לענות
to~AFFLICTION :לעני
to~AFFLICTION~you(ms) :לעניך
to~Esaw :לעשו
to~>~DO(V) :לעשות
to~>~DO(V)~her :לעשותה
to~>~DO(V)~him :לעשותו
to~>~DO(V)~you(mp) :לעשותכם
to~>~DO(V)~them(m) :לעשותם
to~>~make~GIVE.A.TENTH(V) :לעשר
to~DIRT :לעפר
to~Ephron :לעפרון
to~the~TREE~s :לעצים
to~OFFSHOOT :לעקר
to~Eyr :לער
to~Eyriy :לערי
to~CITY~s~her :לעריה
to~CITY~s :לערים
to~Eyran :לערן
to~ONE :לעשתי
to~APPOINTED.TIME :לעת
to~the~EDGE :לפאה
to~MOUTH :לפה
to~Pu'a :לפווה
to~Potiphar :לפוטיפר
to~MOUTH :לפי
to~MOUTH~them(f) :לפיהן
to~MOUTH~him :לפיו

to~WOUND~me :
to~DEPOSITED :
to~OFFENSE~you[mp] :
to~the~FLAX~s :
to~>~much~PERFORM[V] :
to~Palu :
to~FACE~s~me :
to~FACE~s~him :
to~FACE~s~you[ms] :
to~FACE~s :
to~FACE~s~us :
to~the~BULL | to~BULL :
to~the~TENT.CURTAIN | to~TENT.CURTAIN :
to~the~BULL~s :
to~Paroh :
to~Perets :
to~OFFENSE :
to~OPENING :
to~>~GO.OUT[V] :
to~>~GO.OUT[V]~them[m] :
to~the~ARMY :
to~>~make~SWELL[V] :
to~the~FLOCKS :
to~FLOCKS~you[ms] :
to~>~HUNT[V] :
to~>~much~DIRECT[V] :
to~FLOCKS~you[mp] :
to~>~much~LAUGH[V] :
to~ARMY~s~them[m] :
to~Tsiv'on :
to~FRINGE :
to~PERMANENT :
to~>~POUR.DOWN[V] :
to~NARROW~s~me :
to~NARROW~s~him :
to~>~much~SET.APART[V] | to~Qadesh :
to~>~much~SET.APART[V]~him :
to~>~much~SET.APART[V]~them[m] :
to~>~HOLLOW.OUT[V] :
to~the~SPECIAL :
>~TAKE[V] :
to~VOICE :
to~VOICE~you[ms] :
to~VOICE~them[m] :

to~>~RISE[V] :
to~PURCHASE[V]~ing[ms] :
to~Qorahh :
to~much~COLLECT[V] :
he~did~TAKE[V] | ![ms]~TAKE[V] :
she~did~TAKE[V] | he~did~TAKE[V]~her :
they~did~TAKE[V] | they~will~TAKE[V] :
we~did~TAKE[V] :
he~did~TAKE[V]~me :
to~>~TAKE[V] | you[ms]~did~TAKE[V] :
to~>~TAKE[V]~her :
to~>~TAKE[V]~him :
I~did~TAKE[V] :
I~did~TAKE[V]~you[ms] :
you[ms]~did~TAKE[V]~us :
they~did~PICK.UP[V] :
to~Qayin :
to~>~much~BELITTLE[V] :
to~>~much~BELITTLE[V]~you[ms] :
to~>~COME.NEAR[V] :
to~DONATION :
to~the~BOARD :
to~BOARD~s :
to~the~Re'uven~of :
to~>~be~SEE[V] :
to~>~make~SEE[V]~you[mp] :
to~ABUNDANT :
to~FOOT | to~>~much~TREAD.ABOUT[V] :
to~FOOT~me :
to~FOOT~s2~him :
to~FOOT~you[ms] :
to~>~GO.DOWN[V] :
to~the~Re'uven~of :
to~HEAD :
to~>~INCREASE.IN.NUMBER[V] | to~ABUNDANCE :
to~WIND :
to~the~DYSFUNCTIONAL :
to~Rahhel :
to~>~BATHE[V] :
to~the~FIRST :

to~>~BE.SQUARE(V)~her :
to~Rivqah :
to~AROMA :
to~the~EMPTY :
to~>~POSSESS(V)~her :
to~>~POSSESS(V)~you(ms) :
to~the~DYSFUNCTIONAL :
to~DYSFUNCTIONAL :
to~COMPANION~him :
to~DYSFUNCTIONAL~s :
to~COMPANION~you(ms) :
to~SELF-WILL :
to~SHEET :
to~the~LOST :
to~the~>~POSSESS(V) :
to~Sha'ul :
to~the~STAFF :
to~SEVEN :
to~>~SETTLE(V) | to~the~>~SETTLE(V) :
FRESH :
to~the~BREAST~s :
to~the~FALSENESS :
to~>~TURN.BACK(V) :
to~Shuhham :
TONGUE :
TONGUE~him :
to~Shuni :
to~the~OX :
to~OX~you(ms) :
to~Shutelahh :
to~>~much~DAMAGE(V) :
to~>~DAMAGE(V)~her :
to~STAFF~s~you(mp) :
to~SEVEN :
to~>~SETTLE(V)~you(ms) :
to~>~DWELL(V)~him :
to~Shalem :
to~Shimon :
to~Shimon~of :
to~DERISION :
to~Shimron :
to~MAID :
to~>~DWELL(V) :
to~>~DWELL(V)~me :
to~Sheylah :
to~COMPLETENESS :

to~>~much~SEND(V) :
to~>~much~SEND(V)~her :
to~>~much~SEND(V)~him :
to~>~much~SEND(V)~them(m) :
to~>~much~SEND(V)~us :
to~>~MAKE.RESTITUTION(V)~him :
OPAL :
to~DESOLATE :
to~OIL :
to~the~YEAR :
Lesha :
to~GATE :
to~the~FALSE :
to~>~much~MINISTER(V) :
to~>~much~MINISTER(V)~him :
to~>~much~MINISTER(V)~them(m) :
to~SIX :
to~SIX :
to~the~VESSEL :
to~STRAW :
to~BIRTHING~s~them(m) :
to~>~SCOUT(V) :
to~Tahhan :
to~NINE :
to~>~GIVE(V)~her :
to~>~GIVE(V)~me :
to~Tamar :
to~CROCODILE :
to~CROCODILE~s :
to~>~SEIZE.HOLD(V)~her :
to~>~GIVE(V) :
from~FATHER~s~you(ms) :
make~PERISH(V)~ing(ms) :
from~FATHER~them(f) :
from~FATHER~us :
from~STONE~s :
from~Avraham :
from~Agag :
from~LORD~me :
from~HUMAN :
be~much~BE.RED(V)~ing(mp) :
HUNDRED :
from~AFFECTION :

from~Ovot :
MANY :
MANY~you(ms) :
from~TENT :
from~ATTACK(V)~ing(mp)~you(mp) :
ANYTHING :
from~Ur :
LUMINARY~s :
be~much~BETROTH(V)~ing(fs) :
HUNDRED~s :
from~AT.THAT.TIME :
from~UNIT :
from~HOLDINGS :
from~HOLDINGS~him :
from~BROTHER~s~him :
from~to~BROTHER~you(ms) | from~BROTHER~s~you(ms) :
from~AFTER | from~AFTER~me :
from~AFTER~them(m) :
from~AFTER~him :
from~AFTER~you(ms) :
from~AFTER~you(mp) :
from~UNIT :
from~WITHOUT :
from~BUCK :
from~Eyliym :
from~Eylot :
he~did~much~REFUSE(V) :
from~MAN :
from~MAN~her :
from~FIRE.OFFERING~s | from~FIRE.OFFERING~s~me :
from~AT~him :
from~AT~me :
from~AT~you(mp) :
from~AT~them(m) :
NOURISHMENT :
from~MIGHTY.ONE :
from~THESE :
from~Elohiym :
from~Elohiym~you(ms) :
from~Alush :
much~BIND.UP(V)~ing(mp) :

from~THOUSAND~s :
from~OATH~me :
make~SECURE(V)~ing(mp) :
he~did~much~REFUSE(V) | REFUSING | >~much~REFUSE(V) :
from~MAN :
from~MAN~s :
you(ms)~did~much~REFUSE(V) :
you(mp)~did~much~REFUSE(V) :
they~did~REJECT(V) :
much~GATHER(V)~ing(ms) :
I~did~REJECT(V)~them(m) :
you(mp)~did~REJECT(V) :
BAKED :
from~NOSE~you(mp) :
from~Arnon :
from~LAND :
from~LAND~him :
from~LAND~you(ms) :
from~LAND~them(m) :
from~Asher | from~WHICH :
HUNDRED | from~AT :
HUNDRED~s2 :
from~Eytam :
make~SEPARATE(V)~ing(ms) :
ENTRANCE :
FLOOD :
be~much~KNEEL(V)~ing(ms) :
be~much~KNEEL(V)~ing(fs) :
from~be~much~BOIL(V)~ing(ms) :
make~COME(V)~ing(ms) :
make~COME(V)~ing(ms)~you(ms) :
much~SEARCH.OUT(V)~ing(ms) :
much~SEARCH.OUT(V)~ing(mp) :
make~FLEE.AWAY(V)~ing(ms) :
much~KNEEL(V)~ing(mp)~you(ms) :
Magdi'eyl :
much~TAUNT(V)~ing(ms) :
IMMIGRATION~s | IMMIGRATION~s~me :

IMMIGRATION~s~them$^{(m)}$ | IMMIGRATION~them$^{(m)}$: מגוריהם
IMMIGRATION~s~you$^{(ms)}$: מגוריך
make~BE.FACE.TO.FACE$^{(V)}$~ing$^{(ms)}$: מגיד
make~TOUCH$^{(V)}$~ing$^{(ms)}$: מגיע
SHIELD : מגן
PESTILENCE~s~me : מגפותי
>~much~SPEAK$^{(V)}$~ing$^{(ms)}$: מדבר
DISEASE : מדוה
DISEASE~s : מדוי
WHY : מדוע
Medan : מדן
WHAT : מה
from~>~make~COME$^{(V)}$: מהביא
from~>~make~STARE$^{(V)}$: מהביט
from~SPLENDOR~you$^{(ms)}$: מהודך
TUMULT : מהומה
>~HURRY$^{(V)}$ | from~Hor : מהור
from~>~make~DRILL$^{(V)}$: מהחל
Meheytaveyl : מהיטבאל
from~>~self~SOFT$^{(V)}$: מהיתענג
from~>~make~HIT$^{(V)}$: מהכות
from~FURTHER : מהלאה
from~>~WALK$^{(V)}$: מהלוך
Mahalalel : מהללאל
from~them$^{(m)}$: מהם
from~THEY : מהנה
from~the~FLYER : מהעוף
!$^{(ms)}$~much~HURRY$^{(V)}$ | QUICKLY | from~HILL : מהר
QUICKLY : מהרה
!$^{(mp)}$~much~HURRY$^{(V)}$: מהרו
!$^{(fs)}$~much~HURRY$^{(V)}$ | from~HILL~s : מהרי
from~HILL~s : מהררי
Mo'av : מואב
BALANCE~s2 : מואזני
be~make~COME$^{(V)}$~ing$^{(mp)}$: מובאים
BRIDE.PRICE : מוהר
POLE~s : מוטות
be~make~HIT$^{(V)}$~ing$^{(mp)}$: מוכים
SELL$^{(V)}$~ing$^{(ms)}$: מוכר
FOREFRONT : מול
KINDRED : מולדת
KINDRED~him : מולדתו
KINDRED~me : מולדתי
KINDRED~you$^{(ms)}$: מולדתך
BLEMISH : מום
BLEMISH~them$^{(m)}$: מומם
TIME~s : מונים
be~make~GO.AROUND$^{(V)}$~ing$^{(fp)}$: מוסבות
FOUNDATION~s : מוסדי
DISCIPLINE : מוסר
Moseyrah : מוסרה
APPOINTED : מועד
APPOINTED~s : מועדי
Mupim : מופים
WONDER : מופת
WONDER~s~me : מופתי
GOING.OUT : מוצא
FIND$^{(V)}$~ing$^{(ms)}$~him : מוצאו
FIND$^{(V)}$~ing$^{(ms)}$~me : מוצאי
GOING.OUT~s~them$^{(m)}$: מוצאיהם
be~make~GO.OUT$^{(V)}$~ing$^{(fs)}$: מוצאת
be~make~STAND.UP$^{(V)}$~ing$^{(ms)}$: מוצב
make~GO.OUT$^{(V)}$~ing$^{(ms)}$~him : מוציאו
make~GOING.OUT~s : מוציאי
make~GO.OUT$^{(V)}$~ing$^{(ms)}$~them$^{(m)}$: מוציאם
SMOLDERING : מוקדה
SNARE : מוקש
CROP~him : מוראתו
be~make~FRY$^{(V)}$~ing$^{(fs)}$: מורבכת
Moreh : מורה
make~POSSESS$^{(V)}$~ing$^{(ms)}$: מוריש
make~POSSESS$^{(V)}$~ing$^{(ms)}$~them$^{(m)}$: מורישם
FAINT : מורך
POSSESSION : מורשה
GRIEF : מורת
SETTLING : מושב
SETTLING~him : מושבו
SETTLING~s~you$^{(mp)}$: מושבותיכם
SETTLING~you$^{(ms)}$: מושבך
SETTLING~them$^{(m)}$: מושבם
Mosheh : מושה
make~RESCUE$^{(V)}$~ing$^{(ms)}$: מושיע
REGULATE$^{(V)}$~ing$^{(ms)}$: מושל
>~DIE$^{(V)}$ | DEATH : מות

DEATH~him : מותו
DEATH~me : מותי
>~DIE(V)~us : מותנו
WHAT~&~THIS : מזה
DOORPOST~s : מזוזות
EXHAUSTED~s : מזי
make~REMEMBER(V)~ing(ms) : מזכיר
make~REMEMBER(V)~ing(fs) : מזכרת
make~SOW(V)~ing(ms) : מזריע
JOINT~him : מחברתו
PAN : מחבת
>~WIPE.AWAY(V) : מחוה
from~CARVE(V)~ing(ms) : מחוטב
Mehhuya'el : מחויאל
from~Hhawilah : מחוילה
much~TWIST(V)~ing(ms)~you(ms) : מחוללך
be~much~FLAKE.OFF~ing(ms) : מחוספס
from~CUSTOM~s : מחוקות
much~INSCRIBE(V)~ing(ms) : מחוקק
from~Hhor-Hagidgad : מחור הגידגד
from~Hhorev : מחורב
be~much~ATTACH(V)~ing(mp) : מחושקים
VISION : מחזה
make~SEIZE(V)~ing(ms) : מחזיק
much~SEIZE(V)~ing(ms) : מחזק
from~FAILURE~him : מחטאתו
from~FAILURE~him : מחטו
from~BOSOM~him : מחיקו
from~FAT : מחלב
SICKNESS | Mahhlah : מחלה
Mahh'liy : מחלי
much~DRILL(V)~ing(mp)~her : מחלליה
much~DRILL(V)~ing(fs) : מחללת
from~QUARTZ : מחלמיש
from~LOINS~you(ms) : מחלציך
Mahhalat : מחלת
make~BE.SOUR(V)~ing(fs) : מחמצת
from~FIVE : מחמש
CAMP : מחנה
CAMP~him : מחנהו
CAMP~s : מחנות
!(ms)~WIPE.AWAY(V)~me : מחני
CAMP~s~them(m) : מחניהם
Mahhanayim : מחניים
CAMP~s~you(ms) : מחניך
CAMP~you(ms) : מחנך
EXPOSE : מחסוף
LACKING~him : מחסורו
!(ms)~STRIKE.THROUGH(V) : מחץ
ONE.HALF : מחצית
ONE.HALF~her : מחציתה
ONE.HALF~him : מחציתו
from~Hhatsar-Eynan : מחצר עינן
from~Hhatsarot : מחצרות
HALF.THE.SPOILS : מחצת
I~did~STRIKE.THROUGH(V) : מחצתי
TOMORROW : מחר
from~SWORD : מחרב
from~Hharadah : מחרדה
from~FLAMING.WRATH : מחרון
make~TREMBLE(V)~ing(ms) : מחריד
make~KEEP.SILENT(V)~ing(ms) : מחריש
from~Hharan : מחרן
from~KERNEL~s : מחרצנים
from~Hheshbon : מחשבון
INVENTION~s : מחשבות
INVENTION : מחשבת
from~Hhashmonah : מחשמונה
FIRE.PAN~s : מחתות
FIRE.PAN~s~her : מחתותיה
FIRE.PAN~him : מחתתו
BRANCH | make~EXTEND(V)~ing(ms) | BENEATH : מטה
BRANCH~him : מטהו
YARN : מטוה
BRANCH : מטות
BRANCH~s~them(m) | BRANCH~them(m) : מטותם
BRANCH~you(ms) : מטך
TREASURE : מטמון
DELICACY~s : מטעמים
PRECIPITATION : מטר
Matreyd : מטרד
Mey-Zahav : מי זהב
WHO | WATER~s2 : מי
from~B'er-Sheva : מיבאר שבע
from~WELL~s : מיבארות
from~>~COME(V) : מיבוא

from~YOUTH :
CHOSEN :
UTTERANCE :
from~HOUSE :
from~EXCEPT :
from~BETWEEN :
from~Beyt-El :
from~ Beyt-Hayishmot :
from~HOUSE :
from~HOUSE~him :
from~FIRSTBORN :
from~ FIRSTBORN.FEMALE~s :
from~UNAWARE :
from~APART.FROM :
from~SON :
from~DAUGHTER~s :
from~DAUGHTER~s~ him :
from~B'ney- Ya'aqan :
from~SON~s :
from~SON~s~him :
from~SON~s :
from~FLESH :
from~FLESH~him :
from~FLESH~me :
from~FLESH~them(m) :
Mivtsar | FORTIFICATION :
from~Botsrah :
from~CATTLE~you(ms) :
from~HOUSE~s~ you(mp) :
from~BORDER :
BOUNDARY~s :
HEADDRESS~s :
Migdol :
from~REDEEM(V)~ing(ms) :
from~Gil'ad :
from~BEATEN.GRAIN~ her :
from~CAMEL ~s :
from~GARDEN | he~did~ much~DELIVER.UP(V) :
from~GRAPEVINE :
from~IMMIGRANT~you(ms) :
from~FLOOR~you(ms) :
from~Gerar :
OPEN.SPACE :
OPEN.SPACE~s :
OPEN.SPACE~s~ them(f) :
from~>~DRAW.NEAR(V) :
from~HAND :
Meydva :
>~much~SPEAK(V) | WILDERNESS | from~WORD :
WORD~s~you(ms) :
Meydad :
MEASUREMENT :
from~HAND~s2~him | LONG.GARMENT~him | from~ HAND~him :
from~MANDRAKES~s :
from~GENERATION :
MEASUREMENT~s :
from~HAND~me | from~ HAND~s2 | from~SUFFICIENT :
from~Dibon-Gad :
Mid'yan :
Mid'yan~s :
from~HAND~you(ms) :
from~BUCKET~s~him :
from~HAND~them(m) | from~BLOOD :
from~BLOOD~her :
from~BLOOD~him :
from~Daphqah :
STEP | from~ROAD :
from~Yehudah :
from~YHWH :
from~>~EXIST(V) :
you(ms)~did~much~ HURRY(V) :
you(fp)~did~much~ HURRY(V) :
from~DAY :
ALTAR | from~SACRIFICE :
ALTAR~s :
ALTAR~s~ them(m) :
ALTAR~s~them(m) :
ALTAR~me :

ALTAR~you$^{(ms)}$:
from~THIS | Miz'zah :
from~DISCHARGE :
from~DISCHARGE~her :
from~DISCHARGE~him :
from~AGE :
ALTAR~him :
from~SACRIFICE~s :
from~CHOICE.FRUIT :
from~BEARD~s :
from~the~MALE :
SUNRISE :
SUNRISE~unto :
from~SEED :
from~SEED~him :
from~SEED~you$^{(ms)}$:
SPRINKLING.BASIN :
SPRINKLING.BASIN~s :
from~THREAD :
from~OUTSIDE :
REVIVING :
BEST :
RING~s~him :
RING~s~him :
from~Yatvatah :
from~FUNCTIONAL :
from~DIRTY~s :
from~DIRTY~s~him :
from~DIRTY~them$^{(m)}$:
from~DEW :
from~BABIES :
from~PREY :
BED~you$^{(ms)}$:
from~WINE :
WATER~s2 :
from~WINE~him :
from~Yisra'eyl :
Mika'eyl :
from~ARMAMENT :
GRATE :
from~JAR~you$^{(fs)}$:
from~ALL :
from~CRUCIBLE :
SINGE.SCAR :
from~Kineret :
from~ALL :

from~you$^{(mp)}$:
UNDERGARMENT~s :
ROOF.COVERING :
ROOF.COVERING~him :
from~SILVER :
WORTH :
from~ANGER :
from~PALM :
from~>~much~COVER$^{(V)}$:
from~Kaphtor :
!$^{(ms)}$~SELL$^{(V)}$~& :
VALUE~them$^{(m)}$:
STUMBLING.BLOCK :
THING.WRITTEN :
he~did~much~FILL$^{(V)}$:
from~Le'ah :
!$^{(mp)}$~FILL$^{(V)}$:
from~COMMUNITY :
you$^{(ms)}$~did~much~FILL$^{(V)}$:
I~did~much~FILL$^{(V)}$~him :
from~HEART~you$^{(ms)}$:
from~to~STRAND :
from~to~STRAND~him :
from~BOY~s :
from~>~BRING.FORTH$^{(V)}$:
INSTALLATION~s~you$^{(mp)}$:
INSTALLATION~s :
SETTING :
from~LOG :
from~BREAD :
BATTLE :
BATTLE~s :
BATTLE~him :
from~HEART~me :
from~Livnah :
from~BRICK~s~you$^{(mp)}$:
from~to~FACE~s :
from~to~FACE~s~you$^{(mp)}$:
Milkah :
he~did~much~TALK$^{(V)}$:
from~to~BENEATH :
from~to~UPWARD~her | from~to~UPWARD~unto :

from~to~FACE~s~me :
from~to~FACE~s~you(ms) :
from~SEA :
from~PRECIOUS :
from~FOREFRONT :
from~FOREFRONT~me :
from~Moseyrot :
from~SETTLING~s~you(mp) :
from~>~DIE(V)~us :
from~ONE.HALF :
from~ONE.HALF~them(m) :
from~MORROW :
from~BRANCH :
from~BRANCH~s :
from~WATER~s2 | WATER~s2 :
from~WILDERNESS :
WATER~s2~them(m) :
WATER~s2~him :
from~SUNRISE :
WATER~s2~you(ms) :
from~DAY~s :
from~WATER~s2 :
from~RIGHT.HAND :
from~RIGHT.HAND~him :
from~RIGHT.HAND~them(m) :
from~DIRECTIVE~s :
from~DIRECTIVE~s~you(ms) :
from~Mits'rayim :
from~LIVESTOCK :
from~CLAN~s :
from~CLAN :
from~CLAN~him :
from~CLAN~me :
from~Mitqah :
FROM~you(ms) | FROM~you(fs) :
MERCHANDISE :
MERCHANDISE~him :
MERCHANDISE~s~him :
MERCHANDISE :
from~BUSINESS~him :
FROM~her :
FROM~him | FROM~us :
FROM~me :
from~UPRISING :
from~Masreyqah :
from~HABITATION :
from~ABDOMEN~s~you(fs) :
from~ABDOMEN~s~you(ms) :
from~UPWARD :
from~make~GO.UP(V)~ing(mp) :
from~WORK~s~him :
from~WORK~us :
from~TENTH.PART~him :
from~Maqheylot :
from~AREA~him :
from~FOUNTAIN :
from~APPEARANCE :
from~Marah :
from~Mesha :
from~WAIST~s :
FROM :
from~SOUTH :
from~OPPOSITE :
from~RIVER :
DEPOSIT :
from~WADI :
from~INHERITANCE :
DEPOSIT :
DEPOSIT~her :
DEPOSIT~him :
DEPOSIT~me :
DEPOSIT~you(ms) :
DEPOSIT~them(m) :
from~CARCASS~her :
from~CARCASS~them(m) :
from~VOW~s~you(mp) :

make~SUCKLE(V)~ing(fp)
from~>~LIFT.UP(V)
from~YOUNG.AGE~s~him
from~YOUNG.AGE~s~us
SANDAL~s~you(ms)
from~YOUNG.MAN
make~SUCKLE(V)~ing(fs)
from~ALL.AROUND
RIM
from~FIELD
from~RAM
from~Suk'kot
from~FLOUR
>~PLACE(V)~him
from~BURDEN~s~them(m)
TASK.WORK~s
from~Sinai
from~SCROLL~me
from~SCROLL~you(ms)
STOREHOUSE~s
from~WICKER.BASKET
from~CLIFF
from~FLOUR~her
from~LEFT.HAND
from~Se'iyr
LAMENTING
PROVENDER
SCAB
NUMBER
NUMBER~you(mp)
much~CORRECT(V)~ing(ms)~you(ms)
PROPORTION
self~BUILD.UP(V)~ing(ms)
from~Ya'aqov
from~EDGE
from~Padan-Aram
from~Padan
from~Punon
from~AWE
from~MOUTH
from~MOUTH~him
from~MOUTH~you(mp)
from~PRODUCE~him
from~FACE~s | from~FACE~s~me
from~FACE~s~her
from~FACE~s~them(m)
from~FACE~s~him
from~FACE~s~you(ms)
from~FACE~s~you(mp)
from~REGISTER(V)~ed(mp)
from~PRODUCE
from~Paroh
from~Petor
from~OPENING
from~ARMY
from~SIDE
from~FLOCKS~you(ms)
DIRECTIVE~s~me
from~Tso'ar
from~BOULDER
DIRECTIVE~s
DIRECTIVE~him | DIRECTIVE~s~him
DIRECTIVE~s~him
DIRECTIVE~s~you(ms)
FOREHEAD~him
from~GAME
from~SIDE~her
from~GAME~him
from~Tsidon
from~GAME~me
from~SIDE~s~her
from~Tsalmonah
from~RIB~s~him
TURBAN
FEW
Mits'rayim~of
from~NARROW~s~him
Mits'rayim
Mits'rayim~unto
Mits'rayim~s
from~>~BURY(V)

from~EAST :
SANCTUARY | from~ Qadesh :
SANCTUARY~him :
from~SPECIAL~s | SANCTUARY~me | SANCTUARY~s~me :
SANCTUARY~s~you$^{(mp)}$:
from~Qe'hey'latah :
from~SPECIAL :
COLLECTION :
from~SHORTNESS :
from~SMALL :
PLACE.TO.BURN :
from~ Qivrot-Hata'awah :
from~WALL :
from~INSIDE~him :
from~INSIDE~you$^{(ms)}$:
from~METROPOLIS :
REFUGE :
REFUGE~him :
LIVESTOCK :
LIVESTOCK~him :
LIVESTOCK~them$^{(m)}$:
ACQUIRED~s~me :
LIVESTOCK~s~them$^{(m)}$:
LIVESTOCK~you$^{(mp)}$:
LIVESTOCK~you$^{(ms)}$:
LIVESTOCK~us :
ACQUIRED :
ACQUIRED~him :
from~CONCLUSION :
from~EXTREMITY :
MEETING :
MEETING~s :
from~INSIDE :
from~EVENT :
from~NEAR :
BEATEN.WORK :
Mir'yam :
FEEDING.PLACE :
OINTMENT.MIXTURE :
Miysha'eyl :
from~REMAINS :

KNEADING.BOWL~s~them$^{(m)}$:
from~SWEARING~me :
PLAIT~s :
PLAIT~s :
from~>~SETTLE$^{(V)}$:
MISTAKE :
from~OX :
OINTMENT :
from~ THREE.DAYS.AGO :
LYING.PLACE :
LYING.PLACE~s :
LYING.PLACE~you$^{(ms)}$:
!$^{(mp)}$~DRAW$^{(V)}$:
DWELLING :
DWELLING~s~you$^{(ms)}$:
DWELLING~me :
from~DWELLER~her :
SENDING :
from~THERE :
from~TITLE~s~them$^{(m)}$:
from~OIL :
from~OIL~s :
CUSTODY :
CUSTODY~you$^{(mp)}$:
CHARGE :
CHARGE~him :
CHARGE~me :
CHARGE~you$^{(ms)}$:
DOUBLE :
from~TWO :
from~YEAR :
from~SNOOZE~him :
STAVE~him :
from~GATE :
CLAN :
CLAN~s :
CLAN~s~them$^{(m)}$:
CLAN :
CLAN~him :
CLAN~me :
DECISION :
DECISION~s~me :

DECISION~s~him :
DECISION~s~you(ms) :
DECISION~them(f) :
from~Shepham :
WEIGHT~her :
WEIGHT~him :
WEIGHT~them(m) :
JUICE :
you(ms)~did~much~GROPE(V) :
self~CRASH(V)~ing(ms) :
BANQUET :
self~BEND.DOWN(V)~ing(mp) :
self~WALK(V)~ing(ms) :
from~MIDST :
from~MIDST~them(m) :
from~>~SCOUT(V) :
from~UNDER | from~Tahhat :
from~UNDER~s~him :
from~>~GIVE(V)~me :
self~TAKE(V)~ing(ms) :
from~YESTERDAY :
self~ANNOUNCE(V)~ing(mp) :
self~COMFORT(V)~ing(ms) :
from~REMAINDER :
from~Terahh :
STRING~s~them(m) :
STRING~s~him :
>~GIVE(V) :
he~did~BE.LOW(V) :
MISERY~s~him :
make~HIT(V)~ing(ms) | HITTING :
make~HIT(V)~ing(ms)~him :
PEDESTAL :
>~SELL(V) :
HITTING~s :
HITTING~s~you(ms) :
Makhi :
Makhir :
much~FINISH(V)~ing(fp) :
TRIBUTE :
he~did~SELL(V) :
they~did~SELL(V) | he~did~SELL(V)~him :

CAVE~s~them(m) :
he~did~SELL(V)~them(m) :
he~did~SELL(V)~us :
you(mp)~did~SELL(V) :
much~DO.SORCERY(V)~ing(fs) :
FULL | !(ms)~much~FILL(V) | he~did~FILL(V) :
she~did~FILL(V) | FULL :
they~did~FILL(V) :
FULL~s :
FULL~s :
MESSENGER :
BUSINESS :
MESSENGER~him :
MESSENGER~s | MESSENGER~me :
MESSENGER~s~you(ms) :
MESSENGER~s :
BUSINESS :
BUSINESS~him :
BUSINESS~you(ms) :
RIPE.FRUIT~you(ms) :
FILLING :
>~FILL(V) :
SALT :
HEAD.OF.WHEAT :
make~MURMUR(V)~ing(mp) :
KING | >~REIGN(V) :
they~did~REIGN(V) | KING~him :
EMPIRE~him :
KING~s :
KING~s~them(m) :
KING~s :
KING~you(ms) :
much~LEARN(V)~ing(ms) :
BOOTY :
TONG~s~her :
make~IRRITATE(V)~ing(fs) :
be~much~SEASON(V)~ing(ms) :
BASTARD :
make~PRECIPITATE(V)~ing(ms) :
KINGDOM~s :
KINGDOM :
KINGDOM~him :

KINGDOM~me :
Mamre :
make~DISOBEY$^{(V)}$~ing$^{(mp)}$:
much~GROPE$^{(V)}$~ing$^{(ms)}$:
WHAT | Mahn :
much~PROVOKE$^{(V)}$~ing$^{(mp)}$~me :
he~did~RECKON$^{(V)}$:
OASIS :
OASIS :
FLEEING :
LAMPSTAND :
LAMPSTAND :
make~INHERIT$^{(V)}$~ing$^{(ms)}$:
make~SUCKLE$^{(V)}$~ing$^{(fs)}$~/ her :
much~TEST$^{(V)}$~ing$^{(ms)}$:
he~did~WITHHOLD$^{(V)}$:
he~did~WITHHOLD$^{(V)}$~you$^{(ms)}$:
SACRIFICIAL.BOWL~s~him :
Menasheh :
LOAD :
LOAD~him :
UPRISING~s :
LOAD~them$^{(m)}$:
UPRISING :
make~OVERTAKE$^{(V)}$~ing$^{(fs)}$:
Mas'sah :
HOOD :
make~OVERTAKE$^{(V)}$~ing$^{(ms)}$:
CANOPY :
CAST.IMAGE :
PAYMENT~me :
PAYMENT~you$^{(ms)}$:
/ CAST.IMAGE~s~them$^{(m)}$:
IMAGERY~them$^{(m)}$:
IMAGERY :
much~HATE$^{(V)}$~ing$^{(mp)}$~you$^{(ms)}$:
JOURNEY~s :
JOURNEY~s~them$^{(m)}$:
from~SERVANT~s :
from~SERVANT~s~him :
from~SERVANT~s~you$^{(ms)}$:
from~>~SERVE$^{(V)}$~us :
from~SERVICE~you$^{(mp)}$:

from~SERVICE~them$^{(m)}$:
from~>~CROSS.OVER$^{(V)}$:
make~SERVE$^{(V)}$~ing$^{(mp)}$:
make~CROSS.OVER$^{(V)}$~ing$^{(ms)}$:
CROSSING | from~OTHER.SIDE :
from~Evronah :
from~Eden :
TASTY.FOOD :
from~COMPANY :
from~YET.AGAIN~me :
from~YET.AGAIN~you$^{(ms)}$:
>~BE.LESS$^{(V)}$:
from~DISTANT :
from~TWISTEDNESS :
HABITATION :
much~CONJURE$^{(V)}$~ing$^{(ms)}$:
much~CONJURE$^{(V)}$~ing$^{(mp)}$:
from~FLYER :
from~SKIN :
from~>~LEAVE$^{(V)}$:
SMALL.AMOUNT :
make~WRAP.AROUND$^{(V)}$~ing$^{(ms)}$:
from~Iy'yim :
CLOAK :
from~WITH :
from~WITH~him :
from~WITH~me :
from~WITH~you$^{(ms)}$:
from~WITH~us :
from~the~EYE :
SPRING~s :
from~EYE~s2~me | from~EYE~s2 :
from~CITY :
Ma'akhah :
from~UPON | TRANSGRESSION :
make~GO.UP$^{(V)}$~ing$^{(fs)}$ | UPWARD~unto :
they~did~TRANSGRESS$^{(V)}$:
from~UPON~me :
from~UPON~her :
from~UPON~them$^{(m)}$:
from~UPON~him :

from~UPON~you(ms) :
from~UPON~you(mp) :
from~UPON~us :
WORKS~s~you(ms) :
: from~Almon-Divlatayim
make~GO.UP(V)~ing(fs) :
you(mp)~did~TRANSGRESS(V) :
from~PEOPLE :
from~PEOPLE~s~her :
from~PEOPLE~s~him :
from~VALLEY :
from~AFFLICTION :
WORK :
from~>~DO(V) :
WORK~s~him :
WORK~s~you(ms) :
WORK~s~you(mp) :
WORK~s :
WORK~you(ms) :
TENTH.PART :
from~ : TENTH.PART~s~you(mp)
from~DIRT :
from~TREE :
from~Etsi'on- : Gaver
from~Atsmon :
from~BONE~s~me :
PARAPET :
from~EVENING :
from~DESERT~s :
from~Aro'eyr :
from~CITY~s :
from~CITY~s~him :
from~ARRANGEMENT~s :
from~ARRANGEMENT~ : you(ms)
CAVE :
be~much~OPEN(V)~ing(fp) :
make~CLEAVE(V)~ing(ms) :
make~REPRODUCE(V)~ing(ms)~ : you(ms)
make~CLEAVE(V)~ing(fs) :
he~did~FIND(V) :
she~did~FIND(V) | he~did~ : FIND(V)~her

they~did~FIND(V) :
they~did~FIND(V)~me :
we~did~FIND(V) :
you(ms)~did~FIND(V) :
you(ms)~did~FIND(V)~her :
I~did~FIND(V) :
I~did~FIND(V)~her :
she~did~FIND(V)~them(m) :
she~did~FIND(V)~us :
MONUMENT :
MONUMENT~s~ : them(m)
MONUMENT~s~them(m) :
MONUMENT :
UNLEAVENED.BREAD :
much~DIRECT(V)~ing(fs) | much~ : DIRECT(V)~ing(ms)
much~DIRECT(V)~ing(ms)~you(ms) :
be~much~OVERLAY(V)~ : ing(ms)
SMACKED :
be~much~INFECT(V)~ing(fs) :
UNLEAVENED.BREAD~s :
FOREHEAD :
much~LAUGH(V)~ing(ms) :
!(ms)~make~DELIVER(V) :
make~PROSPER(V)~ing(ms) :
I~did~FIND(V) :
make~RECEIVE(V)~ing(fp) :
much~BURY(V)~ing(mp) :
make~SET.APART(V)~ : ing(mp)
much~SET.APART(V)~ : ing(ms)~you(ms)
much~SET.APART(V)~ing(ms)~ : him
from~>~much~ : SET.APART(V)~them(m)
AREA :
AREA~her :
AREA~him :
AREA~me :
AREA~you(ms) :
AREA~them(m) :
FOUNTAIN :
FOUNTAIN~her :
much~COLLECT(V)~ing(ms) :

make~RISE(V)~ing(ms) :
ROD :
make~DRY(V)~ing(ms) :
make~SNAP(V)~ing(mp) :
make~COME.NEAR(V)~ing(ms) :
make~COME.NEAR(V)~ing(mp) :
make~COME.NEAR(V)~ing(mp) :
MYRRH :
APPEARANCE | make~SEE(V)~ing(ms) | be~make~SEE(V)~ing(ms) | APPEARANCE~her :
APPEARANCE~him :
from~>~SEE(V) :
HEADREST~s~him :
from~PRIME :
make~INCREASE(V)~ing(ms) :
make~INCREASE.IN.NUMBER(V)~ing(mp) :
much~TREAD.ABOUT(V)~ing(mp) :
from~>~GO.DOWN(V) :
they~did~REBEL(V) :
Marah :
from~HEAD :
from~HEAD~him :
from~ABUNDANCE :
from~>~INCREASE.IN.NUMBER(V)~you(mp) :
CRUMBLED :
GALL~s :
BITTER.HERBS~s :
from~Rehhovot :
from~DISTANCE :
make~WIDEN(V)~ing(ms) :
from~BOWELS :
much~FLUTTER(V)~ing(fs) :
BOILING.POT :
REBELLIOUS :
from~MYRIAD~s :
CONTENTION | Meriyvah :
Meriyvah :
REBELLIOUS~you(ms) :
BITTER~s | make~RAISE.UP(V)~ing(ms) :

from~Rimon-Perets :
from~Risah :
make~DRAW.OUT(V)~ing(mp) :
HARSH :
you(ms)~did~DISOBEY(V) :
from~Ritmah :
CHARIOT~s :
CHARIOT~s~him :
CHARIOT~him :
PARTNER~him :
from~Ra'meses :
from~Rephiydiym :
Merari :
from~PRIME :
Marah~unto :
LOAN :
make~GO.ASTRAY(V)~ing(ms) :
LOAN :
they~did~MOVE.AWAY(V) :
be~much~WEAVE(V)~ing(mp) :
be~much~RAVE(V)~ing(ms) :
SMEAR(V)~ed(mp) :
>~REGULATE(V) :
be~much~JOINED.TOGETHER(V)~ing(fp) :
much~BE.THREEFOLD(V)~ing(ms) :
much~BE.THREEFOLD(V)~ing(fs) :
be~much~BE.ALMOND.SHAPED(V)~ing(mp) :
be~make~TWIST.TOGETHER(V)~ing(ms) :
he~did~SMEAR(V) :
>~SMEAR(V)~him :
make~DAMAGE(V)~ing(ms) :
make~DAMAGE(V)~ing(mp) :
make~DAMAGE(V)~ing(ms)~them(m) :
you(ms)~did~SMEAR(V) :
>~SMEAR(V)~them(m) | CORRUPTION~them(m) :
make~TURN.BACK(V)~ing(ms) :

I~did~PLUCK.OUT(V)~him :
she~did~DRAW(V) :
much~BE.CHILDLESS(V)~ing(fs) :
PARABLE~him :
much~SEND(V)~ing(ms) :
make~SEND(V)~ing(ms) :
ACQUISITION :
DRINKING | make~DRINK(V)~ing(ms) :
DRINKING~him :
much~MINISTER(V)~ing(ms) :
much~MINISTER(V)~ing(ms)~him :
DIE(V)~ing(ms) | he~did~DIE(V) :
she~did~DIE(V) :
they~did~DIE(V) | DIE(V)~ing(ms)~him :
Metusha'el :
Metushelahh :
DIE(V)~ing(ms)~me | HOW.LONG | MORTAL.MAN~s :
MORTAL.MAN~s~him :
DIE(V)~ing(mp) | MORTAL.MAN~s :
DIE(V)~ing(ms)~you(ms) :
SUM :
CONTRIBUTION | Matanah :
we~did~DIE(V) :
CONTRIBUTION~s | CONTRIBUTION :
CONTRIBUTION~s~you(mp) :
WAIST~s2 :
WAIST~s~you(mp) :
GIFT~them(m) :
PLEASE | RAW :
be~BE.EMINENT(V)~ing(ms) :
be~BE.EMINENT(V)~ing(ms) :
DECLARE(V)~ed(ms) :
we~will~be~AGREE(V) :
we~will~be~AGREE(V)~& :
he~did~be~TAKE.HOLD(V) :
be~SECURE(V)~ing(ms) :
we~will~GATHER(V) :
we~will~GATHER(V) | he~did~be~GATHER(V) :
GROANING :
GROANING~them(m) :
Nevo :
we~will~COME(V) :
BORE.OUT(V)~ed(ms) :
be~ENTANGLED(V)~ing(mp) :
>~FADE(V) :
be~UNDERSTAND(V)~ing(ms) :
ANNOUNCER :
ANNOUNCER~s :
ANNOUNCER~you(ms) :
ANNOUNCER~you(mp) :
Nevayot :
FOOL :
FOLLY | CARCASS :
SOUTH :
SOUTH~unto :
OPPOSITE :
OPPOSITE~you(ms) :
GORER :
he~did~TOUCH(V) | TOUCH :
TOUCH~s :
we~did~TOUCH(V) :
STRIKING :
HEAP :
Nadav | he~did~OFFER.WILLINGLY(V) :
she~did~OFFER.WILLINGLY(V) | FREEWILL.OFFERING :
we~will~much~SPEAK(V) :
WILLING :
WILLING~s :
we~will~KNOW(V) :
VOW :
she~did~MAKE.A.VOW(V) :
VOW~s~her :
VOW~s~you(ms) :
you(ms)~did~MAKE.A.VOW(V) :
you(ms)~did~much~LEAD(V) :
he~did~be~OVERTURN(V) :
RIVER :
we~will~KILL(V) :
RIVER~s~them(m) :
we~will~EAT(V) :
we~did~be~FOOLISH(V) :

we~will~SAY(V) :
Novahh :
PUSH(V)~ing(mp) :
PUSH(V)~ing(mp)~him :
TOUCH(V)~ing(ms) :
SMITE(V)~ing(ms) :
Nod :
he~did~be~KNOW(V) :
I~did~be~KNOW(V) :
ABODE :
FLOW(V)~ing(mp) :
No'ahh :
they~did~be~much~HIT(V) :
IN.FRONT :
we~will~BE.ABLE(V) :
she~did~be~much~HIT(V) :
Nun :
LIFT.UP(V)~ing(ms) :
LIFT.UP(V)~ing(fp) :
LIFT.UP(V)~ing(mp) :
LIFT.UP(V)~ing(mp) :
JOURNEY(V)~ing(ms) :
JOURNEY(V)~ing(mp) :
No'ah :
Nophahh :
TURQUOISE :
FALL(V)~ing(ms) :
FALL(V)~ing(mp) :
FALL(V)~ing(fs) :
we~will~make~GO.OUT(V) :
PRESERVE(V)~ing(ms) :
AVENGE(V)~ing(fs) :
be~FEAR(V)~ing(ms) :
be~SETTLE(V)~ing(fs) :
OVERLOOK(V)~ing(ms) :
be~SLEEP(V)~ing(ms) :
be~SLEEP(V)~ing(fs) :
he~did~be~RESCUE(V) :
GIVE(V)~ing(ms) :
he~did~be~LEAVE.BEHIND(V) :
STEW :
DEDICATED :
DEDICATED~s~her :
DEDICATED~you(ms) :
ORNAMENTAL.RING :
DEDICATION :

you(ms)~did~be~ WITHDRAW(V) :
Nahhbi :
!(ms)~GUIDE(V) :
Nahhor :
COPPER :
you(ms)~did~GUIDE(V) :
WADI :
INHERITANCE | WADI~unto :
WADI~s :
Nahhali'eyl :
we~will~be~EXTRACT(V) :
INHERITANCE :
INHERITANCE~him :
INHERITANCE~you(ms) :
INHERITANCE~them(m) :
INHERITANCE :
INHERITANCE~us :
he~did~GUIDE(V)~them(m) :
be~CRAVE(V)~ing(ms) :
WE :
he~did~GUIDE(V)~me :
be~CONSORT(V)~ing(fs) :
>~much~PREDICT(V) | SERPENT | PREDICTION :
we~did~be~THINK(V) :
Nahhshon :
PREDICTION~s :
Nahhat :
he~did~EXTEND(V) | !(ms)~ EXTEND(V) :
EXTEND(V)~ed(fs) :
you(ms)~did~EXTEND(V) :
he~did~PLANT(V) :
you(ms)~did~PLANT(V) :
NATAPH :
you(ms)~did~ LEAVE.ALONE(V)~me :
she~did~EXTEND(V) :
they~did~much~ PROVOKE(V) :
they~did~be~STIR(V) :
CARCASS~her :
CARCASS~him :
CARCASS~you(ms) :
CARCASS~them(m) :
we~will~BUILD(V) :

she~did~be~BUILD(V) :
they~did~be~CLEAVE.OPEN(V) :
they~did~be~SHAPE(V) :
they~did~be~REMOVE.THE.COVER(V) :
we~will~STEAL(V) :
TOUCH~him :
be~SMITE(V)~ing(ms) :
be~SMITE(V)~ing(mp) :
be~TAKE.AWAY(V)~ing(ms) | we~will~be~TAKE.AWAY(V) :
he~did~be~DRAW.NEAR(V) :
they~did~be~DRAW.NEAR(V) :
FREEWILL.OFFERING~you(mp) :
FREEWILL.OFFERING~them(m) :
FREEWILL.OFFERING :
REMOVAL :
be~DRIVE.OUT(V)~ing(mp) :
be~DRIVE.OUT(V)~ing(ms)~you(ms) :
be~TWIRL(V)~ing(ms) :
VOW~her :
VOW~him :
VOW~s~them(m) :
VOW~s~you(mp) :
be~SEEK(V)~ing(ms) :
REMOVAL :
REMOVAL~her :
he~did~much~DRIVE(V) :
we~will~EXIST(V) :
you(ms)~did~be~EXIST(V) :
she~did~be~EXIST(V) :
we~will~SACRIFICE(V) :
we~will~SACRIFICE(V)~& :
ORNAMENTAL.RING~s :
DEDICATION~him :
we~will~SOW(V) :
SWEET :
SWEET~me :
SWEET~you(mp) :
I~did~be~COMFORT(V) :
I~did~much~PREDICT(V) :

we~will~EXTEND(V) :
they~did~be~EXTEND(V) :
she~did~be~BE.DIRTY(V) :
they~did~be~BE.DIRTY(V) :
you(fs)~did~be~BE.DIRTY(V) :
be~BE.HEAVY(V)~ing(ms) :
IN.FRONT~him :
they~did~much~BE.CRAFTY(V) :
they~will~be~BURN.BLACK(V) :
>~be~CRAVING(V) :
you(ms)~did~be~CRAVING(V) :
we~will~CUT(V)~& :
we~will~MAKE.BRICKS(V) :
be~FIGHT(V)~ing(ms) | he~did~be~FIGHT(V) :
he~did~be~SNIP.OFF(V) :
they~did~be~SNIP.OFF(V) :
be~SNIP.OFF(V)~ing(mp) :
he~did~be~SELL(V) :
he~did~be~FIND(V) | we~will~FIND(V) :
they~did~be~FIND(V) :
Nimrod :
Ninweh :
we~will~INHERIT(V) :
he~did~much~TEST(V) :
he~did~much~TEST(V)~him :
you(ms)~did~much~TEST(V)~him :
you(mp)~did~much~TEST(V) :
POURING~him :
we~will~JOURNEY(V) :
she~did~much~TEST(V) :
we~will~be~HIDE(V) :
she~did~be~RANSOM(V) :
be~PERFORM(V)~ing(fp) :
be~PERFORM(V)~ing(fp)~me :
be~PERFORM(V)~ing(fs) :
she~did~be~SPLIT(V) :
he~did~be~REGISTER(V) :

they~did~be~DIVIDE.APART(V) :
they~did~be~OPEN(V) :
I~did~be~ENTWINE(V) :
be~STAND.UP(V)~ing(ms) :
she~did~be~STAND.UP(V) :
they~did~be~STAND.UP(V) :
be~STAND.UP(V)~ing(mp) :
SHOOT ~her :
we~will~self~BE.STEADFAST(V) :
be~STRUGGLE(V)~ing(mp) :
they~did~be~PIERCE.THROUGH(V) :
we~will~TAKE(V) :
VENGEANCE :
he~did~be~MEET(V) :
he~did~be~MEET(V) :
he~did~be~SEE(V) :
they~did~be~SEE(V) :
he~did~be~HEAL(V) :
be~SINK.DOWN(V)~ing(mp) :
be~REMAIN(V)~ing(ms) | he~did~be~REMAIN(V) :
he~did~be~CAPTURE(V) :
he~did~be~SWEAR(V) :
they~did~be~SWEAR(V) :
you(ms)~did~be~SWEAR(V) :
I~did~be~SWEAR(V) :
he~did~be~CRACK(V) :
she~did~be~DAMAGE(V) :
we~will~SEND(V)~& :
we~will~SAFEGUARD(V) :
he~will~be~HEAR(V) :
BREATH :
we~will~GULP(V) :
he~did~much~DIVIDE.INTO.PIECES(V) :
we~will~self~BE.SKILLED(V)~& :
he~did~be~DROP.DOWN(V) :
we~will~GIVE(V) | be~GIVE(V)~ing(ms) | he~did~be~GIVE(V) :
she~did~be~GIVE(V) | we~did~GIVE(V) :
they~did~be~GIVE(V) :
she~did~be~SEIZE.HOLD(V) :
we~will~make~HIT(V) :
SPICE :
be~PREPARE(V)~ing(ms) :
be~PREPARE(V)~ing(mp) :
we~will~much~KEEP.SECRET(V) :
we~will~make~HIT(V)~him :
FOREIGNER :
FOREIGN :
FOREIGN :
FOREIGN~s :
we~will~STAY.THE.NIGHT(V) :
we~will~WALK(V) :
we~will~WALK(V)~& :
Nemu'eyl :
they~did~be~DISSOLVE(V) :
we~will~DIE(V) :
STANDARD | he~did~FLEE(V) :
he~did~LIFT.UP(V) :
he~did~LIFT.UP(V)~him | they~did~LIFT.UP(V) :
he~did~LIFT.UP(V)~you(ms) :
you(ms)~did~LIFT.UP(V) :
I~did~LIFT.UP(V) :
they~did~be~GO.AROUND(V) :
they~did~FLEE(V) :
>~LIFT.UP(V) :
>~much~TEST(V) :
>~much~TEST(V)~you(ms) :
>~much~TEST(V)~them(m) :
CAPTAIN :
CAPTAIN~s~them(m) :
CAPTAIN~s :
CAPTAIN~s~them(m) :
CAPTAIN~s :
POURED.OUT~you(mp) :
FLEE(V)~ing(mp) :
POURING :
he~did~JOURNEY(V) :
they~did~JOURNEY(V) :
STAGGER(V)~ing(ms) :
we~will~SERVE(V) :
we~will~CROSS.OVER(V) :

we~will~CROSS.OVER$^{(V)}$~& : נעברה
SANDAL : נעל
he~did~be~GO.UP$^{(V)}$ | we~ will~GO.UP$^{(V)}$~& : נעלה
SANDAL~him : נעלו
SANDAL~s~you$^{(ms)}$: נעליך
SANDAL~s~you$^{(mp)}$: נעליכם
Na'amah | she~did~ BE.DELIGHTFUL$^{(V)}$: נעמה
we~will~DO$^{(V)}$ | he~did~be~ DO$^{(V)}$: נעשה
they~did~be~DO$^{(V)}$: נעשו
she~did~be~DO$^{(V)}$: נעשתה
she~did~be~STOP$^{(V)}$: נעצרה
YOUNG.MAN : נער
YOUNG.MAN~s : נערי
YOUNG.MAN~s~him : נעריו
they~did~be~PILE$^{(V)}$: נערמו
we~will~SCATTER.ABROAD$^{(V)}$: נפוץ
they~did~be~ SCATTER.ABROAD$^{(V)}$: נפוצו
Naphish : נפיש
he~did~FALL$^{(V)}$: נפל
she~did~FALL$^{(V)}$: נפלה
they~did~FALL$^{(V)}$: נפלו
she~did~SCATTER$^{(V)}$: נפצה
SOUL : נפש
SOUL~her : נפשה
SOUL~him : נפשו
SOUL~s : נפשות
SOUL~s~you$^{(mp)}$: נפשותיכם
SOUL~s~us : נפשותינו
SOUL~me : נפשי
SOUL~you$^{(ms)}$: נפשך
SOUL~you$^{(ms)}$: נפשכם
SOUL~them$^{(m)}$: נפשם
SOUL~us : נפשנו
Naphtuhh~s : נפתחים
WRESTLING~s : נפתולי
Naphtali : נפתלי
POST : נציב
!$^{(ms)}$~PIERCE.THROUGH$^{(V)}$~& | FEMALE : נקבה
SPECKLED : נקוד
SPECKLED~s : נקודים
>~AVENGE$^{(V)}$ | !$^{(ms)}$~AVENGE$^{(V)}$: נקום
INNOCENT : נקי
INNOCENT~s | INNOCENCE~s : נקיים
VENGEANCE : נקם
LAMP : נר
we~will~GO.DOWN$^{(V)}$: נרד
we~will~GO.DOWN$^{(V)}$~& : נרדה
LAMP~s : נרות
LAMP~s~her : נרותיה
we~will~make~ BE.DYSFUNCTIONAL$^{(V)}$: נרע
we~will~TURN.BACK$^{(V)}$: נשוב
WOMAN~s | WOMAN~s~me : נשי
WOMAN~s~them$^{(m)}$: נשיהם
WOMAN~s~him : נשיו
WOMAN~s~you$^{(mp)}$: נשיכם
WOMAN~s : נשים
WOMAN~s~us : נשינו
USURY | he~did~BITE$^{(V)}$: נשך
BREATH : נשמה
he~did~much~ OVERLOOK$^{(V)}$: נשני
you$^{(ms)}$~did~BLOW$^{(V)}$: נשפת
we~will~make~DRINK$^{(V)}$: נשקה
we~will~make~DRINK$^{(V)}$~ him : נשקנו
EAGLE~s : נשרים
>~GIVE$^{(V)}$: נתון
GIVE$^{(V)}$~ed$^{(fp)}$: נתונות
GIVE$^{(V)}$~ed$^{(mp)}$: נתונים
PIECE~s~him : נתחיו
he~did~GIVE$^{(V)}$ | >~GIVE$^{(V)}$: נתן
Nataneyl : נתנאל
she~did~GIVE$^{(V)}$: נתנה
he~did~GIVE$^{(V)}$~him | they~ did~GIVE$^{(V)}$: נתנו
ERUPTION : נתק
you$^{(ms)}$~did~GIVE$^{(V)}$: נתתה
I~did~GIVE$^{(V)}$: נתתי
I~did~GIVE$^{(V)}$~her : נתתיה
I~did~GIVE$^{(V)}$~him : נתתיו
I~did~GIVE$^{(V)}$~you$^{(ms)}$: נתתיך
I~did~GIVE$^{(V)}$~them$^{(m)}$: נתתים
!$^{(ms)}$~LIFT.UP$^{(V)}$: שא
!$^{(ms)}$~LIFT.UP$^{(V)}$~him : שאהו
!$^{(mp)}$~LIFT.UP$^{(V)}$: שאו
LEAVEN : שאור
!$^{(fs)}$~LIFT.UP$^{(V)}$: שאי

SE'AH~s : 𐤎𐤀𐤉𐤌
>~LIFT.UP$^{(V)}$: 𐤎𐤀𐤕
>~LIFT.UP$^{(V)}$~him : 𐤎𐤀𐤕𐤅
Seva : 𐤎𐤁𐤀
ALL.AROUND : 𐤎𐤁𐤉𐤁
ALL.AROUND~s : 𐤎𐤁𐤉𐤁𐤅𐤕
ALL.AROUND~s~me : 𐤎𐤁𐤉𐤁𐤅𐤕𐤉
ALL.AROUND~her : 𐤎𐤁𐤉𐤁𐤅𐤕𐤉𐤄
ALL.AROUND~s~them$^{(m)}$: 𐤎𐤁𐤉𐤁𐤅𐤕𐤉𐤄𐤌
ALL.AROUND~s~you$^{(mp)}$: 𐤎𐤁𐤉𐤁𐤅𐤕𐤉𐤊𐤌
ALL.AROUND~s~us : 𐤎𐤁𐤉𐤁𐤅𐤕𐤉𐤍𐤅
PLENTY : 𐤎𐤁𐤏
PLENTY~you$^{(ms)}$: 𐤎𐤁𐤏𐤊
she~did~LIFT.HIGH$^{(V)}$: 𐤎𐤂𐤁𐤄
JEWEL : 𐤎𐤂𐤅𐤋𐤄
he~did~SHUT$^{(V)}$: 𐤎𐤂𐤓
they~did~SHUT$^{(V)}$: 𐤎𐤂𐤓𐤅
FIELD : 𐤎𐤃𐤄
FIELD~him : 𐤎𐤃𐤄𐤅
Sedom : 𐤎𐤃𐤅𐤌
Sedom~unto : 𐤎𐤃𐤅𐤌𐤄
FIELD : 𐤎𐤃𐤉
FIELD~you$^{(ms)}$: 𐤎𐤃𐤊
RAM : 𐤎𐤄
>~GO.AROUND$^{(V)}$: 𐤎𐤅𐤁
Sodi : 𐤎𐤅𐤃𐤉
TRADE$^{(V)}$~ing$^{(mp)}$: 𐤎𐤅𐤇𐤓𐤉𐤌
BOOTH~s | Suk'kot : 𐤎𐤅𐤊𐤅𐤕
Suk'kot~unto : 𐤎𐤅𐤊𐤅𐤕𐤄
FENCE.AROUND$^{(V)}$~ing$^{(mp)}$: 𐤎𐤅𐤊𐤊𐤉𐤌
LADDER : 𐤎𐤅𐤋𐤌
FLOUR : 𐤎𐤅𐤋𐤕
>~PLACE$^{(V)}$: 𐤎𐤅𐤌
HATE$^{(V)}$~ing$^{(ms)}$: 𐤎𐤅𐤍𐤀
HATE$^{(V)}$~ing$^{(mp)}$: 𐤎𐤅𐤍𐤀𐤉
HATE$^{(V)}$~ing$^{(mp)}$~him : 𐤎𐤅𐤍𐤀𐤉𐤅
HATE$^{(V)}$~ing$^{(mp)}$~you$^{(ms)}$: 𐤎𐤅𐤍𐤀𐤉𐤊
HATE$^{(V)}$~ing$^{(mp)}$~you$^{(mp)}$: 𐤎𐤅𐤍𐤀𐤉𐤊𐤌
HATE$^{(V)}$~ing$^{(mp)}$~us : 𐤎𐤅𐤍𐤀𐤉𐤍𐤅
HATE$^{(V)}$~ing$^{(ms)}$~you$^{(ms)}$: 𐤎𐤅𐤍𐤀𐤊
HORSE : 𐤎𐤅𐤎
Susiy : 𐤎𐤅𐤎𐤉
HORSE~s : 𐤎𐤅𐤎𐤉𐤌
REEDS : 𐤎𐤅𐤐
>~TURN.ASIDE$^{(V)}$: 𐤎𐤅𐤓
!$^{(mp)}$~TURN.ASIDE$^{(V)}$: 𐤎𐤅𐤓𐤅
he~did~be~much~CREMATE$^{(V)}$: 𐤎𐤅𐤓𐤐
BE.STUBBORN$^{(V)}$~ing$^{(ms)}$: 𐤎𐤅𐤓𐤓
COAT~her : 𐤎𐤅𐤕𐤅𐤄
you$^{(fs)}$~did~GO.ASIDE$^{(V)}$: 𐤎𐤈𐤉𐤕
Si'on : 𐤎𐤉𐤀𐤅𐤍
GRAY-HEADED : 𐤎𐤉𐤁𐤄
BURDEN~s : 𐤎𐤉𐤁𐤋𐤅𐤕
Sevam : 𐤎𐤉𐤁𐤌𐤄
GRAY-HEADED : 𐤎𐤉𐤁𐤕
GRAY-HEADED~me : 𐤎𐤉𐤁𐤕𐤉
RAM~him : 𐤎𐤉𐤅
SHRUB : 𐤎𐤉𐤇
Sihhon : 𐤎𐤉𐤇𐤅𐤍
Sitnah : 𐤎𐤉𐤈𐤍𐤄
he~did~much~CALCULATE$^{(V)}$: 𐤎𐤉𐤊𐤋
!$^{(ms)}$~PLACE$^{(V)}$: 𐤎𐤉𐤌
!$^{(ms)}$~PLACE$^{(V)}$~her : 𐤎𐤉𐤌𐤄
!$^{(mp)}$~PLACE$^{(V)}$: 𐤎𐤉𐤌𐤅
REJOICING~you$^{(mp)}$: 𐤎𐤉𐤌𐤇𐤕𐤊𐤌
APPAREL~s~him : 𐤎𐤉𐤌𐤋𐤅𐤕𐤉𐤅
APPAREL~s~you$^{(mp)}$: 𐤎𐤉𐤌𐤋𐤅𐤕𐤉𐤊𐤌
APPAREL~s~them$^{(m)}$: 𐤎𐤉𐤌𐤋𐤅𐤕𐤌
APPAREL : 𐤎𐤉𐤌𐤋𐤕
APPAREL~him : 𐤎𐤉𐤌𐤋𐤕𐤅
APPAREL~you$^{(ms)}$: 𐤎𐤉𐤌𐤋𐤕𐤊
Sin : 𐤎𐤉𐤍
Sinai : 𐤎𐤉𐤍𐤉
POT : 𐤎𐤉𐤓
POT~s~him : 𐤎𐤉𐤓𐤅𐤕𐤉𐤅
Siryon : 𐤎𐤉𐤓𐤉𐤅𐤍
they~did~much~SHUT.UP$^{(V)}$~them$^{(m)}$: 𐤎𐤉𐤕𐤌𐤅𐤌
HIDING : 𐤎𐤉𐤕𐤓𐤄
>~HIRE$^{(V)}$: 𐤎𐤊𐤅𐤓
HIRELING : 𐤎𐤊𐤉𐤓
WAGE | he~did~HIRE$^{(V)}$: 𐤎𐤊𐤓
WAGE~him : 𐤎𐤊𐤓𐤅
WAGE~me : 𐤎𐤊𐤓𐤉
WAGE~you$^{(ms)}$ | WAGE~you$^{(fs)}$: 𐤎𐤊𐤓𐤊
I~did~HIRE$^{(V)}$~you$^{(ms)}$: 𐤎𐤊𐤓𐤕𐤉𐤊
WICKER.BASKET : 𐤎𐤋
Salu : 𐤎𐤋𐤅𐤀
>~FORGIVE$^{(V)}$: 𐤎𐤋𐤅𐤇
QUAIL~s : 𐤎𐤋𐤅𐤉𐤌
!$^{(ms)}$~FORGIVE$^{(V)}$: 𐤎𐤋𐤇

I~did~FORGIVE(V) :
WICKER.BASKET~s :
Salkah :
OUTER.GARMENT :
OUTER.GARMENT~s~ you(mp) :
OUTER.GARMENT :
PLACE(V)~ing(ms) | he~did~PLACE(V) :
they~did~PLACE(V) :
LEFT.HAND :
LEFT.HAND~him :
REJOICING | !(ms)~REJOICE(V) :
AROMATIC.SPICE~s :
he~did~PLACE(V)~you(ms) | he~ did~SUPPORT(V) :
I~did~SUPPORT(V)~him :
FIGURE :
Samlah :
APPAREL~s :
he~did~PLACE(V)~me :
I~did~PLACE(V) :
I~did~PLACE(V)~him :
he~did~HATE(V) :
you(mp)~did~HATE(V) :
THORN.BUSH :
>~HATE(V) :
HATE(V)~ed(fs) :
Senir :
FIN :
he~did~SKIP.WITH.JOY(V) :
!(ms)~JOURNEY(V) :
BARLEY~s :
Se'iyr | HAIR | HAIRY.GOAT :
Se'iyr~unto :
HAIR~s :
HAIRY.GOAT~s :
HAIRY.GOAT :
HAIR :
HAIR~him :
they~did~STORM(V)~them(m) :
LIP :
BOARDED.UP(V)~ed(ms) :
>~CONSUME(V) :
SCAB :
AFTER.GROWTH :
AFTER.GROWTH~her :
LAPIS.LAZULI :

UPPER.LIP :
SCROLL | >~much~COUNT(V) :
Sephar~unto :
!(mp)~>~much~COUNT(V) :
LIP :
LIP~him :
LIP~s2~her :
LIP~s2 :
LIP~s2~you(ms) :
LIP~them(m) :
SACK :
SACK~him :
>~STONE(V) :
SACK~s~them(m) :
NOBLE | he~did~TURN.ASIDE(V) :
Sered | BRAIDED.WORK :
Sarah | TURNING.ASIDE :
they~did~TURN.ASIDE(V) :
Serug :
OVERHANG(V)~ed(ms) :
LACE :
BE.SUPERFLUOUS(V)~ed(ms) :
Serahh :
SLICING :
Sarai | NOBLE~s :
TWIG~s :
SURVIVOR :
NOBLE~s :
EUNUCH :
EUNUCH~s :
EUNUCH~s~him :
you(ms)~did~TURN.AWAY(V) :
he~did~CREMATE(V) | VENOMOUS :
CREMATING :
they~did~CREMATE(V) :
CREMATING :
you(mp)~did~TURN.ASIDE(V) :
Setur :
SERVANT :
they~did~SERVE(V) | SERVANT~ him :
SERVANT~s | SERVANT~me | SERVANT~s~me :
SERVANT~s~him :
SERVANT~s~you(ms) :
SERVANT~s :

SERVANT~you(ms) | he~did~ SERVE(V)~you(ms) :

SERVANT~you(mp) :

you(ms)~did~SERVE(V) :

I~did~SERVE(V) :

I~did~SERVE(V)~you(ms) :

>~SERVE(V) :

SERVICE :

SERVICE :

SERVICE~him :

SERVICE~me :

SERVICE~you(mp) :

SERVICE~them(m) :

>~MAKE.A.PLEDGE(V) :

!(ms)~CROSS.OVER(V) | >~ CROSS.OVER(V) :

THICK.WOVEN :

THICK.WOVEN~s :

you(ms)~did~BE.THICK(V) :

Ever | he~did~CROSS.OVER(V) | OTHER.SIDE :

>~CROSS.OVER(V)~me :

OTHER.SIDE~them(m) :

>~CROSS.OVER(V)~us :

I~did~CROSS.OVER(V) :

you(mp)~did~CROSS.OVER(V) :

EARRING :

BULLOCK :

HEIFER | CART :

CART~s :

HEIFER :

UNTIL | WITNESS :

Adah | WITNESS :

Adulam~of :

UNTIL~me | UNTIL :

TRAPPINGS~him :

TRAPPINGS~you(ms) :

TRAPPINGS~them(m) | WITNESS~s :

Eden :

PLEASURE :

DROVE :

DROVE~s :

DROVE~s :

LENTIL~s :

COMPANY :

COMPANY~him :

COMPANY~you(ms) :

SERVE(V)~ing(ms) | SERVE(V)~ed(ms) :

SERVE(V)~ing(mp) :

Uval :

CROSS.OVER(V)~ing(ms) :

CROSS.OVER(V)~ing(mp) :

Og :

BAKED.BREAD~s :

YET.AGAIN :

YET.AGAIN~you(ms) :

YET.AGAIN~him :

TWISTEDNESS :

TWISTEDNESS~me :

Uziy'eyl :

BOLDNESS~you(mp) :

Awit :

WICKED | YOKE :

ASCENSION.OFFERING | GO.UP(V)~ing(ms) :

YOKE~him :

ASCENSION.OFFERING~s | GO.UP(V)~ing(fp) | ASCENSION.OFFERING :

ASCENSION.OFFERING~s~ you(ms) :

ASCENSION.OFFERING~s~you(mp) :

GO.UP(V)~ing(mp) :

YOKE~you(mp) :

DISTANT :

ASCENSION.OFFERING :

/ ASCENSION.OFFERING~him :

ASCENSION.OFFERING~you(ms) :

ASCENSION.OFFERING~ them(m) :

STAND(V)~ing(ms) :

STAND(V)~ing(mp) :

OMER | SHEAF :

TWISTEDNESS~her :

TWISTEDNESS~him :

TWISTEDNESS~s :

TWISTEDNESS~s~ you(mp) :

TWISTEDNESS~s~them(m) :

AFFLICTION :

TWISTEDNESS~them(m) :

DO(V)~ing(ms) | DO(V)~ing(fs) :

DO(V)~ing(mp) :
DO(V)~ing(mp) :
FLYER :
Uts :
SKIN :
RAVEN :
SKIN~her :
SKIN~him :
SKIN~s :
SKIN~s~them(m) :
NECK :
BLINDNESS :
STRONG | GOAT :
he~did~LEAVE(V) :
they~did~LEAVE(V) :
you(fp)~did~LEAVE(V) :
you(ms)~did~LEAVE(V)~me :
Ghaza :
>~LEAVE(V) :
BOLDNESS~me :
Azan :
HELP :
HELP~you(ms) :
Atarot :
!(mp)~SERVE(V) :
Eyval :
!(mp)~CROSS.OVER(V) :
Ever~of :
Ever~s :
BLIND :
GOAT~s :
EYE :
Elam :
WITH :
!(mp)~STAND(V) :
BY~me :
WITH~her :
WITH~them(m) :
WITH~him :
WITH~me :
WITH~you(ms) | WITH~you(fs) :
WITH~you(mp) :
WITH~them(m) :
WITH~us :
Eyn-Mishpat :
EYE :
GRAPE~s :

he~did~much~AFFLICT(V) | :
he~did~much~AFFLICT(V)~her | EYE~her
EYE~him :
EYE~s :
EYE~s2 | EYE~s2~me | EYE~me :
EYE~s2~her :
EYE~s2~them(m) :
EYE~s2~him :
EYE~s2 :
EYE~s2~you(ms) :
EYE~s2~you(mp) :
EYE~s2~us :
you(ms)~did~much~AFFLICT(V)~her :
EYE~you(ms) :
Eynan :
ONE.TENTH :
TIRED :
Eyphah :
HARDSHIP~you(fs) :
HEEL~s :
they~did~PLUCK.UP(V) :
CROOKED :
CITY :
Irad :
CITY~her :
CITY~him :
COLT ~him :
NAKED :
NAKED~s :
CITY~them(m) | Iyram :
READY :
Akhbor :
Akhran :
you(mp)~did~DISTURB(V) :
UPON :
LEAF | he~did~GO.UP(V) | !(ms)~GO.UP(V) :
UPON~them(m) :
UPON~them(f) :
!(mp)~GO.UP(V) | they~did~GO.UP(V) :
Alwah | >~GO.UP(V) :
Alwan :
>~GO.UP(V) | GIVE.MILK(V)~ing(fp) :

UPON~me | UPON | !(mp)~GO.UP(V) :עלי
UPON~her :עליה
UPON~them(m) :עליהם
UPON~them(f) :עליהן
UPON~him :עליו
Elyon | UPPER :עליון
UPON~you(ms) :עליך
UPON~you(mp) :עליכם
WORKINGS~s :עלילות
UPON~him :עלימו
UPON~us | we~did~GO.UP(V) :עלינו
you(ms)~did~GO.UP(V) :עלית
you(mp)~did~make~GO.UP(V) :עליתם
UPON~you(mp) :עלכם
she~did~GO.UP(V) :עלתה
PEOPLE :עם
he~did~STAND(V) :עמד
she~did~STAND(V) :עמדה
>~STAND(V)~him :עמדו
you(ms)~did~STAND(V) :עמדת
I~did~STAND(V) :עמדתי
PEOPLE~her :עמה
PEOPLE~him :עמו
PILLAR | >~STAND(V) :עמוד
PILLAR~s :עמודי
PILLAR~s~her :עמודיה
PILLAR~s~them(m) :עמודיהם
PILLAR~s~him :עמודיו
Amon :עמון
Amon~of :עמוני
SUNKEN :עמוק
Ghamorah :עמורה
PEOPLE~me | PEOPLE~s :עמי
Ami'eyl :עמיאל
PEOPLE~s~her :עמיה
Amihud :עמיהוד
PEOPLE~s~him :עמיו
PEOPLE~s~you(ms) :עמיך
PEOPLE~s :עמים
Amiynadav :עמינדב
Amishaddai :עמישדי
NEIGHBOR~him :עמיתו
NEIGHBOR~you(ms) :עמיתך
PEOPLE~you(ms) | PEOPLE~you(fs) :עמך
LABOR :עמל
LABOR ~me :עמלי
LABOR ~us :עמלנו
Amaleq :עמלק
PEOPLE~them(m) :עמם
VALLEY :עמק
Amram :עמרם
GRAPE :ענב
GRAPE~s :ענבים
GRAPE~s~him :ענבמו
Anah | >~much~AFFLICT(V) | he~did~AFFLICT(V) :ענה
GENTLE | !(mp)~ANSWER(V) :ענו
>~FINE(V) :ענוש
>~ANSWER(V) :ענות
>~much~AFFLICT(V)~him :ענותו
>~much~AFFLICT(V)~you(ms) :ענותך
AFFLICTION :עני
AFFLICTION~me :עניי
AFFLICTION~you(fs) :עניך
AFFLICTION~them(m) :ענים
AFFLICTION~us :ענינו
Anam :ענמים
CLOUD :ענן
Anaq :ענק
Anaq~s :ענקים
Aner :ענר
HERB :עשׂב
he~did~DO(V) | !(ms)~DO(V) :עשׂה
he~did~DO(V)~him :עשׂהו
they~did~DO(V) | Esaw | >~DO(V)~him | !(mp)~DO(V) :עשׂו
>~DO(V) :עשׂוה
>~DO(V)~him :עשׂוהו
TENTH.ONE :עשׂור
>~DO(V) :עשׂות
!(fs)~DO(V) :עשׂי
we~did~DO(V) :עשׂינו
TENTH :עשׂירי
TENTH :עשׂירית
you(fs)~did~DO(V) | you(ms)~did~DO(V) :עשׂית
I~did~DO(V) :עשׂיתי
I~did~DO(V)~them(m) :עשׂיתים
/ you(mp)~did~DO(V) :עשׂיתם
you(fp)~did~DO(V) :עשׂיתן
he~did~DO(V)~you(ms) :עשׂך

Eseq :עשק
TEN | >~much~GIVE.A.TENTH(V) :עשר
TEN :עשרה
ONE.TENTH~s :עשרונים
TEN~s :עשרות
TEN~s :עשרים
TEN :עשרת
she~did~DO(V) :עשתה
DIRT :עפר
DIRT~him :עפרו
Ephron :עפרון
TREE :עץ
TREE~her :עצה
NUMEROUS :עצום
>~STOP(V) | STOP(V)~ed(ms) :עצור
COUNSEL~s :עצות
TREE~s :עצי
TREE~s~him :עציו
TREE~s~you(ms) :עציך
TREE~s :עצים
TREE~you(ms) :עצך
BONE :עצם
Atsmon~unto :עצמונה
BONE~s :עצמות
BONE~s~me :עצמותי
BONE~me :עצמי
you(ms)~did~BE.ABUNDANT(V) :עצמת
he~did~STOP(V) :עצר
he~did~STOP(V)~me :עצרני
CONFERENCE :עצרת
HEEL | SINCE :עקב
STRIPED :עקוד
STRIPED~s :עקודים
STERILE :עקר
Aqabariym :עקרבים
STERILE :עקרה
Eyr | Ar :ער
EVENING | he~did~BARTER(V) | MIXTURE :ערב
TOKEN :ערבון
DESERT~s :ערבות
Arad :ערד
HORDE :ערוב
NAKEDNESS :ערוה
SUBTLE :ערום
NUDE~s :ערומים
Aro'eyr :ערוער

NAKEDNESS :ערות
NAKEDNESS~her :ערותה
NAKEDNESS~him :ערותו
NAKEDNESS~you(ms) :ערותך
NAKEDNESS~them(f) :ערותן
CITY~s | Eyriy :ערי
CITY~s~them(m) :עריהם
CITY~s~him :עריו
CITY~s~you(ms) :עריך
CITY~s~you(mp) :עריכם
CITY~s :ערים
BREAD.MEAL~s~you(mp) :עריסותיכם
BREAD.MEAL~s~you(mp) :עריסותכם
BARREN :ערירי
BARREN~s :ערירים
ARRANGEMENT :ערך
ARRANGEMENT~him :ערכו
ARRANGEMENT~you(ms) :ערכך
I~did~ARRANGE(V) :ערכתי
UNCIRCUMCISED :ערל
FORESKIN :ערלה
FORESKIN~s :ערלים
FORESKIN :ערלת
FORESKIN~him :ערלתו
FORESKIN~you(mp) :ערלתכם
FORESKIN~them(m) :ערלתם
MATTRESS :ערש
MATTRESS~him :ערשו
NECK~him :ערפו
NECK~you(ms) :ערפך
OPPRESS(V)~ed(ms) :עשוק
SMOKE | he~did~SMOKE(V) :עשן
SMOKE~him :עשנו
he~did~OPPRESS(V) :עשק
ONE :עשתי
APPOINTED.TIME :עת
NOW :עתה
MALE.GOAT~s :עתודים
PREPARED~s :עתידות
BONNET~s :פארי
Paran :פארן
EDGE :פאת
EDGE~s :פאתי
Pagi'eyl :פגעיאל
I~did~ENCOUNTER(V) :פגשתי

Pedatsur :
Pedah'eyl :
Pedatsur :
>~RANSOM(V) :
REDEEMED~s :
RANSOM :
you(ms)~did~RANSOM(V) :
Padan-Aram~unto :
MOUTH :
HERE :
Potee-Phera :
Putiy'eyl :
Potiphar :
TURN(V)~ing(ms) :
Pu'ah :
REGISTER(V)~ing(ms) | he~did~be~much~REGISTER(V) :
REPRODUCE(V)~ing(ms) :
BURST.OUT(V)~ing(ms) :
BURST.OUT(V)~ing(fs) :
SPREAD.OUT(V)~ing(mp) :
he~did~be~much~SPREAD.OUT(V) :
BE.FRUITFUL(V)~ing(fs) :
INTERPRET(V)~ing(ms) :
AWE~you(ms) :
AWE~you(mp) :
RECKLESS :
WIRE~s :
WIRE~s :
PIT :
BURSTING :
Piy-Hahhiyrot :
MOUTH | MOUTH~me :
FOUL :
CORPSE~s :
CORPSE~s~you(mp) :
RANSOM.PRICE :
SUET~him :
MOUTH~her :
MOUTH~him :
MOUTH~them(m) :
MOUTH~him :
SOOT :
OLIVINE :
BURSTING :
MOUTH~you(ms) :

CONCUBINE :
Pildash :
I~did~much~PLEAD(V) :
Pinon :
CORNER~s~him :
Piynhhas :
I~did~TURN(V) :
LAME :
he~did~much~PEEL(V) :
SEEING :
SEEING~s :
BUD~her :
PRODUCE~her :
PRODUCE~him :
DUNG~her :
DUNG~him :
DUNG~them(m) :
Pishon :
OFFENSE~me :
OFFENSE~s~them(m) :
FLAX~s :
SUDDENLY :
OPEN(V)~ed(mp) :
Pitom :
FRAGMENT~s :
INTERPRETATION~him :
INTERPRETATION~s :
PERFORMANCE :
Peleg :
Palu :
Palti :
Palti'eyl :
ESCAPED~s :
JUDGE~s :
Peleshet~s :
Peleshet :
Pelet :
OTHERWISE :
he~did~TURN(V) :
/ !(mp)~TURN(V) :
Peni'el :
FACE~s | FACE~s~me :
Peni'el :
FACE~s~her :
FACE~s~them(m) :

FACE~s~him :
FACE~s~you(ms) :
FACE~s~you(mp) :
FACE~s :
FACE~s~unto :
he~did~SPREAD.ACROSS(V) :
>~SPREAD.ACROSS(V) :
Pesahh | he~did~HOP(V) :
SCULPTURE~s :
WRIST~s :
SCULPTURE | !(ms)~SCULPT(V) :
she~did~SPREAD.ACROSS(V) :
Pa'u :
MAKE(V)~ed(fs) :
Pe'or :
he~did~MAKE(V) :
DEED~him :
you(ms)~did~MAKE(V) :
BELL :
BELL~s :
FOOTSTEP~s~him :
FOOTSTEP~s2 :
FOOTSTEP~s :
WOUND(V)~ed(ms) :
STRIP :
WOUND :
she~did~PART(V) :
he~did~REGISTER(V) :
they~did~REGISTER(V) :
>~REGISTER(V)~me :
I~did~REGISTER(V) :
>~REGISTER(V) | !(ms)~ REGISTER(V) :
REGISTER(V)~ed(mp) :
REGISTER(V)~ed(mp)~ them(m) :
REGISTER(V)~ed(mp)~him :
REGISTER(V)~ed(mp)~ you(mp) :
OVERSIGHT :
OVERSEER~s :
BULL :
WILD.ASS :
!(ms)~REPRODUCE(V) | COW :
!(mp)~REPRODUCE(V) | they~did~ REPRODUCE(V) :
>~BURST.OUT(V) :

TENT.CURTAIN :
RIP(V)~ed(mp) :
LOOSE(V)~ed(ms) :
COW~s :
he~did~BURST.OUT(V) | BUD :
she~will~BURST.OUT(V) :
PRODUCE :
BULL~s :
Parnakh :
HOOF :
HOOF~s :
LONG.HAIR :
Paroh | he~did~LOOSE(V)~ her :
LONG.HAIR~s :
BREACH | Perets :
you(ms)~did~BREAK.OUT(V) :
/ !(mp)~much~TEAR.OFF(V) :
HORSEMAN~s~him :
HORSEMAN~s :
Perat :
OFFENSE :
FRAGMENT :
OPEN(V)~ed(ms) | >~OPEN(V) :
Petor~unto :
>~CRUMBLE(V) :
OPENING :
CORD :
CORD~s :
ASP~s :
he~did~INTERPRET(V) :
Patros~s :
!(ms)~GO.OUT(V) :
!(mp)~GO.OUT(V) :
>~GO.OUT(V) :
>~GO.OUT(V)~him :
>~GO.OUT(V)~you(ms) :
COVERED :
ARMY :
ARMY~him | they~did~ MUSTER(V) :
ARMY~s :
ARMY~them(m) :
SWELLING :
Tseviim :
Tsedad~unto :

PROVISIONS | he~did~ LAY.IN.WAIT$^{(V)}$:
AMBUSH :
STEADFAST.ONE :
STEADFAST.ONE~s :
STEADFAST :
STEADFASTNESS | she~did~ BE.STEADFAST$^{(V)}$:
YELLOW :
!$^{(ms)}$~much~DIRECT$^{(V)}$:
FLOCKS :
FLOCKS~him :
FLOCKS~me :
FLOCKS~you$^{(ms)}$:
FLOCKS~you$^{(mp)}$:
FLOCKS~them$^{(m)}$:
BACK.OF.THE.NECK~him :
BACK.OF.THE.NECK~s :
BACK.OF.THE.NECK~s~him :
BACK.OF.THE.NECK~you$^{(ms)}$:
GLISTENING :
he~did~be~much~DIRECT$^{(V)}$:
you$^{(ms)}$~did~be~much~DIRECT$^{(V)}$~& :
I~did~be~much~DIRECT$^{(V)}$:
>~much~DIRECT$^{(V)}$~him :
Tsohhar :
LIMP$^{(V)}$~ing$^{(ms)}$:
SPRING.UP$^{(V)}$~ing$^{(fp)}$:
Tso'an :
CRY.OUT$^{(V)}$~ing$^{(mp)}$:
Tso'ar :
Tso'ar~unto :
Tsophim :
SHARP.STONE | Tsur | BOULDER :
Tsuri'eyl :
BOULDER~s :
Tsurishaddai :
Tsurishaddai :
BOULDER~them$^{(m)}$:
PRESS.IN$^{(V)}$~ing$^{(mp)}$~you$^{(ms)}$:
PRESS.IN$^{(V)}$~ing$^{(mp)}$:
LAUGHTER :
she~did~LAUGH$^{(V)}$:
you$^{(fs)}$~did~LAUGH$^{(V)}$:
I~did~LAUGH$^{(V)}$:
ARMY~s :
ARMY~s~me :
ARMY~s~you$^{(mp)}$:
ARMY~s~them$^{(m)}$:
Tsiv'on :
GAME :
PROVISIONS :
Tsidon :
Tsidon~s :
SIDE~s :
SIDE~s~him :
STEADFASTNESS :
STEADFASTNESS~me :
he~did~much~DIRECT$^{(V)}$:
he~did~much~DIRECT$^{(V)}$~him :
I~did~much~DIRECT$^{(V)}$:
I~did~much~DIRECT$^{(V)}$~him :
I~did~much~DIRECT$^{(V)}$~you$^{(ms)}$:
I~did~much~DIRECT$^{(V)}$~them$^{(m)}$:
you$^{(ms)}$~did~much~DIRECT$^{(V)}$~me :
he~did~much~DIRECT$^{(V)}$~you$^{(ms)}$:
he~did~much~DIRECT$^{(V)}$~them$^{(m)}$:
he~did~much~DIRECT$^{(V)}$~us :
he~did~much~DIRECT$^{(V)}$~me :
HUNTER | GAME :
Tsilah :
SHADOW~them$^{(m)}$:
Tsin :
Tsin~unto :
WOVEN.BASKET :
he~did~much~OVERLAY$^{(V)}$:
METAL.PLATING :
BIRD | Tsipor :
Tsiporah :
Tsiphyon :
BIRD~s :
POINT~s~her :
BLOSSOM :
FRINGE :
ROAST :
they~did~BE.OVERSHADOWED$^{(V)}$:

IMAGE~s :
RIB :
RIB~him :
RIB~s :
RIB~s~him :
Tselaph'hhad :
he~did~SPRING.UP(V) :
BRACELET :
BRACELET~s :
WOOL :
WITHER(V)~ed(fp) :
she~did~MARCH(V) :
>~CRY.OUT(V) :
VEIL :
LITTLE.ONE :
CRY | she~did~CRY.OUT(V) :
CRY :
CRY~him :
CRY~them(m) :
Tsepho :
NORTH :
NORTH~unto :
Tsaphnat-Paneyahh :
FROG~s :
NARROW :
SEARING :
INFECT(V)~ed(ms) :
POUCH | >~PRESS.IN(V) :
POUCH~s | PRESS.IN(V)~ed(fp) :
BALM :
NARROW~s~him :
NARROW~s~you(ms) :
NARROW~s~them(m) :
INFECTION :
PERSECUTION :
PERSECUTION~me :
she~did~VOMIT(V) :
!(ms)~HOLLOW.OUT(V)~& :
he~did~HOLLOW.OUT(V)~her :
!(ms)~BURY(V) | >~BURY(V) :
BURIAL.PLACE :
BURIAL.PLACE~her :
BURIAL.PLACE~him :
GRAVE | he~did~BURY(V) :
they~did~BURY(V) | >~BURY(V)~him :

GRAVE~s :
GRAVE~s~us :
I~did~BURY(V) :
STOMACH~her :
UNIQUE :
UNIQUE~s~him :
UNIQUE~s :
she~did~KINDLE(V) :
EAST.WIND :
EAST :
EAST~unto :
Qedeymot :
TOP.OF.THE.HEAD~you(ms) :
TOP.OF.THE.HEAD :
Qadesh | !(ms)~much~SET.APART(V) | PROSTITUTE :
PROSTITUTE | Qadesh~unto :
they~did~SET.APART(V) :
SPECIAL~me | SPECIAL~s :
SPECIAL~s~them(m) :
SPECIAL~s~him :
SPECIAL~s~you(ms) :
SPECIAL~s :
SPECIAL~you(ms) :
ASSEMBLY :
ASSEMBLY :
ASSEMBLY~you(mp) :
Qehat :
>~HOLLOW.OUT(V) :
he~did~be~much~BURY(V) :
SPECIAL :
VOICE :
VOICE~her :
VOICE~him :
VOICE~s :
VOICE~me :
VOICE~you(ms) :
VOICE~them(m) :
VOICE~us :
!(ms)~RISE(V) :
!(mp)~RISE(V)~& :
!(mp)~RISE(V) :
!(fs)~RISE(V) :
VERTICAL :
HANDFUL~him :
HEIGHT~her :
HEIGHT~him :

PURCHASE(V)~ing(ms) :קונה
PURCHASE(V)~ing(ms)~him :קונהו
DIVINE(V)~ing(ms) :קוסם
DIVINE(V)~ing(mp) :קוסמים
BRAMBLE~s :קוצים
Qorahh :קורח
RAFTER~me :קורתי
!(ms)~TAKE(V) :קח
!(ms)~TAKE(V)~& :קחה
!(mp)~TAKE(V) :קחו
!(ms)~TAKE(V)~them(m) :קחם
>~TAKE(V)~you(fs) :קחתך
I~did~BE.SMALL(V) :קטונתי
Qeturah | INCENSE.SMOKE :קטורה
INCENSE.SMOKE :קטורת
SMALL :קטן
SMALL :קטנה
GRAVE~him | !(mp)~BURY(V) :קיברו
Qivrot-Hata'awah :קיברות-התאוה
they~did~much~FACE.TOWARD(V) :קידמו
EASTWARD :קידמת
you(mp)~did~much~SET.APART(V) :קידשתם
I~did~much~BOUND.UP(V) :קיויתי
SMOKING :קיטור
Qayin :קיין
he~did~much~BELITTLE(V) :קילל
ANNOYANCE :קיללת
ANNOYANCE~you(ms) :קיללתך
he~did~much~BE.ZEALOUS(V) :קינא
ZEALOUSNESS :קינאה
they~did~much~BE.ZEALOUS(V)~me :קינאוני
ZEALOUSNESS~me :קינאתי
NEST~him :קינו
NEST~s :קינים
MATERIAL :קינין
MATERIAL~him :קינינו
NEST~you(ms) :קינך
Qeynan :קינן
EXTREMITY~s~him :קיצוותוו
WALL :קיר
!(fp)~CALL.OUT(V) | :קיראן
INSIDE~him | !(mp)~COME.NEAR(V) :קירבו
INSIDE~them(f) :קירבנה
WALL~s~him :קירותיו
METROPOLIS :קיריה
Qiryat-Arba :קירית-הארבע
METROPOLIS :קירית
Qiryatayim :קיריתיים
they~did~BELITTLE(V) :קלו
DRY(V)~ed(ms) :קלוי
ANNOYANCE :קללה
SLING~s :קלעי
SLING~s :קלעים
he~did~RISE(V) :קם
she~did~RISE(V) :קמה
they~did~RISE(V) :קמו
Qemu'el :קמואל
GRAIN.FLOUR :קמח
RISE(V)~ing(mp)~him :קמיו
RISE(V)~ing(mp)~you(ms) :קמיך
GRAIN.STALK :קמת
you(mp)~did~RISE(V) :קמתם
NEST :קן
ZEALOUS :קנא
ZEALOUSNESS~s :קנאות
he~did~PURCHASE(V) | !(ms)~PURCHASE(V) :קנה
he~did~PURCHASE(V)~him :קנהו
>~PURCHASE(V) :קנוה
Qenaz :קנז
STALK~s :קני
STALK~s :קנים
you(ms)~did~PURCHASE(V) :קנית
I~did~PURCHASE(V) :קניתי
he~did~PURCHASE(V)~you(ms) :קנך
Qenat :קנת
JUG :קסות
QESHIYTAH :קסיטה
DIVINATION :קסם
DIVINATION~s :קסמים
TATTOO :קעקע
PLATTER~s :קערות
PLATTER~s~him :קערותיו
PLATTER :קערת
they~did~CURDLE(V) :קפאו
CONCLUSION :קץ
EXTREMITY | he~did~LOATHE(V) :קצה

EXTREMITY~him :קצהו
EXTREMITY~s :קצות
EXTREMITY~s~him :קצותיו
HARVEST :קציר
HARVEST~her :קצירה
HARVEST~you(ms) :קצירך
HARVEST~you(mp) :קצירכם
he~did~SNAP(V) | SPLINTER :קצף
I~will~LOATHE(V) :קצתי
he~did~CALL.OUT(V) | MEETING :קרא
she~did~CALL.OUT(V) :קראה
>~CALL.OUT(V)~us :קראנו
I~did~CALL.OUT(V) :קראתי
I~did~CALL.OUT(V)~you(ms) :קראתיך
he~did~COME.NEAR(V) | !(ms)~ COME.NEAR(V) :קרב
she~did~COME.NEAR(V) :קרבה
they~did~COME.NEAR(V) :קרבו
INSIDE~s :קרבים
DONATION :קרבן
DONATION~her :קרבנה
DONATION~him :קרבנו
DONATION~me :קרבני
DONATION~s~them(m) :קרבניהם
DONATION~you(ms) :קרבנך
DONATION~you(mp) :קרבנכם
DONATION~them(m) :קרבנם
you(ms)~did~COME.NEAR(V) :קרבת
CALL.OUT(V)~ed(mp) :קרואי
NEAR :קרוב
NEAR :קרובה
NEAR~him :קרובו
NEAR~s :קרובים
BALD :קרח
BALD.SPOT :קרחה
CONTRARY :קרי
SELECTED~s :קריאי
he~did~MEET(V)~you(ms) :קרך
he~did~HAVE.HORNS(V) :קרן
HORN~s :קרנות
HORN~s~him :קרנותיו
HORN~s~him :קרניו
HOOK~s :קרסי
HOOK~s~him :קרסיו
they~did~TEAR(V) :קרעו
BOARD :קרש
BOARD~s :קרשי
BOARD~s~him :קרשיו
BOARD~s :קרשים
STUBBLE :קש
HARD :קשה
TIE(V)~ed(fs) :קשורה
HARD~s :קשות
STUBBORNNESS :קשי
BOW :קשת
she~did~BE.HARD(V) :קשתה
BOW~him :קשתו
BOW~me :קשתי
!(ms)~SEE(V) | he~did~SEE(V) :ראה
they~did~SEE(V) | >~SEE(V) | !(mp)~ SEE(V) :ראו
Re'uven :ראובן
>~SEE(V) :ראוה
Re'umah :ראומה
>~SEE(V) :ראות
>~SEE(V)~me :ראותי
>~SEE(V)~you(ms) :ראותך
we~did~SEE(V) :ראינו
you(ms)~did~SEE(V) :ראית
I~did~SEE(V) :ראיתי
I~did~SEE(V)~him :ראיתיו
you(mp)~did~SEE(V) :ראיתם
he~did~SEE(V)~them(m) | RHINOCEROS :ראם
Ramot :ראמות
HEAD~s :ראשי
HEAD~s~them(m) :ראשיהם
HEAD~s~you(mp) :ראשיכם
HEAD~s :ראשים
PRIME :ראשית
PRIME~them(m) :ראשיתם
she~did~SEE(V) :ראתה
ABUNDANT :רב
MYRIAD :רבבה
ABUNDANT | she~did~ INCREASE.IN.NUMBER(V) :רבה
they~did~DISPUTE(V) :רבו
BE.SQUARE(V)~ed(ms) :רבוע
ABUNDANT | >~INCREASE(V) :רבות
NECKLACE :רביד
ABUNDANT~s :רבים
FOURTH :רביעי
FOURTH :רביעית
QUARTER | Reva :רבע

he~did~STRETCH.OUT(V) : רבץ
>~KILL.BY.STONING(V) : רגום
SHAKING : רגז
FOOT : רגל
FOOT~her : רגלה
FOOT~him : רגלו
ON.FOOT : רגלי
FOOT~s~her : רגליה
FOOT~s2~them(m) : רגליהם
FOOT~s2~him : רגליו
FOOT~s2 : רגליים
FOOT~s2~you(ms) : רגליך
FOOT~s2~you(mp) : רגליכם
FOOT~s : רגלים
FOOT~you(ms) : רגלך
FOOT~you(mp) : רגלכם
FOOT~them(m) : רגלם
MOMENT : רגע
!(ms)~GO.DOWN(V) : רד
!(ms)~GO.DOWN(V)~& : רדה
!(mp)~GO.DOWN(V) : רדו
!(ms)~PURSUE(V) : רדוף
they~did~PURSUE(V) : רדפו
they~did~PURSUE(V)~you(ms) : רדפוך
>~GO.DOWN(V) : רדת
SEE(V)~ing(ms) : רואה
SEE(V)~ing(fp) : רואות
SEE(V)~ing(ms)~me : רואי
SEE(V)~ing(mp) : רואים
HEAD | VENOM : רואש
HEAD~her : רואשה
HEAD~him : רואשו
HEAD~me : רואשי
HEAD~you(ms) : רואשך
HEAD~you(mp) : רואשכם
HEAD~them(m) : רואשם
ABUNDANCE : רוב
INCREASE(V)~ing(ms) : רובה
FOURTH.PART : רובע
STRETCH.OUT(V)~ing(ms) : רובץ
STRETCH.OUT(V)~ing(mp) : רובצים
STRETCH.OUT(V)~ing(fs) : רובצת
PURSUE(V)~ing(ms) : רודף
WIND : רוח
WIDTH : רוחב
WIND~him : רוחו
WIND~me : רוחי
RIDE(V)~ing(ms) : רוכב
RIDE(V)~ing(ms)~him : רוכבו
>~RAISE.UP(V) : רום
SPEAR : רומח
TREAD(V)~ing(ms) : רומס
DYSFUNCTIONAL : רוע
FEED(V)~ing(ms) | FEED(V)~ing(fs) : רועה
FEED(V)~ing(mp) | FEED(V)~ing(mp)~me : רועי
FEED(V)~ing(mp)~you(ms) : רועיך
FEED(V)~ing(mp) : רועים
HEAL(V)~ing(ms)~you(ms) : רופאך
MURDER(V)~ing(ms) : רוצח
SPICE.MIXTURE | COMPOUND(V)~ing(ms) : רוקח
EMBROIDER(V)~ing(ms) : רוקם
VENOM : רוש
LEAN : רזה
WIDTH~her : רחבה
WIDTH~him : רחבו
WIDE : רחבת
Rehhov : רחוב
STREET~unto : רחובה
Rehhovot-Ghir : רחובות־עיר
Rehhovot : רחובות
COMPASSIONATE : רחום
DISTANCE : רחוקה
MILLSTONE~s : רחיים
Rahhel : רחל
EWE~s~you(ms) : רחליך
EWE~s : רחלים
BOWELS : רחם
BOWELS~her : רחמה
BOWELS~s~him : רחמיו
BOWELS~s : רחמים
he~did~BATHE(V) : רחץ
FIRST : ריאשון
FIRST : ריאשונה
FIRST~s : ריאשונים
DISPUTE : ריב
MYRIAD~s : ריבבות
DISPUTE~s : ריבות
FOURTH.GENERATION~s : ריבעים
Rivqah : ריבקה
>~GO.DOWN(V)~her : רידתה
AROMA : ריח

AROMA~us :ריחנו
VEHICLE~him :ריכבו
POMEGRANATE~s :רימוני
you(ms)~did~much~ :רימיתני
THROW.DOWN(V)~me
FLAT :ריקועי
EMPTINESS :ריקם
LOST~him :רישעו
WAYWARDNESS~him :רישעתו
TENDER :רך
VEHICLE :רכב
you(ms)~did~RIDE(V) :רכבת
GOODS :רכוש
GOODS~him :רכושו
GOODS~them(m) :רכושם
TENDER~s :רכות
TALEBEARER :רכיל
TENDER~s :רכים
/ he~did~ACCUMULATE(V) :רכש
they~did~ACCUMULATE(V) :רכשו
/ RAISE.UP(V)~ing(ms) :רם
RAISED~ing(fs) | he~did~ :רמה
THROW.DOWN(V)
TREADER :רמס
Resen :רסן
DYSFUNCTIONAL :רע
HUNGER :רעב
FAMINE :רעבון
SHAKING.IN.FEAR :רעד
DYSFUNCTIONAL :רעה
COMPANION~him :רעהו
!(mp)~FEED(V) :רעו
Re'u'eyl :רעואל
DYSFUNCTIONAL~s :רעות
FRIEND~her :רעותה
DYSFUNCTIONAL~s :רעים
COMPANION~you(ms) :רעך
Ramah :רעמה
Ra'meses :רעמסס
FLOURISHING :רענן
DYSFUNCTIONAL :רעת
DYSFUNCTIONAL~him :רעתו
!(ms)~HEAL(V) :רפא
Rapha~s :רפאים
Raphu :רפוא
he~did~RUN(V) :רץ
ACCEPT(V)~ed(ms) :רצוי

SELF-WILL :רצון
ONLY | EMPTY :רק
SHEET :רקיע
Reqem :רקם
he~did~FLOW.OUT(V) :רר
!(ms)~POSSESS(V) :רש
LOST :רשע
SPARK :רשף
NETTING :רשת
Sha'ul | >~INQUIRE(V) | :שאול
UNDERWORLD
UNDERWORLD ~unto :שאולה
he~did~INQUIRE(V) | !(ms)~ :שאל
INQUIRE(V)
you(ms)~did~INQUIRE(V) :שאלת
KIN :שאר
REMAINS~her | KIN :שארה
KIN~him :שארו
REMNANT :שארית
he~did~TURN.BACK(V) | !(ms)~ :שב
SETTLE(V)
Sheva :שבא
!(ms)~SETTLE(V)~& | she~did~ :שבה
TURN.BACK(V)
!(mp)~SETTLE(V) | they~did~ :שבו
CAPTURE(V) | AGATE
WEEK :שבוע
SWEARING :שבועה
WEEK~s :שבועות
WEEK~s2 :שבועיים
SWEARING :שבועת
CRACK(V)~ed(ms) :שבור
CAPTIVITY~you(ms) :שבותך
STAFF :שבט
STAFF~s~you(ms) :שבטיך
!(fs)~SETTLE(V) | CAPTIVE :שבי
we~did~TURN.BACK(V) :שבנו
SEVEN :שבע
GRAIN.SEEDS | SHATTERING :שבר
he~did~CEASE(V) | CEASING | >~ :שבת
SETTLE(V)
she~did~CEASE(V) :שבתה
REST.PERIOD :שבתון
CEASING~s :שבתות
CEASING~s~me :שבתותי
CEASING~s~her :שבתותיה
CEASING~you(mp) :שבתכם

you(mp)~did~TURN.BACK(V) :
he~did~ERR(V) :
ERROR :
BIRTH :
BLAST(V)~ed(fp) :
Shaddai :
Shedeyur :
BREAST~s2 :
FALSENESS :
DRAW.WATER(V)~ing(ms) :
INQUIRE(V)~ing(ms) :
>~TURN.BACK(V) | !(ms)~ TURN.BACK(V) :
!(ms)~TURN.BACK(V)~& :
>~TURN.BACK(V)~him | !(mp)~ TURN.BACK(V) :
!(fs)~TURN.BACK(V) :
>~TURN.BACK(V)~you(ms) :
Shoval :
EXCHANGE(V)~ing(mp) :
Shaweh :
ONYX :
Shu'ahh :
BRIBE :
OFFICER ~ing(mp) :
OFFICER ~ing(mp)~him :
LIE.DOWN(V)~ing(ms) :
DWELL(V)~ing(ms) :
DWELL(V)~ing(ms)~me :
SEND(V)~ing(ms) :
they~did~be~much~SEND(V) :
TABLE :
HEM~s :
HEM~s~him :
HEAR(V)~ing(ms) :
HEAR(V)~ing(mp) :
HEAR(V)~ing(fs) :
SAFEGUARD(V)~ing(ms) :
SAFEGUARD(V)~ing(mp) :
SAFEGUARD(V)~ing(mp) :
Shuni :
SPLIT.IN.TWO(V)~ing(fs) :
Shu'a :
OUTCRY~them(m) :
DECIDE(V)~ing(mp) :
DECIDE(V)~ing(mp)~ you(mp) :

DECIDE(V)~ing(mp) :
POUR.OUT(V)~ing(ms) | POUR.OUT(V)~ed(ms) :
POUR.OUT(V)~ing(ms)~him :
Shophan :
RAM.HORN :
THIGH :
Shur | OX | ROCK.WALL :
OX~him :
OX~you(ms) | OX~s~you(ms) :
ROOT :
Shutelahh :
COAL :
BOILS :
DUST.CLOUD~s :
>~much~DAMAGE(V) :
they~did~GO(V) :
>~SPREAD(V) :
he~did~FLUSH(V) :
STAFF~s :
STAFF~s~you(mp) :
CAPTIVE~her :
CAPTIVE~him :
EAR.OF.GRAIN~s :
SEVEN | Shivah :
SEVEN~s :
SEVEN :
SEVENTH.TIME~ s2 :
he~did~much~CRACK(V) :
!(mp)~EXCHANGE(V) | GRAIN.SEEDS~him :
GRAIN.SEEDS~them(m) :
you(ms)~did~CRACK(V) :
CEASING~him :
ERROR~him :
ERROR~them(m) :
he~did~much~DAMAGE(V) :
ACACIA~s :
!(ms)~LIE.DOWN(V)~& :
!(fs)~LIE.DOWN(V) :
LYING.DOWN :
they~did~much~ BE.CHILDLESS(V) :
you(mp)~will~much~ BE.CHILDLESS(V) :
SHOULDER~her :

SHOULDER~him :
SHOULDER~them(m) :
TRANQUILITY :
SEND.OFF~s~her :
he~did~much~SEND(V) :
!(ms)~SEND(V)~& | he~did~ much~SEND(V)~her :
!(mp)~SEND(V) :
we~did~much~SEND(V) :
you(ms)~did~much~ SEND(V)~me :
you(mp)~did~much~ MAKE.RESTITUTION(V) :
THREE.DAYS.AGO :
THIRD.GENERATION~s :
SAFEGUARDING~s :
TITLE~you(ms) :
!(mp)~HEAR(V) :
Shimon :
REPORT~you(ms) :
Shinav :
TOOTH ~him :
TOOTH ~s~them(m) :
TOOTH ~s :
Shinar :
MAID :
MAID~s~him :
MAID :
MAID~her :
MAID~him :
MAID~me :
MAID~you(fs) :
Shaphtan :
Shiphrah :
FILTHINESS~s~ them(m) :
!(mp)~SING(V) :
!(mp)~SWARM(V) :
SIX :
SIXTH :
SIX~s :
>~SET.DOWN(V)~me :
he~did~LIE.DOWN(V) :
COPULATION~him :
I~did~LIE.DOWN(V) :
COPULATION~you(ms) :
>~LIE.DOWN(V) :

>~FORGET(V) :
I~did~BE.CHILDLESS(V) :
!(ms)~DWELL(V) :
I~did~FORGET(V) :
I~did~BE.CHILDLESS(V) :
SHOULDER | Shekhem :
Shekhem~unto :
he~did~DWELL(V) :
DWELLER~s~him :
LIQUOR :
!(ms)~CAST.OFF(V) :
Sheylah :
>~SEND(V) :
SEND(V)~ing(fs) | SEND(V)~ed(fs) :
COMPLETENESS :
Shelomiy :
Shelumi'eyl :
Sh'lomiyt :
COMPLETENESS~them(m) :
PULL.OUT(V)~ed(fs) :
THREE :
THREE :
THREE~s :
THREE :
!(ms)~much~SEND(V) | he~did~ :
SEND(V) | Shelahh | !(ms)~SEND(V) | >~ much~SEND(V)
she~did~SEND(V) | >~much~ SEND(V)~her :
he~did~SEND(V)~him :
!(mp)~SEND(V)~me :
>~SEND(V)~you(ms) :
>~much~SEND(V)~them(m) :
!(ms)~much~SEND(V)~me | he~did~SEND(V)~me :
you(ms)~did~SEND(V) :
I~did~SEND(V) :
I~did~SEND(V)~you(ms) :
you(mp)~did~SEND(V) :
you(ms)~did~SEND(V)~us :
you(ms)~did~SEND(V)~me :
THIRD :
LIEUTENANT~s~him :
THIRD :
SPOIL :
SPOIL~her :

Shalem | COMPLETENESS | >~ much~MAKE.RESTITUTION(V) : שלם
COMPLETENESS : שלמה
COMPLETENESS~s : שלמות
OFFERING.OF.RESTITUTION~s : שלמי
OFFERING.OF.RESTITUTION~s~them(m) : שלמיהם
OFFERING.OF.RESTITUTION~s~him : שלמיו
OFFERING.OF.RESTITUTION~s~you(ms) : שלמיך
OFFERING.OF.RESTITUTION~s~you(mp) : שלמיכם
COMPLETENESS~s | OFFERING.OF.RESTITUTION~s : שלמים
Sheleph : שלף
THREE : שלש
THREE~you(mp) : שלשתכם
THREE~them(m) : שלשתם
THERE | TITLE | Shem : שם
TITLE~her | THERE~unto | Sham'mah : שמה
TITLE~him : שמו
Shemu'eyl : שמואל
>~RELEASE(V) : שמוט
EIGHT : שמונה
EIGHT~s : שמונים
EIGHT : שמונת
>~HEAR(V) | Shamu'a : שמוע
>~SAFEGUARD(V) : שמור
TITLE~s : שמות
TITLE~s~them(m) : שמותם
TITLE~me : שמי
SKY~s2~him : שמיו
RELEASE : שמיטה
SKY~s2 : שמיים
SKY~s2~you(ms) : שמייך
SKY~s2~you(mp) : שמייכם
TITLE~you(ms) : שמך
TITLE~them(m) : שמם
DESOLATE : שממה
OIL : שמן
OIL | OIL~her : שמנה
you(fs)~did~GROW.FAT(V) : שמנת
he~did~HEAR(V) | !(ms)~HEAR(V) | REPORT : שמע
they~did~HEAR(V) | >~ HEAR(V)~him : שמעו
!(mp)~HEAR(V)~me : שמעוני
!(fp)~HEAR(V) : שמען
!(ms)~HEAR(V)~us | we~did~ HEAR(V) : שמענו
!(ms)~HEAR(V)~me : שמעני
you(ms)~did~HEAR(V) : שמעת
I~did~HEAR(V) : שמעתי
I~did~HEAR(V)~you(ms) : שמעתיך
you(mp)~did~HEAR(V) : שמעתם
he~did~SAFEGUARD(V) | !(ms)~ SAFEGUARD(V) : שמר
they~did~SAFEGUARD(V) : שמרו
SUN : שמש
TOOTH : שן
YEAR : שנה
YEAR~s : שנות
I~did~WHET(V) : שנותי
SECOND | TWO | YEAR~s | SCARLET : שני
TWO~them(m) : שניהם
YEAR~s~him : שניו
SECOND ~s | TWO : שניים
TWO~you(mp) : שניכם
YEAR~s | TWO : שנים
TWO~us : שנינו
SECOND : שנית
YEAR : שנת
YEAR~her : שנתה
YEAR~him : שנתו
SNOOZE~me : שנתי
YEAR~s2 : שנתיים
SPLITTING : שסע
he~did~LOOK.WITH.RESPECT(V) : שעה
LINSEY-WOOLSEY : שעטנז
GATE : שער
GATE~s~you(ms) : שעריך
SHA'AR~s : שערים
Shepho : שפו
>~DECIDE(V) : שפוט
Shaphat : שפט
JUDGMENT~s : שפטים
BARE.PLACE : שפי
ADDER : שפיפון

POUR.OUT(V)~ing(ms) | he~did~POUR.OUT(V) :שפך
she~did~POUR.OUT(V) | PENIS :שפכה
LOW :שפל
Shepham~unto :שפמה
ABOUNDING :שפע
BRIGHT | Shapher :שפר
ALMOND :שקדים
SHEQEL :שקל
SHEQEL~s :שקלים
SPOT~s :שקערורות
FILTHY | >~much~DETEST(V) :שקץ
FALSE :שקר
SWARMER :שרץ
they(m)~did~SWARM(V) :שרצו
CHAIN~s :שרשות
CHAIN~s :שרשרות
LINEN | SIX :שש
Sheyshai :ששי
SIX :ששת
Shet | he~did~SET.DOWN(V) :שת
!(ms)~GULP(V) | he~did~GULP(V) :שתה
they~did~SET.DOWN(V) :שתו
WIDE.OPEN(V) :שתום
TWO :שתי
TWO :שתיים
TWO :שתים
I~did~GULP(V) :שתיתי
you(mp)~did~GULP(V) :שתיתם
he~did~SET.DOWN(V)~them(m) :שתם
you(ms)~will~much~PERISH(V) :תאבדו
you(ms)~will~much~PERISH(V)~must :תאבדון
you(ms)~will~GATHER.FOOD(V) :תאגור
YEARNING | she~will~much~YEARN(V) :תאוה
TWIN~s :תאומים
you(ms)~will~SPIT.UPON(V) :תאור
YEARNING :תאות
you(ms)~will~much~DELAY(V) :תאחר
you(mp)~will~DELAY(V) :תאחרו
she~will~be~EAT(V) :תאכל
you(ms)~will~make~SECURE(V) :תאמין
you(ms)~will~much~BE.STRONG(V) :תאמץ
FIG :תאנה
you(ms)~will~GATHER(V) :תאסוף
she~will~be~GATHER(V) | you(ms)~will~be~GATHER(V) :תאסף
she~will~be~BAKE(V) :תאפה
they(f)~will~be~BAKE(V) :תאפינה
you(ms)~will~make~PROLONG(V) :תאריך
you(mp)~will~make~PROLONG(V) :תאריכו
you(mp)~will~make~PROLONG(V)~must :תאריכון
you(ms)~will~much~BETROTH(V) :תארס
you(ms)~will~make~SEPARATE(V) :תבדיל
you(ms)~will~COME(V) | she~will~COME(V) :תבוא
you(mp)~will~COME(V) :תבואו
PRODUCTION~s :תבואות
they(f)~will~COME(V) :תבואן
PRODUCTION :תבואת
PRODUCTION~her | she~will~COME(V)~& :תבואתה
PRODUCTION~him :תבואתו
PRODUCTION~you(ms) :תבואתך
PRODUCTION~s~him :תבואתנו
you(ms)~will~PLUNDER(V) :תבוז
INTELLIGENCE :תבונה
she~will~be~much~BOIL(V) :תבושל
you(ms)~will~make~COME(V) | she~will~make~COME(V) :תביא
you(mp)~will~make~COME(V) :תביאו
they(f)~will~make~COME(V) :תביאינה
you(ms)~will~make~COME(V)~them(m) :תביאמו
you(ms)~will~make~COME(V)~her :תביאנה
you(ms)~will~make~COME(V)~him :תביאנו
you(ms)~will~make~STARE(V) :תביט
UNNATURAL.MIX :תבל
CATARACT :תבלול
STRAW :תבן
PATTERN :תבנית
you(ms)~will~much~BURN(V) :תבער
Taveyrah :תבערה

you(mp)~will~much~BURN(V) : תבערו
you(ms)~will~much~SEARCH.OUT(V) : תבקש
you(mp)~will~much~SEARCH.OUT(V) : תבקשו
you(ms)~will~SEARCH.OUT(V)~her : תבקשנה
you(ms)~will~much~SEARCH.OUT(V)~him : תבקשנו
you(ms)~will~much~KNEEL(V) : תברך
you(mp)~will~much~KNEEL(V) : תברכו
she~will~much~KNEEL(V)~you(ms) : תברככ
you(ms)~will~much~KNEEL(V)~him : תברכנו
she~will~much~KNEEL(V)~me : תברכני
you(ms)~will~much~BOIL(V) : תבשל
you(mp)~will~much~BOIL(V) : תבשלו
VESSEL : תבת
you(mp)~will~much~CUT.DOWN(V)~must : תגדעון
you(ms)~will~SHEAR(V) : תגוז
you(ms)~will~BE.AFRAID(V) : תגור
you(mp)~will~BE.AFRAID(V) : תגורו
she~will~make~TOUCH(V) : תגיע
you(ms)~will~much~REMOVE.THE.COVER(V) : תגלה
you(ms)~will~much~SPEAK(V) : תדבר
you(ms)~will~much~SPEAK(V)~must : תדברון
you(ms)~will~KNOW(V) : תדע
you(mp)~will~KNOW(V) : תדעו
you(mp)~will~KNOW(V)~must : תדעון
she~will~make~SPROUT(V) : תדשא
you(ms)~will~GIVE.HONOR(V) : תהדר
DEEP.WATER : תהום
DEEP.WATER~s : תהומות
she~will~EXIST(V) : תהי
ADORATION~s : תהילות
ADORATION~you(ms) : תהילתכ
UPSIDE.DOWN~s : תהפוכות
you(ms)~will~KILL(V)~him : תהרגנו
you(ms)~will~KILL(V) : תהרוג
they(m)~will~KILL(V) : תהרוגו
you(ms)~will~CAST.DOWN(V) : תהרוס
you(ms)~will~much~CAST.DOWN(V)~them(m) : תהרסמ
she~will~PERISH(V) : תואבד
you(ms)~will~PERISH(V)~must | you(mp)~will~PERISH(V)~must : תואבדונ
she~will~CONSENT(V) | you(ms)~will~CONSENT(V) : תואבה
you(mp)~will~CONSENT(V) : תואבו
you(ms)~will~EAT(V) | she~will~EAT(V) : תואכל
you(mp)~will~EAT(V) : תואכלו
you(mp)~will~EAT(V)~him : תואכלהו
you(mp)~will~EAT(V)~them(m) : תואכלומ
you(ms)~will~EAT(V)~must : תואכלונ
you(ms)~will~EAT(V)~them(m) : תואכלמ
you(ms)~will~EAT(V)~her : תואכלנה
you(ms)~will~EAT(V)~him | she~will~EAT(V)~us : תואכלנו
BE.DOUBLE(V)~ing(mp) : תואמימ
you(ms)~will~SAY(V) | she~will~SAY(V) : תואמר
you(mp)~will~SAY(V) : תואמרו
you(ms)~will~SAY(V)~must : תואמרונ
you(mp)~will~make~ADD(V)~must : תואסיפונ
you(mp)~will~BAKE(V) : תואפו
FORM : תואר
Tuval-Qayin : תובל-קייננ
THANKS : תודה
THANKS : תודת
CONFUSION : תוהו
MIDST : תוכ
MIDST~him | they~did~be~much~SIT.DOWN(V) : תוכו
you(ms)~will~make~REBUKE(V) : תוכיח
you(ms)~will~BE.ABLE(V) : תוכל
BIRTHING~s : תולדות
BIRTHING~s~them(m) : תולדותמ
you(ms)~will~make~BRING.FORTH(V) : תוליד
Tola : תולע
KERMES~s : תולעימ
KERMES : תולעת
>~BE.WHOLE(V) : תומ
Tumiyim~you(ms) : תומיכ
TWIN~s : תומימ

>~be~BE.WHOLE(V)~them(m) : תומם
you(ms)~will~make~SUPPRESS(V) : תונה
you(mp)~will~make~SUPPRESS(V) : תונו
you(ms)~will~make~SUPPRESS(V)~him : תוננו
she~will~make~ADD(V) | you(ms)~will~make~ADD(V) : תוסיף
you(mp)~will~make~ADD(V) : תוסיפו
you(mp)~will~make~ADD(V)~must : תוסיפון
she~will~make~ADD(V) | you(ms)~will~make~ADD(V) : תוסף
DISGUSTING : תועבה
DISGUSTING~s~them(m) : תועבתם
DISGUSTING : תועבת
WANDER(V)~ing(ms) : תועה
COOKED~s : תופיני
Tophel : תופל
SEIZE.HOLD(V)~ing(ms) : תופס
SEIZE.HOLD(V)~ing(mp) : תופסי
she~will~make~GO.OUT(V) : תוצא
GOINGS~s : תוצאות
GOINGS~s~him : תוצאותיו
you(ms)~will~make~GO.OUT(V) : תוציא
you(mp)~will~make~GO.OUT(V) : תוציאו
she~will~be~make~SMOLDER(V) : תוקד
TURTLEDOVE : תור
TEACHING : תורה
TEACHING~s~him : תורותיו
TURTLEDOVE~s : תורים
you(mp)~will~make~POSSESS(V) : תורישו
she~will~make~POSSESS(V)~them(m) : תורישמו
TEACHING : תורת
SETTLER : תושב
you(mp)~will~make~LEAVE.BEHIND(V) : תותירו
you(ms)~will~make~LEAVE.BEHIND(V) : תותר
she~will~ISSUE(V) : תזוב
you(mp)~will~make~REMEMBER(V) : תזכירו
she~will~make~SOW(V) : תזריע
you(ms)~will~KNOCK(V) : תחבוט
you(ms)~will~TAKE.AS.A.PLEDGE(V) : תחבול
you(mp)~will~HOLD.A.FEAST(V) : תחגוהו
she~will~UNITE(V) : תחד
you(ms)~will~TERMINATE(V) : תחדל
you(ms)~will~HOLD.A.FEAST(V) : תחוג
you(mp)~will~HOLD.A.FEAST(V) : תחוגו
you(ms)~will~SPARE(V) | she~will~SPARE(V) : תחוס
you(ms)~will~PERCEIVE(V) : תחזה
you(mp)~will~SEIZE(V) : תחזקו
she~will~FAIL(V) : תחטא
you(mp)~will~FAIL(V) : תחטאו
you(ms)~will~make~FAIL(V) : תחטיא
you(ms)~will~much~LIVE(V) : תחיה
you(mp)~will~much~LIVE(V)~must : תחיון
she~will~be~DRILL(V) | you(ms)~will~make~DRILL(V) : תחל
SICK~s~her : תחלואיה
you(ms)~will~much~DRILL(V) : תחלל
you(mp)~will~much~DRILL(V) : תחללו
you(ms)~will~much~DRILL(V)~him : תחללנו
you(ms)~will~be~EXTRACT(V) : תחלצו
she~will~be~DISTRIBUTE(V) : תחלק
you(ms)~will~CRAVE(V) : תחמוד
you(ms)~will~SHOW.PITY(V) : תחמול
you(mp)~will~CAMP(V) : תחנו
you(mp)~will~make~BE.FILTHY(V) : תחניפו
you(ms)~will~PROVIDE.PROTECTION(V)~them(m) : תחנם
you(ms)~will~MUZZLE(V) : תחסום
you(ms)~will~DIMINISH(V) : תחסר
you(mp)~will~HASTEN(V) : תחפזו
you(ms)~will~HEW(V) : תחצוב
COLLAR : תחרא
you(ms)~will~SCRATCH(V) : תחרוש
you(ms)~will~make~PERFORATE(V) : תחרים
you(ms)~will~make~PERFORATE(V)~them(m) : תחרימם
you(mp)~will~make~KEEP.SILENT(V)~must : תחרישון
Tahhash | BADGER : תחש
she~will~be~THINK(V) : תחשב

BADGER~s : תחשים
UNDER | you(ms)~will~ BE.SHATTERED(V) : תחת
UNDER~s~her : תחתיה
UNDER~s~them(m) : תחתיהם
UNDER~him | UNDER~s~him : תחתיו
LOWER.PART~s : תחתיים
UNDER~s~you(ms) : תחתיך
LOWER.PART : תחתית
UNDER~them(m) : תחתם
UNDER~her : תחתנה
you(ms)~will~make~EXTEND(V) : תטה
you(ms)~will~much~BE.DIRTY(V) : תטמא
you(mp)~will~much~ BE.DIRTY(V) : תטמאו
you(ms)~will~FADE(V) : תיבול
you(mp)~will~be~ WATCH.OVER(V) : תיבחנו
she~will~SWALLOW(V)~ them(m) : תיבלעמו
she~will~SWALLOW(V)~ us : תיבלענו
you(ms)~will~BUILD(V) | she~ will~be~BUILD(V) : תיבנה
you(ms)~will~FENCE.IN(V) : תיבצור
you(mp)~will~FENCE.IN(V) : תיבצרו
you(ms)~will~PUSH(V) : תיגוס
you(ms)~will~ PLUCK.AWAY(V) : תיגזול
you(ms)~will~be~ REMOVE.THE.COVER(V) : תיגלה
you(mp)~will~YIELD(V) : תיגמלו
you(ms)~will~STEAL(V) : תיגנוב
you(ms)~will~STEAL(V) : תיגנובו
she~will~TOUCH(V) : תיגע
you(mp)~will~TOUCH(V) : תיגעו
she~will~CAST.AWAY(V) : תיגעל
you(ms)~will~TAKE.AWAY(V) : תיגרע
you(mp)~will~TAKE.AWAY(V) : תיגרעו
you(mp)~will~DRAW.NEAR(V) : תיגשו
you(ms)~will~ADHERE(V) : תידבק
you(mp)~will~ADHERE(V)~ must : תידבקון
she~will~ADHERE(V)~ me : תידבקני
you(ms)~will~MAKE.A.VOW(V) : תידור
you(mp)~will~MAKE.A.VOW(V) : תידרו
you(ms)~will~TAKE.STEPS(V) : תידרוך
you(ms)~will~SEEK(V) : תידרוש
you(mp)~will~TAKE.STEPS(V) : תידרכו
you(mp)~will~SEEK(V) : תידרשו
you(ms)~will~SEEK(V)~ him : תידרשנו
you(ms)~will~EXIST(V) | she~ will~EXIST(V) : תיהיה
you(mp)~will~EXIST(V) : תיהיו
you(mp)~will~EXIST(V)~ must : תיהיון
they(f)~will~EXIST(V) : תיהיין
they(f)~will~EXIST(V) : תיהיינה
you(ms)~will~be~CORRECT(V) : תיוסרו
you(ms)~will~be~SNARE(V) : תיוקש
you(ms)~will~be~POSSESS(V) : תיורש
you(ms)~will~SACRIFICE(V) : תיזבח
you(ms)~will~SACRIFICE(V)~ him : תיזבחו
you(mp)~will~ SACRIFICE(V)~him : תיזבחוהו
you(ms)~will~ SACRIFICE(V)~him : תיזבחנו
you(ms)~will~REMEMBER(V) : תיזכור
you(ms)~will~be~ REMEMBER(V) : תיזכר
you(mp)~will~REMEMBER(V) : תיזכרו
she~will~FLOW(V) : תיזל
you(ms)~will~PLUCK(V) : תיזמור
she~will~BE.A.HARLOT(V) : תיזנה
you(ms)~will~SPRINKLE(V) : תיזרוק
you(ms)~will~SOW(V) | she~ will~be~SOW(V) : תיזרע
you(mp)~will~SOW(V) : תיזרעו
you(ms)~will~LIVE(V) : תיחיה
you(mp)~will~LIVE(V) : תיחיו
you(mp)~will~LIVE(V)~must : תיחיון
she~will~BE.CLEAN(V) : תיטהר
you(mp)~will~BE.CLEAN(V) : תיטהרו
you(ms)~will~KEEP(V) : תיטור
you(ms)~will~make~ DO.WELL(V) : תיטיב
she~will~BE.DIRTY(V) : תיטמא
you(mp)~will~self~ BE.DIRTY(V) | you(mp)~will~make~ self~BE.DIRTY(V) : תיטמאו
you(ms)~will~PLANT(V) : תיטע

she~will~BE.HEAVY(V)
she~will~QUENCH(V)
she~will~be~SHAME(V)
you(mp)~will~DIG(V)
you(ms)~will~CUT(V)
you(mp)~will~CUT(V)~must
she~will~be~CUT(V)
you(ms)~will~WRITE(V)
you(ms)~will~WEAR(V)
you(ms)~will~JOIN(V)
you(mp)~will~be~MURMUR(V)
you(mp)~will~be~FIGHT(V)
you(ms)~will~SQUEEZE(V)
you(ms)~will~SQUEEZE(V)~him
you(ms)~will~LEARN(V)
you(mp)~will~PICK.UP(V)~him
you(mp)~will~REJECT(V)
you(ms)~will~WIPE.AWAY(V)
she~will~be~SELL(V)
you(mp)~will~SELL(V)
you(mp)~will~SELL(V)~her
she~will~be~FILL(V)~them(m)
you(ms)~will~REIGN(V)
you(ms)~will~SEASON(V)
Teyman
SOUTHWARD~unto
Timna | you(ms)~will~be~WITHHOLD(V)
Timnat~unto
she~will~TRANSGRESS(V)
you(ms)~will~FIND(V) | she~will~be~FIND(V) | she~will~FIND(V)
you(mp)~will~FIND(V)
you(mp)~will~FIND(V)~him
they(f)~will~FIND(V)
you(mp)~will~REBEL(V)
you(ms)~will~REGULATE(V)
you(ms)~will~SMEAR(V)
you(ms)~will~REGULATE(V)

you(ms)~will~COMMIT.ADULTERY(V)
you(mp)~will~be~SMITE(V)
you(ms)~will~INHERIT(V)
you(ms)~will~be~ACQUIT(V)
you(ms)~will~be~ENSNARE(V)
you(ms)~will~LIFT.UP(V) | she~will~LIFT.UP(V)
you(mp)~will~LIFT.UP(V)
you(mp)~will~BE.SATISFIED(V)
she~will~be~SHUT(V)
she~will~GO.AROUND(V)
you(mp)~will~TRADE(V)
she~will~GO.ASIDE(V)
you(mp)~will~POUR(V)
you(ms)~will~HATE(V)
you(ms)~will~CONSUME(V) | you(ms)~will~be~CONSUME(V)
you(mp)~will~ADD(V)
you(ms)~will~COUNT(V)
you(mp)~will~COUNT(V)
you(ms)~will~CREMATE(V)
you(mp)~will~CREMATE(V)
you(ms)~will~OVERHANG(V)
you(ms)~will~CREMATE(V)
you(mp)~will~CREMATE(V)~must
you(mp)~will~CREMATE(V)~him
you(ms)~will~self~TURN.ASIDE(V)
you(ms)~will~REACH(V)
you(ms)~will~RANSOM(V)
she~will~FALL(V)
you(ms)~will~SHAKE.IN.AWE(V)
she~will~TURN(V)
you(mp)~will~TURN(V)
she~will~SEIZE.HOLD(V)
you(mp)~will~REGISTER(V)
you(ms)~will~REGISTER(V)~them(m)
you(ms)~will~REGISTER(V)
you(ms)~will~REPRODUCE(V)
you(mp)~will~RIP(V)

she~will~BURST.OUT(V) :תיפרח
you(mp)~will~LOOSE(V) :תיפרעו
she~will~OPEN(V) :תיפתח
she~will~PROSPER(V) :תיצלח
you(ms)~will~CRY.OUT(V) :תיצעק
you(ms)~will~GATHER.TOGETHER(V) :תיקבוץ
you(mp)~will~HOLLOW.OUT(V)~him :תיקבנו
you(ms)~will~be~BURY(V) :תיקבר
you(ms)~will~BURY(V)~him :תיקברנו
you(ms)~will~BURY(V)~me :תיקברני
she~will~SET.APART(V) :תיקדש
you(ms)~will~AVENGE(V) :תיקום
you(ms)~will~TAKE(V) | she~will~TAKE(V) :תיקח
you(mp)~will~TAKE(V) :תיקחו
you(ms)~will~TAKE(V)~him :תיקחנו
you(ms)~will~PURCHASE(V) :תיקנה
you(ms)~will~PURCHASE(V) :תיקנו
you(ms)~will~CLOSE(V) :תיקפוץ
you(ms)~will~SNAP(V) :תיקצוף
you(ms)~will~SEVER(V) :תיקצור
she~will~SEVER(V) :תיקצר
you(mp)~will~SEVER(V) :תיקצרו
you(ms)~will~CALL.OUT(V) | she~will~CALL.OUT(V) :תיקרא
you(mp)~will~CALL.OUT(V) :תיקראו
they(f)~will~MEET(V) :תיקראנה
you(ms)~will~COME.NEAR(V) :תיקרב
you(mp)~will~COME.NEAR(V) :תיקרבו
you(ms)~will~FEAR(V) :תירא
you(ms)~will~SEE(V) :תיראה
you(mp)~will~SEE(V) | you(mp)~will~FEAR(V) :תיראו
you(mp)~will~FEAR(V)~them(m) :תיראום
you(mp)~will~FEAR(V)~must :תיראון
you(fs)~will~FEAR(V) :תיראי
you(ms)~will~SEE(V)~him :תיראנו
she~will~INCREASE(V) :תירבה
you(mp)~will~INCREASE(V)~must :תירבון
you(mp)~will~SHAKE(V) :תירגזו
you(ms)~will~RULE(V) :תירדה
you(ms)~will~PURSUE(V) :תירדוף

FRESH.WINE :תירוש
FRESH.WINE~you(ms) :תירושך
you(ms)~will~BE.FAR(V) :תירחק
she~will~TREAD(V) :תירמוס
she~will~DASH.TO.PIECES(V) :תירעץ
she~will~ACCEPT(V) | Tirtsah | you(ms)~will~ACCEPT(V) :תירצה
you(ms)~will~MURDER(V) :תירצח
you(mp)~will~POSSESS(V) :תירשו
you(mp)~will~POSSESS(V) :תירשון
you(ms)~will~INQUIRE(V) :תישאל
she~will~INQUIRE(V)~you(ms) :תישאלך
she~will~be~REMAIN(V) :תישאר
they(f)~will~be~REMAIN(V) :תישארנה
you(mp)~will~CRACK(V) :תישבורו
you(ms)~will~CEASE(V) | she~will~CEASE(V) :תישבות
she~will~CAPTURE(V)~you(ms) :תישבך
she~will~be~SWEAR(V) | you(ms)~will~be~SWEAR(V) :תישבע
you(mp)~will~be~SWEAR(V) :תישבעו
you(mp)~will~CRACK(V) | you(mp)~will~EXCHANGE(V) :תישברו
she~will~CEASE(V) :תישבת
you(mp)~will~CEASE(V) :תישבתו
you(ms)~will~GO.ASTRAY(V) :תישגו
you(ms)~will~SLAY(V) :תישחט
you(mp)~will~SLAY(V) :תישחטו
she~will~be~DAMAGE(V) :תישחת
she~will~LIE.DOWN(V) | you(ms)~will~LIE.DOWN(V) :תישכב
you(ms)~will~FORGET(V) | she~will~be~FORGET(V) :תישכח
you(mp)~will~FORGET(V) :תישכחו
you(ms)~will~SEND(V) :תישלח
you(mp)~will~SEND(V) :תישלחו
you(mp)~will~be~DESTROY(V)~must :תישמדון
you(ms)~will~SAFEGUARD(V) :תישמור
you(mp)~will~SAFEGUARD(V) :תישמורו
you(ms)~will~RELEASE(V)~her :תישמטנה

you(ms)~will~HEAR(V) :
you(mp)~will~HEAR(V) :
you(mp)~will~HEAR(V)~must :
you(mp)~will~SAFEGUARD(V) | you(mp)~will~be~SAFEGUARD(V) :
you(mp)~will~SAFEGUARD(V)~must :
NINE :
NINE~s :
you(ms)~will~DECIDE(V) :
you(ms)~will~POUR.OUT(V) :
you(mp)~will~POUR.OUT(V) :
you(ms)~will~POUR.OUT(V)~him :
you(ms)~will~DEAL.FALSELY(V) :
you(ms)~will~GULP(V) :
you(ms)~will~self~BEND.DOWN(V) :
you(ms)~will~self~YEARN(V) :
you(mp)~will~self~BAND.TOGETHER(V) :
you(ms)~will~self~MEDDLE(V) :
you(mp)~will~self~MEDDLE(V) :
>~GIVE(V)~him :
you(mp)~will~BREAK.DOWN(V) :
you(mp)~will~BREAK.DOWN(V)~must :
you(mp)~will~self~FAIL(V) :
you(ms)~will~self~BE.AN.IN-LAW(V) :
>~GIVE(V)~me :
you(ms)~will~GIVE(V) | she~will~GIVE(V) :
you(mp)~will~GIVE(V) | you(ms)~will~GIVE(V)~him :
you(mp)~will~self~INHERIT(V) :
you(ms)~will~GIVE(V)~her :
you(mp)~will~self~LIFT.UP(V) :
you(ms)~will~self~BUNDLE(V) :
you(mp)~will~THRUST(V) :
you(mp)~will~self~SEE(V) :
you(mp)~will~much~WASH(V) :
you(ms)~will~make~HIT(V) :
you(mp)~will~ESTIMATE(V) :
you(mp)~will~much~DENY(V) :
you(ms)~will~make~PREPARE(V) :
you(ms)~will~make~RECOGNIZE(V) :
you(mp)~will~make~RECOGNIZE(V) :
you(ms)~will~much~FINISH(V) :
you(ms)~will~much~FINISH(V)~her :
BLUE :
you(ms)~will~much~COVER.OVER(V) :
you(ms)~will~much~COVER(V) :
you(mp)~will~make~CUT(V) :
RUIN :
she~will~BRING.FORTH(V) :
you(fs)~will~BRING.FORTH(V) :
he~did~HANG(V) :
HANG(V)~ed(mp) :
you(ms)~will~make~JOIN(V) :
HANG(V)~ed(ms) :
you(mp)~will~be~MURMUR(V) | you(mp)~will~make~JOIN(V)~him :
MURMURING~s | MURMURING :
MURMURING~s~you(mp) :
MURMURING~s~them(m) :
QUIVER~you(ms) :
you(ms)~will~STAY.THE.NIGHT(V) :
you(ms)~will~WALK(V) | she~will~WALK(V) :
you(mp)~will~WALK(V) :
you(mp)~will~WALK(V)~must :
you(fs)~will~WALK(V) :
you(ms)~will~much~LEARN(V)~them(m) :
you(ms)~will~much~PICK.UP(V) :
MATURE | he~did~BE.WHOLE(V) :

they~did~BE.WHOLE(V) :תמו
she~will~TOTTER(V) :תמוט
YESTERDAY :תמול
RESEMBLANCE :תמונה
RESEMBLANCE :תמונת
you(ms)~will~DIE(V) | she~will~DIE(V) :תמות
you(mp)~will~DIE(V) :תמותו
you(mp)~will~DIE(V)~must :תמותון
CONTINUALLY :תמיד
WHOLE :תמים
WHOLE :תמימה
WHOLE~s :תמימות
WHOLE~s :תמימים
you(ms)~will~make~DIE(V) :תמית
they~did~UPHOLD(V) :תמכו
you(ms)~will~much~FILL(V) :תמלא
we~did~BE.WHOLE(V) :תמנו
you(ms)~will~make~BE.LESS(V) :תמעיט
you(mp)~will~make~BE.LESS(V) :תמעיטו
Tamar | you(ms)~will~make~BE.BITTER(V) :תמר
DATE.PALM~s :תמרים
!(ms)~GIVE(V) :תן
!(ms)~GIVE(V)~& :תנה
!(mp)~GIVE(V) :תנו
you(mp)~will~FORBID(V)~must :תנואון
DEFIANCE~me :תנואתי
BOUNTY~s :תנובות
TIP :תנוך
you(ms)~will~FLEE(V) :תנוס
WAVING :תנופה
WAVING~s :תנופות
WAVING :תנופת
OVEN :תנור
you(ms)~will~make~INHERIT(V)~her :תנחילנה
you(mp)~will~much~PREDICT(V) :תנחשו
!(fs)~GIVE(V) :תני
CROCODILE~s :תנינים
you(ms)~will~make~WAVE(V) :תניף
you(mp)~will~TEST(V) :תנסו
you(mp)~will~TEST(V)~must :תנסון
you(ms)~will~much~PICK.OUT(V) :תנקר
you(ms)~will~much~DIVIDE.INTO.PIECES(V) :תנתח
you(ms)~will~make~SHUT(V) :תסגיר
they(f)~did~GO.AROUND(V) :תסובינה
you(ms)~will~POUR.DOWN(V) :תסוך
you(ms)~will~TURN.ASIDE(V) :תסור
you(mp)~will~TURN.ASIDE(V) :תסורו
she~will~make~OVERTAKE(V) | you(ms)~will~make~OVERTAKE(V) :תסיג
you(ms)~will~PLACE(V) :תסים
you(mp)~will~PLACE(V) :תסימו
you(ms)~will~PLACE(V)~must :תסימון
you(mp)~will~make~CALCULATE(V) :תסכילו
you(ms)~did~much~COUNT(V) :תספר
you(mp)~will~SERVE(V)~must :תעבדון
you(ms)~will~be~make~SERVE(V)~them(m) :תעבדם
you(ms)~will~SERVE(V) :תעבוד
you(mp)~will~SERVE(V) :תעבודו
you(ms)~will~MAKE.A.PLEDGE(V) :תעבוט
you(ms)~will~CROSS.OVER(V) | she~will~CROSS.OVER(V) :תעבור
you(mp)~will~CROSS.OVER(V) :תעבורו
you(ms)~will~make~MAKE.A.PLEDGE(V)~him :תעביטנו
you(ms)~will~make~CROSS.OVER(V) :תעבירו
you(ms)~will~make~CROSS.OVER(V)~us :תעבירנו
you(mp)~will~CROSS.OVER(V) :תעברו
you(ms)~will~much~ROLL(V) :תעולל
she~will~be~much~AFFLICT(V) :תעונה
you(mp)~will~much~CONJURE(V) :תעוננו
she~will~FLY(V) :תעוף
she~will~be~LEAVE(V) :תעזב
you(ms)~will~LEAVE(V)~him :תעזבנו
you(ms)~will~LEAVE(V) :תעזוב
you(ms)~will~GO.UP(V) | you(ms)~will~make~GO.UP(V) :תעלה

you$^{(mp)}$~will~make~GO.UP$^{(V)}$ | you$^{(mp)}$~will~GO.UP$^{(V)}$:תעלו
you$^{(ms)}$~will~make~GO.UP$^{(V)}$~us :תעלנו
you$^{(ms)}$~will~STAND$^{(V)}$ | she~will~STAND$^{(V)}$:תעמוד
you$^{(ms)}$~will~AFFLICT$^{(V)}$ | you$^{(ms)}$~will~much~AFFLICT$^{(V)}$:תענה
you$^{(mp)}$~will~AFFLICT$^{(V)}$:תענו
you$^{(ms)}$~will~much~AFFLICT$^{(V)}$~must :תענון
you$^{(ms)}$~will~make~ENCOMPASS$^{(V)}$:תעניק
you$^{(ms)}$~will~AFFLICT$^{(V)}$~you$^{(ms)}$:תענך
you$^{(ms)}$~will~DO$^{(V)}$:תעש
you$^{(ms)}$~will~DO$^{(V)}$ | you$^{(ms)}$~will~DO$^{(V)}$~her | she~will~be~DO$^{(V)}$ | she~will~DO$^{(V)}$ | she~will~DO$^{(V)}$:תעשה
you$^{(mp)}$~will~DO$^{(V)}$:תעשו
you$^{(ms)}$~will~DO$^{(V)}$~must :תעשון
you$^{(fs)}$~will~DO$^{(V)}$:תעשי
they$^{(f)}$~will~be~DO$^{(V)}$:תעשינה
you$^{(ms)}$~will~DO$^{(V)}$~him :תעשנו
you$^{(ms)}$~will~GIVE.A.TENTH$^{(V)}$:תעשר
you$^{(mp)}$~will~be~DISTRESS$^{(V)}$:תעצבו
RAZOR :תער
you$^{(ms)}$~will~BE.TERRIFIED$^{(V)}$:תערוץ
you$^{(mp)}$~will~BE.TERRIFIED$^{(V)}$:תערצו
you$^{(mp)}$~will~BE.TERRIFIED$^{(V)}$~must :תערצון
you$^{(ms)}$~will~OPPRESS$^{(V)}$:תעשוק
you$^{(ms)}$~will~much~DECORATE$^{(V)}$:תפאר
you$^{(ms)}$~will~TURN$^{(V)}$:תפן
you$^{(mp)}$~will~make~LOOSE$^{(V)}$:תפריעו
you$^{(ms)}$~will~much~OPEN$^{(V)}$:תפתח
she~will~GO.OUT$^{(V)}$ | you$^{(ms)}$~will~GO.OUT$^{(V)}$:תצא
you$^{(mp)}$~will~GO.OUT$^{(V)}$:תצאו
you$^{(ms)}$~will~much~DIRECT$^{(V)}$:תצוה
you$^{(ms)}$~will~much~DIRECT$^{(V)}$~them$^{(m)}$:תצוום
you$^{(ms)}$~will~FENCE.IN$^{(V)}$:תצור
you$^{(ms)}$~will~SMACK$^{(V)}$~them$^{(m)}$:תצורם

you$^{(ms)}$~will~make~PROSPER$^{(V)}$:תצליח
she~will~make~SPRING.UP$^{(V)}$ | you$^{(ms)}$~will~SPRING.UP$^{(V)}$:תצמיח
you$^{(ms)}$~will~much~OVERLAY$^{(V)}$:תצפה
you$^{(ms)}$~will~much~OVERLAY$^{(V)}$~him :תצפנו
you$^{(ms)}$~will~SMACK$^{(V)}$:תצר
you$^{(ms)}$~will~make~SET.APART$^{(V)}$:תקדיש
you$^{(ms)}$~will~RISE$^{(V)}$:תקום
HIGH.PLACE :תקומה
CIRCUIT :תקופת
you$^{(ms)}$~will~make~BURN.INCENSE$^{(V)}$:תקטיר
you$^{(mp)}$~will~make~BURN.INCENSE$^{(V)}$:תקטירו
she~will~be~make~BURN.INCENSE$^{(V)}$:תקטר
she~will~make~VOMIT$^{(V)}$:תקיא
you$^{(ms)}$~will~make~RISE$^{(V)}$:תקים
you$^{(mp)}$~will~make~RISE$^{(V)}$:תקימו
you$^{(mp)}$~will~ENCIRCLE$^{(V)}$:תקיפו
you$^{(ms)}$~will~much~BELITTLE$^{(V)}$:תקלל
he~did~THRUST$^{(V)}$:תקע
you$^{(ms)}$~will~make~COME.NEAR$^{(V)}$ | she~will~make~COME.NEAR$^{(V)}$:תקריב
you$^{(mp)}$~will~make~COME.NEAR$^{(V)}$:תקריבו
you$^{(mp)}$~will~COME.NEAR$^{(V)}$~must :תקריבון
you$^{(mp)}$~will~make~BE.HARD$^{(V)}$:תקשו
she~will~be~SEE$^{(V)}$:תראה
you$^{(ms)}$~will~make~INCREASE$^{(V)}$:תרבה
you$^{(mp)}$~will~make~INCREASE$^{(V)}$:תרבו
GREAT.AMOUNT :תרבות
you$^{(ms)}$~will~make~BE.SQUARE$^{(V)}$:תרביע
you$^{(ms)}$~will~make~REPOSE$^{(V)}$:תרגיע
you$^{(ms)}$~will~GO.DOWN$^{(V)}$:תרד
TRANCE :תרדמה
they~did~SCOUT$^{(V)}$:תרו
OFFERING :תרומה

OFFERING~s :תרומות
OFFERING~s~me :תרומותי
OFFERING :תרומת
OFFERING~me :תרומתי
OFFERING~you(mp) :תרומתכם
OFFERING~them(m) :תרומתם
SHOUT :תרועה
Terahh :תרח
you(mp)~will~make~BE.FAR(V) :תרחיקו
you(ms)~will~DISPUTE(V)~him :תריבהו
you(mp)~will~DISPUTE(V)~must :תריבון
you(ms)~will~make~ROAM(V) :תריד
you(mp)~will~make~RAISE.UP(V) :תרימו
you(mp)~will~make~SHOUT(V) :תריעו
she~will~BE.DYSFUNCTIONAL(V) :תרע
you(mp)~will~make~BE.DYSFUNCTIONAL(V) :תרעו
TOPAZ :תרשיש
you(ms)~did~SCOUT(V) :תרתם
you(ms)~will~TURN.BACK(V) | she~will~SETTLE(V) | you(ms)~will~SETTLE(V) :תשב
you(mp)~will~TURN.BACK(V) | you(mp)~will~SETTLE(V) :תשבו
you(ms)~will~make~EXCHANGE(V)~me :תשבירני
you(ms)~will~make~CEASE(V) :תשבית
you(mp)~will~make~CEASE(V) :תשביתו
WOVEN.MATERIAL :תשבץ
you(ms)~will~much~CRACK(V) :תשבר
you(mp)~will~much~CRACK(V) :תשברו
you(mp)~will~much~CRACK(V)~must :תשברון
you(ms)~will~make~OVERLOOK(V) :תשה
you(ms)~will~TURN.BACK(V) | she~will~TURN.BACK(V) :תשוב
you(mp)~will~TURN.BACK(V) :תשובו
you(mp)~will~TURN.BACK(V)~must :תשובון
you(ms)~will~FALL.UPON(V)~him :תשוגנו
FOLLOWING~him :תשוקתו
FOLLOWING~you(fs) :תשוקתך
you(ms)~will~make~DAMAGE(V) :תשחית
you(mp)~will~make~DAMAGE(V)~must :תשחיתון
you(ms)~will~DAMAGE(V) :תשחת
you(ms)~will~BE.UNMINDFUL(V) :תשי
you(ms)~will~TURN.BACK(V) :תשיב
you(mp)~will~make~TURN.BACK(V) :תשיבו
you(ms)~will~make~TURN.BACK(V)~them(m) :תשיבם
you(ms)~will~make~TURN.BACK(V)~him :תשיבנו
you(ms)~will~make~BITE(V) :תשיך
she~will~be~BE.CHILDLESS(V) :תשכל
you(ms)~will~much~SEND(V) :תשלח
you(mp)~will~much~SEND(V) :תשלחו
you(mp)~will~much~SEND(V)~them(m) :תשלחום
you(ms)~will~much~SEND(V)~him :תשלחנו
you(mp)~will~make~THROW.OUT(V)~him :תשליכוהו
you(mp)~will~make~THROW.OUT(V)~must :תשליכון
she~will~make~MAKE.RESTITUTION(V) :תשלים
she~will~DESOLATE(V) :תשם
you(ms)~will~make~RELEASE(V) :תשמט
you(mp)~will~make~DESTROY(V) :תשמידו
NINE :תשע
you(mp)~will~much~DETEST(V) :תשקצו
you(mp)~will~much~DETEST(V)~him :תשקצנו
you(mp)~will~much~DEAL.FALSELY(V) :תשקרו
you(ms)~will~SET.DOWN(V) | you(ms)~will~GULP(V) :תשת
>~GIVE(V) :תת
you(mp)~will~much~POINT(V) :תתאו
you(mp)~will~SCOUT(V) :תתורו
you(ms)~will~much~ABHOR(V) :תתעב
you(ms)~will~much~ABHOR(V)~hi :תתעבנו

Dictionary of Hebrew Words

ABDOMEN (masc. *ma'ah)* The gut, the internal organs of the lower torso, the seat of the unconscious mind. *AHLB:* 1292-H(N) *Strong's:* #4578

ABHOR(V) (*t.ah.b)* To hate something that is disgusting. *AHLB:* 2897(V) *Strong's:* #8581

ABIDE(V) (*n.w.h)* To dwell restfully and peacefully. *AHLB:* 1305-J(V) *Strong's:* #5115

ABODE (masc. *na'weh)* The dwelling place of man (home), god (mountain) *AHLB:* 1305-J(N) *Strong's:* #5116

ABODE.OF.NINUS (masc. *niyn'wah) Strong's:* [Found in names only]

ABOUNDING (masc. *she'pha) AHLB:* 2868(N) *Strong's:* #8228

ABUNDANCE (masc. *rov)* An ample quantity of number (many) *Alternate Translation:* many *AHLB:* 1439-J(N) *Strong's:* #7230

ABUNDANT (masc. *rav fem. ra'bah)* Great plenty or supply of numbers (many) *AHLB:* 1439-A(N) *Strong's:* #7227, #7228

ABUNDANT.ONE (masc. *ats'mon) Strong's:* [Found in names only]

ACACIA (fem. *shit'tah)* A thorny tree commonly found in the Near East. In its plural form can mean wood or boards from the tree. *AHLB:* 1469-A(N1) *Strong's:* #7848

ACCEPT(V) (*r.ts.h)* To receive from the messenger what is given as a message. *AHLB:* 1455-H(V) *Strong's:* #7521

ACCUMULATE(V) (*r.k.sh)* To gather or pile up, especially little by little. *AHLB:* 2772(V) *Strong's:* #7408

ACQUIRED (fem. *miq'nah)* What is obtained as one's own. Often used in the context of purchasing. *AHLB:* 1428-H(h1) *Strong's:* #4736

ACQUIRING (masc. *me'shek) AHLB:* 2358(N) *Strong's:* #4901

ACQUISITION (masc. *me'sheq)* Something gained by purchase or exchange. *AHLB:* 2360(N) *Strong's:* #4943

ACQUIT(V) (*n.q.h)* To declare one innocent of a crime or oath. *AHLB:* 1318-H(V) *Strong's:* #5352

ADD(V) (*y.s.p)* To augment something by increasing it in amount or supply. *Alternate Translation:* more (when written in the participle form); again (when written in the hiphil [active causative] form) *AHLB:* 1339-L(V) *Strong's:* #3254

ADDER (masc. *she'phi'phon)* An unknown species of viper, possibly an adder. *AHLB:* 1477-B(bj) *Strong's:* #8207

ADHERE(V) (*d.b.q)* To join or stick to someone or something. *AHLB:* 2092(V) *Strong's:* #1692

ADMINISTRATION (fem. *ke'hu'nah)* The collective members from the tribe of Levi who administrate over the tent of meeting or the temple. *AHLB:* 1244-G(d1) *Strong's:* #3550

ADMINISTRATOR (masc. כוהן *ko'heyn)* One who manages the affairs and activities of an organization. The administrators (often translated as "priest") *AHLB:* 1244-G(g) *Strong's:* #3548

ADORATION (fem. תהילה *te'hi'lah)* To praise or to be boastful. *AHLB:* 1104-A(ie1) *Strong's:* #8416

ADORN$^{(V)}$ (כהן *k.h.n)* To put on special ornaments or garments for a special office or event. (see Isaiah 61:10). *AHLB:* 1244-G$^{(V)}$ *Strong's:* #3547

ADORNMENT (masc. עדה *od) Strong's:* [Found in names only]

ADVANCE$^{(V)}$ (עתק *ah.t.q)* To bring or move forward; to raise to a higher rank; to make progress. *AHLB:* 2589$^{(V)}$ *Strong's:* #6275

ADVICE (masc. עוץ *uts) Strong's:* [Found in names only]

AFFECTION (fem. אהבה *a'ha'vah)* A moderate feeling or emotion. A tender attachment or fondness. *AHLB:* 1094-C(N1) *Strong's:* #0160

AFFLICT$^{(V)}$ (ענה *ah.n.h)* To oppress severely so as to cause persistent suffering or anguish in the sense of making dark; to be or make humbled. *AHLB:* 1359-H$^{(V)}$ *Strong's:* #6031

AFFLICTION (masc. עני *a'ni)* The cause of persistent suffering, pain or distress. *AHLB:* 1359-A(f) *Strong's:* #6040, #6041

AFRAID (masc. יגור *ya'gor)* The feeling fear; filled with apprehension. *AHLB:* 1066-L(c) *Strong's:* #3016

AFTER (masc. אחר / אחרי *a'hhar / a'hhar'iy)* A time to come beyond another event. *Alternate Translation:* afterward; behind; follow *AHLB:* 1181-C$^{(N)}$ *Strong's:* #0310

AFTER.GROWTH (masc. ספיח *sa'phiy'ahh)* What spreads out by itself rather than sown. *AHLB:* 2496(b) *Strong's:* #5599

AGATE (fem. שבו *she'vo)* Probably the Agate, a variety of quartz that may be gray, light blue, orange, red or black in color. The Septuagint uses achates meaning Agate. *AHLB:* 1462-A(q) *Strong's:* #7618

AGE (masc. זוקן *zo'qen)* The part of existence extending from the beginning to any given time; a period of time marked by a central figure or prominent feature. *AHLB:* 2132(g) *Strong's:* #2207

AGITATED (masc. גתר *ga'tar)* In a state of excitement or disturbance. (A word of uncertain meaning). *Strong's:* [Found in names only]

AGITATION (fem. זועה *z'wa'ah)* An object of terror that causes trembling. *AHLB:* 1154-J(N1) *Strong's:* #2113, #2189

AGONY (masc. חיל *hhil fem.* חילה *hhi'lah)* A state of being in emotional or physical turmoil or pain. *AHLB:* 1173-M$^{(N)}$ *Strong's:* #2427

AGREE$^{(V)}$ (אות *a.w.t)* Two parties to be in concert or concurrence. *AHLB:* 1022-J$^{(V)}$ *Strong's:* #0225

ALL (masc. כול *kol)* The whole of a group. *Alternate Translation:* any; every; among (when followed by the prefix "to~") *AHLB:* 1242-J$^{(N)}$ *Strong's:* #3605

ALL.AROUND (masc. סביב *sa'viv fem.* סביבה *se'vi'vah)* On all sides; enclose so as to surround; in rotation or succession. A circling or bordering about the edge. *AHLB:* 1324-B(b) *Strong's:* #5439

ALLIED (masc. קהת *qe'hat)* To be a joined to another in contract. *Strong's:* [Found in names only]

ALMOND (masc. *sha'qeyd)* The nut or the tree. From the nut's shape like an open eye. *AHLB:* 2872(N) *Strong's:* #8247

ALOE (masc. *a'hal fem.* *a'ha'lah)* Any chiefly shrub belonging to the genus Aloe, of the lily family. The oils or the shrub. *AHLB:* 1104-C(N) *Strong's:* #0174

ALONE (masc. *ba'dad)* One who is separated from the group; solitary; desolate. *AHLB:* 1027-B(N) *Strong's:* #0910

ALONGSIDE (fem. *u'mat)* To stand with, or next to, someone or something. *AHLB:* 1358-J(N2) *Strong's:* #5980

ALSO (masc. *gam)* In addition to. The idea of a gathering of objects or ideas. *Alternate Translation:* and; both; even; should; since *AHLB:* 1059-A(N) *Strong's:* #1571

ALTAR (masc. *miz'bey'ahh)* The place of sacrifice. *AHLB:* 2117(h) *Strong's:* #4196

AMBER (masc. *be'du'lahh)* A fossil gum resin. *AHLB:* 3003 *Strong's:* #0916

AMBUSH (fem. *tse'diy'yah)* A laying down in wait for the purpose of attacking. *AHLB:* 1395-H(f1) *Strong's:* #6660

AMBUSH(V) (*a.r.b)* To lay in wait of another to capture or do harm or injury. *AHLB:* 1439-C(V) *Strong's:* #0693

AMETHYST (fem. *ahh'la'mah)* Probably the Amethyst, a violet form of quartz. (The Septuagint uses Amethystos). *AHLB:* 2164(n1) *Strong's:* #0306

AMPLIFY(V) (*d.g.h)* To expand, multiply or increase. *AHLB:* 1072-H(V) *Strong's:* #1711

ANCIENT (masc. *iy'lam) Strong's:* [Found in names only]

ANGER (masc. *ka'as) AHLB:* 2279(N) *Strong's:* #3708

ANNOUNCE(V) (*n.b.a)* To utter the words or instructions of Elohiym received through a vision or dream. *AHLB:* 1301-E(V) *Strong's:* #5012

ANNOUNCER (masc. *na'vi fem.* *na'vi'ah)* One who utters the words or instructions of Elohiym that are received through a vision or dream. One gifted with more than ordinary spiritual and moral insight. *AHLB:* 1301-E(b), 1301-E(b1) *Strong's:* #5030, #5031

ANNOYANCE (fem. *qe'la'lah)* The act of disturbing or irritating. Something that is light in stature; considered worthless as compared with something of much greater value or importance. *AHLB:* 1426-B(N1) *Strong's:* #7045

ANSWER(V) (*ah.n.h)* Something written or spoken in reply to a question. *AHLB:* 1520-H(V) *Strong's:* #6030

ANSWERED (masc. *a'nah) Strong's:* [Found in names only]

ANTELOPE (masc. *diy'shon)* An unknown species of clean animal. *AHLB:* 1090-M(j) *Strong's:* #1788

ANYTHING (fem. *me'u'mah)* An indeterminate amount or thing. *AHLB:* 1289-D(d1) *Strong's:* #3972

APART.FROM (masc. *bil'a'dey)* At a little distance; away from in space or time; holding different opinions. *AHLB:* 3004 *Strong's:* #1107

APPAREL (fem. *sim'lah)* Something that clothes or adorns. As forming to the image of the body. *AHLB:* 2489(e1) *Strong's:* #8071

APPEARANCE (masc. *mar'e)* What is seen or is in sight. *AHLB:* 1438-H(a) *Strong's:* #4758

APPOINT(V) (*y.ah.d)* To arrange, fix or set in place, to determine a set place or time to meet. *AHLB:* 1349-L(V) *Strong's:* #3259

APPOINTED (masc. *mo'eyd)* A person, place, thing or time that is fixed in place or time; an officially set time or place. *Alternate Translation:* appointment *AHLB:* 1349-L(a) *Strong's:* #4150, #4151

APPOINTED.TIME (fem. *eyt)* A fixed or officially set event, occasion or date. *AHLB:* 1367-A(N) *Strong's:* #6256

APPROACH(V) (*a.n.h)* To come near or nearer to. *Alternate Translation:* delivers (when written in the piel [active intensive] form) *AHLB:* 1014-H(V) *Strong's:* #0579

ARCH (/ *gav / gaph)* A curved object. The bowing of the back as when digging. Also, any high arched or convex thing such as the eyebrow or the rim of a wheel. *AHLB:* 1048-A(N) *Strong's:* #1354, #1610

AREA (masc. *ma'qom)* An indefinite region or expanse; a particular part of a surface or body. A place. *AHLB:* 1427-J(a) *Strong's:* #4725

ARM (fem. *ze'ro'a)* The human upper limb; associated with and representing power. *AHLB:* 2139(c) *Strong's:* #2220

ARM.BAND (masc. *ku'maz)* An insignia or emblem showing loyalty or ownership. *AHLB:* 2263(o) *Strong's:* #3558

ARM.FOR.BATTLE (*hh.m.sh)* To grab weapons in preparation for battle. *AHLB:* 2176(d) *Strong's:* #2571

ARMAMENT (masc. *ka'vod)* The arms and equipment of a soldier or military unit. From a root meaning "heavy" and often paralleled with other weapons. Figurative for power. *AHLB:* 2246(c) *Strong's:* #3519

ARMLET (fem. *ets'a'dah)* An ornament worn on the ankle or wrist that jingles when walking. *AHLB:* 2676(n1) *Strong's:* #0685

ARMY (fem. *tse'va)* A large organized group mustered together and armed for war or service. *AHLB:* 1393-E(N) *Strong's:* #6635

AROMA (fem. *ri'ahh)* A distinctive pervasive and usually pleasant or savory smell or odor. *AHLB:* 1445-M(N) *Strong's:* #7381

AROMATIC.SPICE (masc. *sam)* A spice that is pleasing to the nose. *AHLB:* 1473-A(N) *Strong's:* #5561

AROUND.THE.CORNER (masc. *piy'non) Strong's:* [Found in names only]

ARRANGE(V) (*ah.r.k)* To set something in order or into a correct or suitable configuration, sequence or adjustment. *Alternate Translation:* value, as in arranging a price (when written in the hiphil [active causative] form [see Leviticus 27]) *AHLB:* 2576(V) *Strong's:* #6186

ARRANGEMENT (masc. *ey'rekh)* Set in a row or in order according to rank or age. In parallel. Arranged items in juxtaposition. *Alternate Translation:* valuation (when used in context with make~ARRANGE [see Leviticus 27]) *AHLB:* 2576(N) *Strong's:* #6187

ARRIVE(V) (*a.t.h)* To come to or bring to a destination. *AHLB:* 1022-H(V) *Strong's:* #0857

ARROGANCE (masc. *za'dun)* Feeling pleasure or satisfaction over something regarded as highly honorable or creditable to oneself. *AHLB:* 1142-A(j) *Strong's:* #2087

ARROW (masc. *hheyts)* A missile weapon shot from a bow having a pointed head, slender shaft and feathers at the butt. *AHLB:* 1179-A(N) *Strong's:* #2671

ASCENSION.OFFERING (fem. / *o'lah / go'lah)* An offering that is "brought up" or "lifted up." Also, a burnt offering from the rising smoke of the offering. *AHLB:* 1357-J(N1) *Strong's:* #1473, #5930

ASCENT (masc. *ma'a'leh)* A place of straight or stepped incline. *AHLB:* 1357-H(a) *Strong's:* #4608

ASH (masc. *a'phar)* The solid residue left when material is thoroughly burned. *AHLB:* 1388-C(N) *Strong's:* #0665, #0666

ASP (masc. *pe'ten)* An unknown serpent, from its open mouth. *AHLB:* 2651(N) *Strong's:* #6620

ASSEMBLE(V) (*q.h.l)* To gather together a flock, herd or group of people. *AHLB:* 1426-G(V) *Strong's:* #6950, #7035

ASSEMBLY (masc. *qa'hal fem.* *qa'ha'lah)* A large group, as a gathering of the flock of sheep to the shepherd. *AHLB:* 1426-G(N) *Strong's:* #6951, #3862, #6952

ASSIGN(V) (*hh.r.m)* To be devoted to something special, either for devotion or destruction. *AHLB:* 2206(V) *Strong's:* #2763(x2)

ASSIGNED (masc. *hhey'rem)* What is to be devoted to something special, either for devotion or destruction. *AHLB:* 2206(N) *Strong's:* #2764(x2)

ASSOCIATION (masc. *hhev'ron)* A relationship between two persons, places or objects that connects them. *Strong's:* [Found in names only]

ASTONISHMENT (masc. *tiy'ma'hon)* An overwhelming feeling. *AHLB:* 1496-H(j) *Strong's:* #8541

AT (masc. *et)* A function word to indicate presence or occurrence, a goal of an implied or indicated action, etc. Commonly used as a grammatical tool to identify the direct object of a verb. *Alternate Translation:* by; for; to; upon; with *AHLB:* 1022-A(N) *Strong's:* #0853, #0854

AT.THAT.TIME (masc. *az)* A specified moment or time. *AHLB:* 1007-A(N) *Strong's:* #0227

AT.THIS.POINT (masc. *ha'lom)* To indicate a specific moment or place in time. *AHLB:* 1104-K(p) *Strong's:* #1988

ATONEMENT (masc. *ki'pur)* An act of paying the price to release the debt or person. A covering over of transgression. *AHLB:* 2283(ed) *Strong's:* #3725

ATTACH(V) (*hh.sh.q)* To bring one's self into an association with another. To have an attachment to another. *AHLB:* 2219(V) *Strong's:* #2836

ATTACK(V) (*a.y.b)* To be antagonistic or unfriendly to another. An action taken by an enemy. *AHLB:* 1002-M(V) *Strong's:* #0340, #0341

ATTACK.THE.REAR(V) (*z.n.b)* To slap or strike the part in the back or behind. *AHLB:* 2125(V) *Strong's:* #2179

AUNT (fem. *do'dah)* The sister of one's father or mother. One who is loved. *AHLB:* 1073-J(N1) *Strong's:* #1733

AVENGE(V) (*n.q.m)* To take vengeance for or on behalf of another; to gain satisfaction for a wrong by punishing the wrongdoer; to pursue and kill one who has murdered. *AHLB:* 2433(V) *Strong's:* #5358

AWAKE(V) (*y.q.ts)* To bring sleep to an end; to not be in a state of sleeping. *AHLB:* 1432-L(V) *Strong's:* #3364

AWE (masc. *pa'hhad)* As shaking when in the presence of an awesome sight. *AHLB:* 2598$^{(N)}$ *Strong's:* #6343, #6344

AWL (masc. *mar'tsey'a)* A sharp pointed tool for piercing holes in leather or the skin. *AHLB:* 2791$^{(N)}$ *Strong's:* #4836

AX (masc. *gar'zen)* An instrument with a bladed head on a handle or helve, used for hewing, cleaving, chopping, etc. *AHLB:* 2082(m) *Strong's:* #1631

BABIES (masc. *taph)* Adolescent offspring of the parent or descendents of a patron. More than one child. *AHLB:* 1201-A$^{(N)}$ *Strong's:* #2945

BACK (masc. *a'hhor)* The part of the body that is behind. To be in the rear of or behind something. *AHLB:* 1181-C(c) *Strong's:* #0268

BACK.OF.THE.NECK (masc. *tsa'war)* The nape between the shoulders and the head. *AHLB:* 1411-D(g) *Strong's:* #6677

BACKBONE (masc. *e'tsi'on) Strong's:* [Found in names only]

BACKWARD (fem. *a'hho'ra'niyt)* With the back foremost; in a reverse or contrary way; i.e. To walk backward in the sense of being after oneself. *AHLB:* 1181-C(cm4) *Strong's:* #0322

BADGER (masc. *ta'hhash)* An unknown species of mammal, possibly the badger. *AHLB:* 2891$^{(N)}$ *Strong's:* #8476

BAG (masc. *kiys) AHLB:* 1245-M$^{(N)}$ *Strong's:* #3599

BAKE$^{(V)}$ (*a.p.h)* To cook using dry heat, especially in an oven. *AHLB:* 1017-H$^{(V)}$ *Strong's:* #0644

BAKED (masc. *ma'a'pheh)* What is cooked in a dry heat such as an oven. *AHLB:* 1017-H(a) *Strong's:* #3989

BAKED.BREAD (masc. *og fem.* *u'gah)* A circular loaf of dough that has been baked on hot stones. *AHLB:* 1348-A(N1) *Strong's:* #5692

BALANCE (masc. *mo'zeyn)* A pair of scales used on a balance to weigh an object. *AHLB:* 1152-C(ag) *Strong's:* #3976

BALD (masc. *qey'rey'ahh) AHLB:* 2730$^{(N)}$ *Strong's:* #7142

BALD.SPOT (fem. / / *qar'hhah / qar'ha / qa'ra'hhat) AHLB:* 2730(N1) *Strong's:* #7144, #7146

BALDING (masc. *qo'rahh)* The top of the head void of any hair. *Strong's:* [Found in names only]

BALM (masc. *tse'ri)* An aromatic preparation for a healing ointment. A salve rubbed and pressed into the skin. *AHLB:* 1411-A(f) *Strong's:* #6875

BALSAM בשם ^^ בשם B.S.M) (*B.S.M) AHLB:* 2024$^{(N)}$ *Strong's:* #1313

BAND (masc. *ge'dud)* A gathering of men for attacking or raiding. *AHLB:* 1050-B(d) *Strong's:* #1416

BAND.TOGETHER$^{(V)}$ (*g.d.d)* To gather or assemble as a group for attacking or raiding. *AHLB:* 1050-B$^{(V)}$ *Strong's:* #1413

BANKS (masc. *e'shed)* The banks of a river as a channel for the water. *AHLB:* 1464-C$^{(N)}$ *Strong's:* #0793

BANNER (masc. *de'gel)* An ensign of cloth hung from a pole bearing the emblem of the family. *AHLB:* 2095$^{(N)}$ *Strong's:* #1714

BANQUET (masc. *mish'teh)* An elaborate meal often accompanied by a ceremony. *AHLB:* 1482-H(h) *Strong's:* #4960

BAR (masc. *mot)* The bent bar of the yoke that goes around the neck, also a branch that is used as pole. A slipping or wavering of the foot. *AHLB:* 1285-J(N) *Strong's:* #4132

BARE.ONE (masc. *ey'ran) Strong's:* [Found in names only]

BARE.PLACE (masc. *sh'phiy)* A barren location. *AHLB:* 1477-A(f) *Strong's:* #8205

BARE.SKIN (masc. *ar) Strong's:* [Found in names only]

BARE.SPOT (masc. *gi'bey'ahh fem. ga'ba'hhat)* A lack of hair on the front part of the head. *AHLB:* 2048(N2) *Strong's:* #1371, #1372

BARK(V) (*n.b.hh)* The sound made by a dog. *AHLB:* 2366(V) *Strong's:* #5024

BARLEY (fem. *se'o'rah)* A grain, identified by its hairs, used as food, and for determining the month of Aviv. *AHLB:* 2494(c1) *Strong's:* #8184

BARN (masc. *a'sam) AHLB:* 1335-C(N) *Strong's:* #0618

BARREN (masc. *a'ri'ri)* Incapable of bearing children; childless. *AHLB:* 1365-B(bf) *Strong's:* #6185

BARRENNESS (masc. *a'wen)* Action or thought that is vain or for an improper purpose. *AHLB:* 1014-J(N) *Strong's:* #0205

BARTER(V) (*ah.r.b)* To exchange an item or service for another. *AHLB:* 2573(V) *Strong's:* #6148(x2)

BASE (masc. *keyn)* The bottom or foundation which provides support. A person's home or family as being a base. A species of gnat. *AHLB:* 1244-A(N) *Strong's:* #3653

BASIN (masc. *saph)* A vessel for holding water or other liquid. By extension, the lip of the bason and from this, the lip, or threshold, of a door. *AHLB:* 1339-A(N) *Strong's:* #5592

BASTARD (masc. *mam'zer)* A person born of unmarried parents; an illegitimate child. *AHLB:* 2333(a) *Strong's:* #4464

BAT (masc. *a'a'leyph) AHLB:* 3042 *Strong's:* #5847

BATHE(V) (*r.hh.ts)* To cleanse by being immersed in, or washing with, water. *AHLB:* 2764(V) *Strong's:* #7364

BATTERING.RAM (masc. *m'hhiy)* An engine of war for battering down walls. *AHLB:* 1284-A(f) *Strong's:* #4239

BATTLE (fem. *mil'hha'mah)* A hostile encounter or engagement between opposing military forces. *AHLB:* 2305(h1) *Strong's:* #4421

BE(V) (*h.w.h)* To exist or have breath. That which exists has breath. In Hebrew thought the breath is the character of someone or something. Just as a man has character, so do objects. *AHLB:* 1097-J(V) *Strong's:* #1933

BE.A.HARLOT(V) (*z.n.h)* A woman who practices promiscuous sexual behavior, especially for hire. *AHLB:* 1152-H(V) *Strong's:* #2181

BE.ABLE(V) (*y.k.l)* To successfully prevail, overcome or endure. *AHLB:* 1242-L(V) *Strong's:* #3201

BE.ABUNDANT(V) (*ah.ts.m)* To be strong in might or numbers. From the abundant number of bones in the body. *AHLB:* 2569(V) *Strong's:* #6105

BE.AFRAID(V) (*y.g.r)* Having the feeling fear; filled with apprehension. *AHLB:* 1066-L(V) *Strong's:* #3025

BE.ALMOND.SHAPED(V) (*sh.q.d)* An object that is in the form of an almond. *AHLB:* 2872(V) *Strong's:* #8246

BE.AMAZED$^{(V)}$ (*hh.d.h)* To be overwhelmed with surprise or sudden wonder; astonished greatly. *AHLB:* 1165-H$^{(V)}$ *Strong's:* #2302

BE.AN.IN-LAW$^{(V)}$ (*hh.t.n)* To have a relationship with another through marriage. *AHLB:* 2224$^{(V)}$ *Strong's:* #2859

BE.ANGRY$^{(V)}$ (*k.ah.s)* A strong feeling of displeasure and belligerence aroused by a wrong. *AHLB:* 2279$^{(V)}$ *Strong's:* #3707

BE.ASHAMED$^{(V)}$ (*b.w.sh)* Feeling shame, guilt or disgrace; to be dried up with shame. *Alternate Translation:* refrained (when written in the piel [active intensive] form) *AHLB:* 1044-J$^{(V)}$ *Strong's:* #0954

BE.BITTER$^{(V)}$ (*m.r.r)* Having a harsh, disagreeably acrid taste. One of the four basic taste sensations. *Alternate Translation:* provoke (when written in the hiphil [active causative] form) *AHLB:* 1296-B$^{(V)}$ *Strong's:* #4843

BE.BOLD$^{(V)}$ (*ah.w.z)* To be fearless and daring; courageous. *Alternate Translation:* seek refuge (when written in the hiphil [active causative] form) *AHLB:* 1352-J$^{(V)}$ *Strong's:* #5756

BE.BRIGHT$^{(V)}$ (*y.p.ah) Alternate Translation:* shone (when written in the hiphil [causative] form) *AHLB:* 1384-L$^{(V)}$ *Strong's:* #3313

BE.CHILDLESS$^{(V)}$ (*sh.k.l)* To be without children through miscarriage, barrenness or loss of children. *Alternate Translation:* miscarry (when written in the piel [active intensive] form) *AHLB:* 2836$^{(V)}$ *Strong's:* #7921

BE.CLEAN$^{(V)}$ (*t.h.r)* Free from dirt, pollution or immorality; unadulterated, pure. *Alternate Translation:* declare clean (when written in the piel [active intensive] form) *AHLB:* 1204-G$^{(V)}$ *Strong's:* #2891

BE.CRAFTY$^{(V)}$ (*n.k.l)* The doing of a thing slyly or cunningly. *AHLB:* 2404$^{(V)}$ *Strong's:* #5230

BE.DELIGHTFUL$^{(V)}$ (*n.ah.m)* One of the four basic taste sensations. *AHLB:* 2416$^{(V)}$ *Strong's:* #5276

BE.DIRTY$^{(V)}$ (*t.m.a)* Physically or morally impure; polluted, filthy. *AHLB:* 1197-E$^{(V)}$ *Strong's:* #2930, #2933

BE.DISTINCT$^{(V)}$ (*p.l.h)* To be clearly distinguished. To have a marked difference. To be prominent; separated out completely. *AHLB:* 1380-H$^{(V)}$ *Strong's:* #6395

BE.DOUBLE$^{(V)}$ (*t.a.m)* To have two identical pieces placed together. Also, to bear twins as doubles. *AHLB:* 1496-D$^{(V)}$ *Strong's:* #8382

BE.DRUNK$^{(V)}$ (*sh.k.r)* To be filled with intoxicating drink. *AHLB:* 2839$^{(V)}$ *Strong's:* #7937

BE.DYSFUNCTIONAL$^{(V)}$ (*r.ah.ah)* Impaired or abnormal filling of purpose; to act wrongly by injuring or doing an evil action. *AHLB:* 1460-B$^{(V)}$ *Strong's:* #4827, #7489

BE.EMINENT$^{(V)}$ (*a.d.r)* To be large in size or stature. *AHLB:* 1089-C$^{(V)}$ *Strong's:* #0142

BE.FACE.TO.FACE$^{(V)}$ (*n.g.d)* To face another. *Alternate Translation:* tell (when written in the hiphil [active causative] form) *AHLB:* 2372$^{(V)}$ *Strong's:* #5046

BE.FAR$^{(V)}$ (*r.hh.q)* To be distant, a long way off. *AHLB:* 2765$^{(V)}$ *Strong's:* #7368

BE.FILTHY$^{(V)}$ (*hh.n.p)* To be polluted or dirty. Usually in the sense of immorality. *AHLB:* 2179$^{(V)}$ *Strong's:* #2610

BE.FIRSTBORN[V] (*b.k.r)* To give birth to the first out of the womb or the first produce of the crops. *AHLB:* 2016[V] *Strong's:* #1069

BE.FRUITFUL[V] (*p.r.a)* Abundantly productive. *AHLB:* 1388-E[V] *Strong's:* #6500

BE.GUILTY[V] (*a.sh.m)* To commit an offense, especially consciously. *AHLB:* 1473-C[V] *Strong's:* #0816

BE.HARD[V] (*q.sh.h)* To be difficult; not easily penetrated; not easily yielding to pressure. *AHLB:* 1435-H[V] *Strong's:* #7185

BE.HEAVY[V] (*k.b.d)* To be great in weight, wealth or importance. *Alternate Translation:* honor (when written in the piel [active intensive] form) *AHLB:* 2246[V] *Strong's:* #3513

BE.HIGH[V] (*g.b.h)* To lift up to a greater elevation or stature. *AHLB:* 1048-H[V] *Strong's:* #1361

BE.HUNGRY[V] (*r.ah.b)* To have an urgent craving for food; famished. *AHLB:* 2777[V] *Strong's:* #7456

BE.IMPATIENT[V] (*l.a.h)* Exhausted in strength, endurance, vigor or freshness. *AHLB:* 1258-D[V] *Strong's:* #3811

BE.IN.MISERY[V] (*k.a.b)* A state of suffering and want due to poverty or affliction. *AHLB:* 1232-D[V] *Strong's:* #3510

BE.LAVISH[V] (*z.w.l)* To use or give in great amounts. *AHLB:* 1150-J[V] *Strong's:* #2107

BE.LESS[V] (*m.ah.t)* To be fewer or diminished in size or amount. *AHLB:* 2347[V] *Strong's:* #4591

BE.LET.ALONE[V] (*sh.b.q)* To be let go. *AHLB:* 2810[V] *Strong's:* [Found in names only]

BE.LOW[V] (*m.w.k)* To be brought down low in poverty. *AHLB:* 1287-J[V] *Strong's:* #4134

BE.NUMB[V] (*p.w.g)* Devoid of sensation or emotion. *AHLB:* 1371-J[V] *Strong's:* #6313

BE.OLD[V] (*z.q.n)* To be of an advanced age. *AHLB:* 2132[V] *Strong's:* #2204

BE.OUT.OF.SIGHT[V] (*ah.l.m)* To be hidden or obscured from vision; to be beyond the horizon; to be covered or unknown. *AHLB:* 2544[V] *Strong's:* #5956

BE.OVERSHADOWED[V] (*ts.l.l)* To be sunk down into a dark depth. *AHLB:* 1403-B[V] *Strong's:* #6749, #6750, #6751

BE.RED[V] (*a.d.m)* To be ruddy. To have a dark reddish color. *AHLB:* 1082-C[V] *Strong's:* #0119

BE.RICH[V] (*ah.sh.r)* To have a large accumulation of resources, means, or funds. To be wealthy. *AHLB:* 2585[V] *Strong's:* #6238

BE.SAD[V] (*z.ah.p)* To be in a state of depression. *AHLB:* 2130[V] *Strong's:* #2196

BE.SATISFIED[V] (*sh.b.ah)* To be filled full or to overflowing; to have a complete amount. *AHLB:* 2461[V] *Strong's:* #7646

BE.SHARP.SIGHTED[V] (*ah.q.n)* *Strong's:* [Found in names only]

BE.SHATTERED[V] (*hh.t.t)* To be broken into pieces; to fear; to be in terror. *AHLB:* 1183-B[V] *Strong's:* #2865

BE.SICK[V] (*hh.l.h)* To be twisted through pain. *AHLB:* 1173-H[V] *Strong's:* #2470

BE.SILENT (*d.m.m)* To come to a standstill in speech or deed. To be quiet; refrain from speech or action. *AHLB:* 1082-B[N] *Strong's:* #1826

BE.SKILLED[V] (*hh.k.m)* To be able to decide or discern between good and bad, right and wrong; to act correctly in thought and action. *AHLB:* 2159[V] *Strong's:* #2449

BE.SMALL[V] (*q.t.n)* To have little size or slight dimensions; insignificant. *AHLB:* 2703[V] *Strong's:* #6994

BE.SOFT[V] (*r.k.k)* To be soft. *AHLB:* 1448-B[V] *Strong's:* #7401

BE.SOUR[V] (*hh.m.ts)* To be fermented by adding leaven to bread. Also, sour in taste, thought or action. *Alternate Translation:* leaven (when written in the hiphil [active causative] form) *AHLB:* 2173[V] *Strong's:* #2556

BE.SQUARE[V] (*r.b.ah)* Any four sided object. Also, to go down on the hands and knees, to be on all fours. *AHLB:* 2744[V] *Strong's:* #7250, #7251

BE.STEADFAST[V] (*ts.d.q)* To walk on the right path without losing the way. *AHLB:* 2658[V] *Strong's:* #6663

BE.STRAIGHT[V] (*y.sh.r)* To be in a direct or correct line, path or thought. *AHLB:* 1480-L[V] *Strong's:* #3474

BE.STRANGE[V] (*z.w.r)* To be separated out from others; to be scattered abroad. *AHLB:* 1158-J[V] *Strong's:* #2114

BE.STRONG[V] (*a.m.ts)* To be mentally astute, firm, obstinate or courageous. Having or marked by great physical, moral or intellectual power. *AHLB:* 1294-C[V] *Strong's:* #0553

BE.STUBBORN[V] (/ *s.r.r)* To turn away from the correct path toward another direction. *AHLB:* 1342-B[V] *Strong's:* #5637, #7786

BE.SUPERFLUOUS[V] (*s.r.ah) AHLB:* 2511[V] *Strong's:* #8311

BE.TERRIFIED[V] (*ah.r.ts) AHLB:* 2581[V] *Strong's:* #6206

BE.THICK[V] (*ah.b.h)* To be thick. Thick. *AHLB:* 1508-H[V] *Strong's:* #5666

BE.THREEFOLD[V] (*sh.l.sh)* Being three times as great or as many. *AHLB:* 2847[V] *Strong's:* #8027

BE.UNMINDFUL[V] (*sh.y.h) AHLB:* 1465-M[V] *Strong's:* #7876

BE.WARM[V] (*hh.m.m)* To glow; project extreme heat. To be heated, either internally or externally, such as from the sun or a fire. *AHLB:* 1174-B[V] *Strong's:* #2552

BE.WHOLE[V] (*t.m.m)* To be free of wound or injury, defect or impairment, disease or deformity; physically and mentally sound. *AHLB:* 1496-B[V] *Strong's:* #8552

BE.ZEALOUS[V] (*q.n.a)* To be filled with eagerness and ardent interest in pursuit of something. *Alternate Translation:* envious (when written in the piel [active intensive] form) *AHLB:* 1428-E[V] *Strong's:* #7065

BEARD (masc. *za'qeyn)* The hair that grows on a man's face. A long and gray beard as a sign of old age and wisdom. An elder as a bearded one. *Alternate Translation:* elder (as one with a long beard) *AHLB:* 2132[N] *Strong's:* #2205, #2206

BEARDED.VULTURE (masc. *pe'res)* An unknown bird of prey. *AHLB:* 2640[N] *Strong's:* #6538

BEAST (fem. *be'hey'mah)* An animal as distinguished from man or a plant. A tall or large creature. Also, representative of wealth, as one who is exalted. *AHLB:* 1036-G(N1) *Strong's:* #0929, #0930

BEAT(V) (*p.ah.m)* To strike repeatedly in a rhythm such as a drum. *AHLB:* 2623(V) *Strong's:* #6470

BEAT.OUT(V) (*d.p.q)* To strike something with a sharp blow. *AHLB:* 2109(V) *Strong's:* #1849

BEAT.SMALL(V) (*d.q.q)* To crush or pound something into thin or small particles. *AHLB:* 1080-B(V) *Strong's:* #1854

BEATEN.GRAIN (masc. *ge'res)* Wheat, rye or other seeds that are crushed to make meal. *AHLB:* 2086(N) *Strong's:* #1643

BEATEN.WORK (fem. *miq'shah)* To be shaped into a specific form by an outside force such as a hammer. *AHLB:* 1435-H(h1) *Strong's:* #4749

BEATING (masc. *sav'ta'ka) Strong's:* [Found in names only]

BEAUTIFUL (masc. *ya'pheh)* Generally pleasing. Possessing the qualities of loveliness or functionality. *AHLB:* 1224-H(N) *Strong's:* #3303, #3304

BEAUTY (masc. *hheyn)* A person, place or thing that is graceful and precious; what is worth protecting. *AHLB:* 1175-A(N) *Strong's:* #2580

BED (fem. *mit'tah)* A place for sleeping. Spread out sheet for sleeping. *AHLB:* 1308-A(h1) *Strong's:* #4296

BEE (fem. *d'vo'rah)* An insect that lives in an ordered colony and produces honey. *AHLB:* 2093(c1) *Strong's:* #1682

BEFORE (masc. *te'rem)* What precedes another event. *Alternate Translation:* not yet *AHLB:* 2244(N) *Strong's:* #2962

BEHEAD(V) (*ah.r.p)* To sever the neck from the body. Also, to break the neck. *AHLB:* 2580(V) *Strong's:* #6202

BEING.LOW (masc. *ma'khi) Strong's:* [Found in names only]

BELITTLE(V) (*q.l.l)* To regard or portray as less impressive or important; to be light in weight; to curse or despise in the sense of making light. *AHLB:* 1426-B(V) *Strong's:* #7043

BELL (masc. *pa'a'mon)* An instrument used to call to attention or to a warning. From its rhythmic ringing. *AHLB:* 2623(m) *Strong's:* #6472

BELLY (masc. *ga'hhon)* The undersurface of an animal; the stomach and other digestive organs. *AHLB:* 1054-A(j) *Strong's:* #1512

BELONGING (masc. *put)* To acquire ownership or authority over, something or someone owned by another. *Strong's:* [Found in names only]

BELONGING.TO.NAT (masc. *as'nat) Strong's:* [Found in names only]

BEND.DOWN(V) (*sh.hh.h)* To pay homage to another one by bowing low or getting on the knees with the face to the ground. *AHLB:* 1468-H(V) *Strong's:* #7812

BEND.THE.KNEE (masc. *av'reykh)* A kneeling down, often as a sign of respect to another. *AHLB:* 2039(N) *Strong's:* #0086

BENEATH (masc. *mat'tah)* Below; in a lower place, position or state. As under a stretched out sheet. *Alternate Translation:* bottom; low *AHLB:* 1308-H(a) *Strong's:* #4295

BENEFIT(V) (*s.k.n)* To be of use, service or profit in order that one may benefit from it. *Alternate Translation:* in the habit (when written in the hiphil [active causative] form) *AHLB:* 2478(V) *Strong's:* #5532, #5533

BEQA (masc. *be'qa)* A dry weight measure equal to one-half shekel weight. *AHLB:* 2034(N) *Strong's:* #1235

BESIDE (masc. *e'tsel)* Being next to something. *AHLB:* 1403-C(N) *Strong's:* #0681
BEST (masc. *may'tav)* Excelling all others; most, largest; most productive or good, utility or satisfaction. *AHLB:* 1186-L(k) *Strong's:* #4315
BETROTH(V) (*a.r.sh)* A promise or contract of impending marriage. To request a woman for marriage. *AHLB:* 1458-C(V) *Strong's:* #0781
BETWEEN (masc. *beyn)* In the time, space or interval that separates. *AHLB:* 1037-M(N) *Strong's:* #0996, #1143
BIND(V) (*ah.q.d)* To make secure by tying; to confine, restrain or restrict as if with bonds. bind with a cord. *AHLB:* 2572(V) *Strong's:* #6123
BIND.UP(V) (*a.l.m)* To tie something. The tying of the tongue, silence. *AHLB:* 1266-C(V) *Strong's:* #0481
BINDER (masc. *hha'shuq)* Attached around something. *AHLB:* 2219(d) *Strong's:* #2838
BIRD (fem. *tsi'por)* A creature distinguished by a body covering of feathers and wings as forelimbs. *AHLB:* 2685(c) *Strong's:* #6833
BIRD.OF.PREY (masc. *a'yit)* A carnivorous bird that feeds on carrion or meat taken by hunting. *AHLB:* 1354-M(N) *Strong's:* #5861
BIRTH (fem. *she'ger)* What is brought forth from the womb. *AHLB:* 2816(N) *Strong's:* #7698
BIRTHED (masc. *yi'lud)* What is given birth to; a baby human or animal that is brought from the womb into the open world. *AHLB:* 1257-L(c) *Strong's:* #3209
BIRTHING (fem. *tol'dah)* The act or process of bringing forth offspring from the womb. Total of the children born within an era. *AHLB:* 1257-L(i3) *Strong's:* #8435
BIRTHRIGHT (fem. *be'kho'rah)* Rights, privileges or possessions to which a person is entitled by birth. The rights of the firstborn son (see Deut. 21:17). Also, meaning the firstborn. *AHLB:* 2016(c1) *Strong's:* #1062
BITE(V) (*n.sh.k)* To seize especially with teeth or jaws; to sting, wound or pierce as with a fang. To give usury in the sense of a biting. *AHLB:* 2441(V) *Strong's:* #5391
BITTER (masc. *mar fem.* *ma'rah)* A difficult taste or experience. *AHLB:* 1296-A(N) *Strong's:* #4751, #4752
BITTER.HERBS (masc. *mam'ror)* Edible plants, that when eaten brings tears to the eyes. *AHLB:* 1296-B(ac) *Strong's:* #4472
BITTERNESS (masc. *ma'rar)* Having a harsh, disagreeably acrid taste. *Strong's:* [Found in names only]
BLACK (masc. *hhum)* A dark or darkened color; charcoal color. *AHLB:* 1174-J(N) *Strong's:* #2345
BLACKISH (masc. *kush) Strong's:* [Found in names only]
BLANKET(V) (*hh.p.p)* To cover over. *AHLB:* 1178-B(V) *Strong's:* #2653
BLAST(V) (*sh.d.p)* To blow heavily. *AHLB:* 2817(V) *Strong's:* #7710
BLASTING (fem. *sh'dey'phah)* A strong devastating wind. *AHLB:* 2817(N1) *Strong's:* #7711(x2)
BLAZE(V) (*l.h.t) AHLB:* 1262-G(V) *Strong's:* #3857
BLAZING (masc. *la'hat)* To burn, flash or shine brightly. Also, used for the magic of magicians. *AHLB:* 1262-G(N) *Strong's:* #3858

BLEMISH (masc. *m'um)* A defect or incompleteness that makes on useless or valueless. *AHLB:* 1289-D(d) *Strong's:* #3971

BLIND (masc. *i'weyr)* A darkness of the eye. *AHLB:* 1526-J(N) *Strong's:* #5787

BLIND(V) (*ah.w.r)* To become dark of site through blindness or the putting out of the eyes. *AHLB:* 1526-J(V) *Strong's:* #5786

BLINDNESS (masc. *ey'wa'ron fem.* *a'we'ret) AHLB:* 1526-J(j) *Strong's:* #5788

BLOOD (masc. *dam)* The red fluid that circulates through the body. *Alternate Translation:* bloodshed (when in the plural form) *AHLB:* 1082-A(N) *Strong's:* #1818

BLOOM(V) (*ts.w.ts) AHLB:* 1409-J(V) *Strong's:* #6692

BLOSSOM (masc. *tsits fem.* *tsi'tsah)* The flower of a plant, especially of one producing an edible fruit. *AHLB:* 1409-M(N) *Strong's:* #6731, #6733

BLOW(V) (*n.sh.p)* To expel air from the mouth. *AHLB:* 2444(V) *Strong's:* #5398

BLOW.AWAY(V) (*p.a.h)* To scatter something by blowing. *AHLB:* 1373-D(V) *Strong's:* #6284

BLOWN (masc. *po'ah) Strong's:* [Found in names only]

BLUE (fem. *te'khey'let)* A color that is created with the use of a dye. *AHLB:* 1242-A(i2) *Strong's:* #8504

BOARD (masc. *qe'resh)* A plank of wood often used to wall off an area or restrict access. *AHLB:* 2736(N) *Strong's:* #7175

BOARDED.UP(V) (/ *s.p.n)* To cover as a ceiling or to hide. *AHLB:* 2498(V) *Strong's:* #5603, #8226

BODY (fem. *ge'vi'yah)* The physical form of a person or animal, either alive or dead; a corpse. *AHLB:* 1052-A(f1) *Strong's:* #1472

BOIL(V) (*b.sh.l)* To generate bubbles of vapor when heated; to cook a meat in water; to soften by boiling or ripening. *Alternate Translation:* ripen (when written in the hiphil [active causative] form) *AHLB:* 2043(V) *Strong's:* #1310

BOILED (masc. *ba'sheyl)* Meat or other edible that is cooked in water over a fire. *AHLB:* 2043(N) *Strong's:* #1311

BOILING.POT (fem. *mar'hha'shet) AHLB:* 2766(a2) *Strong's:* #4802

BOILS (masc. *she'hhin)* A festering under the skin. Pits in the skin from disease. *AHLB:* 1468-A(s) *Strong's:* #7822

BOLDNESS (masc. *oz)* Knowing one's position or authority and standing in it. Strengthened and protected from danger. *AHLB:* 1352-J(N) *Strong's:* #5797

BOND (masc. *iy'sar) AHLB:* 1342-C(e) *Strong's:* #0632

BONDWOMAN (fem. *a'mah)* A female slave. One who is bound to another. *AHLB:* 1013-A(N1) *Strong's:* #0519

BONE (masc. *e'tsem)* The hard tissue of which the skeleton is chiefly composed. As a numerous amount. *AHLB:* 2569(N) *Strong's:* #6106

BONNET (masc. *pe'eyr)* A piece of cloth that is wound around the head as a decoration. *AHLB:* 1388-D(N) *Strong's:* #6287

BOOTH (fem. *su'kah)* A temporary shelter; a small enclosure; dwelling place. *AHLB:* 1333-J(N1) *Strong's:* #5521

BOOTY (masc. *mal'qo'ahh)* As tongs for taking food. What is taken. *AHLB:* 2319(ac) *Strong's:* #4455

BORDER (masc. גבול *ge'vul)* The outer edge of a region. Also, the area within the borders. *AHLB:* 2049(d) *Strong's:* #1366

BORE.OUT(V) (נבב *n.b.b)* To form by making something hollow. *AHLB:* 1301-B(V) *Strong's:* #5014

BORE.THROUGH(V) (רצע *r.ts.ah)* To pierce with a sharp object. *AHLB:* 2791(V) *Strong's:* #7527

BORN (masc. יליד *ya'liyid)* Brought forth, as if by birth. *AHLB:* 1257-L(b) *Strong's:* #3211

BOSOM (masc. חק / חוק / חיק *hheyq / hhuq / hheyq)* The human chest, especially the front side. *AHLB:* 1163-M(N) *Strong's:* #2436

BOTTOM (masc. קרקע *qar'qa) AHLB:* 3057 *Strong's:* #7172

BOTTOM.BASE (masc. יסוד *ye'sod fem.* יסודה *ye'so'dah)* A supporting and level base of a building or structure which lies on or in the ground. *AHLB:* 1326-L(c) *Strong's:* #3246, #3247, #3248, #4328

BOUGH (masc. ענף *a'naph) AHLB:* 2558(N) *Strong's:* #6057, #6058

BOULDER (masc. צור *tsur)* A large rock used as a weapon or a rock cliff used as a place of defense. Also, flint, a very hard rock that when fractured forms a razor sharp edge and used for knives, spears or arrowheads. *AHLB:* 1411-J(N) *Strong's:* #6697

BOUND(V) (גבל *g.b.l)* To be defined by a border. *AHLB:* 2049(V) *Strong's:* #1379

BOUND.SHEAF (masc. אלום *a'lum)* Stalks and ears of a cereal grass bound together. A sheaf of grain that is bound. *AHLB:* 1266-C(d) *Strong's:* #0485

BOUND.UP(V) (קוה *q.w.h)* To be confined or hedged in together; to wait or to be held back. *AHLB:* 1419-J(V) *Strong's:* #6960

BOUNDARY (fem. מגבלה *mig'be'let)* Marks the outer edge, the end, of a definite area or region. Idiomatically used for an entire region. *AHLB:* 2049(h1) *Strong's:* #4020

BOUNTY (fem. תנובה *t'nu'vah) AHLB:* 1301-J(i1) *Strong's:* #8570

BOVINE (masc. אלף *e'leph)* An adult male of the bovine family. (In Judges 6:15 this word is used for "family"). *AHLB:* 2001(N) *Strong's:* #0504

BOW (fem. קשת *qe'shet)* A weapon made from a stiff branch to shoots arrows. A bow-shaped object such as a rainbow. *AHLB:* 1435-A(N2) *Strong's:* #7198, #7199

BOW.THE.HEAD(V) (קדד *q.d.d)* To lower the head as a sign of respect. *AHLB:* 1418-B(V) *Strong's:* #6915

BOWELS (masc. רחם *re'hhem)* The belly; the lower portion of the torso. *Alternate Translation:* tenderness *AHLB:* 2762(N) *Strong's:* #7356, #7358

BOWL (masc. גביע *ga'vi'a)* A concave vessel especially for holding liquids. As with high sides. *AHLB:* 2051(b) *Strong's:* #1375

BOX (masc. ארון *a'ron)* A rigid rectangular receptacle often with a cover. Any box-shaped object. *AHLB:* 1020-H(j) *Strong's:* #0727

BOY (masc. ילד *ye'led)* A male child from birth to puberty. *AHLB:* 1257-L(N) *Strong's:* #3206

BRACELET (masc. צמיד *tsa'mid)* An ornamental band or chain worn around the wrist. As the ends joined together. *AHLB:* 2665(b) *Strong's:* #6781

BRAID(V) (ארג *a.r.g)* To twist, entwine or weave several pieces together in parallel to become one. *AHLB:* 1440-C(V) *Strong's:* #0707

BRAIDED.WORK (masc. *se'red)* Articles of clothing made by weaving together fibers. *AHLB:* 2506$^{(N)}$ *Strong's:* #8278, #8279

BRAMBLE (masc. *qots)* A rough, prickly vine or shrub. Thorn. *AHLB:* 1432-J$^{(N)}$ *Strong's:* #6975

BRAMBLE.THORN (masc. *a'tad)* A bush with thorns. *AHLB:* 1188-C$^{(N)}$ *Strong's:* #0329

BRANCH (masc. *ma'teh)* A branch used as a staff. Also, a tribe as a branch of the family. *AHLB:* 1285-H$^{(N)}$ *Strong's:* #4294

BRASS (masc. *na'hhush fem. na'hhu'shah)* From its shine. *AHLB:* 2395(d) *Strong's:* #5153, #5154

BRAVERY (fem. *ge'vo'rah)* An act of defending one's property, convictions or beliefs. Control through physical strength. *AHLB:* 2052(d1) *Strong's:* #1369

BRAWN (masc. *o'tsem fem. a'tsu'mah)* From the strength of the bones. *AHLB:* 2569(g) *Strong's:* #6108, #6110

BREACH (masc. *pe'rets)* A broken, ruptured or torn condition or area; a gap as in a wall made by battering. *AHLB:* 2642$^{(N)}$ *Strong's:* #6556

BREAD (masc. *le'hhem)* Baked and leavened bread primarily made of flour or meal. Also, food in general. *AHLB:* 2305$^{(N)}$ *Strong's:* #3899, #3901

BREAD.MEAL (fem. *a'riy'sah)* Meaning dubious. *AHLB:* 2579(b1) *Strong's:* #6182

BREAK$^{(V)}$ (*p.r.r)* To throw something on the ground and break it by trampling. *AHLB:* 1388-B$^{(V)}$ *Strong's:* #6565

BREAK.DOWN$^{(V)}$ (*n.t.ts)* To demolish an elevated object; to tear down. *AHLB:* 2454$^{(V)}$ *Strong's:* #5422

BREAK.OUT$^{(V)}$ (*p.r.ts)* To be spread out wide or widespread. *AHLB:* 2642$^{(V)}$ *Strong's:* #6555

BREAST (masc. *shad)* Milk-producing glandular organs situated on the chest in the female; the fore part of the body between the neck and the abdomen. Also, a goat-idol from the teats of the goat. *AHLB:* 1464-A$^{(N)}$ *Strong's:* #7699, #7700

BREASTPLATE (masc. *hho'shen)* An ornamental plate worn by the High Priest that held stones representing the twelve tribes of Israel and the Urim and Thummim. *AHLB:* 1182-J(m) *Strong's:* #2833

BREATH (fem. *ne'shey'mah)* Air inhaled or exhaled. The breath of man or god. The essence of life. *AHLB:* 2443(N1) *Strong's:* #5397

BREATHE.DEEPLY$^{(V)}$ (*n.p.sh)* To relax and breath in deeply to refresh oneself. To take a breather. *AHLB:* 2424$^{(V)}$ *Strong's:* #5314

BRIBE (masc. *sha'hhad)* To buy a favor or service that would be otherwise out of reach. *AHLB:* 2822$^{(N)}$ *Strong's:* #7810

BRICK (fem. *le'vey'nah)* A building material typically whitish in color, rectangular and made of moist clay hardened by heat. *AHLB:* 2303(N1) *Strong's:* #3840, #3843

BRIDE.PRICE (masc. *mo'har)* A payment given by or in behalf of a prospective husband to the bride's family. *AHLB:* 1296-G(g) *Strong's:* #4119

BRIGHT (masc. *she'pher)* A radiating or reflective light. As cheerful. *AHLB:* 2869$^{(N)}$ *Strong's:* #8233

BRIGHT.SPOT (fem. *ba'he'ret)* A thin sac or cyst on the skin, containing watery matter or serum, as from a burn or other injury; a possible sign of leprosy. *AHLB:* 1043-G(N2) *Strong's:* #0934

BRIGHTNESS (fem. *shiph'rah)* Harmonized and in balance. Cheerful. *AHLB:* 2869(e1) *Strong's:* #8235

BRIMSTONE (fem. *gaph'rit)* A rock of sulfur that burns. *AHLB:* 2079(N4) *Strong's:* #1614

BRING$^{(V)}$ (*y.b.l)* To cause to come by carrying, leading or dragging. *AHLB:* 1035-L$^{(V)}$ *Strong's:* #2986

BRING.FORTH$^{(V)}$ (*y.l.d)* To issue out; to bring forth children, either by the woman who bears them or the man who fathers them. *Alternate Translation:* act as midwife (when written in the piel [active intensive] form) *AHLB:* 1257-L$^{(V)}$ *Strong's:* #3205

BROKEN (masc. *da'kah)* Something that is struck into fragments. *AHLB:* 1080-E$^{(N)}$ *Strong's:* #1793

BROODING (masc. *de'a'von)* A pining or fainting over something desired or lost. *AHLB:* 1071-D(j) *Strong's:* #1671

BROTHER (masc. *ahh)* A male who has the same parents as another or shares one parent with another. One who stands between the enemy and the family, a protector. *AHLB:* 1008-A$^{(N)}$ *Strong's:* #0251, #1889(x2)

BROTHER-IN-LAW (masc. *ya'vam)* A male sibling of one's spouse. *AHLB:* 1036-L$^{(N)}$ *Strong's:* #2993

BROUGHT.OUT (masc. *ge'resh)* Driven away, expelled, or thrust away. *AHLB:* 2089$^{(N)}$ *Strong's:* #1645

BRUISER (masc. *kiyt) Strong's:* [Found in names only]

BUCK (masc. *a'yil)* The large males of a flock of sheep or heard of deer. By extension, anything of strength including a chief, pillar (as the strong support of a building), or oak tree (one of the strongest of the woods). *AHLB:* 1012-M$^{(N)}$ *Strong's:* #0352, #0353, #0354

BUCKET (masc. *de'liy)* A deep, cylindrical vessel, usually of wood or skin, for collecting, carrying, or holding water; pail. *AHLB:* 1081-H(f) *Strong's:* #1805

BUD (masc. *pe'rahh)* The beginning of a flower that bursts from the plant. *AHLB:* 2636$^{(N)}$ *Strong's:* #6525

BUDDING (masc. *giv'ol)* To sprout flowers or blooms. To come into a fullness. *AHLB:* 3006 *Strong's:* #1392

BUILD$^{(V)}$ (*b.n.h)* To construct a building or home with wood, stone or other material or a family with sons. *AHLB:* 1037-H$^{(V)}$ *Strong's:* #1129

BUILD.UP$^{(V)}$ (*s.l.l)* To raise the elevation of the bank of a river or a highway. To raise one up higher than others. *AHLB:* 1334-B$^{(V)}$ *Strong's:* #5549

BULK (fem. *to'a'phah)* Being immense in size. *AHLB:* 1362-L(i1) *Strong's:* #8443

BULL (masc. *par)* A large male un-castrated bovine. *AHLB:* 1388-A$^{(N)}$ *Strong's:* #6499

BULLOCK (masc. *ey'gel)* A young bull. Also, insinuating strength. *AHLB:* 2524$^{(N)}$ *Strong's:* #5695

BULRUSH (masc. *go'me)* A reed that grows in, or on the edge of, a pond or river. *AHLB:* 1059-E$^{(N)}$ *Strong's:* #1573

BUNCH (fem. *a'gu'dah)* A group of men or things bound together. *AHLB:* 1050-J(n1) *Strong's:* #0092

BUNDLE[V] (*ah.m.r) AHLB:* 2554[V] *Strong's:* #6014

BURDEN (fem. *se'va'lah)* The heavy load carried in bondage. *AHLB:* 2460(N1) *Strong's:* #5450

BURIAL.PLACE (fem. *qe'vu'rah)* The place of interment or deposit of a deceased body. *AHLB:* 2696(d1) *Strong's:* #6900

BURN[V] (*b.ah.r)* To undergo rapid combustion or consume fuel in such a way as to give off heat, gases, and, usually, light; be on fire; have fierce anger; to destroy *Alternate Translation:* ignite (when written in the piel [active intensive] form) *AHLB:* 2028[V] *Strong's:* #1197

BURN.BLACK[V] (*k.m.r)* To char wood in a fire. A passion that burns for another. *AHLB:* 2266[V] *Strong's:* #3648

BURN.INCENSE[V] (*q.t.r)* To light a sacrifice or aromatic plant on fire creating smoke, often aromatic. *AHLB:* 2705[V] *Strong's:* #6999, #7000

BURNING (fem. *be'ey'rah)* Something that is aflame with fire. *AHLB:* 2028(N1) *Strong's:* #1200

BURNING.FLAME (masc. *hhar'hhur)* An inflammation. *AHLB:* 1181-A(l) *Strong's:* #2746

BURNT (masc. *ga'hham)* Something that has been burned. *Strong's:* [Found in names only]

BURNT.VALLEY (masc. *ga'tam) Strong's:* [Found in names only]

BURST.OUT[V] (*p.r.hh)* To be larger, fuller, or more crowded; to break out or break forth as a blooming flower or the wings of a bird. *AHLB:* 2636[V] *Strong's:* #6524

BURSTING (masc. *pe'ter fem. piyt'rah)* A sudden and forceful release or issuing out. *AHLB:* 2604[N] *Strong's:* #6363

BURSTING.FORTH (masc. *giy'hhon)* To break, break open, or fly apart with sudden violence. *Strong's:* [Found in names only]

BURY[V] (*q.b.r)* To dispose of by depositing in the ground. *AHLB:* 2696[V] *Strong's:* #6912

BUSINESS (fem. *me'la'khah)* The principal occupation of one's life. A service. *AHLB:* 1264-D(k1) *Strong's:* #4399

BUT (*u-lam)* On the contrary; an outcome desired. *AHLB:* 1254-J(p) *Strong's:* #0199

BUTCHER[V] (*t.b.hh)* One who slaughters animals or dresses their flesh. *AHLB:* 2227[V] *Strong's:* #2873

BUTTOCKS (masc. *shey'tah)* The posterier part of the body where one sits. *AHLB:* 1482-A[N] *Strong's:* #8357

BUTTRESS (masc. *miq'tso'a)* A support or prop. Wall or abutment built to support another wall on the outside, when very high or loaded with a heavy structure. *AHLB:* 2725(hc) *Strong's:* #4740

BY (masc. *i'mad)* In proximity to. *Alternate Translation:* with *AHLB:* 2550(e) *Strong's:* #5978

CAKE (fem. *de'vey'lah)* A bread made of pressed figs. *AHLB:* 2091(N1) *Strong's:* #1690

CALAMITY (masc. *eyd)* A disaster. *AHLB:* 1004-M[N] *Strong's:* #0343

CALCULATE(V) (*s.k.l)* To comprehend and carefully consider a path or course of action; to determine by deduction or practical judgment. *AHLB:* 2477(V) *Strong's:* #7919

CALL.OUT(V) (*q.r.a)* To raise one's voice or speak loudly and with urgency; to give, a name; to meet in the sense of being called to a meeting; to have an encounter by chance; to read in the sense of calling out words. *AHLB:* 1434-E(V) *Strong's:* #7121

CAMEL (*ga-mal)* Either of two ruminant mammals used as draft animals in the desert. The produce of the fields was tied in large bundles and transported on camels. (Also related in meaning to the original parent root גם as one who gathers at the watering hole). *AHLB:* 2070(N) *Strong's:* #1581

CAMP (masc. *me'hha'neh)* A place suitable for or used as the location of a camp. The inhabitants of a camp. *AHLB:* 1175-H(a) *Strong's:* #4264

CAMP(V) (*hh.n.h)* To erect temporary shelters (as tents) *AHLB:* 1175-H(V) *Strong's:* #2583

CAMPSITE (fem. *ta'hha'nah)* A place suitable for or used as the location of a camp. *AHLB:* 1175-A(i1) *Strong's:* #8466

CANOPY (masc. *ma'sak)* The covering of a temporary shelter. *AHLB:* 1333-A(a) *Strong's:* #4539

CAPTAIN (masc. *na'si)* A military leader; the commander of a unit or a body of troops. The leader of a family, tribe or people as one who carries the burdens of the people. *AHLB:* 1314-E(b) *Strong's:* #5387

CAPTIVE (masc. *she'vi fem. sh'viy'ah)* A person who is enslaved or dominated. *AHLB:* 1462-H(f) *Strong's:* #7628, #7633

CAPTIVITY (fem. / *she'vut / she'viyt)* The state or period of being held, imprisoned, enslaved, or confined. *AHLB:* 1462-H(N3) *Strong's:* #7622

CAPTURE(V) (*sh.b.h)* The act of catching, winning, or gaining control by force, stratagem, or guile; to take one away from his homeland as an involuntary prisoner. *AHLB:* 1462-H(V) *Strong's:* #7617

CARAVAN (fem. *or'hhah)* A traveling company that follows a prescribed path. *AHLB:* 1445-C(g1 & N1) *Strong's:* #0736

CARCASS (fem. *ne'vey'lah)* The remains of a creature or person that has lost its life. *AHLB:* 2369(N1) *Strong's:* #5038

CARNELIAN (fem. *o'dem)* Probably the Carnelian, a reddish-brown gemstone. The Hebrew word is from a root meaning red or reddish. Another possible translation is Jasper. *AHLB:* 1082-C(g) *Strong's:* #0124

CARRY(V) (*s.b.l)* To transfer from one place to another; to transport as by vehicle. *AHLB:* 2460(V) *Strong's:* #5445

CART (fem. *a'ga'lah)* A heavy, two-wheeled vehicle, animal-drawn, used for transporting freight or for farming. *AHLB:* 2524(N1) *Strong's:* #5699

CARTILAGE (masc. *ge'rem)* Translucent elastic tissue that lines the joints of the bony skeleton. *AHLB:* 2084(N) *Strong's:* #1634

CARVE(V) (*hh.t.b) AHLB:* 2154(V) *Strong's:* #2404

CASSIA (fem. *qi'dah)* The tree, wood or spice which is used in anointing oils and perfumes. *AHLB:* 1418-M(N1) *Strong's:* #6916

CAST.AWAY(V) (*g.ah.l)* To throw or hurl. *AHLB:* 2075(V) *Strong's:* #1602

CAST.DOWN(V) (*h.r.s)* To ruin or break into pieces by throwing or pulling down. *AHLB:* 1452-F(V) *Strong's:* #2040

CAST.IMAGE (fem. *ma'sey'khah)* A molten metal that is poured in a cast to form images. *AHLB:* 2412(a1) *Strong's:* #4541

CAST.OFF(V) (*n.sh.l)* To remove with force and intention. *AHLB:* 2442(V) *Strong's:* #5394

CAST.OUT(V) (*g.r.sh)* To forcefully drive away, expel, or thrust away. *AHLB:* 2089(V) *Strong's:* #1644

CATARACT (masc. *te'ba'lul)* The clouding color of the eyes that appear as a mixture. *AHLB:* 1035-B(id) *Strong's:* #8400

CATTLE (masc. / *ba'qar / be'iyr)* Domesticated bovine animals. Strong beasts used to break the soil with plows. *AHLB:* 2035(N) *Strong's:* #1165, #1241

CAULDRON (masc. *ki'or)* A large kettle or boiler, of copper or other metal. A smelting pot. *AHLB:* 1250-J(e) *Strong's:* #3595

CAUSING.TO.OVERLOOK (masc. *man'shah) Strong's:* [Found in names only]

CAVE (fem. *me'khey'rah)* A natural underground chamber or series of chambers that open to the surface. A hole in the rock. *AHLB:* 1250-A(k1) *Strong's:* #4380, #4631

CEASE(V) (*sh.b.t)* To come to an end; to die out; to stop an activity for the purpose of rest or celebration. *AHLB:* 2812(V) *Strong's:* #7673

CEASING (fem. *sha'bat)* A stopping of work or activity; An activity curtailed before completion. The seventh day of the week (often transliterated as Sabbath) *AHLB:* 2812(N) *Strong's:* #7674, #7676

CEDAR (masc. *e'rez)* A coniferous tree from the cyprus family having wide, spreading branches. The wood or tree or something made it. *AHLB:* 1444-C(N) *Strong's:* #0730

CENTER (fem. *hha'tsot)* The middle of something. *AHLB:* 1179-A(N3) *Strong's:* #2676

CEREAL (masc. *da'gan)* Relating to grain or plants that produce it. A plentiful crop. *AHLB:* 1072-A(m) *Strong's:* #1715

CHAIN (fem. *shar'she'rah)* A strand of linked metal loops. *AHLB:* 1480-D(l1) *Strong's:* #8331, #8333

CHAMBER (masc. *hhe'der)* A bedroom; a natural or artificial enclosed space or cavity. Place surrounded by walls. An inner place as hidden or secret. *AHLB:* 2150(N) *Strong's:* #2315

CHAMELEON (masc. *ko'ahh)* An unclean animal of unknown species that is known for its strength. *AHLB:* 1238-J(N) *Strong's:* #3581(x2)

CHANGE(V) (*sh.n.h)* To make radically different; exchange one thing for another. To repeat in the sense of a second time. *Alternate Translation:* repeat (when written in the niphil [passive] form) *AHLB:* 1474-H(V) *Strong's:* #8132, #8138

CHARGE (fem. *mish'me'ret)* A person or thing committed to the care of another. What is given to be watched over and protected. *AHLB:* 2853(h2) *Strong's:* #4931

CHARIOT (fem. *mer'ka'vah)* A light, two-wheeled battle vehicle for one or two persons, usually drawn by two horses and driven from a standing position. *AHLB:* 2769(k1) *Strong's:* #4818

CHEESE (fem. / *hhem'ah / hhey'mah)* A food consisting of the coagulated, compressed and usually ripened curd of milk separated from the whey. *AHLB:* 1174-E(N1) *Strong's:* #2529

CHERISH(V) (*hh.b.b)* To fervently love something. *AHLB:* 1163-B(V) *Strong's:* #2245

CHERISHED (masc. *ya'diyid)* One held or treated as dear; feel love for. *AHLB:* 1073-L(b) *Strong's:* #3039

CHEST (masc. *hha'zeh)* The breast containing heart. What is prominently visible. The breast of an animal used for a sacrifice. *AHLB:* 1168-H(N) *Strong's:* #2373

CHESTNUT (masc. *er'mon)* Probably the chestnut tree but uncertain. *AHLB:* 2908(j) *Strong's:* #6196

CHEW(V) (*g.r.r)* To mash food with the teeth for the purpose of digesting. *AHLB:* 1066-B(V) *Strong's:* #1641

CHEWED (masc. *ga'rar)* What has been mashed with the teeth for the purpose of digesting. *Strong's:* [Found in names only]

CHICK (masc. *eph'ro'ahh)* A young bird that has burst out of the egg. *AHLB:* 2636(N) *Strong's:* #0667

CHIEF (masc. *a'luph)* Accorded highest rank or office; of greatest importance, significance, or influence. The military commander of a thousand men. One who is yoked to another to lead and teach. *AHLB:* 2001(d) *Strong's:* #0441

CHILD (masc. *wa'lad)* A young person, especially between infancy and youth. *AHLB:* 1257-I(N) *Strong's:* #2056

CHILD.OF.THE.SUN (masc. *ra'me'seys)* A word of Egyptian origins. *Strong's:* [Found in names only]

CHIMNEY (fem. *a'ru'bah)* A vertical structure in a building and enclosing a flue or flues that carry off smoke. A hole in the roof where smoke escapes. *AHLB:* 1439-C(d1) *Strong's:* #0699

CHOICE.FRUIT (fem. *zim'rah)* Having qualities that appeal to a cultivated taste. As plucked from the tree or vine. *AHLB:* 2124(N1) *Strong's:* #2173

CHOICE.VINE (masc. *so'reyq fem.* *so'rey'qah)* The best of the vine, the best grapes. *AHLB:* 2513(g) *Strong's:* #8321

CHOICE.VINEYARD (fem. *mas'raq) Strong's:* [Found in names only]

CHOOSE(V) (*b.hh.r)* To select freely and after consideration. *AHLB:* 2012(V) *Strong's:* #0977

CHOSEN (masc. *miv'hhar)* Someone or something that is the object of choice or of divine favor. *AHLB:* 2012(h) *Strong's:* #4005

CINNAMON (masc. *qi'na'mon)* A spice from the bark of a small evergreen tree. The essential oil is of great price. *AHLB:* 2716(j) *Strong's:* #7076

CIRCUIT (fem. *te'qu'phah)* A going around in a circle. To return to a starting point in the sense of going full circle. *Alternate Translation:* end *AHLB:* 1431-J(i1) *Strong's:* #8622

CIRCUMCISION (fem. *mu'lah)* The removal of the front part of the male sexual organ. *AHLB:* 1288-J(N1) *Strong's:* #4139

CISTERN (masc. *bor)* An artificial reservoir for storing water. A hole or well as dug out. *AHLB:* 1250-J(N) *Strong's:* #0953, #2352, #2356

CITY (masc. *ir)* An inhabited place of greater size, population, or importance than a town or village. Usually protected by a wall. *AHLB:* 1526-M(N) *Strong's:* #5892

CITY.OF.JUSTICE (masc. *pi'tom)* A word of Egyptian origins. *Strong's:* [Found in names only]

CLAN (fem. *mish'pa'hhah)* A group of persons of common ancestry. A group of people joined together by certain convictions or common affiliation. *AHLB:* 2863(h1) *Strong's:* #4940

CLASP(V) (*s.p.q) AHLB:* 2499(V) *Strong's:* #5606

CLAY (masc. *hhe'res)* An item made of baked and hardened clay such as a tile or pot. *AHLB:* 2207(N) *Strong's:* #2789

CLAYEY.SOIL (masc. *gash)* Ground that consists of hydrated silicates of aluminum: used for making bricks, pottery, etc. *Strong's:* [Found in names only]

CLEAN (masc. *ta'hor fem. ta'ho'rah)* Someone or something that is free of impurities or is not mixed with any other matter. *AHLB:* 1204-G(c) *Strong's:* #2889, #2890

CLEANLINESS (masc. *to'har)* The act of being free from dirt or immorality. Free from foreign elements. *AHLB:* 1204-G(g) *Strong's:* #2892

CLEANSING (fem. *ta'ha'rah) AHLB:* 1204-G(N1) *Strong's:* #2893

CLEAVE(V) (*p.r.s)* To split in two as the hoofs of a clean animal. *AHLB:* 2640(V) *Strong's:* #6536

CLEAVE.OPEN(V) (*b.q.ah)* To divide by or as if by a cutting blow; to separate into distinct parts; to break, cut or divide something in half. *AHLB:* 2034(V) *Strong's:* #1234

CLEFT (fem. *pis'gah) Strong's:* [Found in names only]

CLIFF (masc. *se'la)* A high rock, cliff or towering rock, as a place of defense. *AHLB:* 2484(N) *Strong's:* #5553

CLING(V) (*b.t.hh)* To grab hold of someone or something that is secure and safe. *AHLB:* 2013(V) *Strong's:* #0982

CLINGING (masc. *ge'shur)* Being joined to someone or something. *Strong's:* [Found in names only]

CLOAK (masc. *me'il)* A loose outer garment worn over other clothes both by men and women. *AHLB:* 1357-M(k) *Strong's:* #4598

CLOD (*r.g.b)* A lump or mass, especially of earth or clay. *Strong's:* [Found in names only]

CLOSE(V) (*q.p.ts)* To draw together to close or shut. *AHLB:* 2722(V) *Strong's:* #7092

CLOTHING (masc. *le'vush)* Garments in general. *AHLB:* 2304(d) *Strong's:* #3830

CLOUD (masc. *a'nan fem. a'na'nah)* A visible mass of particles of water or ice in the form of fog, mist, or haze suspended usually at a considerable height in the air. *AHLB:* 1359-B(N) *Strong's:* #6051, #6053

CLUSTER (masc. *esh'kol)* A number of similar things growing together or of things or persons collected or grouped closely together. A cluster of grapes from the vine or flowers from the plant. *AHLB:* 2836(nc) *Strong's:* #0811

COAL (masc. *sha'hhor)* The dim light before the rising of the sun. As dark in color. *Alternate Translation:* black as coal *AHLB:* 2829(c) *Strong's:* #7838, #7815

COAT (masc. *sut)* An outer garment varying in length and style; the external growth on an animal. *AHLB:* 1344-J[N] *Strong's:* #5497

COHABITATION (masc. *on fem. o'nah)* A place of residence. An abode. *AHLB:* 1359-J(N1) *Strong's:* #5772

COLD (masc. *qar)* A condition of low temperature. *AHLB:* 1434-A[N] *Strong's:* #7119, #7120

COLLAR (masc. *tahh'ra)* The hole in the middle of a rectangular garment for the head to pass through. An area reinforced around the neck opening. *AHLB:* 1181-E(i) *Strong's:* #8473

COLLECT[V] (*q.sh.sh)* To gather up straw, stubble or sticks. *AHLB:* 1435-B[V] *Strong's:* #7197

COLLECTION (masc. *miq'weh)* An accumulation of objects or material. A collection of water (a pool, pond or sea) *AHLB:* 1419-J(h) *Strong's:* #4723

COLT (*ai-yir) AHLB:* 1526-M[N] *Strong's:* #5895

COME[V] (*b.w.a)* To move toward something; approach; enter. This can be understood as to come or to go. *Alternate Translation:* bring (when written in the hiphil [active causative] form) *AHLB:* 1024-J[V] *Strong's:* #0935

COME.NEAR[V] (*q.r.b)* To come close by or near to. *Alternate Translation:* be brought near (when written in the niphil [passive] form); bring near (when written in the hiphil [active causative] form) *AHLB:* 2729[V] *Strong's:* #7126

COME.TO.AN.END[V] (*a.p.s)* To cease. Conclude. *AHLB:* 1383-C[V] *Strong's:* #0656

COME.UP[V] (*z.r.hh)* To rise up, as the sun does at the horizon. *AHLB:* 2135[V] *Strong's:* #2224

COMFORT[V] (*n.hh.m)* Consolation in time of trouble or worry; to give solace in time of difficulty or sorrow. *Alternate Translation:* repent (when written in the niphil [passive] form) *AHLB:* 2392[V] *Strong's:* #5162

COMMIT[V] (*m.s.r) AHLB:* 2345[V] *Strong's:* #4560

COMMIT.ADULTERY[V] (*n.a.p)* To perform voluntary violation of the marriage bed. *AHLB:* 2365[V] *Strong's:* #5003

COMMUNITY (masc. *la'um)* A unified body of individuals; a group of people bound together. *AHLB:* 1266-D(c) *Strong's:* #3816

COMPANION (masc. / *rey'a / rey'ya)* One that accompanies another. *AHLB:* 1453-A[N] *Strong's:* #7453

COMPANY (fem. *ey'dah)* A group of persons or things for carrying on a project or undertaking; a group with a common testimony. May also mean a witness or testimony. *AHLB:* 1349-A(N1) *Strong's:* #5712

COMPARE[V] (*s.l.a) AHLB:* 1334-E[V] *Strong's:* #5537

COMPASSIONATE (masc. *ra'hhum)* Being sympathetic, and understanding. A protecting from harm. *AHLB:* 2762(d) *Strong's:* #7349

COMPEL[V] (*a.w.ts)* To drive or urge forcefully or irresistibly. A pressing into an action or narrow place. *AHLB:* 1018-J[V] *Strong's:* #0213

COMPLAIN[V] (*a.n.n)* To grumble over ones undesired circumstances. *AHLB:* 1014-B[V] *Strong's:* #0596

COMPLAINER (masc. *o'nan)* One who grumbles over his undesired circumstances. *Strong's:* [Found in names only]

COMPLETENESS (masc. */ sha'leym / sha'lom fem. she'ley'mah)* Something that has been finished or made whole. A state of being whole. *AHLB:* 2845(c) *Strong's:* #7965, #8003

COMPLETION (fem. *ka'lah)* The act or process of completing. This can be in a positive sense or negative, such as in a failure. *AHLB:* 1242-A(N1) *Strong's:* #3617

COMPOUND[V] (*r.q.hh)* The combining of two or more ingredients to achieve the desired substance. *AHLB:* 2795[V] *Strong's:* #7543

CONCEAL[V] (*ts.p.n)* To hide to prevent discovery. *AHLB:* 2683[V] *Strong's:* #6845

CONCEIVE[V] (*h.r.h)* To become pregnant with young. *AHLB:* 1112-H[V] *Strong's:* #2029

CONCERNING (fem. *o'dot)* Regarding. Marked interest or regard usually arising through a personal tie or relationship. A turning over and bringing together of a thought. *Alternate Translation:* on account of (when following the word "UPON") *AHLB:* 1004-J(N3) *Strong's:* #0182

CONCLUDED (masc. *go'mer) Strong's:* [Found in names only]

CONCLUSION (masc. *qeyts)* To come to an end. The end of a time period or place or the end of something. The border of a country as its edges. *Alternate Translation:* after (when prefixed with "from~") *AHLB:* 1432-A[N] *Strong's:* #7093

CONCUBINE (fem. *piy'le'gesh)* Cohabitation of persons not legally married; a woman living in a socially recognized state of being a mistress. *AHLB:* 3048 *Strong's:* #6370

CONFERENCE (fem. *a'tsa'rah)* A special occasion as a temporary ceasing of normal activity. *AHLB:* 2570(N1) *Strong's:* #6116

CONFIDENCE (masc. *sod)* Advice given in secret as a result of consultation. *AHLB:* 1326-J[N] *Strong's:* #5475

CONFIDENT[V] (*/ k.s.l / s.k.l)* Always used in a negative sense such as foolish confidence. *AHLB:* 2275[V] *Strong's:* #3688, #5528

CONFIDENT.ONE (masc. *kis'lon) Strong's:* [Found in names only]

CONFUSE[V] (*h.m.m)* To cause trouble and turmoil by the sound of a great noise such as with trumpets. *AHLB:* 1105-B[V] *Strong's:* #2000

CONFUSED (masc. *hiy'mam)* The state of being in trouble or in turmoil. *Strong's:* [Found in names only]

CONFUSION (masc. *to'hu)* To bring to ruin; to make indistinct; to fail to differentiate from an often similar or related other. A barren place. Vanity as a state of waste. *AHLB:* 1488-J(r) *Strong's:* #8414

CONJURE[V] (*ah.n.n)* To call or bring into existence. *AHLB:* 1359-B[V] *Strong's:* #6049

CONSENT[V] (*a.b.h)* To give approval; to be in concord in opinion or sentiment; agreement as to action or opinion; to be willing to go somewhere or do something. *AHLB:* 1028-C[V] *Strong's:* #0014

CONSIDERED.UNCIRCUMCISED[V] (*ah.r.l)* To be uncircumcised. *AHLB:* 2577[V] *Strong's:* #6188

CONSISTENCY (masc. *ey'tan)* Agreement or harmony of parts or features; showing steady conformity to character, profession, belief, or custom. *AHLB:* 1497-C(e) *Strong's:* #0386

CONSORT$^{(V)}$ (*hh.r.p)* To be attached to a husband or wife; to be espoused. *AHLB:* 2208$^{(V)}$ *Strong's:* #2778

CONSUME$^{(V)}$ (*s.p.h)* To eat or drink; with the lips. *AHLB:* 1339-H$^{(V)}$ *Strong's:* #5595

CONSUMING (masc. *ka'leh)* A strong desire or longing. *AHLB:* 1242-H$^{(N)}$ *Strong's:* #3616

CONSUMPTION (fem. *sha'hhe'phet)* A disease making one thin. *AHLB:* 2826(N2) *Strong's:* #7829

CONTENTION (fem. *me'ri'vah)* An act or instance of striving or struggling against great difficulty or opposition. *AHLB:* 1439-M(k1) *Strong's:* #4808

CONTINUALLY (masc. *ta'mid)* Happening without interruption or cessation; continuous in time. *AHLB:* 1280-M(b) *Strong's:* #8548

CONTINUE (masc. *nun)* Maintain the action, to forge ahead with intention. *Strong's:* [Found in names only]

CONTINUOUS (masc. *mat'rad) Strong's:* [Found in names only]

CONTRARY (masc. *qe'riy)* To be in opposition. *AHLB:* 1434-A(f) *Strong's:* #7147

CONTRIBUTION (fem. *mat'nah)* What is given or supplied in common with others. *AHLB:* 2451(a1) *Strong's:* #4979

CONVERT$^{(V)}$ (*m.w.r) AHLB:* 1296-J$^{(V)}$ *Strong's:* #4171

COOKED (masc. *tu'pheyn)* A food that is heated in or over a fire to heat it or make it edible. *AHLB:* 1017-J(is) *Strong's:* #8601

COPPER (fem. *ne'hho'shet)* A malleable, ductile, metallic element having a characteristic reddish-brown color. A precious metal. *AHLB:* 2395(c2) *Strong's:* #5178

COPULATE$^{(V)}$ (*sh.g.l) AHLB:* 2814$^{(V)}$ *Strong's:* #7693

COPULATION (fem. *sh'kho'vet) AHLB:* 2834(c2) *Strong's:* #7903

CORAL (fem. *ra'mah) AHLB:* 1450-D(N1) *Strong's:* #7215

CORD (masc. *pa'til)* A long slender flexible material made of several strands woven or twisted together. Made of twisted fibers. *AHLB:* 2650(b) *Strong's:* #6616

CORIANDER (masc. *gad)* A class of plants with seeds which are in the form of the size of a peppercorn. They are used medicinally and as a spice. Likened to the manna in its form and color. *AHLB:* 1050-A$^{(N)}$ *Strong's:* #1407

CORMORANT (masc. *sha'lakh)* An unknown bird. *AHLB:* 2844$^{(N)}$ *Strong's:* #7994

CORNER (fem. *pin'nah)* The point where two lines meet. *AHLB:* 1382-M(N1) *Strong's:* #6438

CORNER.POST (fem. *me'quts'ah)* The strongest point from where the rest of the structure is built from. As scraped out with a plane. *AHLB:* 2725(ko1) *Strong's:* #4742

CORPSE (masc. *pe'ger)* A dead body. *AHLB:* 2593$^{(N)}$ *Strong's:* #6297

CORRECT$^{(V)}$ (*y.s.r)* To make a preferred change in direction through instruction or chastisement. *AHLB:* 1342-L$^{(V)}$ *Strong's:* #3256

CORRUPTION (masc. *mish'hhat) AHLB:* 2830(h) *Strong's:* #4893

COUCH (masc. *ya'tsu'a)* An article of furniture for sitting or reclining. *AHLB:* 1407-L(d) *Strong's:* #3326

COUNSEL (fem. *ey'tsah)* A giving of advice. *AHLB:* 1363-A(N1) *Strong's:* #6098

COUNT(V) (*s.p.r)* To find the total number of units. Also, to give an account on record. *Alternate Translation:* recount; recounted (when written in the piel [active intensive] form) *AHLB:* 2500(V) *Strong's:* #5608

COUNTRY.OF.TWO.RIVERS (masc. *shiyn'ar) Strong's:* [Found in names only]

COUPLE (masc. *hha'var)* A pair or group that are bound together. *AHLB:* 2143(N) *Strong's:* #2267, #2270, #2271

COUPLE(V) (*hh.b.r)* To bind by joining together. *AHLB:* 2143(V) *Strong's:* #2266

COUPLING (fem. *hho'be'ret)* To bring together as a unit. *AHLB:* 2143(g2) *Strong's:* #2279

COURAGEOUS (masc. *gi'bor)* Having or characterized by mental or moral strength to venture, persevere, and withstand danger, fear or difficulty. *AHLB:* 2052(ec) *Strong's:* #1368

COURTYARD (masc. *hha'tser)* The grounds of a building or group of buildings. Villages outside of the larger cities, as "the yard of the city. " A courtyard as outside the house. *AHLB:* 2197(N) *Strong's:* #2691

COVENANT (fem. *be'rit)* A solemn and binding agreement between two or more parties especially for the performance of some action. Often instituted through a sacrifice. *AHLB:* 1043-H(N4) *Strong's:* #1285

COVER(V) (*k.p.r)* To afford protection or security; to hide from sight or knowledge; to cover over as with a lid; to figuratively cover over an error or failure. *AHLB:* 2283(V) *Strong's:* #3722

COVER.OVER(V) (*k.s.h)* To prevent disclosure or recognition of; to place out of sight; to completely cover over or hide. *AHLB:* 1245-H(V) *Strong's:* #3680, #3780

COVERED (masc. *tsav)* Something laid over something for concealment or protection. *AHLB:* 1393-A(N) *Strong's:* #6632(x2)

COVERING (masc. *ko'pher)* Something that covers or conceals. A covering such as pitch or a monetary covering such as a bribe or ransom. A "village" as a covering. *AHLB:* 2283(g) *Strong's:* #3723, #3724

COW (fem. *pa'rah)* The mature female of cattle. *AHLB:* 1388-A(N1) *Strong's:* #6510

CRACK(V) (*sh.b.r)* To break open, apart or into pieces. *Alternate Translation:* shatter; shattered (when written in the piel [active intensive] form) *AHLB:* 2811(V) *Strong's:* #7665

CRACK.OPEN (masc. *la'sha) Strong's:* [Found in names only]

CRAFTINESS (masc. *ney'khel) AHLB:* 2404(N) *Strong's:* #5231

CRAFTSMAN (masc. *hho'resh)* One who is skilled in the art of engraving wood, stone or metal. *AHLB:* 2211(g) *Strong's:* #2794

CRASH(V) (*sh.a.h)* To break violently and noisily. *AHLB:* 1461-H(V) *Strong's:* #7582, #7583

CRAVE(V) (*hh.m.d)* To have a strong or inward desire for something. *AHLB:* 2169(V) *Strong's:* #2530

CRAVING(V) (*k.s.p)* A great desire or longing. *AHLB:* 2277(V) *Strong's:* #3700

CRAWL(V) (*z.hh.l)* To move on the ground. *AHLB:* 2120(V) *Strong's:* #2119

CREEK (masc. *yu'val)* A flowing body of water. *AHLB:* 1035-L(o) *Strong's:* #3105

CREMATE(V) (/ *s.r.p)* To reduce a dead body, or other object, to ashes by burning. *AHLB:* 2512(V) *Strong's:* #5635, #8313

CREMATING (fem. *se'rey'phah)* The act of burning a dead body to ashes. *AHLB:* 2512(N1) *Strong's:* #8316

CROCODILE (masc. / *tan / ta'nin)* A large creature that lives in the seas and rivers (see Genesis 1:21, Psalm 74:13, Isaiah 27:1, Ezekiel 29:3, Ezekiel 32:2) *AHLB:* 1497-A(N) *Strong's:* #8565, #8577

CROOKED (masc. *iy'qeysh) AHLB:* 2906(e) *Strong's:* #6141

CROP (fem. *mur'ah)* The alimentary canal of a bird. *AHLB:* 1438-L(a1) *Strong's:* #4760

CROP.OFF(V) (*q.t.p) AHLB:* 2704(V) *Strong's:* #6998

CROPLAND (fem. *she'dey'mah)* A level field for growing crops. *AHLB:* 1326-A(p1) *Strong's:* #7709, #8309

CROSS.OVER(V) (*ah.b.r)* To pass from one side to the other; to go across a river or through a land; to transgress in the sense of crossing over. *Alternate Translation:* on account of 'or' in order that (when written in the passive participle and prefixed with the prefix "in~") *AHLB:* 2520(V) *Strong's:* #5668, #5674

CROSSING (masc. *ma'a'var)* A place or structure as on a street or over a river where pedestrians or vehicles pass from one side to the other. In the river for crossing. *AHLB:* 2520(a) *Strong's:* #4569

CROSSING.ONE (masc. *ev'ron fem.* *ev'ro'nah)* One who passes over or through. *Strong's:* [Found in names only]

CRUCIBLE (masc. *kor)* A metal container used for heating substances to high temperatures. *AHLB:* 1250-J(N) *Strong's:* #3564

CRUEL (masc. *akh'zar)* Causing pain or distress. *AHLB:* 2254(N) *Strong's:* #0393

CRUMBLE(V) (*p.t.t) AHLB:* 1390-B(V) *Strong's:* #6626

CRUMBLED (masc. *ma'ro'ahh)* Broken into small pieces. [The meaning of this word is uncertain.] *AHLB:* 2353(c) *Strong's:* #4790

CRUSH(V) (/ *r.ts.ts / r.ah.ah)* To reduce to particles by pounding or grinding. Crush something to pieces. An oppression or struggle as crushing. *AHLB:* 1455-B(V) *Strong's:* #7465, #7533, #7567

CRY (fem. *tse'a'qah)* To utter loudly; to shout; to shed tears, often noisily. A loud crying or calling out. *AHLB:* 2679(N1) *Strong's:* #6818

CRY.OUT(V) (*ts.ah.q)* To cry or call out loudly. *AHLB:* 2679(V) *Strong's:* #6817

CUCUMBER (fem. *qi'shu)* A hard vegetable. *AHLB:* 1435-E(d) *Strong's:* #7180

CUD (fem. *ge'rah)* The portion of food that a ruminant returns from the first stomach to the mouth to chew a second time. *AHLB:* 1066-A(N1) *Strong's:* #1625

CUP (fem. *kos)* A vessel for holding liquids, usually for drinking. *AHLB:* 1245-J(N) *Strong's:* #3563(x2)

CUPPED.HAND (masc. *hho'phen)* The bowl shape of the palm. *AHLB:* 2190(g) *Strong's:* #2651

CURDLE(V) (*q.p.a)* To change into curd; coagulate; congeal. To spoil; turn sour. *AHLB:* 1431-E(V) *Strong's:* #7087

CUSTODY (masc. *mish'mar)* Immediate charge and control exercised by a person or authority. A careful watching over as an office, guard or prison. *AHLB:* 2853(h) *Strong's:* #4929

CUSTOM (masc. *hhuq fem.* *hhu'qah)* A usage or practice common to many or to a particular place or class or habitual with an individual. *AHLB:* 1180-J$^{(N)}$ *Strong's:* #2706, #2708

CUT$^{(V)}$ (*k.r.t)* To penetrate with a sharp-edged instrument. *AHLB:* 2291$^{(V)}$ *Strong's:* #3772

CUT.DOWN$^{(V)}$ (*g.d.ah)* To bring down usually by slicing, hacking or chopping. *AHLB:* 2055$^{(V)}$ *Strong's:* #1438

CUT.IN.TWO$^{(V)}$ (*b.t.r)* To sever into two pieces or parts. *AHLB:* 2047$^{(V)}$ *Strong's:* #1334

CUT.OFF$^{(V)}$ (*n.m.l)* To discontinue or terminate. To sever the tip or end. *AHLB:* 2407$^{(V)}$ *Strong's:* #5243

CUT.PIECE (masc. *be'ter)* A sacrificial animal that has been cut into pieces. *AHLB:* 2047$^{(N)}$ *Strong's:* #1335

CUT.SHARPLY$^{(V)}$ (*hh.r.ts)* To divide or slice with a sharp instrument such as a potsherd or iron blade. To make a decision in the sense of dividing between two choices. To be diligent in the sense of a sharp action. *AHLB:* 2209$^{(V)}$ *Strong's:* #2742, #2782

CUTTING (masc. *ge'rez)* Something cut, cut off, or cut out. *Strong's:* [Found in names only]

DAMAGE$^{(V)}$ (*sh.hh.t)* To bring to ruin by destruction; to destroy through disfigurement or corruption. *Alternate Translation:* destroy (when written in the hiphil [active causative] form) *AHLB:* 2830$^{(V)}$ *Strong's:* #7843

DAMAGING (masc. *mash'hhit)* To completely destroy with force. To tear or bring down. *AHLB:* 2830(ab) *Strong's:* #4889

DANCE (fem. *me'hho'lah)* Twisting, skipping, or leaping with joy. To rejoice in expression of thanksgiving for religious worship or festivity. *AHLB:* 1173-J(k1) *Strong's:* #4246

DANCING.AROUND (masc. *giyl)* A circle of rejoicing. *AHLB:* 1058-M$^{(N)}$ *Strong's:* #1524

DARK (fem. *hha'shey'khah)* Devoid or partially devoid of light; not receiving, reflecting, transmitting, producing or radiating light. As the darkness of a moonless night. *AHLB:* 2215(N1) *Strong's:* #2824, #2825

DARKEN$^{(V)}$ (*hh.sh.k)* To be deprived of light. To be dark as night. *AHLB:* 2215$^{(V)}$ *Strong's:* #2821

DARKNESS (masc. *hho'shekh)* The state of being dark. As the darkness of a moonless night. *AHLB:* 2215(g) *Strong's:* #2822

DASH.TO.PIECES$^{(V)}$ (*r.ah.ts)* To shatter into pieces by force. *AHLB:* 2783$^{(V)}$ *Strong's:* #7492

DATE.PALM (masc. *ta'mar)* The tree that produces the date. An erect tree as a pillar. *AHLB:* 2896$^{(N)}$ *Strong's:* #8558

DAUB$^{(V)}$ (*s.y.d)* To cover or coat with plaster or mud. *AHLB:* 1326-M$^{(V)}$ *Strong's:* #7874

DAUGHTER (fem. *bat)* A female having the relation of a child to parent. A village that resides outside of the city walls; as "the daughter of the city.". *AHLB:* 1037-A(N2) *Strong's:* #1323

DAUGHTER-IN-LAW (fem. *kal'lah)* The wife of one's son. Bride of the son, as brought into the camp. *AHLB:* 1242-B(N1) *Strong's:* #3618

DAWN (masc. *sha'hhar)* To begin to grow light as the sun rises in the east. The place of the rising sun. *AHLB:* 2829(N) *Strong's:* #7837

DAY (masc. *yom)* The time of light between one dusk and the next one. Usually in the context of daylight hours but may also refer to the entire day or even a season. *Alternate Translation:* today (when prefixed with "the~"); daily (when prefixed with "to ~ <the~", or when the word is doubled) *AHLB:* 1220-J(N) *Strong's:* #3117

DAYTIME (masc. *yo'mam)* The time of the day when the sun is shining. *AHLB:* 1220-J(p) *Strong's:* #3119

DEAD (masc. *ra'pha) AHLB:* 1454-E(N) *Strong's:* #7496

DEAL.DECEITFULLY(V) (*h.t.l)* To give as one's portion by a false impression. *AHLB:* 1495-F(V) *Strong's:* #2048

DEAL.FALSELY(V) (*sh.q.r) AHLB:* 2879(V) *Strong's:* #8266

DEATH (masc. *mot)* A permanent cessation of all vital functions; the end of life. *AHLB:* 1298-J(N) *Strong's:* #4192, #4194

DECEIT (fem. *mir'mah)* The act or practice of not being honest. *AHLB:* 1450-A(h1) *Strong's:* #4820

DECEIVE(V) (/ *n.sh.a / n.sh.h)* To cause to accept as true or valid; what is false or invalid; to trick. Also, to extort or to lend. *Alternate Translation:* lend *AHLB:* 1320-E(V) *Strong's:* #5377, #5378, #5383

DECIDE(V) (*sh.p.t)* To make a determination in a dispute or wrong doing; to judge. *AHLB:* 2864(V) *Strong's:* #8199

DECISION (masc. *mish'pat)* A pronounced opinion. *AHLB:* 2864(h) *Strong's:* #4941

DECLARE(V) (*n.a.m)* To make a formal proclamation. Often used for the words of God. *AHLB:* 1312-D(V) *Strong's:* #5001, #5002

DECLINE (*r.p.k) Strong's:* [Found in names only]

DECORATE(V) (*p.a.r)* To apply ornamentation to show distinguishment or distinction. To stand out; being seen in a good light. To boast, in the sense of decorating the self with words. *AHLB:* 1388-D(V) *Strong's:* #6286

DECORATED (masc. *pa'a'ron) Strong's:* [Found in names only]

DECORATION (fem. / *tiph'a'rah / tiph'e'ret)* Ornamentation that shows position, distinguishment or distinction. *AHLB:* 1388-D(i1) *Strong's:* #8597

DECORATIVE.BAND (masc. *hhey'shev)* An adornment with designs used to decorate or tie an article of clothing. *AHLB:* 2213(N) *Strong's:* #2805

DEDICATE(V) (*n.z.r)* To set something apart for a special purpose. *AHLB:* 2390(V) *Strong's:* #5144

DEDICATED (masc. *na'zir)* Devoted to the worship of God. *AHLB:* 2390(N) *Strong's:* #5139

DEDICATION (masc. *ne'zer)* The act of being set apart for a special purpose. Also, a crown of authority as a sign of dedication. *Alternate Translation:* crown *AHLB:* 2390(N) *Strong's:* #5145

DEED (masc. *po'al)* The work or task that is performed in order to produce something. *AHLB:* 2622(g) *Strong's:* #6467

DEEP.BLACK (masc. *iy'shon)* The black of night or the pupil of the eye. *AHLB:* 1021-M(j) *Strong's:* #0380

DEEP.BREATH (masc. *ne'phish) Strong's:* [Found in names only]

DEEP.WATER (fem. *te'hom)* Extending far below some surface or area; in difficulty or distress; a deep and tumultuous water; a subterranean body of water. *AHLB:* 1105-J(i) *Strong's:* #8415

DEFEAT (fem. *hha'lu'shah)* Overcome or weakened by an outside force. *AHLB:* 2168(d1) *Strong's:* #2476

DEFENDER (masc. *gun)* To ward off an attack on another. (A word of uncertain meaning). *Strong's:* [Found in names only]

DEFIANCE (fem. *t'nu'ah) AHLB:* 1300-J(i1) *Strong's:* #8569

DEFORM(V) (*q.l.t)* To be physically deformed in some manner which is usually covered. *AHLB:* 2707(V) *Strong's:* #7038

DELAY(V) (*a.hh.r)* To stop, detain or hinder for a time. *AHLB:* 1181-C(V) *Strong's:* #0309

DELICACY (masc. *mat'am)* The quality or state of being luxurious. Flavorful meat. *AHLB:* 2236(a) *Strong's:* #4303

DELICATE (masc. *a'kad)* Fragile; easily damaged; frail (A word of uncertain meaning). *Strong's:* [Found in names only]

DELIGHT(V) (*hh.p.ts)* To desire something out of pleasure or necessity; to have a high degree of gratification. *AHLB:* 2191(V) *Strong's:* #2654

DELIGHTFUL (fem. *na'a'mah) Strong's:* [Found in names only]

DELIVER(V) (*n.ts.l)* To set free; to take and hand over to or leave for another. *AHLB:* 2428(V) *Strong's:* #5337

DELIVER.UP(V) (*m.g.n)* To hand over to another. (A denominative verb of מגן-a shield). *AHLB:* 2331(V) *Strong's:* #4042

DENY(V) (*k.hh.sh)* To disclaim connection with or responsibility for. Withhold something from another or self as in a lie or submission. *Alternate Translation:* lie (when written in the piel [active intensive] form) *AHLB:* 2257(V) *Strong's:* #3584

DEPART(V) (*r.sh.ah)* To go astray from the correct path and become lost; to act against a law or teaching as one who has gone astray. *Alternate Translation:* convict (when written in the hiphil [active causative] form) *AHLB:* 2799(V) *Strong's:* #7561

DEPART.EARLY(V) (*sh.k.m)* Literally, to put a load on the shoulder to go away or leave early. *AHLB:* 2837(V) *Strong's:* #7925

DEPOSIT (fem. *min'hhah)* The act of making a gift or a free contribution. What is brought to another as a gift. *AHLB:* 1307-A(h1) *Strong's:* #4503

DEPOSIT(V) (*y.n.hh)* To place, especially for safekeeping or as a pledge; to be laid down; to sit down to rest or remain in place. *AHLB:* 1307-L(V) *Strong's:* #3240

DEPOSITED (masc. *piq'don)* Valuables placed for safekeeping. Produce or other stores that are watched over. *AHLB:* 2630(j) *Strong's:* #6487

DEPRESSION (masc. *car)* What is of a concave shape such as a saddle or pasture in a valley. Also, may mean the sheep of the pasture. *AHLB:* 1250-A$^{(N)}$ *Strong's:* #3733

DEPTH (fem. *me'tso'lah)* The bottom of a deep body of water. *AHLB:* 1403-J(k1) *Strong's:* #4688

DERISION (fem. *shim'tsah)* To talk in a low quiet voice. *AHLB:* 2852(e1) *Strong's:* #8103

DESCENDER (masc. *yar'den) Strong's:* [Found in names only]

DESERT (fem. *a'ra'vah)* An expanse of land often barren of vegetation and people. *AHLB:* 2907(N1) *Strong's:* #6160

DESERT.REGION (masc. *tiy'ma) Strong's:* [Found in names only]

DESIRABLE (masc. *tiy'ras) Strong's:* [Found in names only]

DESIRE (fem. *a'wat)* What is good or bad, that is lusted after. *AHLB:* 1006-A(N1) *Strong's:* #0185

DESIRED (masc. *hham'do)* Something that is craved. *Strong's:* [Found in names only]

DESOLATE (fem. *she'ma'mah)* Vacant or void of required sources for life. *AHLB:* 1473-B(N1) *Strong's:* #8047, #8077

DESOLATE$^{(V)}$ (*sh.m.m)* To be devoid of inhabitants or visitors. *AHLB:* 1473-B$^{(V)}$ *Strong's:* #8074

DESOLATE.WILDERNESS (masc. *y'shiy'mon)* A desolate place. *AHLB:* 1473-L(bj) *Strong's:* #3452

DESPAIRING (masc. *la'mad) Strong's:* [Found in names only]

DESPISE$^{(V)}$ (*b.w.z)* To look down on with contempt or aversion. *AHLB:* 1030-J$^{(V)}$ *Strong's:* #0936

DESPISED (masc. *buz)* One who is looked down upon with contempt or aversion. *AHLB:* 1030-J$^{(N)}$ *Strong's:* #0937

DESTROY$^{(V)}$ (*sh.m.d)* To bring to ruin a structure, existence, or condition. *AHLB:* 2848$^{(V)}$ *Strong's:* #8045

DESTRUCTION (masc. *qe'tev) AHLB:* 2701$^{(N)}$ *Strong's:* #6986

DETEST$^{(V)}$ (*sh.q.ts)* To detest that which is filthy. *AHLB:* 2878$^{(V)}$ *Strong's:* #8262

DEVOTE$^{(V)}$ (*hh.n.k)* To set aside for or assign to a specific function, task, or purpose. *AHLB:* 2178$^{(V)}$ *Strong's:* #2596

DEVOTED (masc. *hha'nokh)* Immersed in activity for a specific task. *Strong's:* [Found in names only]

DEVOTION (fem. *hha'nu'khah)* Reserved for a specific use or purpose. *AHLB:* 2178(d1) *Strong's:* #2598

DEVOUR$^{(V)}$ (*hh.s.l) AHLB:* 2183$^{(V)}$ *Strong's:* #2628

DEW (masc. *tal)* Moisture condensed on the surfaces of cool bodies or objects, especially at night. *AHLB:* 1196-A$^{(N)}$ *Strong's:* #2919

DIE$^{(V)}$ (*m.w.t)* To pass from physical life; to pass out of existence; to come to an end through death. *Alternate Translation:* kill or be put to death (when written in the hiphil [active causative] form) *AHLB:* 1298-J$^{(V)}$ *Strong's:* #4191

DIG$^{(V)}$ (*k.r.h)* To break or loosen earth with an instrument or tool. To bargain in the sense of digging. *AHLB:* 1250-H$^{(V)}$ *Strong's:* #3738, #3739

DIG.OUT(V) (*hh.p.r)* To dig something out of the ground. To dig into something as if searching. To confuse in the sense of being dug out. *AHLB:* 2192(V) *Strong's:* #2658, #2659

DIM(V) (*k.h.h)* Emitting a limited or insufficient amount of light; seen indistinctly or without clear outlines or details.. To be dark in the eyes or knowledge. *AHLB:* 1235-B(V) *Strong's:* #3543

DIMINISH(V) (*hh.s.r)* To make less or cause to appear less; to lessen the authority, dignity, or reputation of. Be lacking or to decrease. *AHLB:* 2187(V) *Strong's:* #2637

DIMNESS (masc. *key'heh) AHLB:* 1235-B(N) *Strong's:* #3544

DIP(V) (*t.b.l)* To plunge or immerse momentarily or partially, as under the surface of a liquid, to moisten, cool, or coat. *AHLB:* 2228(V) *Strong's:* #2881

DIRECT(V) (*ts.w.h)* To cause to turn, move, or point undeviatingly or to follow a straight course; give instructions or orders for a path to be taken. *AHLB:* 1397-H(V) *Strong's:* #6680

DIRECTIVE (fem. *mits'wah)* The direction to go. Serving or intended to guide, govern, or influence; serving to point direction. *AHLB:* 1397-H(h1) *Strong's:* #4687

DIRT (masc. *a'phar)* The dust of the ground; a fine powder. *AHLB:* 2565(N) *Strong's:* #6083

DIRTY (masc. *ta'mey fem. ta'mey'ah)* What is morally or physically impure; dirty, filthy. *AHLB:* 1197-E(N) *Strong's:* #2931, #2932

DISCERNMENT (fem. *da'at)* The quality of being able to grasp and comprehend what is obscure. An intimacy with a person, idea or concept. Knowledge. *Alternate Translation:* unknowingly (when following the word "UNAWARE") *AHLB:* 1085-A(N2) *Strong's:* #1847

DISCHARGE (masc. *zuv)* The issue of the sexual organs. *AHLB:* 1140-J(N) *Strong's:* #2101

DISCIPLINE (masc. *mu'sar) mo'sey'rah* Knowledge, information or example imparted to provide guidance, correction and discipline. *AHLB:* 1342-L(a) *Strong's:* #4561, #4148

DISCORD (masc. *m'dan)* A lack of concord or harmony between persons or things. *AHLB:* 1083-A(k) *Strong's:* #4090

DISDAIN(V) (*b.z.h)* A feeling of contempt for what is beneath one; to look with scorn on; to treat something as spoiled or no longer of value. *AHLB:* 1030-H(V) *Strong's:* #0959

DISEASE (masc. *mad'weh)* An incorrectly functioning organ, part, structure, or system of the body that brings on an illness. *AHLB:* 1075-H(a) *Strong's:* #4064

DISGRACE (fem. *hher'pah)* A scorn, taunting or reproach as a piercing. *AHLB:* 2208(N1) *Strong's:* #2781

DISGUSTING (fem. *to'ey'vah)* Something highly distasteful that arouses marked aversion in one. *AHLB:* 2897(g1) *Strong's:* #8441

DISLOCATE(V) (*y.q.ah)* To put out of place; to displace, as to dislocate a joint. Beheading by severing the neck.. *Alternate Translation:* hang (when written in the hiphil [active causative] form) *AHLB:* 1430-L(V) *Strong's:* #3363

DISMAY (fem. *be'ha'lah)* Sudden trouble, terror or ruin. *AHLB:* 1035-G(N1) *Strong's:* #0928

DISOBEY[V] (*m.r.h)* To neglect or refuse to obey; to rebel against. *AHLB:* 1296-H[V] *Strong's:* #4784

DISPERSE[V] (*z.r.h)* To separate or remove to a distance apart from each other; to diffuse or cause to break into different parts. *AHLB:* 1158-H[V] *Strong's:* #2219

DISPUTE (masc. *riv)* Bitter, sometimes violent conflict or dissension. *AHLB:* 1439-M[N] *Strong's:* #7379

DISPUTE[V] (/ *r.y.b / r.w.b)* To engage in argument; to dispute or chide another in harassment or trial. *AHLB:* 1439-M[V] *Strong's:* #7378

DISSOLVE[V] (*m.w.g)* To loose the bonds of something. To make something disappear. *AHLB:* 1279-J[V] *Strong's:* #4127

DISTANCE (masc. *ra'hhoq fem. re'hho'qah)* Separation in space or time. A distant place or time. *AHLB:* 2765(c) *Strong's:* #7350

DISTANT (masc. *o'lam)* A far off place as hidden beyond the horizon. A far off time as hidden from the present; the distant past or future. A place or time that cannot be perceived. *AHLB:* 2544(g) *Strong's:* #5769

DISTRACTED (masc. *pun) Strong's:* [Found in names only]

DISTRACTED.ONE (masc. *pu'non) Strong's:* [Found in names only]

DISTRESS[V] (*ah.ts.b)* The state of being in great trouble, great physical or mental strain and stress. To be in pain from grief or heavy toil. *AHLB:* 2566[V] *Strong's:* #6087

DISTRESSING.PAIN (masc. *e'tsev)* Resulting from grief or heavy toil. This word can also mean an idol or image. *AHLB:* 2566[N] *Strong's:* #6089, #6091, #6092

DISTRIBUTE[V] (*hh.l.q)* To divide and mete out according to a plan among the appropriate recipients. *AHLB:* 2167[V] *Strong's:* #2505

DISTRIBUTION (masc. *hhey'leq)* An individual's part or share of something. The portions dispersed out. *AHLB:* 2167[N] *Strong's:* #2506

DISTURB[V] (*ah.k.r)* To interfere with; to destroy tranquility; to throw into disorder. Agitate or trouble, as when stirring water. *AHLB:* 2541[V] *Strong's:* #5916

DISTURBED.ONE (masc. *akh'ran) Strong's:* [Found in names only]

DIVE[V] (*d.a.h)* To plunge, fall, or descend through the air or water. *AHLB:* 1074-D[V] *Strong's:* #1675

DIVERSE.KIND (masc. *kiy'la)* Something produced by the forbidden practice of crossing together different kinds, such as crossbreeding cattle and the mixing of wool and linen. (This noun is always written in the double plural form). *AHLB:* 1242-E(e) *Strong's:* #3610

DIVIDE[V] (*hh.ts.h)* To separate into two or more parts, areas or groups. To divide in half. *AHLB:* 1179-H[V] *Strong's:* #2673

DIVIDE.APART[V] (*p.r.d)* To separate. *AHLB:* 2634[V] *Strong's:* #6504

DIVIDE.INTO.PIECES[V] (*n.t.hh)* To sever or part into sections To distribute or to bestow in parts or shares. *AHLB:* 2449[V] *Strong's:* #5408

DIVIDED.PART (masc. *ge'zer)* A part of a whole that was split and separated. *AHLB:* 2061[N] *Strong's:* #1506

DIVIDING (masc. *hhats'tsun)* A separating into parts. *Strong's:* [Found in names only]

DIVINATION (masc. *qe'sem) AHLB:* 2718[N] *Strong's:* #7081

DIVINE[V] (*q.s.m)* To practice divination. *AHLB:* 2718[V] *Strong's:* #7080

DIVORCE (fem. *k'riy'tut)* As cut off from the husband. *AHLB:* 2291(b3) *Strong's:* #3748

DO(V) (*ah.sh.h)* To bring to pass; to bring about; to act or make. *Alternate Translation:* make; use *AHLB:* 1360-H(V) *Strong's:* #6213

DO.NOT (masc. *al)* The negative of an alternative choice. To be without; to not be. *AHLB:* 1254-A(N) *Strong's:* #0408

DO.SORCERY(V) (*k.sh.p)* To perform supernatural magic. *AHLB:* 2293(V) *Strong's:* #3784

DO.THE.MARRIAGE.DUTY(V) (*y.b.m)* To perform the duty of the brother-in-law. When a brother dies, it is his brother's responsibility to marry his sister-in-law to provide his brother a child there-by, exalting the woman to her responsibility of bringing a child for her dead husband. *AHLB:* 1036-L(V) *Strong's:* #2992

DO.WELL(V) (*y.t.b)* To do something necessary; to be good. *Alternate Translation:* go well, thoroughly *AHLB:* 1186-L(V) *Strong's:* #3190

DOE (fem. *ay'ya'lah)* The adult female fallow deer. *AHLB:* 1012-M(N1) *Strong's:* #0355

DOG (masc. *ke'lev)* An unclean four-footed animal. Also, meaning contempt or reproach. *AHLB:* 2259(N) *Strong's:* #3611

DOING (masc. *a'sah) Strong's:* [Found in names only]

DONATION (masc. *qor'ban)* Something given to another in devotion. *AHLB:* 2729(gm) *Strong's:* #7133

DONKEY (masc. *hha'mor)* A male ass. *AHLB:* 2175(c) *Strong's:* #2543, #2565

DOOR (fem. *de'let)* A means of access; usually a swinging or sliding barrier by which an entry is closed and opened. *AHLB:* 1081-A(N2) *Strong's:* #1817

DOORPOST (fem. *me'zu'zah)* The vertical supporting frame or post around a door or gate. *AHLB:* 1145-J(k1) *Strong's:* #4201

DOORWAY (masc. *niph'to'ahh) Strong's:* [Found in names only]

DOUBLE (masc. *mish'neh)* To make twice as great or as many. As a second or a multiple of two. *AHLB:* 1474-H(h) *Strong's:* #4932

DOUBLE.OVER(V) (*k.p.l)* To bend at the waist or middle. *AHLB:* 2280(V) *Strong's:* #3717

DOUBLED (fem. *makh'pe'lah) Strong's:* [Found in names only]

DOUGH (masc. *ba'tseyq)* A mass of flour and water that rises when yeast is added and is then baked into bread or cakes. *AHLB:* 2032(N) *Strong's:* #1217

DOVE (fem. *yo'nah)* Any of numerous species of birds, especially a small wild one. *AHLB:* 1221-J(N1) *Strong's:* #3123

DOWRY (masc. *zey'ved)* The money, goods, or estate that a woman brings to her husband in marriage. *AHLB:* 2116(N) *Strong's:* #2065

DRAIN(V) (*m.ts.h)* To squeeze out by wringing. *AHLB:* 1294-H(V) *Strong's:* #4680

DRAW(V) (*m.sh.k)* To pull up or out of a receptacle or place; to draw or pull something out; to prolong in the sense of drawing out time; to draw out a sound from a horn. *AHLB:* 2358(V) *Strong's:* #4900

DRAW.AWAY(V) (*n.t.q)* To draw out or away as a bowstring or to draw a cord to its breaking point. *AHLB:* 2455(V) *Strong's:* #5423

DRAW.NEAR(V) (*n.g.sh)* To bring close to another. *AHLB:* 2379(V) *Strong's:* #5066

DRAW.OUT(V) (*r.w.q)* To empty. To arm oneself by unsheathing a sword in the sense of emptying the scabbard. Acting in vain; empty-handed. *AHLB:* 1456-J(V) *Strong's:* #7324

DRAW.UP(V) (*d.l.h)* To bale up. To lift the bucket out of the well for drawing water. *AHLB:* 1081-H(V) *Strong's:* #1802

DRAW.WATER(V) (*sh.a.b)* To bring up water from a well, usually using a rope and a bucket. *AHLB:* 1477-D(V) *Strong's:* #7579

DRAWING.NEAR (masc. *go'shen)* To come or be brought close. *Strong's:* [Found in names only]

DRAWN.OUT (masc. *mash) Strong's:* [Found in names only]

DREAD (fem. *hhi'tah)* Great fear, especially in the face of impending evil. *AHLB:* 1183-A(N1) *Strong's:* #2847

DREAM (masc. *hha'lom)* A series of thoughts, images or emotions occurring during sleep. *AHLB:* 2164(c) *Strong's:* #2472

DREAM(V) (*hh.l.m)* To see or form a mental image of; to dream dreams. *AHLB:* 2164(V) *Strong's:* #2492

DRIED.OUT (fem. *hhar'bah)* A dry or desolate place. Barren or uncultivated land. Also, a dry land. *AHLB:* 2199(N1) *Strong's:* #2720, #2723, #2724

DRILL(V) (*hh.l.l)* To run into or through as with a pointed weapon or tool; pierce a hole through. *Alternate Translation:* begin, in the sense of pressing in (when written in the hiphil [active causative] form); defile (when written in the hiphil [active causative], piel [active intensive] or niphil [passive] form) *AHLB:* 1173-B(V) *Strong's:* #2490

DRILLED (masc. *hha'lal fem. hha'la'lah)* One who has been run through with a sword. *AHLB:* 1173-B(N) *Strong's:* #2491

DRINK(V) (*sh.q.h)* To swallow liquid, whether of man or of the land. *AHLB:* 1479-H(V) *Strong's:* #8248

DRINKING (masc. *mash'qeh)* The act of swallowing water or other liquid. The drinking of the land in the sense of it being watered or irrigated. *AHLB:* 1479-H(a) *Strong's:* #4945

DRIP(V) (*d.l.p)* To fall in drops. *AHLB:* 2103(V) *Strong's:* #1811

DRIVE(V) (*n.h.g)* To set or keep in motion; to press or force into an activity, course, or direction. *AHLB:* 1302-G(V) *Strong's:* #5090

DRIVE.OUT(V) (*n.d.hh)* To forcefully send someone or something out or away; to drive an axe through wood. *AHLB:* 2381(V) *Strong's:* #5080

DROP(V) (*ah.r.p)* To fall down as rain from the clouds. *AHLB:* 2909(V) *Strong's:* #6201

DROP.DOWN(V) (*n.t.k)* To pour down, pour out to the ground or into a vessel. To pour out anger to another. *AHLB:* 2450(V) *Strong's:* #5413

DROVE (masc. *ey'der)* A group of animals driven or moving in a body. *AHLB:* 2530(N) *Strong's:* #5739

DROWN(V) (*sh.q.ah)* To sink down. *AHLB:* 2876(V) *Strong's:* #8257

DRUNKARD (masc. *sa'va) Strong's:* [Found in names only]

DRY (masc. *ya'veysh fem. ye'vey'shah)* Void of water or moisture. *AHLB:* 1044-L(N) *Strong's:* #3002

DRY$^{(V)}$ (*q.l.h)* To dry foods, grains and meats, to preserve them. Dried foods are carried by the shepherd. To be light in stature, worthless. *AHLB:* 1426-H$^{(V)}$ *Strong's:* #7033, #7034

DRY.GROUND (fem. *ya'ba'shah)* Land that has become parched or void of water. *AHLB:* 1044-L(N1) *Strong's:* #3004

DRY.LAND (fem. *ya'be'shet)* An area void of moisture or water. *AHLB:* 1044-L(N2) *Strong's:* #3006

DRY.OUT$^{(V)}$ (*y.b.sh)* To be withered, ashamed or confused. *AHLB:* 1044-L$^{(V)}$ *Strong's:* #3001

DRY.UP$^{(V)}$ (*hh.r.b)* To be a dry wasteland; to be laid waste and made desolate. *AHLB:* 2199$^{(V)}$ *Strong's:* #2717

DUG.OUT.WELL (masc. *hhe'pher) Strong's:* [Found in names only]

DULL.RED (masc. *hhakh'li'li)* The color of blood and wine. *AHLB:* 2158(lbf) *Strong's:* #2447

DUNG (masc. *pe'resh)* The excrement of animals or humans. Manure or refuse. *AHLB:* 2644$^{(N)}$ *Strong's:* #6569

DUST (masc. *a'vaq)* Fine particles of earth or other material that are easily disturbed to create a cloud. *AHLB:* 1042-C$^{(N)}$ *Strong's:* #0080

DUST.CLOUD (masc. *sha'hhaq)* A mass of fine powder being blown by the wind. *AHLB:* 2828$^{(N)}$ *Strong's:* #7834

DWELL$^{(V)}$ (*sh.k.n)* To remain for a time; to live as a resident; to stay or sit in one location for an indeterminate duration. *Alternate Translation:* place (when written in the infinitive form) *AHLB:* 2838$^{(V)}$ *Strong's:* #7931

DWELLER (masc. *she'khen)* The resident of a region. Also, a habitation, the place of residence. *AHLB:* 2838$^{(N)}$ *Strong's:* #7933, #7934

DWELLING (masc. *mish'kan)* A place of habitation or residence. *AHLB:* 2838(h) *Strong's:* #4908

DYSFUNCTIONAL (masc. *ra fem. ra'ah)* Impaired or abnormal action other than that for which a person or thing is intended. Something that does not function within its intended purpose. *AHLB:* 1460-A$^{(N)}$ *Strong's:* #7451, #7455

EAGLE (masc. *ne'sher)* An unknown bird, but probably a hawk or eagle. *AHLB:* 2446$^{(N)}$ *Strong's:* #5404

EAR (fem. *o'zen)* The organ of hearing on each side of the head. *AHLB:* 1152-C(g) *Strong's:* #0241

EAR.OF.GRAIN (masc. / / *shi'bol / si'bo'let / si'bo'let fem. si'bo'let)* The cluster of seeds found on grass crops. *AHLB:* 2806(ec) *Strong's:* #5451, #7641

EARED.OWL (masc. *yan'shuph)* An unknown bird. *AHLB:* 2444(tc) *Strong's:* #3244

EARRING (masc. *a'giyl)* A circular ornament worn on or hanging from the lobe of the ear. *AHLB:* 2524(b) *Strong's:* #5694

EARTHENWARE (masc. *kiyr)* A hollow box formed out of brick or clay for cooking. *AHLB:* 1250-M$^{(N)}$ *Strong's:* #3600

EAST (masc. *qe'dem)* The general direction of sunrise. As in front when facing the rising sun. Also, the ancient past. *AHLB:* 2698$^{(N)}$ *Strong's:* #6924

EAST.WIND (masc. *qa'dim)* The wind that comes from the east. Toward the east as the origin of the east wind. *AHLB:* 2698(b) *Strong's:* #6921

EASTERN (masc. *qad'mon)* In the direction toward the rising sun. *AHLB:* 2698(j) *Strong's:* #6930

EASTWARD (fem. *qid'mah)* Toward the east. Before another space or time; as the east is in front when facing the rising sun. *AHLB:* 2698(e1) *Strong's:* #6926

EAT(V) (*a.k.l)* To consume food; to destroy. A devouring of a fire. *AHLB:* 1242-C(V) *Strong's:* #0398

EDGE (fem. *pey'ah)* The border or boundary of an object or a region. The thin cutting edge of a blade. *AHLB:* 1369-A(N1) *Strong's:* #6285

EDGING (fem. *gav'lut)* Furnished with a border or trim. Added to a garment for ornamentation. *AHLB:* 2049(N3) *Strong's:* #1383

EGG (fem. *bey'tsah)* The roundish reproductive body produced by the female bird. *AHLB:* 1041-M(N1) *Strong's:* #1000

EIGHT (masc. *she'mo'nah fem.* *she'mo'neh)* A cardinal number eight. May represent fullness from its connection to root meaning fat or rich. *Alternate Translation:* eighty (when in the plural form) *AHLB:* 2850(c) *Strong's:* #8083, #8084

EIGHTH (masc. *she'mi'ni)* An ordinal number. *AHLB:* 2850(bf) *Strong's:* #8066

ELEVATED (fem. *ra'u'mah) Strong's:* [Found in names only]

ELEVATION (fem. *se'eyt)* The height to which something is raised. *AHLB:* 1323-A(N2) *Strong's:* #7613

EMBER (masc. *ge'hhel fem.* *ga'hhe'let)* A small live piece of coal, wood, etc., as in a dying fire. *AHLB:* 2062(N) *Strong's:* #1513

EMBRACE(V) (*hh.b.q)* To clasp in the arms; to cherish or love; to take in or include in a larger group or whole. *AHLB:* 2142(V) *Strong's:* #2263

EMBROIDER(V) (*r.q.m)* To decorate with ornamental and colorful needlework. *AHLB:* 2796(V) *Strong's:* #7551

EMBROIDERY (masc. *re'qem fem.* *riyq'mah)* A decorative work of colorful needlework. *AHLB:* 2796(e1) *Strong's:* #7553

EMERALD (fem. *ba're'qet)* Possibly the Emerald, a green variety of Beryl. The Hebrew word is from a root meaning to flash or shimmer, while the Septuagint uses Smaragdos meaning a 'green stone.' Other possible translations are Beryl or Quartz. *AHLB:* 2041(N2) *Strong's:* #1304

EMINENT (masc. *a'dir)* What exerts power and status. Someone or something that is wide in authority or majesty. *AHLB:* 1089-C(b) *Strong's:* #0117, #0155

EMPIRE (fem. *mal'kut)* The area under the control of a king; a kingdom. *AHLB:* 2340(N3) *Strong's:* #4438

EMPTINESS (masc. *rey'qam)* Lack of contents which should be present. Void of contents or purpose. *AHLB:* 1456-M(p) *Strong's:* #7387

EMPTY (masc. *riyq)* The lack of intelligence or significance in an action. An action or thought with no positive results. To empty by pouring out. *AHLB:* 1456-M(N) *Strong's:* #7385, #7386

EMPTY.OUT(V) (*b.q.q)* To be drained away. *AHLB:* 1042-B(V) *Strong's:* #1238

ENCIRCLE(V) (*n.q.p)* To go around to enclose or go about. *AHLB:* 2435(V) *Strong's:* #5362

ENCOMPASS$^{(V)}$ (*ah.n.q) AHLB:* 2559$^{(V)}$ *Strong's:* #6059

ENCOUNTER (masc. *pe'ga)* A chance meeting. *AHLB:* 2592$^{(N)}$ *Strong's:* #6294

ENCOUNTER$^{(V)}$ (*p.g.sh)* To meet or come in contact with another person. A meeting between two hostile factions; to engage in conflict with. *AHLB:* 2594$^{(V)}$ *Strong's:* #6298

END (fem. *a'hha'rit)* A final point that marks the extent of something. The latter time as coming after everything else. *AHLB:* 1181-C(N4) *Strong's:* #0319

ENDOW$^{(V)}$ (*z.b.d)* To furnish with a dower or payment for a bride. Pay the price for a bride. Give a natural gift. *AHLB:* 2116$^{(V)}$ *Strong's:* #2064

ENEMY (masc. *ar) AHLB:* 1526-A$^{(N)}$ *Strong's:* #6145

ENERGY (fem. *ez'ra)* A power. *AHLB:* 2139$^{(N)}$ *Strong's:* [Found in names only]

ENGRAVE$^{(V)}$ (*hh.r.t)* To mark, scratch, or scrape. To chisel or cut figures, letters, or devices on stone or metal. *AHLB:* 2212$^{(V)}$ *Strong's:* #2801

ENGRAVER (masc. *hhe'resh)* A sculptor or carver who engraves wood, stone or metal. *AHLB:* 2211$^{(N)}$ *Strong's:* #2791, #2796

ENGRAVING (fem. *hha'ro'shet)* A scratching or carving in stone, metal or wood. *AHLB:* 2211(c2) *Strong's:* #2799

ENGRAVING.TOOL (masc. *hhe'ret)* A tool making markings or inscriptions by carving on stone, metal or wood. A stylus for inscribing a clay tablet. *AHLB:* 2203$^{(N)}$ *Strong's:* #2747

ENRAGE$^{(V)}$ (*z.ah.m)* To be extremely angry; to be indignant. *AHLB:* 2129$^{(V)}$ *Strong's:* #2194

ENSNARE$^{(V)}$ (*n.q.sh) AHLB:* 2437$^{(V)}$ *Strong's:* #5367

ENTANGLED$^{(V)}$ (*b.w.k)* Twisted together or interwoven in a confused manner. Involved. *AHLB:* 1034-J$^{(V)}$ *Strong's:* #0943

ENTIRELY (masc. *ka'lil)* A state of being complete. All of it. No missing parts; complete by including everything. *AHLB:* 1242-B(b) *Strong's:* #3632

ENTRANCE (masc. *ma'vo)* A place of entering. Once (Zechariah 8:7) *AHLB:* 1024-J(a) *Strong's:* #3996

ENTRYWAY (masc. *zuz)* A passage for affording entrance. (A word of undertain meaning). *Strong's:* [Found in names only]

ENTWINE$^{(V)}$ (*p.t.l)* To twist together or around; to become twisted. *AHLB:* 2650$^{(V)}$ *Strong's:* #6617

ENWRAP$^{(V)}$ (*ah.t.h)* To tightly wrap something up. *AHLB:* 1354-H$^{(V)}$ *Strong's:* #5844

EPHOD (masc. *e'phod fem. e'phu'dah)* An apron-like vestment having two shoulder straps and ornamental attachments for securing the breastplate, worn with a waistband by the high priest. *AHLB:* 1372-C(c) *Strong's:* #0642, #0646

EPIDEMIC (masc. *de'ver)* A wide spread disease effecting man or animal. A pestilence. *AHLB:* 2093$^{(N)}$ *Strong's:* #1698

EQUAL (masc. *shuh) Strong's:* [Found in names only]

EQUATE$^{(V)}$ (*sh.w.h)* To make something like something else, or to compare it to something else. *AHLB:* 1465-J$^{(V)}$ *Strong's:* #7737, #7738

EQUATED (masc. *shah) Strong's:* [Found in names only]

ERR$^{(V)}$ (*sh.g.g)* To make a mistake in calculation or understanding. *AHLB:* 1463-B$^{(V)}$ *Strong's:* #7683

ERROR (fem. *sh'ga'gah)* A mistake in calculation or understanding. *AHLB:* 1463-B(N1) *Strong's:* #7684

ERUPTION (masc. *ne'teq)* A disease of the skin which breaks open drawing out liquid. *AHLB:* 2455$^{(N)}$ *Strong's:* #5424

ESCAPED (masc. *pa'lit fem.* *pe'ley'tah)* A getting away, especially from confinement. A person or animal that has gotten away. *AHLB:* 2609(b) *Strong's:* #6412, #6413

ESCAPING (masc. *pa'let) AHLB:* 2609$^{(N)}$ *Strong's:* #6405

ESTIMATE$^{(V)}$ (*k.s.s)* To make an approximate count or reckoning. *AHLB:* 1245-B$^{(V)}$ *Strong's:* #3699

EUNUCH (masc. *sa'ris)* A castrated man. As eunuchs were used as officers, may also mean an officer. *AHLB:* 2510(b) *Strong's:* #5631

EVENING (masc. *e'rev)* The latter part and close of the day and the early part of the night. Dark of the evening or dark-skinned people. *AHLB:* 2907$^{(N)}$ *Strong's:* #6153

EVENT (masc. *qa'reh) AHLB:* 1434-H$^{(N)}$ *Strong's:* #7137

EVICTED (masc. *ger'shon)* To be removed or thrown from with force. To dispossess, exile, dismiss. *Strong's:* [Found in names only]

EVIDENCE (fem. *ey'dut)* That which proves or disproves something; something that makes plain or clear; an indication or sign. *AHLB:* 1349-A(N3) *Strong's:* #5715

EWE (fem. *ra'hheyl)* A female sheep. *AHLB:* 2761$^{(N)}$ *Strong's:* #7353

EXAMINE$^{(V)}$ (*hh.q.r)* To intently search or seek for details. *AHLB:* 2198$^{(V)}$ *Strong's:* #2713

EXCEED$^{(V)}$ (*ah.d.p)* Running over, filled beyond capacity. *AHLB:* 2529$^{(V)}$ *Strong's:* #5736

EXCEPT (masc. *bil'ti)* With the exclusion of from the whole. The whole with the exception of one or more. *Alternate Translation:* none; not *AHLB:* 2021(ef) *Strong's:* #1115

EXCHANGE (fem. *t'mu'rah) AHLB:* 1296-J(i1) *Strong's:* #8545

EXCHANGE$^{(V)}$ (*sh.b.r)* The act of giving or taking one thing in return for another. To buy or sell produce, usually grain. Bartering. *AHLB:* 2811$^{(V)}$ *Strong's:* #7666

EXHALE$^{(V)}$ (*n.p.hh)* To give out a breath. To blow on a fire or the boiling water in a pot as an exhale. *AHLB:* 2419$^{(V)}$ *Strong's:* #5301

EXHAUSTED (masc. *ma'zeh)* Drained of strength and energy; fatigued. *AHLB:* 1283-H$^{(N)}$ *Strong's:* #4198

EXIST$^{(V)}$ (*h.y.h)* To have real being whether material or spiritual; to have breath. *Alternate Translation:* come to pass; is; what is needed (when used in the infinitive form and prefixed with "from~") *AHLB:* 1097-M$^{(V)}$ *Strong's:* #1961

EXISTING (masc. *yah) Strong's:* [Found in names only]

EXPERIENCED (masc. *hha'nikh)* Direct observation of or participation in events as a basis of knowledge. Something that is personally encountered, undergone or lived through in its use. *AHLB:* 2178(b) *Strong's:* #2593

EXPIRE$^{(V)}$ (*g.w.ah)* To breathe one's last breath; the last breath of death. *AHLB:* 1062-J$^{(V)}$ *Strong's:* #1478

EXPLAIN$^{(V)}$ (*b.a.r)* To provide a meaning. *AHLB:* 1250-D$^{(V)}$ *Strong's:* #0874

EXPOSE (masc. *mahh'soph)* To cause to be visible or open to public view. *AHLB:* 2186(ac) *Strong's:* #4286

EXTEND[V] (*n.t.h)* To set up camp by stretching out the cover of the tent; to extend or stretch in length. *Alternate Translation:* turn away from (when written in the hiphil [active causative] form) *AHLB:* 1308-H[V] *Strong's:* #5186

EXTRACT[V] (*hh.l.ts)* To pull out or toward. To draw weapons for battle. *Alternate Translation:* arm, in the sense of drawing weapons (when written in the niphil [passive] or the passive participle form) *AHLB:* 2166[V] *Strong's:* #2502

EXTREME.OLD.AGE (masc. *za'qun)* A full and long life. *AHLB:* 2132(d) *Strong's:* #2208

EXTREMITY (masc. *qa'tseh fem.* *qa'tsah)* The most distant end of a place or time; the end, corner or edge. *AHLB:* 1432-H[N] *Strong's:* #7097, #7098

EXUBERANT (masc. *ze'red)* Abounding in vitality; extremely joyful and vigorous. *Strong's:* [Found in names only]

EYE (fem. *a'yin)* The organ of sight or vision that tears when a person weeps. Also, a spring that weeps water out of the ground. *AHLB:* 1359-M[N] *Strong's:* #5869

EYPHAH (fem. *ey'phah)* A dry standard of measure equal to 3 se'ahs or 10 omers. The same as the liquid measure bath which is about 9 imperial gallons or 40 liters. *AHLB:* 1017-M(N1) *Strong's:* #0374

FACE (masc. *pa'neh)* The anterior part of the human head; outward appearance. One present, in the sense of being in the face of another. Often used in the context of being before or in front of. (Always written in the plural form, but usually used as a singular noun) *Alternate Translation:* before; within (when suffixed with "~unto") *AHLB:* 1382-H[N] *Strong's:* #3942, #6440

FACE.TOWARD[V] (*q.d.m)* To face another or meet face to face; to go before someone or something in space or time. *AHLB:* 2698[V] *Strong's:* #6923

FADE[V] (*n.b.l)* To degrade a person, action or object. To droop or pass away. To wither away as a leaf. To wear out of strength. To act unproductively. *AHLB:* 2369[V] *Strong's:* #5034

FAIL[V] (*hh.t.a)* To miss the target, whether a literal target or a goal that is aimed for. *Alternate Translation:* purge; bear the blame or purify (when written in the piel [active intensive] form); purify self (when written in the hitpa'el [reflexive] form *AHLB:* 1170-E[V] *Strong's:* #2398

FAILING (masc. *kiyl'la'yon)* A complete destruction or inability to perform an action. *AHLB:* 1242-A(fj) *Strong's:* #3631

FAILURE (masc. *hha'ta fem.* / *hha'ta'a / hha'ta'at)* An act or condition of ignorant or imprudent deviation from a code of behavior. A missing of the target in the sense of making a mistake. The sacrifice, which by transference, becomes the sin. *AHLB:* 1170-E[N] *Strong's:* #2399, #2400, #2401, #2403

FAINT (masc. *mo'rekh)* From a blow to the loins. *AHLB:* 1448-L(a) *Strong's:* #4816

FAINT[V] (*l.h.h)* Lacking courage and spirit; weak, dizzy and likely to pass out. Lacking distinctness. *AHLB:* 1258-H[V] *Strong's:* #3856

FALCON (masc. *nets)* An unknown unclean bird. *AHLB:* 1317-A[N] *Strong's:* #5322(x2)

FALL (masc. *pa'lal) Strong's:* [Found in names only]

FALL(V) (*n.p.l)* To leave an erect position suddenly and involuntarily; to descend freely by the force of gravity. *Alternate Translation:* throw self (when written in the hitpa'el [reflexive] form) *AHLB:* 2421(V) *Strong's:* #5307

FALL.UPON(V) (*sh.w.p)* To suddenly and forcefully crash upon someone or something. *AHLB:* 1477-J(V) *Strong's:* #7779

FALLEN.GRAPE (masc. *pe'ret)* As broken from the plant and scattered on the ground. *AHLB:* 2637(N) *Strong's:* #6528

FALSE (masc. *she'qer)* A deliberate lie. An expression of a non-truth. *AHLB:* 2879(N) *Strong's:* #8267

FALSENESS (*shu-a) AHLB:* 1461-J(N) *Strong's:* #7723

FAMILY.IDOL (masc. *te'raph)* A household idol of a god, possibly believed to have a healing power. *AHLB:* 1454-A(i) *Strong's:* #8655

FAMINE (masc. *ra'a'von)* An extreme scarcity of food. *AHLB:* 2777(j) *Strong's:* #7459

FAR.BE.IT (fem. *hha'li'lah)* Something least likely to happen. *AHLB:* 1173-B(b1) *Strong's:* #2486

FAR.END (masc. *ey'phes)* The concluding part of an area or extremity. Also, used for the conclusion of a thought; finally, however, but. *Alternate Translation:* in the end *AHLB:* 1383-C(N) *Strong's:* #0657

FASTEN(V) (*ts.m.d)* To be joined to another as in a yoke. *AHLB:* 2665(V) *Strong's:* #6775

FASTENER (masc. *da'vaq)* An item for joining items together. *AHLB:* 2092(N) *Strong's:* #1694, #1695

FAT (masc. *hhe'lev)* Animal tissue consisting of cells distended with greasy or oily matter; adipose tissue. The fat of an animal as the choicest part. Also, milk; A white fatty liquid secreted by cows, sheep and goats, and used for food or as a source of butter, cheeses, yogurt, etc. *Alternate Translation:* milk *AHLB:* 2160(N) *Strong's:* #2459, #2461

FATHER (masc. *av)* A man who has begotten a child. The provider and support to the household. The ancestor of a family line. The patron of a profession or art. *AHLB:* 1002-A(N) *Strong's:* #0001

FATHER-IN-LAW (masc. *hham)* The father of ones wife or husband, father-in-law. *AHLB:* 1174-A(N) *Strong's:* #2524

FATNESS (masc. *da'shan)* An abundance of fat, food or ashes. *AHLB:* 2115(N) *Strong's:* #1879, #1880

FAVORED (masc. *ya'tav) Strong's:* [Found in names only]

FEAR(V) (*y.r.a)* To be afraid of; to have a strong emotion caused by anticipation or awareness of danger; the flowing, or quivering, of the gut from fear or awe; to dread what is terrible or revere what is respected. *AHLB:* 1227-E(V) *Strong's:* #3372

FEARFUL (masc. *ya'rey)* Having great respect; being in a state of awe or fear. *AHLB:* 1227-E(N) *Strong's:* #3373

FEARFULNESS (fem. *yi'rah)* A great respect; a state of awe or fear. *AHLB:* 1227-E(N1) *Strong's:* #3374

FEARING (masc. *mo'ra)* To be in awe, a state of fear or apprehensive. *AHLB:* 1227-E(k) *Strong's:* #4172

FEAST (masc. *hhag)* A commemoration of a special event with dancing, rejoicing, and sharing of food. A ceremony of joy and thanksgiving. A festival with a magnificent meal which is shared with a number of guests. *AHLB:* 1164-A$^{(N)}$ *Strong's:* #2282

FEATHER (fem. *ev'rah)* The principle covering of birds. *AHLB:* 1043-C(N1) *Strong's:* #0084

FED.FAT (masc. *ba'ri)* A member of the livestock that has been fed grains to fatten it for the slaughter. *Alternate Translation:* fattening *AHLB:* 1043-E(b) *Strong's:* #1277

FEED$^{(V)}$ (*r.ah.h)* To give food to; to provide feed or pasture to the flock. Commonly used in the participle form meaning a feeder or shepherd. *AHLB:* 1453-H$^{(V)}$ *Strong's:* #7462

FEEDING.PLACE (masc. *mir'eh)* A place of feeding or grazing. *AHLB:* 1453-H(h) *Strong's:* #4829

FEEL$^{(V)}$ (*m.w.sh)* To handle or touch in order to examine, test or explore some quality. Reach out with the hand to touch. *AHLB:* 1297-J$^{(V)}$ *Strong's:* #3237

FEMALE (fem. *na'qey'vah)* An individual that bears children. Designed with a hollow or groove into which a corresponding male part fits, as with a hole. *AHLB:* 2430(N1) *Strong's:* #5347

FEMALE.OWNER (fem. *ge've'ret)* A female master overseeing slaves or servants. *AHLB:* 2052(N2) *Strong's:* #1404

FENCE (masc. *g'der fem. g'dey'rah)* A wall for enclosing in livestock or garden. *AHLB:* 2057$^{(N)}$ *Strong's:* #1444, #1447, #1448

FENCE.AROUND$^{(V)}$ (*s.k.k)* To surround with a wall of protection or covering. To encompass completely. *AHLB:* 1333-B$^{(V)}$ *Strong's:* #5526

FENCE.IN$^{(V)}$ (*b.ts.r)* A barrier intended to protect, prevent escape or intrusion, or to mark a boundary; to gather together and confine for protection. *AHLB:* 2033$^{(V)}$ *Strong's:* #1219

FERRET (fem. *a'na'qah)* An unclean animal of unknown species. Probably a mammal whose sound is like a cry. *AHLB:* 1318-C(N1) *Strong's:* #0604

FEVER (fem. *qa'da'hhat) AHLB:* 2697(N2) *Strong's:* #6920

FEW (masc. *miz'ar / mits'ar)* Small in number. *AHLB:* 2680(h) *Strong's:* #4213, #4705

FIELD (masc. *sa'deh)* An open land area free of trees and buildings. A level plot of ground. *AHLB:* 1326-H$^{(N)}$ *Strong's:* #7704

FIFTH (masc. *hha'mi'shi)* An ordinal number. *AHLB:* 2176(bf) *Strong's:* #2549

FIFTH.PART (masc. *hho'mesh)* A fifth portion of five equal amounts. *AHLB:* 2176(g) *Strong's:* #2569, #2570

FIG (fem. *te'eyn)* An oblong or pear-shaped fruit from a tree of the fichus genus. *AHLB:* 1014-A(i) *Strong's:* #8384

FIGHT$^{(V)}$ (*l.hh.m)* To make war; to battle as to destruction; to attempt to defeat, subdue, or destroy an enemy by blows or weapons. *Alternate Translation:* wage war (when written in the niphil [passive] form) *AHLB:* 2305$^{(V)}$ *Strong's:* #3898

FIGHTING (masc. *ka'dar) Strong's:* [Found in names only]

FIGURE (masc. *se'mel) AHLB:* 2489$^{(N)}$ *Strong's:* #5566

FILL[V] (*m.l.a*) To occupy to the full capacity. *Alternate Translation:* fulfill; fully; set (the setting of stone) *AHLB:* 1288-E[V] *Strong's:* #4390

FILLING (masc. *me'lo*) An act or instance of filling; something used to fill a cavity, container, or depression. *AHLB:* 1288-E(c) *Strong's:* #4393

FILTHINESS (masc. *shiy'quts*) A dirty, shameful, or detestable action, object or condition. Often used in the context of idols. *AHLB:* 2878(ed) *Strong's:* #8251

FILTHY (masc. *she'qets*) *AHLB:* 2878[N] *Strong's:* #8263

FIN (masc. *s'na'piyr*) The fins of a fish. *AHLB:* 3038 *Strong's:* #5579

FIND[V] (*m.ts.a*) To come upon, often accidentally; to meet with; to discover and secure through searching. *Alternate Translation:* reveal (when written in the hiphil [active causative] form) *AHLB:* 1294-E[V] *Strong's:* #4672

FINE[V] (*ah.n.sh*) A financial penalty made for an offense or damages. *AHLB:* 2560[V] *Strong's:* #6064

FINGER (fem. *ets'ba*) The extension of the hand. Can be used to point. *AHLB:* 2655[N] *Strong's:* #0676

FINGER.SPAN (fem. *ze'ret*) The width of the fingers, often used as a measurement. *AHLB:* 1158-A(N2) *Strong's:* #2239

FINISH[V] (*k.l.h*) To bring to an end; terminate; to complete an action, event. *Alternate Translation:* bring to an end *AHLB:* 1242-H[V] *Strong's:* #3615

FIRE (fem. *eysh*) The phenomenon of combustion manifested by heat, light and flame. *AHLB:* 1021-A[N] *Strong's:* #0784

FIRE.OFFERING (masc. *i'sheh*) A sacrifice that is placed in a fire as an offering. *AHLB:* 1021-H(e) *Strong's:* #0801

FIRE.PAN (fem. *mahh'tah*) A tray for carrying hot coals. *AHLB:* 1183-A(a1) *Strong's:* #4289

FIRMLY.PRESSED (fem. *ma'a'kah*) *Strong's:* [Found in names only]

FIRMNESS (masc. *ey'mun* fem. *e'mu'nah*) Securely fixed in place. *AHLB:* 1290-C(d1) *Strong's:* #0529, #0530

FIRST (masc. *ri'shon*) The head of a time or position. *AHLB:* 1458-D(ej) *Strong's:* #7223

FIRST.RAIN (masc. *yo'reh*) *AHLB:* 1227-H(g) *Strong's:* #3138

FIRST.TIME (fem. *te'hhiy'lah*) The point of time or space at which anything begins. *AHLB:* 1173-A(i1) *Strong's:* #8462

FIRSTBORN (masc. *be'khor*) The first offspring, usually a son, of a man or animal; the prominent one. *AHLB:* 2016(c) *Strong's:* #1060

FIRSTBORN.FEMALE (fem. *be'khi'rah*) The daughter that is born first; the prominent one. *AHLB:* 2016(b1) *Strong's:* #1067

FIRSTFRUIT (masc. *bi'khor*) The first gathered fruits of a harvest; the first results of an undertaking. *AHLB:* 2016(ed) *Strong's:* #1061

FISH (masc. / *dag* fem. *da'gah*) An aquatic animal. Only fish with scales and fins are considered fit for food (clean). *AHLB:* 1072-A[N] *Strong's:* #1709, #1710

FISSURE (fem. *nik'rah*) A division, causing to become two pieces instead of one. A cleft or narrow chasm. *AHLB:* 2436(N1) *Strong's:* #5366

FIST (masc. *eg'roph*) Clenched fingers into the palm of the hand. *AHLB:* 2088(nc) *Strong's:* #0106

FIVE (masc. *hha'mi'shah fem. hha'meysh)* A cardinal number, from the number of fingers on a hand. *Alternate Translation:* fifty (when written in the plural) *AHLB:* 2176(N) *Strong's:* #2568, #2572

FLAKE.OFF (*hh.s.p)* To scale off particles from an object. *AHLB:* 3017 *Strong's:* #2636

FLAME.OF.FIRE (masc. *piyl'dash) Strong's:* [Found in names only]

FLAMING (masc. *hha'ri)* A visible fire, usually used in the sense of a fierce anger. *AHLB:* 1181-A(f) *Strong's:* #2750

FLAMING.WRATH (masc. *hha'ron)* A fierce anger. *AHLB:* 1181-A(j) *Strong's:* #2740

FLANK (fem. *yar'khah)* The hollow of the loins between the legs. *AHLB:* 1448-L(N1) *Strong's:* #3411

FLAPPING.WING (masc. *mam'ra) Strong's:* [Found in names only]

FLARE.UP(V) (*hh.r.h)* To become suddenly excited or angry; to break out suddenly. Burn with a fierce anger. *AHLB:* 1181-H(V) *Strong's:* #2734

FLASH (masc. *ba'raq)* The bright light shining off the edge of a sword. The bright light of lightning. *AHLB:* 2041(N) *Strong's:* #1300

FLAT (masc. *riy'qu'a)* As hammered out flat. *AHLB:* 2797(ed) *Strong's:* #7555

FLAVOR (masc. *ta'am)* The taste of a food or the perception of a person's behavior. *AHLB:* 2236(N) *Strong's:* #2940

FLAX (fem. *pish'teh)* A plant in which its fibers are used in manufacturing articles of clothing. Also, used to make wicks, cords, and bands. Linseed, linseed oil, and oilcake are useful products of the same plant. *AHLB:* 2648(N1) *Strong's:* #6593, #6594

FLEE(V) (*n.w.s)* To run away, often from danger or evil; to hurry toward a place of safety; to flee to any safe place such as a city or mountain. *AHLB:* 1314-J(V) *Strong's:* #5127

FLEE.AWAY(V) (*b.r.hh)* To run away from. *Alternate Translation:* reach (when written in the hiphil [active causative] form) *AHLB:* 2038(V) *Strong's:* #1272

FLEECE (masc. *gaz)* The coat of wool that covers a sheep or a similar animal. Also, the grasses that are sheared off with a sickle in harvest. *AHLB:* 1053-A(N) *Strong's:* #1488

FLEEING (fem. *m'nu'sah) AHLB:* 1314-J(k1) *Strong's:* #4499

FLEET (masc. *iy'rad) Strong's:* [Found in names only]

FLESH (fem. *ba'sar)* The soft parts of a human or animal, composed primarily of skeletal muscle. Skin and muscle or the whole of the person. Meat as food. *AHLB:* 2025(N) *Strong's:* #1154, #1320

FLINT (masc. *ya'ha'lom)* Possibly the flint, a form of quartz of a brown, gray or black color. Other possible translations are onyx and diamond. *AHLB:* 1104-L(qp) *Strong's:* #3095

FLOAT(V) (*z.w.p)* To rest or remain on the surface of a liquid; be buoyant. *AHLB:* 1155-J(V) *Strong's:* #6687

FLOCKS (masc. *tso'neh fem.* / *tson)* Groups of birds or animals assembled or herded together. *AHLB:* 1405-J(N) *Strong's:* #6629, #6792

FLOOD (masc. *ma'bul)* To cover with an overwhelming quantity or volume of water. *AHLB:* 1035-J(a) *Strong's:* #3999

FLOOR (masc. *go'ren)* The level base of a room, barn or threshing floor. *AHLB:* 2085(g) *Strong's:* #1637

FLOUR (fem. *so'let)* Finely ground meal of grain used for making bread. *AHLB:* 1334-J(N2) *Strong's:* #5560

FLOURISHED (masc. *nav) Strong's:* [Found in names only]

FLOURISHING (masc. *ra'a'nan)* A green plant bearing fruit. Also, prosperous. *AHLB:* 2781(m) *Strong's:* #7488

FLOW$^{(V)}$ (*n.z.l)* To stream or gush a liquid substance. To run like water. *AHLB:* 2387$^{(V)}$ *Strong's:* #5140

FLOW.OUT$^{(V)}$ (*r.w.r) AHLB:* 1457-J$^{(V)}$ *Strong's:* #7325

FLUSH$^{(V)}$ (*sh.t.p)* To flow over with copious amounts of water. *AHLB:* 2832$^{(V)}$ *Strong's:* #7857

FLUTTER$^{(V)}$ (*r.hh.p)* To flap the wings rapidly. To move with quick wavering or flapping motions. Shake as a bird in the nest. *AHLB:* 2763$^{(V)}$ *Strong's:* #7363

FLY$^{(V)}$ (*ah.w.p)* To move in or pass through the air with wings; to soar in the air. *AHLB:* 1362-J$^{(V)}$ *Strong's:* #5774

FLYER (masc. *oph)* A flying creature such as a bird or insect. *AHLB:* 1362-J$^{(N)}$ *Strong's:* #5775

FOLLOWING (fem. *te'shu'qah)* To go, proceed or come after. Being next in order or time. Subsequent to. As the river follows the path of its banks. *AHLB:* 1479-J(i1) *Strong's:* #8669

FOLLY (fem. *ne'va'lah)* Lack of good sense or prudence and foresight. In the sense of fading away. *AHLB:* 2369(N1) *Strong's:* #5039

FOOD (fem. *akh'lah)* Something that nourishes, sustains, or supplies. For giving sustenance and making one whole. *AHLB:* 1242-C(N1) *Strong's:* #0402

FOODSTUFF (masc. *o'khel)* A substance that may be eaten for giving sustenance and making one whole. *AHLB:* 1242-C(g) *Strong's:* #0400

FOOL (masc. *na'val)* A silly or stupid person. *AHLB:* 2369$^{(N)}$ *Strong's:* #5036

FOOLISH$^{(V)}$ (*y.a.l)* To be without wisdom. *AHLB:* 1254-L$^{(V)}$ *Strong's:* #2973

FOOT (fem. *re'gel)* The terminal part of the leg upon which the human, animal or object stands. Also, euphemistically for the leg. *Alternate Translation:* times (when in the plural form) *AHLB:* 2749$^{(N)}$ *Strong's:* #7272

FOOTING (masc. *e'den)* Ground or basis for a firm foundation. That which sustains a stable position. *AHLB:* 1083-C$^{(N)}$ *Strong's:* #0134

FOOTSTEP (fem. *pa'am)* A stroke of time as a rhythmic beating of time, one moment after the other. A moment in time. A foot or leg in the sense of stepping. *Alternate Translation:* foot; time; this time (when prefixed with "the~") *AHLB:* 2623$^{(N)}$ *Strong's:* #6471

FOR (masc. *hhey'leph)* An exchange for something else. *AHLB:* 2165$^{(N)}$ *Strong's:* #2500

FORBID$^{(V)}$ (*n.w.a) AHLB:* 1300-J$^{(V)}$ *Strong's:* #5106

FORCE (masc. *hha'yil)* The pressure exerted to make a piercing. *AHLB:* 1173-M$^{(N)}$ *Strong's:* #2428

FORCEFUL (masc. *hha'zaq fem. hha'za'qah)* A strong grip on something to refrain or support. Driven with force. Acting with power. *AHLB:* 2152$^{(N)}$ *Strong's:* #2389, #2390, #2391

FOREARM (fem. *am'mah)* A linear standard of measure equal to the length of the forearm. *AHLB:* 1013-A(N1) *Strong's:* #0520

FOREFRONT (masc. *mul)* In front of or at the head of, in space or time. *Alternate Translation:* in place *AHLB:* 1288-J$^{(N)}$ *Strong's:* #4136

FOREHEAD (masc. *mey'tsahh)* The part of the face which extends from the hair on the top of the head to the eyes. Impudence, confidence, or assurance. The seat of boldness of speech and actions. *AHLB:* 2350$^{(N)}$ *Strong's:* #4696

FOREIGN (masc. *na'khri fem. na'khri'yah)* Situated outside one's own country. Alien in character. A strange person, place or thing as being unrecognized. *AHLB:* 2406(f) *Strong's:* #5237

FOREIGNER (masc. *ney'khar)* A person belonging to or owing allegiance to a foreign country. *AHLB:* 2406$^{(N)}$ *Strong's:* #5235, #5236

FORESKIN (fem. *ar'lah)* A fold of skin that covers the end of the penis. *AHLB:* 2577(N1) *Strong's:* #6190

FOREST (masc. *ya'ar)* A dark place dense with trees. *AHLB:* 1526-L$^{(N)}$ *Strong's:* #3264, #3293

FORGET$^{(V)}$ (*sh.k.hh)* To lose remembrance of; to cease remembering or noticing. *AHLB:* 2835$^{(V)}$ *Strong's:* #7911

FORGIVE$^{(V)}$ (*s.l.hh)* To pardon; to overlook an offense and treat the offender as not guilty. *AHLB:* 2482$^{(V)}$ *Strong's:* #5545

FORK (masc. *maz'leyg fem. miz'la'gah)* An implement, or tool with multiple prongs or tines. *AHLB:* 2122(a) *Strong's:* #4207

FORM (masc. *to'ar)* The outline of an individual. *AHLB:* 1503-D(g) *Strong's:* #8389

FORTIFICATION (masc. *miv'tsar)* A walled place of protection and confinement. *AHLB:* 2033(h) *Strong's:* #4013

FORTIFIED (masc. *kas'lo'ahh) Strong's:* [Found in names only]

FORTRESS.OF.ANU (masc. *kal'nah) Strong's:* [Found in names only]

FORTUNATE (masc. *shun) Strong's:* [Found in names only]

FORTUNE (masc. *gad)* A store of material possessions. *AHLB:* 1050-A$^{(N)}$ *Strong's:* #1409

FORTUNES (masc. *gid'gad fem. gud'go'dah)* Great wealth; ample stock of money, property, and the like. *Strong's:* [Found in names only]

FOUL (masc. *pi'gul) AHLB:* 2591(ed) *Strong's:* #6292

FOUND$^{(V)}$ (*y.s.d)* To lay a foundation of a house, place or plan. *AHLB:* 1326-L$^{(V)}$ *Strong's:* #3245

FOUNDATION (masc. *mu'sad fem. mu'sa'dah)* A supporting and level base of a building or structure which lies on or in the ground. *AHLB:* 1326-L(a) *Strong's:* #4143, #4144, #4145, #4146

FOUNTAIN (masc. *ma'qor)* A spring that comes out of a hole in the ground. The source of water necessary for life in the wilderness. *AHLB:* 1250-J(a) *Strong's:* #4726

FOUR (masc. *ar'ba'ah fem. ar'ba)* A cardinal number. *Alternate Translation:* forty (when written in the plural) *AHLB:* 2744$^{(N)}$ *Strong's:* #0702, #0705

FOURTH (masc. *re'vi'i)* An ordinal number. *AHLB:* 2744(bf) *Strong's:* #7243

FOURTH.GENERATION (masc. ריבע *ri'va)* A great-great grandchild, as a descendant of the fourth generation. *AHLB:* 2744(e) *Strong's:* #7256

FOURTH.PART (masc. רובע *ro'va)* As fourth in the order. *AHLB:* 2744(g) *Strong's:* #7255

FRAGILE (masc. פרנך *par'nakh) Strong's:* [Found in names only]

FRAGMENT (fem. פת *pat)* A part broken off, detached, or incomplete. The removal of a piece resulting in a hole. *AHLB:* 1390-A(N) *Strong's:* #6595

FRAGRANCE (fem. בסמת *bas'mat)* The pleasing aroma of a sweet-smelling spice. *Strong's:* [Found in names only]

FRAGRANT.ONE (masc. זיפרון *ziph'ron)* A person who has a pleasant scent or aroma. *Strong's:* [Found in names only]

FRAIL (masc. רפה *ra'pheh) AHLB:* 1454-H(N) *Strong's:* #7504

FRANKINCENSE (fem. לבונה *le'vo'nah)* A resin or gum that is a residue from the bark of a particular ash or fir tree. Used as incense, perfume, or with an offering. *AHLB:* 2303(c1) *Strong's:* #3828

FREE (masc. חפשי *hhaph'shi)* Released from bondage or burden of obligation. Emancipation. *AHLB:* 2193(f) *Strong's:* #2670

FREE(V) (חפש *hh.p.sh)* To be free from a master or obligation. *AHLB:* 2193(V) *Strong's:* #2666

FREE.FLOWING (fem. דרור *de'ror)* To flow without hindrances. *AHLB:* 1089-B(c) *Strong's:* #1865

FREEDOM (fem. חופשה *hhuph'shah) AHLB:* 2193(o1) *Strong's:* #2668

FREELY (masc. חינם *hhi'nam)* Having no restrictions. A work or action that is performed without wages or without cause. *AHLB:* 1175-A(p) *Strong's:* #2600

FREEWILL.OFFERING (fem. נדבה *ne'da'vah)* A voluntary or spontaneous gift as an offering out of respect or devotion. *AHLB:* 2380(N1) *Strong's:* #5071

FRESH (masc. לשד *l'shad)* Something that is fresh and moist. *AHLB:* 2322(N) *Strong's:* #3955

FRESH.OIL (masc. יצהר *yits'har) AHLB:* 1411-G(t) *Strong's:* #3323

FRESH.WINE (masc. תירוש *ti'rosh)* Newly pressed wine as a desired possession. *AHLB:* 1458-L(ic) *Strong's:* #8492

FRIEND (fem. רעות *re'ut)* A female companion as one who is close. *AHLB:* 1453-A(N3) *Strong's:* #7468

FRINGE (fem. ציצית *tsi'tsit)* A tassel or lock of hair as blossoms. *AHLB:* 1409-M(N4) *Strong's:* #6734

FROG (masc. צפרדע *tse'phar'dey'a)* A four-legged amphibious animal. *Strong's:* #6854

FROM (masc. מני / מן *min / miney)* A function word indicating a starting point or origin. (The short form "מ" is used as a prefix meaning "from") *Alternate Translation:* before (when prefixed with "to~") *AHLB:* 1290-A(h) *Strong's:* #4480

FRUIT.PRESS (masc. דמע *de'ma)* The liquid that seeps out of the fruit and used in making oils and juices. *AHLB:* 2106(N) *Strong's:* #1831

FRUITFUL (fem. ריבלה *riyv'lah)* Bountiful of produce. (A noun of uncertain meaning). *Strong's:* [Found in names only]

FRUITFULNESS (masc. פרת *pa'tar) Strong's:* [Found in names only]

FRY(V) (רבך *r.b.k) AHLB:* 2743(V) *Strong's:* #7246

FULL (masc. *ma'ley fem. me'ley'ah)* Containing as much or as many as is possible or normal. *AHLB:* 1288-E(N) *Strong's:* #4392

FULL.AGE (masc. *ke'lahh)* Advanced in years. *AHLB:* 2260(N) *Strong's:* #3624

FULL.STRENGTH (masc. *tom)* Someone or something that is whole or complete. Full in power or force. One who is mature. *AHLB:* 1496-J(N) *Strong's:* #8537

FUNCTIONAL (masc. *tov fem. to'vah)* Fulfilling the action for which a person or thing is specially fitted or used, or for which a thing exists. A functioning within its intended purpose. *AHLB:* 1186-J(N) *Strong's:* #2896, #2898

FURNACE (masc. *kiv'shan)* An enclosed structure in which heat is produced by burning wood inside. *AHLB:* 2251(em) *Strong's:* #3536

FURROW (masc. *te'lem)* A line scratched in the soil made by oxen while plowing a field. *AHLB:* 1266-A(i) *Strong's:* #8525

FURTHER (fem. *hal'ah)* At a distance beyond the present place or time. *Alternate Translation:* beyond (when prefixed with "from~") *AHLB:* 1104-E(N1) *Strong's:* #1973

FURY (fem. *hha'mah)* Intense, disordered, and often destructive rage. An intense heat from anger. *AHLB:* 1174-A(N1) *Strong's:* #2534

Gain(V) (*y.ah.l)* To profit or benefit. *AHLB:* 1357-L(V) *Strong's:* #3276

GALBANUM (fem. *hhel'be'nah)* An odoriferous resin used in incense. A choice ingredient used in the Temple incense or oil. *AHLB:* 2160(m1) *Strong's:* #2464

GALL (fem. *ma'ro'rah)* The bitter fluids of a serpent. *AHLB:* 1296-B(c1) *Strong's:* #4846

GAME (masc. *tsa'yid)* Animals being pursued or taken in hunting. The produce of the hunt. *AHLB:* 1395-M(N) *Strong's:* #6718

GARDEN (*gan)* A plot of ground where crops are grown. A place for growing crops, and often surrounded by a rock wall or hedge to protect it from grazing animals. *AHLB:* 1060-A(N) *Strong's:* #1588

GARLIC (masc. *shum)* From its strong odor. *AHLB:* 1473-J(N) *Strong's:* #7762

GARMENT (masc. *be'ged)* An article of clothing for covering. *AHLB:* 2004(N) *Strong's:* #0899

GATE (masc. *sha'ar)* The opening in a wall or fence through which livestock or people pass. Can be the gatekeeper. *AHLB:* 2862(N) *Strong's:* #8179

GATHER(V) (*a.s.p)* To bring together; to accumulate and place in readiness. *AHLB:* 1339-C(V) *Strong's:* #0622

GATHER.FOOD(V) (*a.g.r)* To bring together a nourishing substance that is eaten or drunk. *AHLB:* 1066-C(V) *Strong's:* #0103

GATHER.TOGETHER(V) (*q.b.ts)* To come or bring into a group, mass or unit. *AHLB:* 2695(V) *Strong's:* #6908, #6910

GATHERED.UP (masc. *laq) Strong's:* [Found in names only]

GATHERING (masc. *a'siph)* That which has been brought together. [. *AHLB:* 1339-C(b) *Strong's:* #0614

GAZELLE (masc. *ts'viy fem. ts'viy'ah)* A small antelope. *AHLB:* 1393-A(f) *Strong's:* #6643, #6646

GENERATION (masc. *dor)* A body of living beings constituting a single step in the line of descent from an ancestor. *AHLB:* 1089-J(N) *Strong's:* #1755

GENITALS (masc. *ma'vush)* The sexual organs. *AHLB:* 1044-J(a) *Strong's:* #4016

GENTLE (masc. / *a'naw)* A characterstic trait of being meek or humble. *AHLB:* 1359-K(N) *Strong's:* #6035

GERAH (fem. *ge'rah)* A dry weight measure equal to a 20th part of a shekel. *AHLB:* 1066-A(N1) *Strong's:* #1626

GIER-EAGLE (masc. *ra'hham fem.* *ra'hha'mah)* An unknown species of bird, possibly a type of carrion. *AHLB:* 2762(N) *Strong's:* #7360

GIFT (masc. *ma'ten)* To endow with some power, quality, or attribute; the act, power or right of giving. What is given. *AHLB:* 2451(a) *Strong's:* #4976

GIFT.OFFERING (masc. *hav)* A present. *Strong's:* [Found in names only]

GIRD(V) (*a.p.d)* To pull in closely to the body. To wrap around. To tie on the ephod. *AHLB:* 1372-C(V) *Strong's:* #0640

GIRD.UP(V) (*hh.g.r)* To bind the loose portions of clothing into a belt or sash to prepare to go to war; to be bound with arms for war. *AHLB:* 2147(V) *Strong's:* #2296

GIRL (fem. *yal'dah)* A young, unmarried woman. *AHLB:* 1257-L(N1) *Strong's:* #3207

GIVE(V) (*n.t.n)* To make a present; to present a gift; to grant, allow or bestow by formal action. To place in its proper position. *Alternate Translation:* allow; made; make; place *AHLB:* 2451(V) *Strong's:* #5414

GIVE.A.TENTH(V) (*ah.s.r)* To tithe; a tenth part of something given voluntarily for the support of a religious establishment. *AHLB:* 2563(V) *Strong's:* #6237

GIVE.ADVICE(V) (*y.ah.ts)* To assist another by providing wise counsel. *AHLB:* 1363-L(V) *Strong's:* #3289

GIVE.HONOR(V) (*h.d.r)* To ascribe size or majesty to someone or something that is large in stature or position. To puff up. *AHLB:* 1089-F(V) *Strong's:* #1921

GIVE.MILK(V) (*ah.w.l)* To provide nourishment to the young by the female. *AHLB:* 1058-J(V) *Strong's:* #5763

GIVEN.THAT (masc. *ki)* Prone or disposed to according to what preceded. A reference to the previous or following context. *Alternate Translation:* because; but; even; given; if; that; there; when; even though (when attached to the word "WHICH"); except, instead or unless (when followed by the word "IF"); since (when followed by the word "SO") *AHLB:* 1240-A(N) *Strong's:* #3588

GLEANINGS (masc. *le'qet) AHLB:* 2320(N) *Strong's:* #3951

GLIMMER (masc. *la'hav)* The flash of light from a fire or metal. *AHLB:* 1255-G(N) *Strong's:* #3851

GLIMMERING (fem. / / *leh'ha'vah / le'he'vet / lab'bah)* The flash of light from a fire or metal. *AHLB:* 1255-G(N1) *Strong's:* #3827, #3852

GLISTENING (fem. *tso'har)* Emitting or reflecting light. From the glisten of olive oil. Something that shines brightly. Also, noon as the brightest part of the day. *Alternate Translation:* noontime (when in the double plural form) *AHLB:* 1411-G(g) *Strong's:* #6672

GLORIOUS.REST (masc. *pa'nahh) Strong's:* [Found in names only]

GLUTTON(V) (*z.l.l)* A person with a remarkably great desire or capacity for something. *AHLB:* 1150-B(V) *Strong's:* #2151

GNAT (masc. *keyn)* A small flying insect. *AHLB:* 1244-A(N) *Strong's:* #3654

GNAW(V) (*g.r.m)* To chew on something hard such as a bone. *AHLB:* 2084(V) *Strong's:* #1633

GNAWED (masc. *a'raq) Strong's:* [Found in names only]

GO(V) (*sh.w.t)* To go back an forth as a whip. *AHLB:* 1469-J(V) *Strong's:* #7751

GO.ABOUT (masc. *sa'mal) Strong's:* [Found in names only]

GO.AROUND(V) (*s.b.b)* To circle completely around something. *Alternate Translation:* enclosed in (when written in the hophal [passive causative] form) *AHLB:* 1324-B(V) *Strong's:* #5437

GO.ASIDE(V) (*s.t.h)* To turn aside or away. *AHLB:* 1331-H(V) *Strong's:* #7847

GO.ASTRAY(V) (*sh.g.h) AHLB:* 1463-H(V) *Strong's:* #7686

GO.DOWN(V) (*y.r.d)* To go or come lower from a higher place. *Alternate Translation:* come down; bring down (when written in the hiphil [active causative] form) *AHLB:* 1441-L(V) *Strong's:* #3381

GO.OUT(V) (*y.ts.a)* To go, come or issue forth. *Alternate Translation:* bring out (when written in the hiphil [active causative] form) *AHLB:* 1392-L(V) *Strong's:* #3318

GO.RIGHT(V) (/ *y.m.n / a.m.n)* To choose, turn or go to the right hand. *AHLB:* 1290-L(V) *Strong's:* #0541, #3231

GO.UP(V) (*ah.l.h)* To go, come or bring higher. *Alternate Translation:* bring up (when written in the hiphil [active causative] form) *AHLB:* 1357-H(V) *Strong's:* #5927

GOAT (fem. *eyz)* A female domestic animal related to the sheep. *AHLB:* 1513-A(N) *Strong's:* #5795

GOBLET (masc. *a'nan)* A cup for containing liquids. *AHLB:* 1060-C(N) *Strong's:* #0101

GOING.OUT (masc. *mo'tsa)* Coming or issuing out, such as a spring or words from the mouth. *AHLB:* 1392-L(a) *Strong's:* #4161

GOINGS (fem. *to'tsa'ah) AHLB:* 1392-L(i1) *Strong's:* #8444

GOLD (masc. *za'hav)* A malleable yellow metallic element that is used especially in coins, jewelry, and dentures. A precious metal. *AHLB:* 1140-G(N) *Strong's:* #2091

GOODS (masc. *re'khush)* Something that has economic utility or satisfies an economic want; personal property having intrinsic value but usually excluding money, securities and negotiable instruments. *AHLB:* 2772(d) *Strong's:* #7399

GOPHER (masc. *go'pher)* A tree or its wood of an unknown species. *AHLB:* 2079(N) *Strong's:* #1613

GORE(V) (*n.g.hh)* To stab with the horns. *AHLB:* 2373(V) *Strong's:* #5055

GORER (masc. *na'gahh)* An ox that is known to gore with the horns. *AHLB:* 2373(N) *Strong's:* #5056

GOVERNOR (masc. *sha'lit)* An official elected or appointed to act as ruler, chief executive, or nominal head of a political unit. One who has dominion over another; also a rule or law as a master. *AHLB:* 2843(b) *Strong's:* #7989

GRAIN (masc. *bar)* A seed or fruit of a cereal grass. The grain and the field as a place for growing grain. *AHLB:* 1043-A(N) *Strong's:* #1250

GRAIN.FLOUR (masc. *qe'mahh)* Usually finely ground seeds of wheat. *AHLB:* 2711(N) *Strong's:* #7058

GRAIN.SACK (fem. *am'ta'hhat)* A usually flexible container that may be closed for holding, storing, or carrying something; e.g. The mouth is spread apart to put something in or take something out. *AHLB:* 2362(n2) *Strong's:* #0572

GRAIN.SEEDS (masc. *she'ver)* A family of grasses used for food. *AHLB:* 2811(N) *Strong's:* #7668

GRAIN.STALK (fem. *qa'mah)* The tall stem of cereal crops. *AHLB:* 1427-A(N1) *Strong's:* #7054

GRAPE (masc. *ey'nav)* A smooth-skinned juicy greenish white to deep red or purple berry grown on a vine and eaten dried or fresh as a fruit or fermented to produce wine. *AHLB:* 2555(N) *Strong's:* #6025

GRAPE.SKIN (masc. *gaz)* The skin of the berry or fruit that grows in clusters on vines of the genus Vitis. *AHLB:* 1141-A(N) *Strong's:* #2085

GRAPEVINE (masc. *ge'phen)* A woody vine that usually climbs by tendrils and produces fruits that are grapes. *AHLB:* 2078(N) *Strong's:* #1612

GRAPPLE(V) (*a.b.q)* A hand-to-hand struggle. Rolling around in the dust when wrestling. *AHLB:* 1042-C(V) *Strong's:* #0079

GRASP (masc. *hho'zeq)* A firm hold or grip. *AHLB:* 2152(g) *Strong's:* #2392

GRASP(V) (*q.m.ts)* To grab with the hands, to grab a handful. *AHLB:* 2714(V) *Strong's:* #7061

GRASS (masc. *de'she)* Herbage suitable or used for grazing animals. Young green sprouts. *AHLB:* 1090-E(N) *Strong's:* #1877

GRASSHOPPER (masc. *hha'gav)* A species of insect with hind legs used for leaping and mouthparts that chew. *AHLB:* 2146(N) *Strong's:* #2284

GRATE (masc. *mikh'bar)* An agricultural device, like a sieve, used to separate the grain form the stem. *AHLB:* 2250(h) *Strong's:* #4345

GRAVE (masc. *qe'ver)* An excavation for the burial of a body. *AHLB:* 2696(N) *Strong's:* #6913

GRAY (masc. *qa'dar) Strong's:* [Found in names only]

GRAY-HEADED (fem. *si'vah)* One who has gray hair from old age; an old man. *AHLB:* 1324-M(N1) *Strong's:* #7872

GREAT (masc. *ga'dol fem.* *ge'do'lah)* Something with increased size, power or authority. *AHLB:* 2054(c) *Strong's:* #1419

GREAT.AMOUNT (fem. *tar'but) AHLB:* 1439-A(i3) *Strong's:* #8635

GREAT.HOUSE (masc. *par'o)* A word of Egyptian origins. *Strong's:* [Found in names only]

GREAT.NUMBER (fem. *mar'biyt) AHLB:* 1439-A(a4) *Strong's:* #4768

GREAT.TREE (masc. *ey'lon)* A tree made of very dense, hard, wood. *AHLB:* 1012-A(j) *Strong's:* #0436, #0437

GREEN (masc. *ye'req)* A color somewhat less yellow than that of fresh growing grass and of that part of the spectrum between blue and yellow. The color of grasses and herbs as thin. *AHLB:* 1456-L(N) *Strong's:* #3418, #3419

GREEN.GRAIN (masc. *a'viv)* Fresh young stalks of standing grain. Also, the name of a month in the Hebrew calendar. *AHLB:* 1002-B(b) *Strong's:* #0024

GREENISH (masc. *y'raq'raq) AHLB:* 1456-L(l) *Strong's:* #3422

GRIEF (fem. *mo'rah)* Deep and poignant distress caused by or as if by bereavement. As an exchange. *AHLB:* 1296-J(N1) *Strong's:* #4786

GRIND[V] (*t.hh.n)* To reduce to fine particles through abrasion. *AHLB:* 2231[V] *Strong's:* #2912

GROANING (fem. *ne'a'qah)* To voice a deep, inarticulate sound, as of pain, grief, or displeasure. *AHLB:* 1318-D(N1) *Strong's:* #5009

GROPE[V] (*m.sh.sh)* To feel about blindly or uncertainly in search of something. A groping around in the darkness to find something. *AHLB:* 1297-B[V] *Strong's:* #4184, #4959

GROUND (fem. *a'da'mah)* The surface of the earth. From its reddish color. *AHLB:* 1082-C(N1) *Strong's:* #0127

GROUND.TO.PIECES[V] (*d.w.q)* Something that is reduced to fragments. *AHLB:* 1080-J[V] *Strong's:* #1743

GROUSE (fem. *du'khiy'phat)* A species of unclean bird. *AHLB:* 2100(ob2) *Strong's:* #1744

GROVE (fem. *a'shey'rah)* An area of planted trees. Trees planted in a straight line. *AHLB:* 1480-C[N] *Strong's:* #0842

GROW (*sh.b.n) Strong's:* [Found in names only]

GROW.FAT[V] (*sh.m.n)* To be fat or full of oil. *AHLB:* 2850[V] *Strong's:* #8080

GUARD (masc. *shiy'ma'ron) Strong's:* [Found in names only]

GUIDE[V] (*n.hh.h)* One who leads or directs another in his way. *AHLB:* 1307-H[V] *Strong's:* #5148

GUILT (masc. *a'sham)* The fact of having committed a breach of conduct especially violating law and involving a penalty; the state of one who has committed an offense, especially consciously. *AHLB:* 1473-C[N] *Strong's:* #0817, #0818

GUILTINESS (fem. *ash'mah) AHLB:* 1473-C(N1) *Strong's:* #0819

GULP[V] (*sh.t.h)* To drink plentifully; to swallow hurriedly or greedily or in one swallow. *AHLB:* 1482-H[V] *Strong's:* #8354

GUST[V] (*n.sh.b)* A sudden brief rush of wind. The strong blowing of a wind. The wind of a bird's wing when taking flight. *AHLB:* 2440[V] *Strong's:* #5380

GUZZLE[V] (*g.m.a)* To drink greedily, continually, or habitually. A drinking of water as from a pond. *AHLB:* 1059-E[V] *Strong's:* #1572

HABITATION (masc. / *ma'on / ma'iyn fem.* *m'o'nah)* The dwelling place of a god (temple), man (home) *AHLB:* 1359-J(a) *Strong's:* #4583, #4585

HAILSTONES (masc. *ba'rad)* A precipitation in the form of irregular pellets or balls of ice. *AHLB:* 2037[N] *Strong's:* #1259

HAIR (masc. *sey'ar fem.* *sa'ra)* The covering of filaments on a human head or the body of an animal. *AHLB:* 2494[N] *Strong's:* #8163(x2), #8181, #8185

HAIR.FELL.OUT[V] (*m.r.t)* A plucking or falling out of the hair on the head. *AHLB:* 2354[V] *Strong's:* #4803

HAIRY.GOAT (masc. *sa'ir fem.* *se'o'rah)* A breed of goat with an unusual amount of hair. *AHLB:* 2494(b) *Strong's:* #8163(x2), #8166

HALF (masc. *hha'tsi)* An equal part of something divided into two pieces. *Alternate Translation:* middle *AHLB:* 1179-A(f) *Strong's:* #2677

HALF.THE.SPOILS (fem. *me'hhe'tsat) AHLB:* 1179-M(j) *Strong's:* #4275

HALTER (masc. *re'sen)* A device used for leading an animal. *AHLB:* 2776(N) *Strong's:* #7448

HAMMER(V) (*r.q.ah)* To beat a malleable metal with a hammer to make thin sheets. *AHLB:* 2797(V) *Strong's:* #7554

HAND (fem. *yad)* The terminal, functional part of the forelimb. Hand with the ability to work, throw and give thanks. Also, euphemistically for the arm. (Written as יך in error in 1 Samuel 4:13) *AHLB:* 1211-A(N) *Strong's:* #3027, #3197

HAND.OVER(V) (*y.r.t) AHLB:* 1446-L(V) *Strong's:* #3399

HAND.SPAN (masc. *te'phahh)* A linear standard of measure that is equal to the span of the fingers of the hand. *AHLB:* 2238(N) *Strong's:* #2947

HANDFUL (masc. *qo'mets)* As much of or as many as the hand can grasp. *AHLB:* 2714(g) *Strong's:* #7062

HANG(V) (/ *t.l.h / t.l.a)* To suspend with no support from below. *AHLB:* 1495-H(V) *Strong's:* #8511, #8518

HAPPINESS (masc. *o'sher)* A state of well-being and contentment. One who is happy is one whose life is lived straightly. *AHLB:* 1480-C(g) *Strong's:* #0837

HAPPY (masc. *a'sheyr)* A feeling of joy or satisfaction. *AHLB:* 1480-C(N) *Strong's:* #0835

HAPPY(V) (*a.sh.r)* Enjoying well-being and contentment. One who is happy is one whose life is lived straightly. *AHLB:* 1480-C(V) *Strong's:* #0833

HARASS(V) (*ts.w.q)* To press into a tight place, an oppression. *AHLB:* 1402-J(V) *Strong's:* #6693

HARD (fem. *qa'sheh)* Not easily penetrated; resistant to stress; firm; lacking in responsiveness. *AHLB:* 1435-H(N) *Strong's:* #7186

HARDSHIP (masc. *i'tsa'von)* Privation; suffering; something that causes or entails suffering or privation. *AHLB:* 2566(j) *Strong's:* #6093

HARE (masc. *ar'ne'vet) AHLB:* 3059 *Strong's:* #0768

HARM (masc. *a'son)* Physical or mental damage; injury. The pain from the thorn. *AHLB:* 1336-C(c) *Strong's:* #0611

HARNESS שיריון ^^ שיריון shir-yon) (*shir-yon) AHLB:* 1480-A(efj) *Strong's:* #5630, #8302

HARP (masc. *ki'nor)* A stringed musical instrument that is plucked. *AHLB:* 2270(ec) *Strong's:* #3658

HARSH (masc. *m'riy'riy)* A bitter action. *AHLB:* 1296-B(bf) *Strong's:* #4815

HARVEST (masc. *qa'tsir)* The season for gathering agricultural crops. Time when the plants are severed from their roots to be used for seed or food. *AHLB:* 2727(b) *Strong's:* #7105

HASTE (masc. *hhi'pha'zon)* A swift movement or action. *AHLB:* 2188(ej) *Strong's:* #2649

HASTEN(V) (*hh.p.z)* To be in a hurry to move or act. *AHLB:* 2188(V) *Strong's:* #2648

HASTILY (masc. *hho'shem) Strong's:* [Found in names only]

HASTY (masc. *hhush) Strong's:* [Found in names only]

HATE (fem. *sin'ah) AHLB:* 1336-E(N1) *Strong's:* #8135

HATE[V] (*s.n.a)* Intense hostility and aversion, usually deriving from fear, anger, or sense of injury; extreme dislike or antipathy. *AHLB:* 1336-E[V] *Strong's:* #8130

HATED (fem. *sa'niy'ah) AHLB:* 1336-E(b) *Strong's:* #8146

HAVE.COMPASSION[V] (*r.hh.m)* Literally to cradle in ones arms to protect or cherish. By extension to have or show sympathy or sorrow. *AHLB:* 2762[V] *Strong's:* #7355

HAVE.HORNS[V] (*q.r.n)* One of a pair of bony processes that arise from the head of many animals, sometimes used as a wind instrument. The horn-shaped protrusions of the altar or a musical instrument. *AHLB:* 2732[V] *Strong's:* #7160

HAVING.AN.EYE (masc. *ey'nan) Strong's:* [Found in names only]

HAWK (fem. *a'yah)* A bird of prey, probably the hawk, but possibly a kite or vulture. *AHLB:* 1005-M[N] *Strong's:* #0344

HAZEL (masc. *luz)* A light brown to strong yellowish-brown color; small trees or shrubs bearing nuts enclosed in a leafy involucres. *AHLB:* 1260-J[N] *Strong's:* #3869

HE (masc. *hu)* The male who is neither speaker nor hearer. *Alternate Translation:* it; that; this; they (when being used in conjunction with the singular noun PEOPLE) *AHLB:* 1093-J[N] *Strong's:* #1931(x2)

HE.GOAT (masc. *ta'yish)* A male goat. *AHLB:* 1504-M[N] *Strong's:* #8495

HEAD (masc. / *rosh / riysh)* The top of the body. A person in authority or role of leader. *Alternate Translation:* top; beginning; first; chief; best *AHLB:* 1458-D[N] *Strong's:* #7218, #7389

HEAD.OF.WHEAT (fem. *m'liy'lah)* A conglomeration of grain seeds together. *AHLB:* 1288-B(b1) *Strong's:* #4425

HEADDRESS (fem. *mig'ba'at)* A bowl shaped covering for the head. A covering for protection. *AHLB:* 2051(hb2) *Strong's:* #4021

HEADREST (fem. *me'ra'a'shah)* A support for the head. Place where the head is laid. *AHLB:* 1458-D(k1) *Strong's:* #4763

HEAL[V] (/ *r.p.a / r.p.h)* To restore to health or wholeness. *AHLB:* 1454-E[V] *Strong's:* #7495

HEAP (masc. *neyd)* A large pile dirt or rubbish. *AHLB:* 1303-A[N] *Strong's:* #5067

HEAR[V] (*sh.m.ah)* To perceive or apprehend by the ear; to listen to with attention. To obey. *Alternate Translation:* listen (when followed by the preposition TO" or the prefix "to~") *AHLB:* 2851[V] *Strong's:* #8085

HEARER (masc. *shi'mon)* One who listens. The one who acts upon what he has heard. *Strong's:* [Found in names only]

HEARING (masc. *miysh'mah) AHLB:* 2851(h) *Strong's:* #4926

HEART (masc. / *leyv / ley'vav fem. liy'bah)* Literally, the vital organ which pumps blood, but, also seen as the seat of thought; the mind. *AHLB:* 1255-A[N] *Strong's:* #3820, #3824, #3826

HEAT[V] (*y.hh.m)* Natural body warmth, as well as the time of estrous when animals mate. Conception from an animal's mating or through the heat of passion. *AHLB:* 1174-L[V] *Strong's:* #3179

HEAVINESS (fem. *ke'vey'dut)* A physical or spiritual weight. A sadness or burden. *AHLB:* 2246(N3) *Strong's:* #3517

HEAVY (fem. *ka'ved)* Having great weight. Something that is weighty. May also be grief or sadness in the sense of heaviness. Also, the liver as the heaviest of the organs. *Alternate Translation:* heaviness; liver (as the heaviest organ in the body); many *AHLB:* 2246$^{(N)}$ *Strong's:* #3515, #3516

HEAVY.BURDEN (masc. *to'rahh) AHLB:* 2243(g) *Strong's:* #2960

HEEL (masc. *e'qev)* What is restrained when taking a step forward. *AHLB:* 2571$^{(N)}$ *Strong's:* #6119, #6120

HEIFER (fem. *eg'lah)* A young cow, especially one that has not had a calf. *AHLB:* 2524(N1) *Strong's:* #5697

HEIGHT (fem. *qo'mah)* The highest part or most advanced point; the condition of being tall or high. *AHLB:* 1427-J(N1) *Strong's:* #6967

HEIR (masc. *niyn)* The continuation of a lineage through the son. *AHLB:* 1313-M$^{(N)}$ *Strong's:* #5209

HELP (masc. *e'zer fem.* / *ez'rah / ez'rat)* Providing assistance or relief to another. One who comes to assist with a trouble or burden. *AHLB:* 2535$^{(N)}$ *Strong's:* #5828, #5833

HELP$^{(V)}$ (*ah.z.r)* To give assistance or support to. *AHLB:* 2535$^{(V)}$ *Strong's:* #5826

HELPLESS (masc. *dal fem.* *dal)* Unable to care or provide for one's self; one who is weak, sick or poor. *AHLB:* 1081-A$^{(N)}$, 1081-A(N1) *Strong's:* #1800, #1803

HEM (masc. *shul)* The outer edge of a garment. *AHLB:* 1472-J$^{(N)}$ *Strong's:* #7757

HEMLOCK (fem. *la'a'nah)* An unknown bitter plant. *AHLB:* 2316(N1) *Strong's:* #3939

HERB (fem. *ey'sev)* The grasses and plants of the field used for their medicinal, savory, or aromatic qualities. *AHLB:* 2561$^{(N)}$ *Strong's:* #6211, #6212

HERBAGE (masc. *hha'tsiyr)* A plant used as food for men and animals as grown in the yard. *AHLB:* 2197(b) *Strong's:* #2682

HERE (masc. / / *po)* In or at this place. *AHLB:* 1374-A$^{(N)}$ *Strong's:* #6311

HERITAGE (fem. *y'ru'shah) AHLB:* 1458-L(d1) *Strong's:* #3425

HERON (fem. *a'na'phah)* A bird with a large beak (nose). Probably the heron. *AHLB:* 2002(N1) *Strong's:* #0601

HEW$^{(V)}$ (*hh.ts.b) AHLB:* 2194$^{(V)}$ *Strong's:* #2672

HEWN.ONE (masc. *gid'on)* What has been brough down by slicing, hacking or chopping. *Strong's:* [Found in names only]

HEWN.STONE (fem. *ga'zit)* Rocks that are sheared or chipped to form flat sides or an object. *AHLB:* 1053-A(N4) *Strong's:* #1496

HHOMER (masc. *hho'mer)* A dry standard of measurement equal to 65 Imperial gallons. *AHLB:* 2175(g) *Strong's:* #2563(x2)

HIDE$^{(V)}$ (/ *s.t.r)* To put out of sight; to conceal from view; to keep secret. Hide or conceal. *AHLB:* 2516$^{(V)}$ *Strong's:* #5641, #8368

HIDING (masc. *se'ter fem.* *sit'rah)* A shelter or other place of hiding. *AHLB:* 2516$^{(N)}$ *Strong's:* #5643

HIGH (masc. *ga'vo'ah)* Advanced in height such as a wall or hill. *AHLB:* 1048-H(c) *Strong's:* #1364

HIGH.LAND (masc. *a'ra'rat) AHLB:* 4010 *Strong's:* #0780

HIGH.ONE (masc. *si'on) Strong's:* [Found in names only]

HIGH.PLACE (fem. *te'qu'mah)* An elevated area as a place of defense. *AHLB:* 1427-J(i1) *Strong's:* #8617

HIGHWAY (masc. *fem.* *m'siy'lah)* A road constructed above the surrounding area. *AHLB:* 1334-B(ad), 1334-M(k1) *Strong's:* #4546, #4547

HILL (masc. / *har / harar)* An elevation of land such as a hill or mountain. *AHLB:* 1112-A$^{(N)}$ *Strong's:* #2022

HILL.COUNTRY (masc. *har)* A region dominated by hills. *Strong's:* [Found in names only]

HIP (masc. / *ke'sel / se'kel)* The seat of confidence. In a foolish or proper manner. *AHLB:* 2275$^{(N)}$ *Strong's:* #3689, #5529, #5530

HIRE$^{(V)}$ (*sh.k.r)* Payment for labor or personal services; to engage the personal service of another. *AHLB:* 2479$^{(V)}$ *Strong's:* #7936

HIRELING (masc. *se'khir)* One who is hired for service and receives compensation. *AHLB:* 2479(b) *Strong's:* #7916

HIT$^{(V)}$ (*n.k.h)* To deliver a blow by action; to strike with the hand; to clap, kill or harm. *Alternate Translation:* Beat (when written in the pual [passive intensive] form); attack (when written in the hiphil [active causative] form) *AHLB:* 1310-H$^{(V)}$ *Strong's:* #5221

HITTING (fem. *mak'kah)* A striking with a force that destroys or deforms. Also, a plague. *AHLB:* 1310-A(a1) *Strong's:* #4347

HIYN (masc. *hin)* A liquid measure equal to about 5 quarts (6 liters). *AHLB:* 1106-M$^{(N)}$ *Strong's:* #1969

HOARFROST (masc. *ke'phor)* A covering of small ice crystals, formed from frozen water vapor. *AHLB:* 2283(c) *Strong's:* #3713

HOLD.A.FEAST$^{(V)}$ (*hh.g.g)* To commemorate a special event with dancing, rejoicing, and sharing of food.The act of performing a celebration. *AHLB:* 1164-B$^{(V)}$ *Strong's:* #2287

HOLD.A.GRUDGE$^{(V)}$ (*s.t.m)* Be unwilling to give in or admit to. *AHLB:* 2474$^{(V)}$ *Strong's:* #7852

HOLD.BACK$^{(V)}$ (*a.p.q)* To hinder the progress or achievement of; restrain, as the banks of a river hold back the water. *AHLB:* 1387-C$^{(V)}$ *Strong's:* #0662

HOLD.UP$^{(V)}$ (*s.ah.d)* To continue in the same condition without failing or losing effectiveness or force. Be a support or aid for strength or rest. *AHLB:* 2492$^{(V)}$ *Strong's:* #5582

HOLDINGS (fem. *a'hhu'zah)* Property that is held or owned. *AHLB:* 1168-C(N1) *Strong's:* #0272

HOLLOW.OUT$^{(V)}$ (*q.b.b)* To pierce through creating a cavity. *AHLB:* 1416-B$^{(V)}$ *Strong's:* #6895

HONEY (masc. *d'vash)* A sweet material elaborated out of the nectar of flowers in the honey sac of various bees. Also, dates as a thick, sticky and sweet food. *AHLB:* 2094$^{(N)}$ *Strong's:* #1706

HONOR (masc. *ha'dar)* Someone or something that has been enlarged in size, pride or majesty. *AHLB:* 1089-F$^{(N)}$ *Strong's:* #1925, #1926

HOOD (masc. *mas'weh)* A covering of the entire head and face. *AHLB:* 1327-J(a) *Strong's:* #4533

HOOF (fem. *par'sah)* The hard covering of an animal's foot. *AHLB:* 2640(N1) *Strong's:* #6541

HOOK (masc. *qe'res)* A straight piece of wood or metal that is bent at one end. *AHLB:* 2733(N) *Strong's:* #7165

HOP(V) (*p.s.hh)* To jump from one position to another. Also, to be lame, as one who hops on one leg. *AHLB:* 2618(V) *Strong's:* #6452

HOPPING (masc. *pe'sahh)* The feast celebrating the "hopping" (usually called "Passover" but more literally means "hop over"). *Strong's:* [Found in names only]

HORDE (masc. *a'rov)* A large swarm of insects. Also, used for a large group of people. *AHLB:* 2573(c) *Strong's:* #6157

HORN (fem. *qe'ren)* One of a pair of bony processes that arise from the head of many animals and used as a wind instrument. The horns of an animal or a musical instrument in the shape of a horn. *AHLB:* 2732(N) *Strong's:* #7161

HORNET (fem. *tsir'ah)* A flying insect with a stinger that is capable of causing serious injury or death to one that is stung. *AHLB:* 2691(e1) *Strong's:* #6880

HORSE (masc. *sus)* A domesticated animal used as a beast of burden, a draft animal or for riding. *AHLB:* 1337-J(N) *Strong's:* #5483

HORSEMAN (masc. *pa'rash)* One that rides a horse. *AHLB:* 2644(N) *Strong's:* #6571

HOSTILITY (fem. *ey'vah)* Conflict, opposition, or resistance; overt acts of warfare. *AHLB:* 1002-M(N1) *Strong's:* #0342

HOT (masc. / *hhom / hham)* Having a relatively high temperature; eager; passionate. *AHLB:* 1174-A(N) *Strong's:* #2525, #2527

HOUSE (masc. *beyt)* The structure or the family, as a household that resides within the house. A housing. Within. *Alternate Translation:* inside *AHLB:* 1045-M(N) *Strong's:* #1004

HOW (masc. / / *eykh, eykhah, eykhakhah)* In what way or manner; by what means. *AHLB:* 1010-A(N) *Strong's:* #0349

HOW.LONG (masc. *ma'tai)* An unknown duration of time. *AHLB:* 1298-A(f) *Strong's:* #4970

HOWL(V) (*y.b.b)* To utter a loud, prolonged, mournful cry. *AHLB:* 1209-B(V) *Strong's:* #2980

HOWLING (masc. *y'leyl) AHLB:* 1265-L(N) *Strong's:* #3214

HUMAN (masc. *a'dam)* Of, relating to, or characteristic of man. The first man. All of mankind as the descendants of the first man. (Derived from a root meaning "blood" and "of reddish color."). *AHLB:* 1082-C(N) *Strong's:* #0120

HUNCHBACK (masc. *giy'veyn)* A large lump of the back causing one to be bent over. *AHLB:* 2050(e) *Strong's:* #1384

HUNDRED (fem. *mey'ah)* A specific number but also a large amount without any reference to a specific number. *AHLB:* 1277-A(N1) *Strong's:* #3967

HUNGER (masc. *ra'eyv)* A craving or urgent need for food. *AHLB:* 2777(N) *Strong's:* #7457, #7458

HUNT(V) (*ts.w.d)* To attempt to find something with the intent to capture. Hunt in the sense of laying in ambush. *AHLB:* 1395-J(V) *Strong's:* #6679

HUNTER (masc. *tsa'yad)* One who searches for something. Lays in ambush. *AHLB:* 1395-M(N) *Strong's:* #6719

HUNTING (masc. *tsa'yid)* The act of stalking and killing game for the purpose of providing food and skins. *Strong's:* [Found in names only]

HURL[V] (*t.hh.h)* To shoot, throw or cast to a great distance. *AHLB:* 1192-H[V] *Strong's:* #2909

HURRY[V] (*m.h.r)* To carry or cause to go with haste. *AHLB:* 1296-G[V] *Strong's:* #4116, #4117

HUT (fem. *qu'bah)* As a cavity. *AHLB:* 1416-A(o1) *Strong's:* #6898

HYSSOP (masc. *ey'zov)* An aromatic herb whose twigs were used in ceremonial sprinkling. *AHLB:* 1140-C(c) *Strong's:* #0231

I (/ *a-ni, a-no-khi)* A person aware of possessing a personal identity in self-reference. *Alternate Translation:* me *Strong's:* #0589, #0595

IBIS (fem. *tiyn'she'met)* An unknown animal. *AHLB:* 2443(i2) *Strong's:* #8580

ICE (masc. *qe'rahh)* Frozen water. Cold ice, frost or crystals. *AHLB:* 2730[N] *Strong's:* #7140

IDOL (masc. *gi'lul)* The image of a god made from wood or stone that is revered. *AHLB:* 1058-B(d) *Strong's:* #1544

IF (masc. *im)* Allowing that; on condition that. A desire to bind two ideas together. *Alternate Translation:* or; that; therefore (when followed by the word "NOT") *AHLB:* 1013-M[N] *Strong's:* #0518

IGNITING (masc. *ba'ur)* To set on fire. *Strong's:* [Found in names only]

ILL[V] (*d.w.h)* To be of unsound physical or mental health; unwell; sick. *AHLB:* 1075-H[V] *Strong's:* #1738

ILLNESS (masc. *da'veh)* Unhealthy condition; poor health; indisposition; sickness. Also, a woman's cycle. *AHLB:* 1075-H[N] *Strong's:* #1739

ILLUMINATE[V] (*z.h.r)* To give off light; to shine. *Alternate Translation:* warn (when written in the hiphil [active causative] form, in the sense of bringing something to light) *AHLB:* 1158-G[V] *Strong's:* #2094

IMAGE (masc. *tse'lem)* A reproduction or imitation of the form of a person or thing. The form of something as a shadow of the original. *AHLB:* 2663[N] *Strong's:* #6754

IMAGERY (fem. *mash'kiyt)* The casting of an image. *AHLB:* 1410-A(a4) *Strong's:* #4906

IMAGINATION (fem. *sh'riy'rut)* A twisting together of thoughts. *AHLB:* 1480-B(b3) *Strong's:* #8307

IMAGING (fem. *tsal'mo'nah)* A reproduction or imitation of the form of a person or thing. *Strong's:* [Found in names only]

IMBIBE[V] (*s.b.a)* To drink strong drink that can cause intoxication. *AHLB:* 1324-E[V] *Strong's:* #5433

IMITATE[V] (*t.ah.ah)* To follow as a model, pattern or example. *AHLB:* 1499-B[V] *Strong's:* #8591

IMMIGRANT (masc. / *ger / giyr)* A foreigner that permanently or temporarily resides with a native. A person or thing unknown or with whom one is unacquainted. *AHLB:* 1066-A[N] *Strong's:* #1616

IMMIGRATE[V] (*g.w.r)* To dwell as a non-native. Travel in a strange land. Also, the extended meaning of "to be afraid" as an immigrant. *Alternate Translation:* fear *AHLB:* 1066-J[V] *Strong's:* #1481

IMMIGRATION (masc. *ma'gur)* A journey of an immigrant; the course of life on earth. One who travels in a strange land. The dwelling place of an immigrant. *AHLB:* 1066-J(d) *Strong's:* #4033

IMPATIENT (masc. *la'ah) Strong's:* [Found in names only]

IN.FRONT (masc. *no'khahh)* Before or opposite to something. *AHLB:* 2403(g) *Strong's:* #5227

IN.LAW (masc. *hha'tan)* One related by marriage. *AHLB:* 2224[N] *Strong's:* #2860

IN.LINE (fem. *ma'a're'hhet)* a number of things arranged in a row, especially a straight line. *AHLB:* 2576(a2) *Strong's:* #4635

IN.THIS.WAY (masc. / *ko / ka'kah)* To do something in a certain manner; a reference to the previous or following context. *Alternate Translation:* that way; just like this (when prefixed with "like~") *AHLB:* 1235-A[N] *Strong's:* #3541, #3602

INCENSE.SMOKE (fem. / *qe'to'ret / qe'to'rah)* Usually made of several spices and or fruits, etc. To emit a fragrance. Used at the altar as a sweet savor. *AHLB:* 2705(c2) *Strong's:* #6988, #7004

INCREASE[V] (*r.b.h)* To become progressively greater; to multiply by the production of young; to be abundant of number, strength or authority. *Alternate Translation:* great, long *AHLB:* 1439-H[V] *Strong's:* #7235

INCREASE.IN.NUMBER[V] (*r.b.b)* To become progressively greater; to multiply by the production of young. Multiply. Also, meaning "to shoot" from the abundant arrows of the archer. *AHLB:* 1439-B[V] *Strong's:* #7231, #7232

INCREASING (masc. *ka'sad) Strong's:* [Found in names only]

INDEED (masc. *um'nam)* Without any question. *AHLB:* 1290-C(op) *Strong's:* #0552

INFANT (fem. *shiyl'yah)* As drawn out of the mother. *AHLB:* 1472-M(f1) *Strong's:* #7988

INFECT[V] (*ts.r.ah)* To taint or contaminate with something that affects quality, character, or condition unfavorably. To be infected with leprosy, mildew or mold. *AHLB:* 2691[V] *Strong's:* #6879

INFECTION (fem. *tsa'a'rat)* A contaminated substance, such as a disease, mold or mildew, on the skin, cloth or a building. *AHLB:* 2691(N2) *Strong's:* #6883

INFIRMITY (masc. *hha'liy)* A physical weakness or ailment. *AHLB:* 1173-H(f) *Strong's:* #2483

INFLAME[V] (*d.l.q)* To excite to excessive or uncontrollable action or feeling. *AHLB:* 2104[V] *Strong's:* #1814

INFLAMMATION (fem. *dal'le'qet) AHLB:* 2104(N2) *Strong's:* #1816

INHERIT[V] (*n.hh.l)* A passing down of properties, wealth or blessings to the offspring. *AHLB:* 2391[V] *Strong's:* #5157

INHERITANCE (masc. *na'hheyl fem. na'hha'lah)* The acquisition of a possession from past generations. *AHLB:* 2391(N1) *Strong's:* #5159

INNOCENCE (masc. *na'qi'on)* Freedom from guilt or sin through being unacquainted with evil. A state of innocence as an infant. *AHLB:* 1318-A(fj) *Strong's:* #5356

INNOCENT (masc. *na'qi)* Free from guilt or sin. A state of innocence as an infant. *AHLB:* 1318-A(f) *Strong's:* #5355

INQUIRE(V) (*sh.a.l)* To ask about; to search into; to seek to understand what is not known. *Alternate Translation:* grant (when written in the hiphil [active causative] form) *AHLB:* 1472-D(V) *Strong's:* #7592

INSCRIBE(V) (*hh.q.q)* To write, engrave or print as a lasting record. A decree or custom. *AHLB:* 1180-B(V) *Strong's:* #2710

INSIDE (masc. *qe'rev)* The inner or interior part. *Alternate Translation:* among, near *AHLB:* 2729(N) *Strong's:* #7130, #7131

INSTALLATION (masc. *mi'lu)* Placed in its proper and permanent position. *AHLB:* 1288-E(ed) *Strong's:* #4394

INSTANT (masc. *pe'ta)* As a wink of time. *AHLB:* 2652(N) *Strong's:* #6621

INTELLIGENCE (masc. *ta'vun fem. te'vu'nah)* The ability to learn, reason, plan and build. *AHLB:* 1037-J(i) *Strong's:* #8394

INTERCEDE(V) (*ah.t.r)* To intervene between parties to reconcile differences. Supplicate on the behalf of another. *AHLB:* 2910(V) *Strong's:* #6279

INTEREST (fem. *tar'biyt)* From usury. *AHLB:* 1439-A(i4) *Strong's:* #8636

INTERPRET(V) (*p.t.r)* To explain or tell the meaning of. *AHLB:* 2653(V) *Strong's:* #6622

INTERPRETATION (masc. *pit'ron)* The act or result of interpreting. *AHLB:* 2653(ej) *Strong's:* #6623

INTERPRETING (masc. *pe'tor) Strong's:* [Found in names only]

INVADE(V) (*g.w.d)* To enter for conquest or plunder. The slicing through of a band of men. *AHLB:* 1050-J(V) *Strong's:* #1464

INVENTION (fem. *ma'hha'sha'vah)* A product of the imagination. Designing or planning of inventions or plans. *AHLB:* 2213(a1) *Strong's:* #4284

INVESTIGATE(V) (*b.q.r)* To look or search for something. *AHLB:* 2633(V) *Strong's:* #1239

IRON (masc. *bar'zel)* A heavy element frequently used in the making of weapons and tools. The most used of metals. *AHLB:* 3005 *Strong's:* #1270

IRRITATE(V) (*m.a.r) AHLB:* 1296-D(V) *Strong's:* #3992

IRRITATION (masc. *ga'rav)* To have or feel a peculiar tingling or uneasy itch of the skin that causes a desire to scratch the part affected. *AHLB:* 2080(N) *Strong's:* #1618

ISLAND (masc. *iy)* A tract of land surrounded by water. Also, a country in the sense of isolated. *AHLB:* 1014-A(f) *Strong's:* #0336, #0339

ISSUE(V) (*z.w.b)* To flow out; to go, pass, or flow out; emerge. *AHLB:* 1140-J(V) *Strong's:* #2100

ITCH (masc. *hha'res)* A skin irritation. *AHLB:* 2207(N) *Strong's:* #2775

JAR (masc. *kad)* A sudden and unexpected shake; a wide-mouthed container. *AHLB:* 1234-A(N) *Strong's:* #3537

JASPER (fem. *yash'phey)* Probably the Jasper which may be red, yellow or brown in color. The Septuagint uses laspis meaning Jasper. Other possible translations are Ruby, Hyacinth and Emerald. *AHLB:* 1477-L(N1) *Strong's:* #3471

JAW (masc. *l'hhiy)* From the moist cheeks. *AHLB:* 1261-A(f) *Strong's:* #3895

JEWEL (fem. *se'gu'lah)* A precious stone. Something of value. *AHLB:* 2465(d1) *Strong's:* #5459

JOIN(V) (*l.w.h)* To bind together. *Alternate Translation:* loan (when written in the hiphil [active causative] form) *AHLB:* 1259-J(V) *Strong's:* #3867

JOINED.TOGETHER(V) (*sh.l.b)* Two becoming one purposely. *AHLB:* 2840(V) *Strong's:* #7947

JOINING (masc. *law)* The attachment of objects through binding together. *Strong's:* [Found in names only]

JOINT (fem. *mahh'be'ret)* The point at which two opposing objects meet. *AHLB:* 2143(a2) *Strong's:* #4225

JOURNEY (masc. *mas'sah)* The packing up of camp for the purpose of beginning a journey. *AHLB:* 2413(a) *Strong's:* #4550, #4551

JOURNEY(V) (*n.s.ah)* To travel or pass from one place to another; to break camp and begin a journey. *AHLB:* 2413(V) *Strong's:* #5265

JUBILEE (masc. *yo'vel)* A special celebration every fifty years. Also, the jubilee horn of a ram that was used to announce the time of celebration. *AHLB:* 1035-L(g) *Strong's:* #3104

JUDGE (masc. *pa'lil)* One who presides over a dispute. *AHLB:* 1380-B(b) *Strong's:* #6414

JUDGMENT (masc. *she'phet)* Reward for action, good or bad. An aspect of determining the outcome. *AHLB:* 2864(N) *Strong's:* #8201

JUDICIAL (masc. *shaph'tan) Strong's:* [Found in names only]

JUG (fem. *qa'sah)* A vessel used for storage of water, grain, etc. *AHLB:* 1245-A(N1) *Strong's:* #7184

JUICE (fem. *mish'rah)* As loosened from the fruit. *AHLB:* 1480-A(h1) *Strong's:* #4952

JUMP(V) (*z.n.q)* To rise suddenly or quickly. *AHLB:* 2127(V) *Strong's:* #2187

JUNIPER (masc. *re'tem fem. rit'mah)* A species of tree, possibly the Juniper. *AHLB:* 2802(N) *Strong's:* #7574

KEEP(V) (*n.t.r)* To hold onto to preserve, protect or hold in reserve; to hold back. *AHLB:* 2400(V) *Strong's:* #5201

KEEP.BACK(V) (*hh.s.k)* To hold something back or restrain. *AHLB:* 2182(V) *Strong's:* #2820

KEEP.SECRET(V) (*k.hh.d)* To refrain from disclosing information. *Alternate Translation:* hide (when written in the hiphil [active causative] form) *AHLB:* 2255(V) *Strong's:* #3582

KEEP.SILENT(V) (*hh.r.sh)* To stand still and be silent. *AHLB:* 2211(V) *Strong's:* #2790(x2)

KEEP.WATCH(V) (*ts.p.h)* To be on the look-out for danger or opportunity. *AHLB:* 1408-H(V) *Strong's:* #6822

KERMES (masc. *to'la)* The 'coccus ilicis,' a worm used for medicinal purposes as well as for making a crimson or scarlet dye. *Alternate Translation:* crimson *AHLB:* 1269-L(i) *Strong's:* #8438(x2)

KERNEL (masc. *hhar'tsan)* The seed of a grape. *AHLB:* 2209(m) *Strong's:* #2785

KERUV (masc. *ke'ruv)* A supernatural creature, identified in other Semitic cultures as a winged lion, a Griffin. *Strong's:* #3742

KICK(V) (*b.ah.t)* To strike with the foot. *AHLB:* 2026(V) *Strong's:* #1163

KIDNEY (fem. *kil'yah)* An organ of the body. The seat of emotion in Hebraic thought. *AHLB:* 1242-A(f1) *Strong's:* #3629

KIKAR (fem. 𐤊𐤉𐤊𐤓 *ki'kar)* A dry standard of measure. Usually rendered as "talent" in most translations, however the word talent is a transliteration of the Greek word talanton (a Greek coin) *AHLB:* 2258(e) *Strong's:* #3603(x2)

KILL(V) (𐤄𐤓𐤂 *h.r.g)* To deprive of life; to slaughter. *AHLB:* 1440-F(V) *Strong's:* #2026

KILL.BY.STONING(V) (𐤓𐤂𐤌 *r.g.m)* To throw stones to execute. *AHLB:* 2750(V) *Strong's:* #7275

KIN (masc. 𐤔𐤀𐤓 *sha'ar fem.* 𐤔𐤀𐤓𐤄 *sha'a'rah)* A person of close relation. *AHLB:* 1480-D(N1) *Strong's:* #7608

KIND (masc. 𐤌𐤉𐤍 *min)* A category of creature that comes from its own kind as a firm rule. *AHLB:* 1290-M(N) *Strong's:* #4327

KIND.ONE (masc. 𐤇𐤎𐤉𐤃 *hha'siyd)* One who shows favor, mercy or compassion to another. *AHLB:* 2181(b) *Strong's:* #2623

KINDLE(V) (𐤒𐤃𐤇 *q.d.hh)* To kindle a fire. *AHLB:* 2697(V) *Strong's:* #6919

KINDLED (fem. 𐤕𐤁𐤏𐤓𐤄 *tav'ey'rah)* To set fire to or ignite. *Strong's:* [Found in names only]

KINDNESS (masc. 𐤇𐤎𐤃 *hhe'sed)* Of a sympathetic nature; quality or state of being sympathetic. *AHLB:* 2181(N) *Strong's:* #2617

KINDRED (fem. 𐤌𐤅𐤋𐤃𐤕 *mo'le'det)* A group of related individuals. *AHLB:* 1257-L(a2) *Strong's:* #4138

KING (masc. 𐤌𐤋𐤊 *me'lekh)* The male ruler of a nation or city state. *AHLB:* 2340(N) *Strong's:* #4428

KINGDOM (fem. 𐤌𐤌𐤋𐤊𐤄 *mam'la'khah)* The area under the control of a king. *AHLB:* 2340(a1) *Strong's:* #4467

KISS(V) (𐤍𐤔𐤒 *n.sh.q)* To touch together as when kissing with the lips or in battle with weapons. *AHLB:* 2445(V) *Strong's:* #5401

KITE (fem. 𐤓𐤀𐤄 *ra'ah)* An unknown bird of prey with a keen sense of sight. *AHLB:* 1438-H(dm) *Strong's:* #7201

KNEAD(V) (𐤋𐤅𐤔 *l.w.sh)* To work and press dough. Knead dough for bread. *AHLB:* 1274-J(V) *Strong's:* #3888

KNEADING.BOWL (fem. 𐤌𐤔𐤀𐤓𐤕 *mish'eret)* The vessel used for mixing bread dough. *AHLB:* 1342-D(h2) *Strong's:* #4863

KNEE (masc. 𐤁𐤓𐤊 *be'rekh)* The joint between the femur and tibia of the leg. *AHLB:* 2039(N) *Strong's:* #1290

KNEEL(V) (𐤁𐤓𐤊 *b.r.k)* To bend the knee, to kneel in homage or to kneel down to get a drink water. Figuartively, to exalt. *Alternate Translation:* exalt (when written in the piel [active intensive] form) *AHLB:* 2039(V) *Strong's:* #1288

KNIFE (fem. 𐤌𐤀𐤊𐤋𐤕 *ma'a'ke'let)* A cutting instrument consisting of a sharp blade and handle. What is used for preparing and eating food. *AHLB:* 1242-C(a2) *Strong's:* #3979

KNOB (masc. 𐤊𐤐𐤕𐤅𐤓 *kaph'tor)* An ornamental round lump or protuberance on the surface or at the end of something. *AHLB:* 3025 *Strong's:* #3730

KNOCK(V) (𐤇𐤁𐤈 *hh.b.t)* To strike violently or forcefully; to beat a tree to remove its fruit; to thresh. *AHLB:* 2140(V) *Strong's:* #2251

KNOLL (fem. 𐤂𐤉𐤁𐤏𐤄 *giv'ah)* A small round hill. *AHLB:* 2051(N1) *Strong's:* #1389

KNOW(V) (𐤉𐤃𐤏 *y.d.ah)* To have an intimate and personal understanding; to have an intimate relationship with another person, usually sexual. *Alternate Translation:*

reveal self (when written in the hitpa'el [reflexive] form) *AHLB:* 1085-L$^{(V)}$ *Strong's:* #3045

KNOWER (masc. *yid'o'niy)* One with specific and special understanding. *AHLB:* 1085-L(mf) *Strong's:* #3049

LABOR (*a-mal) AHLB:* 2551$^{(N)}$ *Strong's:* #5999, #6001

LACE (masc. *se'rokh)* A cord or string used to draw the edges of shoes or a garment together, as twisted around the foot for attaching sandals. *AHLB:* 2509(c) *Strong's:* #8288

LACKING (masc. *mahh'sor)* Being without; not having; wanting. *AHLB:* 2187(ac) *Strong's:* #4270

LADDER (masc. *su'lam)* Used to raise up. A structure for climbing up or down. *AHLB:* 1334-J(p) *Strong's:* #5551

LAME (masc. *piy'sey'ahh)* As one who hops one leg. *AHLB:* 2618$^{(N)}$ *Strong's:* #6455

LAMENT$^{(V)}$ (*s.p.d)* To mourn aloud; wail. *AHLB:* 2495$^{(V)}$ *Strong's:* #5594

LAMENTING (masc. *mis'peyd)* The act of mourning. *AHLB:* 2495(h) *Strong's:* #4553

LAMP (masc. *ner)* A container for an inflammable liquid, as oil, which is burned at a wick as a means of illumination. *AHLB:* 1319-A$^{(N)}$ *Strong's:* #5216

LAMPSTAND (fem. *me'no'rah)* A platform, sometimes elevated, for holding a lamp. *AHLB:* 1319-J(k1) *Strong's:* #4501

LAND (fem. *e'rets)* The solid part of the earth's surface. The whole of the earth or a region. *AHLB:* 1455-C$^{(N)}$ *Strong's:* #0776

LAPIS.LAZULI (masc. *sa'phir)* Probably the Lapis Lazuli which is similar to the color of the Sapphire. While the Hebrew word is saphiyr, the origin of the word Sapphire, the Sapphire was unknown until the Roman period. *AHLB:* 2500(b) *Strong's:* #5601

LAST (masc. *a'hha'ron fem. a'hha'ro'nah)* In, to or toward the back. To be in back of, at the rear or following after something. *Alternate Translation:* after *AHLB:* 1181-C(j) *Strong's:* #0314

LAST.NIGHT (masc. *e'mesh)* The previous night or a time past. *AHLB:* 1297-C$^{(N)}$ *Strong's:* #0570

LATE (masc. *a'phil)* The latter part of the day, in the sense of night as being dark. The latter part of a season. At or near the end. *AHLB:* 1380-C(b) *Strong's:* #0648

LATE.RAIN (masc. *mal'qush)* A late rain that causes a latter growth of crops. *AHLB:* 2321(ac) *Strong's:* #4456

LAUDANUM (masc. *lot)* An aromatic gum resin obtained from a tree and having a bitter slightly pungent taste. *AHLB:* 1262-J$^{(N)}$ *Strong's:* #3910

LAUGH$^{(V)}$ (*ts.hh.q)* To show mirth, joy, or scorn with a smile and chuckle or explosive sound. *Alternate Translation:* mock (when written in the piel [active intensive] form) *AHLB:* 2660$^{(V)}$ *Strong's:* #6711

LAUGHTER (masc. *tse'hhoq)* The sound of mirth, joy, or scorn with a smile and chuckle or explosive sound. *AHLB:* 2660(c) *Strong's:* #6712

LAW (fem. *dat)* A decree or edict. *AHLB:* 1091-A$^{(N)}$ *Strong's:* #1881

LAWFUL (masc. *do'to)* Pertaining to the law. (A word of uncertain meaning, but closely related in meaning to the parent root). *Strong's:* [Found in names only]

LAY.IN.WAIT(V) (*ts.d.h)* To hide in ambush. *AHLB:* 1395-H(V) *Strong's:* #6658

LAY.WASTE(V) (*b.l.q)* To devestate, destroy or ruin. *AHLB:* 2021(V) *Strong's:* #1110

LEAD (fem. *o'phe'ret)* A very heavy metal that is commonly melted and poured into casts to make statues or other objects. *AHLB:* 2565(g2) *Strong's:* #5777

LEAD(V) (*n.h.l)* To guide on a way, especially by going in advance. The flock directed to the pasture at the end of the journey. *AHLB:* 1311-G(V) *Strong's:* #5095

LEADER (fem. *a'tsil)* One who is in charge or in command of others. *AHLB:* 1403-C(b) *Strong's:* #0678

LEAF (masc. *a'leh)* Foliage of a tree or plant. As high in the tree. *AHLB:* 1357-H(N) *Strong's:* #5929

LEAN (masc. *ra'zeh) AHLB:* 1444-H(N) *Strong's:* #7330

LEAN(V) (*sh.ah.n)* To cast one's weight to one side for support. Lean on something for rest or support. *AHLB:* 2861(V) *Strong's:* #8172

LEAP(V) (*n.t.r)* To spring forward from one position to another. *AHLB:* 2457(V) *Strong's:* #5425

LEAPING.LOCUST (masc. *hhar'gol) AHLB:* 3019 *Strong's:* #2728

LEARN(V) (*l.m.d)* To acquire knowledge or skill through instruction from one who is experienced. *Alternate Translation:* teach (when written in the piel [active intensive] form) *AHLB:* 2311(V) *Strong's:* #3925

LEARNING (masc. *le'qahh)* Teachings and instructions that are received. *AHLB:* 2319(N) *Strong's:* #3948

LEAVE(V) (*ah.z.b)* To go away from; to neglect. *AHLB:* 2532(V) *Strong's:* #5800, #5805

LEAVE.ALONE(V) (*n.t.sh)* To be left behind by those who leave. *AHLB:* 2401(V) *Strong's:* #5203

LEAVE.BEHIND(V) (*y.t.r)* To set aside; to retain or hold over to a future time or place; to leave a remainder. *AHLB:* 1480-L(V) *Strong's:* #3498

LEAVE.IN.PLACE(V) (*y.ts.g)* To put or place something in a specific location. *Alternate Translation:* present (when written in the hiphil [active causative] form) *AHLB:* 1394-L(V) *Strong's:* #3322

LEAVEN (masc. *se'or)* The element that causes bread to rise, such as salt or yeast. *AHLB:* 1342-D(c) *Strong's:* #7603

LEAVENED.BREAD (masc. *hha'mets)* Dough that has had leaven added to make a sour bread. *AHLB:* 2173(N) *Strong's:* #2557

LEFT.HAND (/ / *s.m.a)* To choose the left hand or path. *AHLB:* 3036 *Strong's:* #8040, #8041, #8042

LEG (fem. *ka'ra)* The appendage from the ankle to the hip and bends at the knee. *AHLB:* 2290(N) *Strong's:* #3767

LENGTH (masc. *o'rekh)* A measured distance or dimension. *AHLB:* 1448-C(g) *Strong's:* #0753

LENTIL (fem. *a'dash)* A leguminous plant with flattened edible seeds. *AHLB:* 2531(N) *Strong's:* #5742

LEOPARD (masc. *na'mer fem. nam'rah)* A species of felines. *AHLB:* 2408$^{(N)}$ *Strong's:* #5246

LEVEL.VALLEY (fem. *biq'a)* A depression in the earth's surface between ranges of mountains. Wide level valley as a division between mountains ranges. *AHLB:* 2034(e1) *Strong's:* #1237

LICK$^{(V)}$ (*l.hh.q / l.q.q) AHLB:* 1261-B$^{(V)}$ *Strong's:* #3897, #3952

LID (fem. *ka'po'ret)* The cover of a box or other container. *AHLB:* 2283(c2) *Strong's:* #3727

LIE (masc. *ka'zav)* An untruth. *AHLB:* 2253$^{(N)}$ *Strong's:* #3577

LIE$^{(V)}$ (*k.z.b)* To give a spoken word to deceive, cause failure or disappoint; Not functioning within its intended capacity. *AHLB:* 2253$^{(V)}$ *Strong's:* #3576

LIE.DOWN$^{(V)}$ (*sh.k.b)* To give up; to lie down for copulation, rest or sleep. *AHLB:* 2834$^{(V)}$ *Strong's:* #7901

LIEUTENANT (masc. *sha'lish / sha'losh)* A leader who is responsible for a group of thirty. *AHLB:* 2847(b) *Strong's:* #7991(x2)

LIFT$^{(V)}$ (*r.m.m) AHLB:* 1450-B$^{(V)}$ *Strong's:* #7426, #7318

LIFT.HIGH$^{(V)}$ (*s.g.b)* To be raised up in height; to be exalted. *AHLB:* 2463$^{(V)}$ *Strong's:* #7682

LIFT.UP$^{(V)}$ (*n.s.a)* To raise a burden or load and carry it; to break camp and begin a journey; to forgive in the sense of removing the offense. *AHLB:* 1314-E$^{(V)}$ *Strong's:* #4984, #5375

LIFTED (masc. *ra'ham)* Raised up in position or in exaltation. *Strong's:* [Found in names only]

LIGHT (*or)* The illumination from the sun, moon, stars, fire, candle or other source. *AHLB:* 1020-J$^{(N)}$ *Strong's:* #0216, #0217

LIGHT$^{(V)}$ (*a.w.r)* To shine with an intense light; be or give off light; to be bright. *Alternate Translation:* shine *AHLB:* 1020-J$^{(V)}$ *Strong's:* #0215

LIGHT.BRINGER (masc. *a'ha'ron)* One who carries light into the darkness. *Strong's:* [Found in names only]

LIGHTWEIGHT (masc. *q'lo'qeyl)* Something that is light in weight or position (worthless). *AHLB:* 1426-A(l) *Strong's:* #7052

LIKENESS (fem. *da'mut)* Copy; resemblance. The quality or state of being like something or someone else. *AHLB:* 1082-H(N3) *Strong's:* #1823

LIME (masc. *s.y.d)* A chalky white powder used for making plaster. *AHLB:* 1326-M$^{(N)}$ *Strong's:* #7875

LIMP$^{(V)}$ (*ts.l.ah)* To walk lamely, especially favoring one leg; to go unsteadily; to proceed with difficulty or slowly. From damage to the ridge of the hip. *AHLB:* 2664$^{(V)}$ *Strong's:* #6760

LINEN (masc. *sheysh / shey'shiy)* Fabric made of flax and noted for its strength, coolness and luster. A white cloth. Also, marble from its whiteness. *AHLB:* 1481-A$^{(N)}$ *Strong's:* #7893, #8336

LINGER$^{(V)}$ (*m.h.h)* To be slow in parting or in quitting something. *AHLB:* 1281-B$^{(N)}$ *Strong's:* #4102

LINSEY-WOOLSEY (masc. *sha'at'neyz) AHLB:* 4020 *Strong's:* #8162

LINTEL (masc. *mash'qoph)* A horizontal architectural member supporting the weight above an opening, as a window or a door. *AHLB:* 2877(ac) *Strong's:* #4947

LION (masc. / *ar'yeyh / a'riy)* A large carnivorous chiefly nocturnal cat. A feared animal. *AHLB:* 1442-H(b) *Strong's:* #0738

LION.LIKE (masc. *ar'okh) AHLB:* 4010 *Strong's:* #0746

LIONESS (fem. *la'vi)* A female lion. *AHLB:* 1255-E(b) *Strong's:* #3833

LIP (fem. *sa'phah)* The rim or edge of the mouth or other opening. Language, as spoken from the lips. *Alternate Translation:* edge *AHLB:* 1339-A(N1) *Strong's:* #8193

LIQUOR (masc. *shey'khar)* An intoxicating drink. *AHLB:* 2839$^{(N)}$ *Strong's:* #7941

LITTLE.ONE (masc. / / *tsa'ir / tsa'ur / za'iyr)* Small in size or extent. Something or someone that is smaller, younger or less significant. *AHLB:* 2680(b) *Strong's:* #2191, #6810

LITTLE.OWL (fem. *kos)* An unknown species of bird. *AHLB:* 1245-J$^{(N)}$ *Strong's:* #3563(x2)

LIVE$^{(V)}$ (*hh.y.h)* To be alive and continue alive. Have life within. The revival of life gained from food or other necessity. *Alternate Translation:* keep alive (when written in the piel [active intensive] form) *AHLB:* 1171-H$^{(V)}$ *Strong's:* #2421, #2425

LIVELY (masc. *hhay'eh)* Having the vigor of life. *AHLB:* 1171-H$^{(N)}$ *Strong's:* #2422

LIVESTOCK (masc. *miq'neh)* Animals kept or raised for use or pleasure. What is purchased or possessed. *AHLB:* 1428-H(h) *Strong's:* #4735

LIVING (masc. *hhai fem.* *hhai'ah)* The quality that distinguishes a vital and functional being from a dead body; life. Literally the stomach. Used idiomatically of living creatures, especially in conjunction with land, ground or field. *Alternate Translation:* life (when in the plural form); creature (as a living one) *AHLB:* 1171-A$^{(N)}$ *Strong's:* #2416

LIZARD (fem. *l'ta'ah)* From the camouflaging capability of the lizard to hide. *AHLB:* 1262-E(N1) *Strong's:* #3911

LO (masc. *hey)* To draw attention to something important. *AHLB:* 1093-A$^{(N)}$ *Strong's:* #1887

LOAD (masc. *ma'sa)* Something that is lifted up and carried. The lifting up of the voice in song. *AHLB:* 1314-E(a) *Strong's:* #4853

LOAD$^{(V)}$ (*ah.m.s)* That which is put on a person or pack animal to be carried. *AHLB:* 2552$^{(V)}$ *Strong's:* #6006

LOAN (masc. *fem.* *ma'sha'ah) AHLB:* 1320-E(a1) *Strong's:* #4859, #4874

LOATHE$^{(V)}$ (*q.w.ts)* To dislike greatly and often with disgust. To be sickened as if pierced by a thorn. *AHLB:* 1432-J$^{(V)}$ *Strong's:* #6973

LOBE (fem. *yo'te'ret)* The extended point of the liver. *AHLB:* 1503-L(g2) *Strong's:* #3508

LOCUST (masc. *sal'am)* From its high jumping. *AHLB:* 2484(p) *Strong's:* #5556

LOFT (fem. *a'liy'yah)* A room on top of the house used during hot days of summer. *AHLB:* 1357-H(f1) *Strong's:* #5944

LOG (masc. *lag)* A standard of measure. *AHLB:* 1256-A$^{(N)}$ *Strong's:* #3849

LOIN.WRAP (fem. *hha'go'rah)* A sash or belt that encircles the waist. *AHLB:* 2147(c1) *Strong's:* #2290

LOINS (fem. *hha'rats)* The pubic region; the generative organs. *AHLB:* 2166(N) *Strong's:* #2504

LONG.GARMENT (masc. *mad)* A piece of clothing of unusual length. *AHLB:* 1280-A(N) *Strong's:* #4055

LONG.HAIR (masc. *p'ra)* Hair of an unusual length. *AHLB:* 2641(N) *Strong's:* #6545

LONG.WINGED (masc. *ey'ver)* A large appendage of a bird used for flight. *AHLB:* 1043-C(N) *Strong's:* #0083

LOOK (masc. *hi'ney)* To ascertain by the use of one's eyes. *Alternate Translation:* here; saw *AHLB:* 1106-H(e) *Strong's:* #2009

LOOK.DOWN(V) (*sh.q.p)* To look out and down as through a window. *AHLB:* 2877(V) *Strong's:* #8259

LOOK.FORTH (*s.k.h) Strong's:* [Found in names only]

LOOK.INTO (fem. *hhaz)* To peer toward. *Strong's:* [Found in names only]

LOOK.UPON(V) (*sh.w.r) AHLB:* 1480-J(V) *Strong's:* #7789

LOOK.WITH.RESPECT(V) (*sh.ah.h)* To look upon with high regard. *AHLB:* 1476-H(V) *Strong's:* #8159

LOOP (fem. *lu'lah)* A circular object that is open in the middle. *AHLB:* 1265-E(o1) *Strong's:* #3924

LOOSE(V) (*p.r.ah)* To uncover, remove or let go. Such as to make naked by removing clothing. To uncover the head. *AHLB:* 2641(V) *Strong's:* #6544

LOOSEN(V) (*z.hh.hh)* To make less tight; slacken or relax. To untie or remove. *AHLB:* 1146-B(V) *Strong's:* #2118

LORD (masc. *a'don)* The ruler as the foundation to the community or family. *AHLB:* 1083-C(c) *Strong's:* #0113

LOST (masc. *re'sha)* Departed from the correct path or way, either out of ignorance or revolt. *AHLB:* 2799(N) *Strong's:* #7562, #7563

LOST.THING (fem. *a'vey'dah)* An object that is missing or misplaced. *AHLB:* 1027-C(N1) *Strong's:* #0009

LOT (masc. *go'ral)* Colored stones that are thrown and read to determine a course of action or to make a decision. *AHLB:* 2083(g) *Strong's:* #1486

LOUD.NOISE (masc. *rey'a)* A loud, confused, constant noise or sound. *AHLB:* 1460-A(N) *Strong's:* #7452

LOVE(V) (*a.h.b)* To provide and protect that which is given as a privilege. An intimacy of action and emotion. Strong affection for another arising from personal ties. *AHLB:* 1094-C(V) *Strong's:* #0157

LOW (masc. *sha'phal fem. shaph'lah) AHLB:* 2866(N) *Strong's:* #8216, #8217

LOW.COUNTRY (masc. *de'dan)* A land that is below the general area. *Strong's:* [Found in names only]

LOWER(V) (*k.n.ah)* To be brought down low in humility or submission. *AHLB:* 2268(V) *Strong's:* #3665

LOWER.PART (masc. *tahh'ti)* The part beneath. A low place. *AHLB:* 2892(f) *Strong's:* #8482

LOWERED (masc. *ke'na'an) Strong's:* [Found in names only]

LOWLAND (fem. *sh'phey'lah)* A low place. *AHLB:* 2866(N1) *Strong's:* #8219

LUMINARY (masc. *ma'or)* That which gives off light. *AHLB:* 1020-J(a) *Strong's:* #3974

LYING.DOWN (fem. *she'kha'vah)* A laying with another in copulation. Something spread out. *AHLB:* 2834(N1) *Strong's:* #7902

LYING.PLACE (masc. *mish'kav)* The location one reclines for rest or sleep. *AHLB:* 2834(h) *Strong's:* #4904

LYRE (masc. *ka'ran) Strong's:* [Found in names only]

MADNESS (masc. *shiy'ga'on) AHLB:* 2815(ej) *Strong's:* #7697

MAGGOT (fem. *ri'mah)* The larvae of flies. *AHLB:* 1450-M(N1) *Strong's:* #7415

MAGICIAN (masc. *hhar'tom)* A person skilled in divination. *AHLB:* 2203(qp) *Strong's:* #2748

MAGNIFICENCE (masc. *go'del)* An increase in size power or authority. *AHLB:* 2054(g) *Strong's:* #1433

MAGNIFIED (masc. *ga'deyl)* An increased significance or size. *AHLB:* 2054(N) *Strong's:* #1432

MAGNIFY(V) (*g.d.l)* To increase in size or one's position of honor. *AHLB:* 2054(V) *Strong's:* #1431

MAID (fem. *shiph'hhah)* An unmarried young woman. *AHLB:* 2863(e1) *Strong's:* #8198

MAJESTY (masc. *ga'on)* Elevated to a higher position. Supreme greatness or authority. *AHLB:* 1047-A(j) *Strong's:* #1347

MAKE(V) (*p.ah.l)* To perform a task of physical labor to produce something. *AHLB:* 2622(V) *Strong's:* #6466, #6468

MAKE.A.PLEDGE(V) (*ah.b.t) Alternate Translation:* Lend (when written in the hiphil [causative] form) *AHLB:* 2519(V) *Strong's:* #5670

MAKE.A.VOW(V) (*n.d.r)* To promise solemnly; to make an agreement where one promises an action if the other reciprocates with another action. *AHLB:* 2385(V) *Strong's:* #5087

MAKE.BALD(V) (*q.r.hh)* To shave the hair of the head to make bald. *AHLB:* 2730(V) *Strong's:* #7139

MAKE.BRICKS(V) (*l.b.n)* To shape moist clay or earth into blocks for construction purposes. *Alternate Translation:* Be white (when written in the hiphil [causative] form, from the color of the bricks) *AHLB:* 2303(V) *Strong's:* #3835

MAKE.FAT(V) (*d.sh.n)* To make or become large with fat tissue. *Alternate Translation:* remove the fat (when written in the piel [active intensive] form) *AHLB:* 2115(V) *Strong's:* #1878

MAKE.HASTE(V) (*ah.w.sh / hh.w.sh)* To quickly prepare. *AHLB:* 1527-J(V) *Strong's:* #2363, #5789

MAKE.RESTITUTION(V) (*sh.l.m)* To restore or make right through action, payment or restoration to a rightful owner. *AHLB:* 2845(V) *Strong's:* #7999

MALE (masc. *za'khar)* Being the gender who begets offspring. One who acts and speaks for the family. *AHLB:* 2121(N) *Strong's:* #2145

MALE.GOAT (masc. *a'tud)* A male member of a flock of goats. *AHLB:* 2587(d) *Strong's:* #6259(x2), #6260

MALE.KID (masc. *ge'di)* A young goat. *AHLB:* 1510-A(f) *Strong's:* #1423

MAN (masc. / *iysh / e'nosh)* An adult male human. (Often used to mean "each" in the sense of an individual.) *Alternate Translation:* each; one *AHLB:* 2003(b) *Strong's:* #0376, #0377, #0582

MANDRAKES (masc. *du'dai)* A plant boiled as an aphrodisiac. *AHLB:* 1073-N(o) *Strong's:* #1736

MANE.OF.A.HORSE (fem. *ra'mah) AHLB:* 2780(N1) *Strong's:* #7483

MANY (masc. *me'od)* A large, but indefinite number. An abundance of things (every, many, much, great), actions (complete, wholly, strong, quick) *Alternate Translation:* great; greatly; more; much; very, every *AHLB:* 1004-J(k) *Strong's:* #3966

MARCH$^{(V)}$ (*ts.ah.d)* To move along steadily, usually with a rhythmic stride and in step with others. *AHLB:* 2676$^{(V)}$ *Strong's:* #6805

MARKER (fem. *to'ta'phah)* A mark or emblem used to identify a purpose. *AHLB:* 2233(g1) *Strong's:* #2903

MARRY$^{(V)}$ (*b.ah.l)* To join as husband and wife. *AHLB:* 2027$^{(V)}$ *Strong's:* #1166

MARSH.GRASS (masc. *a'hhu)* The tall grasses that line a body of water as a wall. *AHLB:* 1008-A(r) *Strong's:* #0260

MARVEL$^{(V)}$ (*t.m.h)* Something that causes wonder or astonishment. To see or perceive a full sight, such as a wonder or miracle. *AHLB:* 1496-H$^{(V)}$ *Strong's:* #8539

MASTER (masc. *ba'al)* Having chief authority; a workman qualified to teach apprentices. *AHLB:* 2027$^{(N)}$ *Strong's:* #1167

MATERIAL (masc. *qin'yan)* Something owned, occupied or controlled. The goods and wealth acquired from the idea of acquiring materials for building a nest. *AHLB:* 1428-B(b) *Strong's:* #7075

MATTER (masc. *o'mer)* A word or utterance that is spoken about. *AHLB:* 1288-C(g) *Strong's:* #0562

MATTRESS (fem. *e'res) AHLB:* 2579$^{(N)}$ *Strong's:* #6210

MATURE (masc. *tam)* Having completed natural growth and development. An upright and correct nature. *AHLB:* 1496-A$^{(N)}$ *Strong's:* #8535

MEASURE$^{(V)}$ (*m.d.d)* To determine the length of something by comparing it to a standard of measure. *AHLB:* 1280-B$^{(V)}$ *Strong's:* #4058

MEASURED.AMOUNT (masc. *to'khen)* A calculated measurement of weight. *AHLB:* 2893(g) *Strong's:* #8506

MEASUREMENT (fem. *mi'dah)* A size or distance that is determined by comparing to a standard of measure. *AHLB:* 1280-A(N1) *Strong's:* #4060

MEASURING (masc. *mu'dad) Strong's:* [Found in names only]

MEAT (masc. *ma'zon)* Solid food as distinguished from drink; flesh; a meal. *AHLB:* 1152-J(a) *Strong's:* #4202

MEDDLE$^{(V)}$ (*g.r.h)* To struggle with to gain control over. *AHLB:* 1066-H$^{(V)}$ *Strong's:* #1624

MEDITATE$^{(V)}$ (*s.w.hh)* To engage in contemplation. A sweeping away in thought. *AHLB:* 1330-J$^{(V)}$ *Strong's:* #7742

MEDITATING.ONE (masc. *si'hhon) Strong's:* [Found in names only]

MEET$^{(V)}$ (/ *q.r.h / q.r.a)* To come into the presence of; to go to meet another; to have a chance encounter. *Alternate Translation:* come to meet (when written in the niphal [passive] form) *AHLB:* 1434-H(V) *Strong's:* #7122, #7125, #7136

MEETING (masc. *miq'ra)* To summon; to read. *AHLB:* 1434-E(h) *Strong's:* #4744

MELON (masc. *a'va'tiy'ahh)* A fruit that clings to the vine. *AHLB:* 2013(nb) *Strong's:* #0020

MELT.AWAY(V) (*m.s.s)* To become liquefied by warmth or heat. Also, the dissolving of the heart through fear or discouragement. *AHLB:* 1291-B(V) *Strong's:* #4549

MEMORIAL (fem. *az'ka'rah)* A remembering and action based on a past event. *AHLB:* 2121(n1) *Strong's:* #0234

MEMORY (masc. *zey'kher)* A remembering based on a past event often through an annual festival. *AHLB:* 2121(N) *Strong's:* #2143

MEN (masc. *za'khur)* Male persons. *AHLB:* 2121(d) *Strong's:* #2138

MERCHANDISE (masc. *mim'kar fem. mim'ke'ret) AHLB:* 2337(h) *Strong's:* #4465, #4466

MESSENGER (masc. *mal'akh)* One who bears a message or runs an errand. Walks for another. *AHLB:* 1264-D(a) *Strong's:* #4397

METAL.PLATING (masc. *tsi'phu'i)* Thin layers of metals used to cover materials to give the look of metal. A hammered-out sheet of gold used to overlay something. *AHLB:* 1155-A(rf) *Strong's:* #6826

METROPOLIS (fem. *qir'yah)* A large populace of people; a town or village. A place of meeting and gathering. *AHLB:* 1434-H(f1) *Strong's:* #7151

MIDDLEMOST (masc. *ti'khon)* The absolute center. *AHLB:* 1494-M(j) *Strong's:* #8484

MIDSECTION (fem. *ya'rey'akh)* The lower abdomen and back. *AHLB:* 1448-L(N) *Strong's:* #3409

MIDST (masc. *ta'wek)* The center or middle of the whole. *Alternate Translation:* middle *AHLB:* 1494-J(N) *Strong's:* #8432

MIGHTY.ONE (masc. *el)* One who holds authority over others, such as a judge, chief or god. *AHLB:* 1012-A(N) *Strong's:* #0410

MIGRATION (fem. *sal'kah) Strong's:* [Found in names only]

MILDEW (masc. *yey'ra'qon)* As a thin green film. *AHLB:* 1456-L(j) *Strong's:* #3420

MILLSTONE (masc. *re'hheh)* A large circular stone that is revolved on top of another stone to grind grain into flour. *AHLB:* 1445-H(N) *Strong's:* #7347

MIMIC(V) (*l.w.ts)* To imitate another person's speech as an interpretation or in scorn. *Alternate Translation:* interpret (when written in the hiphil [active causative] form), mocker (when written in the participle form) *AHLB:* 1271-J(V) *Strong's:* #3887

MINISTER(V) (*sh.r.t)* To give aid or service; to be in service to another. *Alternate Translation:* administer *AHLB:* 2884(V) *Strong's:* #8334

MINISTRY (masc. *sh'reyt) AHLB:* 2884(N) *Strong's:* #8335

MIRE (masc. *ya'weyn)* A swamp, bog or marsh. *AHLB:* 1221-J(N) *Strong's:* #3121

MISCHIEF (fem. *zam'mah)* An annoying action resulting in grief, harm or evil. *AHLB:* 1151-A(N1) *Strong's:* #2154

MISCHIEVOUS (masc. *zam'zum)* Maliciously or playfully annoying. *Strong's:* [Found in names only]

MISERY (masc. *makh'ov)* An agony of the heart. *AHLB:* 1232-D(ac) *Strong's:* #4341

MIST (masc. *ad)* A vapor or fine spray. *AHLB:* 1004-A(N) *Strong's:* #0108

MISTAKE (fem. *mish'geh)* An error in calculation or understanding. *AHLB:* 1463-A(h1) *Strong's:* #4870

MIX(V) (*b.l.l)* To combine in one mass; to mingle together. *AHLB:* 1035-B(V) *Strong's:* #1101

MIXED.MULTITUDE (masc. *a'saph'suph)* A gathering of people. *AHLB:* 1339-C(l) *Strong's:* #0628

MIXED.UP (masc. *ba'val)* To be put together indiscriminately or confusedly. *Strong's:* [Found in names only]

MIXTURE (masc. *ey'rev)* Two or more elements to create one new element. Also, the woof in weaving from its mixing of colors. *AHLB:* 2573(N) *Strong's:* #6154

MODERATE(V) (*d.y.n / d.w.n)* To rule over quarrels or other conflicts. *AHLB:* 1083-M(V) *Strong's:* #1777

MODERATOR (masc. *dan)* A judge. One who presides over a dispute. *Strong's:* [Found in names only]

MOIST (masc. *lahh)* Slightly or moderately wet. *AHLB:* 1261-A(N) *Strong's:* #3892, #3893

MOLD(V) (*y.ts.r)* To give shape to; to press or squeeze, as when pressing clay into a shape to form a vessel. *Alternate Translation:* distress *AHLB:* 1411-L(V) *Strong's:* #3334, #3335

MOLDING (masc. *zeyr)* Material used to encompass an area or to enhance or beautify. Spread or scattered over a large area. *AHLB:* 1158-A(N) *Strong's:* #2213

MOMENT (masc. *re'ga)* A single point in time. A wink of the eye. *AHLB:* 2752(N) *Strong's:* #7281, #7282

MONUMENT (fem. *ma'tsey'vah)* A lasting evidence, reminder, or example of someone or something. As standing tall and firm. *AHLB:* 2426(a1) *Strong's:* #4676

MOON (masc. *ye'rey'ahh)* The second brightest object in the sky which reflects the sun's light. Also, a month by counting its cycles. *AHLB:* 1445-L(N) *Strong's:* #3391, #3394

MOREOVER (*aph)* In addition to what has been said. *AHLB:* 1017-H(a) *Strong's:* #0637

MORNING (masc. *bo'qer)* The time from sunrise to noon. Breaking of daylight. *AHLB:* 2035(g) *Strong's:* #1242

MORROW (fem. *ma'hha'ret)* The next day. At a time following. *Alternate Translation:* the next day (when prefixed with "from~") *AHLB:* 1181-A(a2) *Strong's:* #4283

MORTAL.MAN (masc. *mat)* Subject to death. As mortal. *AHLB:* 1298-A(N) *Strong's:* #4962

MORTAR (masc. *hho'mer)* A thick and slimy soil used to join bricks or for making bricks. *AHLB:* 2175(g) *Strong's:* #2563(x2)

MORTAR.AND.PESTLE (fem. *m'do'khah)* *AHLB:* 1080-J(k1) *Strong's:* #4085

MOTHER (fem. *eym)* A female parent. Maternal tenderness or affection. One who fulfills the role of a mother. *AHLB:* 1013-A(N) *Strong's:* #0517

MOUND (masc. *gal)* An artificial hill or bank of earth or stones. A pile of rocks or soil. A spring gushing out of the ground. *AHLB:* 1058-A(N) *Strong's:* #1530

MOUNT (masc. *ha'rar)* To increase in amount or extent; to get up on something above the level of the ground. *AHLB:* 1112-B(N) *Strong's:* #2042

MOUNTAIN-SHEEP (masc. *ze'mer)* An clean unknown species of animal. *AHLB:* 2124(N) *Strong's:* #2169

MOUNTAINSIDE (masc. *ze'dad)* The side or slope of a mountain. *Strong's:* [Found in names only]

MOURN(V) (*a.b.l)* To feel or express grief or sorrow. *AHLB:* 1035-C(V) *Strong's:* #0056

MOURNING (*a-veyl)* A flowing of tears. Also, a meadow as a weeping ground. *AHLB:* 1035-C(N) *Strong's:* #0057, #0058, #0060

MOUSE (masc. *akh'bar)* A small rodent. *AHLB:* 3043 *Strong's:* #5909

MOUTH (masc. *peh)* The opening through which food enters the body. Any opening. *Alternate Translation:* opening, according to *AHLB:* 1373-A(N) *Strong's:* #6310

MOVE.AWAY(V) (*m.w.sh)* To pass from one place or position to another. *AHLB:* 1297-J(V) *Strong's:* #4185

MOVING (masc. *mush)* What has passed from one place to another. *Strong's:* [Found in names only]

MULTITUDE (masc. *ha'mon)* A great number of people. A loud group. *AHLB:* 1105-A(j) *Strong's:* #1995

MURDER(V) (*r.ts.hh)* A killing committed with malice aforethought, characterized by deliberation or premeditation. *AHLB:* 2790(V) *Strong's:* #7523

MURKINESS (fem. *ey'phah) AHLB:* 1523-M(N1) *Strong's:* #5890

MURMUR(V) (*l.w.n)* To make a low or indistinct sound, esp. Continuously. To complain in a low tone, usually in private. *AHLB:* 1451-J(V) *Strong's:* #3885(x2)

MURMURING (fem. *te'lu'nah)* A continuously low or indistinct sound. A complaining in low tones, usually in private. *AHLB:* 1451-J(i1) *Strong's:* #8519

MUSIC (fem. *zim'rat)* An art of sound in time that expresses ideas and emotions in significant forms through the elements of rhythm, melody, harmony, and color. *AHLB:* 2124(e2) *Strong's:* #2176

MUSICIAN (masc. *zim'rah) Strong's:* [Found in names only]

MUSTER(V) (*ts.b.a)* To gather together a group for service, work or war. *AHLB:* 1393-E(V) *Strong's:* #6633

MUTE (masc. *i'leym)* Inability to speak. A bound-up tongue. *AHLB:* 1266-C(e) *Strong's:* #0483

MUZZLE(V) (*hh.s.m) AHLB:* 2184(V) *Strong's:* #2629

MYRIAD (fem. *re'va'vah)* A great abundance in numbers. *AHLB:* 1439-B(N1) *Strong's:* #7233

MYRRH (masc. *mor)* A sweet smelling spice. Used as an exchange due to its monetary value. *AHLB:* 1296-J(N) *Strong's:* #4753

NAIL (masc. *ya'tat) Strong's:* [Found in names only]

NAKED (masc. *ey'rom)* Without clothes. *AHLB:* 1365-A(ecp) *Strong's:* #5903

NAKEDNESS (fem. *er'wah)* The state of being without clothing. Idiomatic for sexual relations. *AHLB:* 1365-K(N1) *Strong's:* #6172

NARROW (masc. *tsar)* Of slender width. A narrow, tight place or situation, a difficulty. An enemy or adversary as one who closes in with pressure. *Alternate Translation:* enemy *AHLB:* 1411-A$^{(N)}$ *Strong's:* #6862

NARROW.WAY (masc. *mish'ol)* A hollow in the land. *AHLB:* 2860(hc) *Strong's:* #4934

NATAPH (masc. *na'taph)* An unknown spice. *AHLB:* 2399$^{(N)}$ *Strong's:* #5198

NATION (masc. *goy)* A community of people of one or more nationalities and having a more or less defined territory and government. The people as the back, or body of the nation. *AHLB:* 1052-A(f) *Strong's:* #1471

NATIVE (masc. *ez'rahh)* Born and raised in the Land. *AHLB:* 2135$^{(N)}$ *Strong's:* #0249

NATIVITY (masc. *lud) Strong's:* [Found in names only]

NEAR (masc. *qa'rov)* Close to; at or within a short distance from. Also, a kin, as a near relative. *AHLB:* 2729(c) *Strong's:* #7138

NECK (masc. *o'reph)* The part of a person that connects the head with the body. *AHLB:* 2580$^{(N)}$ *Strong's:* #6203

NECK.BAND (masc. *a'naq)* An ornamental chain, band or cord worn around the neck. *AHLB:* 2559$^{(N)}$ *Strong's:* #6060

NECKLACE (masc. *ra'vid)* A series of links worn as an ornament or insignia. *AHLB:* 2742(b) *Strong's:* #7242

NECROMANCER (masc. *ov)* One who communicates with the dead (see 1 Sam 28:8). Used once (Job 32:19) *AHLB:* 1002-J$^{(N)}$ *Strong's:* #0178

NEEDY (masc. *ev'yon)* In a condition of need or want. *AHLB:* 1033-C(j) *Strong's:* #0034

NEIGHBOR (fem. *a'miyt) AHLB:* 1358-A(N4) *Strong's:* #5997

NEST (masc. *qeyn)* A bed or receptacle prepared by a bird for its eggs and young. The stall of an animal as a nest. *AHLB:* 1428-A$^{(N)}$ *Strong's:* #7064

NESTING (masc. *qin'yan) Strong's:* [Found in names only]

NET (masc. / *se'vakh)* An open-meshed fabric twisted, knotted, or woven at regular intervals. Also, a thicket as an interwoven network of thorns. *AHLB:* 2459$^{(N)}$ *Strong's:* #5442, #7638

NETTING (fem. *re'shet)* A sheet of meshed fabric, cord or metal. *AHLB:* 1458-A(N2) *Strong's:* #7568

NEVERTHELESS (masc. *a'val)* In spite of that. A flowing of certainty. *AHLB:* 1035-C$^{(N)}$ *Strong's:* #0061

NEW (masc. *hha'dash)* Something that is new, renewed, restored or repaired. *AHLB:* 2151$^{(N)}$ *Strong's:* #2319

NEW.MOON (masc. *hho'desh)* The moon phase when the thin crescent first appears and is perceived as the renewal of the moon. The first day of the month. Also, a month as the interval between crescents. *Alternate Translation:* month *AHLB:* 2151(g) *Strong's:* #2320

NIGHT (masc. / *la'yil / lai'lah)* The time from dusk to dawn. The hours associated with darkness and sleep. *Alternate Translation:* tonight (when prefixed with "the~") *AHLB:* 1265-M$^{(N)}$ *Strong's:* #3915

NIGHT.WATCH (fem. *ash'mu'rah)* An increment of time during the night when guards watch the area. *AHLB:* 2853(nd1) *Strong's:* #0821

NIGHTHAWK (masc. *tahh'mas)* An unclean unknown species of bird. *AHLB:* 2172(i) *Strong's:* #8464

NINE (masc. *tish'ah fem.* *tey'sha)* A cardinal number. The total number of hours in an ancient day or night. *Alternate Translation:* ninety (when written in the plural) *AHLB:* 1476-A(i) *Strong's:* #8672, #8673

NINTH (masc. *t'shiy'iy) AHLB:* 1476-A(bf) *Strong's:* #8671

NOBILITY (masc. *hhiy'rah) Strong's:* [Found in names only]

NOBLE (masc. / *sar)* Possessing outstanding qualities or properties. Of high birth or exalted rank. One who has authority. May also mean "heavy" from the weight of responsibility on one in authority. *AHLB:* 1342-A$^{(N)}$ *Strong's:* #5620, #8269

NOBLEWOMAN (fem. *sa'rah)* A female of authority. *AHLB:* 1342-A(N1) *Strong's:* #8282

NOD$^{(V)}$ (*n.w.d)* A quick downward motion of the head. To shake or wag out of pity, sorrow or wandering. *AHLB:* 1303-J$^{(V)}$ *Strong's:* #5110

NODDING (masc. *nod) AHLB:* 1303-J$^{(N)}$ *Strong's:* #5112

NOMAD (masc. *tsiy)* A member of a people or tribe that has no permanent abode but moves about from place to place, usually seasonally and often following a traditional route or circuit according to the state of the pasturage or food supply. Also, a ship as a nomad of the sea. *AHLB:* 1401-A$^{(N)}$ *Strong's:* #6716

NONE (masc. *bal)* Not any, no part. *AHLB:* 1035-A$^{(N)}$ *Strong's:* #1077

NORTH (fem. *tsa'phon)* The direction of the left hand when facing the rising sun. *AHLB:* 1408-A(j) *Strong's:* #6828

NOSE (masc. *aph)* The organ bearing the nostrils on the anterior of the face. Also, meaning anger from the flaring of the nostrils and the redness of the nose when angry. *Alternate Translation:* nostrils (when in the double plural form) *AHLB:* 1017-A$^{(N)}$ *Strong's:* #0639

NOSE.RING (masc. / *hhahh / hha'hhiy)* A round piece of jewelry, usually of a metal, that is pierced through the nose or lip. *AHLB:* 1169-A$^{(N)}$ *Strong's:* #2397

NOT (masc. / *lo)* A function word to stand for the negative. As being without. *Alternate Translation:* cannot; no; nothing; un-; without; therefore (when preceded by the word "IF"); without (when prefixed with "in~") *AHLB:* 1254-J$^{(N)}$ *Strong's:* #3808

NOURISHMENT (masc. *ma'a'kal)* Food; nutriment. For giving sustenance and making one whole. *AHLB:* 1242-C(a) *Strong's:* #3978

NOW (masc. *a'tah)* At the present time or moment. *AHLB:* 1367-H$^{(N)}$ *Strong's:* #6258

NUDE (masc. *a'rom)* Without clothes. *AHLB:* 1365-A(cp) *Strong's:* #6174

NUMBER (masc. *mis'phar)* A sum of units. Counting as a recording. *AHLB:* 2500(h) *Strong's:* #4557

NUMEROUS (masc. *a'tsum)* Involving more than one. *AHLB:* 2569(d) *Strong's:* #6099

OAK (fem. *ey'lah)* A species of tree with dense, hard, wood. A tough durable wood. *AHLB:* 1012-A(N1) *Strong's:* #0424, #0427

OASIS (masc. *ma'no'ahh fem. me'nu'hhah)* A location where there is freedom from activity or labor; a place for resting or lodging. *AHLB:* 1307-J(a) *Strong's:* #4494, #4496

OATH (fem. *a'lah)* Something corroborated by a vow. A binding agreement, including the curse for violating the oath. *AHLB:* 1012-A(N1) *Strong's:* #0423

OBEDIENCE (fem. *ye'qa'hah)* Submission to the will of another. *AHLB:* 1419-L(N1) *Strong's:* #3349

OFFENSE (masc. *pe'sha)* The exceeding of due bounds or limits. *AHLB:* 2647(N) *Strong's:* #6588

OFFER.WILLINGLY(V) (*n.d.b)* To give from a willing heart. *AHLB:* 2380(V) *Strong's:* #5068

OFFERED.WILLINGLY (masc. *na'dav)* Given of one's free will without recompense. *Strong's:* [Found in names only]

OFFERING (fem. *te'ru'mah)* A donation presented to another. *AHLB:* 1450-J(i1) *Strong's:* #8641

OFFERING.OF.RESTITUTION (masc. *she'lem)* Having all necessary parts, elements or steps. A state of being whole or full. Left unaltered and whole in its original functional state without removing or adding to it. To finish. A sacrifice or offering given to bring about peace. *AHLB:* 2845(N) *Strong's:* #8002

OFFICER (*sh.t.r) AHLB:* 2833(V) *Strong's:* #7860

OFFSHOOT (masc. *ey'qer) AHLB:* 2905(N) *Strong's:* #6133

OH (masc. *oiy)* A passionate cry of desire. *AHLB:* 1006-A(f) *Strong's:* #0188

OIL (masc. *she'men)* A semi-liquid, often oily and thick. Usually olive oil and used as a medicinal ointment. Also, meaning fat or rich. *Alternate Translation:* fat *AHLB:* 2850(N) *Strong's:* #8081, #8082

OINTMENT (fem. *mash'hhah)* An oil or other liquid that is smeared on an animal or person for healing or dedication. *AHLB:* 2357(N1) *Strong's:* #4888

OINTMENT.MIXTURE (fem. *mir'qa'hhat)* A mixture of spices for an ointment or perfume. *AHLB:* 2795(h2) *Strong's:* #4842

OLD.AGE (fem. *ziq'nah)* One up in years. *AHLB:* 2132(e1) *Strong's:* #2209

OLIVE (masc. *za'yit)* The fruit or the tree. The fruit of the olive is used for food and as a source of oil. *AHLB:* 1160-M(N) *Strong's:* #2132

OLIVINE (fem. *pit'dah)* Probably the Olivine, a green gemstone. The Septuagint uses the word topazios, but the Topaz was unknown at the time of the Exodus. Another possible meaning of this word is Chrysolite. *AHLB:* 2603(e1) *Strong's:* #6357

OMER (masc. *o'mer)* A dry measure equal to one tenth of an ephah (about two liters). *AHLB:* 2554(g) *Strong's:* #6016(x2)

ON.ACCOUNT.OF (masc. *ge'lal)* A telling of what occurred previously. Thus used in Hebrew as a rolling back around. (Alwys prefixed with the letter ב). *AHLB:* 1058-B(N) *Strong's:* #1558

ON.FOOT (masc. *rag'li)* A soldier, messenger or traveler who moves on foot. *AHLB:* 2749(f) *Strong's:* #7273

ONE (*ash-tey)* Existing, acting, or considered as a single unit, entity, or individual. *AHLB:* 2586(f) *Strong's:* #6249

ONE.HALF (fem. *ma'hha'tsit)* A portion that is equal to the remainder. *AHLB:* 1179-A(a4) *Strong's:* #4276

ONE.TENTH (masc. *i'sa'ron)* An equal part of something divided into ten parts. *AHLB:* 2563(j) *Strong's:* #6241

ONION (masc. *ba'tsal)* A plant of the amaryllis family, having an edible, succulent, pungent bulb. *AHLB:* 2030(N) *Strong's:* #1211

ONLY (masc. *raq)* A single instance or thing and nothing more or different. *Alternate Translation:* at all *AHLB:* 1456-A(N) *Strong's:* #7535

ONYCHA (fem. *she'hhey'let)* An unknown spice. *AHLB:* 2824(N2) *Strong's:* #7827

ONYX (masc. *sho'ham)* Probably the Onyx, a form of quartz that may be of any color. The Septuagint uses beryllios (Beryl). Another possible translation is the Malachite. *AHLB:* 1473-G(g) *Strong's:* #7718

OPAL (masc. *le'shem)* Possibly the Opal, which may be found in a wide variety of colors. Other possible translates are Amber, Jacinth, Agate or Amethyst. *AHLB:* 2324(N) *Strong's:* #3958

OPEN(V) (*p.t.hh)* To open up as opening a gate or door; to have no confining barrier. *Alternate Translation:* engrave (when written in the piel [active intensive] form) *AHLB:* 2649(V) *Strong's:* #6603, #6605

OPEN.SPACE (masc. *mig'rash fem.* *mig'ra'shah)* A place for grazing livestock, usually on the outskirts of a village or city. *AHLB:* 2089(h) *Strong's:* #4054

OPEN.UP(V) (*p.q.hh)* To make available or accessible. Open the eyes or ears to see or hear. *AHLB:* 2631(V) *Strong's:* #6491

OPENED.WIDE (masc. *pe'or) Strong's:* [Found in names only]

OPENING (masc. *pe'tahh)* Something that is open, as an entrance or opening of a tent, house or city. *AHLB:* 2649(N) *Strong's:* #6607, #6608

OPINION (masc. *da)* To possess an intimate knowledge. An intimacy with a person, idea or concept. *AHLB:* 1085-A(N) *Strong's:* #1843

OPPONENT (masc. *sa'tan)* One who is on the opposing side of an action or thought; an adversary. *AHLB:* 2475(N) *Strong's:* #7854

OPPOSITE (masc. *ne'ged)* Something in front of; on the other side; in the presence of. *Alternate Translation:* before; in the face of *AHLB:* 2372(N) *Strong's:* #5048

OPPOSITION (fem. *sit'nah) AHLB:* 2475(e1) *Strong's:* #7855

OPPRESS(V) (*ah.sh.q)* To press into or on another through force or deceit. *AHLB:* 2584(V) *Strong's:* #6231

OPPRESSION (masc. *o'sheq)* The act of pressing into or on another through force or deceit. *AHLB:* 2584(g) *Strong's:* #6233

OR (masc. *o)* An alternative or optional desire. *Alternate Translation:* whether *AHLB:* 1006-A(N) *Strong's:* #0176

ORDINARY (masc. *hhal)* A place, person or thing that is not set apart for a specific function. *AHLB:* 1173-A(N) *Strong's:* #2455

ORNAMENT (fem. *mig'da'nah)* Something that lends grace and beauty. Precious ornaments probably with gems. *AHLB:* 2329(m1) *Strong's:* #4030

ORNAMENTAL.RING (masc. *ne'zem)* A circular band worn as an adornment on the ear, nose or other part of the body. *AHLB:* 2388(N) *Strong's:* #5141

ORPHAN (masc. *ya'tom)* Having no mother or father. *AHLB:* 1496-L(c) *Strong's:* #3490

ORYX (masc. *t'o)* An unknown animal. *AHLB:* 1484-A(q) *Strong's:* #8377

OSPREY (fem. *az'niy'yah)* An unknown bird of prey. *AHLB:* 2533(f1) *Strong's:* #5822

OTHER (masc. *a'hhar)* One that remains or follows after another. *Alternate Translation:* another *AHLB:* 1181-C(N) *Strong's:* #0312

OTHER.SIDE (masc. *ey'ver)* As being across from this side. *AHLB:* 2520(N) *Strong's:* #5676

OTHERWISE (masc. *peyn)* In a different manner or way. *AHLB:* 1382-A(N) *Strong's:* #6435

OUT.OF.SIGHT (masc. *al'mon) Strong's:* [Found in names only]

OUTCRY (fem. *shaw'ah)* An expression of need, or help or injustice. A loud wail from distress. *AHLB:* 1476-J(N1) *Strong's:* #7775

OUTER (masc. *qi'tson)* The furthest from the center. The end. *AHLB:* 1432-A(ej) *Strong's:* #7020

OUTER.COVERING (masc. *k'su'iy) AHLB:* 1245-A(rf) *Strong's:* #3681

OUTER.GARMENT (fem. *sal'mah)* Garments worn over top of other garments. *AHLB:* 2483(N) *Strong's:* #8008

OUTER.RIM (masc. *kar'kov)* The out edge of something. *AHLB:* 3027 *Strong's:* #3749

OUTSIDE (masc. *hhuts)* A place or region beyond an enclosure or barrier. *AHLB:* 1179-J(N) *Strong's:* #2351

OVEN (masc. *ta'nur)* A chamber used for baking, heating or drying. As a lamp for cooking. *AHLB:* 1319-J(i) *Strong's:* #8574

OVERCOME(V) (*g.b.r)* To get the better of. Be successful in strength or authority. *AHLB:* 2052(V) *Strong's:* #1396

OVERHANG (masc. *se'rahh)* The part that extends out. What is left over. A remnant or residue. *AHLB:* 2507(N) *Strong's:* #5629

OVERHANG(V) (*s.r.hh)* To proceed beyond any given or supposed limit or measure. To extend beyond proper bounds. To be superfluous. *AHLB:* 2507(V) *Strong's:* #5628

OVERLAY(V) (*ts.p.h)* To cover with a different material, usually with gold. *AHLB:* 1408-H(V) *Strong's:* #6823

OVERLOOK(V) (/ *n.sh.a / n.sh.h)* To unintentionaly look past, forget. *AHLB:* 1320-H(V) *Strong's:* #5382

OVERSEER (masc. *pa'qid fem.* *pe'qiy'dot)* One who carefully watches over; a superintendent. *AHLB:* 2630(b), 2630(b3) *Strong's:* #6488, #6496

OVERSIGHT (fem. *pe'qu'dah)* A watching over; the function of the overseer. *AHLB:* 2630(V) *Strong's:* #6486

OVERTAKE(V) (*n.s.g)* To catch up with; to remove in the sense of taking over; to take hold; to acquire wealth *Alternate Translation:* Reach (especially when speaking of the hand reaching out to grab something) *AHLB:* 2410(V) *Strong's:* #5253, #5381

OVERTHROWING (fem. *mah'pey'khah) AHLB:* 1379-F(a1) *Strong's:* #4114

OVERTHROWN (masc. *ri'sah)* To ruin or break into pieces by throwing or pulling down. *Strong's:* [Found in names only]

OVERTOP (*h.g.g)* The covering of a dwelling place. *Strong's:* [Found in names only]

OVERTURN[V] (*h.p.k)* To turn something over or upside down, as if pouring out its contents. *AHLB:* 1379-F[V] *Strong's:* #2015

OVERTURNING (fem. *ha'phey'khah)* The act of turning something over. *AHLB:* 1379-F(N1) *Strong's:* #2018

OWL (fem. *ya'a'nah)* An unknown bird. *AHLB:* 1359-L(N1) *Strong's:* #3284

OWNER (masc. *ge'vir)* Possessor of an article or property. *AHLB:* 2052(b) *Strong's:* #1376

OX (masc. *shor)* A domestic bovine animal used for pulling heavy loads. *AHLB:* 1480-J[N] *Strong's:* #7794

PACK[V] (*t.ah.n)* A bundle arranged for carrying. *AHLB:* 2237[V] *Strong's:* #2943

PALACE (masc. *a'ram)* A large house. *Strong's:* [Found in names only]

PALE (masc. *hhor) AHLB:* 1181-J[N] *Strong's:* #2353, #2715

PALENESS (masc. *hho'ri)* Made with bleached flour. *AHLB:* 1181-J(f) *Strong's:* #2355, #2751

PALM (fem. *kaph)* Part of the hand or foot between the base of the digits and the wrist or ankle; A palm-shaped object. (This word is written in the masculine form in Job 30:6 and Jeremiah 4:29, where it used for "rocks" or a "cliff," a hiding place.) *Alternate Translation:* spoon (from the curved shape being similar to a palm) *AHLB:* 1247-A[N] *Strong's:* #3709, #3710

PALM.GROVE (fem. *da'phaq) Strong's:* [Found in names only]

PAN (fem. *ma'hha'vat)* Any shallow open or closed container used over a fire. *AHLB:* 2145(a) *Strong's:* #4227

PARABLE (masc. *ma'shal)* An illustration of similitude; a story of comparisons; a proverb. *AHLB:* 2359[N] *Strong's:* #4912

PARAPET (masc. *ma'a'qeh)* A place of pressing as one leans on it. A wall that is placed around the roof as this place was occupied because of its coolness in the summer. *AHLB:* 1364-H(a) *Strong's:* #4624

PARCEL (fem. *hhal'qah)* A section or portion of land that has been purchased or aquired. *AHLB:* 2167(N1) *Strong's:* #2513(x2)

PARCHING.HEAT (masc. *hho'rev)* An intense heat that causes shriveling or toasting. *AHLB:* 2199(g) *Strong's:* #2721

PART[V] (*p.ts.h)* To separate. Part the lips to open the mouth. *AHLB:* 1386-H[V] *Strong's:* #6475

PARTNER (masc. *mey'rey'a)* One that shares. A close companion. *AHLB:* 1453-A(k) *Strong's:* #4828

PARTRIDGE (fem. *hhag'lah)* A species of game bird. *Strong's:* [Found in names only]

PASS.OVER[V] (*hh.l.p)* To pass through, by or over something. Also, to change in the sense of going to another one, side or thought. *Alternate Translation:* change (when written in the hiphil [active causative] or piel [active intensive] form) *AHLB:* 2165[V] *Strong's:* #2498

PAST.TIME (fem. *qad'mah)* A time that is before. *AHLB:* 2698(N1) *Strong's:* #6927

PASTE[V] (*hh.m.r)* To smear a paste such as mortar on bricks or tar on a boat. *AHLB:* 2175[V] *Strong's:* #2560

PASTURE (masc. מקהל *maq'heyl fem.* מקהלה *ma'qah'lah)* The grassy place where the flock gathers for feeding. *AHLB:* 1426-G(a) *Strong's:* #4721

PATH (masc. ארוח *o'rahh)* The road or route one travels. *AHLB:* 1445-C(g) *Strong's:* #0734

PATTERN (fem. תבנית *tav'nit)* A model or instructions detailing a construction. *AHLB:* 1037-H(if2) *Strong's:* #8403

PAYMENT (fem. משכרת *mas'ko'ret)* Something that is paid. *AHLB:* 2479(ac2) *Strong's:* #4909

PEASANT (masc. פרז *pa'raz)* One of lower rank, or value, usually dwelling in a town without walls. *AHLB:* 2635[N] *Strong's:* #6518

PEDESTAL (fem. מכונה *me'kho'nah)* A base that is firm and functions as a supports. *AHLB:* 1244-A(kc1) *Strong's:* #4350

PEEL[V] (פצל *p.ts.l)* To strip off an outer layer. *AHLB:* 2626[V] *Strong's:* #6478

PEG (masc. וו *waw)* A peg, nail or hook as used for attaching one thing to another. (The short form "ו" is used as a prefix meaning "and."). *AHLB:* 1121-A[N] *Strong's:* #2053

PELICAN (fem. קאת *qa'at)* An unknown bird that vomits up its food for its chicks. *AHLB:* 1415-A(N2) *Strong's:* #6893

PENIS (fem. שפכה *shaph'khah)* The male reproductive organ. *AHLB:* 2865(N1) *Strong's:* #8212

PEOPLE (masc. עם *am)* A large group of men or women. *AHLB:* 1358-A[N] *Strong's:* #5971

PERCEIVE[V] (חזה *hh.z.h)* To be able to understand on a higher level; to see something that is not physically present. *AHLB:* 1168-H[V] *Strong's:* #1957, #2372

PERFORATE[V] (חרם *hh.r.m)* To fill with holes; to make holes; to destroy. *AHLB:* 2206[V] *Strong's:* #2763(x2)

PERFORATED (masc. חרם *hhe'rem)* Something filled with holes or is perforated. Also, something accursed in the sense of being filled with holes. *AHLB:* 2206[N] *Strong's:* #2764(x2)

PERFORATED.ONE (masc. חרמון *hher'mon) Strong's:* [Found in names only]

PERFORM[V] (פלא *p.l.a)* To do a wondrous action that shows ones might. *Alternate Translation:* too difficult (when written in the niphil [passive] form) *AHLB:* 1380-E[V] *Strong's:* #6381

PERFORMANCE (masc. פלא *pe'le)* A wondrous action. *AHLB:* 1380-E[N] *Strong's:* #6382

PERFORMING (masc. פלוא *pa'lu)* The act of doing, displaying, or creating. *Strong's:* [Found in names only]

PERISH[V] (אבד *a.b.d)* To be deserted or abandoned; separated from the whole, life or functionality. *Alternate Translation:* destroy (when written in the hiphil [causative] form) *AHLB:* 1027-C[V] *Strong's:* #0006, #0008

PERMANENT (fem. צמיתות *ts'miy'tut)* Something that is continual. *AHLB:* 2669(b2) *Strong's:* #6783

PERSECUTION (fem. צרה *tsa'rah)* To agitate mentally or spiritually; worry; disturb. *AHLB:* 1411-A(N1) *Strong's:* #6869

PERSUADE[V] (סות *s.w.t) AHLB:* 1344-J[V] *Strong's:* #5496

PESTILENCE (fem. מגפה *ma'gey'phah)* A plague or other disaster that smites people or beasts. *AHLB:* 2377(k1) *Strong's:* #4046

PICK.OUT[V] (*n.q.r) AHLB:* 2436[V] *Strong's:* #5365

PICK.UP[V] (*l.q.t)* To take hold of and lift up; to gather together. *AHLB:* 2320[V] *Strong's:* #3950

PIECE (masc. *ney'tahh)* A part of the original. What has been cut from the whole. *AHLB:* 2449[N] *Strong's:* #5409

PIERCE[V] (*d.q.r)* To pierce through with a sword or other sharp object. *AHLB:* 2110[V] *Strong's:* #1856

PIERCE.THROUGH[V] (*n.q.b)* To make a hole by puncturing or penetrating; to curse in the sense of piercing through. *AHLB:* 2430[V] *Strong's:* #5344

PIERCED.BREAD (fem. *hha'lah)* Bread that has many holes, as perforated. *AHLB:* 1173-A(N1) *Strong's:* #2471

PIERCING (fem. *sh'niy'nah) AHLB:* 1474-B(b1) *Strong's:* #8148

PILE[V] (*ah.r.m)* To mound up in a heap. *AHLB:* 2578[V] *Strong's:* #6192

PILE.OF.RUINS (masc. *iy) AHLB:* 1516-A[N] *Strong's:* #5856

PILE.UP[V] (*ts.b.r)* To heap something up in a mound. *AHLB:* 2656[V] *Strong's:* #6651

PILLAR (masc. *a'mud)* A standing upright post or column. *AHLB:* 2550(d) *Strong's:* #5982

PILLAR.BASE (masc. *re'phid fem. r'phiy'dah)* The lowest or deepest part of anything. *AHLB:* 2785(b1) *Strong's:* #7507

PISTACHIO (masc. *bo'ten)* A greenish-yellow nut from a small tree of the same name. From its belly shape. *AHLB:* 2015(g) *Strong's:* #0992

PIT (masc. *pa'hhat fem. p'hhe'tet)* A hole in the skin from disease. *AHLB:* 2602[N] *Strong's:* #6354, #6356

PIT.DIGGER (masc. *shu'hham) Strong's:* [Found in names only]

PITCH (fem. *ze'phet)* A sticky substance used to seal wood from water leakage. *AHLB:* 1155-A(N2) *Strong's:* #2203

PITCH.TENT[V] (*a.h.l)* To set up camp. By extension, can also mean a distant shining, such as the moon. *AHLB:* 1104-C[V] *Strong's:* #0166, #0167

PITIED (masc. *hha'mul)* One who deserves pity, sorrow, or regret. *Strong's:* [Found in names only]

PITIFUL (fem. *hhem'lah)* Having or showing sympathetic consciousness of others' distress with a desire to alleviate it. *AHLB:* 2171(N1) *Strong's:* #2551

PLACE[V] (*s.y.m / s.w.m)* To put or set in a particular place, position, situation, or relation. *AHLB:* 1335-J[V] *Strong's:* #3455, #7760

PLACE.OF.LODGING (masc. *ma'lon)* An establishment for lodging and entertaining travelers. A place for spending the night. *AHLB:* 1267-J(a) *Strong's:* #4411

PLACE.TO.BURN (masc. *miq'tar)* A specific location used for burning incense. *AHLB:* 2705(h) *Strong's:* #4729

PLAIN (masc. */ mey'shar / mey'tar)* A level, or straight, place. One who is right or upright. *AHLB:* 1480-L(hc) *Strong's:* #4334

PLAIT (fem. *mish'be'tsah)* A woven or checkered work. *AHLB:* 2809(h1) *Strong's:* #4865

PLANT[V] (*n.t.ah)* To put or set into the ground for growth; to establish plants. *AHLB:* 2398[V] *Strong's:* #5193

PLANTATION (masc. *kar'mel)* A field that produces an abundance of grains, fruit or other crop. By metonymy the crops of the plantation. *AHLB:* 3029 *Strong's:* #3759

PLASTER(V) (*t.w.hh)* To spread a clay and straw mixture out to create a smooth surface. *AHLB:* 1192-J(V) *Strong's:* #2902

PLATFORM (fem. *ba'mah)* A place higher than the surrounding area. Often used in reference to sacred, or exalted, places. *AHLB:* 1036-H(N) *Strong's:* #1116

PLATTER (fem. *qe'a'rah)* A large plate, serving dish. *AHLB:* 2719(N1) *Strong's:* #7086

PLEA (masc. / *diyn / dun)* A request to a person in authority. *AHLB:* 1083-M(N) *Strong's:* #1779, #1781

PLEAD(V) (*p.l.l)* To entreat or appeal earnestly; to fall to the ground to plead a cause to one in authority; prevent a judgment. *Alternate Translation:* Intercede (when written in the hitpa'el [reflexive] form) *AHLB:* 1380-B(V) *Strong's:* #6419

PLEASANT (fem. *hhem'dah)* Having qualities that tend to give pleasure. An object of desire. *AHLB:* 2169(N1) *Strong's:* #2532

PLEASANTNESS (masc. *na'a'man) AHLB:* 2416(m) *Strong's:* #5282

PLEASE (masc. / / *na / a'na / a'nah)* A pleading or request for action from another. *AHLB:* 1300-A(N) *Strong's:* #0577, #4994

PLEASURE (*e-den)* A state of gratification. *AHLB:* 2528(N) *Strong's:* #5730

PLEDGE (masc. *a'vot)* What is given as security for a loan. *AHLB:* 2519(c) *Strong's:* #5667

PLENTY (masc. *sa'va)* A full or more than adequate supply. What is full, satisfied or abundant. *Alternate Translation:* many *AHLB:* 2461(N) *Strong's:* #7647, #7649

PLOT(V) (*z.m.m)* To devise a plan of action, usually with evil intent. *AHLB:* 1151-B(V) *Strong's:* #2161

PLOWING (masc. *hha'rish)* Breaking up the ground in order to plant a crop. The time of plowing. *AHLB:* 2211(b) *Strong's:* #2758

PLOWSHARE (masc. *et)* The cutting point of a plow. *AHLB:* 1022-A(N) *Strong's:* #0855

PLUCK(V) (*z.m.r)* To make music by plucking an instrument. To pick fruit. *AHLB:* 2124(V) *Strong's:* #2167, #2168

PLUCK.AWAY(V) (*g.z.l)* To take off something or someone by force through picking off, robbing or plundering. *AHLB:* 2059(V) *Strong's:* #1497

PLUCK.OUT(V) (*m.sh.h)* To draw or pull out. *AHLB:* 1297-H(V) *Strong's:* #4871

PLUCK.UP(V) (*ah.q.r)* To pull or dig out the roots. *AHLB:* 2905(V) *Strong's:* #6131

PLUCKED (fem. *ge'zey'lah)* To pull with sudden force or with a jerk. *AHLB:* 2059(N1) *Strong's:* #1500

PLUCKED.OUT (masc. *mo'sheh)* What is drawn or pulled out. *Strong's:* [Found in names only]

PLUCKING (masc. *ga'zeyl)* To pull with sudden force or with a jerk. *AHLB:* 2059(N) *Strong's:* #1498, #1499

PLUMAGE (fem. *ni'tsan)* The feathers of a bird. *AHLB:* 1317-M(m1) *Strong's:* #5339

PLUNDER (masc. *baz)* What is seized by war or robbery; prey; booty; spoils *AHLB:* 1030-A(N) *Strong's:* #0957

PLUNDER(V) (*b.z.z)* To commit robbery or looting. *AHLB:* 1030-B(V) *Strong's:* #0962

POINT (masc. *tsiy'po'ren)* The sharp pointed talon of a bird. Also, a fingernail or the sharp point of a flint. *AHLB:* 2685(cm) *Strong's:* #6856

POINT(V) (*t.a.h)* To identify a mark. *AHLB:* 1484-H(V) *Strong's:* #8376

POINT.OUT(V) (*a.w.h)* To show a direction. *AHLB:* 1006-H(V) *Strong's:* #0184

POLE (fem. *mo'tah)* The bent bar of the yoke that goes around the neck, also a branch that is used as pole. *AHLB:* 1285-J(N1) *Strong's:* #4133

POMEGRANATE (masc. *ri'mon)* A sweet deep red fruit prolific with seeds. A symbol of compassion and love. *AHLB:* 1450-A(j) *Strong's:* #7416

POOL (masc. *a'gam)* A collection of water, either natural or manmade. Once (Jeremiah 51:32) *AHLB:* 1059-C(N) *Strong's:* #0098, #0099

POPLAR (fem. *liv'nah)* A tree with white bark. *AHLB:* 2303(e1) *Strong's:* #3839

POSSESS(V) (*y.r.sh)* To come into possession of or receive especially as a right or divine portion; o receive from an ancestor at his death; to take possession, either by seizing or through inheritance. *Alternate Translation:* dispossess (when written in the hiphil [active causative] form) *AHLB:* 1458-L(V) *Strong's:* #3423

POSSESSION (masc. *mo'rash fem. mo'ra'shah)* Something that is personally owned. *AHLB:* 1458-L(a1) *Strong's:* #4180, #4181

POSSIBLY (*u-li)* Being within the limits of ability, capacity, or realization. A possible outcome. To desire what you are without. *AHLB:* 1254-J(f) *Strong's:* #0194

POST (masc. *ne'tsiv)* The place at which a soldier is stationed. As standing tall and firm. A garrison. *AHLB:* 2426(b) *Strong's:* #5333

POSTERITY (masc. *ne'khed)* The offspring of a progenitor to the furthest generation. Continuation through the next generation. *AHLB:* 2402(N) *Strong's:* #5220

POT (masc. *sir)* A vessel used for cooking or storing. *AHLB:* 1342-M(N) *Strong's:* #5518

POUCH (masc. *tse'ror)* A group of things fastened together for convenient handling. Something that is bound up tightly. *AHLB:* 1411-B(c) *Strong's:* #6872

POUR(V) (*n.s.k)* To cause to flow in a stream; to give full expression to. *AHLB:* 2412(V) *Strong's:* #5258, #5259

POUR.DOWN(V) (/ *y.ts.q / y.s.q)* To send a liquid from a container into another container or onto a person or object; to pour molten metal into a cast. *AHLB:* 1410-L(V) *Strong's:* #3251, #3332

POUR.OUT(V) (*sh.p.k)* To let flow a liquid, often the blood of an animal in sacrifice or a man. *AHLB:* 2865(V) *Strong's:* #8210

POURED.OUT (masc. *na'siyk)* A liquid poured out as an offering. *AHLB:* 2412(b) *Strong's:* #5257

POURING (masc. *ne'sak)* A liquid poured out as an offering or the pouring of a molten metal to form images. *AHLB:* 2412(N) *Strong's:* #5262

POVERTY (fem. *mis'key'nut)* Those who rely on benefits from others. *AHLB:* 2478(h3) *Strong's:* #4544

POWDERY (masc. *eph'ron) Strong's:* [Found in names only]

POWER (masc. אלוה *e'lo'ah)* Possession of control, authority, or influence over others; physical might. The power or might of one who rules or teaches. One who yokes with another. Often applies to rulers or a god. Often used in the plural form literally meaning "mighty ones," but often used in a singular sense to mean "The Mighty One.". *AHLB:* 1012-H(c) *Strong's:* #0430, #0433

PRECIOUS (masc. מגד *me'ged)* What is choice or excellent. *AHLB:* 2329^(N)^ *Strong's:* #4022

PRECIOUS.METAL (masc. בצר *be'tser)* Valuables that are stored away and protected. *AHLB:* 2033^(N)^ *Strong's:* #1220, #1222

PRECIPITATE^(V)^ (מטר *m.t.r)* To rain or snow. *AHLB:* 2336^(V)^ *Strong's:* #4305

PRECIPITATION (masc. מטר *ma'tar)* A rain, snow or exceptionally heavy dew. *AHLB:* 2336^(N)^ *Strong's:* #4306

PREDICT^(V)^ (נחש *n.hh.sh)* To foretell what is to come. *AHLB:* 2395^(V)^ *Strong's:* #5172

PREDICTION (masc. נחש *ne'hhash)* A foretelling of what is to come. *AHLB:* 2395^(N)^ *Strong's:* #5173

PREDICTOR (masc. נחשון *nahh'shun)* One who is able to foretell what is to come. *Strong's:* [Found in names only]

PREGNANCY (masc. הריון / הרון *hey'ron / hey'ra'yon)* The quality of containing unborn young within the body. From the mound of the belly. *AHLB:* 1112-H(j) *Strong's:* #2032

PREGNANT (fem. הרי / הרה *ha'reh / ha'riy)* Containing unborn young within the body. *AHLB:* 1112-H(N1) *Strong's:* #2030

PREPARE^(V)^ (כון *k.w.n)* To put in proper condition or readiness. *Alternate Translation:* be ready (when written in the niphil [passive] form); establish (when written in the piel [active intensive] form) *AHLB:* 1244-J^(V)^ *Strong's:* #3559

PREPARED (masc. עתיד *a'tiyd) AHLB:* 2587(b) *Strong's:* #6264

PRESENT (fem. ברכה *be'ra'khah)* A gift given to another in respect as if on bended knee. Also, a pool of water as a place where one kneels down to drink from. *Alternate Translation:* pool (from the idea of kneeling down to drink from it) *AHLB:* 2039(N1) *Strong's:* #1293, #1295

PRESERVE^(V)^ (נצר *n.ts.r)* To watch over or guard for protection. *AHLB:* 2429^(V)^ *Strong's:* #5341

PRESS^(V)^ (שחט *s.hh.t)* Pressure or pushing action. *AHLB:* 2470^(V)^ *Strong's:* #7818

PRESS.FIRMLY^(V)^ (מעך *m.ah.k) AHLB:* 2348^(V)^ *Strong's:* #4600

PRESS.HARD^(V)^ (פצר *p.ts.r)* To push or urge another into an action. *AHLB:* 2629^(V)^ *Strong's:* #6484

PRESS.IN^(V)^ (צרר *ts.r.r)* To confine or restrict in a tight place. *AHLB:* 1411-B^(V)^ *Strong's:* #6887

PRESS.OUT.OIL^(V)^ (צהר *ts.h.r)* Extracting the fluids from the olive. *AHLB:* 1411-G^(V)^ *Strong's:* #6671

PRESUME^(V)^ (עפל *ah.p.l)* To lift up an idea. *AHLB:* 2564^(V)^ *Strong's:* #6075

PREY (masc. טרף *te'reph)* An animal taken as food by a predator. The meat that is torn by the predator. *AHLB:* 2245^(N)^ *Strong's:* #2964, #2965

PRICE (masc. מחיר *m'hhiyr)* The payment for an item. *AHLB:* 2337(b) *Strong's:* #4242

PRICKLY.THORN (masc. צנין / צנן *tsa'niyn)* A sharp thorn that causes pain. *AHLB:* 1336-B(b) *Strong's:* #6796

PRIDE (fem. *ga'a'wah)* A lifting up of one's status in a positive or negative sense. *AHLB:* 1047-K(N1) *Strong's:* #1346

PRIME (fem. *rey'shit)* The first or beginning; the best or most important; the source. *AHLB:* 1458-D(N4) *Strong's:* #7225

PRISON (masc. *so'har)* A place of confinement. *AHLB:* 1342-G[N] *Strong's:* #5470

PRISONER (masc. *a'sir)* One who is bound or confined. *AHLB:* 1342-C(b) *Strong's:* #0615, #0616

PRODUCE (masc. *pe'ri)* Agricultural products, especially fresh fruits and vegetables. The harvested product of a crop. *AHLB:* 1388-H(f) *Strong's:* #6529

PRODUCT (masc. *ye'vul)* The produce of fruits and crops that flourish in fields frequently flooded. *AHLB:* 1035-L(d) *Strong's:* #2981

PRODUCTION (fem. *te'vu'ah)* Total output of a commodity or an industry. An increase of produce, usually of fruit. *AHLB:* 1024-J(i1) *Strong's:* #8393

PROFIT (masc. *be'tsa)* A valuable return; to derive benefit. The taking of money or something of value through force. *AHLB:* 2031[N] *Strong's:* #1215

PROJECTILE (masc. *she'lahh)* A weapon that is sent by the hand. Also, a plant shoot as sent out of the ground. *AHLB:* 2842[N] *Strong's:* #7973

PROLONG[V] (*a.r.k)* To lengthen or delay. *AHLB:* 1448-C[V] *Strong's:* #0748

PROPERTY (fem. *y'rey'shah)* *AHLB:* 1458-L(N1) *Strong's:* #3424

PROPORTION (fem. *miy'sah)* An offering. *AHLB:* 1291-A(N1) *Strong's:* #4530

PROSPER[V] (*ts.l.hh)* To succeed; to move forward in distance, position or in thriving. *AHLB:* 2662[V] *Strong's:* #6743

PROSTITUTE (masc. *qa'deysh fem. qe'dey'shah)* One who exchanges sexual intercourse for payment. *AHLB:* 2700[N], 2700(N1) *Strong's:* #6945, #6948

PROSTITUTION (masc. *za'nun)* The act or practice of engaging in sexual intercourse for profit. *AHLB:* 1152-B(d) *Strong's:* #2183

PROTECTION (masc. *si'tar)* Shielded from harm or destruction. *Strong's:* [Found in names only]

PROTECTIVE (masc. *hha'nun)* Providing a rescue or help to another in distress. *AHLB:* 1175-B(d) *Strong's:* #2587

PROVENDER (masc. *mis'po)* Dry food for domestic animals. A gathering of food. *AHLB:* 1339-E(hc) *Strong's:* #4554

PROVIDE[V] (*y.h.b)* To give what is due; to grant or allow permission. *Alternate Translation:* bring; come *AHLB:* 1094-L[V] *Strong's:* #3051

PROVIDE.FOOD[V] (*l.ah.t)* Supply nourishment. *AHLB:* 2315[V] *Strong's:* #3938

PROVIDE.PROTECTION[V] (*hh.n.n)* To rescue or give help to another, to treat as valuable. *Alternate Translation:* beseech (when written in the hitpa'el [reflexive] form) *AHLB:* 1175-B[V] *Strong's:* #2589, #2603

PROVISIONS (fem. *tsi'dah)* A stock of needed materials. The produce of the hunt. Also, used for "food" in general. *AHLB:* 1395-M(N1) *Strong's:* #6720

PROVOKE[V] (*n.a.ts)* *AHLB:* 1317-D[V] *Strong's:* #5006

PULL.OUT[V] (*sh.l.p)* To pull out, up or off. *AHLB:* 2846[V] *Strong's:* #8025

PULLED.OUT (masc. *sha'laph)* *Strong's:* [Found in names only]

PULVERIZE[V] (*sh.hh.q)* To continually beat something to make it small or turn to powder. *AHLB:* 2828[V] *Strong's:* #7833

PUNISHMENT (fem. *bi'qo'ret) AHLB:* 2633(N1) *Strong's:* #1244

PURCHASE[V] (*q.n.h)* To acquire ownership or occupation through an exchange. *AHLB:* 1428-H[V] *Strong's:* #7069

PURCHASED (masc. *qe'nat) Strong's:* [Found in names only]

PURE.GOLD (masc. *paz) AHLB:* 1375-A[N] *Strong's:* #6337

PURPLE (masc. *ar'ga'man)* A reddish-blue color used to dye yarn and used in weaving. *AHLB:* 1440-C(pm) *Strong's:* #0713

PURSUE[V] (*r.d.p)* To follow in order to overtake, capture, kill, or defeat; to pursue in chase or persecution. *AHLB:* 2755[V] *Strong's:* #7291

PUSH[V] (*n.g.sh)* To drive oxen or men. *AHLB:* 2375[V] *Strong's:* #5065

PUSH.AWAY[V] (*h.d.p)* To drive or force out or away; discharge or eject. *AHLB:* 1086-F[V] *Strong's:* #1920

PUSTULE (fem. *a'va'bu'ah)* A swelling irritation that festers on the skin. An inflammatory pustule as an eruption. *AHLB:* 1039-C(ld1) *Strong's:* #0076

QESHIYTAH (fem. *qe'shiy'tah)* A unit of value, money. *AHLB:* 2739(b1) *Strong's:* #7192

QUAIL (fem. / *se'law)* A small bird used as a food. *AHLB:* 1334-K[N] *Strong's:* #7958

QUANTITY (fem. *m'su'rah)* A large amount. *AHLB:* 1342-J(k1) *Strong's:* #4884

QUARREL (masc. *mid'yan)* A rather loud verbal disagreement. *AHLB:* 1083-A(hb) *Strong's:* #4079

QUARTER (masc. *re'va)* One portion from the whole that has been divided into four equal parts. One side of a four-sided square. A fourth. *AHLB:* 2744[N] *Strong's:* #7252, #7253

QUARTZ (masc. *hhal'la'miysh)* An unknown stone. *AHLB:* 3015 *Strong's:* #2496

QUEEN (fem. *mal'kah)* A female ruler of a region. *AHLB:* 2340(N1) *Strong's:* #4436

QUENCH[V] (*k.b.h) AHLB:* 1232-H[V] *Strong's:* #3518

QUICKLY (masc. *ma'heyr fem. me'hey'rah)* To act on a matter as soon as possible. *AHLB:* 1296-G[N] *Strong's:* #4118, #4120

QUIETNESS (fem. *na'hhat)* Without noise, without making a sound. *AHLB:* 1307-A(N2) *Strong's:* #5183

QUIVER (masc. *te'li)* A case for holding or carrying arrows. As hung over the shoulder. *AHLB:* 1495-A(f) *Strong's:* #8522

RABBIT (masc. *sha'phan)* An unclean animal of unknown species, probably the rabbit. *AHLB:* 2867[N] *Strong's:* #8227

RAFTER (fem. *qo'rah)* The beams which the roof of the house sits on. *AHLB:* 1434-J(N1) *Strong's:* #6982

RAIMENT (fem. *ke'sut)* Clothing; garments. *AHLB:* 1245-A(N3) *Strong's:* #3682

RAIN.SHOWER (masc. *ge'shem)* The rain of the skies. *AHLB:* 2090[N] *Strong's:* #1653, #1730

RAINDROP (masc. *s'iyr)* As the hair from heaven. *AHLB:* 2494(b) *Strong's:* #8164

RAISE.UP[V] (*r.w.m)* To lift something up. *Alternate Translation:* Tall (when written in the participle form) *AHLB:* 1450-J[V] *Strong's:* #7311

RAISED (masc. *ram)* Lifted up in position or in exaltation. *Strong's:* [Found in names only]

RAM (masc. / *seh)* A young male member of a flock of sheep or goats. *AHLB:* 1327-A(N) *Strong's:* #2089, #7716

RAM.HORN (masc. *sho'phar)* The horn of ram made into a trumpet that emits a bright and beautiful sound. *AHLB:* 2869(g) *Strong's:* #7782

RAMPART (fem. *hho'mah)* A fortified enclosure. *AHLB:* 1174-J(N1) *Strong's:* #2346

RANK (fem. *ma'a'ra'khah)* A row, line, or series of things or persons. *AHLB:* 2576(a1) *Strong's:* #4634

RANSOM (fem. *pe'dut)* The act of requiring, or paying, a price for something that was stolen or wrongfully taken. *AHLB:* 1372-A(N3) *Strong's:* #6304

RANSOM(V) (*p.d.h)* To Pay the price stipulated, to retrieve what has been stolen or wrongfully taken. *AHLB:* 1372-H(V) *Strong's:* #6299

RANSOM.PRICE (masc. / *pid'yon / pid'yom)* A stipulated amount given to retrieve what has been stolen or wrongfully taken. *AHLB:* 1372-A(fj) *Strong's:* #6306

RANSOMED (masc. *pe'dah) Strong's:* [Found in names only]

RAPID (masc. *hhiyd'qeyl) Strong's:* [Found in names only]

RASH (masc. *bo'haq)* A harmless eruption of the skin. *AHLB:* 1042-G(N) *Strong's:* #0933

RATTLE (masc. *ney'a) Strong's:* [Found in names only]

RAVE(V) (*sh.g.ah) AHLB:* 2815(V) *Strong's:* #7696

RAVEN (masc. *o'reyv)* A glossy black bird. As black in color. *AHLB:* 2907(g) *Strong's:* #6158

RAVINE (fem. *eysh'dat) AHLB:* 1464-C(N1) *Strong's:* #0794

RAW (masc. *na)* Uncooked meat. Meat that is not fit for consumption. *AHLB:* 1300-A(N) *Strong's:* #4995

RAZOR (*ta-ar) AHLB:* 1365-A(i) *Strong's:* #8593

REACH(V) (*p.g.ah)* To touch or grasp; to get up to or as far as; to come together in meeting by chance; to give or place in the sense of a meeting. *AHLB:* 2592(V) *Strong's:* #6293

READY (masc. *i'tiy)* One whose time has come. *AHLB:* 1367-A(f) *Strong's:* #6261

REASON (masc. *hhesh'bon) AHLB:* 2213(j) *Strong's:* #2808

REBEL(V) (*m.r.d)* To oppose or disobey one in authority or control. *AHLB:* 2352(V) *Strong's:* #4775

REBELLING (masc. *nim'rod) Strong's:* [Found in names only]

REBELLIOUS (masc. *m'riy) AHLB:* 1296-A(f) *Strong's:* #4805

REBUKE(V) (*y.k.hh)* To express disapproval; reprove; reprimand. *AHLB:* 1238-L(V) *Strong's:* #3198

RECEIVE(V) (*q.b.l)* To take or accept what has been given. *AHLB:* 2693(V) *Strong's:* #6901

RECKLESS (masc. *pa'hhaz)* Marked by lack of proper caution. *AHLB:* 2599(N) *Strong's:* #6349

RECKON(V) (*m.n.h)* To appoint, assign, count or number a set of things or people. *AHLB:* 1290-H(V) *Strong's:* #4487

RECOGNIZE$^{(V)}$ (*n.k.r)* To acknowledge or take notice of in some definite way. *Alternate Translation:* make self unrecognizable (when written in the hitpa'el [reflexive] form); pay attention (when written in the hiphil [causative] form); *AHLB:* 2406$^{(V)}$ *Strong's:* #5234

RECOMPENSE (masc. *shiy'leym) AHLB:* 2845(e) *Strong's:* #8005

RECORD (masc. *sa'heyd) AHLB:* 1326-G$^{(N)}$ *Strong's:* #7717

RED (masc. *a'dom fem. a'du'mah)* Of the color red. Ruddy; florid. *AHLB:* 1082-C(c) *Strong's:* #0122

REDDISH (masc. *a'dam'dam fem. a'dam'da'met)* Somewhat red; tending to red; tinged with red. *AHLB:* 1082-C(l) *Strong's:* #0125

REDDISH.GRAY (masc. *tso'hhar)* A dark grayish ruddy color. *Strong's:* [Found in names only]

REDEEM$^{(V)}$ (*g.a.l)* To buy back. Restore one to his original position or avenge his death. In the participle form this verb means "avenger," as it is the role of the nearest relative to buy back one in slavery or avenge his murder. *AHLB:* 1058-D$^{(V)}$ *Strong's:* #1350

REDEEMED (masc. *pa'du'iy) AHLB:* 1372-N(d) *Strong's:* #6302

REDEMPTION (fem. *ge'u'lah)* An act of redeeming or atoning for a fault or mistake, or the state of being redeemed. *AHLB:* 1058-D(d1) *Strong's:* #1353

REDUCED.TO.ASHES (masc. *a'phar) Strong's:* [Found in names only]

REED.PIPE (masc. *u'gav)* A wind instrument made of reeds. *AHLB:* 2523(o) *Strong's:* #5748

REED-BASKET (masc. *te'ne) AHLB:* 1198-E$^{(N)}$ *Strong's:* #2935

REEDS (masc. *suph)* The plants that grow at the edge, or lip, of a river or pond. This word can also mean the edge or conclusion of something. *AHLB:* 1339-J$^{(N)}$ *Strong's:* #5488, #5490

REFINE$^{(V)}$ (*p.z.z)* To reduce to a pure state. *AHLB:* 1375-B$^{(V)}$ *Strong's:* #6338, #6339

REFINED (masc. *zak)* An oil or other substance that is free of impurities. Also, a person without impurities. *AHLB:* 1149-A$^{(N)}$ *Strong's:* #2134

REFLECTION (fem. *mar'ah)* The return of light or sound waves from a surface; production of an image as by a mirror. *AHLB:* 1438-A(a1) *Strong's:* #4759

REFUGE (masc. *miq'lat)* A place one may run to for safety from an avenger. *AHLB:* 2707(h) *Strong's:* #4733

REFUSE$^{(V)}$ (*m.a.n)* To express one's self as being unwilling to accept. *AHLB:* 1290-D$^{(V)}$ *Strong's:* #3985

REFUSING (masc. *ma'eyn)* Rejection of a proposal, denial. *AHLB:* 1290-D$^{(N)}$ *Strong's:* #3986, #3987

REGION (masc. *hhe'vel)* An area surrounded by a specific border. *AHLB:* 2141$^{(N)}$ *Strong's:* #2256

REGISTER$^{(V)}$ (*p.q.d)* To indicate or show acknowledgement of someone or something; to document or count another. *Alternate Translation:* set over (when written in the hiphil [active causative] form) *AHLB:* 2630$^{(V)}$ *Strong's:* #6485, #6486

REGULATE$^{(V)}$ (*m.sh.l)* To govern or correct according to rule; to bring order, method, or uniformity to; to compare one thing to another in the sense of a rule of measurement, often as a proverb or parable. *AHLB:* 2359(V) *Strong's:* #4910, #4911

REGULATION (fem. *mem'sha'lah)* An authoritative rule dealing with details or procedure. The power and authority of one to regulate and control over another. *AHLB:* 2359(k1) *Strong's:* #4475

REIGN(V) (*m.l.k)* To rule over a kingdom as king or queen. *AHLB:* 2340(V) *Strong's:* #4427

REJECT(V) (*m.a.s)* To refuse an action or thought that is not wanted or is despised. *AHLB:* 1291-D(V) *Strong's:* #3988

REJOICE(V) (*s.m.hh)* To be happy, glad. *AHLB:* 2487(V) *Strong's:* #8055

REJOICING (masc. *sa'mey'ahh fem.* *sim'hhah)* A state of felicity or happiness. *AHLB:* 2487(N) *Strong's:* #8056, #8057

RELEASE (fem. *she'mit'tah)* As shaken off. *AHLB:* 2849(N1) *Strong's:* #8059

RELEASE(V) (*sh.m.t)* To let go by dropping or shaking loose. *AHLB:* 2849(V) *Strong's:* #8058

RELIEF (fem. *ye'shu'ah)* A deliverance or freedom from a trouble, burden or danger. *AHLB:* 1476-L(d1) *Strong's:* #3444

REMAIN(V) (*sh.a.r)* To continue unchanged; to stay behind. *Alternate Translation:* leave (when written in the hiphil [active causative] form) *AHLB:* 1480-D(V) *Strong's:* #7604

REMAINDER (masc. *ye'ter)* A group, individual or item that is left behind or set apart. *AHLB:* 1480-L(N) *Strong's:* #3499

REMAINS (masc. *she'ar)* What is left behind, a residue. A relative as a remnant. Flesh as what remains after death. *AHLB:* 1480-D(N) *Strong's:* #7605, #7607

REMEMBER(V) (*z.k.r)* To recall an event or action in memorial or reflection. To speak on behalf of another. To reenact a past event as a memorial. *Alternate Translation:* mention (when written in the hiphil [active causative] form) *AHLB:* 2121(V) *Strong's:* #2142

REMEMBRANCE (masc. *zikh'ron)* A recalling of a past event. Also, an action based on a past event. *AHLB:* 2121(ej) *Strong's:* #2146

REMNANT (fem. *she'ey'rit)* A usually small part, member, or trace remaining. *AHLB:* 1480-D(N4) *Strong's:* #7611

REMOVAL (fem. *niy'dah)* Something that is taken away or thrown out. A menstruating woman that is removed from the camp. *AHLB:* 1303-M(N1) *Strong's:* #5079, #5206

REMOVE.THE.COVER(V) (*g.l.h)* To reveal something by exposing it. Usually from the removal of clothing. *Alternate Translation:* uncover (when written in the niphil [passive] or hiphil [active causative] form) *AHLB:* 1357-H(V) *Strong's:* #1540

REMOVED (masc. *tsu'an)* *Strong's:* [Found in names only]

REPLACEMENT (fem. *hha'li'phah)* That which takes the place of, especially as a substitute or successor. *AHLB:* 2165(b1) *Strong's:* #2487

REPORT (masc. *shey'ma)* An account or statement of an event or happening. What is heard. *AHLB:* 2851(N) *Strong's:* #8088

REPOSE(V) (*r.g.ah)* To stir as in stirring the waters or to stir from sleep. *AHLB:* 2752(V) *Strong's:* #7280

REPRODUCE(V) (פרה *p.r.h)* To produce new individuals of the same kind; to be abundant in fruit. *AHLB:* 1388-H(V) *Strong's:* #6509

REPROVE (fem. מגערת *mig'e'ret)* A communication directed toward a disorderly person to effect a return to their rightful place of order. *AHLB:* 2076(h2) *Strong's:* #4045

REPROVE(V) (גער *g.ah.r)* To communicate toward a disorderly person to effect a return to their rightful place of order. *AHLB:* 2076(V) *Strong's:* #1605

REQUEST (fem. שאלה *sh'ey'lah)* A seeking for what is not known. *AHLB:* 1472-D(N1) *Strong's:* #7596

RESCUE(V) (ישע *y.sh.ah)* To free or deliver from a trouble, burden or danger. *AHLB:* 1476-L(V) *Strong's:* #3467

RESEMBLANCE (fem. תמונה *te'mu'nah)* To be of like kind. Having attributes that are similar in shape, size or value. *AHLB:* 1290-J(i1) *Strong's:* #8544

RESEMBLE(V) (דמה *d.m.h)* To be like, similar or compared to something else. To become silent as one dead. *AHLB:* 1082-H(V) *Strong's:* #1819, #1820

RESERVER (masc. יתרן *yit'ran) Strong's:* [Found in names only]

RESIDE(V) (זבל *z.b.l)* To dwell permanently or continuously. *AHLB:* 2118(V) *Strong's:* #2082

RESIDENT (masc. זבולן *ze'vu'lan)* One who abides or dwells in a place or area. *Strong's:* [Found in names only]

RESPITE (fem. רוחה *re'wa'hhah)* A relief from labor, punishment or trouble. *AHLB:* 1445-J(N1) *Strong's:* #7309

REST (masc. נוח *no'ahh) AHLB:* 1307-J(N) *Strong's:* #5118

REST(V) (נוח *n.w.hh)* Freedom from activity or labor. To rest from trouble or labor. *Alternate Translation:* leave (when written in the hiphil [active causative] form) *AHLB:* 1307-J(V) *Strong's:* #5117

REST.PERIOD (masc. שבתון *sha'ba'ton)* A day when work and normal activities are halted. *AHLB:* 2812(j) *Strong's:* #7677

RESTRAIN(V) (עקב *ah.q.b)* To prevent from doing. Hold back, in the sense of grabbing the heel. *AHLB:* 2571(V) *Strong's:* #6117

RESTRICT(V) (כלא *k.l.a)* To confine within bounds. Hold back or prevent someone or something. *AHLB:* 1242-E(V) *Strong's:* #3607

REVIVING (fem. מחיה *mihh'yah)* Restoring to consciousness or life. *AHLB:* 1171-H(h1) *Strong's:* #4241

RHINOCEROS (masc. ראם *re'eym)* A large land animal where some species have one horn (Latin: unicornis) *AHLB:* 1450-D(N) *Strong's:* #7214

RIB (fem. צלע / צלה *tsa'la / tsey'la)* Any of the paired bony or cartilaginous bones that stiffen the walls of the thorax and protect the organs beneath. A ridge of a hill from its similar shape to a rib. Also, the side. *AHLB:* 2664(N) *Strong's:* #6763

RICH (masc. עשיר *a'shir)* Having wealth or great possessions; abundantly supplied with resources, means, or funds. *AHLB:* 2585(b) *Strong's:* #6223

RICHES (masc. עושר *o'ser)* Wealth. The possessions that make one wealthy. *AHLB:* 2585(N) *Strong's:* #6239

RIDDLE (fem. חידה *hhiy'dah)* A question or statement so framed as to exercise one's ingenuity in answering it or discovering its meaning. *AHLB:* 1165-M(N1) *Strong's:* #2420

RIDE(V) (*r.k.b)* To sit and travel in any conveyance; to sit astride an animal, wagon or chariot. *AHLB:* 2769(V) *Strong's:* #7392

RIGHT (masc. *ye'ma'ni)* A direction as in to the right. *AHLB:* 1290-L(f) *Strong's:* #3233

RIGHT.HAND (fem. *ya'min)* The hand on the right side of a person. Also, a direction as in "to the right.". *AHLB:* 1290-L(b) *Strong's:* #3225

RIM (fem. *mis'ge'ret)* The edge of a region or hole. *AHLB:* 2467(h2) *Strong's:* #4526

RING (fem. *ta'ba'at)* A circular band of metal or other durable material. Also, the signet ring containing the mark of the owner that is sunk into a lump of clay as a seal. *AHLB:* 2229(N2) *Strong's:* #2885

RIP(V) (*p.r.m) AHLB:* 2639(V) *Strong's:* #6533

RIPE.FRUIT (fem. *me'ley'ah)* Fruit that has come to full maturity and fit for eating. *AHLB:* 1288-E(N1) *Strong's:* #4395

RIPEN(V) (*hh.n.t)* To bring to completeness or perfection. Give off the fragrance of the fruit as it ripens. To add spices to a body for embalming. *AHLB:* 2177(V) *Strong's:* #2590

RISE(V) (*q.w.m)* To assume an upright position; to raise or rise up; to continue or establish. *AHLB:* 1427-J(V) *Strong's:* #6965

RISE.UP(V) (*g.a.h)* To lift or grow up high. *AHLB:* 1051-D(V) *Strong's:* #1342

RISING.SUN (masc. *ze'rahh)* The early morning appearence of the sun. *AHLB:* 2135(N) *Strong's:* #2225

RIVER (masc. *na'har)* A natural stream of water of considerable volume. The life-giving water that washes over the soil. *AHLB:* 1319-G(N) *Strong's:* #5104

ROAD (masc. *de'rek)* A route or path for traveled or walked. The path or manner of life. *AHLB:* 2112(N) *Strong's:* #1870

ROAM(V) (*r.w.d)* To wander around restlessly. *AHLB:* 1441-J(V) *Strong's:* #7300

ROAMING (masc. *ra'dah) Strong's:* [Found in names only]

ROAR(V) (*h.w.m)* To make a loud noise. *AHLB:* 1105-J(V) *Strong's:* #1949

ROARING (masc. *ha'mon)* The act of a person, animal, or thing that roars. *Strong's:* [Found in names only]

ROAST (masc. *tsa'li)* A meat that is cooked over a fire. *AHLB:* 1403-H(f) *Strong's:* #6748

ROASTED.GRAIN (masc. / *qa'liy)* Green Grains, which are full of starches and protein, are picked and roasted and can be stored for long periods. *AHLB:* 1426-A(f) *Strong's:* #7039

ROBE (masc. *e'der fem. a'de'ret)* A long flowing outer garment. Wide garment. *AHLB:* 1089-C(N2) *Strong's:* #0155

ROCK.WALL (masc. *shur)* A wall made of rocks or stones for protection. *AHLB:* 1480-J(N) *Strong's:* #7790, #7791

ROD (masc. *ma'qeyl fem. maq'lah)* A long and slender bar of wood. A staff for walking. *AHLB:* 1426-A(a) *Strong's:* #4731

ROEBUCK (masc. *yahh'mur)* An unknown animal, probably of a dark color. *AHLB:* 2175(tc) *Strong's:* #3180

ROLL(V) (*g.l.l)* To move along a surface by revolving or turning over and over, as a ball or a wheel. *Alternate Translation:* glean (when written in the piel [active intensive] form) *AHLB:* 1058-B(V) *Strong's:* #1556

ROLLING.THING (masc. *gal'gal)* The wheel of a cart or a whirlwind. *AHLB:* 1058-A(l) *Strong's:* #1534, #1536

ROOF (masc. *gag)* The covering of a dwelling place. *AHLB:* 1049-A$^{(N)}$ *Strong's:* #1406

ROOF.COVERING (masc. *mikh'seh)* Material used for a top or covering of a building. What covers something. *AHLB:* 1245-H(h) *Strong's:* #4372

ROOFING (masc. *ma'gog)* The act of covering with a roof. *Strong's:* [Found in names only]

ROOT (masc. *sho'resh)* The underground part of a plant. The source or origin of a thing. *AHLB:* 2883(g) *Strong's:* #8328

ROOT.OUT$^{(V)}$ (*n.t.sh) AHLB:* 2456$^{(V)}$ *Strong's:* #5428

ROT$^{(V)}$ (*m.q.q)* To deteriorate, disintegrate, fall, or become weak due to decay. *AHLB:* 1295-B$^{(V)}$ *Strong's:* #4743

ROUND.STONE (masc. *ey'val)* A circular smooth rock. *Strong's:* [Found in names only]

ROUNDED (masc. *u'val)* Of a circular shape. *Strong's:* [Found in names only]

ROUNDNESS (fem. *ki'kar)* A round thing or place. A round loaf of bread. An expanse as a round piece of land. *AHLB:* 2258(e) *Strong's:* #3603(x2)

ROW (masc. *tur)* Set or placed in a line. A mountain range as a row. *AHLB:* 1204-J$^{(N)}$ *Strong's:* #2905

ROW$^{(V)}$ (*t.w.r) Strong's:* [Found in names only]

ROW.OF.TENTS (fem. *ti'rah)* A settlement usually larger than a hamlet and smaller than a town. *AHLB:* 1204-M(N1) *Strong's:* #2918

RUDDY (masc. *ad'mo'niy)* Having a healthy reddish color. *AHLB:* 1082-C(jf) *Strong's:* #0132

RUIN (masc. *tel)* A city that is covered over with dirt or sand forming a large mound. *AHLB:* 1196-A$^{(N)}$ *Strong's:* #8510

RUINED.HEAP (masc. *ey) Strong's:* [Found in names only]

RULE$^{(V)}$ (*r.d.h)* To exert control, direction, or influence over, especially by curbing or restraining; to spread out through a land through authority or by walking among the subjects. *AHLB:* 1441-H$^{(V)}$ *Strong's:* #7287

RULER (masc. *na'giyd)* One who rules or is in charge of others through instructions. *AHLB:* 2372(b) *Strong's:* #5057

RUMP (fem. *al'yah)* The fat part of the hind part of a sheep that is considered an Eastern delicacy. *AHLB:* 1012-A(b1) *Strong's:* #0451

RUN$^{(V)}$ (*r.w.ts)* To go faster than a walk. *Alternate Translation:* quickly bring (when written in the hiphil [active causative] form) *AHLB:* 1455-J$^{(V)}$ *Strong's:* #7323

SACK (masc. *saq)* A bag of cloth or skins for carrying foods or objects. *AHLB:* 1341-A$^{(N)}$ *Strong's:* #8242

SACRIFICE (masc. *ze'vahh)* An animal killed for an offering. *AHLB:* 2117$^{(N)}$ *Strong's:* #2077

SACRIFICE$^{(V)}$ (*z.b.hh)* An act of offering to deity something precious; to kill an animal for an offering. *AHLB:* 2117$^{(V)}$ *Strong's:* #2076

SACRIFICIAL.BOWL (fem. *me'na'qit)* A vessel used to hold the required sacrifice. From the shape of a bowl that holds liquids like a breast that holds milk. *AHLB:* 1318-A(k4) *Strong's:* #4518

SADDLE (masc. *mer'kav) AHLB:* 2769(k) *Strong's:* #4817

SADDLE(V) (*hh.b.sh)* A shaped mounted support on which an object can travel; to bind up with a saddle. *AHLB:* 2144(V) *Strong's:* #2280

SADDLEBAG (masc. *mish'pat)* One of a pair of covered pouches laid behind the saddle. For carrying items. *AHLB:* 2870(h) *Strong's:* #4942

SAFEGUARD(V) (*sh.m.r)* The act or the duty of protecting or defending; to watch over or guard. To keep watch. *Alternate Translation:* guardian (when written in the participle form) *AHLB:* 2853(V) *Strong's:* #8104, #8109

SAFEGUARDING (masc. *shi'mur)* To keep safe. To protect. *AHLB:* 2853(d) *Strong's:* #8107

SAFELY (masc. *be'tahh)* A state or place of safety. *Alternate Translation:* safety *AHLB:* 2013(N) *Strong's:* #0983

SALT (masc. *me'lahh)* An ingredient that adds flavor to food and used in preserving foods. *AHLB:* 2338(N) *Strong's:* #4417, #4419

SANCTUARY (masc. *miq'dash)* A place set apart for a special purpose. *AHLB:* 2700(h) *Strong's:* #4720

SAND (masc. *hhul)* Loose granular material from the disintegration of rocks and consisting of particles not as fine as silt and used in mortar. Sand is used as an abrasive ingredient for drilling by placing it in the hole being drilled. *AHLB:* 1173-J(N) *Strong's:* #2344

SANDAL (masc. *na'al fem. na'a'lah)* A shoe consisting of a sole strapped to the foot. *AHLB:* 2415(N) *Strong's:* #5275

SASH (masc. *av'neyt)* A waistband worn around the waist. *AHLB:* 2022(N) *Strong's:* #0073

SATISFACTION (masc. *so'va)* The state of being content. *AHLB:* 2461(g) *Strong's:* #7648

SAY(V) (*a.m.r)* To speak chains of words that form sentences. *AHLB:* 1288-C(V) *Strong's:* #0559

SAYER (masc. *e'mor)* One who speaks words. Possibly a prophet or psalmist. *Strong's:* [Found in names only]

SCAB (fem. / *mis'pa'hhat)* A sore that spreads. *AHLB:* 2496(N2) *Strong's:* #4556, #5597

SCALES (fem. *qash'qe'shet)* The covering of a fish. Also, the scales of leather armor. *AHLB:* 1245-A(l2) *Strong's:* #7193

SCARLET (masc. *sha'ni)* Any of various bright reds. *AHLB:* 1474-A(f) *Strong's:* #8144

SCATTER(V) (*n.p.ts)* To fling away heedlessly. To separate and go in various directions. *AHLB:* 2422(V) *Strong's:* #5310

SCATTER.ABROAD(V) (*p.w.ts)* To sow, cast or fling widely. *AHLB:* 1386-J(V) *Strong's:* #6327

SCATTERED (masc. *piy'shon) Strong's:* [Found in names only]

SCORCHING (masc. *sa'gan)* Being parched or shriveled from heat or fire. *Strong's:* [Found in names only]

SCORPION (masc. *aq'rav) AHLB:* 3046 *Strong's:* #6137

SCOUR(V) (*m.r.q)* To briskly rub something. *AHLB:* 2356(V) *Strong's:* #4838

SCOUT(V) (*t.w.r)* To travel an area from border to border. *AHLB:* 1503-J(V) *Strong's:* #7788, #8446

SCRAPE.OFF$^{(V)}$ (*q.ts.h)* To cut something out or make short. *AHLB:* 1432-H$^{(V)}$ *Strong's:* #7096

SCRAPED.BARE (masc. *she'pham) Strong's:* [Found in names only]

SCRATCH$^{(V)}$ (*hh.r.sh)* To plow in the sense of scratching a line in the soil; to engrave on wood or stone by scratching. This word can also mean "to hold in peace" or be silent. *AHLB:* 2211$^{(V)}$ *Strong's:* #2790(x2)

SCRAWNY (masc. *daq fem. da'qah)* Wasted away physically. *AHLB:* 1088-A$^{(N)}$ *Strong's:* #1851

SCREAMING (masc. *pa'u) Strong's:* [Found in names only]

SCROLL (masc. *se'pher fem. siph'rah)* A document or record written on a sheet of papyrus, leather or parchment and rolled up for storage. *AHLB:* 2500$^{(N)}$ *Strong's:* #5612

SCULPT$^{(V)}$ (*p.s.l)* To carve or chisel out a figure from wood or stone. *AHLB:* 2619$^{(V)}$ *Strong's:* #6458

SCULPTURE (masc. / *pe'sel / pa'siyl)* A figurine that is formed and shaped from stone, wood or clay. *AHLB:* 2619$^{(N)}$ *Strong's:* #6456, #6459

SEA (masc. *yam)* A large body of water. Also, the direction of the great sea (the Mediterranean), the west. *Alternate Translation:* west (as the Mediterranean Sea is west of Israel) *AHLB:* 1220-A$^{(N)}$ *Strong's:* #3220

SEAGULL (masc. *sha'hhaph)* An unknown bird. *AHLB:* 2826$^{(N)}$ *Strong's:* #7828

SE'AH (fem. *se'ah)* A dry standard of measure equal to 1/3 ephah. *AHLB:* 1323-A(N1) *Strong's:* #5429

SEAL (masc. *hho'tam)* A seal used officially to give personal authority to a document. A signature ring or cylinder with the owner's seal that is pressed into clay to show ownership. *AHLB:* 2223(g) *Strong's:* #2368

SEAL$^{(V)}$ (*hh.t.m)* To close tightly, often marked with the emblem of the owner that must be broken before opening. *AHLB:* 2223$^{(V)}$ *Strong's:* #2856

SEARCH$^{(V)}$ (*hh.p.s)* To look thoroughly in an effort to find or discover something. *AHLB:* 2189$^{(V)}$ *Strong's:* #2664

SEARCH.OUT$^{(V)}$ (*b.q.sh)* To intently look for someone or something until the object of the search is found. *AHLB:* 2036$^{(V)}$ *Strong's:* #1245

SEARCHING (fem. *mahh'te'ret)* A digging up to uncover something hidden. *AHLB:* 2226(a2) *Strong's:* #4290

SEARING (fem. *tsar'vet) AHLB:* 2688(N2) *Strong's:* #6867

SEASON$^{(V)}$ (*m.l.hh)* To season with salt to enhance the flavor. *AHLB:* 2338$^{(V)}$ *Strong's:* #4414

SEAT (masc. *ki'sey)* A special chair of one in eminence. Usually a throne or seat of authority. *AHLB:* 1245-E(e) *Strong's:* #3678

SECOND (*shey-ni) Alternate Translation:* second time *AHLB:* 1474-H(f) *Strong's:* #8145

SECRET (masc. *lat)* That which is unknown or hidden. *AHLB:* 1262-A$^{(N)}$ *Strong's:* #3909

SECURE$^{(V)}$ (*a.m.n)* Solidly fixed in place; to stand firm; not subject to change or revision. *Alternate Translation:* support (when written in the hiphil [active causative] form) *AHLB:* 1290-C$^{(V)}$ *Strong's:* #0539

SECURED (fem. *riyv'qah)* What is firmly attached or tied. *Strong's:* [Found in names only]

SECURITY.DEPOSIT (fem. *te'su'mah) Strong's:* #8667

SEE[V] (*r.a.h)* To take notice; to perceive something or someone; to see visions. *Alternate Translation:* look; watch; appear or seen (when written in the niphil [passive] form); show (when written in the hiphil [active causative] form) *AHLB:* 1438-H[V] *Strong's:* #7200, #7202, #7207, #7212

SEED (masc. *ze'ra)* The grains or ripened ovules of plants used for sowing. Scattered in the field to produce a crop. The singular word can be used for one or more. Also, the descendants of an individual, either male or female. *AHLB:* 2137[N] *Strong's:* #2233

SEED.OF.GRAIN (masc. *ga'ra)* The fertilized, matured ovule of wheat, rye, oats, or millet. (A word of uncertain meaning). *Strong's:* [Found in names only]

SEEING (masc. *pi'qey'ahh)* One who is able to see with the eyes. *AHLB:* 2631[N] *Strong's:* #6493

SEEING.AS (masc. *ya'an)* In the degree that. *AHLB:* 1359-L[N] *Strong's:* #3282

SEEK[V] (*d.r.sh)* To look for or search for something or for answers. *Alternate Translation:* require (when written in the niphil [passive] form) *AHLB:* 2114[V] *Strong's:* #1875

SEIZE[V] (*hh.z.q)* To possess or take by force; grab hold tightly; to refrain or support by grabbing hold. *Alternate Translation:* strengthen (when written in the hiphil [causative] form); strengthen self (when written in the hitpa'el [reflexive] form) *AHLB:* 2152[V] *Strong's:* #2388

SEIZE.HOLD[V] (*t.p.s)* To take hold of something by force. *AHLB:* 2899[V] *Strong's:* #8610

SELECTED (masc. *qa'riy)* Individuals called out for a special purpose. *AHLB:* 1434-E(b) *Strong's:* #7148

SELF-WILL (masc. *ra'tson)* Used to express determination, insistence, persistence, or willfulness. One's desire. *Alternate Translation:* be accepted *AHLB:* 1455-H(j) *Strong's:* #7522

SELL[V] (*m.k.r)* To give up property to another for money or another valuable compensation. *AHLB:* 2337[V] *Strong's:* #4376

SEND[V] (*sh.l.hh)* To cause to go; to direct, order, or request to go. *Alternate Translation:* send off (when written in the piel [active intensive] form) *AHLB:* 2842[V] *Strong's:* #7971

SEND.OFF (masc. *shi'lu'ahh)* To send away a person or gift. *AHLB:* 2842(ed) *Strong's:* #7964

SENDING (masc. *mish'lo'ahh fem. mish'la'hhat) AHLB:* 2842(h2) *Strong's:* #4916, #4917

SEPARATE[V] (*b.d.l)* To set or keep apart. *AHLB:* 2005[V] *Strong's:* #0914

SERPENT (masc. *na'hhash)* A poisonous snake that hisses, creeps and bites. *AHLB:* 2395[N] *Strong's:* #5175

SERVANT (masc. *e'ved)* One who provides a service to another, as a slave, bondservant or hired hand. *AHLB:* 2518[N] *Strong's:* #5650, #5652, #5657

SERVE[V] (*ah.b.d)* To provide a service to another, as a slave, servant or steward; to work at a profession; to serve the land. *AHLB:* 2518[V] *Strong's:* #5647

SERVICE (fem. *a'vo'dah)* The work or labor of a slave, servant or steward. *AHLB:* 2518(c1) *Strong's:* #5656

SET.APART(V) (*q.d.sh)* To move or place someone or something separate from the whole for a special purpose. *AHLB:* 2700(V) *Strong's:* #6942

SET.ASIDE(V) (*a.ts.l)* To reserve or put aside something. *AHLB:* 1403-C(V) *Strong's:* #0680

SET.DOWN(V) (*sh.y.t)* To cause to sit down; to lay down. *AHLB:* 1482-M(V) *Strong's:* #7896

SETTING (fem. *mi'lu'ah)* A recess for filling with a stone or other ornament. *AHLB:* 1288-E(ed1) *Strong's:* #4396

SETTLE(V) (*y.sh.b)* To stay in a dwelling place for the night or for long periods of time; to sit down. *AHLB:* 1462-L(V) *Strong's:* #3427

SETTLER (masc. *to'shav)* One who stays temporarily. Travels from place to place. *AHLB:* 1462-L(i) *Strong's:* #8453

SETTLING (masc. *mo'shav)* The place of sitting, resting or dwelling, usually temporarily. *AHLB:* 1462-L(a) *Strong's:* #4186

SEVEN (masc. *shiv'ah fem. she'va)* A cardinal number. *Alternate Translation:* seventy (when written in the plural) *AHLB:* 2808(N) *Strong's:* #7651, #7657, (x2)

SEVENFOLD (fem. *shiyv'ah)* To do seven times. *AHLB:* 2808(e1) *Strong's:* [Found in names only]

SEVENTH (masc. *she'vi'i)* An ordinal number. *AHLB:* 2808(bf) *Strong's:* #7637

SEVENTH.TIME (fem. *shiy'va'at)* A sequence of events ending with the seventh. *Alternate Translation:* sevenfold (when written in the double plural) *AHLB:* 2808(e2) *Strong's:* #7659

SEVER(V) (*q.ts.r)* To cut short or small; to cut or reap the harvest in the sense of severing the crop from its stalk; to be impatient in the sense of patience being severed. *AHLB:* 2727(V) *Strong's:* #7114

SEW.TOGETHER(V) (*t.p.r)* To join two pieces of cloth with stitches of thread. *AHLB:* 2900(V) *Strong's:* #8609

SHA'AR (masc. *sha'ar)* A standard of measure. *AHLB:* 2862(N) *Strong's:* #8180

SHADOW (masc. *tseyl)* The dark figure cast on a surface by a body intercepting the rays from a light source. *AHLB:* 1403-A(N) *Strong's:* #6738

SHAKE(V) (*r.g.z)* To tremble in fear or anger. *AHLB:* 2748(V) *Strong's:* #7264

SHAKE.IN.AWE(V) (*p.hh.d)* To physically or mentally tremble in amazement or fear. *AHLB:* 2598(V) *Strong's:* #6342

SHAKE.OFF(V) (*n.ah.r)* To violently shake back and forth to throw something off. To overthrow. *AHLB:* 2458(V) *Strong's:* #5286, #5287

SHAKING (masc. *ra'qaz)* A shaking anger. *AHLB:* 2748(N) *Strong's:* #7268

SHAKING.IN.FEAR (masc. *ra'ad fem. re'a'dah)* Being physically effected by shivering or shaking from a dreadful event. *AHLB:* 2778(N) *Strong's:* #7461

SHAME (masc. *bash'nah)* A fact or circumstance bringing disgrace or regret. *AHLB:* 1044-A(m1) *Strong's:* #1317

SHAME(V) (*k.l.m)* To feel pain through something dishonorable, improper or ridiculous. *AHLB:* 2261(V) *Strong's:* #3637

SHAPE (fem. *be'riy'ah)* A unique form. *AHLB:* 1043-E(b) *Strong's:* #1278

SHAPE(V) (*b.r.a)* To fashion or form. *AHLB:* 1043-E(V) *Strong's:* #1254

SHARE (masc. *mahn fem. ma'nah)* A portion that is provided to a group or person to meet their needs. *AHLB:* 1290-A(N1) *Strong's:* #4490

SHARP.SIGHTED (masc. *a'qod) Strong's:* [Found in names only]

SHARP.STONE (masc. *tsor)* A piece of stone from obsidian, flint or chert that forms a narrow and sharp edge when flaked off. *AHLB:* 1411-J(N) *Strong's:* #6864

SHARP.THORN (masc. *tseyn)* A pointed, piercing object. *AHLB:* 1336-A(N) *Strong's:* #6791

SHARPEN(V) (*l.t.sh)* To hone in the sense of narrowing the blade edge by using a whetstone or hammer. To narrow the eyes in the sense of looking sharply, as in squinting. *AHLB:* 2309(V) *Strong's:* #3913

SHARPENED (masc. *la'tash) Strong's:* [Found in names only]

SHATTER(V) (*hh.sh.l) AHLB:* 2216(V) *Strong's:* #2826

SHATTERING (masc. *she'ver)* Suddenly broken or burst into pieces, as with a violent blow. *AHLB:* 2811(N) *Strong's:* #7667

SHAVE(V) (*g.l.hh)* To cut off the hair from the face or another part of the body. *AHLB:* 2065(V) *Strong's:* #1548

SHE (fem. / *hi)* The female who is neither the speaker nor the one addressed. *Alternate Translation:* it; that; this *AHLB:* 1093-J(N) *Strong's:* #1931(x2)

SHEAF (masc. *o'mer) AHLB:* 2554(g) *Strong's:* #6016(x2)

SHEAR(V) (*g.z.z)* To cut or clip wool or hair from something. *AHLB:* 1053-B(V) *Strong's:* #1494

SHE-DONKEY (fem. *a'ton)* A female ass. *AHLB:* 1497-C(c) *Strong's:* #0860

SHEEP (masc. *ke'ves fem. kiv'sah)* A mammal related to the goat and domesticated for its milk, flesh and wool. *AHLB:* 2273(N) *Strong's:* #3532, #3535, #3775

SHEEP.PEN (fem. *bots'rah)* A walled place of protection. *Strong's:* [Found in names only]

SHEET (masc. *ra'qi'a)* A broad piece of cloth or metal. As hammered out flat. *AHLB:* 2797(b) *Strong's:* #7549

SHEPHERD.STAFF (masc. *lam) Strong's:* [Found in names only]

SHEQEL (masc. *she'qel)* A chief Hebrew weight standard of measurement. *AHLB:* 2874(N) *Strong's:* #8255

SHIELD (masc. *ma'gen)* A broad piece of defensive armor carried on the arm. A protective structure. Wall of protection. *AHLB:* 1060-A(a) *Strong's:* #4043

SHINE (masc. *ma'ha'lal)* The emitting of rays of light. Shining brightly. *AHLB:* 1104-B(a) *Strong's:* #4110

SHINE(V) (*h.l.l)* To emit rays of light. Shine brightly. To shine or cause another to shine through one's actions or words. *Alternate Translation:* endorse (when written in the piel [active intensive] form) *AHLB:* 1104-B(V) *Strong's:* #1984

SHINING (masc. *hiy'lul)* The emitting of rays of light. Shining brightly. *AHLB:* 1104-B(bd) *Strong's:* #1974

SHIP (masc. *a'ni'yah)* A large sea-going vessel. As searching through the sea for a distant shore. *AHLB:* 1014-A(f1) *Strong's:* #0591

SHOOT *nets* (fem. *ne'tsah)* The shaft or stem of a plant. *AHLB:* 1317-A(N) *Strong's:* #5322(x2)

SHORE (masc. *hhoph)* The land bordering a body of water. A place covered. *AHLB:* 1178-J[N] *Strong's:* #2348

SHORT (fem. *kiv'rah)* Having little length. A brief distance. *AHLB:* 2250(e1) *Strong's:* #3530

SHORTNESS (masc. *qo'tser)* Short in patience. *AHLB:* 2727(g) *Strong's:* #7115

SHOULDER (masc. *she'khem)* The top of the body where the arms and torso meet; Capable of bearing a task or figuratively a blame. *AHLB:* 2837[N] *Strong's:* #7926

SHOULDER.PIECE (fem. *ka'teyph)* The part of an object that acts like a shoulder. *AHLB:* 2299[N] *Strong's:* #3802

SHOUT (fem. *t'ru'ah)* A great shout of alarm of war or for rejoicing. *Alternate Translation:* alarm *AHLB:* 1460-J(i1) *Strong's:* #8643

SHOUT[V] (*r.w.ah)* To shout an alarm of war or for great rejoicing. *AHLB:* 1460-J[V] *Strong's:* #7321

SHOUT.ALOUD[V] (*r.n.n)* To cry out loudly in triumph or joy. *AHLB:* 1451-B[V] *Strong's:* #7442, #7444

SHOUTING (masc. *o'had)* Raising of the voice to show authority, anger or gladness. *Strong's:* [Found in names only]

SHOUTING.OUT (masc. *shu'a)* *AHLB:* 1476-J[N] *Strong's:* #7769, #7771, #7773

SHOVEL (masc. *ya)* A flat tray attached to a handle for scooping up hot coals. *AHLB:* 1223-A[N] *Strong's:* #3257

SHOW.PITY[V] (*hh.m.l)* To have compassion; to sympathize. *AHLB:* 2171[V] *Strong's:* #2550

SHOWERS (masc. *ra'viyv)* *AHLB:* 1439-B(b) *Strong's:* #7241

SHRUB (masc. *si'ahh)* A low-growing, usually severally stemmed bush or woody plant, as used for making booths. *AHLB:* 1330-M[N] *Strong's:* #7880

SHUT[V] (*s.g.r / s.k.r)* To close or block an opening. *Alternate Translation:* deliver (when written in the hiphil [causative]form) *AHLB:* 2467[V] *Strong's:* #5462, #5534

SHUT.UP[V] (*s.t.m)* To stop by halting or closing. *AHLB:* 2515[V] *Strong's:* #5640

SICK (masc. *ta'hha'lu)* Afflicted with ill health or disease; ailing. *AHLB:* 1173-E(id) *Strong's:* #8463

SICKENED (fem. *ma'hha'let)* To make or become sick. *Strong's:* [Found in names only]

SICKLE (masc. *hhe're'meysh)* *AHLB:* 3020 *Strong's:* #2770

SICKNESS (masc. *ma'hha'leh fem. ma'hha'lah)* A physical or emotional illness. Weakened. *AHLB:* 1173-H(a) *Strong's:* #4245

SIDE (masc. *tsad)* One of the surfaces forming the outside of or bounding a thing; an area next to something. *AHLB:* 1395-A[N] *Strong's:* #6654

SIGH[V] (*a.n.hh)* Exhaling of breath as in relief. To breath out as a desire for rest. *AHLB:* 1307-C[V] *Strong's:* #0584

SIGHTLESSNESS (masc. *sa'gur)* Sightless; unquestioning, as having no regard to rational discrimination, guidance or restriction. As a shutting of the eyes. *AHLB:* 3035[N] *Strong's:* #5575

SIGN (fem. *ot)* The motion, gesture, or mark representing an agreement between two parties. A wondrous or miraculous sign. *AHLB:* 1022-J[N] *Strong's:* #0226

SILENCE(V) (*h.s.h)* To keep quiet by holding the tongue, silent and still. *AHLB:* 1107-H(V) *Strong's:* #2013

SILENCED (fem. *du'mah)* Absence of any sound or noise; stillness. *AHLB:* 1082-J(N1) *Strong's:* #1745, #1822

SILENT (masc. *hhey'reysh)* A state of speechlessness or extreme quiet. *AHLB:* 2211(N) *Strong's:* #2795

SILVER (masc. *ke'seph)* A soft metal capable of a high degree of polish used for coinage, implements and ornaments. A desired and precious metal. *AHLB:* 2277(N) *Strong's:* #3701

SIMMER(V) (*z.w.d / z.y.d)* To cook a soup over a fire. To be heated with pride or anger. *AHLB:* 1142-J(V) *Strong's:* #2102

SINCE (masc. *ey'qev)* From a time in the past until now. *Alternate Translation:* therefore *AHLB:* 2571(N) *Strong's:* #6118

SINEW (masc. *gid)* A tendon of the muscles. *AHLB:* 1050-M(N) *Strong's:* #1517

SING(V) (*sh.y.r / sh.w.r)* To express one's voice in a melody or to music. *AHLB:* 1480-M(V) *Strong's:* #7891

SINGE.SCAR (fem. *mikh'wah) AHLB:* 1235-J(h1) *Strong's:* #4348

SINGEING (fem. *ke'wi'yah)* A burning of the skin or hair. *AHLB:* 1235-J(f1) *Strong's:* #3555

SINGER (masc. *za'mar) AHLB:* 2124(N) *Strong's:* [Found in names only]

SINK(V) (*t.b.ah)* To fall, drop, or descend down to a lower level. *AHLB:* 2229(V) *Strong's:* #2883

SINK.DOWN(V) (*r.p.h)* To drop down; to be slack or idle due to weakness, illness or laziness. *Alternate Translation:* lazy (when written in the niphil [passive] form) *AHLB:* 1454-H(V) *Strong's:* #7503

SINKING (masc. *shuhh) Strong's:* [Found in names only]

SISTER (fem. *a'hhot)* A female who has the same parents as another or shares one parent with another. *AHLB:* 1008-A(N3) *Strong's:* #0269

SISTER-in-law (fem. *ye'va'mah)* A female sibling of one's spouse. *AHLB:* 1036-L(N2) *Strong's:* #2994

SIT.DOWN(V) (*t.k.h)* Meaning dubious. *AHLB:* 1494-H(V) *Strong's:* #8497

SITE (masc. *a'tar)* A site or place that is sought out. The meaning of this Hebrew word is uncertain, but is used in Aramaic and means a site or place that is sought out. *Strong's:* [Found in names only]

SIX (masc. *shi'shah fem. sheysh)* A cardinal number. *Alternate Translation:* sixty (when written in the plural) *AHLB:* 1481-A(N) *Strong's:* #8337, #8346

SIXTH (*shi-shi) AHLB:* 1481-A(ef) *Strong's:* #8345

SKILL (fem. *hhakh'mah)* The ability to decide or discern between good and bad, right and wrong; A deep understanding of a craft. *AHLB:* 2159(N1) *Strong's:* #2451

SKILLED.ONE (masc. *hha'kham)* A person characterized by a deep understanding of a craft; One with the ability to decide or discern between good and bad, right and wrong. *AHLB:* 2159(N) *Strong's:* #2450

SKILLET (masc. *pa'rur)* A flat surface for preparing foods. *AHLB:* 1388-B(d) *Strong's:* #6517

SKIN (masc. *or)* The integument covering men or animals, as well as leather made from animal skins. The husk of a seed. *AHLB:* 1365-J$^{(N)}$ *Strong's:* #5785

SKIN.BAG (fem. *hhey'met)* A container made from the skin of animal, usually a goat or sheep, and used for holding milk, water or other liquid. *AHLB:* 1174-A(N2) *Strong's:* #2573

SKIN.SORE (fem. *ya'le'phet) AHLB:* 1270-L(N2) *Strong's:* #3217

SKIP.WITH.JOY$^{(V)}$ (/ *s.y.s / s.w.s)* To rejoice by moving with quick steps. *AHLB:* 1337-J$^{(V)}$ *Strong's:* #7797

SKULL (fem. *gul'go'let)* The bones of the head. The roundness of the head or skull. Also, a census by the counting of heads. *Alternate Translation:* individual *AHLB:* 1058-A(l2) *Strong's:* #1538

SKY (masc. *sha'mah)* The upper atmosphere that constitutes an apparent great vault or arch over the earth. Place of the winds. *AHLB:* 1473-A$^{(N)}$ *Strong's:* #8064

SLAB (masc. *lu'ahh)* A wood or stone tablet or plank. Often used for writing. *AHLB:* 1261-J$^{(N)}$ *Strong's:* #3871

SLANDER (fem. *di'bah)* Speaking evil of another (usually done quietly). *AHLB:* 1071-A(N1) *Strong's:* #1681

SLAUGHTERING (masc. *te'vahh)* The act of slaughtering, the meat of the slaughter or one who slaughters. Also, an executioner as one who slaughters. *AHLB:* 2227$^{(N)}$ *Strong's:* #2874, #2876

SLAY$^{(V)}$ (*sh.hh.t)* To strike, beat or kill. *AHLB:* 2823$^{(V)}$ *Strong's:* #7819, #7820

SLEEP$^{(V)}$ (*y.sh.n)* To rest in a state of suspended consciousness. Also, supplies being stored through the idea of them sleeping. *Alternate Translation:* Store (To store produce in the sense of sleeping) *AHLB:* 1474-L$^{(V)}$ *Strong's:* #3462

SLEEPING (masc. *ya'sheyn)* The condition of being asleep. Also, storage, in the sense of supplies being in a state of sleep. *Alternate Translation:* Storage (of produce in the sense of sleeping) *AHLB:* 1474-L$^{(N)}$ *Strong's:* #3463, #3465

SLICE$^{(V)}$ (*s.r.t) AHLB:* 2508$^{(V)}$ *Strong's:* #8295

SLICE.OFF$^{(V)}$ (/ *q.ts.ts / q.hh.hh)* To make an end of something by cutting it off. *AHLB:* 1432-B$^{(V)}$ *Strong's:* #7082, #7112

SLICING (masc. *se'ret fem.* *sa're'tet) AHLB:* 2508$^{(N)}$ *Strong's:* #8296

SLICK (masc. *hhey'leq)* The portions dispersed out. *AHLB:* 2167$^{(N)}$ *Strong's:* #2509

SLIME (masc. *hhey'mar)* A thick film of tar or foam that floats to the surface of a liquid. *AHLB:* 2175$^{(N)}$ *Strong's:* #2561, #2564

SLING (masc. *qe'la)* A weapon made of a pouch that is attached to two long cords and used for throwing stones. Also, something that hangs like a sling. *AHLB:* 2709$^{(N)}$ *Strong's:* #7050, #7051

SLIP.AWAY$^{(V)}$ (*m.l.t)* To get away through deliverance or escape. *AHLB:* 2339$^{(V)}$ *Strong's:* #4422

SLOW (masc. *a'reykh)* Capable of calmly awaiting an outcome or result. *AHLB:* 1448-C$^{(N)}$ *Strong's:* #0750

SMACK$^{(V)}$ (/ *ts.w.r / z.w.r)* To strike or push as an attack. *AHLB:* 1411-J$^{(V)}$ *Strong's:* #2115, #6696

SMACKED (masc. / *ma'tsur / ma'zur)* A pressing into a city for conquering it. *AHLB:* 1411-J(a) *Strong's:* #4205, #4692

SMALL (masc. *qa'tan)* Someone or something that is not very large in size, importance, age or significance. *AHLB:* 2703$^{(N)}$ *Strong's:* #6996

SMALL.AMOUNT (masc. *me'at)* Something that is few or small in size or amount. *Alternate Translation:* few, little, small thing; might have (when prefixed with "like~") *AHLB:* 2347$^{(N)}$ *Strong's:* #4592

SMASH$^{(V)}$ *(k.t.t) AHLB:* 1252-B$^{(V)}$ *Strong's:* #3807

SMASHED (masc. *ka'tit)* The pressing of the olive to extract the oil. *AHLB:* 1252-B(b) *Strong's:* #3795

SMEAR$^{(V)}$ *(m.sh.hh)* To overspread with oil for medical treatment or as a sign of authority. *AHLB:* 2357$^{(V)}$ *Strong's:* #4886

SMEARED (masc. *ma'shiy'ahh)* Someone or something that has been smeared or annointed with an oil as a medication or a sign of taking an office. An anointed one; a messiah. *AHLB:* 2357(b) *Strong's:* #4899

SMELL$^{(V)}$ *(r.w.hh)* The odor or scent of a thing. As carried on the wind. To be "refreshed", as when taking in a deep breath. *AHLB:* 1445-J$^{(V)}$ *Strong's:* #7304, #7306

SMITE$^{(V)}$ *(n.g.p)* To deliver a hit with the intent to harm; to bring a plague in the sense of a striking. *AHLB:* 2377$^{(V)}$ *Strong's:* #5062

SMOKE (masc. *a'sheyn)* The gaseous products of combustion. *AHLB:* 2583$^{(N)}$ *Strong's:* #6226, #6227

SMOKE$^{(V)}$ *(ah.sh.n)* To emit a gaseous cloud when burning. *AHLB:* 2583$^{(V)}$ *Strong's:* #6225

SMOKING (masc. *qi'tor)* To burn sluggishly without flame. The smoke of the burning incense or fat. *AHLB:* 2705(ec) *Strong's:* #7008

SMOLDER$^{(V)}$ *(y.q.d) AHLB:* 1418-L$^{(V)}$ *Strong's:* #3344

SMOLDERING (masc. *mo'qeyd fem. mo'qey'dah) AHLB:* 1418-L(a) *Strong's:* #4168, #4169

SMOOTH (fem. *hhal'qah)* Having an even, continuous surface. This word can also mean "flattery" in the sense of being slippery. *AHLB:* 2167(N1) *Strong's:* #2513(x2), #2514

SNAIL (masc. *hho'met)* An unknown creature. *AHLB:* 2170(g) *Strong's:* #2546

SNAKE (masc. *muph) Strong's:* [Found in names only]

SNAP$^{(V)}$ *(q.ts.p)* To make a sudden closing; to break suddenly with a sharp sound; to splinter a piece of wood; to lash out in anger as a splintering. *AHLB:* 2726$^{(V)}$ *Strong's:* #7107

SNAP.OFF$^{(V)}$ *(m.l.q)* To remove the head, usually of a bird, at the neck. *AHLB:* 2342$^{(V)}$ *Strong's:* #4454

SNARE (masc. *mo'qeysh)* A trap laid with bait to capture an animal or person. An entrapment. *AHLB:* 1435-L(a) *Strong's:* #4170

SNARE$^{(V)}$ *(y.q.sh) AHLB:* 1435-L$^{(V)}$ *Strong's:* #3369

SNARER (masc. *yaq'shan) Strong's:* [Found in names only]

SNIP.OFF$^{(V)}$ *(m.w.l)* To cut off the front part (Often used in the context of circumcision). *AHLB:* 1288-J$^{(V)}$ *Strong's:* #4135

SNOOZE (fem. / *shey'nah)* To take a nap. *AHLB:* 1474-A(N1) *Strong's:* #8142

SNORT$^{(V)}$ *(a.n.p)* A heavy breathing through the nose out of anger. *AHLB:* 2002$^{(V)}$ *Strong's:* #0599

SNORTING (masc. *na'hhor)* A forcing of the breath violently through the nostrils with a loud, harsh sound. *Strong's:* [Found in names only]

SNOW (masc. *she'leg)* A precipitation of water in the form of ice crystals. *AHLB:* 2841(N) *Strong's:* #7950

SNOW.MOUNTAIN (masc. *se'nir) Strong's:* [Found in names only]

SO (masc. *keyn)* In a manner or way indicated or suggested. What comes before or after another event. *Alternate Translation:* should; this; thus *AHLB:* 1244-A(N) *Strong's:* #3651

SO.BE.IT (masc. *a'meyn)* An affirmation of firmness and support. *AHLB:* 1290-C(N) *Strong's:* #0543

SOFT (masc. *a'nog fem. a'no'gah) AHLB:* 2556(c) *Strong's:* #6028

SOFT(V) (*ah.n.g)* To be delicate and pleasurable. *AHLB:* 2556(V) *Strong's:* #6026

SOFTLY (masc. *at)* Free from harshness, sternness, or violence. To act softly. A charmer. *AHLB:* 1009-A(N) *Strong's:* #0328

SOLITARY (masc. *ya'hhid)* Separated from the whole of the unit (see Psalm 68:7 [6]). *AHLB:* 1165-L(b) *Strong's:* #3173

SON (masc. *ben)* A male offspring. This can be the son or a later male descendant of the father. One who continues the family line. *AHLB:* 1037-A(N) *Strong's:* #1121, #1248

SONG (masc. *shir fem. shi'rah)* The act or art of singing. *AHLB:* 1480-M(N) *Strong's:* #7892

SOOT (masc. *pi'ahh)* Residue left after burning. *AHLB:* 1376-M(N) *Strong's:* #6368

SORROW (masc. *ya'gon)* Deep distress and regret. *AHLB:* 1210-A(j) *Strong's:* #3015

SORROW(V) (*d.w.b)* Distress caused by loss, affliction, disappointment, etc.; grief, sadness, or regret. *AHLB:* 1071-J(V) *Strong's:* #1727

SOUL (fem. *ne'phesh)* A person or creature; what has breath. The whole of an individual, god or animal including; the body, mind, emotion, character and inner parts. *Alternate Translation:* everyone (when following the word "to~ ALL") *AHLB:* 2424(N) *Strong's:* #5315

SOUTH (masc. *ne'gev)* A cardinal point of the compass lying directly opposite north. Also, the Negev, the desert region in the southern part of Israel. *Strong's:* #5045

SOUTHERN (masc. *da'rom)* A direction lying directly opposite of north. *AHLB:* 2113(c) *Strong's:* #1864

SOUTHERN.REGION (masc. *qat'rus) Strong's:* [Found in names only]

SOUTHWARD (fem. *tey'man)* A cardinal point to the right of east. *AHLB:* 1290-L(i) *Strong's:* #8486

SOW(V) (*z.r.ah)* To spread seeds on the ground; to plant a crop. *Alternate Translation:* Produce a seed (when written in hiphil [active causative] form) *AHLB:* 2137(V) *Strong's:* #2232

SOWN (masc. *z'ru'a)* What is spread like seeds on the ground. *AHLB:* 2137(d) *Strong's:* #2221

SPARE(V) (*hh.w.s)* To forbear to destroy, punish, or harm; give asylum. Give refuge to another. *AHLB:* 1176-J(V) *Strong's:* #2347

SPARK (masc. *re'sheph)* The spark of a fire or thunderbolt. Also, an arrow as a flashing thunderbolt. *AHLB:* 2800[N] *Strong's:* #7565

SPATTER[V] (*n.z.h)* To ceremonially sprinkle water or oil on something that is being dedicated. *AHLB:* 1306-H[V] *Strong's:* #5137

SPEAK[V] (*d.b.r)* A careful arrangement of words or commands said orally. *AHLB:* 2093[V] *Strong's:* #1696

SPEAR (masc. *ro'mahh) AHLB:* 2773[N] *Strong's:* #7420

SPEARHEAD (masc. *qa'yin)* The head of a spear. *AHLB:* 1428-M[N] *Strong's:* #7013

SPECIAL (masc. *qo'desh)* A person, item, time or place that has the quality of being unique; Separated from the rest for a special purpose. *AHLB:* 2700(g) *Strong's:* #6944

SPECKLED (masc. *na'qod)* The spots marking sheep and goats. *AHLB:* 2431(c) *Strong's:* #5348

SPEECH (fem. *am'rah)* The chain of words when speaking. *AHLB:* 1288-C(N1) *Strong's:* #0565

SPELT (fem. *ku'se'met)* A wheat like grain with what looks like trimmed hair. *AHLB:* 2276(o2) *Strong's:* #3698

SPICE (fem. *ne'khot)* Various aromatic vegetable products used to season or flavor foods. *AHLB:* 1310-E(c2) *Strong's:* #5219

SPICE.MIXTURE (masc. *ro'qahh)* A mixture of spices for an ointment or perfume. *AHLB:* 2795(g) *Strong's:* #7545

SPICE.PLACE (masc. *mav'sam)* The location of growing or selling spices. *Strong's:* [Found in names only]

SPIN[V] (*t.w.h)* To revolve in a circle without moving forward. *AHLB:* 1189-J[V] *Strong's:* #2901

SPINE (masc. *a'tseh)* The tree of the body which provides its uprightness. *AHLB:* 1363-H[N] *Strong's:* #6096

SPIT[V] (*y.r.q) AHLB:* 1456-L[V] *Strong's:* #3417

SPIT.UPON[V] (*a.r.r)* To eject saliva, usually on another in spite or disrespect. *AHLB:* 1457-C[V] *Strong's:* #0779

SPITTING (fem. *m'ey'rah) AHLB:* 1457-C(k1) *Strong's:* #3994

SPLASHED (masc. *tsa'va'on)* To appear spattered. *Strong's:* [Found in names only]

SPLENDID (fem. *pu'ah)* Someone or something that is exceptional. A wonder. *Strong's:* [Found in names only]

SPLENDOR (masc. *hod)* Something that is prominent in beauty or action. *AHLB:* 1096-J[N] *Strong's:* #1935

SPLINTER (masc. *qe'tseph)* The sharp flying objects from a snapped piece of wood. Also, wrath as flying splinters. *AHLB:* 2726[N] *Strong's:* #7110

SPLIT[V] (*p.l.g)* To divide lengthwise. *AHLB:* 2606[V] *Strong's:* #6385

SPLIT.IN.TWO[V] (*sh.s.ah) AHLB:* 2857[V] *Strong's:* #8156

SPLITTING (masc. *she'sa) AHLB:* 2857[N] *Strong's:* #8157

SPOIL (masc. *sha'lal)* Plunder taken from an enemy in war or robbery. To impair the quality or effect of. *AHLB:* 1472-B[N] *Strong's:* #7998

SPOKEN (masc. *riy'phat) Strong's:* [Found in names only]

SPOT (fem. *sh'qa'a'ru'ah) AHLB:* 3063 *Strong's:* #8258

SPOT$^{(V)}$ (*t.l.a)* A small area visibly different from the surrounding area. To be covered with spots. *AHLB:* 1196-E$^{(V)}$ *Strong's:* #2921

SPOTTED (masc. *ba'rod)* An animal with white spots which appear as hailstones. *AHLB:* 2037(c) *Strong's:* #1261

SPREAD$^{(V)}$ (*sh.t.hh)* To expand out a great distance. *AHLB:* 2831$^{(V)}$ *Strong's:* #7849

SPREAD.ACROSS$^{(V)}$ (*p.sh.h)* To spread out excessively. *AHLB:* 1389-H$^{(V)}$ *Strong's:* #6581

SPREAD.OUT$^{(V)}$ (*p.r.sh)* To expand beyond a starting point; to be easily and plainly understood. *Alternate Translation:* understood (when written in the pual [passive intensive] form) *AHLB:* 2644$^{(V)}$ *Strong's:* #6566, #6567

SPREAD.WIDE$^{(V)}$ (*p.t.h)* To lay out in a large area. *Alternate Translation:* persuade (when written in the piel [active intensive] form) *AHLB:* 1390-H$^{(V)}$ *Strong's:* #6601

SPRING (masc. *ma'yan)* A source of water issuing from the ground. As the eye of the ground. *AHLB:* 1359-M(a) *Strong's:* #4599

SPRING.UP$^{(V)}$ (*ts.m.hh)* To grow up as a plant. *AHLB:* 2666$^{(V)}$ *Strong's:* #6779

SPRINKLE$^{(V)}$ (*z.r.q)* To drip a liquid, usually water or blood. *AHLB:* 2138$^{(V)}$ *Strong's:* #2236

SPRINKLED (masc. *ka'naz) Strong's:* [Found in names only]

SPRINKLING.BASIN (masc. *miz'raq)* A container of liquid that is used to drip the liquid. *AHLB:* 2138(h) *Strong's:* #4219

SPROUT$^{(V)}$ (*d.sh.a)* To send up or out new growth, as of a plant. Sprout green sprouts. *AHLB:* 1090-E$^{(V)}$ *Strong's:* #1876

SPROUT.UP (masc. *ne'pheg) Strong's:* [Found in names only]

SQUEEZE$^{(V)}$ (*l.hh.ts)* To exert pressure either physically or emotionally. *AHLB:* 2307$^{(V)}$ *Strong's:* #3905

SQUEEZING (masc. *la'hhats)* Pressure being exerted, either physically or emotionally. *AHLB:* 2307$^{(N)}$ *Strong's:* #3906

STACK (masc. *ga'dish)* A pile of grain or dirt. *AHLB:* 2058(b) *Strong's:* #1430

STAFF (masc. *she'vet)* A walking stick made from the branch of a tree. Also, a tribe as a branch of the family. *AHLB:* 2805$^{(N)}$ *Strong's:* #7626

STAGGER$^{(V)}$ (*n.w.ah)* To reel from side to side; to wag or shake back and forth or up and down; to wander as staggering about. *AHLB:* 1322-J$^{(V)}$ *Strong's:* #5128

STAGGERING (fem. *no'ah) Strong's:* [Found in names only]

STAIR.STEP (fem. *ma'a'lah)* A straight or stepped incline for ascending and descending. *AHLB:* 1357-A(a1) *Strong's:* #4609

STALK (masc. *qa'neh)* The main stem and support of a plant. *AHLB:* 1428-H$^{(N)}$ *Strong's:* #7070

STALKER (masc. *qa'naz) Strong's:* [Found in names only]

STAMPED.DOWN (masc. *ya'hats)* A striking or beating with a forcible, downward thrust. *Strong's:* [Found in names only]

STAND$^{(V)}$ (*ah.m.d)* To rise, raise or set in a place. *AHLB:* 2550$^{(V)}$ *Strong's:* #5975, #5976

STAND.UP$^{(V)}$ (*n.ts.b)* To be vertical in position; to stand tall and erect; to set in place. *AHLB:* 2426$^{(V)}$ *Strong's:* #5324

STANDARD (masc. *neys)* A flag that hangs from a pole with the insignia of a tribe or army. Also, a sail. *AHLB:* 1314-A(N) *Strong's:* #5251

STAR (masc. *ko'khav)* A natural luminous body visible in the night sky. *AHLB:* 1232-B(g) *Strong's:* #3556

STARE(V) (*n.b.t)* To carefully look; to make a close inspection. *AHLB:* 2367(V) *Strong's:* #5027

STATEMENT (masc. *a'mar)* A single declaration or remark. *AHLB:* 1288-C(N) *Strong's:* #0561

STATION(V) (*y.ts.b)* To stand firm and in place. *AHLB:* 1393-L(V) *Strong's:* #3320

STATIONED (masc. *ta'rahh) Strong's:* [Found in names only]

STAVE (fem. *mish'ey'nah)* A staff made from a sapling or branch. A support for walking. *AHLB:* 2861(h1) *Strong's:* #4938

STAY(V) (*y.hh.r / y.hh.l)* To remain behind; to wait in anticipation. *AHLB:* 1181-L(V) *Strong's:* #3176, #3186

STAY.THE.NIGHT(V) (*l.w.n / l.y.n)* To remain or stay through the night. *AHLB:* 1267-J(V) *Strong's:* #3885(x2)

STEADFAST (masc. *tse'deq)* The following of the established path or course of action. *AHLB:* 2658(N) *Strong's:* #6664

STEADFAST.ONE (masc. *tsa'diq)* One that makes or sets right. Conforming to fact, standard or truth. *AHLB:* 2658(b) *Strong's:* #6662

STEADFASTNESS (fem. *tse'de'qah)* Being on the correct path; conformity to fact, standard or truth. *AHLB:* 2658(N1) *Strong's:* #6666

STEAL(V) (*g.n.b)* To wrongfully take the property of another; rob. *Alternate Translation:* steal away (when written in the piel [active intensive] form) *AHLB:* 2073(V) *Strong's:* #1589

STEEP.VALLEY (*gai / gai)* An elongated depression between uplands, hills, or mountains. *AHLB:* 1047-M(N) *Strong's:* #1516

STEP (masc. *mid'rakh)* The distance between the feet of a step. *AHLB:* 2112(h) *Strong's:* #4096

STERILE (masc. *a'qar)* Failing to produce or incapable of producing offspring, fruit or spores. Being without children in the sense of being plucked of fruit. *AHLB:* 2905(N) *Strong's:* #6135

STEW (masc. *na'zid)* An edible dish of meat or vegetables cooked in boiling water. *AHLB:* 2386(b) *Strong's:* #5138

STICKERBUSH (masc. *sakh / seykh) AHLB:* 1333-A(N) *Strong's:* #5519, #7899, #7900

STINK(V) (*b.a.sh)* To emit a bad odor or be loathsome. *AHLB:* 1044-D(V) *Strong's:* #0887

STIR(V) (*b.h.l)* To disturb the quiet of; agitate. *AHLB:* 1035-G(V) *Strong's:* #0926

STIR.UP(V) (*ah.w.r)* To shake to awaken. *AHLB:* 1365-J(V) *Strong's:* #5782, #5783

STOMACH (fem. *qey'vah)* As a cavity. *AHLB:* 1416-A(N1) *Strong's:* #6896

STONE (fem. *e'ven)* A piece of rock, often in the context of building material. *AHLB:* 1037-C(N) *Strong's:* #0068

STONE(V) (*s.q.l)* To gather stones for stoning. The act of throwing rocks with the intention of killing. To remove stones from a road or field. *AHLB:* 2502(V) *Strong's:* #5619

STONE.STOOL (masc. אובן *o'ven)* A platform made of stone and used by a potter or a midwife. *AHLB:* 1037-C(N) *Strong's:* #0070

STOOL (masc. כס *keys)* A seat or throne. *AHLB:* 1245-A(N) *Strong's:* #3676

STOOP(V) (כרע *k.r.ah)* To bend the body forward and downward while bending the knees; to stoop or crouch down by bending or getting on the knees. *AHLB:* 2290(V) *Strong's:* #3766

STOP(V) (עצר *ah.ts.r)* To cause to cease; to stop from occurring in the sense of halting, shutting or restraining. *AHLB:* 2570(V) *Strong's:* #6113

STORE(V) (כמס *k.m.s) AHLB:* 2265(V) *Strong's:* #3647

STORE.UP(V) (אצר *a.ts.r)* To keep valuable items or foods in a safe and secure place. *AHLB:* 1411-C(V) *Strong's:* #0686

STOREHOUSE (fem. מסכנה *mis'ke'nah)* Places for storing foods or other items for future benefit. *AHLB:* 2478(h1) *Strong's:* #4543

STORK (fem. חסידה *hha'si'dah)* An unclean bird having long legs and a long neck and bill. Also, the soft feathers of the storks neck. *AHLB:* 2181(b1) *Strong's:* #2624

STORM(V) (שער / סער *s.ah.r)* To be afraid as from a storm. *AHLB:* 2517(V) *Strong's:* #5590, #8175

STRAIGHT (masc. ישר *ya'shar)* Without a bend, angle, or curve. A straight line, path or thought. The cord of the bow as stretched taught. *AHLB:* 1480-L(N) *Strong's:* #3477

STRAIGHT.ONE (masc. ישורון *ye'shu'run) Strong's:* [Found in names only]

STRAIGHT.TRUMPET (fem. חצוצרה *hha'tsots'rah)* A loud wind instrument. *AHLB:* 3018 *Strong's:* #2689

STRAIGHTNESS (masc. יושר *yo'sher) AHLB:* 1480-L(g) *Strong's:* #3476

STRAIT (masc. מצר *mey'tsar)* A narrow tight place or situation. *AHLB:* 1411-A(k) *Strong's:* #4712

STRAND (masc. בד *bad)* A branch (which may be used as a staff or stave), string or filament, as separated from the tree or plant. Linen that is made from the fibers of the flax plant. Often used in the idiom "to his/her own strand" meaning alone or self, stranded. *Alternate Translation:* linen; part; apart; alone; aside; only; self; that alone (when prefixed with "to~"); besides (when prefixed with "from~" and "to~") *AHLB:* 1027-A(N) *Strong's:* #0905, #0906

STRAP (fem. מוסרה *mo'sey'rah)* A long and narrow band. *AHLB:* 1342-L(a) *Strong's:* #4147

STRAW (masc. תבן *te'ven)* Stalks of grain after threshing; dry, stalky plant residue. When more permanent structures were built, they were constructed of stones and bricks made of clay and straw; replacing the tent panels as the main component of construction for dwellings. *AHLB:* 1037-A(i) *Strong's:* #8401

STREAM (masc. יאור *ye'or)* A body of running water; any body of flowing water. *AHLB:* 1227-D(N) *Strong's:* #2975

STREET (fem. רחוב *re'hhov)* A thoroughfare, especially in a city, town or village. *AHLB:* 2759(c) *Strong's:* #7339

STRENGTH (masc. כוח *ko'ahh)* The quality or state of being strong. *AHLB:* 1238-J(N) *Strong's:* #3581(x2)

STRESS (masc. מצוק *ma'tsoq)* Activity or circumstance that causes oppression. *AHLB:* 1402-J(a) *Strong's:* #4689

STRETCH.OUT$^{(V)}$ (*r.b.ts)* To lie or stretch out as to rest; to crouch down to hide for an ambush. *AHLB:* 2745$^{(V)}$ *Strong's:* #7257

STRIFE (masc. *a'saq) Strong's:* [Found in names only]

STRIKE.THROUGH$^{(V)}$ (*m.hh.ts) AHLB:* 2334$^{(V)}$ *Strong's:* #4272

STRIKING (masc. *ne'geph)* The act of being hit. A plague as hitting the people. *AHLB:* 2377$^{(N)}$ *Strong's:* #5063

STRING (masc. *mey'shar / mey'tar)* A cord or rope, as straight. Also, a straight line, path or thought. *AHLB:* 1480-L(k) *Strong's:* #4339, #4340

STRIP (fem. *pe'tsa'lah)* To remove clothing, covering, or surface matter from. *AHLB:* 2626(N1) *Strong's:* #6479

STRIP.OFF$^{(V)}$ (*p.sh.t)* To take off an outer layer; to spread apart; to invade in the sense of spreading out for an attack; to strip off clothing in the sense of spreading the garment for removal. *AHLB:* 2646$^{(V)}$ *Strong's:* #6584

STRIPED (masc. *a'qod)* Having stripes or streaks. As appearing to be whipped with a cord. *AHLB:* 2572(c) *Strong's:* #6124

STRIPED.BRUISE (fem. *hha'bu'rah)* Marks made by ropes binding the wrist or lashes with a rope. *AHLB:* 2143(d1) *Strong's:* #2250

STRIVE$^{(V)}$ (*ah.s.q)* A ground of dispute or complaint. A clash between sides. *AHLB:* 2562$^{(V)}$ *Strong's:* #6229

STRONG (masc. *az)* Having or marked by great physical strength. *AHLB:* 1352-A$^{(N)}$ *Strong's:* #5794

STRONG.ONE (masc. *a'zan) Strong's:* [Found in names only]

STRUGGLE$^{(V)}$ (*n.ts.h)* The act of trying to achieve the goal, but with hindrances. *AHLB:* 1317-H$^{(V)}$ *Strong's:* #5327

STUBBLE (masc. *qash)* What is left after the stalk has been removed. *AHLB:* 1435-A$^{(N)}$ *Strong's:* #7179

STUBBORNNESS (masc. *q'shiy)* As stiff. *AHLB:* 1435-A(f) *Strong's:* #7190

STUMBLING.BLOCK (masc. *mikh'shol)* Used to cause someone to stumble or topple down. *AHLB:* 2292(hc) *Strong's:* #4383

SUBDUE$^{(V)}$ (*k.b.sh)* To conquer and bring into subjection; bring under control. Place the foot on the land in the sense of subduing it. Also, to place one's foot into another nation in the sense of subduing it. *AHLB:* 2251$^{(V)}$ *Strong's:* #3533

SUBDUER (masc. *ka'mush) Strong's:* [Found in names only]

SUBMERGE$^{(V)}$ (*t.m.n)* To hide by burying or covering. *AHLB:* 2234$^{(V)}$ *Strong's:* #2934

SUBMERSION (fem. *a'mo'rah) Strong's:* [Found in names only]

SUBSIDE$^{(V)}$ (*sh.k.k)* Become quiet or less. To calm down or set down. *AHLB:* 1471-B$^{(V)}$ *Strong's:* #7918

SUBSTANCE (masc. *ye'qum)* A fundamental or characteristic part or quality. Any standing thing or person. *AHLB:* 1427-L(d) *Strong's:* #3351

SUBTLE (masc. *a'rum)* Difficult to understand or distinguish. In craftiness or prudence. *AHLB:* 2908(d) *Strong's:* #6175

SUBTLETY (fem. *ar'mah)* Performance that calls no attention to its self. To act in craftiness or prudence. *AHLB:* 2908(N1) *Strong's:* #6193, #6195

SUCKLE$^{(V)}$ (*y.n.q)* To give milk to from the breast or udder. *Alternate Translation:* nurse (when written in the hiphil [active causative] form) *AHLB:* 1318-L$^{(V)}$ *Strong's:* #3243

SUDDENLY (masc. *pit'om)* As a wink of time. *AHLB:* 2652(eqp) *Strong's:* #6597

SUET (masc. *pe'der)* A greasy substance. *AHLB:* 2596(N) *Strong's:* #6309

SUFFICIENT (masc. *dai)* An amount that is not lacking. What is enough. *AHLB:* 1079-A(N) *Strong's:* #1767

SUFFICIENT(V) (*h.w.n)* Adequate for the purpose; enough. *Alternate Translation:* ready (when written in the hiphil [causative] form) *AHLB:* 1106-J(V) *Strong's:* #1951

SUM (fem. *mat'ko'net)* The total amount. An amount weighed out. *AHLB:* 2893(ac2) *Strong's:* #4971

SUMMER (masc. *qits)* The season between spring and autumn. *AHLB:* 1432-M(N) *Strong's:* #7019

SUN (fem. *she'mesh)* The luminous body around which the earth revolves and from which it receives heat and light. *AHLB:* 2854(N) *Strong's:* #8121

SUN.IDOL (masc. *hham'man)* An object of worship representing the sun god. *AHLB:* 1174-A(m) *Strong's:* #2553

SUNKEN (masc. *a'moq) AHLB:* 2553(c) *Strong's:* #6013

SUNRISE (masc. *miz'rah)* When the first light of the sun comes over the horizon. An eastward direction as the place of the rising sun. *AHLB:* 2135(h) *Strong's:* #4217

SUPPLY.HOUSE (masc. *o'tsar)* A place where grain or other items of subsistence are held and protected. *AHLB:* 1411-C(g) *Strong's:* #0214

SUPPORT(V) (*s.m.k)* To uphold or defend; to hold up or serve as a foundation or prop for. *AHLB:* 2488(V) *Strong's:* #5564

SUPPRESS(V) (*y.n.h)* To cause to be brought low by force, hindered. *AHLB:* 1304-L(V) *Strong's:* #3238

SURE (fem. *am'nah)* Safe from danger or harm; marked by or given to feelings of confident certainty. What is firm. *AHLB:* 1290-C(N1) *Strong's:* #0545, #0546, #0548

SURELY (masc. / *a'kheyn / akh)* In a sure manner. To be firm in something. *Alternate Translation:* however; only *AHLB:* 1244-C(N) *Strong's:* #0389, #0403

SURROUNDED.BY.A.WALL (masc. *hhets'ron)* To be surrounded, encompassed, by a wall of stone or thorns for protection. *Strong's:* [Found in names only]

SURVIVOR (masc. *sa'riyd)* What remains from the whole. *AHLB:* 2506(b) *Strong's:* #8300

SUSTAIN(V) (*k.w.l)* To provide what is needed to make someone or something whole or complete. *AHLB:* 1242-J(V) *Strong's:* #3557

SWALLOW(V) (*b.l.ah)* To pass through the mouth and move into the esophagus to the stomach. *AHLB:* 2020(V) *Strong's:* #1104

SWALLOWED (masc. *be'la)* To take in so as to envelope. *AHLB:* 2020(N) *Strong's:* #1105

SWARM(V) (*sh.r.ts)* To move, as a large mass of creatures. *AHLB:* 2881(V) *Strong's:* #8317

SWARMER (masc. *she'rets)* The creature(s) *AHLB:* 2881(N) *Strong's:* #8318

SWARMING.LOCUST (masc. *ar'beh)* A six legged insect having short antennae and commonly migrating in swarms that strip the vegetation from large areas. *AHLB:* 1439-H(N) *Strong's:* #0697

SWEAR(V) (*sh.b.ah)* To completely submit to a promise or oath with words and spoken seven times. *AHLB:* 2808(V) *Strong's:* #7650

SWEARING (fem. *she'vu'ah)* The act of taking an oath. *AHLB:* 2808(d1) *Strong's:* #7621

SWEAT (fem. *ze'ah)* To excrete moisture in visible quantities through the pores of the skin. *AHLB:* 1154-A(N1) *Strong's:* #2188

SWEEP(V) (*g.w.z)* To move or remove (dust, dirt, etc.) *AHLB:* 1053-J(V) *Strong's:* #1468

SWEET (masc. *ni'hho'ahh)* Pleasing to the taste. Not sour, bitter or salty. Something that smells pleasing. *AHLB:* 1310-B(bc) *Strong's:* #5207

SWEET.SPICE (masc. *be'sem)* An aromatic spice that is pleasing to the nose. *AHLB:* 2024(g) *Strong's:* #1314

SWEETNESS (masc. *me'teq fem.* *mit'qah) AHLB:* 2364(N) *Strong's:* #4986

SWELL(V) (*ts.b.h) AHLB:* 1393-H(V) *Strong's:* #6638

SWELL.UP(V) (*b.ts.q)* To rise or increase in size. *AHLB:* 2032(V) *Strong's:* #1216

SWELLING (masc. *tsa'veh) AHLB:* 1393-H(N) *Strong's:* #6639

SWIFTNESS (masc. *pe'let) Strong's:* [Found in names only]

SWINE (masc. *hha'ziyr)* An unclean cloved hoof mammal that does not chew the cud. *AHLB:* 2153(b) *Strong's:* #2386

SWORD (fem. *hhe'rev)* A weapon with a long, possibly curved, blade for cutting or thrusting. *AHLB:* 2199(N) *Strong's:* #2719

TABLE (masc. *shul'hhan)* A flat surface, usually made of wood and with four legs, for laying out the meal to be eaten. *AHLB:* 2842(om) *Strong's:* #7979

TAIL (masc. *na'nav)* The hindmost flexible appendage of an animal. *AHLB:* 2125(N) *Strong's:* #2180

TAKE(V) (*l.q.hh)* To receive what is given; to gain possession by seizing. *AHLB:* 2319(V) *Strong's:* #3947

TAKE.A.FIFTH(V) (*hh.m.sh)* To separate out one equal portion out of five. *AHLB:* 2176(V) *Strong's:* #2567

TAKE.AS.A.PLEDGE(V) (*hh.b.l)* To receive an object in exchange for a promise. *AHLB:* 2141(V) *Strong's:* #2254

TAKE.AWAY(V) (*g.r.ah)* To scrape off or clip. To impair or degrade. *AHLB:* 2087(V) *Strong's:* #1639

TAKE.HEED(V) (*s.k.t)* To be silent. *AHLB:* 2480(V) *Strong's:* #5535

TAKE.HOLD(V) (*a.hh.z)* To have possession or ownership of; to keep in restraint; to have or maintain in one's grasp; to grab something and keep hold of it. *AHLB:* 1168-C(V) *Strong's:* #0270

TAKE.REFUGE(V) (*hh.s.h)* To take shelter or place ones trust in someone or something of support. *AHLB:* 1176-H(V) *Strong's:* #2620

TAKE.STEPS(V) (*d.r.k)* To take a walk or journey. Also, stringing of a bow (from the action of stepping through the bow and using the leg to string the bow). *AHLB:* 2112(V) *Strong's:* #1869

TAKE.UPON$^{(V)}$ (*y.a.l)* The placing of a yoke on the shoulders, literally or figuratively, to perform work or undertake a task. *Alternate Translation:* agree (when written in the hiphil [active causative] form) *AHLB:* 1012-L$^{(V)}$ *Strong's:* #2974

TALEBEARER (masc. *ra'khiyl)* A traveler selling stories and songs. As a talebearer. *AHLB:* 2770(b) *Strong's:* #7400

TALK$^{(V)}$ (*m.l.l)* To deliver or express in spoken words. *AHLB:* 1288-B$^{(V)}$ *Strong's:* #4448

TAMARISK (masc. *a'shal)* The tree or a grove of desert shrubs and trees with masses of minute flowers. *AHLB:* 1472-C$^{(N)}$ *Strong's:* #0815

TAMBOURINE (masc. *toph)* A shallow, one-headed drum with loose disks at the sides played by shaking, striking with the hand, or rubbing with the thumb. *AHLB:* 1500-J$^{(N)}$ *Strong's:* #8596

TASK.WORK (masc. *mas)* A forced labor or service. *AHLB:* 1291-A$^{(N)}$ *Strong's:* #4522, #4523

TASSEL (masc. *ga'diiyl)* An ornament consisting of twisted threads, small cords, or other strands. *AHLB:* 2054(b) *Strong's:* #1434

TASTE.SWEET$^{(V)}$ (*m.t.q)* To have a pleasant taste to the mouth. *AHLB:* 2364$^{(V)}$ *Strong's:* #4985, #4988

TASTY.FOOD (masc. *ma'a'dan)* Having a marked and pleasing flavor. As a pleasurable thing. *AHLB:* 2528(a) *Strong's:* #4574

TATTOO (masc. *qa'qa) AHLB:* 1430-A(l) *Strong's:* #7085

TAUNT$^{(V)}$ (*g.d.p)* To reproach in a sarcastic, insulting, or jeering manner; mock. *AHLB:* 2056$^{(V)}$ *Strong's:* #1442

TEACHING (fem. *to'rah)* Acquired knowledge or skills that mark the direction one is to take in life. A straight direction. Knowledge passed from one person to another. *AHLB:* 1227-H(i1) *Strong's:* #8451

TEAR$^{(V)}$ (*q.r.ah)* To rip into pieces. *AHLB:* 2734$^{(V)}$ *Strong's:* #7167

TEAR.AWAY$^{(V)}$ (*n.s.hh) AHLB:* 2411$^{(V)}$ *Strong's:* #5255

TEAR.INTO.PIECES$^{(V)}$ (*t.r.p)* To tear into pieces as a predator does to its prey; to rip a cloth into pieces. *AHLB:* 2245$^{(V)}$ *Strong's:* #2963

TEAR.OFF$^{(V)}$ (*p.r.q)* To remove reluctantly. *AHLB:* 2643$^{(V)}$ *Strong's:* #6561

TEAT (masc. *dad)* The protuberance on the udder in female mammals, through which the milk ducts discharge. *AHLB:* 1073-A$^{(N)}$ *Strong's:* #1717

TEN (masc. / *a'sa'rah fem.* *e'ser)* A cardinal number. *Alternate Translation:* twenty (when written in the plural) *AHLB:* 2563$^{(N)}$ *Strong's:* #6235, #6240, #6242

TENDER (masc. *rakh fem.* *ra'kah)* Having a soft or yielding texture; easily broken, cut, or damaged. From the tenderness of the loins. *AHLB:* 1448-A$^{(N)}$ *Strong's:* #7390

TENDERNESS (masc. *rokh) AHLB:* 1448-J$^{(N)}$ *Strong's:* #7391

TENT (masc. *o'hel)* A portable shelter made of black goat hair used by the nomads of the Near East. *AHLB:* 1104-C(g) *Strong's:* #0168

TENT.CURTAIN (fem. *pa'ro'khet)* A wall of fabric or hung from the roof to make a dividing of a room. *AHLB:* 2638(c2) *Strong's:* #6532

TENT.PEG (fem. *ya'teyd)* An instrument used to secure the corners and sides of the tent to the ground. *AHLB:* 1487-L$^{(N)}$ *Strong's:* #3489

TENT.WALL (fem. יריעה *ye'ri'a)* The goat hair curtain that forms the walls of the tent. *AHLB:* 1440-L$^{(N)}$ *Strong's:* #3407

TENTH (masc. עשירי *a'si'ri)* An ordinal number. *AHLB:* 2563(bf) *Strong's:* #6224

TENTH.ONE (masc. עשור *a'sor)* That which occupies the tenth position in a sequence. *AHLB:* 2563(c) *Strong's:* #6218

TENTH.PART (masc. מעשר *ma'a'seyr)* One portion of a whole divided into ten equal portions. *AHLB:* 2563(a) *Strong's:* #4643

TERMINATE$^{(V)}$ (חדל *hh.d.l)* To stop or refrain from continuing an action. *AHLB:* 2148$^{(V)}$ *Strong's:* #2308

TERROR (fem. אימה *ey'mah)* A state of intense fear. *AHLB:* 1220-C(N1) *Strong's:* #0367

TEST$^{(V)}$ (נסה *n.s.h)* A critical examination, observation, or evaluation; trial. *AHLB:* 1314-H$^{(V)}$ *Strong's:* #5254

TESTICLES (masc. אשך *e'shekh) AHLB:* 1471-C$^{(N)}$ *Strong's:* #0810

THANKS (fem. תודה *to'dah)* An expression of gratitude or acknowledgement toward another. *AHLB:* 1211-A(i1) *Strong's:* #8426

THANKSGIVING (masc. יהודה *ye'hu'dah)* An expression of thanks through shouting. *Strong's:* [Found in names only]

THAT (masc. מען *ma'an)* The person, thing, or idea indicated, mentioned, or understood from the situation. A close watching. (Always used with the prefix ל meaning "to") *Alternate Translation:* as; on account of, so that, or in order (when prefixed with "to~") *AHLB:* 1359-A(a) *Strong's:* #4616

THAT.ONE (masc. מו *mo)* Being the person, thing, or idea specified, mentioned, or understood. (Always prefixed with the letter ב meaning in, the letter ל meaning to, or the letter כ meaning like.) *Alternate Translation:* as (when prefixed with "like~"); this (when suffixed with "~him") *AHLB:* 1282-A$^{(N)}$ *Strong's:* #1119, #3644, #3926

THEFT (fem. גנבה *ge'ney'vah)* The unlawful taking of another's property. *AHLB:* 2073(N1) *Strong's:* #1591

THEN (masc. אפו *ey'pho)* An inquiry of a time or place. *AHLB:* 1374-C$^{(N)}$ *Strong's:* #0645

THERE (masc. שם *sham)* Used to identify another place. *Alternate Translation:* in *AHLB:* 1473-A$^{(N)}$ *Strong's:* #8033

THERE.IS (masc. אש / יש *yeysh / eysh)* Something that exists. *Alternate Translation:* are; is; will *AHLB:* 1228-A$^{(N)}$ *Strong's:* #0786, #3426

THESE (masc. אלה / אל *el / ey'lah)* The persons, things, or ideas present or near in place, time, or thought or just mentioned. A grammatical tool used to identify something specific in the sense of looking toward a sight. *AHLB:* 1104-A$^{(N)}$ *Strong's:* #0411, #0428

THEY (masc. המה *hey'mah)* The plural of "he." *Alternate Translation:* those, these *AHLB:* 1093-J$^{(N)}$ *Strong's:* #1992

THEY (fem. הנה *hey'nah)* The plural of "she." *Alternate Translation:* those *AHLB:* 1093-J$^{(N)}$ *Strong's:* #2007, #3860

THICK (עב *av) AHLB:* 1508-A$^{(N)}$ *Strong's:* #5645

THICK.DARKNESS (masc. ערפל *a'ra'phel)* A heavy darkness that can be felt. *AHLB:* 3067 *Strong's:* #6205

THICK.GLOOMINESS (fem. *a'phey'lah)* A heavy darkness that brings about sadness or depression. *AHLB:* 1380-C(N1) *Strong's:* #0653

THICK.WOVEN (fem. *a'vot)* A rope or other woven object that is tightly wrapped. *AHLB:* 1508-A(N3) *Strong's:* #5687, #5688

THIEF (masc. *ga'nav)* One who steals the property of another. *AHLB:* 2073(N) *Strong's:* #1590

THIGH (fem. *shuq)* The upper part of the leg of a man or animal. Also, a street. *AHLB:* 1479-J(N) *Strong's:* #7784, #7785

THIGH.MUSCLE (masc. *na'she)* Each side of the trunk formed by the lateral parts of the pelvis and upper part of the femur (thigh bone) *AHLB:* 1320-H(N) *Strong's:* #5384

THIN (masc. *raq)* Not dense in distribution; not well-fleshed. *AHLB:* 1456-A(N) *Strong's:* #7534

THIN.BREAD (masc. *ra'qiq)* Dough that has been spread thin before baked. *AHLB:* 1456-B(b) *Strong's:* #7550

THING.WRITTEN (masc. *mikh'tav)* A composition that has been recorded by the written words. *AHLB:* 2295(h) *Strong's:* #4385

THINK(V) (*hh.sh.b)* To plan or design a course of action, item or invention. *Alternate Translation:* consider (when written in the niphal form); plan (when written in the pi'el form) *AHLB:* 2213(V) *Strong's:* #2803

THIRD (masc. *she'li'shi)* An ordinal number. *AHLB:* 2847(bf) *Strong's:* #7992

THIRD.GENERATION (masc. *shi'leysh)* The third increment within the sequence. *AHLB:* 2847(e) *Strong's:* #8029

THIRST (masc. *tsa'mey fem.* *tsiy'mah)* The lack of sufficient water. *AHLB:* 1404-E(N) *Strong's:* #6771, #6772, #6773

THIRST(V) (*ts.m.a)* To lack sufficient water. *AHLB:* 1404-E(V) *Strong's:* #6770

THIRSTY.LAND (masc. *tsiy'ma'on)* A thirsty land. *AHLB:* 1404-E(ej) *Strong's:* #6774

THIS (masc. *zeh fem.* *zot)* A person, thing, or idea present or near in place, time, or thought or just mentioned. As prominent or pointed out. *Alternate Translation:* that; here (when prefixed with "in~") *AHLB:* 1143-A(N) *Strong's:* #1454, #2063, #2088, #2090, #2097

THIS.ONE (fem. *ha'la'zeh)* The one nearer or more immediately under observation or discussion. *AHLB:* 1260-F(N1) *Strong's:* #1976

THISTLE (masc. *dar'dar)* A prickly plant used by the shepherd to build a corral around the flock at night. *AHLB:* 1089-A(l) *Strong's:* #1863

THORN.BUSH (masc. *se'neh)* A plant, bush or tree, that grows thorns. *AHLB:* 1336-H(N) *Strong's:* #5572

THOUGH (masc. *heyn)* However; nevertheless. In spite of the fact of. A possible or desired location. To bring attention to an event. *Alternate Translation:* but; look; since *AHLB:* 1106-A(N) *Strong's:* #2004, #2005

THOUGHT (masc. *yey'tser)* The forming of ideas in the mind. *AHLB:* 1411-L(N) *Strong's:* #3336

THOUSAND (masc. *e'leph)* Ten times one hundred in amount or number. *AHLB:* 2001(N) *Strong's:* #0505

THREAD (masc. *hhut)* A filament of fibers twisted together by spinning and used for sewing or tying items together. *AHLB:* 1170-J$^{(N)}$ *Strong's:* #2339

THREE (masc. *she'lo'shah fem. she'losh)* A cardinal number. *Alternate Translation:* thirty (when written in the plural) *AHLB:* 2847(c) *Strong's:* #7969, #7970

THREE.DAYS.AGO (masc. *shil'shom)* Literally the day before yesterday, but used as an idiom for the past. *AHLB:* 2847(eqp) *Strong's:* #8032

THRESH$^{(V)}$ (*a.d.sh)* To separate the grain or seeds from a plant by beating with a flail. *AHLB:* 1090-C$^{(V)}$ *Strong's:* #0156

THRESHER (masc. *diy'shan)* One who separates the grain or seeds from a plant by beating with a flail. *Strong's:* [Found in names only]

THRESHING (masc. *da'iysh)* The separating of the grain or seeds from a plant by beating with a flail. *AHLB:* 1090-M$^{(N)}$ *Strong's:* #1786

THROW$^{(V)}$ (*y.r.h / y.r.a)* To propel through the air by a forward motion; to drizzle as a throwing down of water; to teach in the sense of throwing or pointing a finger in a straight line as the direction one is to walk. *Alternate Translation:* point or teach (when written in the hiphil [active causative] form) *AHLB:* 1227-H$^{(V)}$ *Strong's:* #3384

THROW.DOWN$^{(V)}$ (*r.m.h)* To lead astray; to deliver to an enemy by treachery; to reveal unintentionally. *Alternate Translation:* betray (when written in the piel [active intensive] form) *AHLB:* 1450-H$^{(V)}$ *Strong's:* #7411

THROW.OUT$^{(V)}$ (*sh.l.k)* To remove from a place, usually in a sudden or unexpected manner; to cast out, down or away. *AHLB:* 2844$^{(V)}$ *Strong's:* #7993

THROW.THE.HAND$^{(V)}$ (*y.d.h / h.d.h)* To stretch out the hand to grab; to show praise or confession. *Alternate Translation:* thank (when written in the hiphil [active causative] form); confess (when written in the hitpa'el [reflexive] form) *AHLB:* 1211-H$^{(V)}$ *Strong's:* #1911, #3034

THROWING (masc. *miy'dad) Strong's:* [Found in names only]

THRUST$^{(V)}$ (*t.q.ah)* To push or drive with force a pole into the ground, such as when setting up the tent; to blow the trumpet in the sense of throwing out the sound. *AHLB:* 2902$^{(V)}$ *Strong's:* #8628

THUMB (fem. *bo'hen)* The opposable digit of the hand. Also, the big toe of the foot. Perceived as the builder because of its unique abilities. *AHLB:* 1037-G$^{(N)}$ *Strong's:* #0931

TIE$^{(V)}$ (*q.sh.r)* To fasten, attach, or close by means of a string or cord; to tie around; to conspire in the sense of tying up. *Alternate Translation:* robust (when written in the pual [passive intensive] form) *AHLB:* 2740$^{(V)}$ *Strong's:* #7194

TIE.ON$^{(V)}$ (*r.k.s)* To attach or bind one object to another by tying them together. *AHLB:* 2771$^{(V)}$ *Strong's:* #7405

TIE.UP$^{(V)}$ (*a.s.r)* To wrap or fasten with a cord. *AHLB:* 1342-C$^{(V)}$ *Strong's:* #0631

TIGHTLY.WRAPPED (masc. *lut)* To cover or encircle tightly. *AHLB:* 1262-J$^{(N)}$ *Strong's:* #3875

TIME (masc. *mo'neh)* The measured or measurable period during which an action, process or condition exists or continues. A counting or reckoning of time. *AHLB:* 1290-H(g) *Strong's:* #4489

TIME.OF.WEEPING (fem. *be'khit)* A period of sadness or mourning. *AHLB:* 1034-A(N4) *Strong's:* #1068

TIN (masc. *be'diyl)* A metal separated out by smelting. *AHLB:* 2005(b) *Strong's:* #0913

TINY (masc. *tso'ar) Strong's:* [Found in names only]

TIP (masc. *te'nuk)* The pointed end of an object. *AHLB:* 1310-J(i) *Strong's:* #8571

TIRED (masc. *a'yeyph)* Drained of strength and energy; fatigued. *AHLB:* 1362-M$^{(N)}$ *Strong's:* #5889

TITLE (masc. *sheym)* A word given to an individual or place denoting its character. The character of an individual or place. *AHLB:* 1473-A$^{(N)}$ *Strong's:* #8034

TO (masc. *el)* Used as a function word to indicate movement or an action or condition suggestive of progress toward a place, person, or thing reached. *Alternate Translation:* at; by; for; on; into, belonging to *AHLB:* 1104-A$^{(N)}$ *Strong's:* #0413

TO.THIS.POINT (masc. *hey'nah)* A precise moment in time or a specific location. *Alternate Translation:* here *AHLB:* 1106-H$^{(N)}$ *Strong's:* #2008

TOGETHER (masc. *ya'hhad)* In or into one place, mass, collection, or group. *AHLB:* 1165-L$^{(N)}$ *Strong's:* #3162

TOIL (masc. *ye'gi'a)* The act of working one's self to exhaustion. *AHLB:* 1062-L(b) *Strong's:* #3018, #3019

TOKEN (masc. *ey'ra'von)* Something given as a promise as an exchange. *AHLB:* 2573(j) *Strong's:* #6162

TOMORROW (fem. *ma'hhar)* The next day. At a time following. *AHLB:* 1181-A(a) *Strong's:* #4279

TONG (masc. *mel'qahh)* An instrument used for grasping, having two arms working together. A tool for taking coals out of the fire. *AHLB:* 2319(a) *Strong's:* #4457

TONGUE (masc. *la'shon)* A fleshy moveable process on the floor of the mouth used in speaking and eating. Also, language as a tongue. *AHLB:* 2325(c) *Strong's:* #3956

TOOLS (masc. *a'zeyn)* An implement used for agriculture or war. *AHLB:* 1152-C$^{(N)}$ *Strong's:* #0240

TOOTH (*sheyn) AHLB:* 1474-A$^{(N)}$ *Strong's:* #8127

TOP.OF.THE.HEAD (masc. *qad'qod)* The crown of the head. *AHLB:* 1418-A(lc) *Strong's:* #6936

TOPAZ (masc. *tar'shish)* Possibly the Topaz, which may be yellow, gray, white, pink, green or blue in color. Other possible translations are Beryl, Lapis Lazuli, Amber, Jasper, Serpentine, Olivine, or Flint. *AHLB:* 1458-B(ib) *Strong's:* #8658

TOPPLE$^{(V)}$ (*k.sh.l)* To fall over in death or from being pushed. *AHLB:* 2292$^{(V)}$ *Strong's:* #3782

TORCH (masc. *la'pid)* A burning stick of resinous wood. Also, lightning as a torch in the night sky. *AHLB:* 2317(b) *Strong's:* #3940

TORN (fem. *te'rey'phah)* Pulled apart. Flesh that is torn. *AHLB:* 2245(N1) *Strong's:* #2966

TORTOISE (masc. *tsav)* An unknown creature, but probably a turtle or tortoise because of it's protective shell. *AHLB:* 1393-A$^{(N)}$ *Strong's:* #6632(x2)

TOSS[V] (*n.d.d)* To heave or fling about; to throw with a quick, light, or careless motion; to be thrown about or wander around as nodding the head. *AHLB:* 1303-B[V] *Strong's:* #5074

TOSS.OUT[V] (*k.w.r / q.w.r / b.w.r)* To look deeply. *AHLB:* 1250-J[V] *Strong's:* #0952, #6979

TOTTER[V] (*m.w.t)* To waver as a green branch. *AHLB:* 1285-J[V] *Strong's:* #4131

TOUCH (masc. *ne'ga)* A mark as a sign of a touch; a mark indicating a sore, illness or epidemic. *Alternate Translation:* plague *AHLB:* 2376[N] *Strong's:* #5061

TOUCH[V] (*n.g.ah)* To lay hands upon; to touch or strike; to be touched by a plague. *AHLB:* 2376[V] *Strong's:* #5060

TOUGHNESS (masc. *do've)* Strong and durable. [The meaning of this word is unknown, but is translated as "strength" in the Aramaic, Syriac and Greek translations.]. *AHLB:* 1071-E[N] *Strong's:* #1679

TOWER (masc. *mig'dal)* A structure higher than its diameter and high relative to its surroundings. Place of great size. *AHLB:* 2054(h) *Strong's:* #4026

TOWN (fem. *hha'wah)* A small village. *AHLB:* 1167-A(N1) *Strong's:* #2333

TRADE[V] (*s.hh.r)* The business of buying and selling or bartering commodities. To go about as a merchant trading goods. In Psalm 38:11 this word is used for the beating of the heart in the sense of going about to and fro. *AHLB:* 2473[V] *Strong's:* #5503

TRAMPLE.DOWN[V] (*b.w.s)* To purposely destroy by stomping upon to break or smash. *AHLB:* 1038-J[V] *Strong's:* #0947

TRANCE (fem. *tar'dey'mah)* A state of partly suspended animation or inability to function. A deep sleep or unconsciousness. *AHLB:* 2754(i1) *Strong's:* #8639

TRANQUILITY (masc. *shi'loh)* A state of rest. *AHLB:* 1472-H[V] *Strong's:* #7886

TRANSGRESS[V] (*m.ah.l)* To commit an unintentional or treacherous act that results in error. *AHLB:* 2349[V] *Strong's:* #4603

TRANSGRESSION (masc. *ma'al)* An unintentional or treacherous act that results in error. *AHLB:* 2349[N] *Strong's:* #4604

TRAP[V] (*l.k.d)* To forcefully take or seize. *AHLB:* 2310[V] *Strong's:* #3920

TRAPPINGS (masc. *a'di)* Articles of dress or adornment that often witness to a person's position or rank. *AHLB:* 1349-A(f) *Strong's:* #5716

TREAD[V] (*r.m.s)* To trample under foot. *AHLB:* 2775[V] *Strong's:* #7429, #7430

TREAD.ABOUT[V] (*r.g.l)* To be on foot walking through a foreign land, usually in the sense of spying; to trample another with the tongue. *Alternate Translation:* spy (when written in the piel [active intensive] form) *AHLB:* 2749[V] *Strong's:* #7270, #8637

TREADER (masc. *re'mes)* A creature that crawls or creeps on something. *AHLB:* 2775[N] *Strong's:* #7431

TREASURE (masc. *mat'mon)* Wealth hoarded up or stored. What is hidden. *AHLB:* 2234(ac) *Strong's:* #4301

TREASURY (masc. *tsaph'nat) Strong's:* [Found in names only]

TREE (masc. *eyts)* A woody perennial plant with a supporting stem or trunk and multiple branches. *Alternate Translation:* wood (especially when in the plural form, but occasionally, depending on context, in the singular as well) *AHLB:* 1363-A$^{(N)}$ *Strong's:* #6086, #6097

TREMBLE$^{(V)}$ (*hh.r.d)* To shake involuntarily; shiver. *AHLB:* 2201$^{(V)}$ *Strong's:* #2729

TREMBLING (masc. *hha'rad fem.* *hha'ra'dah)* An involuntary shaking or shivering out of fear or awe. *AHLB:* 2201$^{(N)}$ *Strong's:* #2730, #2731

TREMBLING.IN.FEAR (masc. *hhet)* A physical reaction, such as shivering, in fear or dread. *AHLB:* 1183-A$^{(N)}$ *Strong's:* #2844

TRIAL (fem. *ma'sah)* The act of trying, testing, or putting to the proof. *AHLB:* 1314-A(a1) *Strong's:* #4530

TRIBAL (masc. *a'mon) Strong's:* [Found in names only]

TRIBE (fem. *u'mah)* A social group consisting of numerous families, clans or generations together. A family lineage as bound together. *AHLB:* 1013-J(N1) *Strong's:* #0523

TRIBUTARY (masc. *pe'leg)* A dividing of a watercourse into separate branches. *AHLB:* 2606$^{(N)}$ *Strong's:* #6388

TRIBUTE (masc. *me'khes)* An assessment based on a number. *AHLB:* 1245-A(k) *Strong's:* #4371

TRICKLING (fem. *ziyl'pah)* To flow or fall by drops, or in a small, gentle stream. *Strong's:* [Found in names only]

TROUBLE (fem. *te'la'ah)* A difficulty that brings about weariness. *AHLB:* 1258-D(i1) *Strong's:* #8513

TROUBLED (masc. *ze'ah)* To disturb the mental calm and contentment of; worry; distress; agitate. *Strong's:* [Found in names only]

TROUGH (masc. *ra'hat)* A long, shallow often V-shaped receptacle for the drinking water or food of domestic animals. *AHLB:* 1446-G$^{(N)}$ *Strong's:* #7298

TRUTH (fem. *e'met)* The state of being the case. Fact. What is firm. Accurately so. *AHLB:* 1290-C(N2) *Strong's:* #0571

TUMOR (masc. *a'phal)* A mound on the skin. *AHLB:* 2564(g) *Strong's:* #6076(x2)

TUMULT (fem. *m'hu'mah)* A tormenting; trouble; distress; plague; worry. *AHLB:* 1105-J(k1) *Strong's:* #4103

TUMULTUOUS (masc. *) Strong's:* [Found in names only]

TUNIC (fem. *ke'to'net)* A simple slip-on garment with or without sleeves. *AHLB:* 2298(c2) *Strong's:* #3801

TURBAN (fem. *mits'ne'phet)* A cloth that is wrapped around the head. *AHLB:* 2673(h2) *Strong's:* #4701

TURN$^{(V)}$ (*p.n.h)* To rotate or revolve; to face another direction; to turn the face; to turn directions; to turn something back or away. *Alternate Translation:* clear away or clear out (when written in the piel [passive] form) *AHLB:* 1382-H$^{(V)}$ *Strong's:* #6437

TURN.ASIDE$^{(V)}$ (/ *s.w.r)* To change the location, position, station, or residence; to remove. *Alternate Translation:* remove (when written in the hiphil [active causative] form); make self ruler (when written in the hit'pa'el [reflexive] form) *AHLB:* 1342-J$^{(V)}$ *Strong's:* #5493, #7787, #8323

TURN.AWAY$^{(V)}$ (*s.r.h)* To deviate from the correct path toward another direction. *AHLB:* 1342-H$^{(V)}$ *Strong's:* #8280

TURN.BACK(V) (*sh.w.b)* To return to a previous place or state. *Alternate Translation:* return *AHLB:* 1462-J(V) *Strong's:* #7725

TURN.OVER(V) (*ah.t.p)* To turn aside in fainting or hiding. *Alternate Translation:* feeble (when written in the hiphil [active causative] form) *AHLB:* 2537(V) *Strong's:* #5848

TURNING.ASIDE (fem. *sa'rah)* A change in location, position, station or residence, usually as a revolt. *AHLB:* 1342-A(N1) *Strong's:* #5627

TURQUOISE (masc. *no'phek)* Possibly the Turquoise, a blue to green stone that was commonly mined in the Near East. The Septuagint has Anthrax meaning coal. Other possible translations are Carbuncle, Garnet, Emerald and Malachite. *AHLB:* 2420(g) *Strong's:* #5306

TURTLEDOVE (fem. *tor)* A small wild pigeon. *AHLB:* 1503-J(N) *Strong's:* #8449

TWIG (masc. *sa'rig)* A secondary shoot or stem arising from a main trunk or axis.. *AHLB:* 2505(b) *Strong's:* #8299

TWILIGHT (fem. *a'la'tah)* The light from the sky between full night and sunrise; or between sunset and full night. *AHLB:* 2543(N1) *Strong's:* #5939

TWIN (masc. *ta'om)* Born with one other or as a pair at birth. *AHLB:* 1496-D(c) *Strong's:* #8380

TWIRL(V) (*n.d.p)* To toss back and forth. *AHLB:* 2384(V) *Strong's:* #5086

TWIST (fem. *aw'wa) AHLB:* 1511-J(N1) *Strong's:* #5754

TWIST(V) (*hh.w.l / hh.y.l)* A winding or wrapping together; entwined in pain or joy. *AHLB:* 1173-J(V) *Strong's:* #2342

TWIST.AROUND (fem. *hhu'il)* A winding together. *Strong's:* [Found in names only]

TWIST.BACKWARDS(V) (*s.l.p)* A path that winds back on itself. To twist words or actions away from their proper context. *AHLB:* 2485(V) *Strong's:* #5557

TWIST.TOGETHER(V) (*sh.z.r)* To wrap separate pieces together forming one unit. *Alternate Translation:* twisted (when written in the hophal [passive causative] form) *AHLB:* 2821(V) *Strong's:* #7806

TWISTED (masc. *p'tal'tol) AHLB:* 2650(l) *Strong's:* #6618

TWISTEDNESS (masc. *a'won)* Gross injustice; wickedness. The result of twisted actions. *AHLB:* 1512-A(m) *Strong's:* #5771

TWO (masc. *she'na'yim fem. she'ta'yim)* A cardinal number. (Always written in the double plural form) *AHLB:* 1474-H(N) *Strong's:* #8147

ULCER (fem. *ya'be'let)* A flowing or seeping lesion. *AHLB:* 1035-L(N2) *Strong's:* #2990

UNAWARE (masc. *be'li)* Without design, attention, preparation, or premeditation. *Alternate Translation:* not; nothing; lack of (when followed with the word "WITHOUT"); unknowingly (when followed by the word "DISCERNMENT") *AHLB:* 1035-A(f) *Strong's:* #1097

UNCIRCUMCISED (masc. *a'reyl)* A male with a foreskin. *AHLB:* 2577(N) *Strong's:* #6189

UNCLE (masc. *dod)* The brother of one's father or mother; one who is cherished by another. *Alternate Translation:* beloved *AHLB:* 1073-J(N) *Strong's:* #1730

UNCOVER(V) (*ah.r.h)* To remove the covering. *AHLB:* 1365-H(V) *Strong's:* #6168

UNDER (masc. *ta'hhat)* Beneath, below or underneath; a replacement, In the sense of being in place of something else. *Alternate Translation:* by; in place of;

now; underneath; below (when prefixed with "from~"); how long (when attached to the word "WHEREVER"); single one (when followed by the word "UNIT"); because (when followed by the word "WHICH"); *AHLB:* 2892$^{(N)}$ *Strong's:* #8478

UNDERGARMENT (masc. *mikh'nas)* Garment worn under another garment that is bundled up. *AHLB:* 2267(h) *Strong's:* #4370

UNDERSTAND$^{(V)}$ (*b.y.n)* To grasp the meaning of; to have comprehension. *AHLB:* 1037-M$^{(V)}$ *Strong's:* #0995

UNDERSTANDING (fem. *biy'nah)* A comprehension of the construction of a structure or thought. *AHLB:* 1037-M(N1) *Strong's:* #0998

UNDERWORLD (*she-ol) AHLB:* 1472-D(c) *Strong's:* #7585

UNFILLED (masc. *bo'hu)* Empty. As an empty box that needs to be filled. *AHLB:* 1028-J(r) *Strong's:* #0922

UNINHABITED (fem. *ge'zey'rah)* A place barren of people; a place that is cut off. *AHLB:* 2061(N1) *Strong's:* #1509

UNIQUE (masc. *qa'dosh)* Someone or something that has, or has been given the quality of specialness, and has been separated from the rest for a special purpose. *AHLB:* 2700(c) *Strong's:* #6918

UNIT (masc. *e'hhad fem. e'hhat)* A unit within the whole, a unified group. A single quantity. *Alternate Translation:* another; first; one; other; *AHLB:* 1165-C$^{(N)}$ *Strong's:* #0259

UNITE$^{(V)}$ (*y.hh.d)* To put together to form a single unit. *AHLB:* 1165-L$^{(V)}$ *Strong's:* #3161

UNLEAVENED.BREAD (fem. *mats'tsah)* A hard and flat bread or cake made without yeast. *AHLB:* 1294-B(N1) *Strong's:* #4682

UNLESS (masc. / *lu'ley)* Except on the condition that. *AHLB:* 1254-B(o) *Strong's:* #3884

UNNATURAL.MIX (fem. *te'vel)* An action that lacks any results. *AHLB:* 1035-A(i) *Strong's:* #8397

UNPROTECTED (masc. *ar'o'er) AHLB:* 1365-A(cl) *Strong's:* #6176

UNSEASONED (masc. *ta'pheyl) AHLB:* 2898$^{(N)}$ *Strong's:* #8602

UNTIL (masc. *ad)* The conclusion of a determinate period of time or space. Also, again; a repetition of time, either definite or indefinite; another time or place; once more. *Alternate Translation:* again; also; as far as; as well as; before; beyond; by; concerning; even; ever; for; unto; behalf (when prefixed with "in~"); still (when followed by the word "IN.THIS.WAY") *AHLB:* 1349-A$^{(N)}$ *Strong's:* #1157, #5703, #5704

UPHOLD$^{(V)}$ (*t.m.k)* To give support or to steady. *AHLB:* 2895$^{(V)}$ *Strong's:* #8551

UPON (masc. *al)* To be on or over in the sense of the yoke that is placed on the neck of the ox. *Alternate Translation:* about; above; according to; against; also; because; by; concerning; in; in addition; over; with; therefore (when followed by the word "SO"); why (when followed by the word "WHAT"); because (when followed by the word "WHICH") *AHLB:* 1357-A$^{(N)}$ *Strong's:* #5921

UPPER (masc. *el'yon)* Higher than the others. *Alternate Translation:* above (when followed by the word "UPON") *AHLB:* 1357-A(fj) *Strong's:* #5945(x2)

UPPER.LEG (masc. *sho'vel)* The thigh muscle of the lower appendages. *AHLB:* 2806(g) *Strong's:* #7640

UPPER.LIP (masc. *sa'pham) AHLB:* 1339-A(p) *Strong's:* #8222

UPRISING (fem. *ma'se'eyt)* Violence in defiance of something. Something that is lifted up such as a burden, gift or flame. *AHLB:* 1314-E(a2) *Strong's:* #4864

UPSIDE.DOWN (fem. *tah'pu'khah) AHLB:* 1379-F(i1) *Strong's:* #8419

UPWARD (masc. *ma'al)* In a direction from lower to higher. *Alternate Translation:* above; high; top *AHLB:* 1357-A(a) *Strong's:* #4605

USURY (masc. *ne'shek)* The lending or practice of lending money at an exorbitant interest. *AHLB:* 2441(N) *Strong's:* #5392

UTENSIL (masc. *ke'li)* A container for carrying or storing various materials; an implement or weapon. *AHLB:* 1242-A(f) *Strong's:* #3627

UTTER(V) (*b.th.a)* To speak out words. *AHLB:* 1032-E(V) *Strong's:* #0981

UTTERANCE (masc. *miv'tah)* Words that are spoken out. *AHLB:* 1032-E(h) *Strong's:* #4008

VACANT (fem. *bu'qah)* In a state of emptiness, void or waste. *AHLB:* 1042-J(N1) *Strong's:* #0950

VALIANT (masc. *a'vir)* Possessing or acting with bravery or boldness. The mighty power of a bird in flight. Anything or anyone of great mental or physical strength. *AHLB:* 1043-C(b) *Strong's:* #0046, #0047

VALLEY (masc. *ey'meq)* An elongated depression between ranges of hills or mountains. *AHLB:* 2553(N) *Strong's:* #6010, #6012

VALUE (masc. *me'kher) AHLB:* 2337(N) *Strong's:* #4377

VANITY (masc. *he'vel)* The state of being empty of contents or usefulness. *AHLB:* 1035-F(N) *Strong's:* #1892

VEHICLE (masc. *re'khev)* A wheeled transport such as a wagon or chariot used for transportation. Also, the top millstone as a wheel that rides on top of the lower millstone. *AHLB:* 2769(N) *Strong's:* #7393, #7395

VEIL (masc. *tsa'iph)* To cover, provide, obscure, or conceal with or as if with a cloth. *AHLB:* 2678(b) *Strong's:* #6809

VENGEANCE (masc. *na'qam fem. ne'qa'mah)* The desire for revenge. *AHLB:* 2433(N) *Strong's:* #5359, #5360

VENOM (masc. *rosh)* The poison of serpents that comes sacks located in the head. Also, by extension any type of poison. *AHLB:* 1458-D(g) *Strong's:* #7219

VENOMOUS (masc. *sa'raph)* Able to inflict a poisoned bite, sting, or wound. In the Book of Isaiah this is a winged, possibly venomous, creature called a Seraph. *AHLB:* 2512(N) *Strong's:* #8314

VERTICAL (fem. *qom'miy'ut) AHLB:* 1427-J(pf3) *Strong's:* #6968

VESSEL (fem. *tey'vah)* A floating container for holding items. Used for the basket that carried Mosheh down the Nile river and the boat made by Noah. *AHLB:* 1028-A(i) *Strong's:* #8392

VIGOR (masc. *on)* Active bodily or mental strength or force. The power within the belly or loins for reproduction or creative work. *AHLB:* 1014-J(N) *Strong's:* #0202

VILLAGE (masc. *p'ra'ziy fem. p'ra'zah)* A town or village without walls of protection. *AHLB:* 2635(N1) *Strong's:* #6519, #6521

VINE (fem. זמורה *z'mo'rah)* From where grapes are plucked. *AHLB:* 2124(c1) *Strong's:* #2156

VINEGAR (masc. חומץ *hho'mets)* A soured liquid made from grapes. *AHLB:* 2173(g) *Strong's:* #2558

VINEYARD (masc. כרם *ke'rem)* A farm of grapevines. *AHLB:* 2288^(N) *Strong's:* #3754

VINTAGE (masc. בצור *ba'tsur)* The gathered crop of grapes. *AHLB:* 2033(c) *Strong's:* #1208

VIOLENCE (masc. חמס *hha'mas)* Exertion of physical force so as to injure or abuse. A fierce shaking. *AHLB:* 2172^(N) *Strong's:* #2555

VIRGIN (fem. בתולה *be'tu'lah)* An unmarried young woman who is absolutely chaste. *AHLB:* 2045(d1) *Strong's:* #1330

VIRGINITY (masc. בתול *be'tul)* The state of being absolutely chaste; the sign of virginity (Always written in the plural form). *AHLB:* 2045(d) *Strong's:* #1331

VISION (fem. מחזה *ma'hha'zeh)* Something seen in a dream, trance, or ecstasy. *AHLB:* 1168-H(a1) *Strong's:* #4236

VOICE (masc. קול *qol)* The faculty of utterance. Sound of a person, musical instrument, the wind, thunder, etc. *Alternate Translation:* sound; thunder (when in the plural form) *AHLB:* 1426-J^(N) *Strong's:* #6963

VOMIT (masc. זרא *za'ra)* The contents of the stomach when ejected through the mouth; regurgitate. *AHLB:* 1158-E^(V) *Strong's:* #2214

VOMIT^(V) (קיה / קוא *q.w.a / q.y.a) AHLB:* 1415-J^(V) *Strong's:* #6958

VOW (masc. נדר *ne'der)* To promise solemnly. *AHLB:* 2385^(N) *Strong's:* #5088

VULTURE (fem. דאה / דיה *dai'yah / da'ah)* An unknown bird of prey or carrion. *AHLB:* 1074-D(b1) *Strong's:* #1676, #1772

WADI (masc. נחל *na'hhal)* The bed or valley of a stream. A choice piece of land desired in an inheritance because of its fertility. *AHLB:* 2391^(N) *Strong's:* #5158

WAFER (fem. צפיחית *tsa'pi'hhit)* Small thinly baked bread. *AHLB:* 2682(b4) *Strong's:* #6838

WAGE (masc. שכר *se'kher)* The reward or pay the price for one's labor. *AHLB:* 2479^(N) *Strong's:* #7938, #7939

WAGES (masc. אתנן *et'nan)* What is brought to a harlot as a gift. *AHLB:* 1497-C(m) *Strong's:* #0868

WAIST (masc. מתן *ma'ten)* The slender part of the body above the hips. *AHLB:* 2363^(N) *Strong's:* #4975(x2)

WALK^(V) (הלך *h.l.k)* To move along on foot; walk a journey; to go. Also, customs as a lifestyle that is walked or lived. *Alternate Translation:* take (when written in the hiphil [active causative] form) *AHLB:* 1264-F^(V) *Strong's:* #1980, #3212

WALL (masc. קיר *qir)* A permanent upright construction having a length much greater than the thickness and presenting a continuous surface, may be constructed of a curtain, earth, rocks or hewed stones. Used for shelter, protection, or privacy, or to subdivide interior space. *AHLB:* 1434-M^(N) *Strong's:* #2426, #7023

WALLOWER (fem. פלשת *pe'le'shet)* One who rolls around in the dust or ashes. *Strong's:* [Found in names only]

WANDER^(V) (תעה *t.ah.h)* To go astray due to deception or an outside influence. To staggar, as from being intoxicated. *AHLB:* 1499-H^(V) *Strong's:* #8582

WANTING (masc. *hho'ser)* Deficient in some part, thing, or respect. *AHLB:* 2187(g) *Strong's:* #2640

WARP (masc. *sh'tiy)* A tool used for weaving, an activity performed while sitting down. *AHLB:* 1482-A(f) *Strong's:* #8358, #8359

WARRIOR (masc. *ge'ver)* One of great strength in battle, such as a warrior. One who is strong in authority, such as a master. *AHLB:* 2052$^{(N)}$ *Strong's:* #1397, #1399

WASH$^{(V)}$ (*k.b.s)* To immerse articles of clothing into a cleaning solution and agitate them, usually by treading upon them, to clean them; to clean the body. *AHLB:* 2249$^{(V)}$ *Strong's:* #3526

WATCH.OVER$^{(V)}$ (*b.hh.n)* To inspect closely; to test, try or scrutinize. *AHLB:* 2011$^{(V)}$ *Strong's:* #0974

WATCHER (masc. *tsiyph'yon) Strong's:* [Found in names only]

WATCHMAN (masc. *tsaph) Strong's:* [Found in names only]

WATCHTOWER (masc. *mits'peh)* A high place for watching a large area. *AHLB:* 1408-H(h) *Strong's:* #4707

WATER (masc. *mah)* The Liquid of streams, ponds and seas or stored in cisterns or jars. The necessary liquid that is drank. (Always written in the plural form) *AHLB:* 1281-A$^{(N)}$ *Strong's:* #4325

WATERCOURSE (masc. *ya'val)* A flowing body of water. *AHLB:* 1035-L$^{(N)}$ *Strong's:* #2988

WATERED (masc. *ra'weh) AHLB:* 1442-J$^{(N)}$ *Strong's:* #7302

WATERING.TROUGH (fem. *sho'qet)* A trench for bringing water into the village. A place for domestic animals to quench thirst. *AHLB:* 1479-J(N2) *Strong's:* #8268

WAVE$^{(V)}$ (*n.w.p)* To move an object, such as hammer or sacrifice, back and forth; brandish. *AHLB:* 1316-J$^{(V)}$ *Strong's:* #5130

WAVER$^{(V)}$ (*a.z.l)* To go about in a shaking motion. *AHLB:* 1150-C$^{(V)}$ *Strong's:* #0235

WAVING (fem. *te'nu'phah)* The action of moving an object, such as hammer or a sacrifice, back and forth. *AHLB:* 1316-J(i1) *Strong's:* #8573

WAYWARDNESS (fem. *rish'ah) AHLB:* 2799(e1) *Strong's:* #7564

WE (/ / *a-nu, nakh-nu, a-nakh-nu)* I and the rest of a group. *Strong's:* #0580, #0587, #5168

WEAKEN$^{(V)}$ (*hh.l.sh)* To reduce in strength. *AHLB:* 2168$^{(V)}$ *Strong's:* #2522

WEALTHY (masc. *hhash'man fem.* *hhash'ma'nah) AHLB:* 2217(m) *Strong's:* #2831

WEAR$^{(V)}$ (*l.b.sh)* To cover with cloth or clothing; to provide with clothing; put on clothing. *Alternate Translation:* clothe (when written in the hiphil [active causative] form) *AHLB:* 2304$^{(V)}$ *Strong's:* #3847

WEAR.OUT$^{(V)}$ (*b.l.h)* To make useless, especially by long or hard usage. *AHLB:* 1035-H$^{(V)}$ *Strong's:* #1086, #1089

WEARY (masc. *ya'gey'a)* The state of being exhausted from vigorous work. *AHLB:* 1062-L$^{(N)}$ *Strong's:* #3022, #3023

WEASEL (masc. *hho'led)* An unclean animal of unknown species, possibly the weasel. *AHLB:* 2161(g) *Strong's:* #2467

WEAVE(V) (*sh.b.ts)* To interlace (threads, yarns, strips, fibrous material, etc.) *AHLB:* 2809(V) *Strong's:* #7660

WEEK (masc. *sha'vu'a)* A period of time consisting of seven days or seven years. *AHLB:* 2808(d) *Strong's:* #7620

WEEP(V) (*b.k.h)* To express deep sorrow, especially by shedding tears. *AHLB:* 1034-H(V) *Strong's:* #1058

WEEPING (masc. *be'khi)* The act of expressing sorrow by shedding tears. *AHLB:* 1034-A(f) *Strong's:* #1065

WEIGH(V) (*sh.q.l)* To ascertain the heaviness of by a balance or scale. Weigh out, usually of silver for payment. *AHLB:* 2874(V) *Strong's:* #8254

WEIGH.OUT(V) (*a.z.n)* To measure the weight of something; to consider, in the sense of weighing in the mind. *Alternate Translation:* Pay attention, in the sense of giving weight (when written in the hiphil [active causative] form) *AHLB:* 1152-C(V) *Strong's:* #0238, #0239

WEIGHT (masc. *mish'qal)* The amount a thing weighs. Relative heaviness. *AHLB:* 2874(h) *Strong's:* #4948

WELL (fem. *be'eyr)* A dug-out hole, usually a well or cistern. *AHLB:* 1250-D(N) *Strong's:* #0875

WELLNESS (fem. *ya'ta'vah) Strong's:* [Found in names only]

WHAT (masc. *mah)* Interrogative expressing inquiry about the identity, nature, or value of an object. Can also be why, when or how. *Alternate Translation:* how; why (when prefixed with "to~" or preceded by the word "UPON"); how many (when prefixed with "like~"); what is the reason (when prefixed with "to~" and followed by the word "THIS") *AHLB:* 1281-A(N) *Strong's:* #4100

WHEAT (fem. *hhi'tah)* A cereal grain that yields a fine white flour, the chief ingredient of bread. *AHLB:* 2177(e1) *Strong's:* #2406

WHEEL (masc. *o'phen)* A circular frame or disk arranged to revolve on an axis, as on a wagon or chariot. *AHLB:* 1382-C(g) *Strong's:* #0212

WHELP (masc. *gur fem. gu'rah)* Usually a young lion. (May be derived from the sound of the lion). *AHLB:* 1066-J(N) *Strong's:* #1482, #1484

WHERE (masc. / / / *ey, ai'yeh, ey'khoh, ey'phoh)* At, in, or to what place. *Alternate Translation:* why *AHLB:* 1010-A(N) *Strong's:* #0335, #0346, #0351, #0375

WHEREIN (*zu)* A person, thing, or idea present or near in place, time, or thought or just mentioned. *AHLB:* 1143-A(N) *Strong's:* #2098

WHEREVER (masc. / *an, anah)* Anywhere at all. A search for a person, place or time. *Alternate Translation:* how long (when attached to the word "UNTIL") *AHLB:* 1014-A(N) *Strong's:* #0575

WHET(V) (*sh.n.n)* To sharpen a knife or other cutting edge with a stone. *AHLB:* 1474-B(V) *Strong's:* #8150

WHICH (masc. *a'sheyr)* This word links the action of the sentence to the one doing the action. *Alternate Translation:* because; because of what; how; such as; that; what; when; where; who; whoever; whom; whose; whereas (when prefixed with "in~"); just as (when prefixed with "like~"); even though (when attached to the word "GIVEN.THAT") *AHLB:* 1480-C(N) *Strong's:* #0834

WHIP (masc. *pe'rek)* To strike, in punishment or anger with a rope or cord. *AHLB:* 2638(N) *Strong's:* #6531

WHIRLWIND (fem. *su'phah)* A circling wind that devours what is on the land in its mouth. *AHLB:* 1339-J(N1) *Strong's:* #5492

WHIRRING.LOCUST (masc. *tsiyl'tsal)* An unknown species of locust. Also, a cymbal. *AHLB:* 1150-A(el) *Strong's:* #6767(x2)

WHISPER(V) (*r.g.n)* *AHLB:* 2751(V) *Strong's:* #7279

WHITE (masc. *la'van fem.* *le'va'nah)* Free from color, the color of bricks in the Near East. *AHLB:* 2303(N) *Strong's:* #3836

WHITE.ONE (masc. *lev'non)* Of a whitish color. *Strong's:* [Found in names only]

WHO (masc. *miy)* What or which person or persons. *AHLB:* 1286-A(N) *Strong's:* #4310

WHOLE (masc. *ta'mim fem.* *ta'miy'mah)* Free of wound or injury; free of defect or impairment; having all its proper parts or components. *AHLB:* 1496-B(b) *Strong's:* #8549

WHOREDOM (fem. *ze'nut)* The act or practice of engaging in sexual intercourse for profit. *AHLB:* 1152-H(N3) *Strong's:* #2184

WHY (masc. *ma'du'a)* For what cause, purpose or reason for which. *AHLB:* 1085-J(a) *Strong's:* #4069

WICKED (masc. *e'vel fem.* *av'lah)* *AHLB:* 1518-J(N) *Strong's:* #5766, #5767

WICKEDNESS (fem. *al'wah)* *AHLB:* 1518-K(N1) *Strong's:* #5932

WICKER.BASKET (masc. *sal)* A receptacle made of interwoven materials such as reeds. *AHLB:* 1334-A(N) *Strong's:* #5536

WIDE (*ra-hhav)* *AHLB:* 2759(N) *Strong's:* #7338, #7342

WIDE.OPEN(V) (*sh.t.m)* *AHLB:* 2887(V) *Strong's:* #8365

WIDEN(V) (*r.hh.b)* To increase the size of an area wide; large; roomy. *AHLB:* 2759(V) *Strong's:* #7337

WIDOW (fem. *al'ma'nah)* A woman who has lost her husband by death. *AHLB:* 1266-C(m1) *Strong's:* #0490

WIDOWHOOD (fem. *al'me'nut)* In a state of being a widow. *AHLB:* 1266-C(m3) *Strong's:* #0491

WIDTH (masc. *ro'hhav)* Largeness of extent or scope. From the width of a road. *AHLB:* 2759(g) *Strong's:* #7341

WILD.ASS (masc. / *pe're / pe'reh)* A wild animal as prolific. *AHLB:* 1388-E(N) *Strong's:* #6501

WILD.DONKEY (masc. *a'rad)* *AHLB:* 2575(N) *Strong's:* [Found in names only]

WILD.GOAT (masc. *aq'qo)* An undomesticated goat. *AHLB:* 1019-A(q) *Strong's:* #0689

WILDERNESS (masc. *mid'bar)* A tract or region uncultivated and uninhabited by human beings. Place of order, a sanctuary. *AHLB:* 2093(h) *Strong's:* #4057

WILLING (masc. *na'div)* To give honor or offering out of one's own free will. *AHLB:* 2380(b) *Strong's:* #5081

WILLOW (masc. *a'rav)* A species of tree. *AHLB:* 2907(N) *Strong's:* #6155

WIND (fem. *ru'ahh)* A natural movement of air; breath. The breath of man, animal or God. The character. A space in between. *AHLB:* 1445-J(N) *Strong's:* #7305, #7307

WIND.AROUND(V) (*ts.n.p)* *AHLB:* 2673(V) *Strong's:* #6801

WINDOW (*hha-lon)* A hole in the wall that admits light and a view of the other side. *AHLB:* 1173-A(j) *Strong's:* #2474

WINE (masc. *ya'yin)* Fermented juice of fresh grapes. From the mire in the wine. *AHLB:* 1221-M(N) *Strong's:* #3196

WINE.TROUGH (masc. *ye'qev) AHLB:* 1416-L(N) *Strong's:* #3342

WING (fem. *ka'naph)* An appendage that allows an animal, bird or insect to fly. Also, the wings of a garment. *AHLB:* 2269(N) *Strong's:* #3671

WINTER (masc. *hho'reph)* The season between summer and spring. Time of the piercing cold and relative bleakness. *AHLB:* 2208(g) *Strong's:* #2779

WIPE.AWAY(V) (*m.hh.h)* To remove by drying or sweeping away through rubbing; to polish in the sense of a vigorous rubbing; erase. *AHLB:* 1284-H(V) *Strong's:* #4229

WIRE (masc. *pahh)* A slender, string-like piece or filament of relatively rigid or flexible metal often used for snares. *AHLB:* 1376-A(N) *Strong's:* #6341

WITH (masc. *im)* Through the idea of being together in a group. *Alternate Translation:* among, by; away (when prefixed with "from~") *AHLB:* 1358-M(N) *Strong's:* #5868, #5973

WITH.THE.EXCEPTION (fem. *zu'lah)* An exception. *AHLB:* 1150-J(N1) *Strong's:* #2108

WITHDRAW(V) (*hh.b.a)* To take back or withhold what is cherished; to turn away or move back. *AHLB:* 1163-E(V) *Strong's:* #2244

WITHDRAWING (masc. *hhu'vah)* Being withdrawn from view or contact. *Strong's:* [Found in names only]

WITHDRAWN (masc. *nahh'viy)* Removed from view or contact. *Strong's:* [Found in names only]

WITHER(V) (*ts.n.m)* To become dry and sapless; to shrivel. *AHLB:* 2671(V) *Strong's:* #6798

WITHHOLD(V) (*m.n.ah)* To hold back from action. *AHLB:* 2343(V) *Strong's:* #4513

WITHHOLDING (masc. *ma'na) Strong's:* [Found in names only]

WITHOUT (masc. *a'yin)* A lacking of something or the inability to do or have something. The search for a place of unknown origin. *Alternate Translation:* no; not; none; nothing; unable; where *AHLB:* 1014-M(N) *Strong's:* #0369, #0370, #0371

WITNESS (masc. *eyd fem. ey'dah)* Attestation of a fact or event. An object, person or group that affords evidence. *AHLB:* 1349-A(N) *Strong's:* #5707, #5713

WOLF (masc. *ze'eyv)* A yellowish colored animal of the canine family. *AHLB:* 1140-D(N) *Strong's:* #2061

WOMAN (fem. *an'shah)* An adult female person. As mortal. *Alternate Translation:* each; one *AHLB:* 2003(b1) *Strong's:* #0802

WOMB (fem. *be'ten)* An organ where something is generated or grows before birth. *AHLB:* 2015(N) *Strong's:* #0990

WONDER (masc. *mo'phet)* An amazing sight or event that causes one to be dismayed. Something out of the ordinary. *AHLB:* 1390-L(a) *Strong's:* #4159

WOOD.BAR (masc. *be'ri'ahh)* Round wooden dowels. *AHLB:* 2038(b) *Strong's:* #1280, #1281

WOOL (masc. *tse'mer)* The sheared hair from the fleece of a sheep. *AHLB:* 2668$^{(N)}$ *Strong's:* #6785

WORD (masc. *da'var fem. dab'rah)* An arrangement of words, ideas or concepts to form sentences. A promise in the sense of being 'ones word.' An action in the sense of acting out an arrangement. A plague as an act. A matter or thing, as words also have substance in the Hebrew mind. *Alternate Translation:* matter; thing *AHLB:* 2093$^{(N)}$, 2093(N1) *Strong's:* #1697, #1703

WORK (masc. *ma'a'seh)* Activity where one exerts strength or faculties to do or perform something. An action. *AHLB:* 1360-H(a) *Strong's:* #4639

WORK.OVER$^{(V)}$ (*ah.l.l)* To carefully and thoroughly perform a task such as gleaning a field. Also, to mock or abuse in the sense of walking over another. *Alternate Translation:* abused (when written in the hitpa'el [reflexive] form) *AHLB:* 1357-B$^{(V)}$ *Strong's:* #5953

WORKING (masc. *ats'von) Strong's:* [Found in names only]

WORKINGS (fem. *a'liy'lah) AHLB:* 1357-B(b1) *Strong's:* #5949

WORKS (masc. *ma'a'lal)* What is done or performed. *AHLB:* 1357-B(a) *Strong's:* #4611

WORTH (fem. *mikh'sah)* The number assigned according to its amount, importance or need. *AHLB:* 1245-A(h1) *Strong's:* #4373

WORTHLESS (masc. *e'liyl)* A god or being without power. *AHLB:* 1254-B(b) *Strong's:* #0457

WOULD.THAT (masc. / *lu)* A yearning for certain direction or action. *AHLB:* 1254-J$^{(N)}$ *Strong's:* #3863

WOUND (masc. *pe'tsah)* An injury involving rupture of small blood vessels and discoloration without a skin break. The dark coloring of the skin caused by being hit or smashed. *AHLB:* 2628$^{(N)}$ *Strong's:* #6482

WOUND$^{(V)}$ (*p.ts.ah) AHLB:* 2628$^{(V)}$ *Strong's:* #6481

WOVEN.BASKET (fem. *tsin'tse'net)* A container made from multiple pieces of material entwined together into one unit. *AHLB:* 1198-A(el2) *Strong's:* #6803

WOVEN.MATERIAL (masc. *tash'beyts)* Material made from weaving threads of fibers together to become a solid piece. *AHLB:* 2809(i) *Strong's:* #8665

WRAP$^{(V)}$ (*ah.l.p)* To envelop and secure for transport or storage. Also, meaning to faint. *AHLB:* 2547$^{(V)}$ *Strong's:* #5968

WRAP.AROUND$^{(V)}$ (*ah.w.d)* To enclose; to repeat or do again what has been said or done. *Alternate Translation:* warn (when written in the hiphil [active causative] or hophal [passive causative] form) *AHLB:* 1349-J$^{(V)}$ *Strong's:* #5749

WRAPPER (masc. *lu'tan) Strong's:* [Found in names only]

WRATH (fem. *ev'rah)* Strong vengeful anger. As crossing over from peace. *AHLB:* 2520(N1) *Strong's:* #5678, #5679

WREATH (fem. *a'ta'rah) AHLB:* 2538(N1) *Strong's:* #5850

WRESTLING (masc. *naph'tul)* To entwine, such as when twisting cords together to make a rope; to be entwined together when wrestling. *AHLB:* 3034 *Strong's:* #5319

WRIST (masc. *pas)* The joint between the hand and arm. Also, a garment with sleeves that reaches to the wrist. *AHLB:* 1383-A$^{(N)}$ *Strong's:* #6446

WRITE(V) (כתב *k.t.b)* To inscribe a story, thoughts or instructions on in a variety of mediums including stone, papyrus, leather or parchment. *AHLB:* 2295(V) *Strong's:* #3789

WRITING (fem. כתובת *k'to'vet) AHLB:* 2295(c2) *Strong's:* #3793

YARN (masc. מטוה *mat'weh)* Fibers that are spun together to form one strand. *AHLB:* 1189-J(a) *Strong's:* #4299

YEAR (fem. שנה *sha'neyh)* The period of around 365 solar days. *AHLB:* 1474-A(N1) *Strong's:* #8141

YEARN (masc. אוה *e'veh)* To long persistently, wistfully, or sadly. What is desired, whether good or bad. *Strong's:* [Found in names only]

YEARN(V) (אוה *a.w.h)* To have an earnest or strong desire; long. *AHLB:* 1005-J(V) *Strong's:* #0183

YEARNING (fem. תאוה *ta'a'wah)* To long persistently, wistfully, or sadly. What is desired, whether good or bad. *AHLB:* 1005-J(i1) *Strong's:* #8378

YELL (fem. זעק *za'aq)* A vehement protest; a loud cry. *AHLB:* 2131(N) *Strong's:* #2201

YELL.OUT(V) (זעק *z.ah.q)* To call out in a louder than normal voice; to declare; to cry out for help. *AHLB:* 2131(V) *Strong's:* #2199

YELLOW (masc. צהוב *tsa'hov)* A color like that of gold. *AHLB:* 1140-G(c) *Strong's:* #6669

YEMIM (masc. ימים *yeymim)* The meaning of this word is uncertain and it is not known if this is a noun or a name. The Greek Septuagint transliterates this word as Ιαμιν (Iamin). *AHLB:* 1220-B(N) *Strong's:* #3222

YESTERDAY (masc. תמול *te'mul)* On the day last past. Idiomatic for a time past. *Alternate Translation:* previously (when followed by the word "THREE.DAYS.AGO") *AHLB:* 1288-J(i) *Strong's:* #8543

YET.AGAIN (masc. עוד *od)* A repeating of something. *Alternate Translation:* again; also; another; continue; even; ever; more; still; while; yet; whole life (when prefixed with "from~") *AHLB:* 1349-J(N) *Strong's:* #5750

YIELD(V) (גמל *g.m.l)* To produce or be productive. *AHLB:* 2070(V) *Strong's:* #1580

YOKE (masc. עול / על *ol / ul)* A wooden bar or frame by which two draft animals are joined at the heads or necks for working together. *AHLB:* 1357-J(N) *Strong's:* #5923

YOKE.BREAKER (masc. תדעל *da'phaq) Strong's:* [Found in names only]

YOU (masc. אתן *a'ten)* Pronoun, second person, feminine plural. *Strong's:* #0859(x4)

YOU (masc. את *et)* Pronoun, second person, feminine singular *Strong's:* #0859(x4)

YOU (masc. אתם *a'tem)* Pronoun, second person, masculine plural. *Strong's:* #0859(x4)

YOU (masc. אתה *a'tah)* Pronoun, second person, masculine singular. *Strong's:* #0859(x4)

YOUNG.AGE (fem. נעור *na'ur)* A person of short life. *AHLB:* 2418(d) *Strong's:* #5271

YOUNG.BOY (masc. ענר *a'nar) Strong's:* [Found in names only]

YOUNG.CAMEL (masc. בכר *be'kher)* A dromedary of short age. *AHLB:* 2016(N) *Strong's:* #1070

YOUNG.MAIDEN (fem. עלמה *al'mah)* A young female of marriageable age or newly married as at the prime age for work. *AHLB:* 1357-A(p1) *Strong's:* #5959

YOUNG.MAN (masc. נער *na'ar)* A male that has moved from youth to young adulthood. *AHLB:* 2418(N) *Strong's:* #5288, #5289

YOUNG.PIGEON (masc. גוזל *go'zal)* A young featherless bird as plucked. *AHLB:* 2059(g) *Strong's:* #1469

YOUNG.SHEEP (fem. עשתרה *ash'te'rah)* A young one of the flock. *AHLB:* 3047 *Strong's:* #6251

YOUNG.WOMAN (fem. נערה *na'a'rah)* A female that has moved from youth to young adulthood. *AHLB:* 2418(N1) *Strong's:* #5291

YOUTH (fem. בחורות *be'hhu'rot)* The state of being at a young age. *AHLB:* 2012(d3) *Strong's:* #0979

YOUTHFULNESS (fem. צעירה *tse'i'rah)* One who is little in age, a child; one who acts like a child. *AHLB:* 2680(b1) *Strong's:* #6812

ZEALOUS (masc. קנא *qa'nah)* Someone who is insistent on reaching the desired outcome. Single minded. One who is protective over someone or something. *AHLB:* 1428-E(N) *Strong's:* #7067

ZEALOUSNESS (fem. קנאה *qin'ah)* A protective or suspicious nature. *AHLB:* 1428-E(N1) *Strong's:* #7068

Dictionary of Affixes

!(fs)~ Identifies the verb as a feminine singular imperative.
!(mp)~ Identifies the verb as a masculine plural imperative.
!(ms)~ Identifies the verb as a masculine singular imperative.
?~ (*ah)* The interrogative 'Hey' converting the sentence into a question.
~& (*h)* Paragogic 'Hey;' added to the ordinary forms of words, to express additional emphasis, or some change in the sense.
~&~ This symbol is placed between the two words of a compound word or name.
~ed(fp) Feminine plural verb passive participle denoting an action (such as baked).
~ed(fs) Feminine singular verb passive participle denoting an action (such as baked).
~ed(mp) Masculine plural verb passive participle denoting an action (such as baked).
~ed(ms) Masculine singular verb passive participle denoting an action (such as baked).
~her (fem: *ah)* Third person feminine singular pronoun (her) also used as a possessive pronoun (of him or his).
~him (masc: *o)* Third person masculine singular pronoun (him) also used as a possessive pronoun (of him or his).
~ing(fp) Feminine plural verb participle denoting an action (such as baking) or one of action (such as a baking one, or baker).
~ing(fs) Feminine singular verb participle denoting an action (such as baking) or one of action (such as a baking one, or baker).
~ing(mp) Masculine plural verb participle denoting an action (such as baking) or one of action (such as a baking one, or baker).
~ing(ms) Masculine singular verb participle denoting an action (such as baking) or one of action (such as a baking one, or baker).
~me (/ *I / niy)* First person common singular pronoun (me), also used as a possessive pronoun (of me or my).
~must (*n)* Paragogic *'Nun;'* emphasizes the intensity of action of the verb.
~of (*i)* Identifies the noun as singular possessive.
~s (masc: *iym* / fem: *ot)* Identifies the noun as a plural. When attached to the name of a person it identifies the name as plural possessive.
~s2 (*yim)* Identifies the noun as a dual plural.
~them(f) (fem: *hen)* Third person feminine plural pronoun (them) also used as a possessive pronoun (of them or their).
~them(m) (masc: *hem)* Third person masculine plural pronoun (them) also used as a possessive pronoun (of them or their).
~unto (*ah)* Directional 'Hey;' implies movement toward the location identified in the word this suffix is attached to.
~us (*nu)* First person common plural pronoun (we), also used as a possessive pronoun (of us or our).
~you(fp) (fem: *khen)* Second person feminine plural pronoun (you), also used as a possessive pronoun (of you or your).

~you(fs) (fem: *ek)* Second person feminine singular pronoun (you), alsoused as a possessive pronoun (of you or your).

~you(mp) (masc: *khem)* Second person masculine plural pronoun (you), also used as a possessive pronoun (of you or your).

~you(ms) (masc: *kha)* Second person masculine singular pronoun (you), also used as a possessive pronoun (of you or your).

>~ Identifies the verb form as infinitive.

and~ (*we / wa / u)* The conjunction meaning "and." Often used as the *vav* consecutive meaning "that" when prefixed to a verb it will usually reverse the tense of the verb.

be~ Identifies the voice of the verb as passive.

did~ Identifies the tense of the verb as perfect. The perfect tense is a completed action and in most cases is related to the English past tense.

from~ (*me)* A preposition meaning "from."

he~ Identifies the subject of the verb as third person masculine singular.

I~ Identifies the subject of the verb as first person common singular.

in~ (*be)* A preposition meaning in or "with."

like~ (*ke)* A preposition meaning "like."

make~ Identifies the the mood of the verb as causative.

much~ Identifies the the mood of the verb as intensive.

self~ Identifies the voice of the verb as reflexive.

she~ Identifies the subject of the verb as third person feminine singular.

the~ (*ha)* The definite article meaning "the."

they(f)~ Identifies the subject of the verb as third person feminine plural.

they(m)~ Identifies the subject of the verb as third person masculine plural.

they~ Identifies the subject of the verb as third person common plural.

to~ (*le)* A preposition meaning "to" or "for."

we~ Identifies the subject of the verb as first person common plural.

which~ (*she)* A preposition meaning "which" or "who." **!(fp)~** Identifies the verb as a feminine plural imperative.

will~ Identifies the tense of the verb as imperfect. The imperfect tense is an incomplete action and is closely related to the English present and future tenses.

you(fp)~ Identifies the subject of the verb as second person feminine plural.

you(fs)~ Identifies the subject of the verb as second person feminine singular.

you(mp)~ Identifies the subject of the verb as second person masculine plural.

you(ms)~ Identifies the subject of the verb as second person masculine singular.

Dictionary of Hebrew Names

A

Adah (masc: *a'dah)* ADORNMENT *Translation:* Adornment. *Strong's:* #5711
Adbe'el (masc: *ad'be'eyl)* MIST~&~in~MIGHTY.ONE *Translation:* Mist in El. *Strong's:* #0110
Admah (fem: *ad'mah)* GROUND *Translation:* Ground (Or Adamah,). *Strong's:* #0126, #0128
Adonai (masc: *a'do'ni)* LORD~s~me *Translation:* My lords. *Strong's:* #0136
Adulam (masc: *a'du'lam)* WITNESS~&~and~SHEPHERD.STAFF *Translation:* Witness and a shepherd staff. *Strong's:* #5725, #5726
Agag (masc: *a'gag) I~will~*OVERTOP *Translation:* I will be overtop. *Strong's:* #0090
Ahalivamah (masc: *a'ha'li'va'mah)* TENT~of~&~PLATFORM *Translation:* Tent of the platform. *Strong's:* #0173
Ahaliyav (masc: *a'ha'li'av)* TENT~of~&~FATHER *Translation:* Tent of father. *Strong's:* #0171
Aharon (masc: *a'ha'ron)* LIGHT.BRINGER *Translation:* Light bringer (Uncertain meaning, but related to the word for light). *Strong's:* #0175
Ahhi'ezer (masc: *a'hhi'e'zer)* BROTHER~me~&~HELP *Translation:* My brother is help. *Strong's:* #0295
Ahhihud (masc: *a'hhi'hud)* BROTHER~me~&~SPLENDOR *Translation:* My brother is splendor. *Strong's:* #0282
Ahhiman (masc: *a'hhi'man)* BROTHER~me~&~SHARE *Translation:* My brother shares. *Strong's:* #0289
Ahhira (masc: *a'hhi'ra)* BROTHER~me~&~DYSFUNCTIONAL *Translation:* My brother is dysfunctional. *Strong's:* #0299
Ahhiram (masc: *a'hhi'ram)* BROTHER~me~&~RAISED *Translation:* My brother raised. *Strong's:* #0297, #0298
Ahhiysamahh (masc: *a'hhi'sa'mak)* BROTHER~me~&~*he~did~*SUPPORT[V] *Translation:* My brother supports (May also mean "My brother of support."). *Strong's:* #0294
Ahhuzat (masc: *a'hhu'zat)* HOLDINGS *Translation:* Holdings. *Strong's:* #0276
Akad (masc: *a'kad)* DELICATE *Translation:* Delicate (Can also mean 'spark'). *Strong's:* #0390
Akhbor (masc: *akh'bor)* MOUSE *Translation:* Mouse. *Strong's:* #5907
Akhran (masc: *akh'ran)* DISTURBED.ONE *Translation:* Disturbed one. *Strong's:* #5918
Almodad (masc: *al'mo'dad)* MIGHTY.ONE~&~MEASURING *Translation:* El of measuring (The origins of "modad" is uncertain). *Strong's:* #0486

Almon-Divlatayim (masc: דבלתימה *al'mon Divlatayim)* OUT.OF.SIGHT~&~CAKE~s2~unto *Translation:* unto the out of sight of two cakes. *Strong's:* #5963

Alon-Bakhut (masc: *a'lon ba'khut)* GREAT.TREE~&~WEEPING *Translation:* Great tree of weeping. *Strong's:* #0439

Alush (masc: *a'lush) I~will~*KNEAD[V] *Translation:* I will knead. *Strong's:* #0442

Alwah (masc: *al'wah)* WICKEDNESS *Translation:* Wickedness. *Strong's:* #5933

Alwan (masc: *al'wan)* LOFT *Translation:* Loft. *Strong's:* #5935

Amaleq (masc: *a'me'leq)* PEOPLE~&~GATHERED.UP *Translation:* People gathered up. *Strong's:* #6002, #6003

Ami'eyl (masc: *a'mi'eyl)* PEOPLE~of~&~MIGHTY.ONE *Translation:* Peaple of the mighty one. *Strong's:* #5988

Amihud (masc: *a'mi'hud)* PEOPLE~of~&~SPLENDOR *Translation:* Peaple of splendor. *Strong's:* #5989

Amishaddai (masc: *a'mi'sha'dai)* PEOPLE~of~&~BREAST~s~me *Translation:* People of my breasts. *Strong's:* #5996

Amiynadav (masc: *a'mi'na'dav)* PEOPLE~me~&~OFFERED.WILLINGLY *Translation:* My people offered willingly. *Strong's:* #5992

Amon (masc: *a'mon)* TRIBAL *Translation:* Tribal. *Strong's:* #5983, #5984, #5985

Amram (masc: *am'ram)* PEOPLE~&~RAISED *Translation:* People raised. *Strong's:* #6019

Amraphel (masc: *am'ra'phel)* SAYER~&~FALL *Translation:* Sayer of the fall (Can also mean "One that speaks of secrets", "Sayer of darkness" or "Fall of the sayer."). *Strong's:* #0569

Anah (masc: *a'nah)* ANSWERED *Translation:* Answered. *Strong's:* #6034

Anam (masc: *a'nam)* AFFLICTION~&~WATER~s2 *Translation:* Affliction of waters. *Strong's:* #6047

Anaq (masc: *a'naq)* NECK.BAND *Translation:* Neck band. *Strong's:* #6061, #6062

Aner (masc: *a'ner)* YOUNG.BOY *Translation:* Young boy (Meaning and origin are uncertain). *Strong's:* #6063

Aqan (masc: *a'qan)* SHARP.SIGHTED *Translation:* Sharp sighted. *Strong's:* #6130

Aqrabiym (masc: *aq'ra'biym)* SCORPION~s *Translation:* Scorpions. *Strong's:* #4610

Ar (masc: *ar)* ENEMY *Translation:* Enemy (May also mean "city."). *Strong's:* #6144

Arad (masc: *a'rad)* WILD.DONKEY *Translation:* Wild donkey. *Strong's:* #6166

Aram (masc: *a'ram)* PALACE *Translation:* Palace (From a root meaning "a high place," such as used for building palaces and forts). *Strong's:* #0758

Aram-Nahara'im (masc: *a'ram na'ha'ra'yim)* PALACE~&~RIVER~s2 *Translation:* Palace of two rivers. *Strong's:* #0763

Aran (masc: *a'ran) I~will~*SHOUT.ALOUD[V] *Translation:* I will shout aloud. *Strong's:* #0765

Araq (masc: *a'raq)* GNAWED *Translation:* Gnawed. *Strong's:* #6208

Ararat (masc: *a'ra'rat)* HIGH.LAND *Translation:* High land (Meaning uncertain, of foreign origin). *Strong's:* #0780

Ard (masc: *ard) I~will~*GO.DOWN(V) *Translation:* I will go down (Can also mean "I go down"). *Strong's:* #0714

Areliy (masc: *ar'ey'li)* LION~&~MIGHTY.ONE~me *Translation:* Lion of my El. *Strong's:* #0692

Argov (masc: *ar'gov) I~will~*CLOD *Translation:* I will clod. *Strong's:* #0709

Arnon (masc: *ar'non) I~will~*SHOUT.ALOUD(V) *Translation:* I will shout aloud. *Strong's:* #0769

Arodiy (masc: *a'ro'di)* ROAMING~me *Translation:* My roaming. *Strong's:* #0722

Aro'eyr (masc: *ar'o'eyr)* UNPROTECTED *Translation:* Unprotected. *Strong's:* #6177

Arpakhshad (masc: *ar'pakh'shad) I~will~*DECLINE~&~BREAST *Translation:* I declined the breast. *Strong's:* #0775

Arwad (masc: *ar'wad)* ROAMING *Translation:* Roaming. *Strong's:* #0719, #0721

Aryokh (masc: *a'ri'okh)* LION.LIKE *Translation:* Lion like (From a root meaning "long"). *Strong's:* #0746

Ashbeyl (masc: *ash'beyl) I~will~*EXCHANGE(V) *Translation:* I will exchange (Can also mean Fire of Bel). *Strong's:* #0788

Asher (masc: *a'sher)* HAPPY *Translation:* Happy. *Strong's:* #0836

Ashkanaz (masc: *ash'ke'naz)* FIRE~&~SPRINKLED *Translation:* Fire sprinkled. *Strong's:* #0813

Ashterot (masc: *ash'te'rot)* YOUNG.SHEEP~s *Translation:* young sheep. *Strong's:* #6252

Ashterot-Qar'nayim (masc: *ash'te'rot qar'na'yim)* YOUNG.SHEEP~s~&~HORN~s2 *Translation:* Horns of young sheep. *Strong's:* #6255

Ashur (masc: *a'shur)* HAPPY *Translation:* Happy. *Strong's:* #0804

Asiyr (masc: *a'sir)* PRISONER *Translation:* Prisoner. *Strong's:* #0617

Asnat (masc: *as'nat)* BELONGING.TO.NAT *Translation:* Belonging to Nat (Of Egyptian origin). *Strong's:* #0621

Asri'eyl (masc: *as'ri'eyl)* HAPPY(V)~me~&~MIGHTY.ONE *Translation:* My happiness is the mighty one. *Strong's:* #0844, #0845

Atariym (masc: *a'ta'riym)* SITE~s *Translation:* Site. *Strong's:* #0871

Atarot (masc: *a'ta'rot)* WREATH~s *Translation:* Wreaths. *Strong's:* #5852

Atsmon (masc: *ats'mon)* ABUNDANT.ONE *Translation:* Abundant one. *Strong's:* #6111

At'rot-Shophan (masc: *sho'phan)* WREATH~s RABBIT *Translation:* Wreaths of Rabbit. *Strong's:* #5855

Aveyl-Hashit'tim (masc: השטים *a'veyl ha'shiyt'tiym)* MOURNING~&~the~ACACIA~s2 *Translation:* Mourning of the acacias (or "Mourning of Hashit'tim"). *Strong's:* #0063

Aveyl-Mitsrayim (masc: *a'veyl mits'ra'yim)* MOURNING~&~STRAIT~s2 *Translation:* Mourning of two straits (or "Mourning of Mitsrayim"). *Strong's:* #0067

Avida (masc: *a'viy'da)* FATHER~me~&~*he~did*~KNOW(V) *Translation:* My father knows. *Strong's:* #0028

Avidan (masc: *a'vi'dan)* FATHER~me~&~MODERATOR *Translation:* My father is a moderator (May also mean "father of a moderator," "father of Dan," or "My father is Dan."). *Strong's:* #0027

Avihha'il (masc: *a'vi'hha'yil)* FATHER~me~&~FORCE *Translation:* My father is a force. *Strong's:* #0032

Aviram (masc: *a'vi'ram)* FATHER~me~&~RAISED *Translation:* My father is raised. *Strong's:* #0048

Aviyasaph (masc: *a'vi'a'saph)* FATHER~me~&~*he~did*~GATHER(V) *Translation:* My father gathers. *Strong's:* #0023

Aviyasaph (masc: *a'vi'a'saph)* FATHER~me~&~*he~did*~GATHER(V) *Translation:* My father gathers. *Strong's:* #0023

Aviyhu (masc: *a'vi'hu)* FATHER~me~&~HE *Translation:* He is my father. *Strong's:* #0030

Aviyma'el (masc: *a'vi'ma'eyl)* FATHER~me~&~from~MIGHTY.ONE *Translation:* My father is from El. *Strong's:* #0039

Aviymelekh (masc: *a'viy'me'lekh)* FATHER~me~&~KING *Translation:* My father is king (Can also mean "Father of the king."). *Strong's:* #0040

Avraham (masc: *av'ra'ham)* FATHER~&~LIFTED *Translation:* Father lifted. *Strong's:* #0085

Avram (masc: *av'ram)* FATHER~&~RAISED *Translation:* Father raised. *Strong's:* #0087

Awi (masc: *a'wi)* TWIST *Translation:* Twist. *Strong's:* #5757, #5761

Awit (masc: *a'wit)* RUINED.HEAP~s *Translation:* Ruined heaps. *Strong's:* #5762

Ay (masc: *ai)* RUINED.HEAP *Translation:* Ruined heap. *Strong's:* #5857

Ayah (masc: *ai'yah)* HAWK *Translation:* Hawk. *Strong's:* #0345

Ayin (masc: *a'yin)* EYE *Translation:* Eye. *Strong's:* #5871

Azan (masc: *a'zan)* STRONG.ONE *Translation:* Strong one. *Strong's:* #5821

Azazeyl (masc: *a'za'zeyl)* STRONG~&~>~WAVER(V) *Translation:* Strong waver. *Strong's:* #5799

Azni (masc: *az'ni)* EAR~me *Translation:* My ear. *Strong's:* #0241, #0244

B

Ba'al (masc: *ba'al)* MASTER *Translation:* Master. *Strong's:* #1168

Ba'al-Hhanan (masc: *ba'al hha'nan)* MASTER~&~BEAUTY *Translation:* Master of beauty (Can also mean Ba'al is Beauty). *Strong's:* #1177

Ba'al-Me'on (masc: *ba'al me'on)* MASTER~&~HABITATION *Translation:* Master of the habitation. *Strong's:* #1186

Ba'al-Pe'or (masc: *ba'al pe'or)* MASTER~&~OPENED.WIDE *Translation:* Master of the wide open. *Strong's:* #1187

Ba'al-T^{s}ephon (masc: *ba'al tse'phon)* MASTER~&~NORTH *Translation:* Master of the north. *Strong's:* #1189

Balaq (masc: *ba'laq)* *he~did*~LAY.WASTE(V) *Translation:* He laid waste. *Strong's:* #1111

Bamot (masc: *ba'mot)* PLATFORM~s *Translation:* Platforms. *Strong's:* #1120
Barneya (masc: *bar'ney'a)* GRAIN~&~RATTLE *Translation:* Grain rattles. *Strong's:* #6947
Bashan (masc: *ba'shan)* SHAME *Translation:* Shame. *Strong's:* #1316
Basmat (fem: *bas'mat)* FRAGRANCE *Translation:* Fragrance. *Strong's:* #1315
Bavel (masc: *ba'vel)* MIXED.UP *Translation:* Mixed up (From a root meaning "to mix up."). *Strong's:* #0894
Bedad (masc: *be'dad)* ALONE *Translation:* Alone. *Strong's:* #0911
Be'eri (masc: *be'ey'ri)* WELL~me *Translation:* My well. *Strong's:* #0882
Be'er-Lahhiy-Ro'iy (masc: *be'eyr la'hhai ro'iy)* WELL~&~to~LIVING~&~SEE[(V)]~*ing*[(ms)]~me *Translation:* I see a well for life. *Strong's:* #0883
Bekher (masc: *be'kher)* YOUNG.CAMEL *Translation:* Young camel. *Strong's:* #1071
Bela (fem: *be'la)* SWALLOWED *Translation:* Swallowed. *Strong's:* #1106
Beli'ya'al (masc: *be'li'ya'al)* UNAWARE~&~*he*~*will*~Gain[(V)] *Translation:* The unaware will gain. *Strong's:* #1100
Ben-Amiy (masc: *ben a'miy)* SON~&~PEOPLE~me *Translation:* Son of my people. *Strong's:* #1151
Ben-Oni (masc: *ben o'niy)* SON~&~VIGOR~me *Translation:* Son of my vigor. *Strong's:* #1126
Be'on (masc: *be'on)* in~COHABITATION *Translation:* In cohabitation. *Strong's:* #1194
Be'or (masc: *be'or)* IGNITING *Translation:* Igniting. *Strong's:* #1160
B'er (masc: *b'er)* WELL *Translation:* Well. *Strong's:* #0876
Bera (masc: *be'ra)* in~DYSFUNCTIONAL *Translation:* In dysfunction (Can also mean "With shouting", "Son of evil", "A well" or "Declaring."). *Strong's:* #1298
Bered (masc: *be'red)* HAILSTONES *Translation:* Hailstones. *Strong's:* #1260
Beri'ah (masc: *be'ri'ah)* in~COMPANION *Translation:* With a companion. *Strong's:* #1283
B'er-Sheva (masc: *be'er she'va)* WELL~&~SEVEN *Translation:* Seven wells. *Strong's:* #0884
Betsaleyl (masc: *be'tsa'leyl)* in~SHADOW~&~MIGHTY.ONE *Translation:* In the shadow of El. *Strong's:* #1212
Betser (masc: *be'tser)* PRECIOUS.METAL *Translation:* Precious metal. *Strong's:* #1221
Betu'el (masc: *be'tu'eyl)* HOUSE~them[(m)]~&~MIGHTY.ONE *Translation:* Their house is El. *Strong's:* #1328
Beyt-El (masc: *beyt eyl)* HOUSE~&~MIGHTY.ONE *Translation:* House of El. *Strong's:* #1008
Beyt-Haran (masc: *beyt ha'ran)* HOUSE~&~HILL.COUNTRY *Translation:* House of the Hill country. *Strong's:* #1028
Beyt-Hayishmot (masc: הישמות *beyt ha'yish'mot)* HOUSE~&~THERE.IS~&~DEATH *Translation:* House of There is death (or "House of Hayishmot"). *Strong's:* #1020
Beyt-Lehhem (masc: *beyt le'hhem)* HOUSE~&~BREAD *Translation:* House of bread. *Strong's:* #1035

Beyt-Nimrah (fem: *beyt nimrah)* HOUSE~&~LEOPARD *Translation:* House of the leopard. *Strong's:* #1039

Beyt-Pe'or (masc: *beyt pe'or)* HOUSE~&~OPENED.WIDE *Translation:* House of the opened wide one (or "house of Pe'or"). *Strong's:* #1047

Bilam (masc: *bil'am)* NONE~&~PEOPLE *Translation:* None of the people. *Strong's:* #1109

Bilhah (fem: *bil'hah)* DISMAY *Translation:* Dismay. *Strong's:* #1090

Bilhan (masc: *bil'han)* DISMAY~them(f) *Translation:* Their dismay. *Strong's:* #1092

Binyamin (masc: *bin'ya'min)* SON~&~RIGHT.HAND *Translation:* Son of the right hand. *Strong's:* #1144

Birsha (masc: *bir'sha)* in~LOST *Translation:* With the lost. *Strong's:* #1306

B'ney-Ya'aqan (masc: יעקן *be'ney ya'a'qan)* SON~s2~&~*he~will~*BE.SHARP.SIGHTED(V) *Translation:* sons of he will be sharp sighted (or "sons of Ya'aqatan"). *Strong's:* #1142

Botsrah (masc: *bots'rah)* SHEEP.PEN *Translation:* Sheep pen. *Strong's:* #1224

Buqi (masc: *bu'qi)* VACANT *Translation:* Vacant. *Strong's:* #1231

Buz (masc: *buz)* DESPISED *Translation:* Despised. *Strong's:* #0938

D

Dameseq (masc: / / דרמשק / דומשק / *dam'seq / du'me'seq / dar'me'seq)* BLOOD~&~SACK *Translation:* Blood sack. *Strong's:* #1834

Dan (masc: *dan)* MODERATOR *Translation:* Moderator. *Strong's:* #1835

Daphqah (fem: *daph'qah) she~did~*BEAT.OUT(V) *Translation:* She beat out. *Strong's:* #1850

Datan (masc: *da'tan)* LAWFUL *Translation:* Two wells. *Strong's:* #1885

Dedan (masc: / דדנה / *de'dan / de'da'neh)* LOW.COUNTRY *Translation:* Low country (From the root ??. Can also mean breasts or judge). *Strong's:* #1719

De'u'eyl (masc: *de'u'eyl) they~did~*KNOW(V)~&~MIGHTY.ONE *Translation:* They knew the mighty one. *Strong's:* #1845

Devorah (fem: *de'vo'rah)* BEE *Translation:* Bee. *Strong's:* #1683

Dibon (masc: *di'bon)* BROODING *Translation:* Brooding. *Strong's:* #1769

Dibon-Gad (masc: גד *di'bon gad)* BROODING~&~FORTUNE *Translation:* Brooding of fortune (or "Brooding of Gad"). *Strong's:* #1769

Dinah (fem: *di'nah)* PLEA *Translation:* Plea. *Strong's:* #1783

Dinhavah (masc: *din'ha'vah)* PLEA~&~GIFT.OFFERING *Translation:* Plea offering. *Strong's:* #1838

Diqlah (masc: *diq'lah)* PALM.GROVE *Translation:* Palm grove (Meaning and origin are uncertain). *Strong's:* #1853

Dishan (masc: *di'shan)* THRESHER *Translation:* Thresher. *Strong's:* #1789

Dishon (masc: *di'shon)* ANTELOPE *Translation:* Antelope. *Strong's:* #1787

Divriy (masc: *div'riy)* WORD~me *Translation:* My word. *Strong's:* #1704

Di-Zahav (masc: זהב *di za'hav)* SUFFICIENT~&~GOLD *Translation:* Sufficient gold. *Strong's:* #1774

Dodan (masc: רודן / דודן רודן / *do'dan / ro'dan)* LOW.COUNTRY *Translation:* Low country (From the root ??. Can also mean friendship, breast or judge). *Strong's:* #1721

Dotan (masc: דותן *do'tan)* LAWFUL *Translation:* Two wells. *Strong's:* #1886

Dumah (masc: דומה *du'mah)* SILENCED *Translation:* Silenced. *Strong's:* #1746

E

Eden (masc: עדן *e'den)* PLEASURE *Translation:* Pleasure. *Strong's:* #5731

Edom (masc: אדום *e'dom)* RED *Translation:* Red. *Strong's:* #0123, #0130

Ed're'i (masc: אדרעי *ed're'i)* ENERGY~me *Translation:* My energy. *Strong's:* #0154

Ehyeh (masc: אהיה *eh'yeh) I~will~*EXIST(V) *Translation:* I exist (Used only once, Exodus 3:14, where it is used as a proper name). *Strong's:* #1961

Elaley (masc: אלעלא *el'a'ley)* MIGHTY.ONE~&~>~GO.UP(V) *Translation:* The might one goes up. *Strong's:* #0500

Elam (masc: עולם / עילם עולם / *e'lam / o'lam)* ANCIENT *Translation:* Ancient. *Strong's:* #5867

Elasar (masc: אלסר *el'la'sar)* MIGHTY.ONE~&~NOBLE *Translation:* El of the noble (Can also mean "Mighty one is chastiser" or "Revolting from mighty one."). *Strong's:* #0495

Elazar (masc: אלעזר *el'a'zar)* MIGHTY.ONE~&~*he~did~*HELP(V) *Translation:* El helps. *Strong's:* #0499

El-Beyt-El (masc: אל-בית-אל *eyl beyt eyl)* MIGHTY.ONE~&~HOUSE~&~MIGHTY.ONE *Translation:* El of Beyt El. *Strong's:* #0416

Elda'ah (masc: אלדעה *el'da'ah)* MIGHTY.ONE~&~*he~did~*KNOW(V) *Translation:* El knows. *Strong's:* #0420

Eldad (masc: אלדד *el'dad)* MIGHTY.ONE~&~TEAT *Translation:* The mighty one is a teat. *Strong's:* #0419

El-Elohey-Yisra'eyl (masc: אל-אלהי-ישראל *eyl e'lo'hey yis'ra'eyl)* MIGHTY.ONE~&~POWER~s~&~*he~will~*TURN.ASIDE(V)~&~MIGHTY.ONE *Translation:* El of Elohiym of Yisra'el. *Strong's:* #0415

Eli'av (masc: אליאב *e'li'av)* MIGHTY.ONE~&~FATHER *Translation:* The mighty one is father. *Strong's:* #0446

Elidad (masc: אלידד *e'li'dad)* MIGHTY.ONE~me~&~TEAT *Translation:* My mighty one is a teat. *Strong's:* #0449

Eli'ezer (masc: אליעזר *e'li'e'zer)* MIGHTY.ONE~me~&~*he~did~*HELP(V) *Translation:* My El helps (Can also mean "Mighty one of help."). *Strong's:* #0461

Eliphaz (masc: אליפז *e'li'phaz)* MIGHTY.ONE~me~&~PURE.GOLD *Translation:* My El is pure gold. *Strong's:* #0464

Elishah (masc: אלישה *e'li'shah)* MIGHTY.ONE~me~&~EQUATED *Translation:* My El equates or My El resembles (Meaning of the word "shah" is uncertain). *Strong's:* #0473

Elishama (masc: אלישמע *e'li'sha'ma)* MIGHTY.ONE~me~&~*he~did~*HEAR(V) *Translation:* My mighty one heard. *Strong's:* #0476

Elitsaphan (masc: אליצפן *e'li'tsa'phan)* MIGHTY.ONE~me~&~*he~did~*CONCEAL(V) *Translation:* My mighty one concealed. *Strong's:* #0469

Elitsur (masc: *e'li'tsur)* MIGHTY.ONE~me~&~BOULDER *Translation:* My mighty one is a boulder. *Strong's:* #0468

Eliysheva (fem: *e'li'she'va)* MIGHTY.ONE~me~&~*he~did*~SWEAR(V) *Translation:* My El swears. *Strong's:* #0472

Elohiym (masc: *e'lo'him)* POWER~s *Translation:* Powers. *Strong's:* #0430

Elqanah (masc: *el'qa'nah)* MIGHTY.ONE~&~*he~did*~PURCHASE(V) *Translation:* El purchased. *Strong's:* #0511

El-Ra'iy (masc: *el ra'iy)* MIGHTY.ONE~&~*he~did*~SEE(V)~me *Translation:* El sees me. *Strong's:* #0410 & #7200

El'tsaphan (masc: *el'tsa'phan)* MIGHTY.ONE~&~*he~did*~CONCEAL(V) *Translation:* El conceals. *Strong's:* #0469

Elyasaph (masc: *el'ya'saph)* MIGHTY.ONE~&~*he~did*~ADD(V) *Translation:* The mighty one added. *Strong's:* #0460

Elyon (masc: *el'yon)* UPPER *Translation:* Upper. *Strong's:* #5945

Emor (masc: *e'mor)* SAYER *Translation:* Sayer. *Strong's:* #0567

Enosh (masc: *e'nosh)* MAN *Translation:* Man. *Strong's:* #0583

Epher (masc: *e'pher)* DIRT *Translation:* Powder. *Strong's:* #6081

Ephod (masc: *e'phod)* EPHOD *Translation:* Ephod. *Strong's:* #0641

Ephrat (masc: *eph'rat) I~will*~INTERPRET(V) *Translation:* I will interpret. *Strong's:* #0672

Ephrayim (masc: *eph'ra'yim)* ASH~s2 *Translation:* Ashes (Can also mean "fruitful" or "double fruit."). *Strong's:* #0669

Ephron (masc: *eph'ron)* POWDERY *Translation:* Powdery. *Strong's:* #6085

Erekh (masc: *e'rekh)* SLOW *Translation:* Slow. *Strong's:* #0751

Esaw (masc: *e'saw)* DOING *Translation:* Doing. *Strong's:* #6215

Eseq (masc: *e'seq)* STRIFE *Translation:* Strife. *Strong's:* #6230

Eshban (masc: *esh'ban) I~will*~GROW *Translation:* I will grow. *Strong's:* #0790

Eshkol (masc: *esh'kol)* CLUSTER *Translation:* Cluster. *Strong's:* #0812

Etsbon (masc: *ets'bon)* WORKING *Translation:* Working. *Strong's:* #0675

Etsi'on-Gaver (masc: גבר *e'tsi'on ga'ver)* BACKBONE~&~WARRIOR *Translation:* Backbone of the warrior. *Strong's:* #6100

Ever (masc: *e'ver)* OTHER.SIDE *Translation:* Other side. *Strong's:* #5677, #5680, #5681, #5682

Evronah (fem: *ev'ro'nah)* CROSSING.ONE *Translation:* Crossing one. *Strong's:* #5684

Ewi (masc: *e'wi)* YEARN~me *Translation:* My yearning. *Strong's:* #0189

Eyhhiy (masc: *a'hhi)* BROTHER~me *Translation:* My brother. *Strong's:* #0278

Eylah (masc: *ey'lah)* OAK *Translation:* Oak. *Strong's:* #0425

Eyliym (masc: *ey'lim)* BUCK~s *Translation:* Bucks. *Strong's:* #0362

Eylon (masc: *ey'lon)* GREAT.TREE *Translation:* Great tree. *Strong's:* #0356

Eylot (fem: *ey'lot)* DOE~s *Translation:* Does. *Strong's:* #0359

Eyl-Paran (masc: *eyl pa'ran)* BUCK~&~DECORATED *Translation:* Decorated Buck (The word Eyl can also mean ram, hart, tree, lintel, oak, mighty or strength). *Strong's:* #0364

Eym (masc: *eym)* TERROR *Translation:* Terror. *Strong's:* #0368

Eynan (masc: *ey'nan)* HAVING.AN.EYE *Translation:* Having an eye. *Strong's:* #5851

Eynayim (masc: *ey'na'yim)* EYE~s2 *Translation:* Two eyes. *Strong's:* #5879

Eyn-Mishpat (masc: *eyn mish'pat)* EYE~&~DECISION *Translation:* Eye of decision (Can also mean "Spring of judgement."). *Strong's:* #5880

Eyphah (masc: *ey'phah)* MURKINESS *Translation:* Murkiness. *Strong's:* #5891

Eyr (masc: *eyr)* BARE.SKIN *Translation:* Bare skin. *Strong's:* #6147

Eyran (masc: *ey'ran)* BARE.ONE *Translation:* Bare one (May also mean "enemy" or "city."). *Strong's:* #6197

Eyriy (masc: *ey'ri)* BARE.SKIN~me *Translation:* My bare skin. *Strong's:* #6179, #6180

Eyshdat (masc: *eysh'dat)* FIRE~&~LAW *Translation:* Fire Law. *Strong's:* #0799+#1881

Eytam (masc: *ey'tam)* PLOWSHARE~them[(m)] *Translation:* Their plowshare. *Strong's:* #0864

Eytser (masc: *ey'tser) he~did~*STORE.UP[(V)] *Translation:* He stored up. *Strong's:* #0687

Eyval (masc: *ey'val)* ROUND.STONE *Translation:* Round stone. *Strong's:* #5858

G

Gad (masc: *gad)* FORTUNE *Translation:* Fortune. *Strong's:* #1410

Gad'di'eyl (masc: *gad'di'eyl)* FORTUNE~me~&~MIGHTY.ONE *Translation:* My fortune is the mighty one. *Strong's:* #1427

Gad'diy (masc: *gad'diy)* FORTUNE~me *Translation:* My fortune. *Strong's:* #1426

Gahham (masc: *ga'hham)* BURNT *Translation:* Burnt. *Strong's:* #1514

Galeyd (masc: *gal'eyd)* MOUND~&~WITNESS *Translation:* Mound of the witness. *Strong's:* #1567

Gamli'eyl (masc: *gam'li'eyl)* CAMEL~me~&~MIGHTY.ONE *Translation:* My camel is the mighty one. *Strong's:* #1583

Gatam (masc: *ga'tam)* BURNT.VALLEY *Translation:* Burnt Valley. *Strong's:* #1609

Gemali (masc: *ge'ma'li)* CAMEL~me *Translation:* My camel. *Strong's:* #1582

Gera (masc: *gey'ra)* SEED.OF.GRAIN *Translation:* Seed of grain. *Strong's:* #1617

Gerar (masc: *ge'rar)* CHEWED *Translation:* Chewed. *Strong's:* #1642

Gerizim (masc: *ge'ri'zim)* CUTTING~s *Translation:* Cuttings. *Strong's:* #1630

Gershom (masc: *ger'shom)* EVICTED *Translation:* Evicted. *Strong's:* #1647

Gershon (masc: *ger'shon)* EVICTED *Translation:* Evicted. *Strong's:* #1648

Geshur (masc: *ge'shur)* CLINGING *Translation:* Proud beholder. *Strong's:* #1650, #1651

Getar (masc: גתר *ge'ter)* AGITATED *Translation:* Agitation (Can also mean "The vale of trial or searching."). *Strong's:* #1666

Ge'u'eyl (masc: גאואל *ge'u'eyl)* !$^{(ms)}$~RISE.UP$^{(V)}$~&~MIGHTY.ONE *Translation:* The mighty one will rise up. *Strong's:* #1345

Ghamorah (masc: עמורה *gha'mo'rah)* SUBMERSION *Translation:* Submersion. *Strong's:* #6017

Ghaza (masc: עזה *gha'za)* GOAT *Translation:* Goat. *Strong's:* #5804

Gidoni (masc: גדעוני *gid'o'ni)* HEWN.ONE~me *Translation:* My hewn one. *Strong's:* #1441

Gil'ad (masc: גלעד *gil'ad)* DANCING.AROUND~&~WITNESS *Translation:* Dancing around the witness. *Strong's:* #1568

Gilgal (masc: גלגל *gil'gal)* ROLLING.THING *Translation:* Rolling thing. *Strong's:* #1537

Girgash (masc: גרגש *gir'gash)* IMMIGRANT~&~CLAYEY.SOIL *Translation:* Immigrant of clayey soil (Can also mean "dwelling on clayey soil."). *Strong's:* #1622

Giyhhon (masc: גיחון *gi'hhon)* BURSTING.FORTH *Translation:* Bursting forth. *Strong's:* #1521

Golan (masc: גולן *go'lan)* BURNT.OFFERING~them(f) *Translation:* Their burnt offerings. *Strong's:* #1474

Gomer (masc: גומר *go'mer)* CONCLUDED *Translation:* Concluded. *Strong's:* #1586

Goren-Ha'atad (masc: גורן-האטד *goren ha'atad)* FLOOR~&~the~BRAMBLE.THORN *Translation:* Floor of the bramble thorn. *Strong's:* #0329, #1637

Goshen (masc: גושן *go'shen)* DRAWING.NEAR *Translation:* Drawing near. *Strong's:* #1657

Goyim (masc: גוים *go'yim)* NATION~s *Translation:* Nations. *Strong's:* #1471

Gudgodah (fem: גודגודה *gud'go'dah)* FORTUNES *Translation:* Fortunes. *Strong's:* #1412

Guni (masc: גוני *gu'ni)* DEFENDER~me *Translation:* My defender. *Strong's:* #1476

H

Hadad (masc: הדד *ha'dad)* the~TEAT *Translation:* The teat. *Strong's:* #1908

Hadar (masc: הדר *ha'dar)* HONOR *Translation:* Swell. *Strong's:* #1924

Hadoram (masc: הדורם *ha'do'ram)* HONOR~them$^{(m)}$ *Translation:* Their selling. *Strong's:* #1913

Hagar (masc: הגר *ha'gar)* the~IMMIGRANT *Translation:* The immigrant. *Strong's:* #1904

Ham (masc: הם *ham)* ROARING *Translation:* Roaring (From a root meaning "the roar of the sea"). *Strong's:* #1990

Haran (masc: הרן *ha'ran)* HILL.COUNTRY *Translation:* Hill country. *Strong's:* #2039

Hevel (masc: הבל *he'vel)* VANITY *Translation:* Vanity. *Strong's:* #1893

Heymam (masc: הימם *hey'mam)* CONFUSED *Translation:* Confused. *Strong's:* #1967

Hhadad (masc: *hha'dad) he~did~*PARTRIDGE *Translation:* He entered the chamber. *Strong's:* #2316

Hhagi (masc: *hha'gi)* FEAST~me *Translation:* My feast. *Strong's:* #2291

Hhaglah (fem: *hhag'lah)* PARTRIDGE *Translation:* Partridge. *Strong's:* #2295

Hham (masc: *hham)* FATHER-IN-LAW *Translation:* Father in law. *Strong's:* #2526

Hhamat (masc: *hha'mat)* SKIN.BAG *Translation:* Skin bag (Can also mean heat, anger or wall). *Strong's:* #2574, #2575, #2577

Hhamor (masc: *hha'mor)* DONKEY *Translation:* Donkey. *Strong's:* #2544

Hhamul (masc: *hha'mul)* PITIED *Translation:* Pitied. *Strong's:* #2538, #2539

Hhani'eyl (masc: *hha'ni'eyl)* BEAUTY~of~&~MIGHTY.ONE *Translation:* Beauty of the mighty one. *Strong's:* #2592

Hhanokh (masc: *hha'nokh)* DEVOTED *Translation:* Devoted. *Strong's:* #2585

Hharadah (fem: *hha'ra'dah)* TREMBLING *Translation:* Trembling. *Strong's:* #2732

Hharan (masc: *hha'ran)* FLAMING.WRATH *Translation:* Burning wrath. *Strong's:* #2771

Hharmah (fem: *hhar'mah)* ASSIGNED *Translation:* Perforated. *Strong's:* #2767

Hhashmonah (fem: *hhash'mo'nah)* WEALTHY *Translation:* Wealthy. *Strong's:* #2832

Hhatsar-Adar (masc: אדר *hha'tsar a'dar)* COURTYARD~&~*he~did~*BE.EMINENT[(V)] *Translation:* Courtyard of Adar. *Strong's:* #2692

Hhatsar-Eynan (masc: עינן *hha'tsar ey'nan)* COURTYARD~&~HAVING.AN.EYE *Translation:* Courtyard of Having an eye (or "Courtyard of Eynan"). *Strong's:* #2704

Hhatsariym (masc: *hha'tsa'riym)* COURTYARD~s *Translation:* Courtyards. *Strong's:* #2699

Hhatsarmawet (masc: *hha'tsa'ma'wet)* COURTYARD~&~DEATH *Translation:* Yard of death. *Strong's:* #2700

Hhatsarot (masc: *hha'tsa'rot)* COURTYARD~s *Translation:* Courtyards. *Strong's:* #2698

Hhats'tson-Tamar (masc: *hhats'tson ta'mar)* DIVIDING~&~DATE.PALM *Translation:* Dividing the date palm. *Strong's:* #2688

Hhawah (fem: *hha'wah)* TOWN *Translation:* Town. *Strong's:* #2332

Hhawilah (fem: *hha'wi'lah)* TWIST.AROUND *Translation:* Twist around (May have the meaning of "suffers pain" from the idea of twisting). *Strong's:* #2341

Hhawot (fem: *hha'wot)* TOWN~s *Translation:* Towns. *Strong's:* #2334

Hhazo (masc: *hha'zo)* LOOK.INTO~him *Translation:* Look into him. *Strong's:* #2375

Hheleq (masc: *hhe'leq)* DISTRIBUTION *Translation:* Portion. *Strong's:* #2507, #2516

Hhemdan (masc: *hhem'dan)* DESIRED *Translation:* Desired. *Strong's:* #2533

Hhermon (masc: *hher'mon)* PERFORATED.ONE *Translation:* Perforated one. *Strong's:* #2768

Hheshbon (masc: *hhesh'bon)* REASON *Translation:* Reason. *Strong's:* #2809

Hhet (masc: *hhet)* TREMBLING.IN.FEAR *Translation:* Trembling in fear. *Strong's:* #2845, #2850

Hhetsron (masc: *hhets'ron)* SURROUNDED.BY.A.WALL *Translation:* Surrounded by a wall. *Strong's:* #2696

Hhever (masc: *hhe'ver)* COUPLE *Translation:* Couple. *Strong's:* #2268

Hhevron (masc: *hhev'ron)* ASSOCIATION *Translation:* Association. *Strong's:* #2275, #2276

Hheylon (masc: *hhey'lon)* WINDOW *Translation:* Window. *Strong's:* #2497

Hheypher (masc: *hhey'pher)* DUG.OUT.WELL *Translation:* Dug out well. *Strong's:* #2660

Hhideqel (masc: *hhi'de'qel)* RAPID *Translation:* Rapid. *Strong's:* #2313

Hhirot (fem: *hhi'rot)* CISTERN~s *Translation:* Cisterns. *Strong's:* #6367

Hhiw (masc: *hhiw)* TOWN *Translation:* Town. *Strong's:* #2340

Hhiyrah (masc: *hhi'rah)* NOBILITY *Translation:* Nobility. *Strong's:* #2437

Hhor (masc: *hhor)* PALE *Translation:* Pale. *Strong's:* #2752

Hhorev (masc: *hho'rev)* PARCHING.HEAT *Translation:* Parching heat. *Strong's:* #2722

Hhor-Hagidgad (masc: הגדגד *hhor ha'gid'gad)* PALE~&~the~FORTUNES *Translation:* Pale of the fortunes (or "Hhor of Hagidgad"). *Strong's:* #2735

Hhoriy (masc: *hho'ri)* PALENESS *Translation:* Paleness. *Strong's:* #2753

Hhovah (fem: *hho'vah)* WITHDRAWING *Translation:* Hiding place (From a root meaning "bosom," as a place of refuge). *Strong's:* #2327

Hhovav (masc: *hho'vav)* CHERISH(V)~*ing*(ms) *Translation:* Cherishing. *Strong's:* #2246

Hhul (masc: *hhul)* SAND *Translation:* Sand. *Strong's:* #2343

Hhupham (masc: *hhu'pham)* SHORE~them(m) *Translation:* Their shore. *Strong's:* #2349

Hhupim (masc: *hhu'pim)* SHORE~s *Translation:* Shores. *Strong's:* #2650

Hhur (masc: *hhur)* PALE *Translation:* Pale. *Strong's:* #2354

Hhush (masc: *hhush)* HASTY *Translation:* Hasty. *Strong's:* #2366

Hhusham (masc: *hhu'sham)* HASTILY *Translation:* Hastily. *Strong's:* #2367

Hhutsot (masc: *hhu'tsot)* OUTSIDE~s *Translation:* Outsides. *Strong's:* #7155

Hor (masc: *hor)* HILL *Translation:* Hill. *Strong's:* #2023

Hosheya (masc: *ho'shey'a) !*(ms)~*make*~RESCUE(V) *Translation:* Rescue. *Strong's:* #1954

I

I'ezer (masc: *i'e'zer)* ISLAND~&~HELP *Translation:* An Island is help. *Strong's:* #0372, #0373

Irad (masc: *i'rad)* FLEET *Translation:* Fleet. *Strong's:* #5897

Iyey-Ha'a'variym (masc: העברים *i'yey ha'a'va'riym)* PILE.OF.RUINS~s~&~the~OTHER.SIDE~s *Translation:* Pile of ruins of the ones of the other side (or "Pile of ruins of the ones of Eber"). *Strong's:* #5863

Iyram (masc: *i'ram)* CITY~them(m) *Translation:* Their city. *Strong's:* #5902

Iytamar (masc: *it'mar)* ISLAND~&~DATE.PALM *Translation:* Island of the date palm. *Strong's:* #0385

Iy'yim (masc: *iy'yim)* PILE.OF.RUINS~s *Translation:* Pile of ruins. *Strong's:* #5864

K

Kalahh (masc: *ka'lahh)* FULL.AGE *Translation:* Full age. *Strong's:* #3625

Kaleyv (masc: *ka'leyv)* DOG *Translation:* Dog (May also mean "like a heart."). *Strong's:* #3612

Kalneh (masc: *kal'neh)* FORTRESS.OF.ANU *Translation:* Fortress of Anu. *Strong's:* #3641

Kaphtor (masc: *kaph'tor)* KNOB *Translation:* Knob. *Strong's:* #3731, #3732

Karmi (masc: *kar'mi)* VINEYARD~me *Translation:* My vineyard. *Strong's:* #3756

Kasluhh (masc: *kas'luhh)* FORTIFIED *Translation:* Fortified (Can also mean "hopes of life."). *Strong's:* #3695

Kazbi (fem: *kaz'bi)* LIE~me *Translation:* My lie. *Strong's:* #3579

Kedarla'omer (masc: *ke'dar'la'o'mer)* FIGHTING~&~to~the~SHEAF *Translation:* Fighting for the sheaf. *Strong's:* #3540

Kemosh (masc: *ke'mosh)* SUBDUER *Translation:* Subduer. *Strong's:* #3645

Kena'an (masc: *ke'na'an)* LOWERED *Translation:* Lowered. *Strong's:* #3667, #3669

Keran (masc: *ke'ran)* LYRE *Translation:* Lyre. *Strong's:* #3763

Kesed (masc: *ke'sed)* INCREASING *Translation:* Increasing (Appears to be the prefix ? meaning "like" and the root ?? meaning "level field." *Strong's:* #3777, #3778

Keziv (masc: *ke'ziv)* LIE *Translation:* Lie. *Strong's:* #3580

Kineret (fem: *ki'ne'ret)* HARP *Translation:* Harp. *Strong's:* #3672

Kislon (masc: *kis'lon)* CONFIDENT.ONE *Translation:* Confident one. *Strong's:* #3692

Kit (masc: *kit)* BRUISER *Translation:* Bruiser (Can also mean breaking or bruising). *Strong's:* #3794

Kush (masc: *kush)* BLACKISH *Translation:* Black. *Strong's:* #3568, #3569, #3571

L

La'eyl (masc: *la'eyl)* to~MIGHTY.ONE *Translation:* Belonging to the Mighty One. *Strong's:* #3815

Lamekh (masc: *la'mekh)* DESPAIRING *Translation:* Despairing (Can also mean "suffering."). *Strong's:* #3929

Lavan (masc: *la'van)* WHITE *Translation:* White. *Strong's:* #3837

Le'ah (fem: *ley'ah)* IMPATIENT *Translation:* Weary. *Strong's:* #3812

Lehav (masc: *le'hav)* GLIMMER *Translation:* Glimmer. *Strong's:* #3853

Lesha (masc: *le'sha)* CRACK.OPEN *Translation:* Crack open. *Strong's:* #3962

Letush (masc: *le'tush)* SHARPENED *Translation:* Sharpened. *Strong's:* #3912

Le'um (masc: *le'um)* COMMUNITY *Translation:* Community. *Strong's:* #3817
Levanon (masc: *le'va'non)* WHITE.ONE *Translation:* White one. *Strong's:* #3844
Lewi (masc: *le'wi)* JOINING~me *Translation:* My joining. *Strong's:* #3878, #3881
Livnah (fem: *liv'nah)* BRICK *Translation:* Bruick (May also mean "White" or "Moon."). *Strong's:* #3841
Liyvniy (masc: *liv'ni)* WHITE~me *Translation:* My white. *Strong's:* #3845
Lot (masc: *lot)* TIGHTLY.WRAPPED *Translation:* Tightly wrapped. *Strong's:* #3876
Lotan (masc: *lo'tan)* WRAPPER *Translation:* Wrapper. *Strong's:* #3877
Lud (masc: *lud)* NATIVITY *Translation:* Nativity (Can also mean nativity or generation). *Strong's:* #3865, #3866
Luz (masc: *luz)* HAZEL *Translation:* Hazel. *Strong's:* #3870

M

Ma'akhah (masc: *ma'a'khah)* FIRMLY.PRESSED *Translation:* Firmly pressed. *Strong's:* #4601
Madai (masc: *ma'dai)* LONG.GARMENT~s~me *Translation:* My long garments (Can also mean measure, judging, habit or covering). *Strong's:* #4074
Magdi'eyl (masc: *mag'di'eyl)* PRECIOUS~&~MIGHTY.ONE *Translation:* Precious is El. *Strong's:* #4025
Magog (masc: *ma'gog)* ROOFING *Translation:* Roofing. *Strong's:* #4031
Mahalalel (masc: *ma'ha'la'lel)* SHINE~&~MIGHTY.ONE *Translation:* Shining of El. *Strong's:* #4111
Mahhalat (masc: *ma'hha'lat)* SICKENED *Translation:* Sickened. *Strong's:* #4257, #4258
Mahhanayim (masc: *ma'hha'na'yim)* CAMP~s2 *Translation:* Two campsites. *Strong's:* #4266
Mahhlah (fem: *mahh'lah)* SICKNESS *Translation:* Sickness. *Strong's:* #4244
Mahh'liy (masc: *mahh'li)* SICKNESS~me *Translation:* My Sickness. *Strong's:* #4249
Mahn (masc: *mahn)* SHARE *Translation:* Share (The bread-like substance provided to the Israelites while in the wilderness. The actual meaning of this word is uncertain, but can mean "stringed instrument," "from," or "portion." In the Greek *Septuagint* this word is written as 'man' in the book of Exodus and 'manna' in Numbers and Deuteronomy, where the standard transliteration of "manna" comes from). *Strong's:* #4478
Makhi (masc: *ma'khi)* BEING.LOW *Translation:* Being low. *Strong's:* #4352
Makhir (masc: *ma'khir)* PRICE *Translation:* Price. *Strong's:* #4353
Makhpelah (masc: *makh'pe'lah)* DOUBLED *Translation:* Doubled. *Strong's:* #4375
Malki'el (masc: *mal'ki'eyl)* KING~me~&~MIGHTY.ONE *Translation:* My king is El. *Strong's:* #4439
Malkiy-T^{s}edeq (masc: *mal'ki tse'deq)* KING~me~&~STEADFAST *Translation:* My king is steadfast (Can also mean "My king is T^{s}edeq" or "My king is righteousness."). *Strong's:* #4442

Mamre (masc: *mam'rey)* FLAPPING.WING *Translation:* Fatness (From a root meaning "bitter." Can also mean rebellious). *Strong's:* #4471

Manahhat (masc: *ma'na'hhat)* OASIS *Translation:* Oasis. *Strong's:* #4506

Maqheylot (fem: *maq'hey'lot)* PASTURE~s *Translation:* Pastures. *Strong's:* #4722

Marah (fem: *ma'rah)* BITTER *Translation:* Bitter. *Strong's:* #4785

Masa (masc: *ma'sa)* LOAD *Translation:* Load. *Strong's:* #4854

Mash (masc: *mash)* DRAWN.OUT *Translation:* Drawn out. *Strong's:* #4851

Masreyqah (masc: *mas'rey'qah)* CHOICE.VINEYARD *Translation:* Choice vineyard. *Strong's:* #4957

Mas'sah (fem: *ma'sah)* TRIAL *Translation:* Trial. *Strong's:* #4532

Matanah (fem: *ma'ta'nah)* CONTRIBUTION *Translation:* Contribution. *Strong's:* #4980

Matreyd (masc: *mat'reyd)* CONTINUOUS *Translation:* Continuous. *Strong's:* #4308

Medan (masc: *me'dan)* DISCORD *Translation:* Discord. *Strong's:* #4091

Meheytaveyl (masc: *me'hey'tav'eyl)* FAVORED~&~MIGHTY.ONE *Translation:* Favored of El. *Strong's:* #4105

Mehhuya'el (masc: *me'huu'ya'eyl)* BATTERING.RAM~&~MIGHTY.ONE *Translation:* El is a battering ram. *Strong's:* #4232

Menasheh (masc: *me'na'sheh)* CAUSING.TO.OVERLOOK *Translation:* Causing to overlook. *Strong's:* #4519

Merari (masc: *me'ra'ri)* BITTERNESS~me *Translation:* My bitterness. *Strong's:* #4847

Meriyvah (fem: *me'ri'vah)* CONTENTION *Translation:* Contention. *Strong's:* #4809

Mesha (masc: *mey'sha)* TUMULTUOUS *Translation:* Tumultuous. *Strong's:* #4852

Meshek (masc: *me'shek)* ACQUIRING *Translation:* Acquiring. *Strong's:* #4902

Metusha'el (masc: *me'tu'sha'eyl)* DEATH~him~&~*he*~*did*~ENQUIRE(V) *Translation:* His death he enquired (Can also mean "Their death asks."). *Strong's:* #4967

Metushelahh (masc: *me'tu'sha'lahh)* DEATH~him~&~*he*~*did*~SEND(V) *Translation:* His death sends (Can also be "Their death sends."). *Strong's:* #4968

Meydad (masc: *mey'dad)* THROWING *Translation:* Throwing. *Strong's:* #4312

Meydva (masc: *meyd'va)* WATER~&~TOUGHNESS *Translation:* Water of demise. *Strong's:* #4311

Mey-Zahav (masc: *mey za'hav)* WATER~s2GOLD *Translation:* Waters of God. *Strong's:* #4314

Mid'yan (masc: *mid'yan)* QUARREL *Translation:* Quarrel. *Strong's:* #4080

Migdal-Eyder (masc: *mig'dal ey'der)* TOWER~&~DROVE *Translation:* Tower of the drove. *Strong's:* #4029

Migdol (masc: *mig'dol)* TOWER *Translation:* Tower. *Strong's:* #4024

Mika'eyl (masc: *mi'ka'eyl)* WHO~&~like~MIGHTY.ONE *Translation:* Who is like the mighty one. *Strong's:* #4317

Milkah (fem: *mil'kah)* QUEEN *Translation:* Queen. *Strong's:* #4435
Mir'yam (fem: *mir'yam)* BITTER~&~SEA *Translation:* Bitter sea (Can also mean "rebellion."). *Strong's:* #4813
Mishma (masc: *mish'ma)* HEARING *Translation:* Hearing. *Strong's:* #4927
Mitqah (fem: *mit'qah)* SWEETNESS *Translation:* Sweetness. *Strong's:* #4989
Mitspah (masc: *mits'pah)* WATCHTOWER *Translation:* Watchtower. *Strong's:* #4708, #4709
Mits'rayim (fem: *mits'ra'yim)* STRAIT~s2 *Translation:* Two straits (A double plural name). *Strong's:* #4713, #4714
Mivsam (masc: *miv'sam)* SPICE.PLACE *Translation:* Spice place. *Strong's:* #4017
Mivtsar (masc: *miv'tsar)* FORTIFICATION *Translation:* Fortification. *Strong's:* #4014
Miysha'eyl (masc: *mi'sha'eyl)* WHO~&~*he~did*~ENQUIRE$^{(V)}$ *Translation:* Who enquired. *Strong's:* #4332
Miz'zah (masc: *miz'zah)* EXHAUSTED *Translation:* Burnt (Or may mean fear). *Strong's:* #4199
Mo'av (masc: *mo'av)* THAT.ONE~&~FATHER *Translation:* That one is father. *Strong's:* #4124
Molekh (masc: *mo'lekh)* REIGN$^{(V)}$~*ing*$^{(ms)}$ *Translation:* Reigning. *Strong's:* #4432
Moreh (masc: *mo'reh)* THROW$^{(V)}$~*ing*$^{(ms)}$ *Translation:* Teacher (Can also mean rain). *Strong's:* #4176
Moriyah (masc: *mo'ri'yah)* THROW$^{(V)}$~*ing*$^{(ms)}$~me~&~EXISTING *Translation:* Yah is my teacher (Can also mean seen of Yah, chosen of Yah, seeing Yah). *Strong's:* #4179
Moseyrah (fem: *mo'sey'rah)* STRAP~s *Translation:* Strap. *Strong's:* #4149
Moseyrot (fem: *mo'sey'rot)* STRAP~s *Translation:* Straps. *Strong's:* #4149
Mosheh (masc: *mo'sheh)* PLUCKED.OUT *Translation:* Plucked out. *Strong's:* #4872
Mupim (masc: *mu'qim)* SNAKE~s *Translation:* Snakes. *Strong's:* #4649
Mushiy (masc: *mu'shi)* MOVING~me *Translation:* My moving. *Strong's:* #4187

N

Na'amah (fem: *na'a'mah)* DELIGHTFUL *Translation:* Sweetness. *Strong's:* #5279
Na'aman (masc: *na'a'man)* PLEASANTNESS *Translation:* Pleasantness. *Strong's:* #5283
Nadav (masc: *na'dav) he~did*~OFFER.WILLINGLY$^{(V)}$ *Translation:* He offered willingly. *Strong's:* #5070
Nahhali'eyl (masc: *na'hha'li'eyl)* WADI~of~&~MIGHTY.ONE *Translation:* Wadi of the mighty one. *Strong's:* #5160
Nahhat (masc: *na'hhat)* QUIETNESS *Translation:* Quietness. *Strong's:* #5184
Nahhbi (masc: *nahh'bi)* WITHDRAWN *Translation:* Hidden. *Strong's:* #5147
Nahhor (masc: *na'hhor)* SNORTING *Translation:* Snorting. *Strong's:* #5152

Nahhshon (masc: *nahh'shon)* PREDICTOR *Translation:* Predictor. *Strong's:* #5177
Naphish (masc: *na'phish)* DEEP.BREATH *Translation:* Deep breath. *Strong's:* #5305
Naphtali (masc: *naph'ta'li)* WRESTLING~me *Translation:* My wrestling. *Strong's:* #5321
Naphtuhh (masc: *naph'tu'ahh)* DOORWAY *Translation:* Doorway. *Strong's:* #5320
Nataneyl (masc: *na'tan'eyl)* >~GIVE$^{(V)}$~&~MIGHTY.ONE *Translation:* The mighty one gave. *Strong's:* #5417
Nemu'eyl (masc: *ne'mu'eyl)* SEA~&~MIGHTY.ONE *Translation:* Sea of the mighty one. *Strong's:* #5241
Nepheg (masc: *ne'pheg)* SPROUT.UP *Translation:* Sprout up. *Strong's:* #5298
Nephilim (masc: *ne'phi'lim) make*~FALL$^{(V)}$~*ing*$^{(mp)}$ *Translation:* Making fall. *Strong's:* #5303
Nevayot (masc: *ne'va'yot)* FLOURISHED~s *Translation:* Flourishings. *Strong's:* #5032
Nevo (masc: *ne'vo)* FLOURISHED~him *Translation:* His flourishing. *Strong's:* #5015
Nimrah (fem: *nim'rah)* LEOPARD *Translation:* Leopard. *Strong's:* #5247
Nimrod (masc: *nim'rod)* REBELLING *Translation:* Rebelling. *Strong's:* #5248
Ninweh (masc: *nin'weh)* ABODE.OF.NINUS *Translation:* Abode of Ninus (Can also mean handsome). *Strong's:* #5210
No'ah (fem: *no'ah)* STAGGERING *Translation:* Staggering. *Strong's:* #5270
No'ahh (masc: *no'ahh)* REST *Translation:* Rest. *Strong's:* #5146
Nod (masc: *nod)* NODDING *Translation:* Nodding. *Strong's:* #5113
Nophahh (masc: *no'phahh)* EXHALE$^{(V)}$~*ing*$^{(ms)}$ *Translation:* Exhaling. *Strong's:* #5302
Novahh (masc: *no'vahh)* BARK$^{(V)}$~*ing*$^{(ms)}$ *Translation:* Barking. *Strong's:* #5025
Nun (masc: *nun)* CONTINUE *Translation:* Continue. *Strong's:* #5126

O

Og (masc: *og)* BAKED.BREAD *Translation:* Baked bread (The meaning of the feminine Hebrew noun). *Strong's:* #5747
Ohad (masc: *o'had)* SHOUTING *Translation:* Shouting. *Strong's:* #0161
Omar (masc: *o'mar)* MATTER *Translation:* Matter. *Strong's:* #0201
On (masc: *on)* VIGOR *Translation:* Vigor. *Strong's:* #0204
Onam (masc: *o'nam)* COMPLAINER *Translation:* Complainer. *Strong's:* #0208
Onan (masc: *o'nan)* COMPLAINER *Translation:* Complainer. *Strong's:* #0209
Ophir (masc: *o'phir)* REDUCED.TO.ASHES *Translation:* Reduced to ashes (From a root meaning "ashes," "dust" or "powder"). *Strong's:* #0211

Ovot (fem: *o'vot)* NECROMANCER~s *Translation:* Wineskins. *Strong's:* #0088

P

Padan (masc: *pa'dan)* SUET *Translation:* Suet. *Strong's:* #6307

Padan-Aram (masc: *pa'dan a'ram)* SUET~&~PALACE *Translation:* Suet of the palace. *Strong's:* #6307

Pagi'eyl (masc: *pag'i'eyl)* ENCOUNTER~of~&~MIGHTY.ONE *Translation:* Encounger of the mighty one. *Strong's:* #6295

Palti (masc: *pal'ti)* ESCAPING~me *Translation:* My escaping. *Strong's:* #6406

Palti'eyl (masc: *pal'ti'eyl)* ESCAPING~me~&~MIGHTY.ONE *Translation:* My escaping of the might one. *Strong's:* #6409

Palu (masc: *pa'lu)* PERFORMING *Translation:* Performing. *Strong's:* #6396

Paran (masc: *pa'ran)* DECORATED *Translation:* Decorated. *Strong's:* #6290

Parnakh (masc: *par'nakh)* FRAGILE *Translation:* Fragile. *Strong's:* #6535

Paroh (masc: *par'oh)* GREAT.HOUSE *Translation:* Great house. *Strong's:* #6547

Patros (masc: *pat'ros)* SOUTHERN.REGION *Translation:* Southern region (Can also mean "persuasion of ruin."). *Strong's:* #6624, #6625

Pa'u (masc: / פעי / *pa'u / pa'iy)* SCREAMING *Translation:* Screaming. *Strong's:* #6464

Pedah'eyl (masc: *pe'dah'eyl)* RANSOMED~&~MIGHTY.ONE *Translation:* The mighty one ransomed. *Strong's:* #6300

Pedatsur (masc: / פדה-צור / *pe'dah'tsur)* RANSOMED~&~BOULDER *Translation:* Ransomed of the boulder. *Strong's:* #6301

Peleg (masc: *pe'leg)* TRIBUTARY *Translation:* Tributary. *Strong's:* #6389

Peleshet (fem: *pe'le'shet)* WALLOWER *Translation:* wallower. *Strong's:* #6429, #6430

Pelet (masc: *pe'let)* SWIFTNESS *Translation:* Swiftness. *Strong's:* #6431

Peni'el (masc: / פנואל / *pe'ni'eyl / pe'nu'eyl)* FACE~s~&~MIGHTY.ONE *Translation:* Face of El. *Strong's:* #6439

Pe'or (masc: *pe'or)* OPENED.WIDE *Translation:* Opened wide. *Strong's:* #1187, #6465

Perat (masc: *pe'rat)* FRUITFULNESS *Translation:* Fruitfulness. *Strong's:* #6578

Perets (masc: *pe'rets)* BREACH *Translation:* Breach. *Strong's:* #6557

Perez (masc: *pe'rez)* PEASANT *Translation:* Peasant (Meaning one who dwells in a village). *Strong's:* #6522

Pesahh (masc: *pe'sahh)* HOPPING *Translation:* Hopping (The day of deliverance from Egypt. Also, the feast remembering this day and the lamb that is sacrificed for this feast). *Strong's:* #6453

Petor (masc: *pe'tor)* INTERPRETING *Translation:* Interpreting. *Strong's:* #6604

Pikhol (masc: *pi'khol)* MOUTH~&~ALL *Translation:* Mouth of all. *Strong's:* #6369

Pildash (masc: *pil'dash)* FLAME.OF.FIRE *Translation:* Flame of fire. *Strong's:* #6394

Pinon (masc: פינון *pi'non)* AROUND.THE.CORNER *Translation:* Around the corner. *Strong's:* #6373

Pisgah (fem: פיסגה *pis'gah)* CLEFT *Translation:* Cleft. *Strong's:* #6449

Pishon (masc: פישון *pi'shon)* SCATTERED *Translation:* Scattered. *Strong's:* #6376

Pitom (masc: פיתום *pi'tom)* CITY.OF.JUSTICE *Translation:* City of justice (Of Egyptian origin). *Strong's:* #6619

Piy-Hahhiyrot (masc: פי-החירות *pi ha'hhi'rot)* MOUTH~&~the~CISTERN~s *Translation:* Mouth of the cisterns. *Strong's:* #6367

Piynhhas (masc: פינחס *pin'hhas)* MOUTH~&~SERPENT *Translation:* Mouth of the serpent. *Strong's:* #6372

Potee-Phera (masc: פוטי-פרע *po'ti phe'ra)* BELONGING~of~&~LONG.HAIR *Translation:* Belonging of Phera (Of Egyptian origin). *Strong's:* #6319

Potiphar (masc: פוטיפר *po'ti'phar)* BELONGING~of~&~BULL *Translation:* Belonging of Phar. *Strong's:* #6318

Pu'a (masc: פוה / פואה פוה */ pu'ah)* BLOWN *Translation:* Dispersion. *Strong's:* #6312

Pu'ah (fem: פועה *pu'ah)* SPLENDID *Translation:* Splendid. *Strong's:* #6326

Pun (masc: פון *pun)* DISTRACTED *Translation:* Distracted. *Strong's:* #6325

Punon (masc: פונון *pu'non)* DISTRACTED.ONE *Translation:* Distracted one. *Strong's:* #6325

Put (masc: פוט *put)* BELONGING *Translation:* Belonging (Meaning and origin are uncertain). *Strong's:* #6316

Putiy'eyl (masc: פוטיאל *pu'ti'eyl)* BELONGING~of~&~MIGHTY.ONE *Translation:* Belonging of El. *Strong's:* #6317

Q

Qadesh (masc: קדש *qa'desh)* PROSTITUTE *Translation:* prostitute. *Strong's:* #6946

Qadmon (masc: קדמון *qad'mon)* EASTERN *Translation:* Eastern (Can also mean "Easterner."). *Strong's:* #6935

Qayin (masc: קין *qa'yin)* SPEARHEAD *Translation:* Spearhead. *Strong's:* #7014, #7017, #8423

Qedar (masc: קדר *qe'dar)* GRAY *Translation:* Gray. *Strong's:* #6938

Qedeymot (masc: קדמות *qe'dey'mot)* PAST.TIME~s *Translation:* Past times. *Strong's:* #6932

Qedmah (masc: קדמה *qed'mah)* PAST.TIME *Translation:* Past time. *Strong's:* #6929

Qehat (masc: קהת *qe'hat)* ALLIED *Translation:* Allied. *Strong's:* #6955

Qe'hey'latah (masc: קהלתה *qe'hey'la'tah)* ASSEMBLY~her *Translation:* Her assembly. *Strong's:* #6954

Qemu'el (masc: קמואל *qe'mu'eyl) I*[(ms)]~RISE[(V)]~&~MIGHTY.ONE *Translation:* Ell will rise. *Strong's:* #7055

Qenat (masc: קנת *qe'nat)* PURCHASED *Translation:* Purchased. *Strong's:* #7079

Qenaz (masc: קנז *qe'naz)* STALKER *Translation:* Stalker. *Strong's:* #7073, #7074

Qeturah (masc: קטורה *qe'tu'rah)* BURN.INCENSE[(V)]~*ed*[(fs)] *Translation:* Incense smoke. *Strong's:* #6989

Qeynan (masc: קינן *qey'nan)* NESTING *Translation:* Nesting. *Strong's:* #7018

Qiryat-Arba (masc: *qir'yat ar'ba)* WALL~&~FOUR *Translation:* Four walls. *Strong's:* #7153

Qiryatayim (masc: *qir'ya'ta'yim)* METROPOLIS~s2 *Translation:* Two metropolises. *Strong's:* #7156

Qivrot-Hata'awah (masc: *qiv'rot ha'ta'a'wah)* GRAVE~s~&~the~YEARNING *Translation:* Graves of the yearning. *Strong's:* #6914

Qorahh (masc: *qo'rahh)* BALDING *Translation:* Balding. *Strong's:* #7141

R

Rahhel (fem: *ra'hheyl)* EWE *Translation:* Ewe. *Strong's:* #7354

Ramah (masc: *ra'mah)* MANE.OF.A.HORSE *Translation:* Mane of a horse. *Strong's:* #7484

Ra'meses (masc: *ra'me'ses)* CHILD.OF.THE.SUN *Translation:* Child of the sun (Of Egyptian origin). *Strong's:* #7486

Ramot (fem: *ra'mot)* CORAL~s *Translation:* Corals. *Strong's:* #7216

Rapha (masc: *ra'pha)* DEAD *Translation:* Dead. *Strong's:* #7497

Raphu (masc: *ra'phu)* HEAL(V)~*ed(ms)* *Translation:* Healed. *Strong's:* #7505

Ravah (fem: *ra'vah)* ABUNDANT *Translation:* Abundant. *Strong's:* #7237

Rehhov (masc: *re'hhov)* STREET *Translation:* Street. *Strong's:* #7340

Rehhovot (masc: *re'hho'vot)* STREET~s *Translation:* Streets. *Strong's:* #7344

Rehhovot-Ghir (masc: *re'hho'vot ghir)* STREET~s~&~CITY *Translation:* Streets of the city. *Strong's:* #7344, #5892

Rephiydiym (masc: *re'phi'dim)* PILLAR.BASE *Translation:* Bottom. *Strong's:* #7508

Reqem (masc: *re'qem)* EMBROIDERY *Translation:* Embroidery. *Strong's:* #7552

Resen (masc: *re'sen)* HALTER *Translation:* Halter. *Strong's:* #7449

Re'u (masc: *re'u)* COMPANION *Translation:* Companion. *Strong's:* #7466

Re'u'eyl (masc: *re'u'eyl)* COMPANION~&~MIGHTY.ONE *Translation:* Companion of El. *Strong's:* #7467

Re'umah (fem: *re'u'mah)* ELEVATED *Translation:* Elevated. *Strong's:* #7208

Re'uven (masc: *re'u'veyn) !(ms)*~SEE(V)~&~SON *Translation:* See a son. *Strong's:* #7205

Reva (masc: *re'va)* QUARTER *Translation:* Quarter. *Strong's:* #7254

Rimon-Perets (masc: פרץ *ri'mon pe'rets)* POMEGRANATE~&~BREACH *Translation:* Pomegranate of the breach. *Strong's:* #7428

Riphat (masc: / ריפת / *di'phat / ri'phat)* SPOKEN *Translation:* Spoken (Can also mean remedy, medicine, release or pardon). *Strong's:* #7384

Risah (masc: *ri'sah)* OVERTHROWN *Translation:* Overthrown. *Strong's:* #7446

Ritmah (fem: *rit'mah)* JUNIPER *Translation:* Juniper. *Strong's:* #7575

Rivlah (fem: *riv'lah)* FRUITFUL *Translation:* Fruitful. *Strong's:* #7247

Rivqah (fem: *riv'qah)* FATTENING *Translation:* Fattening. *Strong's:* #7259

Rosh (masc: *rosh)* HEAD *Translation:* Head. *Strong's:* #7220

S

Salkah (fem: *sal'kah)* MIGRATION *Translation:* Migration. *Strong's:* #5548
Salu (masc: *sa'lu)* COMPARE(V)~*ed*(ms) *Translation:* Compared. *Strong's:* #5543
Samlah (masc: *sam'lah)* APPAREL *Translation:* Apparel. *Strong's:* #8072
Sarah (fem: *sa'rah)* NOBLEWOMAN *Translation:* Noblewoman. *Strong's:* #8297
Sarai (fem: *sa'rai)* RULER~s~me *Translation:* my rulers. *Strong's:* #8283
Savtah (masc: / סבתא / *sav'tah)* GO.ABOUT *Translation:* Go about. *Strong's:* #5454
Savtekha (masc: *sav'ke'kha)* BEATING *Translation:* Beating. *Strong's:* #5455
Sedom (masc: *se'dom)* SCORCHING *Translation:* Scorching (Can also mean "burning" or "cement."). *Strong's:* #5467
Se'iyr (masc: *se'ir)* HAIRY.GOAT *Translation:* Goat. *Strong's:* #8165
Senir (masc: *se'nir)* SNOW.MOUNTAIN *Translation:* Snow mountain. *Strong's:* #8149
Sephar (masc: *se'phar)* SCROLL *Translation:* Scroll. *Strong's:* #5611
Serahh (masc: *se'rahh)* OVERHANG *Translation:* Overhang. *Strong's:* #8294
Sered (masc: *se'red)* BRAIDED.WORK *Translation:* Braided work. *Strong's:* #5624
Serug (masc: *se'rug)* TWIG *Translation:* Twig (From a root meaning "to be intertwined"). *Strong's:* #8286
Setur (masc: *se'tur)* HIDE(V)~*ed*(ms) *Translation:* Hid. *Strong's:* #5639
Seva (masc: *se'va)* DRUNKARD *Translation:* Drunkard. *Strong's:* #5434
Sevam (masc: *se'vam)* BALSAM *Translation:* Balsam. *Strong's:* #7643
Shaddai (masc: *shad'dai)* BREAST~s~me *Translation:* My breasts. *Strong's:* #7706
Shalem (masc: *sha'lem)* OFFERING.OF.RESTITUTION *Translation:* Complete. *Strong's:* #8004
Sham'mah (masc: *sham'mah)* DESOLATE *Translation:* Desolate. *Strong's:* #8048
Shamu'a (masc: *sha'mu'a)* HEAR(V)~*ed*(ms) *Translation:* Heard. *Strong's:* #8051
Shaphat (masc: *sha'phat) he~did*~DECIDE(V) *Translation:* He decided. *Strong's:* #8202
Shapher (masc: *sha'pher)* BRIGHT *Translation:* Bright. *Strong's:* #8234
Shaphtan (masc: *shiph'tan)* JUDICIAL *Translation:* Judicial. *Strong's:* #8204
Sha'ul (masc: *sha'ul)* ENQUIRE(V)~*ed*(ms) *Translation:* Enquired. *Strong's:* #7586
Shaweh (masc: *sha'weh)* EQUAL *Translation:* Resembling. *Strong's:* #7740
Shaweh-Qiryatayim (masc: *sha'weh qir'ya'ta'yim)* EQUAL~s~&~WALL~s *Translation:* Resembling walls. *Strong's:* #7741
Shedeyur (masc: *she'dey'ur)* BREAST~s~&~LIGHT(V) *Translation:* Breasts of light. *Strong's:* #7707
Shekhem (masc: *she'khem)* SHOULDER *Translation:* Shoulder. *Strong's:* #7927, #7928
Shelahh (masc: *she'lahh)* PROJECTILE *Translation:* Projectile. *Strong's:* #7974

Sheleph (masc: *she'leph)* PULLED.OUT *Translation:* Pulled out. *Strong's:* #8026

Shelomiy (masc: *she'lo'miy)* COMPLETENESS~me *Translation:* My completeness. *Strong's:* #8015

Shelumi'eyl (masc: *she'lu'mi'eyl)* COMPLETENESS~of~&~MIGHTY.ONE *Translation:* Completeness of the mighty one. *Strong's:* #8017

Shem (masc: *shem)* TITLE *Translation:* Title. *Strong's:* #8035

Shemever (masc: *shem'ey'ver)* TITLE~&~LONG.WINGED *Translation:* Title of the long winged (Can also mean "lofty flight."). *Strong's:* #8038

Shemida (masc: *she'mi'da)* TITLE~me~&~OPINION *Translation:* My title is an opinion. *Strong's:* #8061, #8062

Shemu'eyl (masc: *she'mu'eyl)* TITLE~him~&~MIGHTY.ONE *Translation:* His title is the mighty one. *Strong's:* #8050

Shepham (masc: *she'pham)* SCRAPED.BARE *Translation:* Scraped bare. *Strong's:* #8221

Shepho (masc: / שפי / *she'pho / she'phiy)* BARE.PLACE *Translation:* Bare place. *Strong's:* #8195

Sheshupham (masc: *she'phu'pham)* ADDER *Translation:* Adder. *Strong's:* #7781, #8197

Shet (masc: *shet)* BUTTOCKS *Translation:* Buttocks. *Strong's:* #8352

Sheva (masc: *she'va)* SEVEN *Translation:* Seven. *Strong's:* #7614

Sheylah (masc: *shey'lah)* REQUEST *Translation:* Request. *Strong's:* #7956

Sheyshai (masc: *shey'shai)* LINEN~s~me *Translation:* My linens. *Strong's:* #8344

Shilem (masc: *shi'lem)* RECOMPENSE *Translation:* Recompense. *Strong's:* #8006

Shimon (masc: *shi'mon)* HEARER *Translation:* Hearer. *Strong's:* #8095

Shimron (masc: *shim'ron)* GUARD *Translation:* Guard. *Strong's:* #8110

Shinar (masc: *shi'nar)* COUNTRY.OF.TWO.RIVERS *Translation:* Country of two rivers (Can also mean "sleeps"). *Strong's:* #8152

Shinav (masc: *shi'nav)* TOOTH~&~FATHER *Translation:* Tooth of father (Can also mean "Changing father" or "Splendour of father."). *Strong's:* #8134

Shiphrah (fem: *shiph'rah)* BRIGHTNESS *Translation:* Brightness. *Strong's:* #8236

Shitiym (masc: *shiy'tiym)* ACACIA~s *Translation:* Acacias. *Strong's:* #7851

Shivah (masc: *shi'vah)* SEVENFOLD *Translation:* Sevenfold. *Strong's:* #7656

Shiymiy (masc: *shi'mi)* REPORT~me *Translation:* My report. *Strong's:* #8096

Sh'lomiyt (masc: *sh'lo'miyt)* OFFERING.OF.RESTITUTION~of *Translation:* One of Shalem. *Strong's:* #8019

Shoval (masc: *sho'val)* UPPER.LEG *Translation:* Upper leg. *Strong's:* #7732

Shu'a (masc: *shu'ahh)* SHOUTING.OUT *Translation:* Shouting out. *Strong's:* #7770

Shu'ahh (masc: *shu'ahh)* SINKING *Translation:* Sinking. *Strong's:* #7744

Shuhham (masc: שוחם *shu'hham)* PIT.DIGGER *Translation:* Pit digger. *Strong's:* #7748, #7749
Shuni (masc: שוני *shu'ni)* FORTUNATE~of *Translation:* One of Shun (May also mean "my sleep."). *Strong's:* #7764
Shur (masc: שור *shur)* ROCK.WALL *Translation:* Rock wall. *Strong's:* #7793
Shutelahh (masc: שותלח *shu'te'lahh)* SET.DOWN(V)~*ed*(ms)~&~MOIST *Translation:* Moistness sat down. *Strong's:* #7803, #8364
Sidim (masc: סידים *si'dim)* FIELD~s *Translation:* Fields. *Strong's:* #7708
Sihhon (masc: סיחון *si'hhon)* MEDITATING.ONE *Translation:* Meditating one. *Strong's:* #5511
Sin (masc: סין *sin)* SHARP.THORN *Translation:* Sharp thorn. *Strong's:* #5513
Sinai (masc: סיני *si'nai)* SHARP.THORN~s~me *Translation:* My sharp thorns. *Strong's:* #5514
Si'on (masc: סיאון *si'on)* HIGH.ONE *Translation:* High one. *Strong's:* #7865
Siryon (masc: סיריון *sir'yon)* HARNESS *Translation:* Harness. *Strong's:* #8303
Sitnah (masc: סטנה *sit'nah)* OPPOSITION *Translation:* Opposition. *Strong's:* #7856
Sitriy (masc: סיתרי *sit'ri)* PROTECTION~me *Translation:* My protection. *Strong's:* #5644
Sodi (masc: סודי *so'di)* CONFIDENCE~me *Translation:* My confidence. *Strong's:* #5476
Suk'kot (masc: סוכות *suk'kot)* BOOTH~s *Translation:* Booths. *Strong's:* #5523
Suphah (fem: סופה *su'phah)* WHIRLWIND *Translation:* Whirlwind. *Strong's:* #5492
Susiy (masc: סוסי *su'siy)* HORSE~s *Translation:* My horse. *Strong's:* #5485

T

Tahhan (masc: תחן *ta'hhan)* CAMPSITE *Translation:* Camp. *Strong's:* #8465, #8470
Tahhash (masc: תחש *ta'hhash)* BADGER *Translation:* Badger. *Strong's:* #8477
Tahhat (masc: תחת *ta'hhat)* UNDER *Translation:* Under. *Strong's:* #8480
Talmai (masc: תלמי *tal'mai)* FURROW~s~me *Translation:* My furrows. *Strong's:* #8526
Tamar (fem: תמר *ta'mar)* DATE.PALM *Translation:* Date palm. *Strong's:* #8559
Tarshish (masc: תרשיש *tar'shish)* TOPAZ *Translation:* Topaz. *Strong's:* #8659
Taveyrah (fem: תבערה *tav'ey'rah)* KINDLED *Translation:* Kindled. *Strong's:* #8404
Terahh (masc: תרח *te'rahh)* STATIONED *Translation:* Stationed. *Strong's:* #8646
Tevahh (masc: טבח *te'vahh)* SLAUGHTERING *Translation:* Slaughtering. *Strong's:* #2875
Teyma (masc: תימא *tey'ma)* DESERT.REGION *Translation:* Desert region. *Strong's:* #8485
Teyman (masc: תימן *tey'man)* SOUTHWARD *Translation:* South. *Strong's:* #8487, #8489
Tidal (masc: תדעל *ti'dal)* YOKE.BREAKER *Translation:* Yoke breaker (Meaning and origin are uncertain). *Strong's:* #8413
Timna (masc: תימנע *tim'na)* WITHHOLDING *Translation:* Withholding. *Strong's:* #8555
Timnat (masc: תימנת *tim'nat)* SOUTHWARD *Translation:* South. *Strong's:* #8553

Tiras (masc: *ti'ras)* DESIRABLE *Translation:* Desirable (Meaning and origin are uncertain). *Strong's:* #8494

Tirtsah (fem: *tir'tsah) you$^{(ms)}$~will~*ACCEPT$^{(V)}$ *Translation:* You will accept. *Strong's:* #8656

Togarmah (masc: *to'gar'mah) you$^{(ms)}$~will~*GNAW$^{(V)}$~her *Translation:* You will gnaw her. *Strong's:* #8425

Tola (masc: *to'la)* KERMES *Translation:* Kermes. *Strong's:* #8439

Tophel (masc: *to'phel)* UNSEASONED *Translation:* Unseasoned. *Strong's:* #8603

T^{s}almonah (fem: *tsal'mo'nah)* IMAGING *Translation:* Imaging. *Strong's:* #6758

T^{s}aphnat-Paneyahh (masc: *tsaph'nat pa'ney'ahh)* TREASURY~&~GLORIOUS.REST *Translation:* Treasury of the glorious rest. *Strong's:* #6847

T^{s}aphon (masc: *tsa'phon)* NORTH *Translation:* North. *Strong's:* #6827

T^{s}edad (masc: *tse'dad)* MOUNTAINSIDE *Translation:* Mountain side. *Strong's:* #6657

T^{s}elaph'hhad (masc: *tse'laph'hhad)* SHADOW~&~AWE *Translation:* Shadow of awe. *Strong's:* #6765

T^{s}emar (masc: *tse'mar)* WOOL *Translation:* Wool. *Strong's:* #6786

T^{s}epho (masc: / צפי / *tse'pho / tse'phiy)* WATCHMAN~him *Translation:* His watchman. *Strong's:* #6825

T^{s}idon (masc: *tsi'don)* HUNTING *Translation:* Hunting. *Strong's:* #6721

T^{s}ilah (masc: *tsi'lah)* SHADOW *Translation:* Shadow. *Strong's:* #6741

T^{s}in (masc: *tsin)* FLOCKS *Translation:* Flocks. *Strong's:* #6790

T^{s}iphyon (fem: *tsiph'yon)* WATCHER *Translation:* Watcher. *Strong's:* #6837

T^{s}ipor (masc: *tsi'por)* BIRD *Translation:* Bird. *Strong's:* #6834

T^{s}iporah (fem: *tsi'po'rah)* BIRD *Translation:* Bird. *Strong's:* #6855

T^{s}iv'on (masc: *tsiv'on)* SPLASHED *Translation:* Splashed. *Strong's:* #6649

T^{s}o'an (masc: *tso'an)* REMOVED *Translation:* Removed. *Strong's:* #6814

T^{s}o'ar (masc: *tsu'ar)* TINY *Translation:* Tiny (Meaning "insignificant."). *Strong's:* #6820, #6686

T^{s}ohhar (masc: *tso'hhar)* REDDISH.GRAY *Translation:* Reddish gray. *Strong's:* #6714

T^{s}ophim (masc: *tso'phim)* KEEP.WATCH$^{(V)}$~*ed$^{(mp)}$ Translation:* Kept watch. *Strong's:* #6839

T^{s}ur (masc: *tsur)* BOULDER *Translation:* Boulder. *Strong's:* #6701

T^{s}uri'eyl (masc: *tsu'ri'eyl)* BOULDER~me~&~MIGHTY.ONE *Translation:* My boulder is the mighty one (May also mean "Boulder of El."). *Strong's:* #6700

T^{s}urishaddai (masc: / צורי-שדי / *tsu'ri'sha'dai)* BOULDER~me~&~BREAST~s~me *Translation:* My boulder is my breasts (This name may also be written as T^{s}ur of Shaddai). *Strong's:* #6701

T^{s}'vo'yim (masc: / צבויים / *tse'vi'im / tse'vo'iym)* GAZELLE~s *Translation:* Gazelles. *Strong's:* #6636

Tumiym (masc: *tu'mim)* FULL.STRENGTH~s *Translation:* Full strengths. *Strong's:* #8550

Tuval (masc: תובל *tu'val) you$^{(ms)}$~will~*BRING$^{(V)}$ *Translation:* You will bring. *Strong's:* #8422

Tuval-Qayin (masc: תובל-קין *tu'val qa'yin) you$^{(ms)}$~will~*BRING$^{(V)}$~&~SPEARHEAD *Translation:* You will bring the spearhead. *Strong's:* #8423

U

Ur (masc: אור *ur)* LIGHT *Translation:* Light. *Strong's:* #0218

Uriy (masc: אורי *u'ri)* LIGHT~me *Translation:* My light. *Strong's:* #0221

Uriym (masc: אורים *u'rim)* LIGHT~s *Translation:* Lights. *Strong's:* #0224

Uts (masc: עוץ *uts)* ADVICE *Translation:* Advise. *Strong's:* #5780

Uval (masc: עובל *u'val)* ROUNDED *Translation:* Rounded. *Strong's:* #5745

Uzal (masc: אוזל *u'zal) I~will~*BE.LAVISH$^{(V)}$~*ed*$^{(ms)}$ *Translation:* I will be lavished. *Strong's:* #0187

Uziy'eyl (masc: עוזיאל *u'zi'eyl)* BOLDNESS~me~&~MIGHTY.ONE *Translation:* My boldness is El. *Strong's:* #5816

W

Waheyv (masc: והב *wa'heyv)* and~GIFT.OFFERING *Translation:* And a gift offering. *Strong's:* #2052

Waphsi (masc: ופסי *waph'si)* and~WRIST~me *Translation:* And my wrist. *Strong's:* #2058

Y

Ya'aqov (masc: יעקוב *ya'a'qov) he~will~*RESTRAIN$^{(V)}$ *Translation:* He restrains. *Strong's:* #3290

Yaboq (masc: יבוק *ya'boq) he~will~*EMPTY.OUT$^{(V)}$ *Translation:* He will fail. *Strong's:* #2999

Yagbahah (fem: יגבהה *yag'ba'hah) he~will~*BE.HIGH$^{(V)}$~her *Translation:* He will be her highness. *Strong's:* #3011

Yagli (masc: יגלי *yag'li) he~will~*REMOVE.THE.COVER$^{(V)}$ *Translation:* He will remove the cover. *Strong's:* #3020

Yah (masc: יה *yah)* EXISTING *Translation:* Existing (The actual pronunciation of this name is not certain but probably "Yah."). *Strong's:* #3050

Yahats (masc: יהץ *ya'hats)* STAMPED.DOWN *Translation:* Stamped down. *Strong's:* #3096

Yahh'le'el (masc: יחלאל *yahh'le'eyl) he~will~*STAY$^{(V)}$~&~MIGHTY.ONE *Translation:* El will stay. *Strong's:* #3177, #3178

Yahhtse'el (masc: יחצאל *yahh'tse'eyl) he~will~*DIVIDE$^{(V)}$~&~MIGHTY.ONE *Translation:* El will divide. *Strong's:* #3183

Ya'ir (masc: יאיר *ya'ir) he~will~make~*LIGHT$^{(V)}$ *Translation:* He will make light. *Strong's:* #2971

Yakhin (masc: יכין *ya'khin) he~will~*PREPARE$^{(V)}$ *Translation:* He will prepare. *Strong's:* #3199

Yalam (masc: יעלם *ya'lam) he~will~*BE.OUT.OF.SIGHT[V] *Translation:* He will be out of sight. *Strong's:* #3281

Yamin (masc: ימין *ya'min)* RIGHT.HAND *Translation:* Right hand. *Strong's:* #3226

Yaphet (masc: יפת *ya'phat)* WONDER *Translation:* Wonder. *Strong's:* #3315

Yaq'shan (masc: יקשן *yaq'shan)* SNARER *Translation:* Snarer. *Strong's:* #3370

Yaqtan (masc: יקטן *yaq'tan) he~will~*BE.SMALL[V] *Translation:* He will be small. *Strong's:* #3355

Yarden (masc: ירדן *yar'den)* DESCENDER *Translation:* Descender. *Strong's:* #3383

Yared (masc: ירד *ya'red) he~will~*GO.DOWN[V] *Translation:* He will go down. *Strong's:* #3382

Yashuv (masc: ישוב *ya'shuv) he~will~*TURN.BACK[V] *Translation:* He will turn back. *Strong's:* #3437

Yatvatah (fem: יטבתה *yat'va'tah)* WELLNESS~her *Translation:* Her wellness. *Strong's:* #3193

Yaval (masc: יבל *ya'val)* WATERCOURSE *Translation:* Watercourse. *Strong's:* #2989

Yawan (masc: יון *ya'wan)* MIRE *Translation:* Mire (Closely related to the Hebrew word yayin meaning "wine"). *Strong's:* #3120

Yazeyr (masc: יעזר *ya'zeyr) he~will~*HELP[V] *Translation:* He will help. *Strong's:* #3270

Yegar-Sa'haduta (masc: יגר-שהדותא *ye'gar sa'ha'du'ta)* AFRAID~&~RECORD *Translation:* Afraid of the record. *Strong's:* #3026

Yehoshu'a (masc: יהושע *ye'ho'shu'a)* EXISTING~&~*he~will~*RESCUE[V] *Translation:* Yah will rescue. *Strong's:* #3091

Yehudah (masc: יהודה *ye'hu'dah)* THANKSGIVING *Translation:* Thanksgiving. *Strong's:* #3063

Yehudit (fem: יהודית *ye'hu'dit)* THANKSGIVING *Translation:* Thanksgiving. *Strong's:* #3067

Ye'ish (masc: יעוש / יעיש יעוש / *ye'ish / ye'ush) he~will~*MAKE.HASTE[V] *Translation:* He will hasten. *Strong's:* #3274

Yemu'el (masc: ימואל *ye'mu'eyl)* DAY~&~MIGHTY.ONE *Translation:* Day of El. *Strong's:* #3223

Yephunah (masc: יפונה *ye'phu'nah) he~will~be~*TURN[V] *Translation:* He will be turned. *Strong's:* #3312

Yerahh (masc: ירח *ye'rahh)* MOON *Translation:* Moon. *Strong's:* #3392

Ye'rey'hho (masc: ירחו *ye'rey'hho)* MOON~him *Translation:* His moon. *Strong's:* #3405

Yeshurun (masc: ישורון *ye'shu'run)* STRAIGHT.ONE *Translation:* Straight one. *Strong's:* #3484

Yeter (masc: יתר *yeter)* REMAINDER *Translation:* Remainder. *Strong's:* #3500

Yetet (masc: יתת *ye'tet)* NAIL *Translation:* Nail. *Strong's:* #3509

Yetser (masc: יצר *ye'tser)* THOUGHT *Translation:* Thought. *Strong's:* #3337

Yetur (masc: יטור *ye'tur) he~will~*ROW[V] *Translation:* He will row. *Strong's:* #3195

Yevus (masc: יבוס *ye'vus) he~will~*TRAMPLE.DOWN[V] *Translation:* He will trample down. *Strong's:* #2982, #2983

YHWH (masc: *yhwh) he~will~*BE$^{(V)}$ *Translation:* He is (The actual pronunciation of this name is not certain). *Strong's:* #3068

YHWH-Nisiy (masc: *yhwh ni'si) he~will~*BE$^{(V)}$~&~STANDARD~me *Translation:* Yhwh is my standard. *Strong's:* #3071

YHWH-Yireh (masc: *yhwh yi'reh) he~will~*BE$^{(V)}$~&~*he~will~*SEE$^{(V)}$ *Translation:* Yhwh will see. *Strong's:* #3070

Yidlap (masc: *yid'lap) he~will~*DRIP$^{(V)}$ *Translation:* He will drip. *Strong's:* #3044

Yigal (masc: *yig'al) he~will~*REDEEM$^{(V)}$ *Translation:* He will redeem. *Strong's:* #3008

Yimnah (masc: *yim'nah) he~will~*RECKON$^{(V)}$ *Translation:* He will reckon. *Strong's:* #3232

Yish'baq (masc: *yish'baq) he~will~*BE.LET.ALONE$^{(V)}$ *Translation:* He will be let alone. *Strong's:* #3435

Yishma'el (masc: *yish'ma'eyl) he~will~*HEAR$^{(V)}$~&~MIGHTY.ONE *Translation:* El will hear. *Strong's:* #3458

Yishwah (masc: *yish'wah) he~will~*EQUATE$^{(V)}$ *Translation:* He will equate or He will resemble. *Strong's:* #3438

Yishwiy (masc: *yish'wi) he~will~*EQUATE$^{(V)}$~me *Translation:* He will equate me or He will resemble me. *Strong's:* #3440, #3441

Yiskah (fem: *yis'kah) he~will~*LOOK.FORTH *Translation:* He will look forth. *Strong's:* #3252

Yisra'eyl (masc: *yis'ra'eyl) he~will~*TURN.ASIDE$^{(V)}$~&~MIGHTY.ONE *Translation:* He turns El aside. *Strong's:* #3478

Yis'sas'khar (masc: *yeysh'sa'khar)* THERE.IS~&~WAGE *Translation:* There is a wage. *Strong's:* #3485

Yitran (masc: *yit'ran)* RESERVER *Translation:* Reserver. *Strong's:* #3506

Yitro (masc: *yit'ro)* REMAINDER~him *Translation:* His remainder. *Strong's:* #3503

Yits'har (masc: *yits'har) he~will~*PRESS.OUT.OIL$^{(V)}$ *Translation:* He presses out oil. *Strong's:* #3324

Yits'hhaq (masc: *yits'hhaq) he~will~*LAUGH$^{(V)}$ *Translation:* He laughs. *Strong's:* #3327

Yokheved (fem: *yo'khe'ved)* EXISTING~&~HEAVY *Translation:* Yah is heavy. *Strong's:* #3115

Yoseph (masc: *yo'seph)* ADD$^{(V)}$~*ing*$^{(ms)}$ *Translation:* Adding. *Strong's:* #3130

Yov (masc: *yov)* HOWLING *Translation:* Howling. *Strong's:* #3102

Yovav (masc: *yo'vav)* HOWL$^{(V)}$~*ing*$^{(ms)}$ *Translation:* Howling. *Strong's:* #3103

Yuval (masc: *yu'val)* CREEK *Translation:* Creek. *Strong's:* #3106

Z

Za'awan (masc: *za'a'wan)* TROUBLED *Translation:* Troubled. *Strong's:* #2190

Zakur (masc: *za'kur)* REMEMBER$^{(V)}$~*ed*$^{(ms)}$ *Translation:* Remembered. *Strong's:* #2139

Zamzum (masc: *zam'zum)* MISCHIEVOUS *Translation:* Mischievous. *Strong's:* #2157

Zerahh (masc: *ze'rahh)* RISING.SUN *Translation:* Rising sun. *Strong's:* #2226, #2227
Zered (masc: *ze'red)* EXUBERANT *Translation:* Exuberant. *Strong's:* #2218
Zevulun (masc: *ze'vu'lun)* RESIDENT *Translation:* Resident. *Strong's:* #2074
Zikh'riy (masc: *zikh'ri)* MEMORY~me *Translation:* My memorial. *Strong's:* #2147
Zilpah (fem: *zil'pah)* TRICKLING *Translation:* Trickling. *Strong's:* #2153
Zimran (masc: *zim'ran)* MUSICIAN *Translation:* Musician. *Strong's:* #2175
Zimri (masc: *zim'ri)* SINGER~me *Translation:* My singer. *Strong's:* #2174
Ziphron (masc: *ziph'ron)* FRAGRANT.ONE *Translation:* Fragrant one. *Strong's:* #2202
Zuz (masc: *zuz)* ENTRYWAY *Translation:* Entryway. *Strong's:* #2104

www.ingramcontent.com/pod-product-compliance
Lightning Source LLC
Chambersburg PA
CBHW031233090426
42742CB00007B/175
* 9 7 8 1 9 4 9 7 5 6 5 2 4 *